HISTORY OF FLORENCE

VIEW OF FLORENCE FROM THE CONVENT OF SAN FRANCESCO ABOVE FIESOLE (ALINARI).

HISTORY OF FLORENCE
from the Founding of the City
through the Renaissance

BY FERDINAND SCHEVILL

WITH ILLUSTRATIONS AND MAPS

NEW YORK : HARCOURT, BRACE AND COMPANY

Designed by Robert Josephy
PRINTED IN THE UNITED STATES OF AMERICA
BY QUINN & BODEN COMPANY, INC., RAHWAY, N. J.

To Clara

FOR WHOM THIS BOOK WAS BEGUN

AND TO WHOSE BRIGHT AND GALLANT SPIRIT

IT IS DEDICATED

CONTENTS

iv CONTENTS

LIST OF ILLUSTRATIONS

LIST OF ILLUSTRATIONS

LIST OF MAPS

Introduction: On Florentine Historiography

FIRST legend, then history—that is the inevitable succession among all groups and peoples which, by steadily advancing in the command of themselves and their environment, at last achieve a notable civilization. On reaching the stage at which history definitely rules, they usually give evidence of an increased self-esteem by somewhat contemptuously affixing to the version of the past, so long the cherished possession of their ancestors, the label "legend" and by dismissing it from consideration as the negligible offspring of ignorance and fancy. At the very least they develop a certain skepticism regarding it, simultaneously welcoming the factual and critical version of their past put forth by the representatives of the new culture. This they affirm to be history, meaning thereby a product which, in distinction from legend handed down by word of mouth and reshaped by each narrator according to his pleasure, is reliable, accurate, and certain because based on the facts as revealed by the surviving records. In short, the position of the later, more enlightened generations is that legend is fiction, history truth, and that whereas men were once content to receive the story of their past from their dreamers and poets, they now take it from their scholars and historians in command of a method of investigation calculated to yield a full and satisfying knowledge.

Although such is the view advanced societies usually entertain regarding the distinction between legend and history, it errs by drawing too absolute a line between them. This will become apparent the moment we take up an individual instance like that of Florence. In the thirteenth century when the Arno city was making rapid strides toward the conquest of that power and civilization on the strength of which it was destined in the succeeding century to become a leading world-center, the citizens were in possession of a version of their past which, to their as yet simple and untutored understanding, was a truthful record of events and therefore authentic history. It is this history which Dante Alighieri learned when he was a boy and which, never challenging, he closely reflects in his great poem. It circulated in the poet's youth in many slightly different versions, some of which have come down to us and have been made accessible in our time in printed form.

Whoever is curious about Dante's historical background cannot overlook these ancient compilations. Taking up the one which goes under the name of *Il Libro Fiesolano*,[1] we are struck at once by its palpably fabulous character. Plainly the unknown author was utterly ignorant of the Florentine past but, possessed of the literary and chivalric culture of his century, was prompted in the spirit of the contemporary romancers to entertain his audience with war and adventure on a heroic scale. So completely does the taste of readers change from age to age that it is hard for us of the twentieth century to believe that this sort of uncontrolled invention was ever considered to be entertaining. The evidence to the contrary is, however, so abundant that there is no rejecting it. With frank delight, then, the medieval reader learned from the old story-teller how Fiesole was the first town to be built after the universal flood, how the son of the first sovereign pair of Fiesole was Italo who gave his name to Italy, how a second son migrated to the east and founded Troy, how Troy was destroyed owing to the sinful love of Paris and Helen, how Aeneas made his escape from the captured city and came to Italy, how the descendants of Aeneas founded Rome, mistress of the world, and how the Romans, after taking and destroying Fiesole, laid the foundations in the plain below Fiesole of Florence, building it as the exact counterpart of their own proud capital upon the Tiber. The invention, wholly literary and fantastic, would seem to carry no single element suggestive of a genuine popular tradition.

While, owing to its total lack of verisimilitude, this version fusing universal and local history into a comprehensive unit fails to impress the living generation, we should be making a mistake to dismiss it from our attention without noting that it contains an impalpable something which should not be overlooked. Closely scanned, it communicates what to the early Florentines was without doubt the outstanding feature of their moral and political world. The young and struggling city in the valley was completely dominated by the older Fiesole on its lofty eminence, and before ambitious Florence could expand and spread its wings the dangerous rival would have to be brought low. Therefore the venerable but inconveniently close neighbor became the object of a passionate hatred; and as at the same time the memory had not died out that Fiesole was of Etruscan origin, it followed that the Florentines, so radically different in their own estimate from their despised rivals as to impose the assumption of another and a nobler race of men, were necessarily identified with the Romans,

---

[1] Published with two similar compilations under the comprehensive title, *Chronica de Origine Civitatis,* by O. Hartwig, *Quellen und Forschungen zur aeltesten Geschichte der Stadt Florenz.* Marburg, 1875. See also on legends and early chronicles, Santini, *Quesiti e Ricerche di Storiografia Fiorentina.* Florence, 1903.

proud conquerors in their day of Fiesole and all Etruria. In short, the Arno city was the beloved daughter and potential heir of the imperial city on the Tiber. This flattering descent the eager dreamers of the rising town pondered and poetically embroidered until it became the first and outstanding article of the civic faith with which Florence began her existence.

In the face of this patriotic kernel of the *Libro Fiesolano,* a kernel containing in terms of the imagination the most immediate and pressing reality of the youthful town, it is impossible to maintain that the past which Dante absorbed from the writings current in his day must be rated as pure romance without a shadow of historical value. On the contrary, the assertion, strengthened by picturesque particulars, of the noble Roman origin of the Florentines and of the vileness of the adder brood of the Fiesolan neighbors is without the least doubt an appreciable moral factor in that amazing energy with which medieval Florence pushed and hacked her way across every obstacle to a lofty, distant goal. Indisputably the legend carries a body of events which, historically considered, have little value or even no value at all; however, by revealing a state of mind, a psychological slant, it throws a not unimportant light on the early history of the town. We must conclude that, inasmuch as legend and history, at least in the instance under consideration, possess in certain imponderable psychological data a common denominator, they are not, as is often affirmed, two wholly diverse worlds separated by a clear-cut dividing line.

This conclusion is confirmed when we examine the Florentine work wherein for the first time and in the most decisive manner legend was replaced by history. Immediately after Dante's day, or rather while Dante was still alive, a somewhat younger contemporary, Giovanni Villani, began writing his famous chronicle.[2] We have already suggested that history as distinct from legend is at all times and everywhere recognizable by a simple criterion: it reconstructs the events with which it deals not from hearsay and dream-stuff but from the facts transmitted by the records. This test Villani successfully meets, although not consistently throughout his narrative. Leaving to one side those sections of his work which deal with the world in general and concentrating on the parts devoted to Florence—a procedure to which no one will object since it is to the Florentine material that Villani owes his fame—we are struck with the circumstance that what he has to offer of copious and well-sifted information belongs overwhelmingly to the period of his own lifetime. For this period his records or sources were his own intelligent and inquiring self, other living witnesses of the events described, and numerous official documents to which he had access. But when by way of introduction to what occurred in his day he undertook

---

[2] *Cronica di Giovanni Villani.* Ed. Franc. Gherardi Dragomanni. 4 vols. Florence, 1844-45.

to add the story of the birth and childhood of his beloved commonwealth, he found little else to fall back on save the legend on which he, and Dante before him, had been brought up; and having nothing better in hand, he incorporated it in his work.

In following this course Villani was troubled by no sense of incongruity. Scholars are universally agreed that his distinction as a chronicler lies in a feeling for factual reality which no medieval writer before his time possessed in the same degree. It was natural for a man so endowed to be guided by the evidence, and this was Villani's actual procedure subject to limitations beyond his control. When the records were plentiful, as in his own age, he used as many as were immediately available; and when, as for early Florence, he had access to no other records than such legendary tales as the *Libro Fiesolano,* he let himself be governed by them. In either case his method was much the same; and if he did not instinctively balk at what we recognize at once as the transparent and monstrous absurdities of the legend, we may explain this credulity in the main by his medieval simplicity. But without the least doubt it is also referable to the tone and background of the legend, which with its declaration of the Roman origin of Florence fell in exactly with his own ruling patriotic bias.

The deduction to be drawn from this kinship of Villani, first authentic historian of Florence, to the Florentine legend is so important that we must pause to elaborate it. Not only in legend but also in veritable history as well there is unmistakably something personal or subjective which is woven into the events described and is recognizable by the intelligent reader as a prejudice or a point of view or a supporting mental substructure. Even when history is composed with the most wholehearted submission to the evidence, aspiring, according to the demand of some of its most recent hierophants, to a coldly scientific attitude toward its material, the ideal is never realized. For, when the mastery of the evidence has been effected, it must, in order to be converted into a history, be shaped in the mind of the investigator; and in that process it will inevitably acquire something of the form and color of the vessel in which it was prepared. Moreover, this personal contribution is not personal in the sense of being wholly original with the chronicler or historian under consideration. As an ephemeral, and, let us add, an eminently social creature, he is the child of his environment and exhibits innumerable earmarks indicative of his particular time and place. It is for this reason we are obliged to inquire with regard to every history that comes into our hands: Who wrote it? When and where did the writer live? With what particular outlook or religion or philosophy did he face the problems of history and of life? And we shall invariably find that the answers to these questions defining the historian's individuality always enter, though not regularly in the same degree, into works passing as histories. They may have been composed with the most devoted attention to the facts, but the facts on getting themselves ordered in a logical or a chronological series have had something extraneous imposed on them, something that is not native to them as mere facts. Call this addition form, mind, interpretation—there it is! He who lacks the skill or penetration to detect this often hidden agent with his quiet manipulations and directive comment, he who reads history, any history, as if it were something impersonal communicating an absolute and final truth has never reflected on the necessary limitations of this department of literature and is likely in the end to take from it more injury than profit.

By insisting at the outset on the human equation as an ever-present element in the vast mass of Florentine historiography beginning with the earliest legend extant, we are providing ourselves with a taper calculated to shed a serviceable light throughout our journey. Although the writer of the *Libro Fiesolano* must be rated as a mere entertainer, while the first chronicler, Villani, fairly qualifies as a historian, the two have a common background of patriotic sentiment and become related to each other by this emotional tie. Nonetheless we emphatically enter with Villani into a new world which he creates by his command of the facts and his power of critically evaluating them. His immense achievement, for which we of a later period can never be too grateful, is the accurate description of the town under his eyes, his story of its trade, its industry, its social classes, its religious customs, its relation to its neighbors, its ceaseless and passionate domestic conflicts. But pulsating with life as the picture is, it is not the last word on the subject. In fact, if we have made our point, there is never any last word or final truth on any historical subject; for, even should a mistaken and self-satisfied generation think itself in possession of this truth, its successor will not fail, or at least up to the present has never yet failed, to replace it with a truth of its own.

What happened in Villani's case was that he scrutinized the Florentine scene before his eyes with a novel and amazing degree of directness and candor. While that is the first and most essential point to be noted, it is also true that his viewpoint was that of the merchant group to which he belonged and whose passionately papal or Guelph sentiments he fully shared. His whole heart goes out to the burgher republic of the merchants and artisans constituted in his impressionable youth after a long and bloody conflict with an older governing group of aristocratic and landowning families. Although his burning patriotism is rooted in class prejudice, it loses none of its sincerity on that account. This Florence, his beloved city, in becoming a merchant republic has acquired just the right constitution for its needs, although

Villani does not go the uncritical length of asserting that the individual merchants who appropriated the offices were necessarily impeccable. Living in the first half of the fourteenth century, when the new constitution was at the height of its vigor, and identifying himself with it inwardly by a solemn act of faith, he pictured it in operation with an incomparable vivacity and freshness. Because of these various circumstances weaving like a shuttle between the describer and the thing described, he created an advanced type of medieval chronicle, a chronicle which is undoubtedly on the way to becoming a coherent and critical history, although it does not quite attain its goal.

Considerable as Villani's achievement was, there is nothing mysterious or inexplicable about it. The advance signalized by him was in the air, as an examination of the work of the contemporary chroniclers throughout Italy would easily establish. In a sketch limited to Florence it will suffice to adduce the case of another Florentine, Dino Compagni. Dino wrote in Villani's day— around 1310—a chronicle [3] which represents an even more radical departure from the traditional limitations of the chronicle type than the work of his more famous fellow-citizen. In fact Dino's work, though bearing the name chronicle, is, in respect to its form, already a full-fledged history since it presents, in intention if not always in execution, a reasoned exposition of events befalling in Florence during the passionate struggle for political power between the Blacks and the Whites. Its most notable drawback is that, in contrast to the broad sweep of Villani's work, it strictly confines itself to the incidents just before and after the year 1300 in which Dino participated as a leading White. However, remarkable as the production is in itself and invaluable as throwing light on the spirit of the age, it exercised no influence on the development of Florentine historiography. For reasons of political expediency Dino's history was both during his own life and for some generations after his death kept jealously from the public eye. Even two and three hundred years after it had been penned, it circulated only privately and in manuscript form. For the world in general it cannot be said to have existed till 1726 when it was published by the great Muratori. Throughout the long period of the unfortunate suppression of Dino's amazingly original and stirring work the chronicle of Villani was in everybody's hand and was broadly utilized both for reference and imitation.

Two or three generations elapsed after Villani and Dino before the writing of history took a new turn in Florence. By that time not only had Florence reached another stage of political development but the Florentine mind, as reflected by the educated class, was dominated by very different trends.

[3] The standard edition is by I. Del Lungo, *Dino Compagni e la sua Cronica*. 3 vols. Florence, 1879-80.

Between 1400 and 1450 the movement we know as humanism had become the ruling influence among the cultivated circles on the Arno and, on the side of history, humanism in its early phase signified the conscious imitation of the classical historians, particularly those of Rome. That statement puts in a nutshell why the new or humanistic school of Florentine historiography has never been highly regarded except by its contemporaries blindly enamored of antiquity. Since it was content to imitate it took over the external characteristics of the ancients rather than their impalpable spirit and produced works which weary to exhaustion the present-day reader with their descriptions of battles, their invented rhetorical speeches, and their general failure to get below the surface of events and come to grips with reality. Two outstanding humanists tried their hands at a history of Florence. They were Leonardo Bruni and Poggio Bracciolini; and, although they deservedly hold a high place as classical scholars, by either ancient or modern standards they rate as very mediocre historians. Their accounts of Florence do not stand out by reason of new facts drawn into the light of day or of any intellectual distinction imparted to the traditionally accepted facts. As we have seen, unless the historian shines in one or the other or, better still, in both of these particulars, he will have labored in vain. Nothing illustrates more strikingly the tendency of Bruni and Poggio to succumb to false values than that, born to the racy Tuscan speech, they chose to write in the stilted Latin which the intelligentsia of their day considered a more dignified and worthy vehicle of expression. Except to pin on them their appropriate historiographical tag, there is no reason to drag them from the limbo to which they consigned themselves by their own deliberate vacuity.

The third period of Florentine historiography makes a clean break with the barren tradition of the early humanists by re-establishing an immediate contact with life. Chronologically the third period falls within the first half of the sixteenth century and is culturally identified with the later humanism of the full Renaissance. At the same time it embraces, politically, the last and dying phase of the Florentine republic. Pre-eminent among the names of the period are two that will always have a place on Clio's golden roll of honor, Niccolò Machiavelli and Francesco Guicciardini. But let us never forget that these leaders appeared among a host of hardly lesser men. Besides them, Nardi,[4] Nerli,[5] Vettori,[6] Varchi,[7] Segni,[8] and Pitti,[9] directed their considerable

---

[4] J. Nardi, *Istorie della Città di Firenze dall'anno 1494 fino al 1531.* 2 vols. Florence, 1858.
[5] F. Nerli, *Commentari dei Fatti Civili occorsi nella Città di Firenze.* Augsburg, 1728.
[6] F. Vettori, "Sommario della Storia d'Italia dal 1511 al 1527," *Arch. Stor. It.,* Vol. VI (1848), Appendice.
[7] B. Varchi, *Storia Fiorentina.* Per cura di L. Arbib. 3 vols. Florence, 1838-41.
[8] B. Segni, *Istorie Fiorentine dall'anno 1527 al 1555.* Florence, 1857.
[9] J. Pitti, "Istoria Fiorentina," *Arch. Stor. It.,* Vol. I (1842).

talents upon the spectacle under their eyes of the struggling but doomed commonwealth of which they were living, passionate, and suffering members. Whoever looks about to discover another city or nation which within the spread of approximately half a century harbored an equally brilliant array of historians will be put to a long and probably futile search.

Naturally this group of writers has much in common. To begin with, they all have a share, though in different degree, in the advanced thought of the Renaissance. No longer worshiping the ancients as unapproachable models, as had their predecessors of the early humanistic school, they have by reason of this very independence learned some of the finest secrets of their classical exemplars, above all, their sharp analysis of human motive. Moreover, by being confronted in their day by the extraordinary spectacle of an Italy culturally predominant but politically too feeble successfully to defend itself against the attack and invasion of the two great powers of France and Spain, they found themselves thrust, as it were, into a political laboratory in which all the doctrines of the ancients and their own as well were put to the test of practice. It was of course a terribly painful experience, this watching the slow and fateful enslavement of their country to foreigners rated by them with their greater refinement of mind and manners as rude barbarians. The spectacle wounded them profoundly and each reacted to his wound, according to his temperament and social standing, by boiling indignation, or loss of faith, or weak dejection, or frigid cynicism, or by all these moods in varying combination. But, in addition to the depressing drama of general Italian subjection, this group of Florentine historians was confronted with the no less tragic experience of Florence itself. This is particularly important, for in an Italy partitioned among a host of little states and not yet disposed seriously to entertain the thought of national unity, these men were Florentines before they were Italians. When it came to choosing a historical field on which to exercise their literary and reasoning powers, they therefore showed a preference for the theme nearest their heart and focused their attention on their narrow actual rather than on their broad ideal fatherland. In one form or another they all produced histories of Florence. This holds even of Guicciardini, although it is a notable circumstance distinguishing him that, after writing a history of Florence in his youth, he undertook in his mature years—and he was the first man who ever did so— to write a history of Italy as a political whole.[10] With the widest practical experience in political affairs of any member of the Renaissance group he came to see that, after the invasion of Italy by Charles VIII in 1494 and the consequent destruction of the old Italian balance of power, the developments in the city of Florence were unintelligible save within the frame

[10] F. Guicciardini, *La Storia d'Italia* . . . a cura di A. Gherardi. 4 vols. Florence, 1919.

of the forces operating throughout the peninsula. Machiavelli, too, rose occasionally to this larger vision as is witnessed by his famous study in contemporary government, *The Prince*. But only Guicciardini gave it expression in the novel form of a general Italian history.

Citizens of Florence and essentially contemporaries, the historians we are considering were confronted with political fluctuations in their native town involving two leading problems which never ceased to press upon and puzzle them. What were the weaknesses of the old republican constitution which had enabled the Medici gradually to replace it with their tyranny? And why, when the Medici were overthrown, for the first time in 1494 and again in 1527, had it been impossible to find a new and satisfactory constitution of a popular kind? Without an inkling of the modern view of the state as a slow and cumulative organic growth, they all regarded government as mere machinery, that is, as a product of human craftsmanship, skilled or unskilled as the case might be. It followed that they believed it could be carried to something like perfection by untiring thought and ever-renewed experimentation. They were prompted to this view, to a certain extent, by their classical exemplars, but in the main they came to it from the actual, perplexing developments of their own country. For several generations, indeed ever since the collapse of feudalism in the thirteenth century, governments devised by individuals or groups had been hopefully set up at one point or another throughout Italy only to be replaced by a fresh and more promising invention before as much as a year or even a month had gone round.

It is because of this intense preoccupation with government in general and with the Florentine government in particular that the Renaissance historians have been characterized as *statisti* (statesmen) and *politici* (politicians). Each had his own political viewpoint and in both practice and theory traveled his individual path; nonetheless they had so much in common that, by examining the procedure of one, we become measurably familiar with the leading characteristics of them all. Doubtless their most brilliant representative and certainly the one who most deeply impressed the succeeding generations down to our own time was Machiavelli. To his countrymen of the Fascist Italy of today he is more emphatically than at any earlier period *il nostro più grande politico*. While his living admirers usually base their high estimate of his talents on *The Prince,* so closely devoted to government as to be classifiable as essentially a treatise in political science, they cannot afford not to take account of his more purely narrative work, the *History of Florence*. Although indisputably a history and not a political essay, its assumptions and teachings are in no way at variance with those of *The Prince*. Having space for only a single example of Renaissance historiography, let us turn to this able, powerfully reasoned, and, in spite of innumerable errors of fact and feeble documentation, still invaluable book.[11]

Machiavelli's general attitude toward the Florentine republic during its career of several centuries is highly characteristic. He contends that the goal of every political community is unity, and that, if unity is difficult to achieve, it is because of the constant formation in the midst of every society of *sette* or parties. Parties are an affliction capable of being mastered only by good laws, from which, should they become successfully established, there results not only unity but that special reward of unity and highest goal of struggling mankind, civil liberty. To this goal the Florentines had persistently aspired, but as they had never been able to overcome the pest of parties, they had never quite achieved their aim. True, they had clung to their purpose longer than the other Italian cities, but in the end, like every community unable to cure its internal divisions, they had succumbed to the intervention of the tyrant. Between the two poles of liberty (the dream) and tyranny (the actuality) hangs suspended the world of Machiavelli's thought. Brought up in the Florentine republican tradition, he could not help putting a lingering faith in the corrective power of wise laws; but faced with the periodic and, finally, the permanent anarchy which overtook every Italian city-republic (with the exception of Venice), he was obliged by his clearness of vision and uncompromising rectitude of mind to justify the armed enforcer of laws and destroyer of parties, the prince. This meant, in the case of Florence, to declare for the Medici, certainly with no touch of enthusiasm, and just as certainly on no ground of vulgar self-interest, as has frequently been charged. The incisive but passionate thinker that Machiavelli was contented himself to present the facts as he found them and resolutely to stand by the consequences.

While Machiavelli's views on law, liberty, and parties are far from identical with those of Guicciardini, Nerli, Varchi, or any other Renaissance writer, for each of these masters reflects a very personal attitude toward the troublesome problems of Florence, nonetheless his thought and method enable us to establish the intellectual kinship existing among all the members of the group. They all saw history as limited to politics and wrote of Florence accordingly, weaving into the political narrative that particular compound of personal feeling and scientific detachment resulting from the sum of each one's qualities. Less narrators, however, than political philosophers, they accompanied the events they describe with copious reflections on governments and parties and on the actions of leaders diversely moved by jealousy, zeal, ambition, and all the other passions to which man is heir. Whoever in our day reads their books, no longer

[11] Niccolò Machiavelli, *Istorie Fiorentine*. Testo critico con Introduzione e Note per cura di Plinio Carli. 2 vols. Florence, 1927.

does so for their factual content, which is admittedly uneven and far from trustworthy, but for this savory by-product of their comment. By means of it they have thrown, as the ancients did before them, a sharp light on the personal agencies and accidents which now as then make and unmake governments and on the hidden psychological twists which have prompted and will always prompt the actions of men. And let it be once more said that although their procedure co-ordinates them historically with the ancients, they are no miserable apprentice group like the early humanists but, owing to the native vigor of their minds, a body of masters in their own right.

In the centuries that have elapsed since the Renaissance and particularly in the most recent century, the conception of history has undergone a great change. History, as the living generation understands it, embraces immense bodies of subject matter besides politics, and this enlargement of scope has brought it about that the narrowly focused Renaissance histories strike us as thin and, from the point of view of the invisible and truly determinative forces in Florentine development, as even lacking in relevance. This change in evaluation may be adduced as further proof of the theory, expounded in connection with Villani and underlying this whole historiographical survey, that each age or stage of civilization weaves a logic and mentality peculiar to itself into the texture of the facts, thus producing the history suitable to its own level of taste and experience but certain to be revised, if not rejected altogether, when another level has been reached. To the Machiavelli-Guicciardini school of thinkers the definition of history as past politics was so entirely satisfactory that they would have been unable even to conceive of a criticism inspired by another view of what it is important to know about the past. And yet another view is precisely what did come about, though only as the result of a development covering many generations. Consequently the Renaissance historians have gradually lost their vogue until at the present day they are but rarely taken from the shelves for the reason, against which there is no appeal, that they fail to supply the kind of information concerning Florence we moderns are resolved to have.

Long before rejection went this length, however, the school was subjected to adverse criticism on a ground other than that of scope. Engrossed with political reflections, deductions, and apothegms, it had only a secondary interest in the accuracy of its facts, taking them generally with the greatest unconcern and often without changing a single word from earlier authors who had gone over the same ground. Even Machiavelli and Guicciardini followed a practice which by our present standards would lay them open to a clear charge of plagiarism.[12]

[12] The habit of transcribing entire passages has been proved in the case of Guicciardini by Ranke in his *Zur Kritik neuerer Geschichtschreiber* and for Machiavelli by P. Villari in Vol. III, chaps. XII, XIII, XIV, of his *Niccolò Machiavelli e i suoi Tempi*. Florence, 1877-82.

We might not trouble ourselves about a transgression which did not rank as such in the eyes of their contemporaries were it not for important implications of the practice incapable of being overlooked. By taking much of their material bodily from selected predecessors, the Renaissance historians failed to subject their always prejudiced and often thoroughly unreliable authorities to the cleansing process of a healthy criticism; and even worse, they failed to cultivate and deepen a conviction which, astir in them, though in rudimentary form, counseled them to set the evidence of the original documents above the convenient but unsafe manuals at their elbow. We may therefore say sweepingly of them, not only that they did not go back to the primary sources, but also that they did not apply the sharp scalpel of criticism to the secondary authorities on which in the main they relied.

We must be careful to distinguish, in the case of these incisive political thinkers, between a sense of reality in which they abounded and a sense of valid historical proof in which they were conspicuously deficient. This contradiction has served to bring it about that, while their incisive intelligence has tended to secure them continued consideration, their shortcomings as investigators have raised a demand for a fuller and more reliable treatment of events. As a matter of fact it was not till the seventeenth and even the eighteenth century that such a demand made itself generally felt. Its appearance was undoubtedly owing to a novel and increasing appreciation of the value of primary sources. But so many difficulties had to be overcome before primary sources could be made broadly available that students of history only very gradually abandoned the traditional authorities and the slipshod method of getting at the facts which these authorities had hallowed. Not that there was or ever had been any lack of original documents. They were known to exist in great quantities in state, municipal, and ecclesiastical archives; but as these crowded repositories had been permitted to fall into an appalling confusion, there was required as a preliminary measure a long and costly labor of archival reorganization. Then, with the documents catalogued according to classes and periods, the difficult and interminable work of deciphering, editing, and interpreting them could at last be inaugurated. All this was something new: it was scholarship, and scholarship would have to develop its numerous special divisions and techniques before a new kind of history, consciously and solidly founded on scholarship and its inexhaustible resources, could come to birth.

It was in the seventeenth century that the vast possibilities for history of a scholarship dedicated to the recovery and interpretation of the records first dawned, not only on the Italian, but on the European mind in general. The new trend made its first appearance in the field of ecclesiastical history. This was as might be expected, since with the Reformation attacking the Catholic church on the score of its alleged perversion of the teachings of the early saints and holy doctors, the most effective defense against the charge would be an appeal to the original records. Zealous and learned Catholic champions, therefore, launched the publication of diverse bodies of ecclesiastical data such as the *Annales Ecclesiastici* undertaken by Baronius just before the close of the sixteenth century and the *Acta Sanctorum,* which began to appear in 1643. The service rendered to the Roman church by these and similar collections of source materials can hardly be exaggerated. They buttressed its weakened foundations and enabled it triumphantly to resist all later Protestant attacks. That was their immediate practical value; but, in the light of the historiographical development we are engaged in tracing, they possess the additional merit of having blazed the path for historical scholarship in general.

As soon as the value of documents for ecclesiastical history was recognized, it was inevitable that they should be demanded also for a fuller understanding of civil and secular history. Here and there throughout western Europe scattered individuals gradually caught the scent and published, at first rather as antiquarians than as scholars (for scholarship required time to develop its strict tenets), some of the secular manuscripts which they found buried in the private libraries of great lords or in neglected public archives. In Italy more than elsewhere men were carried off their feet by this novel antiquarian passion, and among its earliest evidences was a new history of Florence. Its authors were the two Ammirati, father and son, and so numerous were the new facts they succeeded in abstracting from hitherto neglected documents that their book, a recognizably novel departure, won a standing which it retained far into the nineteenth century.[13] The devotedly Christian spirit of these two sons of the Counter-Reformation is in the sharpest possible contrast to the largely pagan attitude of their Renaissance predecessors. This is worth noting as marking the effects of time; but it is more important still to take due account of their meticulous antiquarianism, which moved them to pile up their novel data in a shapeless mass instinctively repugnant to the order and clarity of the classical tradition.

Though enterprising and earnest devotees of learning, the Ammirati and the many imitative dilettanti scattered over Italy who followed in their footsteps failed to make a deep impression until that rarity, a genuinely creative scholar, came along whose genius first succeeded in giving significance to the new studies. This was the famous Muratori, who in the second quarter of the eighteenth century issued his magnificent collection of the medieval sources of

---

[13] S. Ammirato, *L'Istorie Fiorentine.* Con le Giunte di Scipione Ammirato il Giovane. 3 vols. (folio). Florence, 1647.

his country.[14] If his work set a scholarly mark for the other nations to aim at, that fact states its European importance; its main significance for Muratori's own people was that it made accessible for the first time and in an orderly form a sizable portion of the vast body of raw material on which a deep-delving and thoroughgoing history of medieval Italy and, above all, of that renowned medieval institution, the free commune, would have to be based. Of course even Muratori's *Scriptores* no more than blazed a trail, though a trail pointing in the right direction; and it should cause no surprise that it was only after some further generations of at first rather poorly correlated efforts that Italian and European scholarship awakened to its full responsibilities as the gateway to a new and modern type of history-writing completely liberated from the hampering conventions of the classical method and resting on its own deliberately developed preconceptions.

But this is not the place to unfold the story and analyze the stages in the development of modern historical scholarship. It is not even the intention of this Introduction to treat in exhaustive detail of Florentine historiography since from the start we have pursued no other end than the indication of the chief phases of its ebb and flow. On looking back over the road traveled thus far, we note again that a long period of flighty myth-makers was followed in the fourteenth century by a realist group of honest chroniclers, of whom the forth-right, inquisitive Villani was the leading spirit. Then in the next century came the early humanists, hollow imitators of Livy and the other Roman masters, to be followed after another century by the great Renaissance writers, Machiavelli and the rest, who, while they continued to tread in the footsteps of the ancients, won a place at their side as their not unworthy compeers. But was this the end of desire? Not in a civilization which, like that of western Europe, is always pushing on to new horizons! Owing to the expansive nature of western culture and its amazing ability ever to renew itself, the seventeenth and eighteenth centuries, as we have seen, glimpsed fresh possibilities by the use of a more comprehensive and critical method than the one employed by the historians of Greece and Rome. These pioneering centuries uncovered the value of original documents and in the course of their long-continued occupation with them gradually shaped the numerous techniques which in their sum constitute our vaunted modern scholarship.

But let us make no mistake: scholarship is a portal, not a goal. It deals with the records left behind by the past, not as though they were an end in themselves, but in order that the unusual and rare scholar who combines creative gifts of mind with the stern discipline of research may set forth a more accu-

---

[14] *Rerum Italicarum Scriptores ab Anno Aerae Christianae 500 ad 1500.* Edited by L. A. Muratori. 25 vols. Milan, 1723-51. Completed by his *Antiquitates Italicae Medii Aevi.* 6 vols. Milan, 1738-42.

rate and authentic version of the past. Hence the modern historian, though he must be refreshed at the well of scholarship and emancipated from the narrow older methods, is still required, like the classical historians, the original inventors of this form of literature, to prove himself an artist. It is his task to take over the voluminous and sifted data of innumerable scholarly helpers and to give them an order and a meaning, rendering them intelligible and quickening to his generation. Thus both consciously and unconsciously (for much of the labor of every artist is of the unconscious kind), he impresses a particular stamp on his work which is not native to the facts. "It dates" is the current phrase by which we admit the presence in every literary production, including history, of characteristics which do not derive from the material itself but from its treatment by an individual mind. Did we not detect mind behind the legend, behind Villani's candid narrative, behind the writings of both the earlier and the later humanists? Undoubtedly we did; and when in due course modern historiography based on modern scholarship began its sway, mind or viewpoint or an underlying norm of judgment—call it what you will —continued to figure in every separate production exactly as before.

This needs expressly to be said because of the contrary claim regarding history-writing in our day which has recently been advanced by some historical practitioners and their attendant band of scholars. Conscious of the greater fullness and accuracy made possible by the vast accumulations of tested data put at their disposal through systematic research, they have set up as their ideal the history which represents the complete recovery of the past and is therefore that final and conclusive thing, the truth. They may admit that the truth has as yet in no single instance been attained; still they declare its mastery to be possible by reason of their confidence in the elaborate and impressive machinery of modern scholarship. Indeed so great is their faith in this tool that they frequently call their improved method of investigation "scientific," boldly equating it with the method of the natural sciences and claiming for it an effectiveness that is bound to find its culmination in the discovery of a body of historical laws sweepingly descriptive of the past and valid for the whole future of our human kind.

As this is not the place for a searching theoretical discussion on the nature of history, we shall content ourselves with two declaratory statements which, if they prove nothing, at least make clear the position taken by the writer with regard to the above-mentioned claim. First, we agree with the champions of the "scientific" school that modern historians enjoy an immense advantage over their predecessors through the abundant factual resources made available by the extraordinarily fruitful activities of scholarship. Secondly, we flatly reject the assertion that scholarship has put us in possession of a method capable of

replacing our doubts and uncertainties about the past and our incurable ignorance touching the future with a revelation carrying with it the implication of
a final truth; and consequently we categorically refuse to assign to history,
which has always been and must needs remain a very personal art, the status
of an abstract science. It is our opinion that these statements will be established
beyond reasonable doubt by the review of the last and modern phase of Florentine historiography which we shall now undertake.

Modern Florentine historiography dates from the beginning of the nineteenth century and Sismondi is its first notable representative. Although of
remote Italian ancestry, J. C. L. Simonde de Sismondi was a Genevan by birth
who wrote his famous *History of the Italian Republics* in his native language,
that is, in French.[15] While he treated of Florence in this work, he treated of
it along with all the other Italian city-republics since he was prompted to
undertake his work by a very definite idea or theme. This was that the Italian
communes mark the rise of human liberty out of the muck of feudal degradation and tyranny. In this general story the Arno town was no more than a
link in a connected chain. When Sismondi began to write, a modern tyrant,
the Emperor Napoleon, dominated Europe; and since the Genevan's work
with its libertarian theme had a subtle relevance to contemporary conditions,
it aroused considerable interest and was widely read. But before long the critics
began to busy themselves with its shortcomings and had no difficulty in demonstrating that they were neither few nor unimportant. To begin with, there was
the inevitable subjective contribution. Sismondi was intellectually the child of
the French Revolution and a passionate partisan of its concept of liberty. This
was decidedly in his favor so far as those readers were concerned who sub-
scribed to the current revolutionary doctrine; but the conservatives, who, especially after 1815, were for a time in the ascendant, were repelled by an attitude
which presented itself to them as a detestable mental squint. Between the two
hostile camps, which respectively extolled and damned the new work, stood a
small band of scholars who, dedicated to the ideal of fair play, were able without fear or favor to point out the extravagances and anachronisms into which
Sismondi's libertarian enthusiasm had led him. In the course of time their
moderate view gradually prevailed with the result that no one now disputes
that Sismondi's work exhibits all the hallmarks of the political philosophy
which dominated his own and the succeeding generation and which is loosely
subsumed under the term liberalism. Liberalism still enjoys support in considerable present-day circles, but it would not occur to any living man capable

15 J. C. L. Simonde de Sismondi, *Histoire des Républiques Italiennes du Moyen Age.* 16 vols.
Paris, 1809-18.

of detached reflection to conceive of it as other than the mental product of a particular and limited phase of human experience.

Even more vigorously the critics of Sismondi's work exposed its weakness on turning to its cargo of facts. Multiplied knowledge verified by authentic documents was the shibboleth of the new school of erudition, and, although Sismondi had not failed to profit from the labors of the eighteenth-century investigators, he could not foresee the discoveries subsequent to his date of publication. But such discoveries followed without interruption, stimulated in part by his own work and the numerous historical controversies which it succeeded in stirring up. Among other questions the origin of the commune treated by him raised the issue in a nationalist-minded Europe whether the new and promising self-government of the twelfth and thirteenth centuries was the child of the free institutions carried into the Italian peninsula by the Germanic invaders or whether it was nothing other than the return to life of the Roman municipal institutions supposed long since to have perished. Scholars of great renown such as Savigny, Leo, Hegel, and Troya were drawn into this fundamental debate, and, while they were not able to bring the quarrel to a speedy settlement, they succeeded in drawing into the light of day a body of hidden material concerning the rise of the Italian communes which added invaluable details to our knowledge of the subject. The long-drawn-out battle between the champions respectively of the Roman and the German schools constitutes one of the most brilliant episodes of modern scholarship and undoubtedly carried Italian studies to a higher plane. Its leading result was that to a considerable extent the conviction gained ground that the demand of the hour was not so much a new history either of Florence or of any other medieval commune as a continued exploitation of the archives along the line of Muratori's pioneer labors. Not, however, without a different emphasis from Muratori. As the very title, *Scriptores,* of Muratori's leading work shows, the eighteenth century had given a preference to the evidence supplied by forgotten medieval chroniclers, and Sismondi had built his communal edifice largely on this class of evidence. The vigorous controversy that followed had shown the superiority of documents, which were the immediate impersonal records of political and juridical acts or of commercial transactions, over chronicles with their inevitable errors of fact and their element of personal bias. What we may call the later or nineteenth-century phase of scholarship gave precedence to documents with an official character and in the discovery, cataloguing, and interpretation of them developed an intensity and professional severity which left the scholars of Muratori's day far behind.

While no one will expect an exact date of birth to be assigned to this more intensive scholarship dedicated to sources incontestably primary, it is proper

to bring out that one of its attendant features was the appearance and multiplication of professional journals. In 1842 such a journal, the *Archivio Storico
Italiano,* saw the light at Florence. Planned as a co-operative enterprise for the
promulgation of unpublished manuscripts and records and for minute critical
monographs by and for a limited circle of experts, it scored an immediate success and has now for almost a hundred years served as a rallying-point, especially for scholars interested in Tuscan and Florentine developments. For to
this field it has largely confined its attention, leaving the other provinces of
Italy to other journals of a similar nature which presently sprang up. But let
no one imagine that the *Archivio* sufficed as a repository for the special studies
on Florence to which the confident and prolific nineteenth-century phase of
scholarship gave rise. Interest in Florence became an unquenchable enthusiasm
and, spreading to every country of Europe, produced a steady stream of studies,
brochures, and books on every phase of the town's activities. Since, let us say,
the middle of the nineteenth century these specialized contributions, which,
were this Introduction a systematic historiographical survey, would have to be
examined in detail, have grown to such dimensions that justice could not be
done to them short of a ponderous volume. And the great flood of these pub-
lications has shown no sign of abatement to the present day.

We are but holding ourselves to our self-imposed limitations if, after indicating the nature and mass of the output of a numerous, widely scattered,
and narrowly focused body of scholars, we return to our central argument and
raise the question whether this devotion to the minutiae of the past has checked
the production of general histories dealing with Florence. For, occupied solely
with them, we have attempted to define their tendencies since the first appearance of the genre. A general history, in distinction from the highly specialized
product which has without question been the most characteristic feature of
history-writing in the reigning era of scholarship, represents an attempt at an
intellectual synthesis of a larger or shorter period of Florentine experience, and
practically all of the earlier Florentine historical literature from the birth of
the legend to the rise of modern scholarship falls by our definition under this
particular head. When, following the rise of a meticulous scholarship, Sismondi
presented the first synthesis of the communal movement, he revealed the heavy
risks to which histories of the general type would henceforth be exposed. For,
owing to the rapid and ceaseless accumulation of new data, a general history
was not likely to enjoy authority for any considerable length of time. But it is
also true that by or shortly after Sismondi's day, Florence had taken possession
of the consciousness of all educated people as a prime factor in the development of our occidental culture. This is all-important and must never be forgotten. For it was the passionate curiosity focusing on Florence that made the

production of further syntheses inevitable, no matter how vigorously some per-fectionists might argue that all such attempts should be abandoned until schol-arship had completed its work of assembling and sifting all the available docu-mentary material. The weakness of the perfectionist argument lies, on the one hand, in the circumstance that the labors of scholarship in their very nature can never be terminated, and, on the other hand, in the inconclusiveness of the facts, however well established, considered by themselves. Regarding this latter peculiarly important point, we must again insist that a written history is the product of an individual mind selecting and arranging the facts and that every community and generation imperatively needs such a history as an aid to its orientation in an ever-changing world. Moreover, varying and even contradictory versions arising out of varying and contradictory viewpoints are as desirable as they are unescapable. From this need and habit of a continuous working over of the past, it follows that more especially in the recent decades of accelerated change it is not uncommon for a history, which on its appear-ance was greeted with enthusiasm, to be regarded after the lapse of a relatively short span of years as stale, pointless, and outmoded.

We should now be prepared to understand why, even if some specialists have frankly deprecated the writing of further histories of Florence until scholarship shall have written finis under its labors, the writing of such his-tories has gone on in response to an ever-present demand of the human spirit. In concluding our review by considering these productions of the new age of scholarship we shall glance only at the outstanding works in order to deter-mine their character and value. Exactly as throughout our sketch, our aim will continue to be illustrative rather than exhaustive; above all, we shall dis-regard every work, no matter how much esteemed in lay circles, which does not meet modern professional standards by being a significant synthesis resting solidly on the great body of minute analytical studies.

In the seventies the Frenchman Perrens began the publication of a history of Florence which was planned on a larger scale than had ever been essayed before. It appeared in two parts, the first part reaching to the Medicean domi-nation, the second part covering the rule of the Medici to the fall of the republic in 1531.[16] At about the same time a descendant of an ancient Florentine family, Gino Capponi, put out his history representing a labor of love sustained through many decades.[17] Both of these men were able and diligent students, but diligence, however great, could not save them, as it has not saved any of their predecessors and will not save any of their successors, from being over-

---

[16] F. T. Perrens, *Histoire de Florence* (from the origins to 1434). 6 vols. Paris, 1877-83. F. T. Perrens, *Histoire de Florence depuis la domination des Médicis jusqu'à la chute de la République (1434-1531).* 3 vols. Paris, 1888.
[17] Gino Capponi, *Storia della Repubblica di Firenze.* 2 vols. Florence, 1875.

taken before long by a tireless scholarship. Since the day their works first saw the light the specialists have succeeded in uncovering such a wealth of data touching every stage, and especially the earliest stages of Florentine history, that the information conveyed by Perrens and Capponi has become either partially or wholly obsolete. That it took only some fifty years to bring about this result conveys a vivid impression of the tempo of modern discovery. A more melancholy implication of this accelerated motion is that all works of history produced under modern conditions are destined to have but a short life and that a literary form, which in its classical representatives still enjoys high authority, has recently taken on a tragically ephemeral aspect.

Threatened with oblivion because their scholarship is no longer abreast of the times, Perrens and Capponi have not suffered eclipse to the same extent on account of their viewpoint. True, their peculiar ideology no longer rules the day, but it is characteristic of mental formulas that they command scattered intellectual support even after they have gone, generally speaking, out of fashion. Nonetheless the outlook of each of these historians is for us of a later age very definitely the product of a "dated" mind. Perrens was close enough to Sismondi to be swayed by the same nineteenth-century philosophy of liberalism and he employed it just as confidently and jubilantly as had his predecessor for the framework of his story. As for Capponi, the born Florentine, he was the natural heir of the powerful Guelph tradition native to his city. He was the less moved to question its validity as he wrote expressly for his fellow-townsmen in their own plain speech with no other purpose than that of producing a work which they would gladly read ("una storia tutta popolana"). Capponi is throughout his narrative as consistently a Florentine Guelph as Perrens is a pugnacious, mid-century European liberal. And while each viewpoint still has followers, it no longer carries as much weight as it once did.

While these men were still engaged on their respective tasks it happened that the concept of history experienced that final expansion at which we have already glanced. In the view of the ancients history was concerned with affairs of state, and this view, taken over by the humanists, long continued to dominate the moderns. Even after the startling conquests of an enterprising scholarship and the concomitant decline of the prestige of the ancients, historians were reluctant to abandon the classical models in the matter of the definition and scope of history and continued to follow them in these particulars far into the nineteenth century. Indeed up to the very threshold of the twentieth century, Thucydides and Tacitus have in some quarters been extolled as the unrivaled and never-to-be-surpassed exponents of the literary genre called history. In the meantime, however, political economy, sociology, anthropology, and psychology had come strongly to the fore with their special discoveries regarding man and society which the historians, enamored though they might be of diplomacy and war, could not in the long run ignore. First here, then there, protests against the weight of a dead tradition made themselves heard. They swelled to an academic storm, a much more frightful phenomenon than the innocent words suggest, and, when toward the close of the nineteenth century the atmosphere began to clear, the time-honored political conception had been discarded in favor of the broader view that history should and must take account not only of government but also of commerce, industry, communications, social classes, juridical theory and procedure, the progress of the arts, and every other matter shaping the life of men. In the eyes of the reformers classical history and its more recent derivates became Old History, while the New History, offered as a substitute, proposed to regard politics as no more than the surface manifestation of much more fundamental forces stirring at the heart of the world. Interpreted in connection with the whole movement of civilization during the last half of the nineteenth century, the New History was essentially an attempt on the part of its adepts to put themselves in step with their time. Influenced though these adepts were by the important developments in both the social and the natural sciences, they were particularly impressed with the enormous and revolutionary advances made by the allied biological studies. In this connection it will serve to clarify the perspective if we remind ourselves that Darwin's epoch-making *Origin of Species* came from the press in 1859. Under the general conceptions which this book more than any other helped to popularize, government came to be viewed as a biological organism engaged in gradual evolutionary transformation; at the same time it came to be rated as a rather minor organism embraced within the much vaster social organism which gave it birth. Slowly but inevitably the attention of the historian swung from the less inclusive to the more inclusive entity, from government to society, while the purpose of the historian came with mounting insistence to define itself as the tracing of the ceaseless biological changes of the particular social organism under consideration.

The enlarged societal view of history which naturally invaded and took possession also of the Florentine field was in the nineties voiced vigorously for the first time by Pasquale Villari in the most penetrating study of the origins of the Arno town which had thus far appeared.[18] With the aid of the preparatory labors of a group of contemporary scholars he was able to go beyond any of his predecessors in reducing the struggles, triumphs, and institutions of the young commune to an intelligible unity. As is usual with fertile and original works, his book did not go unchallenged and led to an intensified exploration

[18] P. Villari, *I Primi Due Secoli della Storia di Firenze.* 2 vols. Florence, 1893-94. New edition, 1905.

of the archives and to better co-ordinated projects of publication. In fact, materials of such importance and variety were brought to light that they made possible a complete reshaping of Florentine history in accordance with the modern social and evolutionary emphasis. Prominent among this recent group of scholars working on a broader system were men such as Paoli, Gherardi, Hartwig, Santini, and Salvemini.[19] And no sooner did the older members of this group begin to pass from the scene than they were replaced by eager disciples such as Ciasca, Sapori, Ottokar, in whom the fires of politico-social research burned with undiminished ardor.

Agreeable as it would be to define the learned and often creative contribution of these contemporary or all but contemporary scholars, we shall have to content ourselves with singling out the monumental work of the greatest master of them all, Robert Davidsohn.[20] There are those who do not hesitate to hail in Davidsohn the most fruitful scholar among the many who since the revolution inaugurated by Muratori have made Florentine history their specialty. They would accord him this distinction on the strength of the vast amount of new material touching every phase of Florentine development he has uncovered not only in Florentine and Tuscan but in Italian archives in general. For within the whole peninsula there is no notable repository of materials bearing on Florentine affairs to which he has not resorted in his search for first-hand information. But if, as has happened in some cases, the critics extol his scholarship only to belittle his historical art, it is impossible to subscribe to this judgment, at least without important reservations. For Davidsohn, thoroughly imbued with the spirit of his generation, is dominated by the organic conception of society and has consistently striven to utilize the innumerable fresh data discovered by himself and others for the better understanding of the slow unfolding through the ages of the Arno commonwealth. Aiming to present an intelligible and unique whole engaged in an unbroken development under environmental stimulus as well as under its own indefinable impulsion, he has so well succeeded that, although many problems, as might be expected, have continued to baffle him, he has far surpassed in the close weave of his fabric his predecessors of every historiographical period. Indeed they make an almost painfully threadbare showing beside him enveloped in his sturdy, full-bodied garment. As the work has to date not advanced beyond the early decades of the fourteenth century, it remains to be seen if the

---

[19] Some of their labors may be here listed for purposes of illustration: C. Paoli, *Il Libro di Montaperti*. Florence, 1889. P. Santini, *Documenti dell'Antica Costituzione del Comune di Firenze*. Florence, 1895. A. Gherardi, *Le Consulte della Repubblica Fiorentina*. Florence, 1896. G. Salvemini, *Magnati e Popolani in Firenze dal 1280 al 1295*. Florence, 1899.

[20] R. Davidsohn, *Geschichte von Florenz*. 4 vols. Berlin, 1896-1927. Also *Forschungen zur Geschichte von Florenz*. 4 vols. Berlin, 1896-1908.

later volumes will prove equally substantial. The central organic viewpoint re-enforced by the disclosures resulting from a better co-ordinated attack on the documents was certain to prove particularly valuable for the earlier and rela-tively neglected stages of Florentine development. The great Renaissance writers took very slight account of these remoter phases and were content to limit their consideration of Florence to the Medicean rule. Should Davidsohn ever get to the Medici, a possibility which in view of his advanced years and the deliberate pace of publication hitherto maintained, is doubtful, he will enter more immediately into rivalry with this group of his predecessors and will find his own originality matched, on different and therefore essentially incomparable lines it is true, by theirs.

However, criticisms have been voiced against the work and may not be overlooked; for instance, against its immense, its positively astronomical scale. Although the author exercised in this respect a privilege within his choice, it committed him to a work of such spread and weight that other than specialists are not likely to read it without indulging in liberal omissions. This is regret-table, because if history is to maintain a secure position as a department of literature, it must not close the door upon the general reader. The cause of Davidsohn's imposing bulk is the absorption into his text of an immense num-ber of details accumulated to illustrate a story of slow growth. Although from his point of view these tiny multiplied data possess each one a distinct im-portance, they bring it about that the large structural lines of the work at times completely disappear. While this is a drawback and a flaw, it is only inter-mittently disturbing, for in the long run the organic pattern, central to the whole composition, never fails to arise again from the mass, binding the pro-fuse and usually significant matter into a finely integrated whole.

Even if Davidsohn's great work did not suffer from overspecialization and even if it went beyond the early fourteenth century to the fall of the republic, thus filling out its natural framework, it would not be the final history of Florence. For, let it be said once more, the final record of anything having, like the Arno town, a cultural significance the index of which changes with each new generation of men is an impossibility. There have therefore been histories since Davidsohn's which, though they are deeply in debt to both its facts and its viewpoint, take rank as independent works and are not just a rehash of the master-work. Perhaps the best of them is that of Romolo Cag-gese.[21] It exhibits a modern approach and critical spirit and, in spite of a self-satisfied and irritating dogmatism, comes off with a considerable sparkle. More-over, it traces the story of Florence from beginning to end and even, as might

[21] R. Caggese, *Firenze dalla Decadenza di Roma al Risorgimento d'Italia.* 3 vols. Florence, 1912-21.

be objected, beyond the end, since in the last volume it covers the wearisome and irrelevant stages of decay subsequent to the heroic demise of the republic in 1530. If the modern outlook requires that Florence be viewed as a social organism sustained by its native energy, there can be no valid argument for dissecting the remains after life has fled.

We have reached the end of our historiographical note, which was not intended to be and must not be confused with a bibliographical guide. Such a guide which, if ever undertaken, would win the gratitude of all serious students, will have to set itself a very broad task. Besides tracing, and far more fully than we have done, the general movement of Florentine historiography, it will have to classify, describe, and evalue all writings of every sort connected with the diverse fortunes and manifold achievements of Florence; and, because of the recent expansion of scholarly inquiry, it will have to give particular attention to the innumerable detailed studies of the last two or three generations. Our historiographical sketch was planned as an introduction to and, in a certain sense, as an explanation of, the present work. It is in no sense an apology, for an apology, if the purpose of history has been correctly set forth in the foregoing pages, is not necessary, since there is always room in a growing world for a new historical synthesis. If the synthesis is lacking in significance, the new version of an old story will quickly reveal itself as a work of supererogation. The simple criterion by which the reader of the present work may decide for himself the issue of its worth is to ask the question whether these pages revive or fail to revive the incomparable chapter of human experience that goes by the name of Florence. If the Arno city does not emerge from between the covers of this book as a living reality, if its noble civilization does not take on a fresh meaning, the author will and should be judged to have labored in vain. In that case he will have no reason to complain if his book should swiftly make its way into the capacious limbo reserved for literary efforts which have missed fire and serve no discoverable purpose.

HISTORY OF FLORENCE

I. Etruscan and Roman Florence

THERE is no better introduction to Florence than to mount one of the many hills by which it is surrounded and to let the quickened eye take in the noble physical setting in which the town is framed. For in the close relation of city, river, plain, and mountains lies the earliest and the most abiding clue to the history with which we are about to concern ourselves. Let us, therefore, after settling among a dozen possible lookouts on ancient Fiesole as our objective, ascend to this venerable forerunner of the more famous city lying at its foot, and having reached the wide piazza with its austere Romanesque cathedral, take the steep path that leads to the summit of the adjoining height. Here in remote Etruscan days rose Fiesole's arx or citadel. It has long since disappeared, but by a happy stroke of the magician Time its site is now occupied by the church, dormitories, and enchanted gardens of a Franciscan monastery, which, itself centuries old, goes back almost to the days of the Assisan saint.

From this incomparable outlook we command the whole dominion ruled by the Arno from the river's source in the lofty mountains of the Casentino to its junction with the Mediterranean at its journey's end. First in abrupt descents, then by more gradual inclines the crowded highlands fall away, hiding from sight the rushing river until it reaches the foothills directly under our eye and again disappears among the dense mass of roofs, domes, and towers constituting Florence. Beyond the city the valley gradually widens and the hills decline in height, though their march in ordered double file continues westward as far as the eye can reach. Between the diminishing elevations we trace the narrow ribbon of the Arno, flashing silver as it picks up the sun and sky, and visible almost to the western sea.

Turning again to the east, we note that the great chain of the Apennines, of which the Casentino range, the birthplace of the Arno, is but the central link, sweeps on proudly, not only to the south but to the north as well, curving westward around Fiesole until its columns encounter the north-south line of the marble-bearing Carrara group raising their sharp peaks along the Mediterranean shore. And suddenly we become aware that all this land of Tuscany, of which the Arno is the vivifying artery and Florence the natural focus, is a well-marked geographic unit constituting a broken plateau declining gently from the towering bastion of the Apennines to the low-lying Mediterranean Sea. While the Arno is the main stream, it has many tributaries coming from both north and south and, as the laughing landscape declares at a glance, the province is the home of a numerous and energetic farming population. An intense cultivation, conducted by means of terraces on which the vine and olive flourish, often extends to a considerable altitude before the too precipitous plunge of the upper levels with their mass of sliding rock defeats the effort of the industrious peasants to gain a living from the soil. However, only the summits of the high mountains are as a rule entirely barren, having ages ago been stripped of their waving forest crown by the improvident inhabitants. But who has time for economic regrets in the face of all this beauty? In spite of the arid mountain peaks, this Tuscany with its fertile bottom-lands, with its opulent vineyards and olive groves climbing every slope, with its industrious cities strung along the Arno from Arezzo at the source to Pisa at the mouth, with gracious Florence spread beneath our feet, with Pistoia and Lucca nestling unseen among the northern foothills, and with invisible Siena crowning the blue upland to the south over which runs the road to Rome—this seductive and infinitely various Tuscany, we are moved gladly to declare, is one of earth's garden spots in which God still walks as in the days of creation.

When in the distant ages we call prehistoric men first settled in this segment of the Italian peninsula, it was an untamed wilderness without a suggestion of its present evidences of an intense cultivation and multifold communications. Recent excavations have uncovered burial finds which make it certain that man's presence in Tuscany goes back many thousands of years. We know absolutely nothing of these first settlers of the Stone Age apart from the scant information disclosed by occasional tombs owing their discovery to the chance action of a peasant's pick or plow. The earliest inhabitants of whom we have a definite and relatively abundant knowledge are the Etruscans who have given the land and its dwellers the names whereby they have been known ever since. There is considerable likelihood that the Etruscans came to Italy by sea from Asia Minor. Supposing this migration to be a fact and to have taken place around 1000 B.C., we can without difficulty picture to ourselves the main conditions and stages under which the occupation took place. At that remote time dense forests affording excellent hunting covered all the uplands; and the many affluents of the Arno, which now are but torrents and disappear or almost disappear from view in summer, ran lustily the year round, while the Arno, itself at present no more than the ghost of a river in the torrid season, perennially rolled a broad sheet of water to the sea. There was fine fishing in these abundant streams which, in addition, served the descendants of the newcomers, as soon as they had acquired a firm footing along the bottom-lands, to float the products of the forests as well as the wheat, wine, and olive oil which they soon learned to grow to the Mediterranean Sea. Therewith the Etruscans touched a highway which they shared with many other peoples and by which they were free to exchange their native goods for the iron of Spain and the gold, silver, jewels, and pottery of those old and famous eastern centers of civilization, Egypt, Syria, and Greece.

These statements are not merely speculative; they are based on very considerable archaeological and even on some definite literary evidence. The scattered data permit us categorically to affirm not only that the ancient Etruscans were active farmers but also that they plied a busy trade with all the peoples of the Mediterranean littoral. There must too have been much warfare, for the settlers showed a decided preference for planting their towns on inaccessible hills and fortified each town with a powerful ring of masonry. At the side of this wall there regularly rose a soaring citadel. Fiesole, one of more than a score of characteristic Etruscan sites that can still be identified, bears witness in the massive remnants of its cyclopean wall to the political divisions as well as to the engineering skill and moral resolution of the Etruscan folk. A few hundred years after their arrival they had become sufficiently strong, or, to put it more correctly, a loose federation effected among some of their cities had become sufficiently strong, to assume the role of conqueror and to bring large sections of Italy, in addition to Tuscany, and more particularly Latium and Campania to the south, under their yoke. Recent investigations have established that they extended their rule over the young Latin settlement on the Tiber, called Rome, and that the kings with whom Roman history is inaugurated were probably nothing other than Etruscan tyrants who lost their throne when the Roman people rose against them and, casting them out, established a republic.

From this time on there was unceasing war between the vigorous, self-confident Roman republic and its former masters holding the hilly region to the north. For several centuries the battle swayed to and fro; but in the long run the Romans triumphed and by approximately 300 B.C. the Etruscan towns had one after the other been reduced to subjection. Thus the power of Etruria was broken and its independence came to an end. Naturally so striking a reversal may be set down as an important milestone in the resolute march of the Romans to complete domination in Italy. For us, however, who are concerned with Tuscany and not with Rome, its significance lies rather in the proof which it supplies that the old military prowess of the Etruscans had markedly declined. Their well-attested material prosperity, on the other hand, did not immediately follow the same downward curve. Indeed, owing to the greater measure of security which the firm Roman rule brought to Etruria and to the rest of the peninsula as well, production and exchange took on new life and the subjugated province became an important factor in the economic system of the expanding Roman republic.

It was under these general conditions that Florence was born. Around the year 200 B.C. the people of Fiesole, who had hitherto prudently clung to their fortified hilltop, made up their mind, since trade was now protected by a powerful central government and moved with the security provided by Roman military might along the convenient valley levels, to found a colony directly on the Arno. Somewhat to the east of the later historical Florence but within the range of its present suburban extension they built a small, strictly Etruscan settlement which prospered notably until Rome, seized with the digestive troubles growing out of its many too rapidly appropriated conquests, was convulsed with the violence of civil war. The Etruscans, among whom the memory of their former independence still lingered, sided very generally against the narrow nationalist and aristocratic faction headed by Sulla; and when Sulla was victorious they had to pay the price of defeat. For having offered a particularly stubborn resistance to the conqueror, youthful Florence, the infant of the Etruscan family of towns, was singled out as an example and in the year 82 B.C. was leveled with the ground. So complete was the destruction that it is only in recent times that the site of this first, short-lived, and Etruscan Florence has been definitely established.[1]

When after a brief interval the town arose again it was not as a colony of Etruscan Fiesole but of Latin Rome and with the conscious purpose on the part of the Latin founders of undoing the havoc caused by the recent devastating civil war. In the year 59 B.C. there was passed during the consulship and under the auspices of Julius Caesar an agrarian law which goes by his name (lex Julia) and which sketched a vigorous program of civic restoration throughout Italy. The Florentines of the poet Dante's day fondly believed that their city owed its existence to the personal intervention of the great Julius. That was a legendary exaggeration born of the desire of the medieval citizenry to be associated not only with conquering Rome but also with Rome's greatest son. However, since the founding undoubtedly took place in consequence of the reconstruction policy championed by Caesar, the medieval tradition was much less removed from the truth than most of the stories regarding the origins of the city believed in Dante's time and firmly rooted in Florentine consciousness to this very day.

The second Florence was not erected on the ruins of the first but somewhat farther downstream on the very ground which it still occupies. As no very great future was anticipated for the new venture, the ground plan, in the shape of the familiar square favored for the Roman camp, exhibits very modest proportions.[2] Its sides measured no more than five hundred meters, that is, hardly one-third of a mile. There was a wall with four main gates, one in the approximate center of each side, through which ran the north-south and east-west highways traversing the town. At their intersection and therefore in the approximate middle of the plan lay the forum or market, which for the convenience of traffic was relatively spacious. This forum corresponds to the Mercato Vecchio or Old Market of medieval times and in our day, although much enlarged by the ruthless destruction of a dark, picturesque tangle of adjoining streets, presents itself to view as the commonplace but spacious Piazza Vittorio Emanuele. The Romans erected a bridge across the Arno which, although in the course of time it had to be frequently rebuilt, is identical with the venerable, still existent Ponte Vecchio. The Ponte Vecchio served to conduct across the Arno the great northward road from Rome, the Via Cassia, which in passing through the town followed the line indicated by the

---

[1] The site of Etruscan Florence has been the subject of an acrimonious archaeological dispute which, in spite of the literary dust it has thrown up, is not very important. I have accepted the view of Davidsohn propounded in Vol. I, pp. 4-6, and supported by impressive evidence assembled in *Forschungen,* Vol. I, pp. 1-6. Davidsohn's opinion runs counter to the traditional view which identifies the site of Etruscan Florence with that of the later Roman Florence. Most of the local scholars such as Milani, Villari, and Santini have chosen on the basis of arguments which deserve respectful attention to adhere to the tradition. An eminently fair statement of their case is given by Villari, *I Primi Due Secoli della Storia di Firenze,* p. 61 note. New edition (1905). Santini indorses Villari in a review, *Arch. Stor. It.,* Serie 5, Vol. XXXV (1905), p. 453.

[2] A detailed plan of Roman Florence is attached to Davidsohn, Vol. I.

street now called Por Santa Maria and its prolongations. It is thus clear that Roman Florentia can still be traced in important topographical features of present-day Florence and, above all, in many of the north-south and east-west street lines.

Interesting as these identifications are, they do not permit us to deduce that the Roman town ever rose to be more than an unimportant provincial center of the greatest empire of antiquity. Like every other daughter of the great capital on the Tiber, it boasted, in imitation of the mother-city, an aqueduct, baths, a theater, and various temples to the gods. They have all completely disappeared, although their location has been determined and sections of their foundations have been uncovered by careful excavations conducted in the eighties and nineties of the nineteenth century. In the course of time and in proof of a certain modest expansion Florentia developed suburbs extending beyond each of the four main gates, and in the eastern, apparently thickly populated, suburb there was erected an amphitheater for the gladiatorial games and animal hunts which were a characteristic expression of the hard-featured warrior civilization of Rome. As the line followed by the circular outer wall of this rather ambitious monument can in part still be traced in the curve of certain house fronts in the neighborhood of the present Piazza Peruzzi, we may regard these crumbling segments of brick masonry as the most consid-erable single relic of the Roman city which has come down to us. In spite of the evidence that Roman Florence presented itself to view as a small-scale copy of the greatest capital of antiquity, it remains true that so long as the mother-city continued to dominate the world Florence played a humble, provincial role and fell with hardly perceptible weight into the political scales. It was rarely even as much as mentioned by the historians of the empire. Concerned with recounting the great affairs of state, they had no occasion to rescue from oblivion the happenings in the obscure and sleepy market center on the middle Arno.

On the strength of the decidedly meager body of evidence which has come down to us, we may think of Roman Florence as reaching its greatest bloom and prosperity during the early period of the empire and as then participating in the startling general decline of the Roman state and society. This was already so far advanced by the fourth century after Christ that the Romans themselves lost hope and ceased to struggle against fate. Consequently when with the fifth century there came the determined onslaught of the German tribes, the already demoralized empire went down before it like a spent fighter. It was in the year 405 A.D. that Florence experienced its first siege at the hands of an army of marauding barbarians under a Gothic leader named Radagasius. The invaders were beaten off and a great victory was won, but it is eloquent evidence of the hopeless Roman decline that the imperial armies were not led by a man of Roman birth but by Stilicho, a German tribesman in Roman employ. What is even more significant, Stilicho's victorious forces were made up entirely of hireling Goths and Huns. The battle fought on the broken ter-rain between Florence and Fiesole turned out to be the last crushing defeat Rome succeeded in administering to the barbarian invaders of Italy; and the only unequivocally Roman feature about the event was that of the two contending barbarian hosts the Roman state was the paymaster of the victors. Having long ago ceased to take any interest in their government, the timorous and despicable Romans had of course also broken with the custom of serving their country by enlisting in the army. This fact alone, although it appears concomitantly with a score of other evidences of moral and civic exhaustion, would serve to explain the catastrophe which overtook them and their moribund civilization. The unexampled decline constitutes an epic of disaster that concerns us only insofar as it reveals what happened in Tuscany and Florence when the last remnant of the old imperial authority broke down and successive German tribes attempted to set up their own rude barbarian government on the ruins.

But before in the following chapter we focus on these groping labors of political reconstruction under barbarian leadership, we must take account of the last great event which befell within the Roman world before its dissolution and which, because it gradually drew the conquering German tribes within its orbit, is absolutely basic to the whole subsequent development of Italy and Europe. This monumental event is the coming of Christianity. After slowly gaining a footing in the Mediterranean world, where it was obliged to meet the competition of a large number of rival oriental faiths, Christianity in the fourth century won a complete victory and swept not only its other eastern rivals but also ancient Roman paganism from the field. Three landmarks may be set down here to help us recall the almost vehemently sudden triumph. In 313 A.D. the new faith was for the first time conceded complete toleration by an imperial decree (Edict of Milan); a little more than a decade later, in the year 325, the first General Council of the Christian church met at Nicaea in Asia Minor under the presidency of Constantine the Great, the first Roman emperor to profess Christianity; and before the close of this same century the Christian victory achieved its logical conclusion in the outlawry of every other form of divine worship. While the rival faiths, and especially Roman paganism, undoubtedly continued to thrive under cover for a long time to come, Christianity had gained a legal monopoly which gave it an incontestable authority and prestige.

Contrary to the flattering legend which gained currency among the Florentines in the Middle Ages, the new faith did not establish itself solidly on the banks of the Arno till at a relatively late period and long after the days of the apostles. Moreover, the first authentic Christians who appear as residents of the provincial Roman city were not even native Florentines but itinerant traders from the eastern Mediterranean. They were either Greeks or Hellenized Asiatics from Syria and Asia Minor. This closely falls in with what we might expect when we recall that Christianity came to birth in a small Jewish community of the east and that it gained its gentile following by gradually spreading into the surrounding areas of Greek culture. It was the slow but steady expansion of the gentile element that before long made Christianity a formidable influence. Under these circumstances we need feel no surprise to learn that it was Greek, Syrian, and Jewish merchants who, having adopted the new faith, first carried it, along with their more material wares, into the Latin west. Wherever, in pursuit of profit, these easterners formed a commercial settlement, they created a Christian nucleus which acted as a more or less power-ful center of attraction on the Italian, Spanish, and Gallic natives among whom they dwelt. That the probably feeble Greek colony in pagan Florence for a long time had very little success in making converts is indicated by the fact that in the persecution of the Emperor Decius in 250 A.D. the single Arno inhabitant to suffer martyrdom was Minias—a Greek. He was buried on the hill to the east of the town which afterwards received his name (San Miniato). To him and to his place of burial we shall have occasion to return in connec-tion with the medieval awakening of the city.

It took another hundred years after the martyrdom of Minias before native Florentines were won to the novel oriental faith in large numbers; and it was not till the end of the fourth and the beginning of the fifth century that paganism was sufficiently discredited to be completely routed from the town. The leading figure in this final stage of the Christian triumph was none other than the most vigorous and shining exponent of Christianity in that period, Bishop Ambrose of Milan. In 393 A.D. this great man, distinguished among his contemporaries as both a practical statesman and a fiery Christian evan-gelist, fled from Milan, owing to a conflict in which he had become involved with the reigning emperor, and sought refuge in Florence until the storm had blown over. During his stay on the Arno of over a year he performed a his-toric act of which we have accurate knowledge: he dedicated the church of San Lorenzo, the simple forerunner of the church of that name which still stands.[3] Furthermore, he consecrated as bishop of the city a certain Zenobius, who is sometimes called the first bishop of Florence, although this honor can hardly, strictly speaking, be his, since for the year 313 there is mention of an earlier bishop by the name of Felix. If the document which mentions Felix is authentic, Florence already had a Christian bishop some eighty years before the time of Zenobius. Be that as it may, the Florentine bishopric was in all probability not solidly established until Zenobius became its incumbent and made the newly dedicated church of San Lorenzo his episcopal seat. This view is strengthened by the circumstance that his fellow-citizens so fondly cherished the memory of Zenobius that his fame survived the obliterating darkness which after his time descended on Florence and all Italy in the train of the rude Germanic invaders. The victorious persistence of the bishop's reputation can best be explained on the hypothesis of his services to the en-feebled city. More particularly it may have sprung from his having been still in office as the spiritual ruler of Florence during the terrifying first siege, in the year 405, which the hitherto safe town underwent from a mixed army of pillagers under Radagasius. The long period of Roman decline preceding the siege had been an age of waxing superstition and miraculous interventions. Consequently when, as already noted, the plunderers were disastrously beaten in battle, the good bishop, who, as the story went, had promised his people rescue through divine intervention, was, together with the God whom he worshiped, given full credit for the outcome. Although almost everything connected with Zenobius remains conjectural, it is clear that Christianity was

[3] On St. Ambrose's Florentine sojourn see Davidsohn, Vol. I, pp. 34-36.

so greatly strengthened during his incumbency that shortly after the beginning of the fifth century we may regard paganism as having become virtually extinct on the Arno.

Under these prospering circumstances the location of the episcopal seat outside the city, at San Lorenzo, where the great Ambrose had consecrated Bishop Zenobius, was bound to be challenged. Clearly a cathedral church ought to lie within the town serving as the capital of the diocese. Nothing was done to mend the awkward situation until the seventh century when a bishop, whose name has not come down to us, boldly transferred his seat from San Lorenzo to the newly risen church and baptistery of San Giovanni, just inside the city wall. At the same time he established his personal residence among the ruins of a Roman bath directly west of San Giovanni on what is now, owing to the leveling of the original building, an open piazza serving as approach to the present episcopal palace. When San Giovanni (which still stands) became too small for the growing town and in its turn failed to satisfy the needs of a new age, the cathedral was again moved. This time the church of Santa Reparata was selected as the central church of the Florentine diocese, and Santa Reparata, afterward rebaptized Santa Maria del Fiore, has retained its primacy to this day.

The three successive seats of the Florentine episcopal see, San Lorenzo, San Giovanni, and Santa Reparata, are enumerated at this place chiefly for the purpose of calling attention to the inconspicuous saint for whom the first small church to occupy the site of the present imposing cathedral was named. It was because the later Florentines knew nothing whatever of Santa Reparata and became secretly ashamed of having their leading house of worship named for an insignificant and unfamiliar resident of heaven that they renamed their cathedral after the most popular intercessor of the culminating Middle Ages, the Virgin Mary.[4] The interesting fact for us, who are engaged in tracing the earliest beginnings of Christianity in the Arno city, is that the historical Reparata was a lady who at a very early date suffered martyrdom in distant Caesarea in Asia Minor. If she was held in high esteem in Florence and, as can still be proved, in a large number of other trading centers of Italy and southern France, that was because the men who dedicated churches to her were visitors from the orient, fellow-countrymen of hers, who came to the Latin west to earn a living by trade but who at the same time, as sincere Christians, erected the first churches to serve the religious needs of themselves and of such native converts as they might succeed in bringing into the fold.

That Christianity was first brought to Florence by Greek, Syrian, and Jewish merchants is an interesting but relatively unimportant fact. What alone really matters is that Florence became wholeheartedly and unanimously Christian at the very time when the Roman state crashed to the ground. Rome perished, but Christianity, the youngest child of Rome, survived. The cultural catastrophe was therefore not so complete as appeared at first glance. For

---

[4] Villani, VIII, 9, tells us that the church of Santa Reparata received its new name of Santa Maria del Fiore in the year 1294 (actually 1296), but that the common people continued to cling to the familiar name. It took more than a hundred years for the new name to displace its homely predecessor.

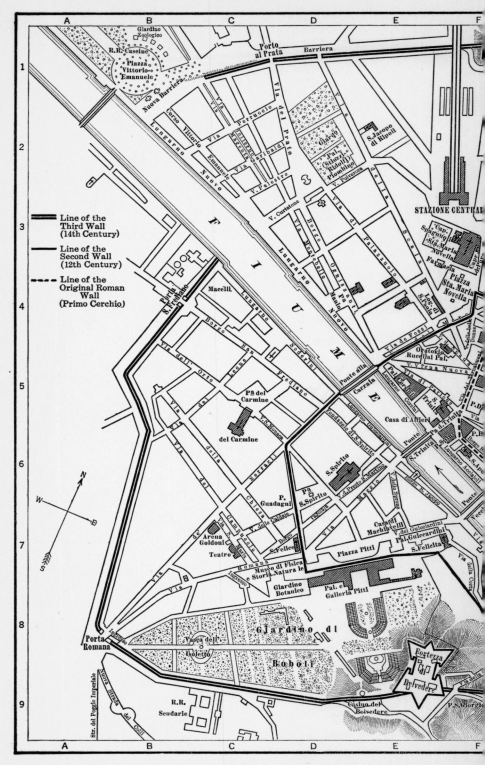

FLORENCE SHOWING ITS THREE WALLS AND THE LEADING PUBLIC BUILDINGS

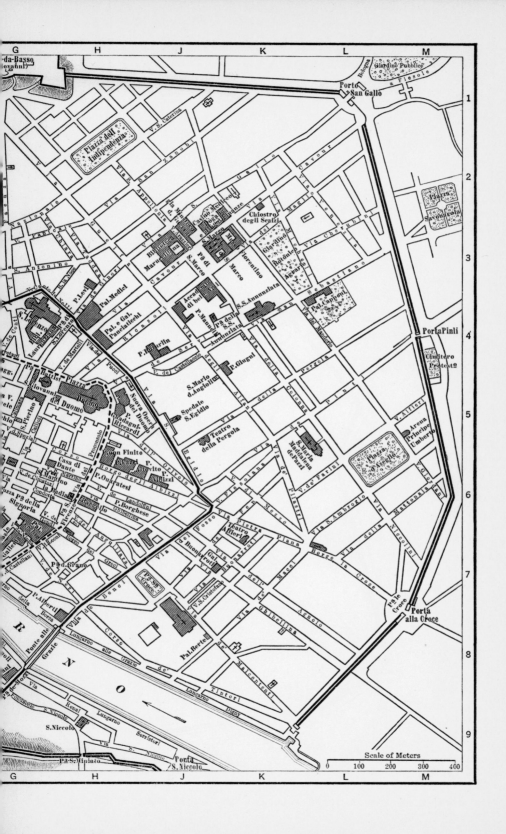

Christianity, beginning, like all other mystery religions, as a faith and an aspiration, had under Roman legal influence expanded into a vast organization, a universal church, in which important elements of Mediterranean civilization were incorporated and by which they were cherished and preserved. The energetic new institution, famous as the Roman Catholic church, became the point of departure of the new or western civilization destined in the course of time to take over and develop the Mediterranean heritage. In the creation of the new culture the city of Florence, whose role in the vanished classical world had been entirely negligible, took a most active part. Indeed so significant was the Florentine contribution that to define and appraise it is the leading purpose of this book. We may therefore agree that the true starting-point of our venture is the Germanic conquest of Italy by which Roman Florence was engulfed and in the course of which it physically disappeared. But in taking leave of Roman Florence we should never forget that from the dying civilization to which it belonged was salvaged the youngest and sturdiest feature of the Roman state, the Christian faith and church. It was with this singularly fruitful endowment that Florence entered on the new or medieval phase of its existence, a phase destined to lift it to a place of unsurpassed distinction among the famous cities of the world.

II. Italy and Her Invaders

I F DURING the Etruscan and Roman periods Florence led an obscure provincial existence, the situation for a long time experienced no substantial change when the coming of the German barbarians put an end to the Roman empire in the west and inaugurated the new period of history we call the Middle Ages. This meaningless term has got itself so firmly established in the English as well as in all the other European tongues that it is futile to attempt to displace it. However, from any angle taking account of fundamental social processes it is clear that what we call the Middle Ages is nothing other than the first stage of a new civilization, which slowly got under way on the dissolution of the great classical civilization and which, by a steady unfolding of its energies through the succeeding centuries, has culminated in that occidental or western civilization which, for better or for worse, has in the course of the most recent generations spread over the whole world. Although the expression Middle Ages will have to be retained, it is important to understand that it will be used here to designate a period in which the birth and death of social forms mingled as they always do, but in which, from the viewpoint of the subsequent development of Europe, the significant and outstanding feature is the appearance of vigorous, fresh shoots destined to become a magnificent and richly individual growth on the imperishable tree of life.

In thus asserting in regard to the Middle Ages that they are the earliest phase of the new civilization which arose on the ruins of the Roman empire, we date them as beginning approximately with the fifth century and as continuing into the eleventh century, that is, we hold that they embrace the years from about 500 to 1000 A.D. These five centuries, constituting the deep Middle Ages, are followed by the later Middle Ages which extend from about 1000 to 1300. They may be considered a period of transition as they prepare the ground for what is commonly called the Renaissance. The Renaissance is, organically considered, the second main stage of western civilization and may be held to cover the period from 1300 to 1550. Because the precise division into periods here suggested is likely to give a distorted picture of the nature of social change, it should not be taken too seriously. The excuse for it is that for both historian and reader it constitutes a useful and even indispensable chronological device.

Now during the five hundred years of the deep Middle Ages our city of

Florence remains as completely hidden from view, and may therefore be presumed to have been as unimportant a human center, as during the preceding
five hundred years constituting its Roman period. But in the case of this second
five-hundred-year period we cannot with the same ease of conscience evade
the obligation of attempting to penetrate behind the veil. For during the deep
Middle Ages there took place the events and there were generated the forces
which prepared the ground for the emergence of Florence not only as a powerful political entity but also as one of the leading agents of the new civilization which was slowly disengaging itself from the turmoil of the times. It is
the Florence rising into view after 1000 A.D. with which this book is mainly
concerned, and a close scrutiny of the slight data bearing on its dark gestation
during the immediately preceding period becomes as legitimate as it is unescapable. But before we embark on this task it will be necessary to accept the
obligation of presenting in swift, summary form the vicissitudes of the whole
peninsula of Italy following the Germanic conquest. It is this conquest which
contributed important elements to medieval society, more particularly by introducing those politico-social changes which alone made it possible for Florence to rise from impotence to power, from the darkness of obscurity into the
light of fame.

The mixed army of barbarians led by the Goth, Radagasius, which in 405 A.D.
was defeated outside Florence, was the forerunner of a long succession of German invaders whom the enfeebled Roman empire, never again defeating,
proved itself unable to resist. Like the provinces of Gaul, Spain, and Britain
and simultaneously with them, Italy fell gradually a prey to the barbarians.
After seventy years, in 476, a crisis was reached in this process of barbarization
which cannot be overlooked. In that year Romulus Augustulus, the last Roman
emperor of the West, was forced to yield his shadowy authority into the hands
of a German chief, Odoacer, and was peremptorily ordered by him to descend
from the throne. True, the Roman emperor of the East, seated in his capital
of Constantinople, entertained the view that the western provinces were by
this usurpation only temporarily alienated and that, ideally at least, they still
belonged to the one and indivisible *imperium romanum,* of which he was the
lawful head. If, owing to pressing difficulties nearer home, he did not promptly
defend his constitutional rights, that would not hinder a successor from defending them the moment a more favorable opportunity should arise. Under
Emperor Justinian, as we shall see, that auspicious day dawned, and Italy became once again by conquest through an imperial army an immediate province
of the Roman realm. Justinian's triumph turned out to be ephemeral and the
barbarians speedily retrieved their fortunes. Nonetheless, it is a fact of the
greatest importance for the history of medieval Italy first, that the empire of
the East did not for many centuries cease to lay claim to the peninsula, and
second, that for many generations after Justinian's time it retained within its
grasp, even though that grasp was steadily weakening, scattered segments of
the Italian coastal area. In short, in one way or another the Eastern empire
continued to figure as an element in the complicated play of Italian medieval
forces which must always be reckoned with.

Brushing aside the detailed comings and goings of the roving barbarian hordes who plundered Italy at will during the harassed fifth century, we shall come at once to the Ostrogoths, who in the year 489 crossed the northeastern Alps under their king, Theodoric. They are important for us because, coming less to plunder than to colonize, they set up the first Germanic state on Italian soil. They succeeded in this purpose because they had at their head a sovereign who, in addition to being the typical brave warrior of the period of the migrations, was a man of such exceptionally broad and enlightened views that he may without fear of contradiction be called a statesman. That Theodoric, the Ostrogoth, should have succeeded in mounting to a political level high above the average barbarian chieftain, he probably owed to his having been exposed by a long residence at Constantinople during his youth to the declining but still irresistible attractions of Roman civilization. In this manner, while continuing to share the contempt with which every German leader regarded the decadent Romans, he acquired a feeling almost akin to religious awe for the great organized structure of the Roman state. His highest ambition came to be to enter the service of this majestic creation and to perpetuate its power. It throws an interesting light on his attitude that he did not enter Italy with his swarming followers till he had received a formal commission to this effect from Emperor Zeno. Thus fortified, he successfully disposed of Odoacer, the German tribal chief who since the usurpation of 476 had been holding the land in subjection, and set up his own rule at Ravenna. He chose Ravenna as his seat because during the final phase of the Western empire it had served as the administrative capital of Italy and further, because by means of this residence, he could palpably present himself before the inhabitants of the peninsula as the representative of the legal sovereign. Far from irregularly robbing the natives and subjecting them to the capricious violence of his warriors, as all his German predecessors had done, he honestly and sincerely desired to bring them peace and security. In this he succeeded so well that during the thirty-odd years that his reign lasted his Roman subjects enjoyed an ordered existence such as they had not known for several generations. To effect this considerable change he was obliged, as the first item of his policy, to put an end to the long succession of raids which in recent decades had been devastating the peninsula. The only available instrument for bringing this about was his own Gothic host. According to the program which he put into effect, his stalwart people were to be the missing army of the Roman community of Italy. With protective garrisons stationed at all the strategic points the peninsula would be secured against further Teutonic invasions, thus permitting the natives to go peacefully about their various occupations much as in the great days of the empire.

It was a program devised to bring into a practical interdependence the two realities of contemporary Italy, the Roman state and society which was without military might, and German military might which, in a civilized sense, was neither a state nor a society. Theodoric was the point of junction of the two realities which otherwise had nothing in common and were by their nature mutually exclusive. As soon as the occupation was effected the king provided for his land-hungry Goths by assigning to them for their support a third of the property of the great landowners. That was an incisive but not an unreasonable measure when we consider that the Goths, though technically *hospites* (guests), were in reality conquerors, that they had to be provided for some-how, and that in return for a regulated maintenance they were required to render a primary social service. Having satisfied the demand of his warriors for an adequate means of support, Theodoric refused to entertain any further dispossession of his Roman subjects. In fact he did not scruple to use his prac-tically unlimited power as commander-in-chief to keep his Goths strictly within their assigned bounds. They were the military arm of the state living on Roman soil by the labor of Roman hands. Their continued separateness as a people was indicated by their subjection not to Roman but to the tribal Gothic law which they had brought with them. The civilized Romans on the other hand lived under the familiar Roman law administered by Roman judges. It will be readily believed that the two juxtaposed but distinct societies regarded each other with spontaneous aversion. And it will also be conceded that they would not have remained harnessed together for a day, had it not been for the genius of their common sovereign. No sooner therefore had the great Theod-oric died in 526, leaving his power to his grandson, a boy of ten years for whom his mother acted as regent, than this very personal system disastrously collapsed.

The minority of the new king and the clamorous incongruity of the Roman and Gothic societies were not the only factors in the overthrow. Although the Goths had been converted to Christianity even before they entered Italy, they were Christians of the Arian sect and, branded as heretics by the dominant Catholic church, invited the scorn and hatred of the Catholic Romans. This religious division was another and very potent influence accounting for the Gothic disaster. The final and most decisive factor in their overthrow, how-ever, was the Emperor Justinian, a man of great energy and far-ranging views, who had mounted the throne of the Eastern empire a year after Theodoric's demise. Gazing intently westward, Justinian came to the conclusion that the moment had come for reassuming the direct rule of Africa, Italy, and, if pos-sible, of the other alienated western provinces as well. Accordingly, he em-barked on a policy of conquest which put a sudden end to such pacification as had been achieved by Theodoric's system and which transformed Italy into a bloody battlefield for the next twenty years. Successful beyond expectation in his first assault on the Goths, Justinian learned to his sorrow that his opponents were a sturdy people of undaunted courage and abundant resilience. Again and again he had to send his armies, first under the famous general, Belisarius, and then under the even more capable Narses against the dwindling but stubborn hosts of the enemy; and when finally, a little past the middle of the sixth cen-tury, the last remnant of the Goths had been annihilated, it was a ravaged, depopulated, and tragically exhausted Italy which had been brought back into the Roman fold.

Even so, not for long. From a country reduced to the utmost misery by the terrible Gothic war, Narses, the emperor's viceroy and alter ego, had to extract the taxes necessary to pay for a costly army and administration. As a devoted servant of a distant and autocratic master he wished to prove not only that conquered Italy was self-supporting, but that it could even contribute to the maintenance of the luxurious imperial court on the Bosporus. To this end he unscrupulously applied the tax-screws; and as he could not count overmuch on the fidelity of the native Italians, he employed, especially in the upper categories of his administrative service, a host of imported Greek officials. It was frankly a Greek or Byzantine, that is, a foreign government that Narses conducted at the capital city of Ravenna. Undeniably the fast-ebbing Roman civilization was benefited by the influences which radiated from the Greek officials, who still moved on a culture level high above the debased Latin west. The churches of San Vitale and San Apollinare in Classe, which still adorn the now shrunken and provincial city by the Adriatic, furnish impressive evidence of a creative vigor which continued to characterize the east at a time when the west had already definitely lost its moral, intellectual, and artistic energy. But it may be doubted that the Italians took pleasure in the cultural superiority of the new rulers. Brought forcibly back into the empire, they learned that they had merely exchanged a Byzantine for a Gothic master and that they were no better off than before.

Then with the suddenness that had marked the long series of their sufferings since the first failure of the Roman strength, a new catastrophe befell. The great statesman, Emperor Justinian, died in 565, leaving the throne to his nephew, Justin II. Almost the first act of the new sovereign was to supplant the victorious and too self-reliant Narses with a more pliant tool. Encouraged by the confusion caused by this change of governors, another mass of German barbarians gathered behind the curtain of the Alps and in 568 descended into the northeastern plain. The new invaders were the Lombards, one of the most backward, undisciplined, and brutal of the northern peoples. For some generations before their appearance in Italy they had been pushing gradually southward from their home along the shores of the North and Baltic seas in the hope of casual loot and, more important still, of fertile lands capable of furnishing them with a steady and abundant supply of food.

The story of the Lombard conquest raises many puzzling questions which can only be answered partially or not at all. Since these newest Germans were a poorly organized horde constantly threatened with falling into independent units under rebel leaders, how did they have any success at all? And having gained a foothold at one or another point of the valley of the Po, how did they with their meager administrative experience manage to keep control? Why did the Byzantine army content itself with a purely defensive policy and from first to last offer so despicable a resistance? Putting these questions to one side as incapable of better than a speculative answer, let us note that the conquest was like the inundation of a river which floods a considerable area and, after an occasional halt or even a recession, against every reasonable expectation begins to mount again. In simple truth the capricious Lombard inundation of the Italian peninsula continued for generations and at no time, not even at its height some two centuries after its beginning, did it ever completely cover the land from the passes of the Alps to the straits of Messina. The feature above all others that needs to be observed about this particular and doubtless most important of all the German invasions is its geographic limitations. Starting at the foothills of the Alps the Lombards gradually occupied the Po Valley and on reaching the Apennines pushed along their ridges far into the south. Be-

cause they constituted a primitive army ill equipped to carry on siege operations and, owing also to their lack of ships, they were unable to capture any
seaport which offered resolute resistance. Unexpectedly feeble as the Byzantines proved themselves on land, they possessed the valuable asset of a fleet
and were thus able to maintain themselves in the Venetian lagoons, at their
capital of Ravenna, at Rome and its environs, at Naples, and around the whole
bend of the southern coast. The aim of the Lombards from the first was and
never ceased to be the possession of the whole peninsula; but even under their
greatest king, Liutprand, who reigned from 712 to 744, they did not gain control of the coveted coastal areas. True, shortly after Liutprand's death they had
the satisfaction of capturing Ravenna and its dependent district, thus bringing
almost all of northern and central Italy into the kingdom. The duchy of Rome
held by the pope and serving as the capital of Christendom they never brought
under their yoke. And they never acquired Naples and the stretch of seacoast
that outlines the foot of the long Italian boot. Because the Lombard conquest
thus fell short of its object, it divided Italy—tragically as most Italian historians
affirm—into three political areas which it is startling to observe remained separate and distinct throughout the medieval and modern periods down almost
to our own day. There was first the Lombard kingdom comprising the bulk
of the peninsula; next came the duchy of Rome, nucleus of the later State of
the Church ruled by the pope; and finally there was the south, where the
Greeks long continued to hold sway and where, after the dislodgment of the
Greeks, a succession of other conquering powers, of which we need not take
account at this point, gained control.

If the Lombard conquest was geographically less extensive than that of the
Ostrogoths, even a superficial investigation will serve to show that it had social
and economic consequences which were far more profound and lasting. To
begin with, the Lombards did not, like the Goths, come to Italy as allies of the
Roman emperor to settle and rule the peninsula with his consent. On the contrary, they came as his enemies and, being ruthless barbarians, who, unlike the
Goths, had not previously experienced any of the refining (and enfeebling) influences of Mediterranean culture, they were prompted by no higher motive
than the gross desire to possess themselves of the lands and chattels of their
victims. To them the Roman state, more enduring than brass according to its
classical encomiasts, appeared as a thing of lath and plaster, and they swept it
aside more from a childlike passion for destruction than from any deep-laid
political plan. In effect they wrote finis under the long and impressive history
of Roman civil administration. But if this administration now disappeared
from public view, that does not necessarily mean that it was utterly destroyed
in all its numerous ramifications. Haphazard survival at scattered places of
some of its institutions is more than probable; but in view of the mental back-
wardness of the Lombards and of the furious war they waged with the Roman
empire represented by Byzantium, it is certain that they did not repeat the
Gothic experiment of two juxtaposed societies, each supreme in its own field.
Italy was their prize and by means of sword and fire they broke down every
resistance to their will in order to get and retain possession.

The chief objective of the barbarians was the land, for the land would support them by the labor of the slaves and serfs (*coloni*), who, under the long imperial regime, had cultivated it for the benefit of the great landlords. We must understand that these three terms, slaves, serfs, landlords, describe the outstanding social elements of the late-Roman agrarian system. The Lombards had only to get rid of the landlord class, either by outright murder or by driving its members into exile, and success was theirs. Without further ado they would acquire title to the expropriated fields, while the slaves and serfs, left undisturbed, would work the farms exactly as before except that the surplus product of their labor would now go to another set of masters. That this social revolution was attended by horrible excesses against the Roman upper class is attested by the echo still audible in the records which have come down to us; but it is more than probable that the Lombard violence hardly touched the great mass of the agricultural population. The rude government which the barbarians set up in measure as they took over the control of the country was founded wholly on Lombard experience and Lombard tribal law. According to this law only the Lombards were free, that is, they alone enjoyed full citizen rights. The former Roman freemen, the landowners, no longer cumbered the earth, or, if they did, can only have escaped destruction by absorption into the class below them, the lowly coloni. Under the Roman system there had been of course a legal distinction between this agricultural group, which may be broadly described as serfs, and the still lower group of the slaves. While the imposed Lombard law did not fail to take account of this distinction, nonetheless both classes were bondsmen in its eyes, and the sole body in the state enjoying the rights of freemen were the victorious invaders. The quality of freedom pertained to the individual Lombard by virtue of his twofold capacity of warrior and landlord.

The Lombard state signified the forceful imposition on Italy of a harsh, cruel, and primitive politico-social system under which the peninsula made its final plunge into barbarism. The conquered Romans themselves became barbarized and the last dim tapers of classical culture guttered and went out. Then, after a hundred years of all but complete darkness, there came, hardly perceptible at first, a turning-point. When after three generations of practically continuous warfare with the invaders the Byzantine empire had failed to cast them out, the eastern government declared itself ready to make peace on the basis of each warring party keeping as its own what it happened at the time to hold. The treaty—it was signed around 677—for the first time gave the Lombard conquest an unambiguous legal standing and by encouraging personal and commercial intercourse among the hitherto hostile groups closed the first and utterly brutal period of Lombard history. Another circumstance tending to improve peninsular conditions was that after a hundred years of residence on Italian soil the Lombards themselves were no longer what they had been when they first arrived. Under the immediate pressure of geographic conditions they had at a relatively early stage accommodated their northern dress and diet, unsuited to the Italian climate, to the native standards. Soon after this change they became bilingual; and after a further lapse of time they replaced their Germanic tongue entirely with the more cultured and flexible Latin idiom of their subjects. Already very dissimilar from its classical prototype, this idiom was rapidly assuming the characteristics of that offshoot of the Latin speech which came to be known as Italian.

But the circumstance offering the most convincing indication that the Lombards were being slowly reshaped by their social environment was their gradual absorption into the fold of the Catholic church. Before coming into Italy, like many of the other wandering German tribes, they, too, had become converted to Christianity. Superficial Christians no doubt, they were—a much more serious failing according to current views—also false Christians of the same Arian type as their Germanic predecessors, the Ostrogoths. In the eyes of the Italian natives, who were Catholics, and especially and implacably in the eyes of the Catholic pope, their heterodoxy was a heinous offense. Even before the important accommodation with the emperor of 677 the Lombard royal family had become persuaded that it was the part of political wisdom to abandon a faith productive of the rancorous resentment aroused by Arianism. With the rulers making spiritual submission to the pope, their Lombard subjects speedily followed the same road. By 700 A.D. at the latest, the Lombard state had become organized ecclesiastically in dioceses under orthodox Catholic bishops who accepted the pope as their divinely appointed head.

These developments, considered in their totality, permit us to conclude that by the eighth century a fusion between conquerors and conquered was definitely under way. It took the form of the gradual absorption of the thin upper stratum of the ruling Lombards by their more numerous subjects in town and country. In short, the Lombards went through a process of Romanization or, since they in their turn helped impress a changed physical and moral character upon the natives, we may with even greater propriety speak of an amalgamation effected between the two groups. The product of the fusion was essentially a new people, the medieval Italians. It would be rash to say that by the eighth or even the ninth century this new people has stepped upon the scene invested with all the characteristics that afterwards distinguished it; but it is entirely permissible to insist that by the above-mentioned centuries all the forces were already busily at work from the interplay of which the medieval Italians arose. Undoubtedly they would owe most of their traits to the Roman side of their inheritance. Their speech and their religion and all the subconscious habit-elements that these subsume derived exclusively from that source. Moreover, under King Liutprand (of the first half of the eighth century) the submerged Roman law began to reassert its latent energy. Since it had never been relinquished as the basis of its organization by the Catholic church, it followed that when the Lombards finally adopted Catholicism they were obliged to accord the Roman law formal recognition by permitting the Catholic clergy to live under it. A close scrutiny of the juridical situation reveals that in other ways besides ecclesiastical usage the Roman law experienced a revival, for the statutes issued by King Liutprand accepted it as the personal law of occasional individuals among his subjects who were not of clerical standing. Thus by almost imperceptible stages it took its place at the side of the hitherto exclusively dominant Lombard law. While this revival of Roman legal norms indicates conclusively that by Liutprand's time the Lombard kingdom had broadened its cultural basis, it becomes clear from other evidence which

has reached us that it was also becoming politically stronger and better consolidated. Under King Liutprand there functioned an improved administrative
machine which gave him for the first time since the coming of his people into
Italy an effective sovereignty over his state.

Without the least doubt it was precisely this auspicious development of the
Lombard state which caused its overthrow. For, prompted by a sense of increased authority, King Liutprand took the natural but hazardous step of resuming the interrupted conquest of Italy. His immediate goal became the old
imperial and present papal capital, the city of Rome. In spite of repeated attacks
he did not succeed in capturing this august center, but he imposed his design
as a primary duty to the state on all the sovereigns that came after him. Theoretically in King Liutprand's day Rome and its immediate environment constituted a duchy subject to the Eastern or Byzantine emperor; but as the
enfeebled emperor was no longer able to protect his dependency, its defense
against Lombard aggression fell automatically to the lot of the leading local
figure, who was, of course, the pope. But the pope, too, lacked the means with
his own unaided strength to resist a long-continued Lombard pressure; and
when he became persuaded that the Eastern emperor either would or could not
help him, he appealed for succor to the most powerful of the Germanic kingdoms founded on Roman soil, the kingdom of the Franks.

Therewith we encounter a turning-point in early medieval history, for we
have reached the famous alliance between the popes and the Frankish mayors
of the palace for their mutual advantage. In return for the pope's crowning
the great palace official, Pippin, king of the Franks, thereby enabling him to
displace the legitimate Merovingian line, the usurper twice crossed the Alps
with an army and obliged King Liutprand's successor, Aistulf, to desist from
his stubbornly renewed attacks on the papal capital. As an additional measure
of punishment Pippin took from the defeated Aistulf the province of Ravenna
and presented this territory, familiarly called the exarchate, to his papal ally
(756). The famous so-called donation of Pippin has ever since been regarded
as the rock on which the popes were enabled to erect their temporal power.
When a new king, Desiderius by name, mounted the Lombard throne, he
stubbornly resumed the now traditional anti-papal policy of his predecessors.
The new attack on Rome drew Pippin's son and successor, Charles, across the
Alps; and Charles, determined to have done with half-measures, continued the
war against Desiderius until he had forced him to abdicate the throne. In 774
the Lombard kingdom passed into Charles's hands, and thus, after two hundred years, the Lombard chapter of the German invasions of Italy came to
an end.

The victory of Charles the Great—the towering Charlemagne of medieval
poetry and legend—inaugurated the Frankish phase of Italian subservience.
The new sovereign saw no reason to change greatly the administration which
the Lombards had gradually evolved. Originally the kingdom had been divided
into provinces ruled over by local leaders called dukes or *duces*. They exercised such extensive power within their respective jurisdictions that whenever
the Lombard king was lacking in initiative, they comported themselves as
practically independent rulers. For this reason the later and stronger sover-

eigns attempted to supplant the dukes by means of officials called *gastaldi* more immediately under royal control. Dukes and gastalds remained a characteristic feature of Lombard administration till the conquest effected by the Franks. Unhurriedly and by degrees the great Charles replaced both types of officials with Frankish counts (*comites*), in whom as his personal appointees he naturally had more confidence than in Lombard agents inherited from a discredited regime. Behind the new king and his administrative representatives Frankish adventurers poured into Italy in such numbers that some historians feel justified in speaking of a new and appreciable Germanic influx. In any case, the Franks, who, like all the barbarian peoples, carried their native law with them wherever they went, brought it about that with their advent to power the Frankish law was accorded an equal standing in the kingdom with the ruling Lombard and Roman codes.

The vigorous personality and rare executive ability of the Frank conqueror brought Italy a greater measure of peace and prosperity than it had enjoyed since the days of Theodoric. Charles continued to extend his power in Europe until the new Germanic kingdoms had one after the other passed under his control. It was his unchallenged authority over most of the former Roman provinces seized by the barbarian conquerors that now precipitated an event of the greatest significance for all subsequent history. This was the coronation of the king of the Franks as Roman emperor of the West. On Christmas Day of the year 800 Pope Leo III performed at Rome in the church of St. Peter the coronation ceremony conferring this high title on the Frankish chief. In so doing, Pope Leo set a precedent from which in later centuries his successors on St. Peter's chair drew sweeping claims of supremacy over the restored empire. Although the papal assumptions were never fully accepted by the emperors and were even frequently and emphatically denied, the popes, supported by their vast spiritual prestige, succeeded in keeping them alive. The fatal result of Leo's famous act was that pope and emperor became entangled in a relationship which made them, in spite of their theoretic partnership in the rule of Christendom, bitter and, in the end, irreconcilable enemies.

In some quarters the renewal of the Roman empire brought about by the coronation of Charles the Great has been represented as a historical delusion and absurdity. While there is much to be said against any attempted revival of a dead past, it has been argued in this particular instance that, since Charles had gained actual possession of the bulk of the western lands, he might without conspicuous impropriety employ a title which had once served to express a commensurate authority. Be that as it may, it was an unfortunate circumstance that the vast political edifice of the Frank sovereign was a personal creation which, even before he died (814), exhibited unmistakable signs of a threatening dissolution. Under his son and successor, Louis the Pious (814-40), the disintegration proceeded apace and at Louis' death led to a complete and startling collapse. This emperor had three sons who, after coming to blows over the paternal inheritance, with better sense than might be expected of their very mediocre endowment agreed to partition it among them. In 843, by the treaty of Verdun, they carved the vast Frankish state into three areas, two of which approximately corresponded to the regions later identified as France and

Germany. The third area was composed of the former Lombard kingdom with the addition of a broad belt of transalpine territory (Lotharingia) lying between the two northern shares. This third share, the largest and most important of the three, was accorded to Lothar, who, as the deceased Louis' oldest son, had already been permitted to assume the imperial crown. In this manner the Carolingian house, fallen into three branches, continued to rule over western Europe. As for the imperial title, inhering as it did in Lothar's line, the view became current and gradually hardened into a tradition that its employment was dependent on the control of Italy and the consequent coronation by the pope in the historic capital of Rome.

By his general ineffectiveness Emperor Lothar I proved himself a typical Carolingian degenerate. Already during the reign of his vacillating father, Louis, the Saracens, who for some generations had been swarming over the Mediterranean Sea, had taken to harrying the Italian coasts. For their ravages, which steadily grew worse, Lothar was unable to find a cure, and under his successors an even less effective resistance was made against the enterprising pirates than by himself. Let us be just to Lothar and remember that such strength as he and his successors might unfold depended on the concurrent action of their great feudal subjects. But these proud and selfish aristocrats refused to yield obedience to their sovereign and mockingly left him in the lurch. In 875, amidst ominous signs of waxing political chaos, the line of Italian Lothar became extinct. Thereupon the two remaining Carolingian branches, the French and the German, promptly urged their claims to the Italian crown. Representatives of these lines even crossed the Alps in the hope of adding luster to their names; but when it came to the defense of Italy against the pestilential Saracens, they refused to assume this heavy responsibility and pusillanimously retired to the safer ground of their respective northern homes. We may regard the feeble gestures they made in Italy as so much shadow-boxing and agree that the Carolingian rule of Italy terminated with Lothar's line. Through good and evil fortune it had lasted almost exactly one hundred years (774–875).

There followed a period of outright anarchy which in its turn lasted for something rather less than a hundred years. It was the mark of this perturbed era that a crass feudalism gained the upper hand, prompting every ambitious duke and count to pluck at the Italian crown. In connection with this royal symbol the interesting fact calls for notice that it was at this time, that is, it was during the latter part of the ninth century that what had thus far figured as the Lombard crown came to be designated by the more inclusive name of the Italian crown. By a related change in phraseology and thought the term *regnum lombardicum* began to yield its place in official documents to the term *regnum italicum*. We have given due weight to the fusion which, already during the Lombard period, was being effected of the diverse racial elements of which the population of the peninsula was composed. Of this uninterrupted assimilation the slight but significant modification of traditional legal forms may be adduced as effective additional evidence. Recent Italian historians have gone so far as to attribute to this period of desperate social degradation the symptoms of a dawning sense of what they call *italianità*. Italianità is not quite patriotism, much less is it what we moderns signify by the term national-ism. It is admittedly a rather indefinite sentiment, which, however, by grad-ually gaining ground, encouraged the inhabitants of Italy, regardless of origin, to think of themselves as a single and separate European group. The assertion in however feeble a form of italianità in the anarchic interlude we are treating is a decidedly interesting phenomenon.[1]

More immediately important than this faint flicker of a unifying purpose within the legal-minded administrative class of the peninsula are the continued devastating invasions which in this period of the utmost feudal anarchy afflicted the unhappy land. To the Saracen inroads, of which we have already heard, were now added those of another people, the Magyars. If the later Carolingians, who, in spite of their decline, still possessed some authority, had proved them-selves incapable of defending the coasts, what happened during the terrible post-Carolingian confusion may be left to the imagination. With no one to oppose them, the plundering corsairs came and went at will. Established along the coasts of Africa and Spain, the Saracen pirate communities were in pos-session of all the western areas submerged by the great flood of conquest which in the seventh century issued from Arabia, and which in the following century brought and for many generations to come kept the Mediterranean Sea under Moslem control. It was not till around the year 1000, that is, it was not till two hundred years had passed, that the Italians set about remedying the intolerable situation by the only available means, which was to provide themselves with a navy. When that time came, it was not, as we shall learn hereafter, the central government but the maritime cities, organized as self-governing republics, which put an end to Moslem encroachments and inaugurated a new era for the commerce and shipping of Christendom.

The other body of invaders, the Magyars, represent a crisis which, though fully as sharp as that associated with the Saracens, was of far shorter duration. Not till the end of the ninth century (899), in the very midst of the period of anarchy we are here considering, did they make their appearance on the Italian scene. Swift-moving horsemen, hailing originally from Asia, they had only recently pushed into Europe, where they had taken possession of the mid-Danubian plain which their descendants, commonly called Hungarians, still occupy. Using these rich grasslands as their base, they pushed their raids fre-quently far into Germany and also poured periodically across the Alpine passes to burn and plunder at pleasure the villages and towns of northern and north-central Italy.

For the disastrous civil strife among the great feudality, which by paralyzing the action of the central government was chiefly to blame for the Saracen and Magyar incursions, no cure was found until one of the baronial factions drew King Otto I of Germany into Italy by appealing to him for succor against a rival group. This Otto belonged to the Saxon line which had succeeded to the German crown after the dying-out, early in the tenth century, of the German branch of the Carolingians. In response to the invitation of the Italian mag-

[1] For a suggestive discussion of these matters see L. Chiappelli in *Arch. Stor. It.*, Serie 7, Vol. X ("La Formazione Storica del Comune Cittadino"), and P. S. Leicht in *Rivista di Storia del Diritto Italiano*, Vol. III (1930), pp. 5-20.

nates he came to Italy, first experimentally in 951, and with a more clearly
defined program ten years later. On this second occasion he succeeded in making himself undisputed master of what since Carolingian times was called the
Italian kingdom, and with complete propriety he could therefore request the
pope to invest him with the imperial crown. The ceremony which duly followed has been hailed as a second restoration of the Roman empire of the
West. In close imitation of the first renewal under Charlemagne the coronation of Otto was performed at Rome in the central church of Christianity, the
basilica of St. Peter.

However, it was not the Roman empire, it was not even the empire of
Charlemagne that was revived on that February day of the year 962 when Pope
John XII anointed Otto I and proclaimed him the successor of the Caesars.
Otto already bore the title German king and, ruling Germany, possessed a
land which was no more than a fraction of the vast territory subject to Frankish Charles when, over a century and a half before (800), he had been invested
with the same crown. In point of power, therefore, Otto was a much less imposing figure than the towering Charles. Indeed on close scrutiny and in spite
of the imperial title, Otto had accomplished no more than to bring Germany
and Italy under a single scepter. Consequently the leading historical result of
Otto's conquest of Italy, a conquest which logically entailed the coronation
ceremony at St. Peter's, was that it inaugurated still another chapter of the
long subjection of Italy to her invaders. The new chapter may be called the
German phase which, beginning with Saxon Otto in 962, was, if not juridically,
at least effectively terminated in 1250 with the defeat and death of the greatest
of all the German medieval sovereigns, the Hohenstaufen emperor, Frederick II.

The union of the crowns of Germany and Italy effected by Otto I in 962
goes commonly under the name of the Holy Roman empire. It is a peculiarly
apt designation for the political creation of the great Saxon sovereign since it
takes cognizance of the fact that the new polity was sufficiently different from
both its immediate Carolingian and its more distant Augustan predecessor to
deserve a special appellation. The tenth century successor of the Roman empire
came to be so closely tied up with concepts and conditions peculiar to the
Middle Ages that this revived empire was necessarily different from its earlier
manifestations. Moreover, the difference resulted so largely from the close association of the resurrected empire with the church and Christianity, that to
qualify it as holy was unescapable. At the time of Charles the Great the interaction of state and church, though close, had not yet assumed the later intimacy, and consequently the revival of the Roman empire connected with his
name did not quite achieve the character of sacredness associated with its
Ottonian offspring. Essentially, however, this talk of holy and less holy is
beside the mark. The distinction between the two Roman revivals is a matter
of power and reduces itself in substance to the circumstance that Charles's authority was so great that he dominated both state and church, while Otto's
position was much weaker, especially in regard to the state. While he may be
said to have kept the church in considerable dependence, he was obliged to
share the civil power with the great feudatories; and not very long after his

death the popes began to grow so strong that the unchallenged control of the church gradually passed into their hands. For all its "holiness," in fact even because of it, Otto's empire was a far less vigorous entity than that of Charles. But this admission should not blind us to the circumstance that the Holy Roman empire was a towering structure which for almost three centuries dominated the European scene.

If long before its fall the Italians began to turn against the Holy Roman empire, that was because they had been brought to see it in its true light as a foreign conquest and were determined to be free of its control. Concomitantly with its decline in Italy the empire lost its grip also in Germany; but there, owing to its being after all the national kingdom of the Germans, it managed to survive the thirteenth century and was not finally swept into the limbo of dead dreams till the vast European revolution connected with the name of Napoleon. The successive stages of its long decline interest us, for the present at least, little if at all. We are about to concern ourselves and we shall be occupied for a long time to come with the Holy Roman empire when it was the leading power of Europe and territorially embraced both Germany and Italy. But the equality between the two members implied in this statement did not conform with the facts. In reality Germany had effected the conquest of Italy, and the complicated situation which resulted for the peninsula from this enforced foreign control justifies our calling the period from 962 to 1250 the German or Holy Roman empire phase of Italian history.

The great event of the German phase dwarfing all others is the slow rise of Italian national feeling resulting at last in the overthrow of the German domination. The political instrument through which the national victory was brought about was the self-governing town, called by the Italians the commune. The multiplication of communes, the growth of their commerce and industry, the increase of their wealth and power enabling them to challenge the emperor and his feudal followers, constitute the central feature of this age. But not only does the commune signify a political and social revolution of the first order, but from it sprang also an admirable intellectual and artistic culture, the rise of which put an end to the long medieval night into which ignorance and barbarism had plunged the land. No wonder that the question as to how this dynamic institution originated became in after days an issue exciting the most passionate curiosity. From the fifteenth century, intellectually dominated by the humanists, and more decidedly from the eighteenth century, overshadowed from the point of view of historical inquiry by the great Muratori, the commune has been in the forefront of Italian medieval studies. And although only the origin of the single commune of Florence is our concern in this book, the general issue is so engrossing and at the same time so appropriate to this summarizing chapter projected as a background for the origins of Florence that a brief indication of the line which the communal inquiry has taken, especially since the rise with the labors of Muratori of modern scholarship, is indispensable.

For Muratori the question took the form of whether the Italian commune, which becomes faintly visible about the time of Otto I and multiplies rapidly after the year 1000, should be ascribed to a resurrection of the vanished Roman

municipal institutions or should rather be regarded as an outgrowth of the free
institutions of the Lombard and the other German invaders. Declaring in favor
of a Germanic origin, Muratori took a position which was generally accepted
till the beginning of the nineteenth century when it was challenged by the
German historian, Savigny.[2] This scholar attempted to establish the unbroken
continuity of Roman municipal institutions (and of Roman law as well). His
thesis was sharply disputed by a number of German and Italian historians,
among whom Troya[3] and Hegel[4] stand out most prominently. So successfully did the proponents of the Germanic origin of the free commune establish
their case that their results were not called into question for several decades.

We thus come to the close of the nineteenth century when historical scholarship entered on that more intensive phase described in our introductory historiographical sketch. The new phase was made possible by the accumulation
of a vast wealth of fresh documentary material and by the closer focusing by
scholars on much more narrowly circumscribed bodies of fact. Under these
circumstances detailed information became available that made the earlier results appear incomplete and gradually aroused the suspicion that the problem
had been attacked from a wrong angle. For Muratori as well as for the investigators of the first half of the nineteenth century the question had been
posed in such a way that they were bound to declare for one of two possible
answers. That was the kind of simplification to which human nature is prone
but which regularly fails to square with the discoveries of a more microscopic
scholarship. What began to appear, first vaguely, then with more and more
definiteness, was that the communes when studied individually and not in the
mass failed to range themselves meekly in one or the other of two indicated
categories. In point of fact it became increasingly clear that the new municipalities were not so much either Roman or German as the substantially original
creations of the new era which began with Otto I and the formation of the
Holy Roman empire. Since this revised position has resulted from a general
movement of recent critical thought, it would be vain to attribute priority to
one or another of its many representatives. But it is wholly permissible to affirm
that the foremost champion of the new attitude was Robert Davidsohn. It was
in 1891 that Davidsohn published his epochal article on the origin of the consulate[5] and five years later followed it up with his presentation of the origin
of the Florentine commune in his *Geschichte von Florenz.*

As we shall in due time deal in some detail with Florentine origins as por-
trayed by Davidsohn it will suffice at this juncture if Davidsohn's contention
in regard to the rise of free communal institutions in general is made clear.
His starting-point is the undeniable fact that, owing to the extremely primitive
conditions that prevailed in Italy during the long centuries of barbarian rule,
the central government was always weak and functioned feebly or not at all
in local matters. Consequently all purely local affairs, involving such indispen-

[2] F. C. von Savigny, *Geschichte des Roemischen Rechts im Mittelalter.* 7 vols. Heidelberg,
1834-51.
[3] C. Troya, *Storia d'Italia del Medio Evo.* 17 vols. Naples, 1839-59.
[4] K. Hegel, *Geschichte der Staedteverfassung von Italien.* Leipzig, 1847.
[5] R. Davidsohn, "Entstehung des Konsulats," *Zeitschrift fuer Geschichtswissenschaft,* Vol. VI
(1891), pp. 22 ff.

sable immediate concerns as the upkeep of roads, bridges, and fountains, and the repair of the parish church, were left to the restricted group directly interested. This is the *vicinia* or *vicinanza,* the association of the neighbors of the countryside, which took these affairs into its own keeping and thus in an inconspicuous and almost invisible manner assumed a modest measure of self-government. In the once flourishing towns of the Roman period which had long ago dwindled to mere villages and market-places the same process is observable as in the country districts. The most familiar unit of organization within the town was the parish, and in town as well as country it was usually the parish members who made up a particular vicinia. When neighboring town parishes had common interests to debate, they would be moved to hold a general meeting, and on coming to a decision as to the action to be taken they would entrust a committee from their number with its execution. The committee members were called *boni homines* and were in effect a skeletal municipal government. With the slow but steady growth of the towns in the eleventh century the boni homines acquired a longer tenure and a greater dignity. This fresh advance was marked by the assumption on their part of the sonorous title of consuls. If we accept the advent of the consuls as a conclusive sign not only that the commune is born but that it is now a going concern, the theory of Davidsohn is that the new government springs from the earlier institution of the boni homines, who in their turn point to the neighborhood groups, the vicinie, as their vital germinal principle.

The books and monographs which during the last forty years have wrestled with Italian communal origins are literally legion. They are almost without exception well disposed to the Davidsohn theory of the commune being an original creation based on the self-help of the vicinie, but they often hesitate to accept the boni homines as the universal precursors of the consuls. And in point of fact instances have been found which do not permit the assigning to the boni homines of this decisive chrysalis role. Over and over again when the investigation focuses on a single commune some element appears which, if not entirely novel, represents a departure from the pattern characteristic of the other communes. Thus it has gradually become clear that in consequence of the barbarian invasions the conditions in Italy became so chaotic and varied so widely from point to point of even the same province that a general formula describing the evolution of communal liberty is unattainable and should be given up. The tendency prevailing at the present time is to insist on a multiple origin, that is, on the view that every commune owes its free institutions to a combination of conditions peculiar to itself. But this is not to abandon the inquiry or to leave it where it started. The gains since the famous work of Savigny have been enormous. In the first place no one any longer dreams of referring the commune flatly to either a Roman or a German origin.[6] It is admitted that Roman and German administrative institutions co-existed on Italian soil and may or rather must have entered into the new creation in a measure which it is the business of scholarship to determine in each instance.

[6] This is too absolute. Old theories die hard. Not so long ago the Roman thesis was very vigorously renewed by E. Mayer, *Italienische Verfassungsgeschichte von der Gothenzeit bis zur Zunftherrschaft.* 2 vols. Leipzig, 1909.

However, the decisive factor in the birth of the commune is a historical *novum* testifying to the emergence of a new vigor in Italian medieval society. It is this fresh biological energy that counts and not the occasional borrowing of Roman or Germanic forms that contended for supremacy during the dark centuries of unrelieved barbarism. And when we look for the invariable central germ of the new energy we regularly find it in the resumption of immediate self-help by small voluntary groups.[7]

This chapter has been an excursus into general Italian history planned to supply a convenient background for the unfolding of medieval Florence. Admittedly we have oversimplified, overschematized. The generous provisional acceptance by the reader of the periodization here suggested will have the advantage of enabling us to go ahead with our strictly local undertaking without too many interruptions to explain the developments within the whole peninsula.

[7] It will not be possible to do more than list a few of the works illustrative of this recent phase of the communal investigation. Davidsohn, *Geschichte von Florenz*, Vol. I, chap. 8. A. Solmi, *Le Associazioni in Italia avanti le Origini del Comune*. Modena, 1898. A. Solmi, *Il Comune nella Storia del Diritto*. Milan, 1922. L. von Heinemann, *Zur Entstehung der Staedteverfassung in Italien*. Leipzig, 1896. P. Sella, *La Vicinia come Elemento Costitutivo del Comune*. Milan, 1908. G. Volpe, *Questioni Fondamentali sull'Origine e Svolgimento dei Comuni Italiani*. Pisa, 1905. G. Volpe, *Il Medio Evo*. Florence, 1926. G. Mengozzi, *La Città Italiana nell'Alto Medio Evo*. Rome, 1914. F. Schneider, *Die Entstehung von Burg und Landgemeinde in Italien*. Berlin, 1924. L. Simeoni, *Le Origini del Comune di Verona*. Venice, 1913. L. M. Hartmann, *Geschichte Italiens im Mittelalter*. 4 vols. Leipzig, 1897-1915. L. Chiappelli, "La Formazione Storica del Comune Cittadino in Italia (Territorio Lombardo-Tosco)," *Arch. Stor. It.*, Serie 7, Vols. VI, VII, X, XIII, XIV.

III. Darkness over Florence

THE deep Middle Ages, which we have agreed cover the five centuries following on the collapse of the Roman empire of the West, constitute the long incubation period of our western civilization. During all that time Florence drowsed in the obscurity of an all but impenetrable barbarism. It was not till around the year 1000 that the darkness over the town began to lift and that the new life commenced to stir which launched Florence on its historical career. In this chapter it is proposed to treat briefly the five-hundred-year period of gloom. Fortunately it has recently been pierced by a few scattered rays from various sources enabling us to arrive at some sort of an idea of what was going on behind the veil. Outstanding among these sources is archaeology with its sheaf of very definite revelations touching the physical vicissitudes of the town. Next, there is our general knowledge of Italy and Tuscany during the Germanic invasions which permits the drawing of inferences securely applicable to our particular municipality. Finally, a few documents, chiefly of an ecclesiastical order, have been recovered yielding information of a slight but direct and indubitable nature.

Because these scattered facts have only rather recently become available, the older writers resorted to free invention to fill the gap. According to the first local chronicler of merit, Villani, Florence was, toward the middle of the sixth century, completely destroyed by Totila, one of the later kings of the Ostrogoths. As an almost incredible confusion characterizes Villani's story of the event, it is not to be wondered at that he identifies Totila, who was a man and sovereign of parts, with the much earlier Attila, king of the Huns, the terror-inspiring *flagellum dei* of his age. Following its overthrow, when "not a stone was left upon another," Florence—still according to Villani—lay in undisturbed ruin throughout the Lombard period and was not rebuilt till the time of the Franks, when none other than Charlemagne himself took the good work in hand. These statements of the chronicler are unequivocally false, for neither was Florence destroyed by a barbarous Goth nor was it rebuilt after some two hundred and fifty years of extinction by a somewhat less barbarous Frank. Villani took over the story from his immediate predecessors, the fanciful myth-makers, and they were stirred to free invention due to the circumstance that no information whatever regarding Florence during the dark period of the Germanic invasions had come down to them. Pressed to explain the puzzling

29

silence, they postulated a dramatic Gothic cataclysm, followed, after a sleep of almost three centuries, by an equally dramatic resurrection.

What really happened at Florence during the Gothic and Lombard periods was the very opposite of striking drama, for the town obscurely vegetated in slow, uninterrupted decay. Never very important during the Roman era, it sank even lower in the social scale during the invasions, when the urban civilization of Italy, so long a-dying, went finally to pieces and the whole peninsula reverted to a rude, impoverished agrarianism. Florence repeated the experience of every town of the peninsula. The local stream of trade dried up, the population declined, the Roman public buildings, the temples, baths, and theaters were abandoned and crumbled to dust, and gardens and fields made their incongruous appearance within the narrow circuit of the walls. Too indolent and discouraged to remove the débris, the few remaining inhabitants raised such new shops and shelters as they might require on the steadily accumulating rubbish piles, until every trace of the Roman buildings had been covered up and the slowly rising medieval town was lifted to a level anywhere from four to ten feet above the level of its Roman predecessor.

All this has been fully demonstrated in recent generations by the labors of expert archaeological and historical scholars. They have established the sites of all the more important Roman buildings and have made it clear that the Roman walls, far from being leveled with the ground, as would have been the case if the reported destruction by King Totila had occurred, stood whole and unimpaired till as late as the twelfth century. Having by that time lost their usefulness, they were ordered removed because the town, now embarked on a career of rapid expansion, had burst its bounds and required for the protection of its citizens and their houses and property a second and ampler circle of walls. We may therefore fall in with Villani, after all, and agree that in the early Middle Ages Roman Florence all but completely disappeared from the face of the earth. However, instead of being destroyed by a Germanic conqueror, it perished painlessly from waxing senility, very much like the Roman civilization with which it was identified. As for the new, the medieval town, which slowly rose on the scrambled classical remains, it was for many centuries as inconspicuous and unimportant as the new European culture just beginning to rear its head.

We have already learned that it was the Lombard conquest which had more important consequences for Italy than any other German invasion. Next to the fertile valley of the Po, which from the completeness of its subjection to the newcomers came to be called Lombardy, a name it has retained to this day, it was the province of Tuscany which figured as a leading Lombard center. We have learned that these particular invaders were ferocious, plundering barbarians with no experience whatever of civilized ways, and that consequently they were slow in giving their conquest an even rudimentary organization. When something akin to order gradually emerged, we get a picture not without distinct and interesting political contours. It presents a king and court at the head of the state and residing commonly in the city of Pavia. The king was usually no more than a figurehead except in the rare instance when, endowed with great natural gifts, he was also favored by fortune. Immediately under him were dukes and gastalds presiding over the provinces and districts into which the kingdom was divided. The only difference between these two types of high officials seems to have been that the dukes, as the older dignitaries dating from the conquest, claimed the provinces under them by hereditary right, whereas the gastalds arose later and, serving as the personal appointees of the sovereign, were removable at his pleasure. We may fairly conclude that the gastalds indicate an attempt on the part of the later Lombard kings to acquire a more effective control of their kingdom. In Tuscany both dukes and gastalds occur and the Lombard folk took firm root in the province on the strength of a considerable influx. The invaders constituted an upper class of landholders and warriors who at the bidding of their military leaders, the king, duke, and gastald, followed them into the field.

That Florence, like every other Tuscan town, became a center of Lombard activity does not admit of the least doubt. Near the east wall, on land where now stands that majestic symbol of municipal liberties, the Palazzo Vecchio, there rose the characteristic watch-tower or Gardingo of the Lombards. Its existence till a time long after the Lombard period is amply attested. Its frowning presence overlooking the approaches from the east proves incontestably that Florence was one of the forts or military centers maintained by the Lombards to secure their rule. Other documents establish the erection under Lombard patronage of several churches, conspicuous among them the original Or San Michele, predecessor of the existing church of that name. If the theory warmly defended by Davidsohn is correct, no less an ecclesiastical edifice than the baptistery of St. John, one of the most famous as well as one of the most beautiful buildings still adorning the town, was erected in the Lombard era.[1] In no case is it possible to maintain that the two-hundred-year rule of the Lombards passed over Florence without leaving behind as much as a trace.

When in the year 774 the rule of the Franks superseded that of the Lombards, the administration of Tuscany underwent some changes which, at least for a time, made for a greater effectiveness. The Lombard dukes and gastalds were swept aside in favor of Frankish appointees, an official called a count being set over each town and its dependent district. Among his other functions the count, who represented the sovereign, acted as judge, and in connection with his judicial service we learn that, associated with him in finding the verdict, were a number of local assessors called *scabini*. The scabini were chosen from among the free residents of the town and it was by virtue of their free status that they shared in the administration of justice. They may be accepted as incontrovertible evidence of the achievement of a modest measure of municipal self-government as early as the Frankish period. In the age of anarchy following the extinction of the Carolingian line the scabini are still encountered here and there, although plainly they were no longer functioning regularly. With the advent to power (962) of Saxon Otto they vanished entirely from the scene. We can hardly be mistaken in referring these important municipal officials to a movement of political self-help which manifested itself

[1] Davidsohn, Vol. I, p. 72; *Forschungen*, Vol. I, p. 24. For a detailed discussion of the origins of San Giovanni, see chap. XV.

in the Frank period. Defeated by the spread of an anarchic feudalism, the movement could be counted on to reappear with the coming of more favorable conditions, when it would dig other and more permanent channels for itself.

Another important administrative feature appearing in Tuscany during the Frank period and probably ascribable to the enfeeblement of the central power under the later Carolingians was the rise of a dignitary bearing the title of margrave. Not only did the margrave exercise rule over all Tuscany, but so powerful was he that, as had been the case in the days of the Lombard dukes, he made, or at least aspired to make, the margravial dignity hereditary in his family. For over two hundred years, till the death in 1115 of the *gran contessa,* Matilda, of whom there will be much to say hereafter, the Tuscan margraves were the most powerful feudatories of the Italian kingdom. They usually made their residence in Lucca, which by being thus distinguished became the leading town of their territory; and they preserved their margravial authority from diminution by serving as count for every town of the margraviate. However, as they could not be present in all of the Tuscan towns at the same time, they had themselves represented in the towns other than Lucca by agents who appropriately bore the designation of vice-counts.

Under the administrative system established by the Frank conquerors each town was the head of the surrounding territory, town and territory together constituting a county (*comitatus, contado*). This division of Tuscany into counties is exceedingly important for the whole later development of the province. It certainly goes back to the Frank, quite possibly it goes back to the Roman period, when an identical unit of city and outlying district was called *civitas* and constituted the basis of the old imperial administration. The cropping up after a long lapse of time of an element of the Roman system (civitas) under a name (comitatus) having reference to a Germanic administrative division may serve to remind us how Roman and Germanic elements merged in the Middle Ages, and how mistaken it is to assert categorically that the free municipal institutions which appeared later are either wholly Roman or wholly German. Much more probably, when they are not an entirely fresh growth, they represent a fusion of both traditions.

In the ninth century, toward the close of the Frank period, when wildly anarchic conditions were rapidly gaining the upper hand, there took place an event which at a later time proved very advantageous for Florence. Under the Frank system Fiesole was one of the Tuscan towns which served as the administrative center of a dependent territory or county. For reasons which thus far have completely eluded the investigators, around the middle of the ninth century and certainly by the year 854 the county of the old Etruscan hill town was merged with that of Florence. Thenceforward Fiesole was a town without a county, while Florence commanded the largest contado in Tuscany.[2] The puzzling event, which apparently caused no stir, had no immediate consequences. There were as yet no municipal liberties and neighbor towns were not yet locked in mortal combat over markets and trade routes. However, when, two centuries later, municipal competition had reached this stage of ferocious

2 Davidsohn, Vol. I, p. 85; *Forschungen,* Vol. I, p. 27.

rivalry, it appeared at once that, as against not only nearby Fiesole but every other Tuscan town as well, Florence enjoyed a considerable advantage by finding itself provided with a larger dependent territory than any municipal competitor.

Admittedly the foregoing scattered data on Florence during the first five medieval centuries are too slight to give the town even the semblance of a physiognomy. Any disappointment a reader may feel will disappear when he reflects that the shrunken and barbarized Florence of that period can have had no features worth recovering. We are aiming in this book at the Florence that came to vigor after the year 1000; and the only valid reason for glancing at the stagnant period that went before is to arrive at some conception as to what the situation on the Arno may have been when the town at last awakened from its sleep and girded its loins for the race. Knowledge on this head is pertinent and even necessary; but more than from such isolated facts as those already enumerated, it will result from a general acquaintance with the conditions of the tenth century, out of which Florence, like all the other free communes, arose. To put the case as precisely as possible, we want to know the outstanding characteristics of Italian society at the time of Emperor Otto I and his immediate successors, and particularly we want to know the leading aspects of the two ruling institutions, the church and the state.

By way of introduction to such a survey we shall have to inquire how feudalism developed in Italy and what specific forms it assumed in the old core of the Latin world. Some writers are inclined to refer its origin back to the Lombards or even back of their time to the last phase of the Roman empire. In a strictly technical sense this is inadmissible, although the disorder of both the late-Roman and the Lombard period produced a condition favorable to novel and incipiently feudal practices with regard to land tenure. However, feudalism could not fully triumph until the central power had declined to the point of paralysis, and under the last Roman emperors as well as under the Lombard kings this was never quite the case. When Charles the Great took over the Lombard kingdom, the central power even experienced an increase, as appears from the merest glance at his remarkably vigorous administration. As we are already aware, his Italian kingdom was divided into counties under leading officials called counts. Not only were they appointed and removed by Charles at his pleasure, but they were also subjected to the periodic inspection of his famous traveling agents, the *missi dominici,* who were sent on their rounds for the very purpose of holding the counts in due submission to the crown.

Under the puny successors of Charles, his system of government rapidly crumbled and, before long, was succeeded by an unqualified anarchy. Then, and not till then, the last barriers of order broke down and the very complicated system of self-help we call feudalism came into being. It is not our business to describe it in this book in its innumerable ramifications. It will serve our limited purpose to call attention to some of the outstanding features of the appalling ninth- and tenth-century confusion. While there was still usually an administrative head or king, there was no king strong enough to enforce obedience. The consequence was that his local representatives, the counts, felt encouraged to make their power personal and hereditary. From having been officials subject to recall by their sovereign they aspired to become landed proprietors in their own right in enjoyment of as many farms, fields, and fortified castles as they could successfully appropriate. Voluntarily abandoning the towns or else driven out of them by the rebellious citizens, they settled in the countryside, where the estates and castles which they coveted were mainly located. Automatically by this development the church dignitaries, the bishops, became the leading personages of the towns. Without necessarily resorting to violence and often even at the pressing request of the townsmen deprived of their customary ruler, they assumed, in addition to their ecclesiastical duties, the public functions of the vanished counts. It was in the tenth century that the revolution culminated which made the spiritual lords, the bishops, also the civil rulers of the towns; and the movement, though general, was particularly characteristic of the northern, the Lombard, area of the kingdom.

In Tuscany the development took a different turn. There, as already noted, a great noble, probably himself originally a count, had succeeded during the declining years of Frank rule in bringing under his sole control the counties of Lucca, Pisa, Pistoia, Siena, and Florence. Owing to his exceptional position, he aspired to a more honorable designation than to the familiar one of count and either took, or by one of the shadowy sovereigns of the time was given, the title of margrave.[3] From the moment that he had gained a firm footing in Tuscany, the margrave exercised an authority hardly distinguishable from unqualified sovereignty. If, as happened from time to time even in the age of anarchy, an emperor-king held the throne who was strong enough to impose respect, the margrave would prudently agree to recognize him as his superior and to exercise the authority he held in the royal name. The statement holds also for the counts and bishops throughout the extent of the kingdom: they practiced independence, but if the suzerain chanced to command military resources, they did not hesitate to make a harmless profession of submission.

Now this breakdown of the central authority coupled with the rise of usurping local powers is not in itself feudalism. Feudalism is a system of order in disorder, and it arose from certain practices which the unutterably confused public situation just described brought in its wake. One of these practices is known as commendation. When the smaller landholders became aware that they were no longer protected in their rights by the king, they "commended" themselves to a more powerful neighbor, that is, in return for protection they offered the neighbor more vigorous than themselves certain specified services, above all, of a military nature. In due course the compact came to be sanctified by the ceremony and vows of homage, from which the superior emerged as "lord" and the inferior as "man" or "vassal." In measure as the great landholders, both lay and ecclesiastical, received the submission of their lesser neighbors, they acquired the character of local potentates, each potentate

---

[3] Not unlikely the early margraves were the counts also of the two remaining Tuscan counties of Arezzo and Volterra. That these two towns were not subjected to the rule of their bishops till around the middle of the eleventh century would appear from evidence presented by Davidsohn, Vol. I, pp. 198-99. Until subjected to their bishops, we may think of them as in all probability included in the margraviate.

commanding a company of vassals practiced in arms and prepared to follow him into the field.

The rivalry among these numerous new wielders of power was intense, the disturbances among them perennial. As is ever the case when society dissolves into its constituent atomic parts, a situation was created which cannot be better described than as a war of all against all. The conflict, turning around lands and vassals, involved the bishops no whit less than the lay lords. Possessed of vast properties, which they were obliged to defend, the bishops developed the same martial outlook as the nobles and were consequently threatened with estrangement from their original spiritual functions. And to this peril, let it be observed, the bishops of Tuscany, although they did not acquire the civil powers of the counts, were just as much exposed as the bishops of Lombardy, who in most instances did acquire them. In either case a bishop was a great landowner capable of giving protection to a smaller neighbor. That, as a great Catholic prelate, he had also a hallowed character would very probably incline the frightened possessor of a small freehold to consider that his act of submission was likely to bring him a double security.

Simultaneously with commendation feudalism took on another feature to which it chiefly owed such local vigor as it succeeded in acquiring—the feature of immunities. In measure as the central government broke down, the usurping lords took over many of its functions, especially those pertaining to war and justice. This deadly mischief the weak kings who played at royalty during the post-Carolingian anarchy were utterly unable either to hinder or undo. Indeed, in return for the small benefit of a formal recognition of their crown, they repeatedly found themselves obliged to legalize the seizure of public functions which had taken place. The usual procedure for doing this was to issue a royal charter enumerating the privileges (or immunities) of which a particular lord stood possessed. Clearly by such grants the ruler stripped himself of many essential features of sovereignty. Himself mortised henceforth into the crude system of feudalism, he exercised so strictly limited an authority that he was condemned to an all but complete impotence unless he happened to be a man of unusual ability. Ability of course performs wonders under any circumstances. In sum, power was no longer with the king but with the great landholders, lay and ecclesiastical. And because the age was characterized by religious zeal, a leading expression of which was the foundation of great monasteries, the heads of these monasteries, the staff-and-scepter-bearing abbots, also presented themselves to view as ecclesiastical landlords. Profiting by commendation and demanding and receiving immunities like the bishops, they were in every respect the peers of these older ecclesiastical dignitaries.

Such was the fluid and desperate Italian situation, when in 962 Otto I of Germany became king of Italy and Holy Roman emperor. Without any doubt he would, if he could, have re-established the vanished royal power. A real statesman, vigorous but prudent, he recognized that in the altered political circumstances such an attempt on his part would be fantastic, and that the only course open to him was to accept the accomplished feudal revolution.

Accordingly, he came to terms with the territorial magnates, the bishops, abbots, counts, and margraves, by formally enfeoffing them with their lands. In the northern or Po area he lent his support to the movement which had not yet exhausted its strength and which was pushing the bishops into civil authority in the towns. He must have reflected that with bishops who held office only for life he would not run the risk he did with lay counts of having the appointment take on a hereditary character. In consequence of Otto's policy it became the rule rather than the exception for a northern bishop to be also a civil ruler, a count. As Tuscany was under a margrave, Otto, following his policy of subscribing to the *status quo,* acknowledged the margrave, even though this nobleman, on the Saxon's descent into Italy, had sided against him. On being received back into favor, the margrave, Hubert by name, remained faithful to the new dynasty, as did his son after him. Of this son, Margrave Hugo, we shall hear later on, for it was during his reign that Florence emerged definitely into the light of history.

If it must be denied that Otto I built up in Italy an effective royal administration, he may without challenge be said to have given the troubled peninsula a greater security than it had enjoyed for over a century and a half before his advent. His most distinguished single service was to put an end to the devastating raids of the Magyars. In the year 955 he administered so capital a defeat to them on the Lechfeld in southern Germany that they lost their taste for the nomadic way of life and settled down to an agricultural existence on the Hungarian plain. Even before their incursions into Italy had ceased, we get evidence of a timid revival of trade coupled often with almost startling manifestations of fresh life in the towns. Left to themselves during the anarchy of the period preceding Otto, the towns had on several occasions given proof that they were no longer willing to play the role of mere passive victims of circumstance. After all, the ancient Roman walls, though in decay, could be restored and, in default of help from an impotent ruler, needed only to be manned by a resolute citizenry to foil the assault of the Hungarian nomads, invincible in the open country but incapable of conducting patient and extended siege operations. The habit of self-defense, once resumed, grew until it led to the creation of an organized town militia. Plainly Italian citizens who risked their lives in their own cause and who, as soon as they met encouragement from Otto's revived central government, began again to spin the threads of trade, were recovering from the cowardly dejection which had been the unbroken rule during the many centuries of the barbarian invasions. As social good and evil are in the last analysis alike referable to the quality and temper of the human spirit, we are well inspired to take account of the novel military and commercial activities manifesting themselves in the Italian towns. Without any doubt they may be signalized as marking the earliest dawn of that great communal era which was to challenge the dominant feudal order and bring it to its fall.

During Otto's reign, however, as well as during that of his successors for a long time to come, feudalism remained the characteristic institution of society and completely overshadowed the life of the peninsula in both its public and private aspects. So decisive was its dominance that it even threatened to denature and absorb the venerable and far more ancient institution of the church. For by imperceptible stages the church had become integrated with the ruling system to such an extent that bishops and abbots, and the pope as well, were no longer particularly distinguishable from the great lay nobles. By reason of their immunities they enjoyed temporal authority, and because of the conditions connected with its exercise they were involved in unceasing quarrels over lands and vassals. No wonder that, accommodating their conduct to the prevailing pattern, they assumed the brutal manners and purely military outlook of their lay rivals.

And yet the great feudalized prelates were in the first instance representatives of holy church and presumable exemplars of Christian piety and faith. True, this faith had long ceased to be the simple and naïve body of religious practices it had been in the age of the Fathers. It had become embodied in a church and, obliged to wrestle with practical necessities, it had learned that in order to carry out the vast social and religious program with which it had charged itself, it would have to have ample material resources at its disposal. This signified the possession of landed estates; and wealth in the form of land had for ages past been poured into the lap of the church as from a streaming horn of plenty. Touching these vast possessions the authoritative spokesmen of the church had never ceased to proclaim that they were under no circumstances to be understood as belonging to the clergy, the functionaries of the church, as individuals. The revenues the estates yielded were to be devoted to the maintenance of the ecclesiastical establishment, and whatever surplus there might be was supposed to be distributed among the poor. From the humblest priest to the highest prelate life was to be lived simply, even ascetically, detached from the pursuit of riches, personal ambition, and carnal delights. Such was the official doctrine, and to enforce it the popes and the councils had for centuries past enacted innumerable ordinances against every form of worldliness, and above all, against two evils to which the clergy had been found most commonly to succumb, the evils of bribery and of the flesh. Accordingly, all priests were strictly required to take the vow of celibacy and to eschew every semblance of traffic in clerical office. The latter practice was stigmatized as simony and denounced as one of the most heinous of sins.

Now it is easy to see how the clerical ideal embodied in the twofold solemn command to shun simony and fleshly concupiscence fared in the feudal age. Practically indistinguishable from their lay rivals, the great prelates tossed to the winds the obligations of their clerical status, lived in unashamed concubinage with one or more women, begot sons and daughters, for whom, as fond parents, they provided by robbing the endowments intrusted to their care, and at their death left behind a miserably depleted ecclesiastical domain. To be sure, whenever a resolute emperor assumed the scepter, and with the advent of the Saxon house there was for a time an unbroken succession of capable rulers, he would, as the official protector of the church, cancel the acts whereby an unscrupulous bishop had dispersed his possessions among relatives and favorites. Only through these repeated imperial interventions did the ecclesiastical foundations retain their character of vast landed units. That the emperor had also a personal interest in keeping them intact will be understood if we recall that they were essential elements of his power and that whenever death removed the reigning bishop or abbot, it fell to the sovereign to appoint the successor. As soon as such a demise occurred, a horde of ambitious aspirants hurried to the emperor's court and by a lavish expenditure of money and promises attempted to wring from him the coveted appointment. Not only did simony thus show its face openly, but the successful appointee would be almost sure to be a wholly worldly individual. His thought would revolve habitually around politics and war; he would make mock of his vows of celibacy; he would follow the emperor into the field clad in costly armor and attended by a clanking company of vassals; and in the occasional intervals of peace he would divert himself with the characteristic aristocratic amusement of the hunt. By the tenth century the misgoverned church had reached a degree of corruption that cried to heaven and threatened the ancient organization with an early dissolution. The very sentiment of religion, the most precious heritage of the common man and the rock on which the vast ecclesi- ·astical superstructure ultimately rested, was threatened with complete disintegration by the spectacle of the great clerical titularies shamelessly wallowing' in the black morass of a degrading materialism.

In this extremity and just in the nick of time the church was saved by one of those remarkable revivals that have been a feature of its history down to our day. That, divorced from the spirit which gave it birth, the church is no better than an empty husk will be readily admitted even by devoted churchmen; but why that spirit has repeatedly through the ages been threatened with extinction only promptly to be born again is something of a riddle. Be the cause what it may, the church has always been subject to this tidal movement. We have in this chapter dealt with a dying and dishonored church not without indicating some of the causes of its disease and shame. But around the year 1000 a revival set in which, before it had spent its force, gave Italy, and all Europe for that matter, a new religious aspect. Of particular interest to the lover of Florence is the circumstance that our town rose first and definitely into the view of history by championing the movement of ecclesiastical purification.

IV. Florence and the Religious Revival of the Eleventh Century

THE religious revival, the seeds of which were sown in the tenth and germinated in the eleventh century, was a movement as wide as the dominion of the Roman Catholic church. As this universal aspect is not our concern, as even the phenomena peculiar to Italy do not touch us except insofar as they happen to involve Tuscany, we are free to concentrate our attention on the neighborhood of Florence and to become acquainted with the character and *modus operandi* of the great revival by examining a particular instance.

Since the revival was a spontaneous movement of revulsion against the gross and palpable worldliness of the church, it was but natural that it should have had as its leaders and prophets individuals for whom the unworldly and ascetic features of Christianity constituted its vital core. Such men were likely, nay, almost certain, to be monks and hermits, that is, Christian believers who, after cutting the ties binding them to family and community, had in proof of their sincerity devoted themselves single-mindedly to the search for God. Even in the tenth century with its very general corruption men of this sort were not uncommon. To escape the temptations of the flesh they sought the solitude of mountain and forest; but often in their retreat they were visited by dreams and visions which obliged them to seek the crowded centers in order to call sinners to repentance and to proclaim the divine purpose of the Lord.

The first of these strange evangelists of whom we hear in the corrupt tenth century as carrying his message from city to city in Tuscany was a certain Romuald. Not a Tuscan by birth but a native of the Romagna, he was possessed of the fiery temper which has always distinguished the sons of this harsh Apennine soil. As is not uncommon with such enthusiasts, he had in his undisciplined youth yielded to every impulse of his passionate nature until, overwhelmed by a sense of sin, he had sought escape by prayer and flagellation. To complete his conversion from the world and the flesh he had buried himself in the savage mountains. But when, after a season devoted to his purification, he had become full to overflowing with the conviction of his mission, he was moved to seek the company of his fellows in order, like his ancient forerunners of the hills of Judaea, to discharge the burden of God's love or, in case he found his hearers disinclined to listen, again like his Judaean exemplars, to annihilate them with the thunders of God's wrath. It was in his own

39

Romagna that Romuald first testified against the terrible corruption of the clergy; but before long he crossed the mountains to carry his angry gospel along the highways of Tuscany. It is not recorded that he won any of the sin-hardened bishops to his views. But he did gradually gain a following among the common people; and surprisingly, and against all probability, he celebrated a triumph at the political and social apex of the province by bringing under his influence the margravial family.

Because of the relatively few documents which have come down to us, the line of Tuscan margraves beginning with the declining age of the Franks is imperfectly known, and those margraves whose names have been recovered pass before us like a procession of insubstantial shadows. The margrave of Romuald's day was Hugo, who held his post from about 970 to his death in the year 1001. With Hugo we come for the first time upon a margrave of whom we learn enough to arrive at some sort of opinion as to what manner of man he was.[1] His mother, Willa, on being left a widow had sought comfort in religion, and probably it was she who, first of her family, fell under the influence of the fiery hermit. A cure of the contemporary corruption much recommended by him and his like was the rearing of monasteries charged with reviving Christian zeal and serving as a retreat for holy men; and in the year 978 we hear of Willa founding at Florence, hard by the eastern wall and at the exact spot where it still stands, the famous abbey, La Badia (the abbey). It came to be called *the* abbey by the Florentines because it was for a long time the only creation of the kind within the city. Two decades after Willa's initial act Margrave Hugo in an outburst of generosity made over vast properties to his mother's foundation. As he was equally free-handed or, as we may even say, spendthrift in providing for the monastery of St. Michael at Marturi in the Elsa Valley, we may conclude that, as his life drew toward its close, he identified himself with increasing fervor with Romuald and the ascetic movement. So great was the gratitude felt for the magnanimous Hugo by the monks of the Badia that in a spirit in which we sense a somewhat too ready servility they elevated him, in the place of his mother, Willa, to the distinction of founder.

Margrave Hugo died on December 21, 1001, and was buried near the high altar of the church of the monastery which he had so richly endowed. The beautiful tomb which invites the admiration of the present-day visitor was erected almost five hundred years later. It ranks among the finest work of Mino da Fiesole. The original tomb was on a more modest but not unimpressive scale, for Hugo was laid to rest in an ancient Roman sarcophagus. The grateful brothers at once adopted the day of the margrave's death, which, the shortest of the year, was sacred to St. Thomas, for the annual memorial service of the founder. They have celebrated the event, without a single interruption, for now over nine hundred years. Dante, born within the shadow of the Badia, must have often witnessed the ceremony in his impressionable youth, for he saw fit to recall it in his immortal poem.[2]

In this same passage the poet celebrates Hugo, whom he admiringly calls *il gran barone,* as the stout trunk of the many-branched chivalry of Florence.

[1] A. Falce, *Il Marchese Ugo di Tuscia.* Florence, 1921.
[2] *Paradiso,* XVI, 128.

Doubtless the margrave, who, as his office required, was a great warrior, served in his day as the focal point of those influences from which sprang afterward the ideal of knighthood. The note of love and gratitude sounded by the verses is re-enforced from other sources. The fact is that both to Dante and to Dante's contemporaries Hugo was the earliest character of Florentine history to stand out with definite personal traits. During his long rule he had endeared himself to the citizens not only by reason of his munificence to a foundation of which they were justly proud, but also because he had given proof of a special affection for Florence by preferring it as his residence to Lucca, the traditional seat of the margraviate. Immediately after his death, stories began to circulate in his praise. In some of them he was even assigned the role, rare to the point of incredibility in a ruler of those brutal times, of champion of the humble classes against the violence of the strong. In short, since no people can flourish without heroes, as soon as the Florentines had advanced sufficiently to imagine a great future for themselves, they scanned their obscure beginnings and discovered just enough vitality in the scattered recollections of the Margrave Hugo to enable them to put his name at the head of the roster of great men required to feed their patriotic pride and spur them to great deeds.

The next name to emerge from the darkness of the age with definite individual characteristics is that of the Bishop Hildebrand. As there were excellent reasons for not hailing him as a hero, he was not, like Hugo, adopted into the official patriotic cult. Nevertheless we have such revealing information regarding him and he is so richly characteristic of his time that we cannot but profit greatly by subjecting him to a close scrutiny.

Hildebrand became bishop of Florence around the year 1008 in the manner and under the conditions inherent in the evil practice of episcopal immunities. By Bishop Hildebrand's time immunities were already of almost hoary antiquity. So far as the Florentine bishopric is concerned, we learn that as early as 874 or 875 a Bishop Andrew acquired a *privilegium* from Emperor Louis II, by which the episcopal estates were detached from the margraviate and subjected to Andrew and his successors.[3] The usual consequences put in a prompt appearance. The bishopric became the prize of ambitious, worldly men who spent their days in riotous living and squandered the possessions intrusted to their care among favorites and harlots. If the sovereign had not interfered from time to time to oblige the despoilers to return the alienated goods, the impoverished Florentine see would not have been able to fulfil its obligations to its subjects by discharging its spiritual duties. Such an imperial restorer was Otto I, who intervened vigorously against the bishop of his time, Raimbald by name, in order to force him to end his scandalous dilapidations.[4] Of course Otto was not moved by exclusively ecclesiastical considerations, for the episcopal lands constituted a fief which it was the emperor's secular interest to keep intact. In neighboring Fiesole the bishops had proved themselves even worse wolves than those of Florence, for by Otto's time the dispersion of the episcopal resources had become so complete that, in spite of his efforts and those of many of his successors, the bishopric was never restored to financial

[3] Davidsohn, *Forschungen,* Vol. I, p. 173.
[4] Davidsohn, Vol. I, p. 107.

solvency. Twenty years after Otto interfered to straighten out the tangled affairs of the Florentine church his son, Otto II, gave voice (983) to his indignation over the fresh misappropriations of Raimbald's successor, a certain Sichelmus.[5] So long as the bishops remained the frank worldings they were, it was apparently impossible to bring the episcopal finances back to health.

Steeped to their necks in feudal politics and utterly estranged from their spiritual functions, the bishops of Florence were not likely to lend an ear to the preachment of rude, skin-clad hermits who, like Romuald, descended on them from the wilderness of the Apennines. And so we come to Bishop Hildebrand, who was a most worthy successor of his immediate predecessors in that he bribed his way to office, did homage to his lord, the emperor, as though the bishopric were nothing other than an imperial fief, and played the absorbing role of feudal magnate by pursuing plans of personal grandeur and giving himself heartily to all the carnal delights forbidden to his cloth. Surviving documents inform us that whenever the emperor appeared in Italy the magnificent Hildebrand rode out to meet him at the head of his armed retainers, and that he dutifully performed all the acts required of a direct vassal of the crown. It is evident that he loved martial pomp and was insensible to the corruption with which he and his fellow-prelates were so manifestly spotted. For while he distinguished himself honorably from many of his colleagues by failing to maintain a whole harem of concubines, he did live with a woman in so frank and unconcealed a manner that he did not hesitate to sanctify his relation with her by the sacrament of marriage. The name of his wife was Alberga and she, the bishop, and their numerous sons lived together as a happy family in the *episcopium,* predecessor of the existing episcopal palace and, like it, directly west of the baptistery of St. John. Alberga must have been a woman of parts, a veritable virago. She took a passionate personal interest in all the problems of her husband's diocese. Whenever the bishop, conducting court for the purpose of giving audience to petitioners or of pronouncing judgment in quarrels brought to his attention, sat enthroned among his spiritual and temporal attendants, called in feudal language his *fideles,* Alberga brazenly took her seat at her lord and master's side. A very precious memory of such a court session has been preserved and illuminates for us as by a flash of lightning the crisis precipitated by the spreading activity of the reformers.

The scene falls approximately in the year 1020 and carries Alberga and a certain Guarinus as its leading dramatis personae. Guarinus was the abbot of a recently established monastery at Settimo, which, some five miles down the Arno, lay within the boundaries of the Florentine diocese. Bishop Hildebrand was therefore Abbot Guarinus's superior. But let the chronicler have the floor:[6]

This Guarinus made a practice of speaking openly against simoniacs and clerics living in concubinage [the regular two-point program of the reformers!]. On one occasion, having some business in hand, he sought the presence of the bishop of Florence, Hildebrand by name, and having presented his case, awaited the episcopal decision. Thereupon the wife of the bishop, Alberga, who was seated at his side,

---

[5] Davidsohn, Vol. I, pp. 111-12.

[6] *Vita Johannis Gualberti.* Davidsohn, *Forschungen,* Vol. I, p. 56. The *vita* is an invaluable document, owing to its preservation of the opinions current among the reformers.

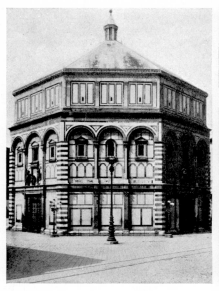

left: BAPTISTRY OF SAN GIOVANNI, EXTERIOR (ALINARI). *right:* BAPTISTRY OF SAN GIOVANNI, INTERIOR (ALINARI).

left: SAN MINIATO, FAÇADE (ALINARI). *right:* SAN MINIATO, INTERIOR (ALINARI).

THE PONTE VECCHIO, LOOKING DOWNSTREAM. THE MODERN SUSPENSION BRIDGE IN
THE DISTANCE HAS RECENTLY BEEN REPLACED BY A STONE BRIDGE (ALINARI).

left: THE BARGELLO, FORMERLY PALAZZO DEL PODESTÀ (ALINARI). *right:* THE BAR-
GELLO, THE COURT (ALINARI).

made answer: "My lord abbot, concerning this business you have brought forward, my lord the bishop has not yet been advised. He will take counsel with his *fideles* and inform you of his pleasure." At these words the abbot, fired with the zeal of God, poured out vehement maledictions on her, saying: "You accursed, sinful Jezebel, how do you dare open your mouth before this assembly of chosen representatives (*boni homines*) and priests? You ought to be burned at the stake for having presumed to asperse a creature and priest of God."

A tumult followed these wild words, but the chronicler drops the curtain and leaves us in doubt as to the issue. He does, however, vouchsafe the information that Abbot Guarinus fled to Rome and succeeded in persuading the pope to withdraw the abbey of Settimo from Florentine episcopal jurisdiction by subjecting it directly to himself. We may therefore conclude that Guarinus was not punished for his audacity; and we are justified in drawing the further deduction that reform was sweeping in like a tide and that, ominous evidence of its waxing strength, priests and leading clerics were beginning to identify themselves with the movement.

Possibly the stout old sinner on the cathedral chair began himself to be troubled, if not by mounting moral compunctions, at least by the increasing hostility of his subjects. Be that as it may, the time came when he resolved to found a monastery. It comports best with his character to refer his resolution to his active self-esteem and love of splendor, but, like other medieval men, doubtless he also hoped to have the reckoning of his sins reduced or even canceled out entirely by so signal a service to the Christian faith as the founding of a monastery was universally held to be. Although the exact moment of Bishop Hildebrand's determination to win renown as an ecclesiastical benefactor cannot be ascertained, it is certain that it antedates by some years the above-recorded outbreak against himself and his august lady. His first step was to choose as the site for his establishment the low hill overlooking Florence from across the Arno to the east and designated by tradition as the burial place of the first—and apparently only—Florentine martyr, San Miniato.

As we are aware, Minias or Miniato suffered death in 250 A.D. in the persecution of the Christians instituted by the Emperor Decius and was buried on the slope of the hill that afterward received his name. When, in the following century, Christianity was legalized, a small chapel was erected over the confessor's grave. The Minias worship, however, never became popular, for, when some five or six centuries later we get news of the chapel, we learn that it had been permitted to fall into decay and the instituted service to be neglected. Let the fact remind us that the Italians by no means uniformly cherished the memory of the early heroes of the faith. In the case of Miniato neglect and indifference went the extraordinary length of permitting, apparently without a protest, a relic-hunting German bishop of the entourage of Otto I to exhume the bones of Miniato and carry them off in triumph to distant Metz in Lotharingia.[7] In the countries north of the Alps, where martyrs were relatively few, they enjoyed an esteem in inverse ratio to their number. In consequence of this unfortunate abduction, Bishop Hildebrand faced a serious difficulty as soon as he

[7] Davidsohn, Vol. I, pp. 110-11. The removal took place about 968.

approached the execution of his grandiose design. A monastery dedicated to the
Florentine saint must imperatively possess his sacred remains. For a less resourceful man than Hildebrand the problem might have proved unsolvable.
He was favored by the circumstance that the saint's removal by the Lotha-
ringian bishop half a century before had caused so little stir that either it had
never become known or else it was no longer remembered. When, therefore,
the cunning bishop ordered a search for Miniato's bones to be conducted over
the hillside, his pick-and-shovel squad found them without any difficulty.
While the initial act connected with the great project was thus a pious fraud,
that did not fall heavily into the scales in an age which, gladly credulous, was
not troubled by a scrupulous sense of fact.

Planning an abbey on a truly liberal scale, the powerful patron endowed it
richly with possessions. The dormitory was intended to serve a goodly body of
monks, and the adjoining church was to be the most imposing edifice to be
found within the whole Florentine diocese. After a few years construction had
gone far enough to permit the buildings to be put to use. Consequently, on
April 27, 1018, the church was formally consecrated. This dates the famous
structure which, still standing on its lovely hill, holds an important place in
the history of medieval architecture. However, the edifice was far from finished
at the time of dedication. With building operations continuing during the
following decades in measure as funds became available, it was not till past the
middle of the century that the church of San Miniato presented itself to view
essentially as we see it today.

As Bishop Hildebrand appears in the records for the last time in 1024, in
which year we may assume he died, we have the assurance that he lived long
enough to see his undertaking well established. The credit for this pioneering
work in medieval architecture is therefore indisputably his. His largeness of
view arouses even greater respect when we recall that maritime Pisa, the most
populous and opulent town of Tuscany at this time, did not feel prompted till
half a hundred years later to undertake in its celebrated cathedral a comparable
monument. While the cathedral of Pisa marks a striking advance in scale,
daring, and beauty, to concede as much is not to deprive San Miniato either
of its historic or its aesthetic distinction. Not its least merit is that it was a
courageous venture undertaken at a time when Florentine society was still
unbelievably poor, crude, and backward. Undoubtedly eager for the sumptuous effect produced by polished marble, the bishop to his regret found marble
too expensive a material to use other than sparingly. Accordingly we find it
employed in but two places, on the façade and along the inner wall of the apse,
and there only as a thin covering or veneer. Conclusive evidence of the reigning poverty is furnished by the fact that the walls were erected throughout
of irregularly sized blocks of stone. Even the tall columns of the nave were
built up with these same small blocks, although, having at a later time been
given a coat of marbled stucco, they deceive unwary present-day visitors into
thinking that they are marble. Once again we may convince ourselves that the
vanished Roman Florentia had been a mean city, since its ruins, which we may
be sure were diligently combed for suitable remains, yielded the builders of
San Miniato only the scantiest harvest in the form of a few undistinguished

columns and capitals. They were incorporated in the lofty choir and in the low crypt beneath the choir, where they can still be identified.

An act of the doughty warrior-bishop, which still remains to be mentioned, was his appointing as the first abbot of his proud establishment a priest, Drogo by name, whom he instructed to prepare a life worthy of the holy proto-martyr supposedly buried under the high altar. As the only biographical material at Drogo's disposal were a few scant notices touching the saint handed down from the distant past, the task assigned to him was, historically speaking, incapable of solution. But Abbot Drogo had a mind above evidence. As he was also very proud of his Latin learning, he looked upon his commission primarily as a call to exercise his rhetorical powers. The result was a biography of San Miniato in which every son of the Arno city could take legitimate pride. To this day the popular histories of Florence, and often the so-called scientific histories as well, purvey Drogo's fables as the unvarnished truth. As might be expected, such works recount with particular unction the wonderful concluding feat of the martyr, who, when his head had been cut off outside the east gate of the town, picked it up with the greatest composure and, flying with it across the river, deposited it, together with himself, on the exact spot where he wished to be buried. The colorless original, from which Drogo was supposed to derive his facts, had the saint decapitated on the hill and prosaically buried where he fell.[8]

The biography of Abbot Drogo supports the contention put forward in the Introduction of this book that legend is the forerunner of history, and that what is properly called history is not born until society develops the habit of critical and analytic thought. Although legend and history are thus sharply distinguished, they stem from a common mental root and are both divisions of literature. For this reason Drogo's biography of San Miniato, while pretending to be history, which it is not, is, as a work of the imagination, indubitably literature. Viewed in this light, it is not without distinction. For as the first literary work accredited to a Florentine citizen, it stands at the head of a magnificent tradition culminating three centuries after Drogo in the famous trinity of Dante, Petrarch, and Boccaccio.

The events clustering around Bishop Hildebrand can leave no doubt in our minds that Florence had awakened from its long, medieval sleep, that it had in fact become a leading center of the impending spiritual conflict. In the years following the splendor-loving founder of San Miniato the conflict grew steadily more intense until it became the central concern of the citizens and drew Florence into the vortex of world-happenings. Nothing demonstrates the uninterruptedness of the movement better than the appearance, not long after the magnificent prelate had passed from the scene, of a man resolved to carry on the war against all that the bishop had stood for with as much and more of the vehemence of the Abbot Guarinus. The new head of the reform movement was Giovanni Gualberti.

Giovanni was the son of a small nobleman of the Pesa Valley and, like the ruling class throughout Europe, was brought up to the profession of arms. If

[8] Davidsohn, Vol. I, p. 135; *Forschungen*, Vol. I, p. 34. Consult also *Acta Sanctorum*, Octobris Tomus Undecimus, pp. 415-32.

we place his birth around the year 1010, we become aware that he grew up in the atmosphere dominated by the engrossing issue of ecclesiastical reform. The wind raised by the heated conflict between the saints and the sinners stirred his susceptible spirit to its depths. Therefore, no sooner had he attained manhood than he decided to abandon the military life and become a monk. As a resident of the countryside about Florence he shared with his countrymen their pride in the new foundation of San Miniato. He turned his footsteps thither and assumed the cowl.

The monk Giovanni at once gave evidence that his was the active, not the contemplative, religious temper. For, although self-condemned to a cell, he could no more avoid a life of combat than if he had never abandoned sword and buckler. At the head of San Miniato at this time was a successor of the literary Drogo, the Abbot Hubert. He owed his appointment to his patron, the bishop of Florence, to whom he had made the usual "presents" in recognition of the honor conferred on him. As soon as the militant Giovanni gained positive assurance that his spiritual chief had thus tainted himself with simony, he began to denounce him; and when the Florentine bishop, Hatto by name, himself a simoniac like the long line of his immediate predecessors, sided with the abbot as he was in duty bound, Giovanni without hesitation attacked Hatto also. It took a courageous fanatic to challenge these two dignitaries, mighty men in the first place and, in addition, the young monk's ecclesiastical superiors. Grimly resolved to see the struggle through to whatever issue it might bring, he determined to draw the people into the controversy by haranguing them at street-corners about the sins of their spiritual leaders. In an uprising produced by him in the heart of Florence, in the Mercato Vecchio, he received a severe beating at the hands of the partisans of the bishop and betook himself in search of convalescence to the solitudes of Vallombrosa (1035?). This was, and in part still is, a densely wooded mountain district of the Arno Valley to the east of Florence. Joined before long by numerous youthful enthusiasts, he collected them into a monastic foundation of his own. It grew rapidly in the following years until, under the name of the Vallombrosan Order, it had spread in numerous dependencies throughout Tuscany and central Italy. Thus was the rebel of a corrupt monastery visibly rewarded from on high by becoming the father of a whole congregation of monasteries dedicated to purity and incorruption.[9]

As head of a powerful order called into being by his religious ardor, the Abbot Giovanni was able to carry the campaign against simony and clerical concubinage far and wide in Tuscany and, like many another hard, uncompromising fighter, lived to see the triumph of his cause. Long before his death

[9] My account has omitted the celebrated story of Giovanni Gualberti's conversion, according to which he spared an enemy delivered into his hands by an accidental encounter, when the frightened victim threw himself on the ground and with extended arms presented the figure of a cross. On going, deeply stirred, into a nearby church to pray, the crucifix over the altar solemnly inclined its head in sign of approval of his generous act. The upshot was that he renounced the world and became a monk. This impressive story was cut out of whole cloth by Giovanni's first hagiographer. Taken in connection with Drogo's free inventions in behalf of Miniato, it drives home the point that we are dealing with a credulous age endowed with the will to believe and as yet undisturbed by intellectual doubt. On the several "Lives" of Giovanni Gualberti see Davidsohn, *Forschungen*, Vol. I, pp. 50 ff.

the movement had spread into every corner of Italy, arousing repercussions that made themselves felt through the length and breadth of Christendom. However, to achieve this universal character it had to be taken up by a man of greater reach and stature than distinguished an, after all, purely provincial personage like Gualberti. This champion was none other than that fearless and towering pontiff, the famous Gregory VII. In the next chapter we shall hear how the reform movement came to a head under him, challenged the current ecclesiastical abuses in the person of their main supporter, the emperor, and filled the church in every country of Europe with new life. To our Giovanni may be conceded the by no means inconsiderable honor of being a forerunner, who with other forerunners in other parts of the world prepared the way for the triumphant Gregory. That he died in the very year of Gregory's elevation to the chair of St. Peter (1073) may be taken as the conclusive confirmation of his pioneership. Shortly before he died he enjoyed a success that must have given him immense satisfaction, for he won it in the strenuous local war, with the declaration of which he had inaugurated his religious career. The story sheds so much light on the religious situation in Florence that it cannot be passed over.

In spite of the agitation for reform, the bishopric of Florence long remained entangled in the corrupt practices which had become traditional. However, by the middle of the century the monkish party had acquired a considerable following among both laity and clergy. It had gained a foothold even in the capital of Christendom and, with occasional support from Rome itself, the agitators were able to make the situation of a proved simoniac in possession of the Florentine see highly uncomfortable. It was around the year 1061 that a certain Peter Mezzabarba became bishop of Florence through appointment by the imperial court. Unfortunately for him the usual "presents" by which he paved his way became a matter of public knowledge. The incident constituted so flagrant a case of the forbidden sin that it lashed the reformers to an unexampled outburst of fury. Immediately the alert Gualberti, now the powerful head of the Vallombrosan Order and a lifelong fighter for ecclesiastical purity, took command of the opposition. The new battle developed into the severest conflict of his career, for the erring bishop was not without numerous supporters among his fellow-bishops (like himself simoniacs almost to a man), besides having many lay noblemen and particularly the powerful Margrave Godfrey of Tuscany on his side. But Gualberti was equal to the occasion. He mobilized his ecclesiastical troops, the devoted Vallombrosan monks, and had them carry on such a frenzied campaign in Florence and throughout the diocese that the population was fanned into a white heat of religious zeal.

Thereupon the agitators played their trump card in the form of the demand that Bishop Peter submit himself to the judgment of God. That meant, according to the juridical ideas of the day, a trial by fire. When the indignant bishop refused the test, his persecutors went the length of ordering a boycott of the churches served by priests of his appointment who refused to repudiate their sinful chief. So terrible was the pressure exercised under the generalship of the fanatical Vallombrosan chief that parish after parish fell away from Peter until he stood on his episcopal eminence a man marked with a public stigma and—

alone. To clinch the now certain victory the Abbot Giovanni resolved to conduct the fire test, even though the accused party refused to participate. The excited people imperatively demanded a spectacle and, talented impresario that Gualberti was, he was more than willing to serve them.

The fighting abbot had conducted his campaign from the monastery at Settimo as his base, and it was Settimo he chose as the scene of the trial. When we remember that Settimo had been the home of that Abbot Guarinus who had begun the war against simony by attacking Bishop Hildebrand, we must concede that there was an eminent fitness in its selection, for now, after half a century of conflict, Guarinus was to receive his reward. The ordeal took place on February 13, 1068, and an incident more dramatic and at the same time more illuminative of certain dark areas of the medieval mind cannot be imagined. As soon as day dawned long lines of people from Florence and the countryside began to pour over all the roads that led to Settimo. They gathered in a dense, expectant mass around two piles of wood somewhat less than man-high with a narrow path left open between them. To represent the prosecution and bear the burden of the trial the Abbot Giovanni had chosen one of his Vallombrosan monks, Peter by name, who, as might be expected, was the most simple, guileless, and devoted member of the band. Then, after the brothers had chanted their litanies, the two piles of wood were set aflame and the great moment of Peter's life had come. He took the path indicated, was swallowed from view among the enveloping smoke and flames, and a few seconds later reappeared safe and sound. The enthusiasm of the spectators was indescribable. Their cries of thanksgiving rose to heaven and in their rush to kiss the hem of the poor monk's garment they almost trampled him to death. From that moment Peter became Fiery Peter (Petrus Igneus) for his admiring contemporaries. Before many years had passed, he was made a cardinal, and when he died he was widely adored as a saint. As for the controversy between Abbot Gualberti and Bishop Peter, which had for years turned the Florentine diocese topsyturvy, it was over, for further resistance was impossible after God himself had pronounced in favor of the abbot and against the wicked prelate. Driven from the city by a popular uprising, Peter was deposed by a papal synod and a successor ordered to be elected in strict accordance with the canons of the church.

If success ever brings happiness to men, Giovanni Gualberti must have felt richly blessed during the five years of life still vouchsafed him. Then, at the close of his days he experienced a final triumph, for he lived just long enough to see that man elevated to the chair of St. Peter who had become the champion of reform at Rome itself and who was destined to make Gualberti's Tuscan struggle as universal as the church.

V. The Countess Matilda and the Emergence
of Communal Autonomy in Tuscany and Florence

THE movement of ecclesiastical reform, spontaneously inaugurated at many centers of Italy and Europe though it was, would never have acquired a unified and irresistible character if it had not been taken up by the central institution of the church, the papacy. But that the papacy of that period would ever champion the cause of reform must have seemed utterly improbable even to its most sanguine supporters, for, during the first half of the eleventh century, it was passing through one of the blackest phases of its history. True, almost from its foundation it had experienced these sudden and overwhelming calamities. They issued in the main from the circumstance that the papacy had its seat in feudalized medieval Rome, in whose passionate local issues it became inextricably entangled. Repeatedly in the past it had succumbed so completely to its environment that, in spite of its universal claim and mission, it sank lower and lower in the scale until it was, in effect, no more than a Roman municipal office, over the possession of which rival feudal families fought and intrigued without respite and without shame.

Precisely this was the situation in the days of Giovanni Gualberti's youth. Never had the chief office of Christendom reached a lower moral depth; and Gualberti and all the other leaders of the ascetic movement, anxiously noting every ailment of the church, did not fail to give moving expression to their sorrow and indignation over the disgraceful spectacle presented by the capital of Christianity. However, the spirit of reform was abroad and was spreading, and presently the reformers had the satisfaction of winning to their side a discontented element of the Roman clergy. This was an indispensable preliminary to a revolution at the corrupt heart of the Christian system. But before a moral movement of irresistible momentum could get under way, the Augean stable that Rome and the papacy had become would have to be swept clean with an iron besom. And as matters stood in the world in the first half of the eleventh century, the only possible wielder of that besom was the emperor.

The Saxon line of emperors inaugurated by Otto I came to an end in the person of Henry II in the year 1024 and was followed by the Franconian line, of which the second and greatest representative was Henry III. Raised to the throne in 1039, he did not make his first descent into Italy till seven years later. Like all the finer-fibered individuals of his age, he too had been deeply troubled by the corruption of the church, and under the influence of the reformers who, for Europe north of the Alps, had their vital center in the great monastery of Cluny, he was resolved to do everything in his power to bring the ailing institution back to health. That meant specifically that he would lend his aid in imposing celibacy on the clergy and in eliminating the worst abuses connected with nomination to clerical office. However, he would not surrender blindly to the movement of reform. While honestly resolved to serve religion and the church, he would refuse to impair his royal prerogative by giving up his customary right to appoint the great prelates. For, under the system of immunities, bishops and abbots were his immediate political subordinates, the nomination of whom he could not surrender without giving up the very substance of his power. His reform activity would therefore be strictly accommodated to his conception of his imperial authority. He would forbid "gifts" and other corrupt practices; he would have only tried and worthy men intrusted with the great ecclesiastical dignities; but he would hold fast to the view that it was his right and privilege to appoint these fit candidates and to invest them with office. Immediately on mounting the German throne he had elaborated these principles for Germany and now, on crossing the Alps, he resolved to apply them also in Italy.

On arriving in Italy Henry made his way to Rome to be crowned emperor by the pope, as custom demanded. It was the very moment the papacy had reached its most scandalous decline, for as many as three rival popes were attempting to drape themselves in the seamless mantle of Christ. The indignant and energetic Henry made short shrift of their conflicting claims. Although not clothed with such supervising powers by any ordinance of the church, he deposed all three contestants tainted alike with simony, and seated on the papal throne a German bishop, whom he could trust to live up to the obligations of his new office. It was from this personal appointee, Clement II, that he received the imperial crown. When Clement II died after a few weeks, the all-powerful emperor raised his successor to office; and he continued to exercise this unwarranted authority till a total of four popes owed their elevation to his intervention. The issue of simony was not raised nor can it be said to have been involved, for he exacted no money from his appointee. Nonetheless there was a new abuse of the greatest gravity in that the church had at its very crown and apex been brought under the control of a temporal lord. If this usurpation aroused at first only secret clerical opposition, the adversaries were the more dangerous as they were the very reformers whom the honest intentions of the sovereign had for the first time put in the saddle at the capital of Christendom.

As long as the formidable Henry dominated the scene, his opponents hesitated to show themselves in the open. Hardly had he died (1056), however, at the early age of thirty-nine, when the reformers were encouraged to repudiate the imperial hegemony and to carry through the reorganization of the church according to their own views and under their own authority. The bold resolution was greatly favored by the troubles which impaired the royal power in Germany immediately on Henry's death. As his son and heir, Henry IV, was only six years old, his mother exercised the rule in the capacity of regent. Not only was she too feeble to keep the reins firmly in her hands but, like all the German sovereigns before and after her, she suffered from the geographical nandicap of being too far removed from Italy to bring such power as she had to bear upon the situation. When, before long, Germany was convulsed with a succession of revolts that paralyzed the central authority, the Roman reform party recognized that its hour had come and set about the execution of its plans without concerning itself further with the shaky pretentions to ecclesiastical supremacy of the distant German court.

The head of the Roman clerical party and formulator of its independent policy was a man who by all but universal consent is the greatest figure of his century. Hildebrand, born of an obscure family of southern Tuscany, had as a youth gone to Rome and become a monk in response to an urge of purification shared by so many of his best contemporaries. Joining at once the as yet insignificant party of the reformers, he succeeded in acquiring a much wider survey of the human scene than was common among his Roman friends by visiting the monastery of Cluny beyond the Alps and making his home for a while in that most dynamic of all the centers of the religious revolution. While the heart of Hildebrand glowed with religious zeal, he also felt strongly the need to busy his mind with practical affairs. This preoccupation with both heaven and earth is his outstanding characteristic and supplies us with the key to his historic eminence. Pushed by his rare executive ability into the fields of diplomacy and administration, he gradually gained such considerable influence over the far-flung business of the papacy that, long before the world in general had heard his name, he was recognized at Rome as the most important member of the papal court, the invisible director concealed under the mantle of the successive popes who sat upon St. Peter's chair following the death of Henry III. It was Hildebrand who, during the eclipse of the imperial power, took the reform movement in hand and gave it its final expression. It had started with a passionate outcry against simony and concubinage, and from these demands, received from his predecessors, Hildebrand never departed. But because of his long and agitated personal experience at the capital of Christendom he now added a specifically papal feature to the program which pushed the reform into the arena of European politics and ended by making the pope the arbiter of the western world.

While living in Rome as a young monk, Hildebrand had been outraged by the spectacle of the papacy perpetually fought over by rival feudal factions immediately on the ground. This condition was made possible by the traditional manner of election, according to which each new incumbent of St. Peter's chair owed his elevation to the action of the clergy and people of Rome. So loose an arrangement was bound to produce disturbances, and in point of fact a papal election regularly gave rise to political machinations, armed intervention, and bloody riots. To a man of Hildebrand's temper a system provocative of such ever-recurrent evils was monstrous and unbearable. Therefore, when Henry III put an end to it, the reformers applauded him to the echo; but on the emperor's then arrogating to himself the right to appoint the pope, he aroused an opposition which was no less vigorous for being kept discreetly under cover so long as his power lasted. He had hardly departed this life, leaving, as we have seen, the imperial power in a paralyzed condition, when Hildebrand came forward with an electoral plan of his own. By it each new pope was to be chosen by a small number of the higher clergy of Rome distinguished by the title of cardinals. Intrusted to a limited body of churchmen of high station, the election was to be taken entirely out of lay hands, whether those hands belonged to a base Roman mob, to a junta of feudal conspirators, or to a single grasping potentate.

It was in 1059, during the reign of Pope Nicholas II, that Hildebrand promulgated the decree establishing the new electoral system. Its striking success is witnessed by its having lasted in its essential features through all the succeeding centuries down to our day. But to admire the new electoral machinery is far from doing justice to the scope and logic of Hildebrand's papal program. While he desired passionately to free the papacy from the non-clerical influences which had brought confusion on its head, his leading purpose was to make it more supreme over the Christian church than it had yet been and, with the vast ecclesiastical power concentrated in its hands, to bring all temporal potentates, great and small alike including the emperor, under the control of the pope. The universal monarchy of Rome was to be revived, but not in the manner of Charlemagne or Otto. Recalled to life in a world that had become passionately Christian, it was to be identified with the church, the venerable and authoritative association of true believers. It followed unescapably that the head of the new universal state must be the pope, vicegerent of Christ and successor of the apostle Peter. But not for his personal satisfaction and aggrandizement was the Holy Father to be raised to his unrivaled eminence. He was to exercise his vast authority in order to bring God's great purpose to fulfilment by leading mankind to salvation.

Although Hildebrand did not at once publish his revolutionary program to the world, the mere fact that he nursed it, shaping every measure of the Roman court in accordance with its terms, signified that a life-and-death struggle with the emperor could not be avoided. It did not actually break out till Hildebrand himself mounted the papal throne as Gregory VII. In the year 1073 the man who for several decades had been serving as the masterful counselor of popes stepped at last into the open by himself assuming the highest Christian office. He promptly brought to a head the conflict with the temporal power for which he had been so long preparing by having a Roman synod sweepingly enact the whole reform program into law. Accordingly, the papal anathema, which already on previous occasions had been fulminated against simony and concubinage, was renewed in the most vigorous terms, while bishops and abbots who should receive their offices from lay hands, and every emperor, king, and temporal ruler who should presume to invest bishops and abbots with office were threatened with excommunication. From the Pandora's box of the papal synod of 1075 there issued for the first time in definite form the fateful issue which goes under the name of "lay investiture." Although we may agree that it was implied in the problem of ecclesiastical reform from the start, we must insist that it did not actually leap to the front till Hildebrand, become pope, made it the pivotal item in his program.

Since the time of the great Otto the emperors, practically without exception, had been extremely well disposed to the church. They had been particularly interested in providing the great body of the laity with a purer Christian ministry. But when, as now appeared, the purer ministry, to which they had given their support, was to be achieved by the abolition of lay investiture, that is to say, by the annihilation of their power, the reigning emperor, Henry IV, registered an immediate and violent protest. For throughout alike his German and Italian lands bishops and abbots ruled over vast territories, and if they were no longer to be invested with their domains by their sovereign, they would be released from his control and he, for his part, would no longer in any effective sense be a sovereign. When Pope Gregory VII promulgated the audacious decree of 1075 Henry IV was ruling Germany in his own name with all the arrogance and caprice of an undisciplined young man. Without hesitation he tossed his gauntlet to Gregory by declaring him deposed from office. The pope's answer was as prompt as it was uncompromising. He in his turn deposed Henry and, in addition, laid him under the curse of excommunication. The war for supremacy between the two claimants to the power of ancient Rome had begun. Never again would there be a durable peace between empire and papacy until one had defeated and humbled the other.

In this fateful conflict our concern is limited to the part played in the drama by Florence and Tuscany. It happens to be important largely for the reason that the ruler of Tuscany, who was the most powerful vassal of the emperor in all Italy, sided unreservedly with the opponent of the emperor, the pope. In order to appreciate the full significance of this action we must briefly bring the story of the Tuscan margraviate down to Gregory's time.

The Margrave Hugo, who looms so large in Florentine myth and story, died without offspring in 1001 and was succeeded by a number of imperial appointees with whom we need not concern ourselves till we reach Boniface II. This Boniface was invested with office by Emperor Conrad II in 1027. The new provincial chief was head of the Canossa family, already abundantly endowed with lands extending from the northern slopes of the Apennines all the way across Lombardy to the foothills of the Alps. The family took its name from the castle of Canossa, which from its bold Apennine rock looked threateningly across the smiling plain of the Po stretching northward as far as the eye could reach. With Tuscany added to his strength by Conrad's munificence the Margrave Boniface completely dominated central and northern Italy; and since he clung to his superior, the emperor, with more consistency than was usual among feudal magnates, he served as the main pivot of the imperial power in Italy in his day.

However, while giving the emperor his support, Margrave Boniface was not minded to let any opportunity slip by calculated to promote his personal interests. He was a grasping, iron-fisted lord who oppressed his subjects and steadily increased his possessions at the expense of both clergy and laity.[1] One gets the impression that he was an admirable embodiment of the feudal spirit in its crudest form. Before his death a little past the middle of the century (1052), he had raised his house to a position which caused it to be regarded on all hands with mixed awe and dread. His widow Beatrice undertook to carry

---

[1] Falce, *Bonifazio di Canossa*. 2 vols. Reggio Emilia, 1926. The first volume is a biography of the dubious, "reconstructed" sort. The second volume, entitled *Regesto,* is a valuable digest of relevant documents.

on the government in behalf of her infant son and, when her son died prematurely, in behalf of the sole surviving heir, a daughter, Matilda. From fear that she, an unarmed woman in a turbulent, arms-bearing world, would not be able to cling to the precarious summit to which Boniface had climbed, she contracted a second marriage, choosing as her husband Godfrey, duke of Upper Lotharingia. This Godfrey, every whit as lordly a man as Boniface, championed her cause so effectively that, on his death in 1069, she felt sufficiently strong to try the experiment of ruling without masculine support, in association with her vigorous and rarely capable daughter. Until Beatrice herself died in 1076 mother and daughter shared the reins in unbroken harmony. These bare facts needed to be enumerated because they explain how it happened that a woman came into possession of the margraviate of Tuscany and the vast Canossa heritage in Lombardy as well. The Countess Matilda was still young in office when by his bold prohibition of lay investiture Pope Gregory VII precipitated the epic struggle with the emperor.

Counting Matilda's accession to the margraviate from the death of her stepfather (1069), we note that she dominated Tuscany and central Italy for almost half a century. To voice their feeling of respect, her contemporaries called her the great countess (*la gran contessa*). What particularly impressed them, as it continues to impress us, was her clear-cut character, which, having prompted her to side with Gregory the moment war was declared between him and the emperor, kept her unalterably faithful to the papal cause. And let it not be forgotten that her decision imperiled both her life and her possessions, since the emperor commanded great resources and was, in addition, her lawful overlord. The danger left her unperturbed. By taking her stand at the side of Gregory she became the strong shield without which he might easily have gone down to defeat; and as if to make it clear that she was fighting, less for a person than for a cause, when Gregory died she made an equally uncompromising fight in behalf of his three immediate successors on St. Peter's throne. By thus bracketing her name with that of the church without regard to personal consequences, she appeared to the party of reform as a heaven-sent champion fighting in shining armor on the side of Christ and righteousness against the forces of the world and Satan. Beginning even before her death, these partisans made a myth of the great countess until they had transformed her into a holy virgin in complete accord with the colorless feminine ideal cherished by all preachers of a perverse asceticism. This legendary portrait still looks out at us from most of even the recent histories. It is, if not false, at least so one-sided that it invites correction by the rehearsal of some of the actual circumstances of Matilda's life, in the light of which she again becomes an actual woman in a living world.

Although we may assume that Matilda was born with a tender religious conscience, we have no evidence to indicate that the reformers enjoyed her support in the days of her youth. In the rude society in which she lived young women accepted in public and private matters alike the guidance of their male relatives, and Matilda was no exception to the rule. Almost the first fact we know of her is the marriage to which she was obliged to submit to her stepfather's son and heir, the younger Godfrey. She dutifully followed her husband to his home beyond the Alps, to the duchy of Upper Lotharingia, and there an emotional crisis occurred which the few shadowy details that have come down to us suffice to make reasonably clear. She was not fond of her husband who, though a famous fighter, was a hunchback and hideous to look upon. When the child born to them died almost at birth, she could not bear to continue life at his side and returned to her native land. Thenceforth husband and wife lived apart, and when in 1076 the hunchback perished at an assassin's hand, Matilda must have felt that she had been liberated from an odious yoke.

We can hardly doubt that her unhappy marriage dropped a blight into the young countess's soul, which drove her to seek refuge in religion and which, at least in part, explains how she became the devoted and ever-obedient daughter of the church. But stalwart as that devotion was, she never permitted it to interfere with the secular duties imposed upon her as the heir of a great house. She was a powerful feudal sovereign, the chief Italian vassal of her liege, the emperor, and in her public and private character she consistently maintained the style appropriate to her station. Contemporaries tell us that, clad in helmet and coat of mail, she led her forces in person into the field and that, when she required relaxation, she would eagerly indulge herself, like all the members of the ruling class, in the pleasures of the hunt. It accords well with this picture of her in her worldly aspect that in her court, famous throughout Europe for its feudal magnificence, her vassals were wont to address her on their knees. In short, to think of her, as the hagiographers would have us do, as a closeted nun exclusively occupied with thoughts of salvation, does her a wrong by blotting out her role as a great secular power.[2]

The struggle between Gregory VII and Henry IV, inaugurated by their furious declarations of war in 1075, came to a swift climax in the scene of Canossa which held and still holds captive the imagination of the world. By the universal defection of his own countrymen the conceited young sovereign of Germany was apprized that he had challenged a power before whose moral authority the sword broke in his hand. When presently he stood alone, ejected from Christian society and facing deposition, he hazarded as a last resource the journey that brought him as a humble seeker for forgiveness to the feet of his papal adversary. In the bitter month of January of the year 1077 he waited for three days in the cold and snow to be admitted to Gregory's presence. The memorable scene was laid at Canossa, the Apennine stronghold of Matilda and the home from which her race drew its name. Canossa testified to the world that the gran contessa, the most powerful sovereign of Italy, stood behind, not the emperor, but the emperor's adversary, the pope, and that she stood behind him with all her castles and all her armed men. If we agree, as agree we must, that Henry, the barefoot petitioner at the barred gate of Canossa, was not dragged from his pedestal by a manifestation of material power, we should nonetheless be blind not to perceive that Matilda's presence at her ancestral castle with Gregory was at least a not insubstantial factor in his terrible humiliation.

[2] The literature on Matilda is very considerable. A good recent work is by L. Tondelli, *Matilda da Canossa*. Reggio Emilia, 1926. The best biography in English is by Nora Duff, *Matilda of Tuscany*. London, 1909. The earliest monkish biography, an invaluable source, is by a younger contemporary of Matilda, Donizone by name. It will be found in Muratori, *Scriptores*, Vol. V.

Instead of the end, Canossa turned out to be no more than the prologue to the great struggle over lay investiture. Henry and Gregory conducted the conflict so long as they lived; and when they had departed this life, it was continued by their respective successors. When both sides at last resolved to negotiate and effected an accommodation of their claims in the Concordat of Worms (1122), the movement of reform had passed its apex and the world, as has been its capricious way from the beginning, had turned to other interests. The document signed at Worms accorded the victory to neither combatant. To the pope it conceded the right to invest the bishops and abbots with spiritual authority; to the emperor, the right to invest them with their lands. So lame a compromise was possible only because, after fifty years of warfare, the reform movement had exhausted its energy. Before its ardor was extinguished, however, it had expressed itself in a movement of such importance for the civilization of Europe that it cannot be overlooked. In the year 1095, at a General Council of the church held at Clermont in France, the reigning pope, Urban II, had the happy inspiration of reviving the religious fervor, which by its nature requires constant feeding with fresh fuel, by directing it upon a new enterprise. He proposed a war of the united Christian west against the Moslems to wrest from them the Holy Places of Palestine. His project was wildly acclaimed by a vast multitude and led to the launching of the First Crusade. Without any doubt the stirring war between Cross and Crescent must be accepted as the astonishing final fruitage of the religious reform inaugurated over a hundred years before by puritanical monks and hermits roused to indignation by the scandalous degradation of the church.

We have lingered over the world-issues of the last quarter of the eleventh century largely for the purpose of supplying something of the background of Matilda's personal thought and feeling. This greatest personality that had thus far sprung from Tuscan soil will remain a stranger to us unless we grasp that the two materially distinct but spiritually related movements of the investiture struggle and the crusades utterly filled her being. Just as certainly as the interminable war between pope and emperor wrung her soul with agony, the war between Christian and Moslem released a holy joy, even though, as a woman, she was hindered from joining the crusading host. And yet, overshadowing as the religious movement in its several aspects seemed to her, it was not and could not be more than a segment of the age in which she lived. Numerous other interests were arising, which even in her day were slowly pushing the religious issue into the background, and which in the century after her reign succeeded in greatly altering the face of Europe. While Matilda did not comprehend these novel agencies, they already so fully dominated the new generation which confronted her in her old age that often she must have seemed to herself to be living among strangers. In sober fact in her last phase the aging countess was as much of an anachronism as her tough, simoniac father, the Margrave Boniface, had been an anachronism in the atmosphere of religious purification steadily gaining ground during the last years of his reign.

The new forces announcing a new age were secular in their nature and may all, in last analysis, be referred to the revival of commerce. In now turning to this engrossing movement we are obliged to make those enemies of Christendom, the Moslems, our starting-point and to recall how, after converting the Mediterrean Sea into a Moslem lake, they had filled the measure of their iniquity to overflowing by periodically harrying the coasts of Italy with fire and sword. Not till the time of Otto I and his successors did the situation register a gradual improvement. Even so, it was noticeable rather within the peninsula than upon the sea, owing to the fact that the emperors, commanding an army but not a navy, could not make their power felt beyond the shore. Indeed under an agrarian system, like feudalism, it was unlikely that the rulers would ever come into possession of a navy; and consequently, if the Moslem pirates were ever to be tamed, it would devolve upon the maritime towns to take the business in hand by means of a navy built and manned by themselves.

The Mediterranean shore of Tuscany is lacking in good natural harbors. The only seaport of any consequence it boasted at that time was Pisa, which, at the mouth of the greatest Tuscan river, the Arno, enjoyed a dominant position. With no aid to be had from the land-minded emperor, it behooved the Pisans themselves to terminate the calamities from which they suffered along with all the other dwellers on the coast. In their feebleness they made but slow headway for a long time. Both before and after the year 1000 the occasional chroniclers continue to report destructive raids on the part of the pirates against the Tuscan littoral. Conscious, however, that resistance to their encroachments was gradually becoming more resolute, the Saracens determined to nip the recovery movement in the bud by seizing the island of Sardinia, from which rising Pisa and all western Italy for that matter could be kept under convenient control. Its successful capture by the Moslems spurred the Pisans to the greatest effort they had made so far and they drove the enemy from the neighboring island. The startling victory, won in 1016, marks the turning of the tide. Encouraged by success, the Pisans now began to extend their cruises. They traded boldly along the whole Italian coast and, before many decades had passed, demonstrated their growing confidence by assuming the offensive. They leaped upon the Moslem corsairs wherever they found them, in the waters of Spain and Sicily and along the coast of northern Africa. After some generations, by the time, let us say, of the reign of the Countess Matilda, Pisa had become a thriving community steadily extending its range at sea at the expense of the Moslems and sharing with Genoa on the adjoining Ligurian shore an already all but assured primacy over the western Mediterranean.

The remarkable initiative manifested by the Pisans was no isolated phenomenon. All the other Tuscan towns, beginning with Pisa's nearest neighbor, Lucca, before long exhibited similar signs of vitality attended by an enlarged exchange of goods. But no sooner was the commercial movement well under way than the towns became aware of a monster in their path in the form of the feudal system. This so-called system was, as we are aware, a makeshift born of anarchy and never free from manifestations of war and violence. Incapable of giving security, it was bound to disintegrate the moment that groups it oppressed acquired the courage and developed the resources successfully to organize themselves against it. Throughout Italy the most characteristic single feature of the established social order were the great lordships made up of a widely scattered aggregation of estates and castles. Under the novel conditions brought to birth by the eleventh century these vast properties were exposed to the attack, first, of the rising townsmen and, second, of the lower nobility, the *milites,* as impatient in their way as the townsmen of their dependence on the caprice and wilfulness of their hard masters. The century was not far advanced when townsmen and lesser nobility occasionally joined forces against the common enemy; and although they by no means uniformly scored a victory, they remained in touch with each other, prepared to renew the struggle the moment the occasion seemed auspicious. The best evidence of this trend is seen in the growing habit of the lesser gentry to take up their residence in the towns, where they became an upper layer of privileged, fighting citizens. Starting with the immediate practical demand of open communications for their goods and the cessation of capricious taxes levied along the highways, the townsmen before long moved on from this modest program to fairly ambitious projects of self-government. In point of fact, they began on their own authority to organize such simple municipal services as their most pressing needs required; and almost before they were themselves aware of it, they were practicing a limited municipal autonomy, for which there was as yet no basis in either law or custom.

Need we go farther to indicate the main aspects of the complex social upheaval which went on under the eyes of the Countess Matilda not only in Tuscany but at an even accelerated rate among her northern, her Lombard dependencies? And need we marvel that she, who took so clear and confident a stand in the great religious issue of the day, looked in a kind of daze on economic phenomena wholly beyond her narrow, aristocratic comprehension? Jealously bent on preserving her inherited rights, she was instinctively hostile to political change of every kind and particularly critical of what to her mind were the insolent demands and actions of the upstart townsmen. She would have preferred—this meek virgin of the legend—to lay her powerful sword to their backs, but the delicate situation stayed her hand; she had cast her fortunes with the pope and, except for some truce-like intervals devoted to negotiations, she was permanently at war with her powerful suzerain, the emperor. The merchants in control of the towns would have been obliged to deny their sharp, bargaining natures if they had not taken advantage of this conflict between their two feudal superiors. The opportunity was theirs to side with either Matilda or the emperor, depending on which was willing to pay the price. And the price, in view of the usurpation of municipal authority of which in varying measure they were all guilty, could not be other than the legalization by description in a formal charter of as much of the usurped authority as countess or emperor could be induced to concede.

The struggle between the two overlords, between emperor and countess, explains the famous charters which Henry, he of the memorable Canossa incident, issued in 1081 to Lucca and Pisa respectively.[3] Being at war with the pope and the countess, Henry badly needed the help which two such prosperous towns as Lucca and Pisa could bring to his cause. Therefore, with many com-

---

[3] For the charter to Lucca see Ficker, *Forschungen zur Reichs und Rechtsgeschichte Italiens,* Vol. IV, p. 124. For the Pisan charter see Muratori, *Antiquitates,* Vol. IV, p. 19.

punctions, as we may be sure, he agreed to put the seal of his approval on the municipal activities by which the two towns had partially lifted themselves out of the frame of feudalism and taken their first uncertain steps toward self-government. What Henry had thus granted, his vassal, the countess, did not have the power to revoke. To be sure, Pisa and Lucca might not, under all circumstances, be able to enforce their proud new status, but since it had been confirmed by the fountainhead of feudal law, it was difficult to see how it could ever again be successfully nullified.

In the light of these general Tuscan developments we are now prepared to narrow our inquiry to Florence and to take note of its fortunes during the long reign of the great countess. The first circumstance to leap to view is that throughout the life of Matilda the cordiality existing between her and her town on the middle Arno was never broken. Florence approved of the Matildan policy of supporting the pope and, alone of Tuscan cities, refused to listen to the overtures repeatedly made by Henry IV with a view to drawing it to his side. We shall not be making a mistake if we ascribe this fidelity to the countess as owing, in the first instance, to the devotion to the papal cause that the townsmen shared with their valiant ruler. They had become identified with religious reform in the pre-Gregorian days of Giovanni Gualberti's missionary labors, and their fervor had given their city a moral energy permitting it to radiate an influence which made itself felt far and wide over Italy. To compare it with the influence exercised by Cluny over the lands beyond the Alps is by no means an exaggeration. Then, too, there was a strong personal attachment to Matilda and her house. A little past the middle of the century, in 1057, Florence had been made the center of the margravial administration, thereby replacing Lucca as the capital of the province.[4] This was a great material advantage, and the honor that went with it was underscored by the open preference repeatedly exhibited by Matilda for the City of the Baptist. Although, like all feudal sovereigns of wide sway, she engaged in constant travel and lived in many castles, she resided for sufficiently long periods in her palace at Florence to be regarded affectionately by the inhabitants as their fellow-citizen. On the strength of this emotional bond there was gradually happening to her what had already happened to the Margrave Hugo and Giovanni Gualberti. Even before her end she was being incorporated in the steadily expanding patriotic legend of the town.

Cordial as were the relations between ruler and ruled, they did not hinder Florence from experiencing the commercial impact of the age. Somewhat more tardily than Pisa and Lucca, it is true, but no less surely, the town was going through all the changes making for burgher self-esteem and calling for the creation of new commercial, juridical, and political institutions. It is not to be supposed for a moment that the Florentine merchants nursed a greater indulgence toward the oppressive feudal system than the merchants of the other Tuscan towns or that they were less eager to promote their selfish interests. Inevitably therefore they began to perform individual acts of autonomy, with no

---

[4] Chiapelli, "La Formazione Storica del Comune Cittadino." *Arch. Stor. It.,* Serie 7, Vol. XIII (1930), p. 7 (footnote). My date (1057) is supplied from Davidsohn, Vol. I, pp. 203-5.

idea in their heads at first beyond the limited one of solving the problem lying immediately across their path. The haphazard procedure is illustrated by a few isolated facts of which we have certain knowledge. Thus by the year 1079 the Florentines already had their own system of weights and measures.[5] Perhaps they had acquired this privilege through a diploma issued by their friend, the countess. No document to that effect has come down to us; indeed the extraordinary dearth of documents for this period makes it impossible to come to other than very tentative conclusions regarding the advance of the movement of self-government. However, the above-mentioned proved use of municipal weights and measures signifies the exercise of a sovereign act, which, if not ascribable to a margravial concession, must be regarded as an out-and-out usurpation. A little later (1090), we hear of the city collecting a feudal due throughout its county (*comitatus*), which again signifies the assumption of a right ordinarily reserved to the margravial power. Since only a few years before this event Henry IV had so conspicuously honored Pisa and Lucca with the ample privileges of 1081, Matilda may have felt obliged to make some equivalent concession to her subjects of Florence in order to command their continued loyalty. And whether she made the concession or not, the Florentines, whose faithfulness to the countess was entirely compatible with a strong sense of their own rights, would not in the least be minded to let their political development lag behind that of the other Tuscan towns.

That, in point of fact, it did not so lag was conclusively proved not long after by the exercise of an authority entirely impossible in the old days of feudal submissiveness. Of all the symbols of sovereignty, the most imposing from the beginning of history has been the right to make war and peace. Should we therefore learn that Florence undertook to levy war without the consent of its overlord and in its own exclusive interest, we would be justified in declaring that a very respectable measure of practical independence has been won. And an unequivocal declaration to this effect is made possible by an event recorded by the earliest Florentine chronicler whose meager assortment of happenings in the life of the young commune has come down to us. In the year 1107, according to this unknown annalist, "the Florentines destroyed the castle of Monte Gualandi." [6] This castle lay some eight miles down the Arno on a hill above the existing village of Lastra and belonged to a branch of the Conti Alberti. The Alberti (or Counts Alberti) were one of the great feudal families of the Florentine county; and when we are told that a citizen army destroyed one of their castles lying along the road to Pisa, we are obliged to deduce that Florence had been annoyed by a barrier to its commerce and had leveled it with the ground. Like all the rising communes of Italy, the Florentines recognized that the prime obstacles to their development were the great feudal families and that they and their castles would have to be cleared from the path if the city was to enjoy the unhampered growth to which it aspired. The destruction of Monte Gualandi was the first step in a policy which did

---

[5] Davidsohn, Vol. I, p. 270. The author's interesting discussion concerning the coming of autonomy is supported by evidence in *Forschungen*, Vol. I, pp. 62-3.

[6] Annales Florentini, II. Hartwig, *Quellen und Forschungen*, Vol. II, p. 140.

not rest until, though only after several centuries, there was not an independent feudal stronghold left in Tuscany.[7]

Some years later (1114) the same nameless annalist reports the destruction by the Florentines of another castle, Monte Cascioli. It lay on the left bank of the Arno only a short distance from the recently destroyed Monte Gualandi. The complicated provincial situation which led to this new aggression has been reconstructed by the historians of the period, such as Santini and Davidsohn. It will satisfy our limited purpose if we content ourselves with two remarks. The first is that by the early twelfth century Florence had manifestly become an aggressive community regarding war in its own interest as its legitimate province; the second makes the point that the first wars of Florence had as their objective the numerous nearby castles from which the feudal lords threatened the rising commerce of the town. It is quite improbable that the Countess Matilda was consulted in connection with these actions, which were a concern not of hers but of the trading burghers. Clearly in Florence, as everywhere else, the floodlike movement of events was pushing her aside. She may not even have been fully conscious that her power was on the wane; but such facts as these here recorded permit us to affirm that, with or without her consent, Florence, like every other city of her realm, was exercising rights which in their sum signify the assumption of a liberal measure of administrative and political autonomy.

Should anyone require additional proof regarding the decline of Matilda's authority during the latter half of her reign, let him consider an outstanding event of her very last years. In the year 1113 Pisa, risen a hundred years after its capture of the island of Sardinia to the status of a bustling and irrepressible commonwealth, organized a crusade against a band of Saracen corsairs who, from the Balearic Islands as a base, ventured to reassert an ascendancy which they had never entirely surrendered. Since the crusade, if successful, would destroy a vicious nest of pirates, all the neighboring ports and the inland Tuscan towns as well were invited by Pisa to join in the enterprise. Many towns, including Florence, responded to the call, with the result that a magnificent armada sailed westward over the sea and, after a campaign which cost three years of strenuous endeavor, captured Majorca, the main Moslem fortress.[8] True, when, with their object gained, the crusaders returned home, fresh Moslem bands from Spain resettled the islands. We hear of them as an unabated nuisance for a long time to come. Nonetheless a glorious victory had been won, bringing honor to the Tuscan towns but chiefly to sea-faring Pisa, which had captained the enterprise. A notable feature that will not escape the student attentive to political change was that the ruler of Tuscany, whose participation in such an enterprise might well be taken for granted, shone by her absence. In an expedition affecting the welfare of the whole province, the famous and authoritative Matilda had no share. Apparently no one consulted her about the venture nor did she feel a pressing desire to take charge. Perhaps her ad-

[7] The attack on Monte Gualandi was part of a complicated series of actions arising from a new phase in the war between emperor and pope. Whoever is interested in these larger implications may consult Santini, "Studi sull'Antica Costituzione del Comune di Firenze," *Arch. Stor. It.*, Serie 5, Vol. XXV.

[8] For the Balearic crusade see Heywood, *A History of Pisa*, chap. V. Cambridge, 1921.

vanced years—she was nearing seventy—caused her to be less eager than had once been the case to assert her power. In any event she does not figure in the greatest armed feat in which her Tuscan subjects had thus far engaged. On July 24, 1115, only a few months after the capture of Majorca and before the Tuscan rejoicings over the great triumph had subsided, she died at Bondeno, one of her many castles in Lombardy. Who can doubt that the church bells rung at her funeral sounded also the knell of an epoch?

We cannot close this chapter without referring to a memorial of the Balearic crusade which to this day intrigues the visitor of the Arno city. On either side of the main door of the baptistery of St. John he sees a much damaged porphyry column securely fastened to the wall by iron hoops. These two not unimpressive shafts were among the booty brought from Majorca by the Florentine contingent in that expedition and were triumphantly set up in the as yet mean and undistinguished town to commemorate the victory. After some generations had passed the ever-exuberant fancy of the burghers busied itself to twine a vine of legend around the damaged trophies. According to this invention, which has enjoyed an unchallenged currency down to our own day, the columns represented a fraud practiced by the treacherous Pisans on their unsuspecting Florentine friends and allies. Perhaps the battered appearance of the shafts suggested to a later generation that there must have been some deception, and the theory the more readily gained ground as there had meanwhile sprung up a passionate ill-will between the two towns. The fact to which to hold fast, however, is that the ill-will and hatred did not develop till a hundred years after the Balearic expedition and that they were completely nonexistent when the blackened relics first made their appearance in Florence. Instead of commemorating Pisan bad faith, they undoubtedly celebrate a mutually advantageous friendship. However, that there could ever have been a time when trust and friendship ruled between them and the Pisans, the Florentines of the subsequent centuries absolutely refused to credit; and to justify their invincible aversion of their neighbors they spun a malicious tale illustrative of the well-known and ingrained Pisan treachery.

VI. The Twelfth Century: The Consular Phase of Communal Autonomy

IN TRACING the history of Florence during the investiture struggle we learned that the town, still in shadow, though the shadow was lifting, had assumed either with or, as is far more likely, without margravial authority certain self-governing functions, and had thereby constituted itself as a commune. As at the same time many other towns in Tuscany and many scores of towns throughout Italy had done the same thing, we are confronted with the famous communal period of Italian history and, by way of overture, with the much agitated issue of communal origins. While there is no need to repeat what has already been said on the score of origins,[1] it is permissible once more to point out that the nineteenth-century conflict between the followers of the German and the Roman schools was based on what to us of a later day is a historical misconception. Inspired by a simple faith in the effectiveness of institutions in themselves, the scholars took them as their point of departure. Institutions were regarded as the deliberate invention of men, subject to modification by other men as intelligence and self-interest directed. With the adoption of the genetic approach to history characteristic of the present time the older view gradually lost favor, since the contemporary historian inclines to look behind institutions to the general social conditions producing them. He tends to regard society as an organism which periodically runs with fresh sap obliging the organism to express itself in novel forms. The sap which in the eleventh century began to fill the Italian towns was the revival of commerce; and it no sooner ran, magically multiplying both private and public activities, than it was sluiced into numerous appropriate channels. In other words, as has been the case from the beginning of time, the quickening social energies called into being the new economic, juridical, and political forms they needed in order to function. They may in some instances have utilized either a Roman or a German form, which happened to have survived and lay conveniently at hand. In that case they made institutional borrowings, but the borrowings, however definite and provable, are relatively unimportant. What alone greatly matters is the coming of new life, which, like the season of spring in the world of nature, is far more a mysterious and unfathomable process than it is a rational and analyzable one. Working with unabated but capricious energy, the commercial revival brought into being such institutions of law and government as were capable of serving its ends. This is an organic view of social

---

[1] Chap. II.

processes, and in its light the commune, the sum of the institutions slowly rising to view in the eleventh century, is not the revival of a dead past, Roman or German, but essentially an original creation.

However, just as spring comes slowly and hesitantly, the communal institutions had a very gradual unfolding and their hidden beginnings go far back of the eleventh century, when the commune first made its appearance as a going concern. For our town of Florence the increasing activities of the eleventh century and the barely perceptible movements of a still earlier time have been so thoroughly investigated by Davidsohn that every subsequent student must needs follow the trail he has blazed.[2] Davidsohn, with his eye directed on Florence, and the numerous scholars who, taking their cue from him, have undertaken similar investigations covering the length and breadth of the peninsula, have shown beyond challenge that in the anarchic period following the Carolingian dissolution the central government practically ceased to function and that men were obliged to shift for themselves or perish. As a result neighbors banded together to perform the absolutely indispensable services pertaining to the business of living on its simplest conceivable level. Such voluntary groups, called *vicinie* or *vicinanze,* arose spontaneously here, there, and everywhere, indicating that, just as social dissolution had reached its lowest point, a fresh and narrowly local start toward organization was made in response to such pressing necessities as could not be evaded if life was to go on. In lieu of the vainly implored help from above, the neighbors, abandoned by the government, undertook to help themselves.

If we try to picture the combined county of Florence-Fiesole during the anarchic ninth and tenth centuries, we must begin by conceiving of Florence itself as still inclosed within its Roman walls but in other respects hardly more than a village, whose usually deserted streets were brought to a certain moderate animation on the customary market days. The hilly country round about was still heavily wooded, with its extensive clearings worked by peasants who were held in the many degrees of dependence characteristic of serfdom by a thin upper layer of feudal lords. The status of these latter as a ruling class of warriors is indicated by the fact that they bore arms and were housed for safety in rude castles of stone. It is still possible to prove from documentary references that even after the communal age had got well under way, in the twelfth century, there existed in the single contado of Florence as many as one hundred and thirty castles. The actual number at that time and during the immediately preceding centuries, which we are here considering, must have been far greater. In fact, there is every reason to believe that our rolling comitatus and, for that matter, the whole variously contoured province of Tuscany carried a castle on every hill offering a fair prospect of safety from marauders. But these rude defensive structures were not for the lords alone. A castle consisted of a tower with barns and stables inclosing one or more open courts and with a sturdy wall, unscalable except with ladders, enveloping the whole compound. To this fortress-like residence, as soon as an enemy appeared, the cultivators of the surrounding fields flocked for safety, bringing with them all they held dear, their families, their animals, and their chattels. In the frequent, sudden emer-

2 Davidsohn, Vol. I, chap. VIII.

gencies of that lawless epoch the peasants of whatever degree served as the garrison of the castle, performing the military duties required by the occasion; and in return for this service they were endowed with a number of rights, among them the very important right to appoint a gateman or *portinarius* to act as caretaker of their goods. Here, then, in connection with the castle of the countryside we encounter one of the earliest forms of the vicinia: agricultural neighbors resorting to military self-help in times of unusual stress.

Another form of the vicinia may be noted in connection with the *populus* or parish. The well-knit ecclesiastical organization of Italy did not break down when the civil administration failed. Indeed, with other institutional props disastrously giving way, men looked with increased affection to the parish church, which with its solemn ceremonies of baptism, marriage, and burial gave spiritual strength and moral sanction to the primal social unit, the family. After celebration of the mass on Sunday or on holidays, the neighbors of the parish would meet in the open space in front of the church and take council together concerning the repair of God's house, or the maintenance of paths and roads, or the upkeep and increase of the water supply.

In Florence too, ecclesiastically divided from the early days of Christianity into parishes, the parish neighbors on coming together after mass would deliberate concerning their common interests. However, when it came to defense against a sudden assault upon the town, the parish meeting was not the proper court of appeal. To meet a situation of equal importance to all the parishes there had sprung into being an organization expressive of the circumstance that Florence was a walled town entered by four dangerously exposed gates. In case of attack every male inhabitant was required to report with such arms as he possessed at the gate to which he belonged in order to render military service as the member of a gate company. Like the meeting of the parish neighbors, who would name a committee to carry out the measures they had adopted, the four gate companies would intrust the conduct of their business to leaders or captains elected by the group. Such agents were commonly called *boni homines* and, after performing the service for which they were appointed, these true and honorable men would report to their respective assemblies and, if their service was approved, would be discharged with thanks.

When this extremely primitive social situation experienced the economic recovery setting in with the eleventh century, the first effect was a rapid increase in the neighborhood activities attended by the need of their better coordination from the point of view of the town as a commercial and political unit. Neighboring parishes or neighboring gate companies would find themselves obliged to act together in a matter of common concern. To this end they would consult regarding the appointment of boni homines of broader scope than had hitherto been usual until this development would inescapably terminate in boni homines representative of the whole town. We should not think of these representatives of wider scope as acquiring at once a permanent character. They long continued to function as a purely provisional executive and, their task completed, they would vanish from the scene. Let us never forget that everything was fluid, experimental, and haphazard in this inchoate and still profoundly disturbed society. On this very account, however, the advantages of a firmer organization would not fail to impress themselves, and uncertain steps aiming at a continuous and improved control would be gradually taken, although it is no longer possible to trace them in detail. With commerce steadily expanding and bringing up new problems we cannot doubt that officials uninterruptedly engaged upon their growing tasks became an urgent necessity. There would have to be—to mention only the most indispensable requirements—a secretary to keep the communal records, a treasurer to assemble and disburse the communal funds; and there would also have to be a town hall to house these earliest officials of the emerging commonwealth, even though at the beginning it might be represented by nothing more than a single rented room in a private house.

Municipal rudiments of the haphazard and experimental order indicated were probably in existence in Florence by the middle of Matilda's reign. They can be proved for other Tuscan towns, such as Pisa and Lucca, where organization had already by that time gone so far as to give the central executive committee of boni homines something more than a purely temporary, *ad hoc* character. As soon as this particular advance had been made, whether in Tuscany, Lombardy, or elsewhere, it became customary to call the boni homines by a more dignified name, by the name of consuls. The title, harking back to the republican days of Rome, stirred a proud, never wholly forgotten memory in Italian bosoms and gained an immediate popularity throughout the communal area. Without hesitation the rising towns fastened on the Roman term; and its adoption appeared so significant to later generations that it became usual to date the achievement of full self-government on the part of any town from the first accredited use of the consular title. This was anything but a sound procedure, for while, on the one hand, self-government of a loose provisional sort antedated by a good deal the appearance of consuls, on the other hand, the presence of these officials is no assurance of autonomy, much less of sovereignty, fully achieved, since for a long time after consuls can be proved for a given commune, the commune was still, both theoretically and practically, dependent on the emperor and, on the rare occasions when the emperor was strong, might actually find itself thrust back into full feudal subjection.

Provided we make due allowance for the constant fluctuations and incurable uncertainties inherent in the communal situation, there is no reason why we should not join in celebrating the institution of the consuls as a considerable political advance indicative of a new and higher stage of municipal organization. But at this point we are met by a fresh difficulty springing from our inability to date exactly the arrival of consuls in even a single instance. The best we can do is to fall back on their earliest mention in a document. Thus in the case of our town of Florence the first authoritative reference to consuls belongs to the year 1138.[3] For Siena we have documentary proof of their existence by 1125;[4] and for Pisa and Lucca the evidence reaches well back into the previous century. As there was, in spite of the admittedly

[3] Hartwig, *Quellen und Forschungen*, Vol. II, p. 185. Santini, *Documenti dell'Antica Costituzione*, etc., Introduzione (p. XXVI).
[4] Pasqui, *Documenti per la Storia della Città di Arezzo*, p. 573.

earlier self-governing activity of Pisa and Lucca, an essentially parallel political development of all the Tuscan towns, we may safely affirm that Florence had consuls for some time before 1138, probably from the death of Matilda in 1115, and not improbably even before that.

Once established, the consular executive, generally speaking, lasted well through the twelfth century. While many details regarding the consular system as operated in Florence and Tuscany remain a complete puzzle, we know enough confidently to essay a general description. The consulate is always a multiple executive, twelve being the more usual number of consular associates. They served commonly for one year and were invested with the power to negotiate treaties, to lead the urban host in war, and to preside at the highest municipal court. The method of election is wholly conjectural. The consular system recognized a general meeting of the citizens called *parlamentum* or *contio* or *arringhum* and presided over by the consuls. This was its democratic feature, of which a great deal has always been made by passionate proponents of the democratic principle. But although the parlamentum was commonly asked to approve treaties and to acclaim the new consuls on their assumption of authority, it is not at all likely that it had a hand in electing these officials. Consuls issued so regularly from the highest stratum of the citizens that we are obliged to define the consulate as an essentially aristocratic institution carefully manipulated in the interest of the leading families. In the unwieldiness of the parlamentum lies the probable explanation of its largely ornamental character. No orderly election of executive officials is possible in a mass meeting nor can a mob function as a satisfactory legislature. Therefore, if the Florentine or any other Tuscan parliament ever had any legislative authority, it yielded it at an early date to a council (*concilium, consiglio*) of approximately one hundred and fifty members. As the council, too, was drawn regularly from the same well-to-do element as manned the consulate, we can hardly escape the conclusion that, contrary to a still prevalent fiction, the consular constitution of the young communes did not have its root in the people but functioned as an oligarchy coated with a thin democratic veneer. Owing to the fact that many generations passed before the town equipped itself with adequate public buildings, the early parlamentum of the Arno town met either in the cathedral or on a public square under the open sky, while the early council assembled in one of the lesser churches such as San Piero Scheraggio. At an early date it became customary to define the authority committed to the consular officials in a *breve consulum*. On this document the incoming consuls took the oath of office for their term. Periodically revised and enlarged, the breve grew until it became, but not till the following century, a fully elaborated constitution.[5]

An examination of the social structure of Florence in the twelfth century makes it absolutely clear why the political government could not be other than aristocratic. The most conspicuous social group were the lesser nobles, the knights or *milites*. Endowed with lands in the immediate vicinity of the town, they had probably always lived within the walls. However, during the con-

[5] A breve consulum for Florence cannot be proved before 1159. As to the certainty of earlier brevi and the manner of their expansion into a constitution see Davidsohn, Vol. I, p. 665.

sular regime their number steadily increased by the policy of the victorious commune to oblige the conquered possessors of more distant castles to become Florentine citizens and to manifest their acceptance of the new situation by residing for at least a part of each year in the town. Immediately after this dominant group came the prosperous merchants. Their wealth enabled them to intermarry with the knights so that they became imperceptibly merged with them in a single class of the rich. The knights for their part made fusion easy since, having breathed town air from their birth, they were far from exhibiting any insuperable aversion for trade. In possession of all the wealth there was, in possession of both fixed and fluid capital, this upper crust enjoyed a prestige which made it possible for them to monopolize the communal offices without any difficulty. There would have to be a large and active population of shop-keepers and artisans before the political control of the oligarchs could be challenged with any chance of success. And as yet these two classes were extremely feeble. Indubitably they had begun to increase in the century under discussion, but their number did not reach a sufficient figure to unsettle the social balance. The remaining elements composing the population were the clergy, the physicians, the men of law, and the common laborers. The clergy were a numerous and highly respected class made up of the bishop and the cathedral canons, the parish priests, and a great variety of monks and nuns. As members of the Roman Catholic church, an institution which had achieved a status on a par with and outside of civil society, they were indeed sheltered and protected by the commune, but they were not a political part of it. Physicians were as yet few in number; men of law, made up of notaries and judges, were far more plentiful. Rapidly gaining in authority, they will by the following century have become an indispensable adjunct of a society given to an ever-increasingly eager pursuit of wealth. As to the laborers, dependent for a living on daily wages, while their number was undoubtedly expanding through immigration from the farms, neither now nor as long as Florence continued to figure as an independent commonwealth did they exercise an influence remotely commensurate with their numbers.

The associative impulse, which had given birth to the commune in the first place, long continued to manifest itself as the fundamental energy of society. Until a strong government had arisen, prepared to guarantee life and property, individuals would be prompted to make agreements with other individuals to gain security for their persons and to promote their material interests. Hence the extraordinarily complicated network of social, economic, and religious bonds which underlies medieval society everywhere. Throughout the twelfth century Florence gave birth to new and ever newer associative phenomena. Very early in that century, perhaps even in the previous century, the resident knights constituted themselves as a *societas militum,* to which members of well-established merchant families were after a delay admitted on a basis of equality. Although the miles or knight was originally a lesser nobleman, a sub-vassal who rode to war in the service of a greater lord, by the consular age any citizen rich enough to own a helmet, spear, sword, coat of mail, and of course a horse, might aspire to qualify as a miles. While the Florentine knights, accoutered in the manner indicated, have the look of a military aristocracy and were pleased to display the martial manners of such a class, let us never forget that from a purely economic angle they were simply the men of means, the rich.

The remaining citizens, naturally the vast majority of the population, made up the foot-soldiers, the *pedites*. They were originally assembled in companies according to the parish in which they resided. In the course of time, but not till the next, the thirteenth, century, they were amalgamated into a *societas peditum,* which, under the more expressive term of a *societas populi,* was destined to challenge and, in the end, to overthrow the military aristocracy. Cavalry and infantry together made up the communal army which, when an expedition was ordered, took the field under the command of the consuls. Of course the cavalry, composed of men dedicated to arms as a profession, were a far more effective force than the infantry, who, called from their shops and benches by the ringing of a bell, fought without armor and with such improvised, casual weapons as their slender means permitted them to provide. The greater value on campaign of the well-born and wealthy horsemen must be set down as a weighty factor in their long-continued political ascendancy. It is highly characteristic of the still purely private nature of the public activities of the citizens in the consular age that, while the obligation to serve in the army was general, and while the army was the most perfect expression of the unitary will of the new political entity, the commune, each inhabitant provided his own military equipment and was a horseman or a foot-soldier according to his private resources.

When the communal army was mobilized for war it took with it into the field as a symbol of the new and precious union of the citizens the car of state, the *caroccio*. This consisted of a platform on four wheels carrying suspended from a mast the banner of the commune, not yet the famous Red Lily on a white field but a simple cloth of two stripes, one red, the other white.[6] The car was drawn by one or more pairs of white oxen which, like the vehicle itself and its troop of attendant grooms, were swathed in rich crimson stuffs. Since the caroccio, far from being a destructive engine of war, was a cumbersome contraption which seriously interfered with the mobility of the citizen army, we can account for its existence only by referring it to the zest and swagger which were the pardonable accompaniment of the commune's adolescence. Around the caroccio, far visible with its waving communal banner, the youth of Florence gathered, when the battle raged, prepared to defend this ark of the covenant with the last drop of their blood.

The massing of the milites, the men on horseback, in a single society conveys the impression of a unity among them which was clamorously denied by the facts. Nothing was more characteristic of the upper class than their implacable feuds. On account of the strong call of the blood among medieval men they accepted the family bond as something irrevocable and hallowed. Long after the commune with its public responsibilities had raised its head the family with its ancient obligations of a private nature exercised an undiminished sway. Therefore whenever a quarrel occurred between two young swordsmen and braggarts, it automatically involved their respective families; and if it chanced that blood had been spilt in the course of the argument, blood was

[6] Villani, IV, 7; also VI, 43.

called for in return. Love of fighting for its own sake, fortified by the solemn family obligation of vendetta, explains a type of association interesting in itself and doubly interesting because it provided twelfth-century Florence with its most characteristic physical feature. Still an almost unbelievably primitive community, the town boasted, with the exception of the handsome baptistry of St. John, not a single church conspicuous for either size or beauty; it had not a single civic building, for civic organization had not yet advanced to the point of requiring a special structure; and it housed its poor, which means the overwhelming majority of the population, in wretched wooden hovels among conditions of indescribable squalor. But if from a neighboring hill, like San Miniato, we could have looked down on this Florence contained as yet within the narrow circuit of its Roman walls and presenting to view a huddle of mean structures, largely of wood and dangerously inflammable, we would have broken into a spontaneous cry of surprise over the sight of scores of towers of brick and stone soaring high above the surrounding roofs.[7]

These towers were the property of related groups of noble families or, in a few instances, of a single particularly powerful family. Without any doubt whatever they originally served as residences, although in the course of time the families that owned them commonly provided themselves with more habitable quarters erected at the side of the towers. In that case the tower became the fortress whither the family retreated the moment that a vendetta developing with a rival family precipitated private war. Families sharing the possession of a tower formed a tower association (*consorteria*), and the towers, constituting a series of town castles, served as military supports in the battles that periodically raged up and down the narrow streets. Throughout the twelfth century, and for most of the following century as well, the municipal government was far too feeble to suppress the savage extravagances perpetrated by the upper class in pursuit of mere private hate and vengeance. For many generations it did not even try to do so, for the communal government itself at first had the character of a private association exercising strictly limited local powers, among which the dissolution of the consorterie did not figure. Besides, the government was in the hands of the very people who gloried in the towers as an expression of class and family pride. Under these circumstances the towers may be thought of as symbols of a lawless upper caste ruling the town in its own interest and indulging itself in practices which were a constant menace to the safety of the common people. We may conclude without fear of contradiction that if Florence was ever to be established as an orderly burgher community, the towers, the tower associations, and the nobles themselves would have to disappear. A clean sweep would have to be made and indeed was made, as we shall learn; but happily, we are moved to declare, it was not so clean a sweep that numerous towers, prudently deprived of their threatening upper stories, have not survived. In the consular age the towers rose thick as a canebrake, especially in the Mercato Vecchio and along the street leading to the Old Bridge, called Por (for porta) Santa Maria. Along this street and its lateral feeders, streets which in our day better than any other

---

[7] Davidsohn is of the opinion that around 1180 the towers of Florence numbered over one hundred. Davidsohn, Vol. I, p. 554.

surviving Florentine district preserve the peculiar aspect of the medieval town, many of these towers may still be identified by the attentive visitor. They will appeal to his awed imagination as the impressive remains of an age when the recently formed commune was governed by a feudal caste and was exposed daily and even hourly to the shock of arms.[8]

If the tower associations enshrined an important aspect of the feudal governing class, the newly risen classes, falling in with the active spirit of the age, formed equally characteristic associations of their own. Since the main transforming influence of society was commerce, the merchants were the outstanding *novi homines* and to protect their interest formed a *societas mercatorum*, in sum, a merchant gild. While the records are too defective to permit any positive assertions, it is not open to dispute that from an early time there existed a powerful gild of merchants, on whose shoulders rested the rising prosperity of the town.[9] Its members, either as individuals or through partnerships, dealt indiscriminately in all the goods which were in demand, particularly in cloth, dyes, hides, and spices. With money coming more and more into use as the medium of exchange, they concerned themselves also with the current coins, the silver *denarii* (pennies), put out by the various governments of Europe, as well as with the practice of borrowing and lending. Thus almost unconsciously they launched into the business of banking. Since these rising merchant-bankers, when they were rich enough, intermarried with the knights, and since, owing to this relationship, the knights established a direct contact with trade, it commonly happened that the merchant gild bore on its roster the names of numerous members of the tower families. Let the fact confirm the fusion, already noted in the case of the societas militum, of the two urban groups possessed of wealth; and let it at the same time serve to refute the hoary fiction, imbedded in all the older histories of Florence, that the citizens who comported themselves as feudal lords proudly spurned the vulgar allurements of commerce. True, this stubborn aloofness does seem to have characterized the leading noble family, the rather grandiose Uberti; certainly the rest of the local gentry showed no aversion whatever to participating in merchant enterprises in the hope of sharing the consequent profits. In the consular age and for the following ages as well it is quite impossible to draw a sharp dividing line between a nobility concerned alone with fighting and a bourgeoisie devoted exclusively to trade.

With trade breathing life into the activities of the town, the crafts came into being; and no sooner were there crafts than there were also craft gilds or, to use the Italian term for gilds, there were *arti* (arts). In attributing craft gilds to the Florence of the twelfth century we are obliged to resort to conjecture or else to argue from analogous data supplied by other towns. However, just before the close of the century, in 1193, we get an unmistakable notice proving

---

[8] The many interesting aspects of the tower societies and, above all, their legal aspect, are treated by Santini, "Società delle Torri in Firenze," in *Arch. Stor. It.,* Serie 4, Vol. XX, pp. 25-58, 178-204.

[9] Davidsohn, Vol. I, p. 667. The earliest surviving reference to a merchant gild belongs to the year 1182. It occurs in the submission to Florence of Empoli. Santini, *Documenti dell'Antica Costituzione,* etc., No. XII.

the existence of an undetermined number of craft gilds.[10] It has been assumed that their number in the above-mentioned year was seven, but the probability is great that they ran to a much higher figure. Be that as it may, the total importance of these minor gilds, compared with that of the single powerful merchant gild, remained small for long years to come.

The summary information supplied in this chapter on the political, social, and economic developments in Florence during the twelfth century is intended to serve a double purpose. While the reader has been made acquainted with the main domestic concerns of the still embryonic commonwealth, a picture worth getting for its own sake, he has also been provided by means of a body of social-economic data with the leading clue to Florentine foreign policy. To this policy we shall now turn and begin with the assertion that, from the moment the Arno city became autonomous, it aimed at something better than autonomy: it aimed at complete independence. It did not take this stand from any abstract love of freedom, but because in its immediate practical affairs it found itself obstructed at every point by the feudal system in which it was imbedded. Feudalism was an agrarian development with no comprehension for, nor sympathy with, trade; and when Florence, the very life of which was commerce, discovered that feudalism regarded commerce as an upstart to be kept down and exploited without mercy, the resolution gradually took shape that feudalism would have to go. Under these circumstances the main feature of Florentine foreign policy became a relentless combat with this proved and self-confessed enemy.

Now the visible representatives of the feudal system were the emperor, the margave of Tuscany, and the nobles, great and small alike, but more particularly the great nobles since the sub-vassals were often so hostile to their superiors that they did not hesitate to seek the protection of the towns in the vicinity of which their possessions lay. We have seen that Florence had an upper layer of nobiliary citizens and we have not failed to note that most of these had made submission to the commonwealth of their own volition in the hope of escaping the exactions of their immediate overlord. It need hardly be expressly said that the conflict between vassals and sub-vassals was of decisive advantage to the towns. Even more advantageous was the falling out, already mentioned, between the emperor and the margrave over the investiture issue. However, the death of Countess Matilda in 1115 created a new situation. With it as our starting-point, we shall resume our interrupted political narrative and carry it through the century under consideration.

Emperor Henry V, son of the man who had stood as a humble penitent at the gate of Canossa castle, was not minded to let the new margrave, whom the death of Matilda gave him the right to appoint, play the same hostile role as the great countess. To this end he adopted a new policy. He was the more inclined to consider a change as Matilda, being the last of her race, had made a testament, transferring all her allodial property to the chair of St. Peter, that is, to the pope.[11] In this she was acting entirely within her rights, although we

[10] A. Doren, *Entwickelung und Organisation der Florentiner Zünfte in 13. und 14. Jahrhundert* (Schmoller's *Forschungen,* Vol. XV), pp. 8-11.

[11] Matilda made two testaments to the above effect dated respectively 1077 and 1102. Davidsohn, Vol. I, pp. 259, 290.

must understand that she could not—and did not—assign to the pope the estates with which she had been enfeoffed by the emperor and which were attached to the margravial office. True, there might be a difficulty in distinguishing in every case between what was feudal and what was allodial property, but the difficulty did not at once put in an appearance. It failed to do so because Emperor Henry V completely ignored the testament and appropriated the whole inheritance for himself. The papacy, temporarily enfeebled, did not even register a protest. But when its fortunes rose again in the eternal ebb and tide of Italian politics, it presented its claim, and the later emperors, enfeebled in their turn, were obliged to reopen the question. There can be no doubt that the Matildan inheritance added fuel to the always either smoldering or blazing fire lit by the irreconcilable ambitions of the two heads of Christendom, but that it was to any considerable degree a determining factor in the conflict which, off and on, raged between them for another two hundred years must be denied. The vicissitudes of the inheritance have been carefully traced by Overmann.[12] Whoever is interested may follow them in minute detail under his guidance. For the general reader it will suffice to learn that, while the quarrel between the two contestants of the will dragged on interminably, a third party—the usual mischievous *tertium gaudens*—with no claim at all except his strong right arm, possessed himself of the lion's share of the prize. That third party was, for the Lombard properties, the various Lombard communes; for the Tuscan properties, the various Tuscan communes. In the course of the many years during which the quarrel continued the masterful young republics quietly appropriated by far the greater portion of the margravial estates, whether feudal or allodial, thus clearly revealing not only the strength of the communal movement but the relative political weakness compared with it of both pope and emperor.

No less than in the absorption of Matilda's inheritance Emperor Henry V was interested in a successor to the margraviate who would prove steadily subservient to his authority. With this object in mind he resolved to replace the hereditary margraves of Italian nationality with German appointees removable at his pleasure. The very first German, a certain Rabodo, transferred the margravial administration from Florence, where it had rested since 1057, to San Miniato situated on a hill high over the junction of the Elsa with the Arno, in the very center of Tuscany. Owing to its association in the mind of the natives with a foreign domination the new capital acquired the designation of San Miniato del Tedesco, under which name it still lifts a tall, dark tower, like a warning finger, over the smiling valley at its foot. Rabodo had no luck in enforcing his authority, for when, in the name of the empire, he occupied Monte Cascioli, recently taken by the Florentines, their citizen army descended on him, retook the castle by assault, and buried Rabodo among the ruins (1119).

Thereupon another margrave was sent from Germany, indeed a long succession of them, of all of whom it may be reported that they had as little success as the unfortunate Rabodo in maintaining the imperial authority

[12] Overmann, *Gräfin Matilde von Tuscien: Geschichte ihres Gutes von 1115-1230*. Innsbruck, 1895.

against the rising communes. Whenever the emperor himself appeared at the head of an army, as he did from time to time, it was, to be sure, a different story. Before this exhibition of irresistible force the young republics drew in their horns. But no sooner had he vanished behind the snows of the Alps than they showed renewed disrespect for his representative by refusing to pay him the monies which were his due or to make war at his bidding. Under the circumstances the margrave dwindled to a pallid and harmless official without a following in the province; and although it is a fact that he figures in Tuscan history to the end of the century and that a succession of German margraves has been recovered from the documents as long and shadowy as the line of kings following in the wake of Banquo's ghost, we are justified in thinking of the margravial office as having the great countess as its last effective occupant.

The practical disappearance of the margrave left the emperor and the great nobles as the sole defenders of the feudal system and opponents of the revolutionary communes. And again these latter greatly profited from the fact that, owing to the only occasional presence of the emperor in Italy, the feudal defenders did not steadily and solidly stand together. Except under the emperor's immediate command the self-willed feudatories could not be persuaded to present an undivided front to the enemy. In spite of poor team play, however, they continued to wield a considerable power which, whenever it was co-ordinated by the emperor's personal intervention, swelled to formidable proportions. It is therefore proper that we look somewhat more closely at the great feudality; but as we wish to view them from the angle of our city of Florence, we shall take as our point of departure the doctrine firmly held at Florence in the communal age regarding the normal relationship between town and countryside.

Every Tuscan town of the eleventh century thought of itself as identified with its county, in spite of the fact that actually the county was and had been for some time past in the hands of the great feudality. Perhaps a memory persisted of the comitatus of the Franks, perhaps even an older memory of the civitas of the Romans had again come to life in the hearts of the townsmen. It was the special feature of both of these former administrative units that they emphasized the identity of the town and its immediate countryside. However, should the memory of the Frank and Roman divisions have dropped from the mind, there, in effective visible operation, were the dioceses of the church, which in the main still followed the boundaries of the old Roman civitates. Since the town, in the person of the bishop, ruled the contado ecclesiastically, it seemed logical that, as soon as the town became a responsible governing entity, it should rule the contado also politically. On this consummation the townsmen of the twelfth century had so set their hearts that war between them and the feudal powers in actual possession of the contado was unavoidable.

The outstanding feature which met the eye, scanning not only the Florentine diocese but also that larger unit born of an obscure event of the ninth century, the united county of Florence-Fiesole,[13] was that diocese and county

13 See chap. III, p. 32.

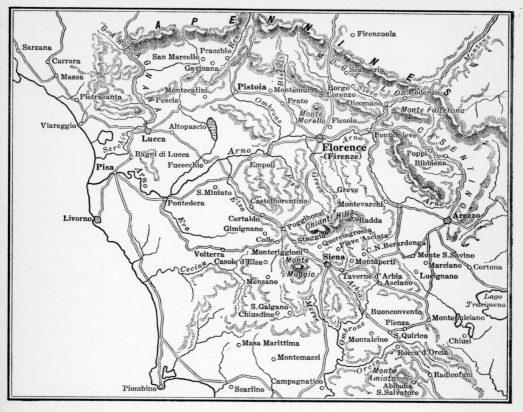

TUSCANY SHOWING THE CHIEF TOWNS, RIVERS, ROADS, AND MOUNTAINS

were dominated by three great feudal magnates. One of these was the bishop himself; the other two were the respective heads of the great Guidi and Alberti families.[14] If not the immediate, the ultimate aim of the townsmen was to destroy the long string of castles by which the lords maintained their power and to draw their innumerable estates within the jurisdiction of the commune. But from the first a distinction was made between the bishop and the two lay rulers. We are aware that the bishop, owing to the system of immunities, was also a lay ruler; but not for a moment are we permitted to doubt that his newer, political power was less essential to him than his older, spiritual power, sole source of his vast moral authority. In his spiritual capacity the Florentines sincerely venerated their bishop and had no desire to deprive him of the revenues which he drew from his estates. He was the most distinguished resident of the town and was expected to maintain a dignified court in his spacious palace lying just west of the baptistery. But the Florentines also contended, and with the greatest vigor, that civil rule over his estates was not inherent in his episcopal office and that it rightfully belonged to them. With astonishingly little conflict, at least of an open nature, their viewpoint gradually prevailed. In the course of the twelfth century the bishop let himself be divested of the civil jurisdiction over his lands for reasons which are not difficult to recover. For one thing, he lacked the military strength necessary to meet the communal challenge; and for another, as long as the townsmen guaranteed him his undiminished revenues, he may even have welcomed a development that enabled him to devote himself exclusively to his strictly clerical duties.

Not content with dealing with their bishop in the cavalier manner indicated, the Florentines resolved to use him as a cloak to hide their policy of expansion. A difficulty in which this policy entangled them from the start was that they obliged such lords as they conquered to become their subjects, although these lords were legally the subjects of the margrave and the emperor. The subjection was therefore an offense to the constituted powers, whose wrath it was to the advantage of the burghers to avert until the time when they had become strong enough no longer to fear it. To this end they bethought themselves of a fiction by which they might give a certain air of respectability to their bold usurpations. In the charter of surrender they would require the conquered nobleman to certify his submission, not to themselves, but to the cathedral church and to its patron saint, St. John the Baptist; and further, in visible sign of his submission, they would require him to make an offering of wax candles on the Baptist's annual festival. As this fell on the twenty-fourth of June it came about that once every year Florence witnessed a spectacle that swelled the bosom of the citizens with barely controllable pride. For, forming a line which grew longer with every decade, on each St. John's day the conquered noblemen of the contado, in gala raiment and bearing lighted candles in their hands, presented themselves in solemn procession at the portal of San Giovanni to signify their subjection to the victorious commune.

[14] Santini, "Studi sull'Antica Costituzione del Comune di Firenze," *Arch. Stor. It.,* Serie 5, Vol. XXV (1900). An accompanying map shows the location of the many fiefs of the three lords in question.

It cannot be said that the emperor or anyone else was deceived by the subterfuge. However, as it was employed not only by Florence but by all the other Tuscan communes as well, it must have had some value as a legal device to bridge over the gap between a society that was slowly dying and its successor that was just as slowly coming to birth.

The bishop, then, in spite of his numerous well-distributed estates, was no obstacle to the plan of the citizens to govern their county. The opposition came, in the main, from the two ancient and powerful families, the Guidi and Alberti, with their literally scores of castles scattered chiefly over the county of Florence but to be found also, especially in the case of the Guidi, the more formidable of the two clans, in many adjoining counties. In sign of their ancient blood and long exercise of authority the members of both families bore the title of count. As the Alberti owned many castles almost within sight of Florence, the earliest clashes of the ambitious commune befell with them. When in the year 1107 the Florentines inaugurated, so far as we can now see, their expansion policy, they captured Monte Gualandi, a castle of the Alberti; and when, six years later, they celebrated a second triumph of this sort at Monte Cascioli, they moved against a family with which the Alberti were closely leagued. Thus reluctantly were these counts moved to acquire respect for the upstart commune, an attitude greatly furthered by the circumstance that the new German margraves sent to Tuscany as successors to the Countess Matilda were without adequate resources and the emperor too far away to give effective aid. Consequently the Alberti were often in a mood to seek an accommodation with the Florentines; and as the Florentines, for their part, were frequently in serious straits because of having too many irons in the fire, they welcomed intervals of peace in their relations with the counts. This must be grasped if we are to understand the bewildering surface changes in the attitude of Florence toward the Alberti. Without ever losing sight of its fixed purpose, the prudent commune was prepared to reckon with the shifting currents of practical politics and to reach the goal of its ambition slowly and by devious paths. To follow the perpetual alternations of good and bad neighborhood relations between the commune and the Alberti would lead us into a maze as confusing as it is unprofitable. Suffice it that the Alberti, although often defeated by the commune and manifestly on the wane, continued to cut an important figure in Florentine and Tuscan politics throughout the consular age.

The same is true of the Guidi, a family credited at the meridian of its power with the possession of three hundred castles distributed, we should never forget, almost as widely over the Romagna as over Tuscany. The Guidi were perhaps the greatest feudal family of all central Italy. Hostilities with them did not become chronic until the Alberti were already hard pressed; but, the battle once joined, it never again rested, although it was not continuously waged and was even punctuated with intermittent periods of amity. On purely rational and material grounds the two great clans should always have stood shoulder to shoulder, but there was too much jealousy between them for this to be effected. Of this extremely fortunate division Florence took full advantage by frequently using one group against the other. However, as often as the emperor arrived in Tuscany, Alberti and Guidi alike crowded to his service, whereupon the stock of the feudality would suddenly rise, while that of the communes would score a corresponding decline.

The emperors who immediately followed Henry V were Lothar III (1125–37) and Conrad III (1138–52). They showed less interest in their Italian kingdom than their immediate predecessors had done; and although they visited it, largely to effect the coveted imperial coronation at Rome, they did not linger long and, giving only half-hearted attention to the problem created by the rising communes, avoided precipitating the conflict between the old and new order which, in the long run, was inevitable. Not till the reign of Frederick I was the rising new order effectively challenged. Elevated to the German throne in 1152, Frederick came to Italy two years later. Before considering the activist policy which he at once adopted and which precipitated a tremendous convulsion, we shall have to give attention to a factor in the program of Florence which was coming more and more to the front, and which loomed as large as and, finally, even larger than its animosity against the two great feudal families.

In the very year (1107) in which Florence embarked on the conquest of the feudal castles lying athwart its road, she also made a descent on the inconspicuous, close by town of Prato and destroyed it.[15] Although Prato, a very recent creation, bore witness to the commercial spirit abroad in the world, it came into existence under the fostering care of the Alberti, who owned a castle at that point. While hostility to the Alberti doubtless figured in the Florentine attack, the destruction of the little market town was induced, at least preponderantly, by the unwillingness of the Arno city to have a possible trade rival grow up at its doorstep. That Prato lay just outside the county of Florence, in the county and diocese of Pistoia, made no difference to the merchants in control of Florentine policy. When, owing to one of the sudden, kaleidoscopic changes usual in Tuscan politics, the attention of the Florentines was drawn elsewhither, Prato was rebuilt and Florence did not again interpose its veto. For one thing, the governing class may have convinced itself that tiny Prato was not a real commercial menace; and for another, the rulers had made the agreeable discovery that Prato was a still greater annoyance to Pistoia than to themselves. Lying at the foot of the Apeninnes, Pistoia commanded the immensely important road that led to Bologna; and Florence, obliged to use that road for her steadily broadening enterprises, instinctively sensed in Pistoia a dangerous future rival. For its part, Pistoia, following the same policy regarding its county as did Florence and every other town, wanted to keep Prato in close subjection. Consequently, as soon as the Florentines discovered that the Pratesi were a major thorn in the side of Pistoia, they completely changed their attitude by lending support to their little neighbor. In their eyes the real opponent in this quarter was not Prato but Pistoia. Besides illustrating the passionate flare-up of jealousy among communal neighbors, which at an early date started dangerous fires all over Tuscany, the episode shows how the general Tuscan situation tended to become complicated by the con-

---

[15] Annales Florentini, II. Hartwig, *Quellen und Forschungen*, Vol. II, p. 40.

flict of every town with its town neighbors, great and small, and by the rapidly shifting alignments among the towns, which made and unmade treaties with an entire lack of scruple and with an eye directed solely to the main chance.

That the animosities among neighboring towns, largely over trade advantages, date from the very beginning of the communal movement, and that they at once assumed perfectly fantastic proportions could not be better proved than by a glance at the case of Pisa and Lucca. These two towns were the first in Tuscany to respond to the commercial stimulus, and they no sooner aimed at a greater volume of trade than they engaged in ferocious warfare with each other. Their wars ended only to begin again, and so passionate and spontaneous did the hatred between Pisans and Lucchese become that we are prepared to believe, as contemporary writers solemnly report, that they imbibed it as babes with their mother's milk. Before the twelfth century, covering the first phase of the communal revolution, was over, the Pisan-Lucchese feud had been duplicated by literally scores of similar feuds, usually between large-town neighbors, but not infrequently also between small-town neighbors and even between neighboring villages. Wherever the tide of trade flowed, there envy and jealousy raised their ugly heads. While we are concerned only with Tuscany, the statement applies with equal force to Lombardy, Venetia, Emilia, Umbria—in short, to all northern and north-central Italy. To all this area the communal spirit came with a rush indistinguishable from frenzy. Unless we steadily keep both the extent and the vehemence of the movement in mind, we shall be tempted to make the mistake of regarding Florence as a unique and monstrous instance.

We are now prepared to understand the next peculiarly ferocious act of the youthful republic. On a hill to the north and in full sight of the town on the bank of the Arno stood ancient Fiesole. There is no evidence of any rivalry between the two neighbors before the communal era; but no sooner had commerce begun to bring its benefits, and to scatter its terrible dragons' teeth as well, than Florence visited Fiesole with an inextinguishable hatred. Its echoes can still be heard in the legend which Florentine mothers of later generations recounted to the children at their knees. According to this hate-inspired invention the Fiesolans were a vile Etruscan breed, which could not possibly be permitted to exist on the same earth with Florentines, who, as authentic descendants of the conquering Romans, were manifestly a chosen people. While the legend has been completely discredited by modern scholarship, it is not wholly without significance, since it tells us of an unreasoning aversion which, itself a historical fact of no mean order, we are free to explain in our own way. For us, familiar with the behavior pattern of the rising communes, it is clear that Florence resolved to bring Fiesole under its control. Indeed, owing to the physical closeness of Fiesole, the Florentine determination would be among the earliest manifestations of its budding sovereign will.

After much precedent petty bickering, in the year 1123 the Florentines, mobilizing their citizen army of cavalry and infantry, climbed up the hill to Fiesole and laid siege to it. The first campaign was a failure, owing to an inherent weakness of the communal forces. Composed largely of shopkeepers and artisans, they could not be kept long in the field. When Fiesole did not promptly surrender, the Florentines went home. The war was renewed in the following year and in the year after that; and it was not till this third campaign that Fiesole was taken (1125). The vengeance of the victors was terrible. Not only were the Fiesolans slaughtered almost to a man, but the little town was utterly destroyed. Especial animosity was directed to the protective girdle of its walls. These went back to Etruscan days, as every visitor can still convince himself by inspecting the small section to the north which was happily spared and has survived to this day. These immense, these cyclopean blocks of stone, here as wherever we encounter them in central Italy, betray Etruscan origin and workmanship. In order not to offend the pope unnecessarily the fine Romanesque cathedral, a creation of the previous century, was also spared. All around the cathedral the ruthless victors spread a desert; and if, some years afterward, they permitted the few Fiesolan survivors to crawl back and to provide a miserable shelter for themselves among the ruins, they did so on the condition that the walls and the citadel above the town should never under any circumstances be rebuilt. Fiesole never again raised its head and to this day conveys to every sensitive visitor the impression of a community stricken with a mysterious blight.

The next stage of the Florentine advance brought the commune face to face with Siena. This town owed its commercial importance to its location on one of the main roads leading to the capital of Christendom, to Rome. At the very first appearance of communal self-consciousness it resolved, like all its neighbors, to gain the control of its county; and presently, on this very score, it came into conflict with Florence. While county boundaries coincided in the main with diocesan boundaries, this was not always the case, and in these exceptional instances the county boundary was certain to be a matter of dispute. When Florence pressed the claim that its county line toward the south reached within a few miles of Siena's northern gate, the Sienese protested, partly because the issue was in doubt, and partly because they did not feel safe with a neighbor of the mettle of Florence camped almost under the shadow of their wall.[16] The resulting animosity was stimulated by commercial rivalry until it led unescapably to war. The first certain armed conflict between the two communes occurred in 1129, four years after the destruction of Fiesole; and the fire lighted on that occasion was not effectively extinguished for many hundred years. The famous Florence-Siena feud will force itself on our attention again and again in the course of this history. It reached a degree of ferocity that obliges us to list it among the most embittered communal feuds of the period, with neither the monstrous Pisa-Lucca nor the equally terrible Pisa-Genoa feud surpassing it in implacability.

In the early twelfth century the struggle between the two towns was as yet in its infancy. Much remains dark about this phase, but it is certain that the initial conflict of 1129 was followed at irregular intervals by many others. While the issues involved have been touched upon and require no further

16 A map throwing light on the boundary dispute will be found in Schevill, *Siena: The Story of a Medieval Commune*, p. 178. New York, 1909. The wars of the two communes are related with some detail in chap. VI.

clarification, we must understand that Siena and Florence were not concerned to bring them to a decision in single combat like a pair of duelists. As soon as a fresh conflict threatened, each contestant searched the horizon feverishly for allies and indicated a willingness to accept support from every available quarter. The two towns therefore turned for help not only to other towns within the orbit of their trade and politics but also to the surrounding feudal lords. Naturally Siena, threatened by Florence, turned to the clans of the Guidi and Alberti, who might be expected to hail with delight this opportunity to lower the pride of their communal enemy, while Florence responded in kind and sought the alliance of the great feudal clans of the Sienese contado, such as the Cacciaconti and the Aldobrandeschi. It may be left to the imagination to what an extent this situation pumped fresh blood into the veins of the declining feudatories. Just as they seemed to be doomed by the communal movement, the movement dissolved itself into a number of separate units, and against the threat of the enemy commune the magnates found unexpected protection in that commune's political rival.

If we now remind ourselves that the policy adopted by Florence and Siena closely resembled that of every other commune in Tuscany, we are prepared for a wild confusion of wars and alliances. Luckily there is no need whatever to plunge into the maze and to disengage its intolerably tangled threads. It will suffice if we master the leading forces and motives, which, operative in the case of Florence and Siena, repeated themselves at a score of other points over the face of Tuscany. The commune, every commune, had as its enemy the feudal lords and desired to destroy them; the commune, every commune, came to grips with as many of its neighbor communes as seemed to obstruct its commercial and political development. Communes and feudal lords alike invariably followed the line of immediate advantage, changing partners with the greatest ease and with an entire lack of scruple. But—and herewith we broach a matter of the greatest consequence—while fighting and intriguing among themselves without interruption, they did not fail to turn an uneasy eye in the direction of their distant common master, the emperor. For during the first half of the twelfth century the emperor was still strong enough to inspire his subjects with respect and fear. However, as we have seen, the emperors of the period, Lothar and Conrad, did not happen to spend much time in Italy; and when they came, they were too much perplexed by the situation and its infinite ramifications to attack it with vigor. As a result the local forces fought it out among themselves as best they could under the anarchic slogan of everyone-for-himself. No one won a decisive victory, but the trend of events imposed the certain conclusion that the feudal clans were a declining, the communes, in spite of their paralyzing differences, an advancing power. At this point the situation took on a new aspect by the appearance on the scene of an emperor who was resolved to break with the do-nothing policy of his immediate predecessors and to make the empire again an active force in Italian affairs.

The new emperor was Frederick I of the house of Hohenstaufen. Intelligent, vigorous, and authoritative, he had complete faith in the feudal system in which he had been brought up in Germany, where it had not yet been disrupted by the rising power of the towns. On crossing the Alps in 1154, he set foot first in Lombardy, from the point of view of urban development the most advanced section of his Italian kingdom. To his surprise and indignation he noted that the many prosperous towns sown along the valley of the Po had all become self-governing under a regime of elected consuls. This to his simple, feudal mind was rank rebellion, which he was resolved to crush without delay. He would bring the towns back to their old dependence and rest the imperial administration, in the future as in the past, on the great body of his vassals, the lords, lay and spiritual. How this reactionary policy, backed by an apparently irresistible army, at first overawed the Lombard towns; how Milan, the leading commune, on trying to resist, was obliged to surrender; how, here and there, the resistance continued to push spasmodically to the surface; how Milan, on venturing to revolt a second time, was punished by being leveled with the ground (1162)—all this is a passionately interesting story which we cannot follow in detail, but which concerns us deeply because, without it, the Tuscan developments must remain entirely unintelligible.

Triumphant in Lombardy in his early years by a policy of war and terror, Frederick I, whom, because of his luxuriant, flame-colored beard the Italians called Barbarossa (Redbeard), discovered even in this period of comparative felicity that he had to reckon with the ancient rival and enemy of the empire, the papacy. The emperor was engaged in making himself the unchallenged master of the peninsula, and no incumbent of St. Peter's chair could accept that prospect unless he was prepared to surrender all the ecclesiastical and political advantages gained since the great Hildebrand. As no true pope would make that sacrifice, Frederick encountered papal opposition from the first, which with the elevation to the pontifical office of Alexander III (1159–81) became open and unflinching. Aware of Alexander's enmity, Frederick met it by inducing a minority group in the college of cardinals to set up a rival pope, thereby precipitating a religious schism. The device proved unavailing. The world in general paid homage to Alexander III, who both by his character as a man and by his gifts as a diplomat proved himself worthy of his most capable predecessors. His keen penetration enabled him to see that the Lombard cities needed only to stand firmly together under the patronage of an unyielding pope, and the battle would be won, though it might be hard fought and long drawn out. He advocated this associative policy year in, year out, until he overcame all effective opposition to his plan. Under papal inspiration the Lombard towns at last agreed to form a single overwhelming league; and in 1176, a date so important for Italian communal history that it deserves to be inscribed in brass, they won a crushing victory over Frederick at Legnano.

Unable after Legnano to offer further resistance, the red-bearded emperor was obliged to come to terms with both his adversaries, the pope and the Lombard communes. The negotiations which he spun with Alexander III led in 1177 to a peace congress at Venice. It was opened by an act of formal reconciliation between emperor and pope in the atrium of the great church of St. Mark. Prostrating himself before his adversary to kiss his foot, the humbled Barbarossa presented a picture to the world which in the long gallery of medieval spectacles takes its place beside the memorable scene enacted at

Canossa exactly one hundred years before. In distinction from the earlier, still exclusively feudal scene, there were present at Venice representatives of the Lombard communes, to whom on this occasion the papacy in large part owed its victory. To these spokesmen of a new social and political order the defeated sovereign was not obliged to prostrate himself as a measure preliminary to a settlement; but he had to accept a truce with them on terms which, six years later, were converted into the Peace of Constance (1183). As this treaty confirmed to the Lombard towns all the essential rights of self-government, it may, though it did not quite ring the death knell of feudalism, be hailed as a fundamental charter legalizing the new urban civilization.

In the epochal Lombard struggle covering over a quarter of a century (1154–83) the Tuscan communes took no part. Neither now nor afterward did there ever develop a sense of solidarity among the Italian towns; and a national sentiment, as we understand the term, was not born till the nineteenth century. As for the emperor, engaged during this period with all his resources in the struggle with the pope and the Lombard communes, he was obliged to maintain an attitude of conciliation toward Tuscany by leaving it largely to itself. Thus to be left alone was all that the Tuscan communes desired. They had their mind set on continuing the struggle among themselves and with the great barons in their midst without interference from above; and out of necessity, certainly not from choice, Frederick I gratified their wish.

An exception to this imperial aloofness cannot, however, be passed over in silence. When in the year 1162 the emperor had destroyed Milan, he entered on an interval of comparative peace and authority in the north, which at last enabled him to take a more lively interest in Tuscany. Under the inspiration of his chancellor, Rainald, who was also archbishop of Cologne, he worked out a plan of imperial control in this province which Rainald in person undertook to carry out. While attempting to establish a kind of balance between the warring communes and the feudality, it presented as its major feature the creation of an imperial administration composed of a network of agents (*potestates*) of the sovereign spread over the whole province. The potestates were intrusted with the collection of monies owing to the sovereign and with the maintenance of peace and were responsible to an imperial governor residing at San Miniato del Tedesco. Ever since the death of Matilda this little hill town over the Arno had been the capital designate of Tuscany, but not till Frederick I called into being a German bureaucracy to rule the land did it figure as the capital in a real and practical sense. The distinction thus won it retained as long as any trace of imperial authority survived in Tuscany.

Since for the brief number of years it lasted the reorganization effected by Chancellor Rainald reduced, if it did not terminate, the anarchic confusion of Tuscany, we may fairly affirm that it sprang from a sound idea. That idea may be defined as provincial pacification brought about by means of an authoritative central administration; and no student of history will fail to note that this was the road afterward traveled by every state of Europe which found an effective cure for feudalism. Rainald was therefore on the right track so far as his leading principle was concerned. But he loaded it with too many liabilities. In the first place, his plan was not radical enough, since he joined it with an anachronistic attempt to preserve the feudality in all its ancient rights; in the second place, its execution was put into the hands of a body of foreigners without any support in the country. While pointing to a possible solution, his scheme was imperfectly conceived and executed and began to go to pieces as soon as the Lombard provinces braced themselves to resume the intermitted struggle with the emperor. The new conflict, dating from 1167, was not closed till the victory of Legnano (1176) had been crowned by the Peace of Constance. As soon as, beginning in 1167, the emperor was once more obliged to concentrate his strength on Lombardy, he had no way of hindering the breakdown of his Tuscan experiment. His potestates, no longer obeyed, ceased to function and gradually withdrew from the province. Thereupon the various local powers eagerly resumed an independence which the irrepressible mutual animosities promptly turned into the previous mad-house war of all against all.

The story of Florence may and should be seen as an illuminating instance of the general Tuscan turmoil. The moment that Barbarossa's bureaucratic program collapsed, the liberated town returned to its previous policy of self-aggrandizement, snarling and snapping at every foe whom the current atomization of society planted across its path. Successes, often astonishing in their promptness and magnitude, were scored in every direction. As the conquest of Fiesole had clearly shown, Florence was grimly resolved not to permit any of its small neighbors to develop into possible future rivals. Consequently such inconspicuous urban nuclei as Figline and Empoli, lying somewhat farther afield than Fiesole, were now brought into a desired subjection.[17] In its set purpose to control its county the town was not minded to let even the smallest fish slip through the meshes of its net.

And naturally the close watch kept since the very beginning of the consular period on the great feudal families, the Guidi and Alberti, suffered no relaxation. After the collapse of their suzerain's authority at Legnano, both families were drawn into the Florentine system, though with a difference, owing to the greater subtlety of the reigning head of the Guidi clan. This was Count Guido Guerra, who had been a most active partisan of the emperor during the recent attempt to impose an imperial administration on the province. Sensing his danger under the altered circumstances, he entered into relations of amity with the burghers which, while leaving him ostensibly free, reduced him to something suspiciously close to subjection. In his attempt to achieve a cessation of the warfare so destructive of his rights he even condescended (1180) to ask for the hand of Gualdrada,[18] daughter of a leading citizen, Bellincione Berti. The marriage succeeded in creating a kindlier atmosphere between count and commune, and as long as the husband of Gualdrada lived, the ancient feud with the Guidi seems actually to have rested. As the more rancorous and, therefore, more foolish head of the Alberti tribe refused to abate his hostility in any way, the citizen army in 1184 stormed his great castle of Mangona in the Apennines and took the count himself prisoner. He was not released till

[17] The subjection of Figline on the Arno above Florence occurred in 1168; Empoli on the Arno below Florence was subjected in 1182.

[18] Gualdrada was admired for her beauty and delicate Tuscan speech. Elevated to the highest feudal rank by her marriage, the *buon Gualdrada* was promptly absorbed into the Florentine patriotic legend and, generations later, was respectfully saluted by Dante and Villani.

he had signed a sweeping submission acknowledging the jurisdiction over his estates of the victorious republic. With the fall of the Alberti the last impediment had broken down, and Florence had achieved the ambition with which she had embarked on her consular career: she was the unchallenged mistress of her county, with noblemen and small towns alike acknowledging her supremacy.

A characteristic act of this period of swelling confidence must not be overlooked. It consisted in Florence providing itself with a second and ampler circle of walls. As originally laid out by the Romans, Florentia took the shape, as we know, of a small, irregular square penetrated by four gates. In spite of the shrinkage of the population during the early Middle Ages, the Roman wall did not disappear. Not till the consular age did the revival of commerce bring about a noticeable increase of population, from which fact it followed that suburbs, called *borghi* in Italian, began to extend along all the roads issuing from the gates. By the reign of Emperor Frederick I the borghi had become so considerable that an enemy by attacking and setting fire to them might inflict a very serious loss on the community. In 1172 the citizens set about correcting this alarming situation by undertaking a new girdle of walls planned to embrace the exposed suburbs. They took four years to complete the very considerable enterprise. As eloquent evidence of the commune's physical growth let us note that the new wall inclosed three times the area of the first circuit and, what is particularly deserving of remark, by taking in a segment of the left bank it established Florence on both banks of the river. The increased traffic of the communal age is indicated by the circumstance that, whereas four gates had originally met existing needs, three times that number of gates were required to serve the enlarged town.[19]

At this point all the success and glory harvested by a policy of stealthy, sleepless encroachment upon its neighbors and competitors were imperiled by one of those sudden turns of the wheel of fortune so characteristic of the fluid Italian situation. In the year 1184 the Emperor Frederick, now an old man whose famous golden beard had long since turned silver, came again to Italy; and this time he came on a mission which, at least on the surface, was eminently peaceful. He crossed the Alps in order to marry his son and successor, Henry, to Constance, heiress of the kingdom of Sicily. There was to be no war, if possible not even any friction, between him and his Italian subjects until the union had been effected which would establish the Hohenstaufen family in southern Italy, thus enabling its chief effectively to straddle the peninsula and keep it in secure subjection. On passing through Lombardy the emperor was received with rejoicing by the communes, which since the Peace of Constance were in legal possession of full, self-governing rights. From Lombardy Frederick pressed southward into Tuscany, where, to his chagrin and indignation, he found the communes practicing the same freedom as their sisters in the plain of the Po. To his conservative, legalistic mind the distinction between the two cases was that between law and rebellion; for, what the Lombard towns were doing, had been conceded to them by charter, whereas

[19] See map on p. 10. Attached to Davidsohn, Vol. I, is a map which traces in detail the first and the second circle of walls.

the Tuscan towns, with the exception of Pisa,[20] could point to no document from him to justify their usurpation. In his view the only valid system for Tuscany was the one set up by his chancellor, Rainald of Cologne, some twenty years before, and he proceeded straightway to put it again in operation. The surprising thing is that the cities, of whose pride and daring we can have no doubt, yielded without a struggle. But the surprise evaporates when we consider the situation. Owing to their implacable divisions, the communes were utterly incapable of forming a union against their suzerain on the model of the successful Lombard league. Consequently, each town was obliged to deal with Frederick separately and, as he was now at peace with the Lombard communes, he was for the time being irresistible.

In the course of the two years following the royal visit to Tuscany of 1185 Frederick and, after him, his son Henry, reordered the government of the province along the lines with which we are familiar. A body of imperial officials, called *potestates* or *teutonici,* radiating from San Miniato del Tedesco as their capital, took over the collection of taxes and the administration of justice; the nobles, great and small alike, were reinstated in their undiminished rights and possessions; and the communes, while confirmed in their local self-government, were limited in its exercise to the actual town area or, as a special act of imperial grace, they were permitted to include within their subject territory the immediate countryside to an average depth of five or six miles.[21] In 1189, on the death of the childless King William of Sicily, Henry and his queen, Constance, succeeded to William's throne. Then in the following year Henry also succeeded his father as Holy Roman emperor. Never before had an emperor possessed Sicily and Naples, and therefore never before had an emperor dominated Italy so completely as did Henry VI. The ancient rival of the emperor, the pope, found himself tragically eclipsed in his capital at Rome and, at least for the time being, did not venture to offer resistance. If we remember the conjunction of compelling circumstances which raised Henry to such heights, we cannot fail to understand how it came about that an administration of authoritative imperial agents could be reimposed on Tuscany to remain intact as long as the towering Henry lived.

A factor which came to the aid of Frederick, and to Henry after him, in pacifying Tuscany according to their conservative prescription remains to be mentioned. At precisely this time a new wave of crusading fervor poured over western Christendom, owing to the arrival of gravely disturbing information from the east. It was in the autumn of 1187 that the news of the capture by the Saracens of Jerusalem the Holy spread like wild fire through the countries of the occident. Won a hundred years before by the knighthood of the First Crusade, Jerusalem had come to be regarded as the supreme shrine of the faith

[20] Pisa is a special case among the Tuscan communes for the simple reason that Pisa possessed a navy. From an early time the emperors were prepared to make considerable concessions to Pisa in return for support at sea. We have seen (p. 58) that Pisa got a charter of liberties from Henry IV as early as 1081. In 1162 it got a still ampler privilege from Frederick I conferring the fullest self-government as well as complete jurisdiction over its county. *Mon. Ger. Hist. Legum,* Sectio IV, Tomus I, p. 282. For significant comment see Davidsohn, Vol. I, p. 478.

[21] The charter which Henry, in the name of Frederick, conceded to Florence may be found in Ficker, *Forschungen,* Vol. IV, p. 213. It is dated June 24, 1187, and is notable as the first imperial privilege ever issued to Florence conferring a limited self-government.

which the infidels must under no circumstances be permitted again to ravish. At the report of its fall such a sea of warrior enthusiasm washed over the European peoples that their sovereigns, bowled over by its impetuous onset, were obliged to head the movement of retaliation and assume the cross. Together with the kings of France and England the now venerable Emperor Frederick was sucked into the maelstrom. In 1189, attended by a great army, he set out for the east from Regensburg in Germany. Following the land route, he got as far as Asia Minor, where his fate overtook him, for he was drowned while crossing a small stream. Although the German host melted away at this misfortune, the kings of France and England persisted in the enterprise. However, beyond capturing (1191) the port of Acre after a long siege, nothing of note was accomplished. Jerusalem was not even threatened and continued to rest securely in the hands of the Saracens.

In the emotional crisis represented by these events our Florentines were as deeply entangled as the rest of the western world. The crusade turned their eyes to a considerable degree away from the distressing domestic situation. Seizing upon this outlet for their suppressed emotions, they threw themselves with passionate fervor into the war for the delivery of Jerusalem. In such numbers did they volunteer for the crusade that, when they arrived by sea in Syria, they were permitted to constitute a separate division of the Christian army drawn in a besieging ring around Acre. Without any doubt they had an honorable part in the capture of this seaport, thereby spreading the fame of their growing city over Europe. But that their share was as decisive as their chroniclers were afterward so unanimous in telling the world may be doubted without the least injury to the reputation of a brave and devoted band.

Henry, who had stayed behind as regent when his father went on crusade, ruled the empire as Emperor Henry VI for the brief period of seven years (1190–97). Energetic, unscrupulous, and vastly ambitious, he overawed his enemies both in Germany and Italy and did not meet with any serious opposition from his obedient province of Tuscany. Florence in particular seems to have made up its mind that it was useless to kick against the pricks, although there is evidence of occasional local disturbances indicating that the citizens did not bear the imperial yoke without a protest. In the main, very much like the rest of Tuscany and Italy, the commune adopted a waiting attitude. Suddenly, in the autumn of the year 1197, the whisper went from mouth to mouth that the all-powerful emperor, the ferocious tyrant, had died of a fever at Messina. It was true: Henry VI had expired, hardly thirty years of age, leaving behind as his heir a boy, Frederick by name, aged three years. Henry's power had manifestly been a personal power and was laid with him into the grave. Nobody knew this better than the oppressed communes of Tuscany and without delay they determined to act.

VII. The Tuscan League of 1197; Replacement of the Consuls by the Podestà; The Religious Revival of the Begging Friars

THAT the Tuscan communes lost no time to act on hearing of the death of Henry VI is indicated by their sending delegates to San Genesio to take counsel together within a few weeks after the event. San Genesio was a small open town in the plain below San Miniato del Tedesco, and because of its central location had already on earlier occasions served as meeting-place for the Tuscan republics. And now it was seen that Henry's iron yoke had caused the bitter local feuds to be at least momentarily forgotten, for a Tuscan league, which it had never been possible to realize in the past, came into spontaneous existence. It was born too, exactly like its Lombard predecessor, under the auspices of the papacy. Two cardinals attended the sessions of the congress and committed the church to loyal support of the liberation movement. The sessions were still proceeding when in January, 1198, a new pope mounted the throne, who, under the name of Innocent III (1198–1216), revived the most exaggerated claims of his predecessors to universal empire. His accession guaranteed an alliance as firm as that famous older union between the Lombard league and Alexander III which had brought about the triumphant settlement of Constance. An immense advantage enjoyed by the latest alliance between pope and towns was that the war with the empire, which seemed to be a certain consequence of its action, did not materialize. A disputed election in Germany had carried two candidates, Otto of the house of Guelph and Philip, brother of the late emperor, into the lists against each other, and until they had settled their differences the empire was paralyzed. As this condition lasted for ten years, the Tuscan league was never subjected to the supreme test, the test of war against its feudal chief.

Even though the expected war with the empire did not take place, there was abundant work for the league of another kind. Each commune wished to get back its freedom of action and, above all, to recover the lost control of its county. Though in guarded language, this purpose was written into the agreement of November 11, 1197, which every town, nobleman, and castle was invited to sign. Even Pisa was summoned to subscribe, although it already enjoyed by imperial charter all the advantages the other Tuscan communes were combining in order to achieve. But except Pisa, which felt it had nothing to gain, the others did, either at once or in the course of the winter, attach their signatures till the document bore the names of Florence, Siena, Lucca, Arezzo, and the bishop of Volterra (signing for the town of which he was the lord).[1] What is more surprising at first blush, it bore the names also of the heads of the two great feudal families, the Guidi and Alberti. Only with the greatest reluctance could these counts have presented themselves at San Genesio to make their submission to the communes under a deceptive formula of amity. It proves that they themselves no longer entertained any doubt that the emperor was their sole support and that, on his failing them, their best course was to adjust themselves to the altered circumstances and to save what they could from the wreck. Exactly as under the similar situation of twenty years before, the Guidi fared better than the Alberti. Without a struggle they yielded the civil jurisdiction over their castles in the Florentine contado to the triumphant commune. Apparently they solaced themselves with the thought that, owing to their large holdings beyond the reach of Florence on either side of the Apennines, they could still comport themselves as imperial magnates and unfold a baronial grandeur. The Alberti, more narrowly a family of the Florentine contado and more hateful to the citizens because of their long and unconcealed hostility, were subjected to a grinding humiliation. By a series of acts of the year 1200 they surrendered to Florence all the castles and way-tolls the commune demanded of them and, in substance, submitted to be rated as Florentine citizens.[2]

In the years immediately following the formation of the Tuscan league each commune tried to realize its fixed and burning ambition to conquer and rule its contado. While the feudal nobility, as the case of the Guidi and Alberti shows, was obliged at least to pretend to accept this program, this was not yet the case with the many small urban settlements scattered over the countryside. The free winds blowing vigorously over Italy had created a passion for liberty in which every hamlet, regardless of its size, had a share. It often required more than threats on the part of Florence before towns like Figline and Certaldo, of small circumference but swelling with a fresh, communal pride of their own, agreed to curb their necks under the yoke of their larger neighbor. And one of these small towns had the effrontery to put up such an audacious resistance that it obliged Florence to conduct a war requiring five campaigns before it was crowned with success. This town was Semifonte. As it presents an instance strikingly illustrative of the selfish and headstrong resolution of our pushing community of traders, the story of Semifonte is worth recounting.

The venomous character of Florentine hostility to Semifonte is not a political enigma. Semifonte was an artificial creation of those dangerous and persistent enemies of the Arno commonwealth, the Counts Alberti. Engaged in a bitter contest with a commercial community that was notably adding to its strength with every passing decade, the Alberti bethought themselves of erecting a town on land of their own which should develop into a rival of Florence and draw off some of the Florentine profits into their pockets. They selected for this purpose a high hill near Certaldo; and in the decade of imperial control coincident with the rule of Henry VI they built a town on that summit with a strong wall around it and called it Semifonte. It bloomed astonishingly to the immense disgust of its Florentine neighbors, who would

[1] Santini, *Documenti dell'Antica Costituzione*, etc., No. XXI.
[2] *Ibid.*, Nos. XXVII, XXVIII, XXIX.

have gone into action against it at once with sword and fire, had it not been for Henry's imperial officials, effective guardians of the peace of Tuscany. Then with dramatic suddenness came Henry's death, the collapse of his administration, and the Tuscan league. Therewith Semifonte, as lying in the contado of Florence, was delivered into that commune's hands as completely as the Alberti magnates themselves. It is interesting to note that many of the small neighbors of Semifonte in the Elsa Valley, such as Colle and San Gimignano, either secretly or openly encouraged it to offer resistance to the town that claimed the undisputed headship of the county. Instinctively these little communities sensed that their own independence was tied up with that of Semifonte. However, such slight help as they managed to provide was unavailing; and although the Semifontians proved themselves a race of heroes and held the Florentines at bay for five campaigning seasons, at last, in the year 1202, they were obliged to surrender. While the inhabitants saved their lives in return for a promise to disperse, the town itself, delivered over to the mercy of the conquerors, was destroyed even more completely than that earlier thorn in the Florentine flesh, Fiesole. So thoroughly was the work of demolition carried out that before many generations had passed there was no longer any memory in the neighborhood that such a town as Semifonte had ever existed. In an effort to locate the vanished community modern antiquarians have diligently searched the reputed site without recovering as much as a single stone that might with certainty be ascribed to the short-lived, upstart rival of Florence.

The immediate effect of the league of San Genesio was a general civil war in Tuscany, or rather, in view of the permission granted each leading commune to possess itself of its county, a series of separate and distinct civil wars between each county capital and its dependent countryside. In spite of the valiant resistance of obstinate little centers like Semifonte, the work of subjection was completed after a few seasons, with the result that the great communes achieved a domination which was nonetheless real for its manifest lack of a legal basis. Then with the end gained, for the sake of which the league in the first instance had been formed, the federation flew violently apart. All the terrible interurban feuds that had come to birth in the consular age flamed up anew exactly as if there had not been a sworn alliance and a quinquennium of ostensible brotherhood. What else was to be expected? As soon as Florence or Siena or any other town had mastered its particular contado, it faced its neighbor across a boundary which was sometimes in dispute— the Siena-Florence boundary was such a case—and which, whether in dispute or not, was regularly without any geographical significance. From an economic or a political point of view it was difficult, if not impossible, to call a halt at so purely artificial a line; and young exultant organisms, like the Tuscan communes, could not be expected to do so. As a result Florence clashed with Siena and Pistoia, Siena with Florence and Arezzo, Lucca with Pisa and Pistoia; in short, all the wars broke loose again which we have already noted in our record of the previous century and which were bound to continue until one commune would prove itself stronger than the others and by conquering them in turn would at last impose an enforced peace upon the province. That one and only solution was not even remotely in sight at the beginning of the thirteenth century. The Tuscan towns were approximately as yet of the same size and strength and the prospect immediately ahead was a planless, internecine struggle conducted with blind impulsiveness and without so much as a trace of either faith or scruple.

As long as Florence had not set its heel on Semifonte, it was at some pains to keep on speaking terms with Siena. However, hardly had Semifonte been converted into a dust heap when the old bickerings were renewed over the disputed boundary. In the hope of having the ancient quarrel adjudicated without war, Siena in 1203 agreed to submit the case to an arbiter and to accept the podestà of Poggibonsi in that capacity. The result was a judgment or *lodo* which drew the boundary in every respect in accordance with the pretensions of Florence.[3] More exacerbated than ever the Sienese nursed a rage in their hearts which led shortly to a new war, in fact to a long succession of wars, with the details of which we shall not concern ourselves. Such significance as they have lie in the fact that the expanding Arno city proved itself to be no longer interested in merely its own county; it desired to extend its control into the neighboring Sienese county by lending aid to small towns in this area like Montepulciano and Montalcino in their efforts to preserve their liberties against the encroachments of Siena. Plainly the ambition of Florence was bursting its early, self-imposed bounds and taking a broader survey of the Tuscan scene.

The deliberate selection by Florence of centers of political support in Sienese territory was duplicated by similar action in the counties of Pistoia and Arezzo; and inescapably this reaching out farther and farther over Tuscany would before long carry the Florentines to the sea. Begun modestly as purely overland trade, their commerce had hardly got under way when the crusades opened up golden opportunities in the east. In view of their amazing energy, the Florentine merchants would not be inclined for long to leave the immense profits of this oversea traffic in the hands exclusively of the towns planted on the coast. During the twelfth century, when Florence, not yet having acquired much momentum, was necessarily humble in manner and restricted in outlook, it had maintained the most friendly relations with Pisa, at the mouth of its river, content to accept such commercial favors as the much more powerful maritime community might concede. Pisa, in its turn, did not fail to see the advantage of having a friend and ally in inner Tuscany. This sense of mutual dependence led to the treaty of 1171, as important politically as it was commercially, for, after establishing an offensive and defensive alliance between Pisa and Florence to run for forty years, it laid down a series of trade provisions of inestimable advantage to the inland town. The most important of these was the obligation assumed by Pisa that Florentine merchants and their goods should enjoy the same rates in Pisan vessels as native goods and merchants.[4] There can be no doubt whatever that Florence benefited immensely from this concession, on the strength of which it was enabled to extend its commercial operations over the whole Mediterranean Sea. The unchecked arrogance noticeable in the conduct of the government in the early thirteenth

---

[3] Date of lodo, June 3, 1203. Davidsohn, Vol. I, pp. 640-1.
[4] Santini, *Documenti*, No. IV; Davidsohn, Vol. I, p. 518.

century is referable to a large extent to the ever-widening range of Florentine enterprise. Slowly but decisively the earlier attitude of deference to the great seaport began to disappear; and so slight an incident as the clash in 1220 between the Florentine and the Pisan delegations attending the coronation festival of Frederick II at Rome sufficed to release an animosity which was never again composed. The war born of this Roman episode is a milestone in Tuscan history, for with it the Florentines turned their attention to the control of the coast of their province in their own interest. With this enlargement of their already ambitious program they produced a political alignment among the Tuscan communes which remained characteristic for a long time to come. Inevitably on the transformation of Florence from a friend to an enemy, Pisa sought the company and support of Siena, while Florence, in its turn, edged close to Lucca, the ancient and uncompromising foe of Pisa. It followed from other circumstances to be recounted hereafter that Pisa and Siena with their following came to be bracketed as the imperial (later to be called Ghibelline) powers of Tuscany, while Lucca and Florence with such adherents as they commanded served as the pillars of the ecclesiastical (later to be called Guelph) cause. We shall pass over the dark intrigues and incessant, petty wars among the Tuscan towns till toward the middle of the century when they became tied up with a world-situation which has a genuine claim on our attention.

In the period of the Tuscan league and the renewed conquest by the towns of their contado, there occurred a change in their constitutional structure which has been given different and even radically opposed interpretations. The multiple executive of the consuls was replaced by a single executive called *podestà*. The word is derived from the Latin *potestas,* and potestas owed its contemporary currency to the circumstance that it was the name given by the Emperor Barbarossa to the imperial agents he established in Tuscany and elsewhere. The change from consuls to podestà was not effected at once but carried out over a period of years and had at the beginning plainly an experimental character. In Florence, for example, as early as 1193 a single Florentine citizen served as head of the government in place of the consuls.[5] After thus giving the podestàship a trial, the citizens reverted to the familiar multiple consulate. Then, as a further experiment, they summoned a foreigner to serve as podestà; and before the first decade of the new century had elapsed, the foreign podestà had won such general approval that he became a fixture. At the same time the conditions under which he served took definite shape. On assuming office for his term, which usually ran for a year, he took a solemn oath to fulfil the duties specified in the constitution and to execute that document in every particular. When his year was over, he agreed to submit, before leaving for home, to an audit (*sindicato*) and to have deducted from his salary any fines for which he may have made himself liable by transgressing his authority.[6]

Simultaneously with the change in the chief executive the whole constitution suffered certain rather minor modifications. They deserve, however, to be recorded since they mark a departure from the established consular usage. As the fruitful source of political disturbances the public assembly or parlamentum,

---

[5] Santini, *Documenti*. Catalogo degli Ufficiali del Comune di Firenze, p. XLI.
[6] Full details of the close supervision exercised over the podestà in Davidsohn, Vol. I, p. 697.

in which we detected the democratic base of the consular government, had already during the consulate been permitted to fall more and more into disuse. This tendency continued under the podestà. In measure as the parlamentum declined the council rose in authority, not only because it lent itself better to orderly debate, but pre-eminently because it rested securely in the hands of the leading citizen groups exercising control of the town. However, with the coming of the podestà the council experienced a bifurcation into a general and a special council. This involved no change in the ruling system since both councils continued to be recruited from the same upper strata of society. The creation of a smaller special council strengthened, if anything, the control of the government by the well-to-do, as the foreign podestà could undertake nothing without the preliminary consent of this more intimate body.

It has been hotly debated whether or not these changes may be interpreted as a democratic advance. Any question posed in this way permits the adducing of arguments favorable to either side. If, on the other hand, we drop the dogmatic point of view and agree to study the communal constitution genetically, we shall be content to see what actually happened without feeling obliged to evaluate the happening in terms of a particular theory. Proceeding in this manner and directing our attention to the special instance of Florence, we observe that the consular executive, composed usually of twelve men, had by the second half of the twelfth century developed serious imperfections. In the first place, government by a large board has always and everywhere proved unwieldy, and Florence was no exception to the rule. Next, the consular posts having become from the outset the prerogative of the leading families, two opposed high-born cliques developed, each of which tried to monopolize the consulship and to exclude from power the members of the rival clique. On the occasion of the annual elections there was in consequence a tension in the city which threatened civil war. In the year 1177, for instance, the group of consular families which cohered around the Uberti rose in rebellion against the group of which the Giandonati were the head and which had managed in the immediately preceding years to attribute the consular offices exclusively to its members. The resulting civil war lasted three years.[7] The inflamed local passions could be most satisfactorily appeased by a single executive, who, drawn from another town and province, might be expected to hold the balance between the warring groups. The single head, charged, among other duties, with the task of maintaining peace among the noble factions, would have the further advantage of appealing to the trading elements who were gaining in numbers every year and who were instinctively averse to the nobiliary excesses. Finally, since the podestà was a paid official, called by the council and responsible to it by his obligation to submit to an audit, he was under much more effective control than had ever been the case with the consuls. Whether in view of these circumstances, all of which may be thought of as having conduced to the replacing of the consuls with the podestà, the new official is to be rated as a democratic felicity or as an aristocratic menace is essentially unimportant. It is enough that the consuls had proved themselves an unsatisfactory executive and that their successor, the podestà, offered the possibility of termi-

---

[7] Davidsohn, Vol. I, pp. 553-59.

nating the civil war to which the local consular elections periodically gave rise. Finally, the foreign podestà was summoned as a specialist in administration and justice and filled the chief magistracy much more effectively than the consuls had done.[8]

While these developments were taking place in Tuscany, the empire was in one of its periodic swoons, owing to the disputed election following the death of Henry VI. The crisis was not terminated till 1208, when the murder of Philip of Suabia, brother of the late emperor, left his rival, Otto of Saxony, in unchallenged control. The two men represented respectively the great German houses of Hohenstaufen and Guelph (Welf), the irrepressible conflict between which was now in the third generation. For the moment at least success smiled on Guelph Otto and, securely in possession of the German throne, he set out for Italy, where, in 1209, he was crowned emperor by Pope Innocent III. This pontiff needed all his ability to steer his course safely amid the rocks that threatened him and his office. Like all his immediate predecessors he was averse to the Hohenstaufens because of the unyielding obstinacy with which since the advent to the throne of Frederick I in 1152 they had upheld the authority of the civil power against the claims of the church. The bitterness had reached its highest stage when the family, through the marriage of Henry VI with the heiress of Sicily, had gained possession of this flourishing southern kingdom. During his short reign Henry, with one foot planted in northern, another in southern, Italy, straddled Rome like a colossus and held the pope at his mercy. Without any doubt the emperor's premature death was a lucky stroke for the papacy. In fact it gave back to the head of Christendom his full freedom of action, for not only was Frederick, the three-year-old heir of Henry, eliminated, on account of his immaturity, from among the candidates for the German throne, but, on the death of his mother, which followed quickly on that of his father, he fell into unqualified dependence on the pope by becoming his ward. At this point we must recall that when the Normans conquered the Italian south back in the eleventh century, they agreed to rule it as a papal fief. Among the rights of the pope as acknowledged suzerain of the kingdom of Sicily was the exercise of wardship over a king who was an orphan and a minor. A thoroughly honorable man, the reigning pope, Innocent III, was at pains to give young Frederick a careful bringing-up; but he was equally determined that the dangerous situation in which the papacy had found itself in Henry's time should under no circumstances be permitted to return. For this reason, while prepared to let Frederick, on coming of age, mount the Sicilian throne, he was pleased to have the implacable enemy of the Hohenstaufens, Guelph Otto, wear the German and imperial crowns. Moreover, being a clever and far-seeing statesman, Innocent was resolved to make himself as sure as possible of the perpetual separation of the Sicilian and imperial scepters. Therefore, before placing the crown on Otto's head, he made him take a solemn oath that he would respect all the traditional rights of the church and particularly that he would never attempt to add Sicily to the empire.

[8] Since the towns wanted the podestàs whom they called as executives to be as expert as possible, young men began to prepare themselves for the office as for a profession. On the professional aspect, see Davidsohn, Vol. I, p. 695. It is not an exaggeration to think of some of the podestàs, the best of them, in terms of a present-day city-manager.

Following his coronation, the new emperor, Otto IV, retired to Tuscany and immediately again set up in that province the imperial administration which had collapsed so promptly and ignominiously at the death of Henry VI. If in this respect he scored an ephemeral success, he owed it, as his predecessors had done, to his military power. The communes had just finished repossessing themselves of their counties and regarded their acquisition as the apple of their eye. But there was no legal basis for the seizures they had effected; they failed to stand shoulder to shoulder, owing to their fatal disagreements; and on sober second thoughts they chose not to measure their strength at this time against that of their imperial master. It is these considerations that explain how it happened that Otto was able to call back to life a system which only ten years before, in the first flush of the triumphant Tuscan league, had seemed to have been swept away forever. From the battlements of the great tower at San Miniato del Tedesco the imperial banner with its heraldic eagle again fluttered in the wind, and from and to this tower imperial agents (*potestates, teutonici*) were in constant movement on errands of their once more triumphant lord, the emperor.

It was a triumph brief as summer lightning, owing in large measure to Otto's unfathomable falsity and folly. No sooner was he safely possessed of Tuscany than he undertook to do the very thing he had renounced under the most solemn vows. He resolved to conquer Sicily on the certainly very debatable ground that it was a subject-land of the empire. We can imagine Innocent's indignation at this base betrayal. Not only did he promptly excommunicate the perjurer, but he prepared to punish him in a more effective manner still by starting a backfire in Germany. He summoned his Suabian charge, now a youth of eighteen, to Rome and, forgetting in his wrath at Otto his fear of the Hohenstaufens, he dispatched young Frederick across the Alps to win the German throne from the Guelph incumbent (1212). At the mere prospect of this move Otto hurriedly withdrew from Italy; and hardly had his army left the Tuscan soil when the imperial administration in Tuscany once more broke down and the towns again resumed the interrupted rule of their counties. Italy was left to itself, while the Guelphs and the Hohenstaufens renewed their ancient and disastrous feud for the possession of the German crown. On this occasion it was the Hohenstaufen champion who gained the victory and in 1215 young Frederick was crowned German king at Aachen. It was only now that Pope Innocent's normal caution reasserted itself; and during the negotiations with the young sovereign in regard to his future coronation as emperor he insisted that, as an indispensable preliminary to that ceremony, Frederick would have to renounce the earlier, the Sicilian crown. The negotiations on this head were still proceeding when the masterful pope died (1216). As Germany continued to seethe with disorder, Frederick was obliged to linger in the north. Not till 1220 did he reappear in Italy, when he immediately betook himself to Rome to be formally invested with the empire. The new pope, Honorius III, a gentle soul, the exact opposite in temper to his lordly predecessor, was content to leave Frederick's renunciation of the kingdom of Sicily involved in verbal ambiguities. All his thoughts and hopes were set upon a new crusade to liberate Jerusalem; and when he had exacted a promise from Frederick to lead a Christian host against the infidel, he placed the crown upon the Hohenstaufen's head.

With the accession to the empire of Frederick II there began a new chapter in the long struggle of the Italian communes for self-determination, for Frederick did not scruple to renew the attempts of his father and grandfather to subject them to imperial control. The fresh effort to turn back the wheel of time ended in failure like all its forerunners, but it was made forever memorable by the extraordinary character and talents of the imperial incumbent. It has, besides, a special claim on our attention because of the prominent part taken in the struggle by our town of Florence. Reserving this climax of the long conflict between the two opposed systems of agrarian feudalism and urban self-government to the following chapter, we shall take up a change in the religious temper of Christianity befalling at this time which greatly contributed to the failure of Frederick II by once more endowing the church with irresistible energy. As it is the unfolding civilization and not merely the political evolution of the Arno town which is our goal, we are certainly on the right track when we propose to keep in touch with the ever-changing phases of Christian thought and feeling. For religion provided the climate in which the society of the Middle Ages had its being to a degree which the present generation can only realize by a lively effort of the imagination.

The religious movement inaugurated with the beginning thirteenth century flows from many sources and gathers around many champions; but with all due respect to its complicated character we commit no violence if we refer its decisive manifestations to the pontificate of Innocent III (1198–1216). Innocent was a sanguine, intelligent, and irrepressibly energetic man, who subordinated his ambition to his office, but whose ambition *for* his office absolutely knew no bounds. Like all the great medieval popes, practically without exception, far from falling under the type of mystic and dreamer, he was primarily an administrator, a jurist, and a statesman. He had studied canon law at the University of Bologna and his training, added to the hard, metallic quality native to his mind, inspired him with the desire to have the still frequently fluctuating practices and doctrines of the church cast into rigorous, legal form. There, for instance, was the unsettled and ever cantankerous question of the church and the state. The theory commonly held in the early Middle Ages was that church and state were independent of each other, that each was supreme in its own field, and that both derived directly from God. However impressive on paper, this equalitarian, this dualist theory had worked out very badly in practice; and church and state, instead of living peacefully side by side as partners in a common enterprise, had been perpetually at each other's throat. Under these distressing circumstances an ecclesiastical school of thought came to the front, beginning with the famous Gregory VII, which contended that the church was superior to the state and that, whenever a conflict threatened, the state must yield to the institution which possessed the greater authority because it boasted Christ himself as its founder. While this conception may be said to have been in the air since Hildebrand's time, it had never been pressed, never even been more than tentatively formulated. To Innocent's juristic temper this wavering condition was unendurable, and he resolved to put an end to it by making the church unquestionably supreme both in fact and in theory. In numerous letters and addresses he insisted that the pope was the vicar of God on earth and that, as such, he towered over all civil rulers, who henceforth would be considered to be exercising their authority subject to good behavior and at the pope's pleasure. The goal of his policy was the control by his office of all the sovereigns of Europe, and it is amazing to what an extent he realized his purpose. He made and unmade emperors, as the cases of Otto IV and Frederick II show; he obliged the king of France meekly to take back the wife whom he had repudiated; and he brought the kings of Portugal, Aragon, and England so completely to heel that they made a gift to him of their respective kingdoms and received them back at his hands as papal fiefs.

Never since its origin had the church with the tiara-crowned pope at its head been more unquestionably the ruling institution of the west than under Innocent III. But if one looked behind the brilliant façade at the Christian congregation which it hid from view, he became aware of conditions calculated to startle and alarm him. Ever since the eleventh century, which had inaugurated the revival of commerce, this congregation had been involved in a vast social and economic upheaval. The statement applies to the whole west without exception, but it is particularly true of Italy and southern France, which undoubtedly marched in the European van in respect to urban development. When the religious reform of the eleventh century declared war upon the gross worldliness which was undermining the church, it drew its main support from the new and restless elements gathered in the towns. But such success as the reform achieved rapidly evaporated in the following century. The church of the twelfth century pursued wealth, power, and display more openly and eagerly than ever, and a striking feature of the revived worldliness was that the papacy itself took the lead in the movement. The immediate successors of the ascetic Gregory VII found their main satisfaction in increasing the revenues of the Roman see and in tightening their hold on the universal church of which they were the visible head. More and more definitely they assumed the character of absolute monarchs. When at the close of the century Innocent III in characteristically arrogant terms proclaimed this achieved absolutism to the world, far from proving himself an innovator, he did no more than bring a movement of long and slow gestation to its inevitable issue.

The splendid edifice of papal power did not, however, overawe the enemies of ecclesiastical worldliness. On the contrary, more fervidly than before they uttered their protest against a development which, according to them, offended both the original spirit of Christianity and the multitude of God's poor, for whom, according to the declaration of the Fathers, the church had in the first place been established. The masses of the needy were by the twelfth century congregated in the rising towns and, frequently unemployed and always miserable, they were only too ready to listen to a preachment which fell with a peculiar flattery on their ears. When the bolder critics of the prelatical magnificence at last very positively demanded that the church divest itself of its wealth in favor of the poor and return to the simplicity and poverty of apostolic times, the great dignitaries became alarmed and promptly communicated their alarm to the pope. In the hope of silencing the opponents of the ruling trend, not one but several popes of the twelfth century publicly and unambiguously condemned as false the teaching that it was sinful for the church to be endowed with worldly goods. And when Innocent III in his day renewed the anathema in a particularly rigorous form, he was again doing no more than following in the footsteps of his predecessors. By the repeated papal declarations every preacher of, and believer in, apostolic poverty for the church automatically became a heretic.

From its earliest days Christianity had been obliged to wrestle with opinions which, failing to square with the orthodox viewpoint, were condemned as heretical and called for extirpation, at need with fire and sword. Nonetheless the sects charged at one time or another with nursing false doctrines had by no means all disappeared. Some of the more vigorous heretical groups, such as the Cathari, the Manichaeans, the Paulicians, maintained a secret, underground existence throughout the Middle Ages. When the popes of the twelfth century, culminating in the mighty Innocent III, made advocacy of ecclesiastical poverty a heresy, they rendered the older heresies, which though invisible were still alive, an unexpected service. For immediately the indignant new heretics allied themselves with the more ancient outlaws, and a fusion of forces of such dimensions took place that it became a serious threat to the church. More particularly in the flourishing town area of southern France did the movement assume alarming proportions. So numerous and confident did its followers become that they dared go so far as openly to profess their divergent faith. Called Albigenses from the town of Albi, one of the centers of their worship, the rebel believers seemed to be on the point of superseding orthodox Christianity throughout a wide section.

When Pope Innocent III became aware of the crisis which had arisen in southern France, he met it in a manner befitting the unflinching devotee of the law. Heresy had become rampant because the church had been too lenient; the quickest, the only, cure was to pluck it up root and branch. Scorning negotiations, he proclaimed a crusade against the Albigenses under the leadership of the orthodox princes of northern France; and hounded to the attack by the vicar of Christ, these warriors of the Cross turned the blooming cities of Languedoc into a shambles. However, believing also in persuasion, Innocent at the same time under the name of inquisitors dispatched missionaries into the infected area to attempt to win the heretics back to the fold by argument; and this missionary work continued long after the crusade had scored its bloody triumph. When the satisfied pope reviewed his victory, he could persuade himself that in the crusade and inquisition he commanded two tools admirably suited for dealing with religious perversity. He resolved to make the inquisition permanent and to extend its operations to the whole dominion of the church. In 1215 at a General Council held at Rome this body obediently and enthusiastically indorsed the project.

In connection with the traveling missionaries who labored in behalf of orthodoxy in southern France, a Spaniard by the name of Dominic had greatly distinguished himself. He shared the pope's horror of heresy and, like him, was not averse to employing the sword against it; but he also held that force was not enough for the work in hand and that it should not be employed at all until persuasion had been tried and had failed. Since the heretics had been manifestly led astray by evil counselors, Dominic thought it reasonable to suppose that they could be won back to the fold by the sounder arguments of the true believers. What the errant sectaries therefore supremely needed was divinely inspired teaching and preaching. To this end the eager and indefatigable Spaniard gradually gathered a company of like-minded men about him. They became the nucleus of his famous Order of the Preaching Friars. The new society won the approval of the pope, who welcomed it as a valuable ally in his declared war on heresy. As enthusiasm begets enthusiasm, recruits flowed in on Dominic from all sides. In a surprisingly short time his order had spread to every country of the west. Than these blindly devoted brothers no fitter body could be found to give effect to Innocent's expertly devised institution of the inquisition. Accordingly, it was intrusted to their care, and in every country of Europe and particularly in every commune of Italy troubled by the presence of heretics the local Dominican group was charged with a supervision of speech and conscience planned to hold the inhabitants to an unvarying orthodox course. The inquisition long retained something of the idealism associated with a missionary enterprise. More and more, however, it resorted to torture and the faggot and became a ferocious and purely repressive agency. Let no one say that force wins no victories, for after the systematic application through several generations of the inquisitorial horrors heresy lost its hold on the Italian urban elements. While uprooted in Italy, it did, to be sure, persist in other countries assuming ever novel forms determined by the place and hour. Centuries passed before it gained an irresistible momentum and scored a supreme triumph in the movement called the Protestant Reformation. All these subsequent manifestations are a separate story and do not concern us here.

While the sweeping thirteenth-century victory of orthodoxy may be attributed to the inquisition and its watchful special police, the Dominican friars, there remain other factors to be considered. They come into play because medieval Christianity was a highly complex phenomenon. Insofar as it was a church based on law and organization, the inquisition and the Dominican order, which emphasized the ecclesiastical aspect, were notable additions to its strength. But Christianity was also a sum of sentiments and aspirations turning about the love of God; in fact these sentiments constituted the original Christian core, to which the organized church had been afterward added as a convenient practical means of perpetuating the Christian community. It follows therefore that an attack on heresy to be completely successful would have to be conducted with due regard for both the church and the faith. The inquisition and the Dominicans represent the ecclesiastical attack; they signify an action by organization in behalf of organization and their achievement on the strength of the evidence must be admitted to have been remarkable. But had this been all, had the inquisition not been supplemented by a campaign of an emotional and religious character, it is highly doubtful that its success would have been other than temporary and that heresy would have been driven from the field.

And so we come to St. Francis of Assisi, the man who completed the work of St. Dominic by remembering that Christianity was not only an institution but also an unceasing personal search for God. The sole inspiration of St. Francis was the gospels. From beginning to end they spoke to him of divine love, spoke to him indeed so intimately and persuasively that he completely identified himself with their message. When followers gathered about him, they pressed him for a *regula* or rule by which to guide their footsteps. Hesitantly consenting to their request, he drew up a document to which the successor of Innocent, Pope Honorius III, gave his blessing. Thus was founded the Order of the Brothers Minor, commonly called the Order of St. Francis. Taking, like the Dominicans, the three vows of obedience, chastity, and poverty, the Franciscans indicated by the assumption of these pledges their effective derivation from the monastic movement reaching back to the distant days of St. Benedict. But, in spite of this descent, they blazed an entirely fresh trail by aiming at a very different objective from their monastic predecessors. Far from fleeing the haunts of men to seek God in the solitude of forest or desert, the brothers who wore the rough brown garb of St. Francis sought the crowded towns in order to tend the sick, to distribute alms, and to perform the many other services of Christian charity. Since the Dominicans in their earliest phase directed their efforts to preaching and instruction, there was thus a distinct dividing line between the original purposes of the two orders. In point of fact the dividing line soon disappeared, because a rivalry sprang up between them which, on the one hand, pushed the Dominicans into the service of the poor and, on the other hand, induced the Franciscans, but not till after their noble founder's death, to concern themselves with instruction and to seek the honors of scholarship. Already by the second half of the thirteenth century the rivalry was at white heat, and, although each continued to exhibit the characteristic stamp of the genius who had called it into being, both orders were by that time moving along substantially parallel lines of endeavor.

In spite of this close duplication of effort every penetrating consideration of the two orders confirms the opinion that it was not Dominic but Francis who with his message of love made religion again a living force in a doubt-troubled world. If ever teaching was evangelical, it was his, for he tried to live his life from day to day in literal imitation of the Lord Jesus. He was particularly enamored of poverty and never spoke more movingly than when engaged in its praise. But preaching poverty for his friars, he did not preach the poverty of the church, and thus avoided falling under its anathema. He had nothing but reverence for the ecclesiastical order with the pope at its head and unquestioningly held to the belief that there was ample room for his great missionary work within the church as it existed. Therefore without arousing hostility in high places he brought evangelicalism, a strictly limited evangelicalism, it is true, back into favor. In this way he did the church an inestimable service, for the masses who had become estranged from a ceremonial church ruled by great dignitaries separated from themselves by an unbridgable chasm, welcomed in St. Francis and his followers a body of lesser clerical servants, who descended to their own level and preached and practiced love of God and neighbor as the core of Christianity. It was only because the church had become empty of comfort that the people had ever turned against it; but now that comfort was again dispensed, a comfort exactly adjusted to the needs of the lowly and the overburdened, they again made their peace with the church, accepting it as the sure gate to salvation.

As the spirit of Francis shines in all he said and did, it shines also in an act by which he attached great bodies of the laity to his ideals. Not all men, even if they heard the inner call, could abandon shop and family and join the Order of St. Francis; nor could all women join the Order of St. Clare, founded by Clara, the friend and Assisan neighbor of Francis, as the female counterpart of the male order. To meet the case of innumerable devotees who could not leave the world, Francis had the happy inspiration to create a lay adjunct of the two regular Franciscan orders. It is popularly called the Third Order and its members, Tertiaries. It was open to both men and women. Tertiaries did not take the vows prescribed for the regular brothers and sisters, nor did they leave their work or surrender their place in society. They pledged themselves simply to be guided by the spirit of the founder, to live frugally, distribute alms, and love their fellow-men. Large numbers of the laity were in this manner again brought into touch with the original spirit of Christianity as unfolded in the gospels. There is no telling how much the Tertiaries added to the religious fervor of the thirteenth century, although we may guess that the contribution was large. Since the rivalry between Franciscans and Dominicans moved them to copy each other in every possible respect, it followed that the Dominicans were not slow to create a Third Order of their own. Doubtless it did its share to popularize religion and to bring it about that the Christian church of the thirteenth century was probably closer to the hearts of the people of all classes, high and low, than ever before or since.

For us engaged in tracing the many lines of Florentine development, it is a matter of no slight interest to learn how the Florentines were affected by the religious revival connected with the two great orders of begging friars. Over a hundred years earlier they had shown their susceptibility to religious emotions when, carried away by the ascetic preaching of Giovanni Gualberti, they had become the most important Italian center of the reform movement headed in its final phase by Pope Gregory VII. Since all emotions exhibit a tidal action, alternately rising and receding, we are prepared to hear that the ecclesiastical enthusiasm fanned by Gualberti gradually subsided. In the century following the struggle over lay investiture, the church came in for much criticism in the Arno city and many different kinds of heresy won a foothold within the circle of its walls. It was this ecclesiastical rebelliousness, become common throughout Italy, that both Dominic and Francis were prompted to seek out; and as their active missionary spirit kept them in almost uninterrupted movement through the cities of the peninsula, it happened that they brought their message also to Florence. Dominic entered the city apparently only once; of Francis we know with certainty that he was a frequent visitor of the City of the Baptist. It was in the year 1219 that the famous Spanish preacher entered the gates and immediately his magnetic personality caused a Dominican community to spring to life. Two years later it was put in possession of a little insignificant church, Santa Maria Novella, located in the western section of the town just outside the recently completed second circle of walls. The settlement grew rapidly in numbers, riches, and influence so that dormitories and cloisters had to be added and repeatedly enlarged. From practically the day of its founding its friars were intrusted by the pope with the work of the inquisition for the Florentine area, and by their persistent fanatic zeal they gradually overcame the early reluctance of the commune and people to approve of the eradication of dissident opinion by violent means. Before the end of the thirteenth century the Florentine Dominicans had waxed so great that they undertook to replace the inconspicuous original Santa Maria Novella with the magnificent church of that name which still stands. Its scale and grandeur may be accepted as a just index of the importance within the Florentine world which the Dominicans had by that time acquired and which they retained unimpaired for several centuries. From the great Dominican compound there radiated influences which profoundly affected the Florentine religious, moral, intellectual, and artistic development, as we shall have frequent occasion to see. Florentine politics, too, did not escape the Dominican impact. For, as devoted sons of the papacy, the brothers of Santa Maria Novella were the willing channel by which the popes brought a powerful influence to bear in their own behalf on the Arno government.

Although Francis visited Florence many times to bring to it his message of divine love, there is no record of the creation of a Franciscan community in the Arno city till two years after his death. It was in 1228 that a band of Franciscan brothers took over the church of Santa Croce for the preaching of a simple, popular character which was one of their most cherished purposes. Santa Croce was a small, undistinguished building in the eastern part of town just beyond the new or second wall. The local branches of the two great begging orders were thus as far removed from each other physically as possible. But as both equally enjoyed the favor of the citizens, the Franciscan nucleus expanded no less rapidly than the rival organization. Cloisters and dormitories were presently constructed, and just before the end of the thirteenth century the friars were able to replace their first extremely modest house of worship with the famous Gothic structure which is still one of the landmarks of the city. The significance for Florentine civilization of the great Franciscan settlement yields in no respect to that of its Dominican counterpart. Florentine manners and morals and, above all, the Fine Arts were affected at every turn by the congregation of brothers who made their home at Santa Croce. For the pope it became a second center of political support within the town. For, rivals in everything, the Franciscans did not let themselves be outdone by the sons of Dominic in unhesitating devotion to the chair of St. Peter.

From the second quarter of the thirteenth century onward we must think of Florence as provided with two new dynamic centers of religion, the one in the eastern, the other in the western, section of the town. An electric current passed from each of them to the citizen body and from the citizen body flowed back to the two centers. It was a religious and a cultural exchange of great energy which continued unabated for many generations. While both groups of friars put themselves, each in its own way, at the service of the people of Florence, they did not put themselves, at least with anything like the same devotion, at the service of the Florentine government. For, as members of the church, they enjoyed ecclesiastical immunity and dwelt outside the civil order. From the point of view of organization they looked upon themselves, and indeed were, each one a papal citadel within the rising commonwealth. From this Rome-ward orientation there arose no difficulty so long as the papal and the Florentine governments lived in peace and harmony; but when they disagreed, as they very often did, a grave local tension could not be avoided.

VIII. The Buondelmonte Murder; Guelphs and Ghibellines; Triumph and Failure of Frederick II

THE coming of the podestà at the beginning of the thirteenth century signified a revolution within the consular system. While its meaning has been disputed, it is reasonably clear that it represented an attempt to put an end to the ferocious factional warfare for consular honors among the upper order of the citizens, the milites. We have seen that the great body of the Florentines made up the foot-soldiers or pedites, and that through the public assembly, or parlamentum, the pedites brought a faint flavor of democracy into the consular system. Throughout the consular period, however, the political power was virtually monopolized by the wealthy burghers who rode to war on horseback and were carried on the urban muster rolls as milites. It was human, intensely human, that factions should develop among this ruling class; and in view of the vendetta obligation, which no miles could escape, and of the numerous tower associations admirably suited to give vendetta a prompt effect, it was inevitable that upper-class rivalry in connection with the annual consular elections should lead to ever-recurring civil disturbances. They became more and more numerous toward the turn of the century until a solution had somehow to be found. As other towns in the same case tried the arbiter from without, the foreign podestà, Florence tried him too. By 1207 the new era, the era of the podestà, was well under way.

We may agree that the new chief executive was in more than one respect an improvement on the consuls. That he would suddenly patch up the ancient quarrels among the magnates was not to be expected and did not follow. The quarrels, as part of the long established habits of a group feudally oriented, obstinately continued; in fact, through various circumstances to be presently related, they grew steadily more embittered until, toward the middle of the thirteenth century, a factional conflict had developed of so passionate a nature that it defied every attempt at compromise. Over this inner division the societas militum, representing the unity of the old ruling class, went to pieces; and although one of the nobiliary factions was in the end victorious over the other and the nobles as a class were not immediately wiped out, the ruin of their society must, from their class point of view, be accounted a loss which it was impossible ever again to make good.

For the common people, on the other hand, the disappearance of the society that gave the milites the character of a unified order was bound to prove an immeasurable gain. Unfortunately in the case of our city of Florence we have

103

no evidence covering the early decades of the thirteenth century which tells us just how the pedites reacted in the face of the irritating arrogance and the civic misbehavior of their social superiors. To supply the missing information recourse may fairly be had to neighboring towns, such as Lucca and Siena, where essentially identical social conditions obtained; and in these nearby communes we learn from authentic records that the pedites developed the necessary spirit to take the protection of their interests into their hands. They did so by forming a political society of their own, a *societas populi*. Therewith they declared in substance that their numbers and importance justified their claiming a larger share in the government than had thus far been accorded them. Even though the Florentine popular movement cannot be proved to have reached this fighting stage till some decades later, we know beyond a doubt that Florence experienced a social and economic development identical with that of its Tuscan neighbors. Exactly like them, it boasted throughout the twelfth century a waxing trade, an uninterrupted increase of occupational activities, and an expanding population. Consequently there took place a steady strengthening of the common people throughout the consular age. With the advent of the podestà the Florentine popular elements may quite possibly have tried the experiment of a society of their own, which, quickly quashed by the governing group, has happened to leave no record behind. Be that as it may, at the exact middle of the century (1250) the foot-soldiers of the Arno city did at last form a societas populi of which we have definite news and which developed such amazing power that it ventured to set up a revolutionary government on the basis of its exclusive rule. True, under the stress of unexpected and incalculable forces which, after 1250, overwhelmed Florence and all Tuscany, the first Florentine democracy, celebrated in Florentine annals as *Il Primo Popolo,* lasted only a decade. How it arose and how it fell will be told in the following chapter. At this juncture we are interested in establishing nothing more than this: that the first half of the thirteenth century witnessed a significant social revolution exhibiting two distinct but subtly interrelated phenomena. The first of these was the intensification of faction among the well-to-do, the horsemen (milites), to a point which destroyed their class coherence and brought them to the verge of ruin; the second was the slow rise and gradual emancipation of the common people till with a sudden rush they were able to take over the government. It is this exciting social-political upheaval among the milites and pedites during the first half of the thirteenth century on which our interest will be centered in this chapter.

It lay in the nature of the case that the blood-feuds among the upper class were constantly nursed by fresh episodes, sometimes of a political, sometimes of a personal, character. The podestà had not long replaced the consuls when such an episode befell. Beginning as a purely personal quarrel, it took on a political color, as personal quarrels among a governing group have the habit of doing, and blazed up so prodigiously that the early chroniclers—and the poet Dante as well, who received his local history from these chroniclers—represented it as the prime cause, the veritable *fons et origo* of all the unhappy civil broils in which the town became subsequently engulfed. This is of course an exaggeration, since, conflicts among the nobility being no novelty in Florence, the new outburst was no more than a fresh link in a long chain of incidents reaching back far into the past. Nonetheless the Buondelmonte murder of the year 1216 took hold of the imagination of the citizens to such an extent that, on this ground alone, it is impossible to pass it by. We shall present it in the version of a chronicler who wrote about one hundred years after the event. His story has so authentic a ring that it has been suggested that he must have drawn upon the family records, the *ricordanze,* as they are locally called, of some memoirists close to the main participants. A notable quality of the account that no one will overlook derives from the vivid glimpses it affords of contemporary feudal manners.

A few explanatory words may bring the feudal manners revealed by our selection somewhat more into the open. The story begins with a feast offered by a new-made knight at his country seat some six miles to the west of the city. In this connection we should remind ourselves that knights were a product of the movement of chivalry which originated in northern France about the time of the First Crusade and promptly imposed itself as its most handsome decoration on the rough feudal society characteristic of the whole European west. While every Florentine who was rich enough to own a horse from the angle of civic organization ranked as a miles, not every miles by any means was a knight, that is, an accredited member of the high, informal order of European chivalry. Eligible to knighthood, like the miles of every other country the Florentine miles had to satisfy certain indispensable tests before he could be promoted to the honor to which he aspired. He might then be struck knight after appropriate games and ceremonies of which he and his family were obliged to bear the costs. As not many could afford the heavy expense of these formalities, comparatively few Florentine milites ever gained the knightly dignity; but having gained it, we may be sure that they bore themselves with an added touch of arrogance toward their humbler fellow-citizens. Since a knight continued to be carried on the Florentine official register as a miles, a certain confusion has arisen in regard to the term, as it designates both a horseman and a horseman become a knight. We need not let that particularly disturb us. For us the milites are a social order which includes the knights, the knights being just the more eminent milites who have achieved the honors of chivalry.

At the feast described by our chronicler the food was doubtless plentiful, though by our contemporary standards greatly lacking in variety; and a poverty and simplicity characteristic of the age were indicated by the circumstance that the knights at table were grouped in pairs so that a single plate might do service for two guests. This must be kept in mind if we are to understand why it was that two knights were insulted when a plate was suddenly snatched from under the nose of one of them. It was seized by a clown, one of a large company of mimes, acrobats, and minstrels who in that roving age were wont to make an appearance wherever and whenever invitations to a wedding or a knighting or any gathering whatever of notables had gone forth. If much of the fun of these wandering entertainers was extremely unrefined, its broad note harmonized admirably with the rude tone of the feudal rulers, whose chief idea of amusement was a rough horseplay calculated to evoke a side-splitting laughter. And finally we come face to face with an instance of the terrible vendetta custom. We are aware that spilt blood called for blood and that the obligation rested less on the injured individual than on the individual's family or on the group of associated families to which he belonged. By the time of the murder about to be related, an accommodation of a feud had become permissible. The compounding often took the form of a marriage arranged between members of the aggrieved families. To exorcise hatred and enmity by the merry peal of wedding bells looks like a wildly romantic undertaking. Over and over again it ended dismally in failure, but in the instance under consideration the failure assumed nothing less than tragic proportions bringing death to many and widespread ruin to the town. And now let the unknown chronicler have the floor:[1]

In the year 1216, when Messer Currado Orlandi was podestà, Messer Mazzingo Tegrimi of the family of the Mazzinghi had himself struck knight at a place called Campi, some six miles from Florence, and invited thither all the best people (*tutta la buona gente*) of the town. And when all the knights had sat down to meat, a buffoon snatched away the full plate set before Messer Uberto dell' Infangati, who was paired at table with Messer Buondelmonte de' Buondelmonti. That angered Messer Uberto greatly, and Messer Oddo Arrighi de' Fifanti, a man of valor, roughly reproved him on this account. In reply Messer Uberto told him he lied in his throat, at which Messer Oddo Arrighi tossed a plate full into his face. And the whole assembly was in an uproar. When the tables had been removed, Messer Buondelmonte struck at Messer Oddo Arrighi with a knife and wounded him severely.

As soon as all the company had returned to their homes Messer Oddo Arrighi took counsel with his friends and relatives, among whom were the counts of Gangalandi, the Uberti, the Lamberti, and the Amidei; and their advice was that peace should be concluded over the issue and that Messer Buondelmonte should take for wife the daughter of Messer Lambertuccio de' Amidei, who lived at the head of the bridge. The bride-to-be was the niece of Messer Oddo Arrighi. Accordingly, the marriage contract was drawn up and the peace arranged and on the following day the wedding was to be celebrated. Thereupon Madonna Gualdrada, the wife of Messer Forese Donati, sent secretly for Messer Buondelmonte and when he came spoke to him as follows: knight, you are forever disgraced by taking a wife out of fear of the Uberti and the Fifanti; leave her you have taken and take this other [i.e., her own daughter whom we must imagine her bringing forward at that moment] and your honor as knight will be restored. As soon as he had heard, he resolved to do as he was told without taking counsel with any of his kin. And when on the following day, the morning of Thursday, February 11, the guests of both parties had assembled, Messer Buondelmonte passed through the gate of Santa Maria and went to pledge troth with the girl of the Donati family; and her of the Amidei he left waiting at the church door.

This insult enraged Messer Oddo Arrighi greatly and he held a meeting with all his friends and relatives in the church of Santa Maria sopra Porta. When all were assembled he complained in strong terms of the disgrace put upon him by Messer Buondelmonte. Some counseled that Buondelmonte be given a cudgeling, others that he be wounded in the face. At this spoke up Messer Mosca de' Lamberti: whoever

---

[1] His chronicle goes under the name of *Pseudo-Brunetto Latini* and has been published by Hartwig, *Quellen und Forschungen*, Vol. II, pp. 221 ff. The translated passage begins on p. 223. The dates, given in the document in accordance with the Florentine calendar, have been accommodated in the translation to the current Christian calendar. The Florentine year began not on January 1 but on the twenty-fifth of March, the reputed day of the Annunciation.

beats or wounds him let him first see to it that his own grave has been dug; what this case requires is not half measures but clean work [*cosa fatta capo ha,* the famous phrase quoted by Dante and destined to become proverbial in the language. An equally terse translation is impossible]. Thereupon they decided that the vendetta was to be carried out at the very place where the injury had been done, when the parties had gathered for the exchange of the marriage vows. And thus it came about that when on Easter morning [with his bride at his side] Messer Buondelmonte in doublet of silk and mantle and with a wreath about his brow came riding over the bridge, no sooner had he arrived at the statue of Mars than Messer Schiatta degli Uberti rushed upon him and, striking him on the crown with his mace, brought him to earth. At once Messer Oddo Arrighi was on top of him and opened his veins with a knife. And having killed him, they fled. The ambush had been in the houses of the Amidei [who, as we have learned, lived at the head of the bridge].

Immediately there was a tremendous tumult. The body of the murdered man was placed on a bier and the bride took her seat on the bier, holding the head in her lap and weeping aloud. And in this manner the procession moved through all Florence.

Before night fell on that bloody Easter day the hostile families had taken up arms and war raged as so often before from tower to tower and street to street till the podestà interfered and imposed a truce. There was nothing particularly novel in the situation, unless it be that the incidents leading to this latest nobiliary brawl presented so many picturesque and romantic features that they became indelibly impressed on the minds of the citizens. The peace patched up by the podestà would last till a fresh event caused the slumbering passions again to flare up. Thereupon local fighting would be renewed, sometimes with the same, sometimes with a different, cast of characters. The podestà proved to be a restraining and moderating influence, and the nobles themselves, especially the older and more judicious elements among them, were loath to let the divisions in their class become irreconcilable. For, should that come about, the societas militum, the organization through which they exercised a dominant political influence, would necessarily suffer shipwreck. However, they were swept along by a current difficult, if not impossible, to control. We get a hint of the danger lying ahead from the chronicler on whom we have just drawn. He concludes his account of the Buondelmonte murder with the following startling words: "On this day . . . for the first time new names were heard, to wit, Guelph party and Ghibelline party." In sum, he lets us know that the traditional upper-class altercations were threatening to take on the character of a permanent schism; and without his expressly telling us, we are instinctively aware that, should distinct parties replace the haphazard divisions which had thus far been the rule among the magnates, their common politico-military society would have to go by the boards.

The names Guelph and Ghibelline loom so large in Italian history for more than two hundred years after this event that we must imperatively look into their origin and significance. We shall assume the obligation the more readily, as the story has its start at Florence where, exactly as the chronicler indicates, the names were first employed. This has been established in so indisputable a fashion by recent investigation that the tale can now be presented without any apologies for regrettable lacunae.[2] Let us imagine ourselves at Florence in the year 1212, some four years before the above-related murder, when Pope Innocent III, having excommunicated Otto IV, dispatched the young king of Sicily, Frederick of Hohenstaufen, to Germany to claim the crown. As to all the other Italian principalities and cities, so also to Florence Innocent issued the strict command to repudiate Otto and acknowledge Frederick. However, the Florentines were slow to obey the papal order, owing to the lively recollection among them of how shabbily they had been treated by the father and grandfather of Frederick. They felt themselves much less threatened in their self-governing aspirations by Otto, at whose hands they had recently enjoyed some not inconsiderable favors. Quite naturally therefore there formed itself in Florence a party of Otto which, since Otto was of the Welf or Guelph family, took the name of the party of the Guelph (*parte del Guelfo*). Contrariwise, those who bowed to the pope's orders and accepted Frederick as sovereign called themselves party of the Ghibelline (*parte del Ghibellino*). The Hohenstaufen family had been long associated with the castle of Waiblingen in Suabia so that "Waiblingen, Waiblingen," was one of the battle-cries with which their followers were wont to charge the enemy. Transformed by the Italian tongue into Ghibellino, this name made an appearance in Florence contemporaneously with Guelfo. Before a generation had passed both names had spread like a ripe contagion into every town and hamlet of Italy. And when the dissemination was complete the Guelphs had become aligned with the church and the Ghibellines with the empire. This is of course the familiar identification of the two terms; but in view of this very familiarity, it is rather startling to observe that on their first raising their heads at Florence the Guelphs were in opposition to the pope, while the Ghibellines, as supporters of the pope's candidate for the empire, enjoyed his hearty indorsement. We may regard this as an accidental quirk or twist resulting from Innocent's momentary support of a young and unknown Hohenstaufen against an unmasked and treacherous Guelph. On the very day on which Frederick, after winning the German crown, made it clear that he would continue the policy of his ancestors, the papal quirk disappeared. No other than the ancestral policy was open to the young Hohenstaufen, who, unless he were prepared to betray his office, would imperatively have to maintain the independence of the state against the church. However, from the moment Frederick showed his true colors, he and his supporters, the Ghibellines, were promptly denounced by the successors of Pope Innocent as persecutors of the church. At this turn of affairs the Guelphs, as opponents of Frederick, gathered under the banner of the papacy. The grouping thus achieved remained characteristic of Italian political life for all the years to come.

But this is only one aspect of the story of the Guelph and Ghibelline partisanship. It would be a grave mistake to think of the Guelphs, whom already by the middle of the thirteenth century we encounter in practically every Italian town, as organized primarily to support the church; and it would be just as erroneous to think of the equally universal party of the Ghibellines as

---

[2] Davidsohn, *Forschungen,* Vol. IV, pp. 29 ff. "Die Entstehung der Guelfen und der Ghibellinen Partei."

created for the single purpose of serving the empire. Deeply considered, the two parties owed their existence to the communal revolution, the problems of which were much closer to the inhabitants of the towns, and much more real to them, than the relatively remote issue of supremacy so ferociously argued and fought over by empire and church. The point we are trying to make is strikingly illustrated by the case of our very city of Florence. For a hundred years before the conflict between Otto and Frederick, and for over a hundred years after that conflict, the leading issue in Florence was without any question the purely communal problem of political independence. Throughout the consular period there had already been a citizen group which cherished independence as its dearest goal and which, recognizing the empire as the main obstacle to its ambition, opposed the emperor openly when he was feeble and secretly whenever he visited Tuscany with an irresistible army. As at the time of the conflict between Otto IV and Frederick II the imperial authority was negligible, its Florentine enemies did not hesitate to assume a bold front. By supporting Frederick's opponent and calling themselves Guelphs after him, they could even give their boldness an appearance of legality. Their intimate thoughts, we may be sure, turned, not about Otto and Frederick, but about Florence and the increase of their local authority likely to result from the success of their imperial candidate. In the same way their political opponents, the Ghibellines, were concerned, first and foremost, with the enlargement of their power at home. In Ghibelline eyes the empire was still a power to be reckoned with and in the hope of obtaining Frederick's aid for their plan of controlling the city, they ostentatiously tendered him their allegiance.

At the head of the local group of nobles which already during the consular period had built its plans of domination on Hohenstaufen support was the oldest and haughtiest family of the town, the Uberti. Never did a quarrel break out in Florence in the ranks of the governing class without their taking a hand, partly because of their violent feudal manners, partly because of their many ramifications with other leading families either through marriage or by reason of partnership in one of the soaring towers. We have just learned how the head of the house, Schiatta degli Uberti, participated in the Buondelmonte murder, although he was not immediately involved in the offense which had led to the vendetta. His action injected a non-personal, a distinctly political element into the assassination. Moreover, following the murder, the Uberti, we learn, at once took up arms; and with civil war on their hands, they would not fail to see the advantage of adding to their strength by identifying themselves with the cause of Frederick. This decision by the Uberti would of itself suffice to persuade the Buondelmonti and the Buondelmonti adherents to seek the advantage certain to accrue from adopting the opposite or Guelph cause. It will not do to press these tentative political alignments too closely. The situation was as fluid as water and long continued to remain so. But it is fairly clear that it was over nothing other than the issue of local control that the two factions of the nobility, which had so dramatically collided in 1216, tended to consolidate into parties, although the final step, from which there was no retreat, was not taken till several decades later. Only when the division had at length reached that decisive point do we find the Uberti faction definitely organized as the Ghibelline party and the Buondelmonte faction just as uncompromisingly identified with the Guelphs. Each party, though essentially local, was ready at any time to accept help from without the town, the Uberti from the emperor and his allies, the Buondelmonti from the pope and such friends as the papacy commanded; and in return for help received from outside partisans each party was of course prepared to come to the aid of these outsiders. Undoubtedly therefore both the Guelphs and Ghibellines of Florence had a foreign policy and made their influence felt beyond the limits of their city. Just the same the most ardent concern of both parties was always the domestic situation, for each aimed at the exclusive rule of the passionately loved town.

The rapid radiation of the Guelph-Ghibelline animosity from Florence over Tuscany and thence over Italy, though puzzling at first sight, is easily explained on the ground of the essentially identical conditions among all the young city-republics. In every Italian commune the governing group around the year 1200 had fallen into two rival factions; and in their struggle for supremacy each local faction eagerly sought the support of some power stronger and more permanent than itself. Within the whole peninsula there were just two powers of this kind available, the empire and the papacy. It is the tie-up effected between an infinity of circumscribed local interests and the issue of church and state, general to the whole peninsula, that gave the two parties their broadly national character. Far more surprising, on the whole, than the ubiquity of Guelphs and Ghibellines is the extraordinary rancor that marked their rivalry. Partisanship is so unfailing a feature of every great historical development that, within limits, we are prepared to accept it as a positive sign of health. But partisanship in the Italian city-republics reached such a height and frenzy of virulence that life must have been conducted perpetually at wasteful fever heat. Not content with civil warfare with its but too familiar accompaniment of riot, arson, and murder, Guelphs and Ghibellines carried their differences into every conceivable field of human expression. You knew a Guelph from a Ghibelline by the cut of his doublet, by the angle at which he wore the feather in his cap, by the shape of the battlements that crowned the family tower. Luckily these extravagances, like the parties themselves, were largely limited to the upper order; also they did not reach their climax till the passage of one or more generations had permitted the movement to gather momentum. We are here dealing with its infancy and have still to show how in this phase it was deeply affected by a great, a masterful individual. This was the Emperor Frederick II, to whom an all but universal opinion points as the outstanding personality of his age.

When, after an absence of eight years in Germany, Frederick II returned to Italy and in 1220 was crowned emperor at Rome by Pope Honorius III, he was a vigorous, self-assured young man of twenty-six. He had just assumed toward the pope, and in the most solemn manner, the obligation of leading a crusade to the Holy Land; but before setting out for the east, he obtained permission to visit his kingdom of Sicily, where his presence was required in order to revive the royal authority seriously impaired through his long absence in the north. Once in his native kingdom, he resolved to engage on a far-reaching reorganization. This domestic program of his revealed his vigorous political initiative, for it signified nothing less than the replacement of the anarchic self-government of the feudal barons with a centralized bureaucracy under royal control. So radical an undertaking could not be carried through under many years. On being reminded by the pope from time to time of his crusading vow, he excused himself by the pressure of work in his Sicilian home as well as throughout his kingdom of Italy. However, to placate Honorius he met the wishes of the Holy Father in other respects, less immediately important to himself. He agreed, for instance, to satisfy a papal demand of long standing by bringing the civil authorities into line with the ecclesiastical rulers in the uprooting of heresy. Thus it came about that Frederick became the sponsor of the most rigorous criminal code *contra hereticos* that was ever devised; and repeatedly during his reign he issued peremptory orders to the governments of all the Italian communes to incorporate this ferocious legislation in their local constitutions. It is impossible to explain this hearty seconding of the papal inquisition by a man of Frederick's skeptical and secular outlook except on the ground of political opportunism.

In the year 1227 the mild and conciliatory Honorius died and was succeeded by Gregory IX, a man no whit less imperious than the fiery Innocent III. In the new pope's view his predecessor had been trifled with by the slippery young man on the imperial throne; and when Frederick seemed to be at his old tricks with him too, Gregory promptly banned him from the Christian fold. Without waiting to have the ban removed, Frederick in June, 1228, set sail for the east, thereby affording the world the curious spectacle of an excommunicated Christian prince faring on crusade to wrest the Holy Land from an infidel foe. Europe was even more dumbfounded when, without fighting a single battle, this strange crusader, whom all the faithful were ordered to avoid like the plague, gained what thousands of earlier crusaders under the special blessing of the church had died in a vain effort to achieve. In simple fact, and in spite of his expedition in behalf of the Cross, Frederick did not at any time have his heart in the enterprise. He was just a calculating diplomat governed by common-sense considerations and, on finding the Moslem ruler over Syria disposed to come to terms, he promptly signed a treaty with that sovereign by which Jerusalem and a few adjoining districts were delivered into his hands. Thereupon he crowned himself king of Jerusalem and, with fame sounding its trumpets before him, returned to Italy. Many were rejoiced by his success but the head of Christendom was not among them. As there was no denying, however, that Frederick had brought the Holy Places of Palestine back into Christian possession, Gregory let himself be gradually drawn into negotiations. They ended in his cancelling his curse and signing a general treaty of reconciliation (1230).

The new peace between pope and emperor soon proved a sham, as had the long roster of its predecessors. So long as the empire made claims that the church would not recognize and vice versa, every treaty signed between the two adversaries could be nothing better than a truce. The new peace would last, exactly like the many that had gone before, until some fresh event deeply affected the relationship of the two parties and made them disposed to have recourse to war in the hope of improving their position. The rupture of the treaty of 1230 did not occur till almost a decade later in consequence of the open and avowed renewal, on the part of Frederick, of his grandfather's attempt to bring the Lombard cities under the imperial yoke. Without any question he had been pondering the reopening of this crucial issue ever since his coronation in 1220; but the complicated business of reorganizing Sicily and, afterward, the innumerable troubles released by the crusade absorbed his energy and he had been obliged to curb his impatience.

Frederick II was a man so responsive to the new modes of thought and feeling beginning to stir in Europe in his day that in many respects he would seem to have stepped across the threshold of the Middle Ages into the modern world. Child of a Sicilian mother and brought up in southern Italy, where Christian and Moslem influences met and mixed, he had developed an intellectual skepticism which rendered him completely immune to the religious fervor characteristic of an age of faith. Far from being a help to him as a ruler, his critical attitude of mind proved to be a heavy liability in a society which, still medieval, was just then passing through a vast religious revival championed by the two begging orders. Both Dominicans and Franciscans instinctively sensed the emperor's intellectual emancipation and worked against him secretly and openly by every means at their disposal. From pulpit and street-corner they denounced him—and in so doing they were probably not far from the truth—as a secret follower of the Arab philosopher, Averroes, and consequently as an infidel and a rationalist. Again, on grounds no less valid, they poured the vials of their wrath over him as an Epicurean and a sensualist. For, endowed with delicate senses as well as with an alert mind, Frederick delighted in all the refinements and luxuries with which the west had become acquainted since it had re-established contact with the east through the crusades. He made his court the most elaborate and exquisite of his age. In his palaces and gardens knights and ladies joined in pleasant intercourse and listened to those alluring entertainers out of the Provence, the troubadours, who sang the love of woman and gloried in the beauty of the earth. Frederick himself wrote verses in the Provençal manner and is deservedly celebrated as one of the earliest adepts of Italian lyric poetry. It was in the realm of sex that the oriental influences which he had assimilated manifested themselves in the most conspicuous manner. For by openly maintaining a harem he revealed that he had succumbed to the sensuous languors of another and a softer civilization.

This fluid individual, who succeeded in bursting through so many of the current medieval limitations, is immediately important to us only on the side of his political activity. That Frederick was capable of thinking just as fresh thoughts in the political field as in philosophy and poetry was proved by the reform he carried through in Sicily. It amounted to nothing less than replacing the loose and wasteful feudal system with an efficient monarchical absolutism. When, many generations later, absolutism revealed itself throughout the extent of Europe as the common remedy for feudal anarchy, Frederick had been long forgotten; but that cannot deprive him of the honor of having been perhaps the first European, certainly the first Italian, ruler, not merely to project, but actually to create a modern state. We hail him therefore as a political innovator but—and here we encounter one of those contradictions which no complex character seems to be able to escape—when he faced the issue raised by the prosperous north Italian towns, he was incapable of seeing it in any other than in the conservative light in which it had presented itself to his father and grandfather before him. To him, as to them, the communes were exercising or attempting to exercise self-governing rights which were an infringement on the sacred imperial authority. To be sure, the Lombard group of towns had secured an acknowledgment of their freedom in the victorious treaty of Constance (1183) and were therefore fairly within their rights; but the indisputable legality of their very substantial independence did not make it any more agreeable to contemplate. Frederick pondered the situation in the spirit of an obstinate aristocrat, whose heart stirred with contempt for upstart traders and craftsmen daring to challenge the long-established authority of their betters; and following his reconciliation with Pope Gregory IX in 1230, he made up his mind that the time had come to take the matter actively in hand. As the Lombard cities commanded great resources and were well armed, he was obliged to proceed with a considerable measure of caution. And when he was at last ready and about to strike, he was checked by a revolt which broke out in 1235 in Germany. Hurrying thither to suppress it, he did not return to Italy till two years later. Then at last the storm broke with extraordinary fury. As it broke in Lombardy, its details do not concern us. It will suffice if we trace the general course of Lombard events in order to understand the important repercussions they produced in Tuscany.

On November 27, 1237, Frederick unexpectedly fell upon the army of the Lombard league at Cortenuova and defeated it utterly. In his exultation he imagined he had reversed the decision of Legnano and had made himself master of northern Italy. He soon learned he was mistaken, for, in spite of defeat, first one town and then another defied him, obliging him continuously to hold the field and spend his energy on a succession of tedious and wasteful sieges. In this manner years passed during which the terror spread by the Cortenuova triumph gradually evaporated. Besides, in 1239 Pope Gregory terminated his neutrality and actively entered the game. We cannot but agree that it was normal for the papacy to join whatever agency was resisting its ancient enemy, the empire; and Gregory, secretly rejoicing over Frederick's waxing difficulties in Lombardy, stepped out into the open against him just as soon as the moment seemed auspicious. Less than two years after Cortenuova the pope stiffened the ranks of the Lombard opposition by once more excommunicating the emperor. At the same time those formidable cohorts of the papacy, the Dominicans and Franciscans, went up and down the land inflaming the common people against the Hohenstaufen sovereign, whom they denounced in unbridled language. They called him a heretic and limb of Satan and in their frenzy even spread the ominous whisper that he was that most fearful of all visitations, the anti-Christ, forerunner of the Last Judgment.

The considerable military power commanded by Frederick was bound in the long run to exhaust itself against the combination of Lombard resolution,

papal authority, and religious fanaticism. Slowly but inexorably his cause
turned to its setting. When Gregory died in 1241, he was succeeded by Innocent IV, and the new pontiff, even more grimly hostile than his predecessor,
resolved to make the chasm between himself and his opponent absolutely un-
bridgeable. At a General Council of the church, which he summoned to meet
him at Lyons in France, not only did he excommunicate the emperor anew
but, as earlier popes had done with earlier emperors, he went further and declared him deposed from office (July 17, 1245). Misfortunes now crowded on
the unhappy man in a bewildering succession. The pope succeeded in setting up
a rival king in Germany; Frederick's army suffered a crushing defeat at Parma
at the hands of the Lombards; the Bolognese captured his favorite son, Enzio,
and clapped him in prison. He bore the multiplied blows of fate with unshaken fortitude and till death visited his tent kept his banners waving in
the wind.

Before coming to this closing scene we must catch up with the very important developments in Tuscany and Florence. From the day of his accession
to the empire, Frederick had been in the habit of sending representatives to
Tuscany to exercise the rights which were his traditional due in that province.
Conspicuously ignored by the expanding towns and, more particularly, by
Florence, these agents led an obscure existence, far from calculated to enhance
their master's credit. The terror produced by Cortenuova, however, changed
this ignominious situation almost over night. A new emissary, a certain Gebhard of Arnstein, issued the command to the Tuscan towns to acknowledge the imperial authority without more ado; and the bitterly divided communes, unable to agree on united action, were obliged to obey. Proud Florence was no exception to the rule. Gebhard wisely made its submission easy
by refraining from excessive demands. The Arno city was permitted to retain
its constitution with the provision that the podestà, before entering on office,
should receive the indorsement of the emperor (1238). Presently Gebhard was
replaced as legate in Tuscany, and with each new year his successors clipped
from the Florentines one or another of their cherished liberties. The insidious
process continued till all the boasted gains since the Tuscan league of 1197
had been cancelled and the town had been unequivocally subjected to the
emperor. Florence had become a humbled Ghibelline community.

The acceptance by Florence as podestà of Frederick's illegitimate son, Frederick of Antioch, marks the culmination of the disastrous development. It
was in 1246 that the younger Frederick became ruler of the city. Since his
father appointed him at the same time as vicar-general in Tuscany, his rule
extended over the whole province. By taking up his residence in Florence,
he automatically made this city, in place of the historic San Miniato del
Tedesco, the focus of the imperial administration. In the name of the emperor
the son, whose talents and gallantry made him a representative worthy of
his famous father, appointed the podestàs, the judges, and the notaries throughout his territory. So far as it is possible to penetrate into the secret places of
the emperor's mind, he seems to have planned to provide Tuscany with a
bureaucratic government fashioned after the regime he had introduced into
his kingdom of Sicily. If that is true, he failed to take account of the fact

that Tuscany and Sicily were two entirely distinct societies. While the southern kingdom was still overwhelmingly agrarian and feudal, Tuscany had
become revolutionized by commerce and took its political tone from a flourishing body of irrepressible towns. From the day of his assumption of the imperial scepter in 1220 the weakness of Frederick's statesmanship was and
remained that he failed to appreciate the vigor, the valor, and the ultimate
necessity of the new burgher society volcanically pushing upward through the
feudal crust. Indeed his blindness to this complex of irresistible energies gives
him, who was in so many respects aware of psychological realities hidden from
his contemporaries, something of the air of a misguided Don Quixote. It is
certainly necessary to search far and wide in history before finding anything
more fantastically quixotic than Frederick's lifelong labor to build a dam
against the vast new forces that were in his day engaged in reshaping the
world. They might delay their action in the deceptive manner of such forces;
but in their own good time they would with an explosive energy that could
not be checked sweep the emperor's puny obstructions, together with his person, out of their path.

When Frederick of Antioch became the all-powerful vicar-general of Tuscany, he found that he faced a Florentine opposition which was no less alive
for having gone temporarily into hiding. We have learned that the local
Guelphs were a group of the nobility who favored the independence of their
city from the empire, and who in pursuit of this bold policy sought the support of the papacy. The Ghibellines, on the other hand, leaned toward the
empire in the hope of being rewarded for their fidelity with the rule of the
city. We have seen that the two distinct trends went back at least to the latter
half of the consular era, and that since the Buondelmonte murder of 1216 the
animosities that gave them birth had steadily increased. Notwithstanding, up
to the appearance in Florence of Frederick of Antioch in 1246, the Guelph-
Ghibelline quarrel had not yet been carried to a final and irrevocable schism.
That schism was now to take place; and at the same time the common people,
long disaffected toward the lawless and high-handed nobles in their midst,
were to be prompted to rise in an attempt of their own to free the city from
foreign control and by that act to secure its government for themselves. As
to the common people or *popolani,* they were not, at least not yet at this time,
either Guelph or Ghibelline. This distinction had arisen in the upper order
and long remained peculiar to it. However, as the Florentine commoners also
favored the liberation of their city from the imperial yoke, they clearly nursed
sentiments of a general Guelph nature. Consequently, in the struggle between
the two groups of nobles for control they leaned, though somewhat hesitantly
at first, toward the Guelph side. In the course of time and in measure as the
Ghibellines more and more flagrantly offended the burgher passion for independence, the merchants and craftsmen turned their backs on them, until the
hour came when *guelfismo,* that is, a settled Guelph disposition of mind,
became characteristic of the whole population. Therefore in the days ahead,
when Florence, having disfranchised the nobles, became a democratically
oriented society, it consistently comported itself as a Guelph commonwealth.
But this historical Guelphism must not be thought of as going back to the

first half of the thirteenth century nor should it be regarded as a blind submission to the papacy. Essentially it was a passionate patriotism expressing itself in frenzied hatred of every individual or party threatening the city's independence.

On the emperor's young son taking over the reins in Florence, he found himself enthusiastically but interestedly supported by the Ghibelline faction headed by the great family of the Uberti. To put their services in the best light they lost no opportunity to denounce their Guelph enemies as secretly nursing treasonable projects. And while these Guelphs may have been quiet for the moment, it was certain, even though the charge might not be possible to prove, that they were in touch with the papal court and its army of belligerent friars spread over Italy and sleeplessly busy at stirring up the excitable masses against the excommunicated emperor. In so nervous an atmosphere clashes between the two magnate groups within the city walls were inevitable. Whenever they occurred, young Frederick regularly sided with the Ghibellines. After a particularly severe brawl at the beginning of 1248 the Guelphs, in a state of panic, on Candlemas Day (February 2), abandoned the city. They retired to the hills, where they had castles and retainers, and where they were better prepared to offer resistance than in their crowded city quarters. Whenever the Ghibellines organized an expedition to pursue their foes to one or another of their many retreats, a combat flared up which threw the whole countryside into confusion. In connection with these violent new disorders we have mention for the first time of *capitani dei Guelfi*. The title admits of no other interpretation than that the exiles had given themselves a party organization under elected officials. And if the Guelphs now went this length, the Ghibellines must be supposed to have done the same. The division in the magnate group, which had repeatedly threatened during recent decades but which had always been patched up again, thus became final, and the old *societas militum*, sign and guaranty of magnate solidarity, came to an end. When we reflect that the nobles had been able to exercise their political preponderance in the past through this class organization, we realize what a fatal blow they struck their own ascendancy by their incurable partisan hatred. And since it is pertinent to our understanding of the situation, let us not fail to note that even though the *societas militum* now vanished from the scene, the obligation of the individual *miles* to serve in the citizen army remained unimpaired. Henceforth the nobles still rode to war, the Guelphs under Guelph captains, the Ghibellines under Ghibelline captains, but, thus divided, they weighed considerably less both in war and in politics.

In connection with the Candlemas Day exodus of their enemies, the Ghibellines were guilty of an act of vengeance which constituted an innovation in the practices of local warfare, and which was destined in the end to be visited on their own heads with compound interest. Unable to lay their hands on the persons of the Guelphs, the victors vented their spite on their foes' inanimate possessions. Some thirty-six structures, most of them towers, belonging to the exiles were in blind fury leveled with the ground. Among them was a tower of the Adimari over two hundred feet high. As it stood near the graveyard adjoining the baptistry of St. John, it was called *Il Guardamorto* (Guardian of the Dead); and when it was brought down without damage to the town's most beloved ecclesiastical monument, excited citizens with Guelph sympathies who witnessed the destruction declared that they saw the falling tower deflected in mid-course by the miraculous intervention of the Baptist himself.[3]

Owing to the manifest decline of the emperor's fortunes in the late forties, spasmodic revolts multiplied all over Tuscany and obliged the vicar-general, Frederick of Antioch, to spend much of his time in the field away from Florence. One of these absences in the autumn of 1250 led to momentous consequences. By suddenly attacking the Ghibelline host encamped at Figline above Florence, the exiled Guelphs won a notable victory. No sooner had the news of this rout reached the city than it encouraged the people to attempt to regain their freedom. In the course of the last decade not only had they been saddled with every form of vexatious taxation, but they had also been obliged to surrender their hard-won independence and humbly bend their necks under an imperial governor. To the cry *Viva il Popolo* they gathered in the streets and churches, resolved to recover their liberty. Before the absent vicar-general could assemble the necessary forces to crush the revolt he was reached by information which struck the sword from his hand. On December 3, 1250, the Emperor Frederick had died in southern Italy. Like the rest of the world, the son saw at once that with the death of his father the whole artificial Frederician system was doomed and, bowing to the will of the gods, he put the spurs to his horse and rode away. Florence was therefore left in the hands of its rebellious inhabitants, and without risk of interference from on high they set about giving themselves the kind of government they desired. As the revolution was the work exclusively of the people, and as neither the Guelph nor the Ghibelline faction of the nobles had had a hand in it, the triumphant commoners provided themselves with a constitution in which for the first time since the rise of the commune the decisive influence was attributed to themselves. The period thus inaugurated goes by the name of the First Democracy (*Il Primo Popolo*).

The new government was characterized by two outstanding features. Since the people had made the revolution, and since they were aware that they could not retain their power except by military means, they formed themselves into twenty companies under a single leader. This was the *capitano del popolo,* who could mobilize his companies instantly at the ringing of a bell. The capitano was by no means to replace the traditional ruler, the podestà, but was to function at his side as the special protector of the people. Indeed the traditional government of the podestà was left substantially intact on the understanding that it should henceforth be more responsive to the people, who, organized into a military society under an elected head, had risen to a novel position of authority. It was wholly in the spirit of this experimental age not to evolve an entirely new government from preliminary theoretical considerations, but, taking over the old core, to add to it the features expressive of the newest energies of the commonwealth. This viewpoint accounts for the second important element of the new constitution. Since the civil powers inherent in the office of the podestà were hardly, if at all, diminished by the rise of a popu-

[3] Villani, VI, 33.

lar official like the capitano, the sponsors of the revolution, convinced that they needed an office capable of acting as a check on the podestà, created the *anziani* (ancients). This was a body of twelve good and true men of the people, two for each of the *sesti* (sixths) into which the city was divided. They were charged with the general supervision of the state and its finances. Above all, they were expected to breathe a vivifying democratic spirit into the revolutionary system. And that they actually did so is proved by the fact that ever afterward the twelve anziani signified to the Florentines the very substance of their first democratic venture.[4]

Before taking up the exciting and colorful career of the new government we may pause to consider the death of the sovereign, on whom rumor fed so busily in his day that he threatened to become a legend while still in the flesh. Extraordinary and amazing rather than great, Frederick puzzled his contemporaries with his many unresolved contradictions, as he has continued to puzzle all the later generations. Even with his death he added to the mixture of terror, awe, and bewilderment with which he was generally regarded. He died at Fiorentino in Apulia; and fifty years later, when Villani wrote his chronicle, there still circulated a tale regarding his demise which is so revealing in respect both to Frederick's unfathomed character and to the murky atmosphere of an age whose religion was shot through with the weirdest superstitions that we must imperatively give it our attention. In spite of Frederick's rationalism, which liberated him from many of the prejudices of his time, he continued to hold firmly that the stars controlled the lives of men and, consequently, he governed himself as far as possible in accordance with the prognostications of his court astrologers. Now these magi of his had frequently warned him against Florence (Fiorenza), because in Florence he would meet his death. He scrupulously obeyed the admonition; and although he moved tirelessly up and down Italy throughout his life and was repeatedly in Tuscany, it is an established fact that he never set foot within the Arno town. But no one can escape his destiny. Consequently when the emperor died, it was indeed not in the Tuscan commune but in a small Apulian town with an all but identical name (Fiorentino). Good old Guelph Villani fully believed the current tale, especially as he too had complete faith in the astrological mysteries. He took exception, however, to one point. Instead of the emperor's receiving the warning from honorable astrologers, he had received it from one of the demons with whom he, as an indubitable son of Satan, habitually consorted. And the chronicler closes his account with this gloating comment: "Ill did he understand the lying word of the demon, which bade him beware of dying in Fiorenza but not of dying in Fiorentino."[5]

---

[4] The constitution of 1250 has not survived. It has been carefully reconstructed from other documents by Davidsohn, Vol. II¹, pp. 367-73.

[5] Villani, VI, 41.

IX. Il Primo Popolo or The First Democracy (1250–60)

EMPEROR FREDERICK II had filled so large a place during his life that his death created an immense vacuum. It was as if he had taken the empire with him into his tomb; and although he was survived by one legitimate and several illegitimate sons, so complete was the collapse of his power that few contemporaries believed it could ever, even in part, be revived. His legitimate son and acknowledged heir was a young man, who, having been crowned king of Germany in Frederick's lifetime, was known as Conrad IV. During his father's last phase he had represented the emperor in the northern kingdom. But the excommunication and deposition of Frederick decreed by the council of Lyons had broken Germany into factions and rocked it to its foundations. Conrad might conceivably have triumphed over his many difficulties, had he not preferred to rush to Italy on his father's death in order to assume the Sicilian inheritance. Sicily, too, was in turmoil, owing to a baronial uprising provoked by the pope. Conrad had a difficult fight on his hands; and hardly had he mastered the situation when he died (May 21, 1254), a victim, like his grandfather, the mighty Henry VI, of the fever which has frequently been the best ally of this southern people against an intruder from the north. While Conrad's son and heir, Conradin, a mere babe in arms, was growing up in Germany, the maintenance of the Hohenstaufen cause in Sicily devolved on Manfred, the emperor's illegitimate son and uncle of the distant Conradin. Manfred's position, however, was highly precarious, for, more firmly than ever, the pope was resolved to transfer the crown of Sicily to some other house than that of Suabia. Therefore, under the most favorable circumstances, a struggle awaited the Hohenstaufen champion which would engage his attention for years to come. The bare facts here recited should make it clear that for some years following the demise of Frederick II the imperial cause was prostrate throughout Italy, and that Florence, the great rebel community of mid-Italy, was free to realize its ambitions without interference from above.

Although the new Florentine government was a democratic innovation and represented a revolt against the traditional ascendancy of the nobles, it took over the foreign policy of its predecessor without changing it by a hair's breadth. That policy went back in a straight line to the earliest days of the commune. In the initial stage its aim had been the mastery of the Florentine county by clearing it of the oppressive feudal lords. But no sooner had this purpose been achieved than, the appetite growing with what it fed on, the neighboring counties began to look desirable; and by the time the podestà replaced the consuls Florentine ambition ventured to lift its eyes to Tuscany itself as the goal of its endeavor. Toward the middle of Frederick II's reign and just before that emperor, following the battle of Cortenuova, turned his attention to the control of Tuscany, Florence had already won a dominant position in the Arno Valley. When this not only had to be given up but was replaced by an abject subservience to the emperor's agents, a despair settled on the city which at last found vent in the explosion of 1250. Taking over at once and without opposition the rule of its county, the new government, which from the first day exhibited an amazing daring and vitality, returned to the program of the pre-Frederician period and resumed the struggle, to which Frederick had put a stop and which aimed to bring all Tuscany under Florentine control.

In our own time we call such a policy imperialism and recognize that it is primarily prompted by the energy of an expanding commercial community. It is therefore highly probable that what we may call the Florentine imperialism of this and the subsequent centuries was a response primarily to the demands of an enterprising merchant class. However, as the imperialist trend goes back to the consular age, although in those early days it was but a feeble plant, we are driven to the conclusion that, in spite of the prevalence of nobiliary names at the head of the government, the great merchants were already at that time the hidden directive force of the state. When after the revolution of 1250 the victorious democracy without delay struck out on the same path, we must again conclude that, the new popular apparatus notwithstanding, it was still the bankers and foreign traders who imposed their policy on the government. If this is true, the continuity of Florentine foreign policy, just noted, loses its quality of mystery. Regardless of the forms successively assumed by the government, the merchants would seem to have been and, as we shall have occasion to see hereafter, would seem to have remained, the controlling factor. In the case of the Primo Popolo, with which we are dealing in this chapter, the artisans and shopkeepers undoubtedly shared in the government and thereby gave it a popular character; but there was nothing in the system to keep the great bankers and merchants from exercising hidden, essential control and, in the sacred name of home and country, persuading the whole citizen body to make the merchant policy its own.

By its very first act in the foreign field the new government committed itself to a policy of bold aggression. It persuaded a count of the great Aldobrandesca family, which held a position in the Sienese region analogous to that of the Guidi clan around Florence, to lease the port of Talamone to the Arno city. True, Talamone was a miserable little village with a silted harbor which has defied the many efforts made in the course of the ages to render it practicable; but its obstinate resistance to improvement had not yet been established, when in the spring of 1251 a sudden diplomatic stroke established Florence on the coast of the Maremma. While the action was particularly resented by Siena, which on geographic grounds regarded the Maremma coast as lying within its sphere of influence, it also alarmed Pisa with the prospect of the creation of a rival port to its immediate south. The prompt result was a defensive league of the two towns, to which Pistoia, perpetually threatened by nearby Florence, joined itself as a third member. Inasmuch as these three towns had usually in the past sided with the empire, theirs was naturally a Ghibelline league, to which Florence, the confirmed enemy of the empire, opposed just as naturally the Guelph league of itself and Lucca. Since Ligurian Genoa was always ready to unite in any action aimed at its maritime rival, Pisa, no difficulty was encountered in adding Genoa to the Guelph combination. Tuscany, thus divided, was threatened with a struggle which would not leave the remotest village undisturbed.

The war broke out at once and lasted for four years. Its most outstanding feature was the unbounded energy displayed by democratic Florence. Although neither Lucca nor Genoa withheld their aid, Florence engaged in the conflict with such sustained fervor that the victories won over each of the Ghibelline foes in turn or over all of them in combination were primarily the work of the Arno city. From the start it aimed its attack at the weakest link in the Ghibelline chain, at Pistoia. Blockading the town and cruelly harrying the countryside, the Florentines usually waited till the Sienese and Pisans brought up a relieving army, when they would throw themselves on the advancing forces with ferocious impetuosity. It was the tactics of an unwavering offensive admirably expressive of the indomitable mood of the people. Under these circumstances little Pistoia was after a few campaigns reduced to the last extremity and obliged to sue for peace. Signed on February 1, 1254, the treaty spelled, in substance, submission to Florentine control.

It was now Siena's turn. The Florentines invaded the Sienese contado and systematically laid waste its fields and olive orchards. After appealing in vain to Pisa which, caught in a vise between Lucca and Genoa, was unable to render help, the exhausted Sienese offered to come to terms some five months after the surrender of Pistoia. The main demand of the Florentines was that the small hill towns of Montalcino and Montepulciano, lying in the southern part of Siena's county, should be given their independence. The stipulation admits of no other interpretation than that the victors planned to use the two liberated communities as points of support for their own ultimate expansion into southern Tuscany. Thus only Pisa remained to be dealt with. Cruelly pressed by her three enemies without and paralyzed by an outbreak of factions within, Pisa broke down in its turn, hardly more than a month after Siena had yielded to Florentine might. The leading article of the treaty signed with Pisa was a plain indication that Florence had already convinced itself of the vanity of its Talamone plans; for, by this article Florence fastened on Pisa as its best possible outlet to the Mediterranean markets by acquiring the privilege of importing and exporting its goods *via* Pisa free from all customs dues. For the elated Florentines the year 1254 became and remained ever afterward "the year of victory." It did not detract from the glory won in that *annus mirabilis* that the Pisans, consumed by chagrin, delayed the execution of the peace for a number of years. In the end they had to swallow their pride and acknowledge that the hegemony in Tuscany, so long enjoyed by them, had passed to the upstart inland rival.

On the inauguration of the war in 1251 Florence had attempted to win the support of the common people throughout the Tuscan world by proclaiming that she was fighting the battle of democracy. By coming to the aid of Montalcino and Montepulciano in their struggle against Siena she could with a certain plausibility establish the added claim that she was the champion of the small Tuscan towns against the greed of their larger neighbors. In a struggle for power an alert and unscrupulous opponent will not neglect to avail himself of the imponderable moral values. When, however, with the victory won, Florence surveyed a submissive Tuscany, she cast the mask aside and frankly revealed her plan of complete Tuscan control. With the large towns prostrate, the small towns, at least all those within convenient reach, were absolutely at her mercy. At a nod from the imperious democracy they came to terms; and when a nod did not suffice, they yielded precipitately before the threat of military action. The most important single area of small towns was the hill region of the Elsa Valley, where the spheres of influence of Pisa, Florence, and Siena met and overlapped. Here three towns, Poggibonsi, San Gimignano, and Volterra had taken advantage of the balance hitherto maintained among their three large neighbors to set up independent governments, behind which they put all the unreasoning fervor characteristic of the communal age. In the eyes of their citizens life without independence or, as they preferred to call it, liberty, lost half its value. However, when victorious Florence had become queen of Tuscany, the independence could not be sustained, and the three towns were obliged, with what deep heart-burnings the future would reveal again and again, to accept their fate.

For the Arno city, still young in conquest, it now became imperative to work out a method of control for its dependencies. It is interesting to observe how the early measures dealing with this problem had a purely empirical character and differed considerably in detail. A usual requirement was that the subject town should accommodate itself to the Florentine political system, preferably by taking over bodily the constitution of 1250. It was an ingenious procedure calculated to make Tuscany, along with Florence, safe for democracy. Another demand commonly imposed was that the chief local official, the podestà, should be selected from among the citizens of Florence. Finally, as a safeguard against rebellion, which had always to be reckoned with, the dependent community was required either to demolish its walls or to suffer a fortress, a so-called cassero, to be built at a strategic point within the walls and to be garrisoned by Florentine troops. The latter measure was imposed on Volterra, the former on Poggibonsi and San Gimignano.[1] One procedure was probably as successful as the other so long as the hegemony of Florence remained unchallenged; but let her rule appear to be shaken and straightway hope would visit the unreconciled spirits of her subjects and move them, regardless of the risk they ran, to attempt to strike off their chains.

The triumphs of 1254 were still on every tongue when Florence supplemented the peace treaty with Siena by a treaty of alliance (1255). By its terms the City of the Virgin, as the Sienese delighted to call their town, accepted

[1] Davidsohn, *Forschungen*, Vol. IV, p. 115. "Die erste Unterwerfung von Pistoia, Poggibonsi, Volterra und San Gimignano (1253-57)."

left: SANTA MARIA NOVELLA, LOOKING TOWARD THE HIGH ALTAR (ALINARI). *right:* THE CATHEDRAL OF SANTA MARIA DEL FIORE, LOOKING TOWARD THE HIGH ALTAR (ALINARI).

left: SANTA CROCE, LOOKING FROM THE HIGH ALTAR (ALINARI). *right:* THE PALAZZO VECCHIO, FORMERLY THE PALACE OF THE PRIORS (ALINARI).

left: THE CAMPANILE OF GIOTTO. *upper right:* THE LOGGIA DEI LANZI, FORMERLY THE LOGGIA DEI SIGNORI. *center:* OR SAN MICHELE. *lower right:* OR SAN MICHELE. INTERIOR, SHOWING THE TABERNACLE BY ORCAGNA (ALINARI PHOTOGRAPHS).

every detail of the Tuscan reorganization which Florence had recently effected. Furthermore, the two towns agreed to come to each other's help in time of war and in time of peace to live on such good terms that neither would receive the political exiles (*fuorusciti*) of the other. In short, the upland town bound itself to undertake nothing calculated to disturb the achieved ascendancy of its lowland rival. Immense must have been the prestige of the City of the Baptist and great the terror that went before its name for Siena ever to have been induced to sign a paper testifying to the abdication of its ancient claims to political equality.

To its achievements in politics and war the Florentine democracy added in this triumphant period a no less notable body of achievements in the broad civil field. Our concern being with the total cultural activity of Florence, they may by no means be overlooked. Up to this point the emergence of the political sovereign unit has chiefly engaged our attention. With the advent of the democratic regime, however, a change may be noted, and so many evidences of an uncommon mental and spiritual vigor began to accumulate that we must needs take account of them, partly for their own sake and, even more, as an earnest of the far greater developments to follow. Agreeing that they are of varying importance, we shall set them down in the haphazard way in which they thrust themselves into the situation.

One of the first acts of the proud and self-conscious democracy was to give to Florence the famous coat-of-arms which is its emblem to this day: the red lily on a white field. The adoption was occasioned by an incident which carries to a striking degree the peculiar flavor of the age. We have heard that when the caroccio was decked out for war, it bore suspended from a tall mast two long, narrow stripes of silk, one red, the other white. This simple device was the earliest banner of the young commonwealth and remained in use as long as the caroccio itself was mobilized for war. But in an age given to colorful self-expression in heraldic language, this single banner was not enough, and the rising commune had adopted, as a second emblem, a white lily on a red field. This, as abundantly picturesque, had swiftly gained the general favor. Now in the year 1251, when the war for the control of Tuscany began, the Florentine Ghibellines committed an open act of treason by joining the enemies of their native city. The motive for their act was not Ghibelline in the generally accepted sense of the word, for the empire had vanished from the scene at the death of Frederick. What irked these noble gentlemen was the triumph of democracy in their home town; and they calculated that if Florence were defeated in the field, they might come back into power on the wave of an emotional reaction. Accordingly, they rode forth from the city, and on the arrogant assumption that they were the legitimate commune, they took along with them the municipal banner, displaying it vaingloriously at the head of their cavalcade. The undismayed democracy met the challenge with inventive promptness. Abandoning the white lily on a red field to the noble traitors, it reversed the color scheme and declared that henceforth the red lily on a white field should be the emblem of the commune. At the same time the common people, who, as we are aware, had organized themselves as a militia under the capitano del popolo, adopted the lion (*marzocco*) as their particular group device; and lion and red lily from this time on served as the beloved symbols by which the Florentine commoners demonstrated to themselves and to the world their devotion to their city.

To complete the tale of the Ghibelline exodus with its attendant theft of the town banner we must not omit to note the complete failure of the action. Unable to stay the Florentine tide of victory, which set in with the very first year of the war, the Ghibellines, prompted by discretion, offered to come to terms, and a year after their treason to their home town committed a second treason by deserting the Pistoia-Siena-Pisa alliance, to which they were under solemn engagement. It obliges us to hold the shrewdness of the commoners in high regard that they were willing to let by-gones be by-gones in the hope— vain as it turned out to be—of welding the citizen body into a solid unit. Re-admitted to favor (1252), the Ghibellines returned to Florence, although it was perfectly clear that, unless they should cease thinking of themselves as a caste born to rule, they would repeat their felony at the earliest opportunity.

One of the signs in every river town of a growing animation is the multipli-cation of bridges. The oldest bridge across the Arno, the famous Ponte Vecchio, went back to Roman times. On its solid Roman foundations it rested immut-able till 1178; at least there is no record of a collapse until that year when, as an annalist informs us, it was washed away in a frightful inundation. On being rebuilt it lasted for one hundred and fifty years, when it again col-lapsed (1333), owing to torrential rains, which almost drowned the whole population and of which we shall hear later on. Not till the first half of the thirteenth century did the need of crossings over the Arno supplementary to the Ponte Vecchio make itself felt. In 1218 a second bridge, afterward known as Ponte alla Carraia, was undertaken; it was followed in 1237 by a third bridge, originally called Rubaconte, in honor of the podestà under whose rule it was begun, but familiar to later generations as Ponte alle Grazie. To these three bridges, already in existence at the time of the revolution, the new democratic government added, in 1252, a fourth bridge, which from its vicinity to the church of that name was called Ponte Santa Trinità. It gives a measure of the rapid advance made by Florence in the first half of the thirteenth century to be reminded that by 1252 the City, once of the White, but now of the Red, Lily, was already provided with all the bridges it ever boasted during the period of its greatness. Of the four the Ponte Vecchio still is nearest the heart of the Florentines because, as the oldest bridge, it is en-veloped with a particularly luminous mist of memories. Strangers, too, are greatly drawn to it, more especially by reason of the quaint shops with which it is lined. In medieval times this was not the unusual feature it has become in our day, since shops were often installed on Italian bridges and, for that matter, on bridges throughout Europe. The Florentine commune, eager for revenue, did not feel it could forgo the rentals accruing to it from the wooden *botteghe* which, if picturesque, were far from safe and not infrequently were swept by a devastating fire.

Of all the domestic measures of the Primo Popolo none added so much to the reputation of the city as the issuance of a new and famous coin, the gold florin. The history of Tuscan money is a story which this is not the place to unfold in detail.[2] Suffice it for the present to relate that the current coin of medieval Tuscany was the silver penny (*denarius*). It was minted first at Lucca, the margravial capital, and later at Pisa and other places on the strength of an imperial privilege. In view of the fact that coinage was a prerogative of the crown, a town could not issue its own money without a document affirming the consent of the sovereign. Although Florence, so generally in opposition to the emperor, never gained the concession, nonetheless a little before or after 1235, having for the time being nothing to fear from Frederick II, it boldly usurped this right and issued as its first coin not a silver penny but a silver florin. This, let it be observed, was an innovation, for the silver florin was worth twelve silver pennies. Commerce which had by this time far outstripped the penny stage, so heartily welcomed the newer and more convenient unit that the silver pennies of Lucca, Pisa, and Siena, hitherto dominating the Tuscan markets, lost much of their prestige. Not only did the minting of the new coin, in view of its illegality, reveal the daring of the Florentines, but it also disclosed the commercial sagacity of a people who, when the traditional monetary unit proved inadequate in the face of the increasing magnitude of commercial transactions, invented a more suitable coin twelve times the value of its Tuscan predecessors.

Continuing on the bold path blazed by the government of the podestà, the new democratic government resolved to carry Florentine initiative to a still higher level and in 1252 began the issue of the gold florin. It bore the image of the lily on one side and, on the other, that of John the Baptist, patron saint of the city. Before this time only the Emperor Frederick II among occidental sovereigns had issued a gold coin, and with his death his mint had completely shut down. With merchants confronted with the difficulties caused by innumerable pennies of varying silver content, we need not wonder that the appearance of the gold florin, a beautiful shapely coin, studiously kept by an enlightened government at its full value, was hailed as a light shining in darkness. Here was the stable standard which commerce imperatively required for the handling of the steadily increasing volume of international trade. The new gold florin was worth twenty silver florins, and since a silver florin (or *solidus*) was the equivalent of twelve silver pennies, the gold florin had a value of two hundred and forty pennies. In a surprisingly short span of time the gold florin was adopted as the coin in which prices were quoted and transactions consummated throughout the western world. For several centuries its authority was much like that of the English pound in the period before the World War. As indicative of how fame in a world dedicated to and living by trade grows out of economic prestige, we note, not without a measure of dismay, that neither Dante nor Giotto nor the whole succession of quattrocento painters did so much to carry the name of the City of the Red Lily to the ends of the earth as the little, convenient invention, the *fiorino d'oro,* which commerce hailed as a compass incomparably useful in helping it to steer its difficult, international course.[3]

[2] For a fuller account see chap. XVII.
[3] Davidsohn, Vol. II[1], p. 411.

As our last evidence of the vitality of this government we point to the new official home it erected for itself and which, begun in 1255, was brought to completion in the course of the next few years. Up to this time the podestà had been quartered in a private dwelling rented for the purpose, while the councils had utilized the various churches as their meeting-places. The proud democracy in control of the town felt that this haphazard method of housing its representatives no longer satisfied the dignity of the commonwealth and erected the impressive Palazzo del Popolo which still stands. For Florentines of a later period it became the Bargello; and Bargello it is still called in spite of its conversion, in the second half of the nineteenth century, into a National Museum of Sculpture. Ecclesiastical construction had begun long before in Florence, as such buildings already in existence as San Giovanni and San Miniato al Monte sufficiently disclose. Private building was as yet represented by nothing better than the rude palaces and soaring towers of the military families. With the new communal residence, the Palazzo del Popolo, civic architecture came to life, producing as its first handiwork an impressive, fortress-like structure crowned with battlements and tower. The Italian towns had arisen as a protest against the feudal system, but in Florence as everywhere else, the earliest expression of their spirit in stone and mortar took rather incongruously the form of a feudal castle.

Florence had for some years ruled a largely dependent Tuscany, when what had been long a faint vapor to the south began to darken and fill the sky with warnings of a storm. We left Manfred, Frederick's illegitimate son, charged with defending the claims of the Suabian house to the kingdom of Sicily. Difficult as his situation was in the face of the always recalcitrant barons, it was rendered almost untenable by the resolution of the papacy at all costs to dispossess the family from which it had suffered so many indignities. In pursuit of this aim, in the year 1255, the pope offered the Sicilian crown to the king of England. This was Henry III, who not only promptly accepted it for his second son, Prince Edmund, but agreed besides to aid the pope in squeezing vast sums out of the English church with which to fit out a papal army of conquest. Manfred had a hard stand, but was so consistently successful against the invaders that by the summer of the year 1258 he felt strong enough to crown himself king at Palermo. In doing so, he ignored the rights of his nephew, the boy Conradin, possibly, as his enemies declared, owing to his vaulting ambition, but possibly too because he believed he had won the realm for himself by force of arms. In any case it was far more likely that the barons would be faithful to him than to a distant boy relative, whose German bringing-up made him a complete stranger to the south.

The effect on Tuscany of Manfred's coronation was electric. The animosities secretly nursed against the hegemony won by the Florentine democracy ventured into the open and one of the earliest evidences of the hopes awakened by the *biondo e bello* son of the unforgotten Frederick was furnished by the ever-restive Ghibellines of Florence. Although they had been forgiven their treason of 1251, they had not renounced any of their aristocratic pretensions. They were Ghibellines, not, or at least not primarily, because they were attached to the empire but because they regarded the empire as the most likely means to

win back their privileged position in their native town. We shall see later on
that the Florentine Guelphs dwelt on no higher moral plane, since they were
Guelphs mainly by reason of their expectation of realizing their dream of
Florentine ascendancy through the backing of the pope. In the summer of 1258
the Florentine Ghibellines, wildly elated by the rise of Manfred, made an attempt to overthrow the hated democratic government and, on failing to realize
their aim, promptly withdrew from the town. This time the aroused citizens,
egged on by the Guelph faction, knew no mercy. Throwing moderation to
the winds, they decreed the destruction of the houses and towers of the Uberti,
Lamberti, and the other fuorusciti, thereby dotting the town with unsightly
rubbish heaps that long remained untouched in order to serve as a warning to
traitors. For the Guelph nobles it was the revenge long overdue for the destruction wrought on their houses by the Ghibellines some ten years before. The
largest single area of destruction was the site once covered by the houses of the
proudest of the magnate families, the Uberti. When after more than a generation it was at length cleared of its ruins, it was converted into a magnificent
central square, the present Piazza della Signoria.

Exiled a second time the Florentine fuorusciti withdrew as before to Siena;
and, in spite of the fact that since 1255 Siena and Florence had been allies and
that one article of the treaty expressly forbade either town to give shelter to the
rebels of the other, when the fugitives, headed by the bold Farinata degli
Uberti, knocked at the Sienese gate, they were promptly admitted. Here was
a most acceptable *casus belli,* in case the Florentines were looking for one. On
second thoughts they preferred to ignore the incident, possibly on the calculation that Manfred's swollen power would collapse as rapidly as it had gathered.
The Sienese, on the other hand, reckoned with the opposite probability and
looked upon the Sicilian sovereign's south Italian dominance as the certain
herald of an early Tuscan intervention. More hotly than ever they avowed their
Ghibellinism for the reason, the sole reason, that the representative of the Hohenstaufen cause was the only means at hand for overthrowing the hated
primacy of Florence. It is as foolish to predicate of the Sienese a love of the
empire for its own sake as it is absurd to credit the Florentines with a blind
devotion to the church. We are dealing with two young sovereignties, each of
which was supremely concerned with its own selfish ends and each of which
hated the other with elemental fury because it lay across the path of its ambition.

Impatient to inaugurate its war of liberation against Florence, Siena sent an
embassy to Manfred's court which engaged to swear fealty to him in return
for the promise of military aid. Manfred accepted the offer and in May, 1259,
dispatched a first small troop of horsemen, Germans and South Italians, to
Siena as an earnest of his good will. When these were followed in December
by an impressive force of German mercenaries under Manfred's relative, Count
Giordano, the cup of the Sienese overflowed and they gave the stalwart band
a delirious welcome. Giordano displayed a patent from his master naming
him vicar-general of all Tuscany. With Siena as his rallying-point he was empowered to assemble the scattered supporters of the empire throughout the
province in the hope of putting an end to Florentine control.

Even now, when it was plain that war was no longer avoidable, the Florentines, instead of striking at once, displayed an unusual hesitation. They permitted the Sienese, aided by Giordano's cavalry, to assume the offensive by attacking the small towns and castles in their neighborhood devoted to the Florentine interest. Several of these, including the important Grosseto in the Maremma littoral, had fallen before the Florentine host, in April, 1260, was at last mobilized to check the Sienese action. At that moment the main body of the auxiliaries under Count Giordano, supported by a section of the Sienese militia, was laying siege to the strong fortress of Montemassi, not far to the north of vanquished Grosseto. Entering the Elsa Valley, the Florentines pushed on as if bent on the relief of the beleaguered Montemassi. Suddenly they swerved from their track and struck straight at Siena in the hope of taking the city by surprise. On May 17 they made their appearance on the heights to the west of the town; but when on the next day they pushed forward against the Porta Camollia, they were thrown into great confusion and all but routed through a sudden furious sortie conducted by a small band of German troopers who had been left behind to guard the town when Count Giordano departed on the Montemassi expedition. The failure of their ruse discouraged the Florentine leaders, and in an access of caution they led the army home. It had been a typical democratic campaign in that, begun with enthusiasm, its energy rapidly evaporated on meeting with unexpected difficulties. No matter how loudly the good burghers crowed victory on their return to their wives and children, the spring offensive had been an expensive failure.

The first effect of the Florentine retreat was that the defenders of Montemassi surrendered. This gave Siena unchallenged control of the Maremma. Her next step was to bear down on the small towns of Montalcino and Montepulciano, particularly hateful because, although lying in the Sienese contado, they were always treacherously leagued with Florence. In July Montepulciano yielded, making the best terms it could; but Montalcino, sending up sharp cries to heaven and to Florence for aid, stubbornly continued to resist the Sienese assault. In order to provision the beleaguered town and balk the Sienese of their prey the Florentines during the summer prepared a new campaign, and toward the end of August started from their city. No pains were spared to provide the most elaborate equipment with which a Florentine army had ever yet set forth. The details are preserved for us in the famous official record, the *Libro di Montaperti*.[4] Its abundant documents afford a degree of illumination touching the art of war as practiced by communal Florence which leaves little to be desired. The whole male population between the ages of fifteen and seventy, with the exception of the sick, the disabled, and certain exempt groups required for necessary work at home, was liable to service in the field; and on a typically hot, late summer day the burgher host, fully mobilized, marched out of the southern gate. At places appointed beforehand the Florentine forces were swelled by the contingents of the allied and subjected towns, Lucca, Pistoia, Prato, Arezzo, Volterra, San Miniato, and San Gimignano. We get a vivid impression of the authority enjoyed by Florence when we hear that

[4] *Il Libro di Montaperti*. Per cura di Cesare Paoli. *Documenti di Storia Italiana,* Vol. IX.

Bologna and Orvieto, lying well beyond the confines of Tuscany, were prompt, at the bidding of the Red Lily, to come to her assistance and make a stipulated contribution to her masterful host. An army of probably seventy thousand fighting men moved on Siena, without comparison the largest force medieval Tuscany had yet seen in action. Indeed this army *was* Tuscany, which under the guidance of its foremost town marched forth resolved to coerce its one erring member into joining the provincial fold. For, excepting the eight hundred horsemen under Count Giordano, the handful of Florentine Ghibellines under Farinata degli Uberti, and the contingents of a few small dependent neighbors, Siena stood absolutely alone. Even Pisa, as consistently Ghibelline as Siena and ever ready in the past to side with the City of the Virgin, on this occasion either refused or was unable to render aid.

On the closest possible calculation the Sienese must have been outnumbered some two or three to one. Owing probably to this circumstance the Florentines considered that they ran no risk of being attacked if they passed under the very nose of Siena on their way to Montalcino. For the reprovisioning of that hill town and for the support of the great army on its march the fighting forces were attended by an immense train of twenty thousand pack animals. With all this unexampled magnificence—the numerous allied contingents under their waving banners, the rich equipment of arquebuses and other war machines, the countless beasts of burden laden with supplies—the Florentines hoped to overwhelm the imagination of the Sienese when they mounted their walls and other vantage points to watch the enemy file by. Some of the more sanguine leaders of the Arno town seem even to have entertained the delusion that their discouraged antagonists would in the face of all this *pompa e grandigia* surrender without more ado. May the purpose of the march past Siena have been what it will, on the afternoon of September 3, 1260, the allied Tuscan army pitched camp among the bare, chalk hills of the Arbia Valley, only a few miles distant from the eastern gate of Siena. It was a dangerously exposed position, only slightly improved by the seizure and occupation of Montaperti, the only fortified castle of the immediate neighborhood. As the sun went down the Florentines could see the towers of lofty Siena silhouetted like serried spears against the sky and its formidable, rose-tinted walls of brick rising and dipping with the undulations of the ground.

If anything was needed to convert the normal courage of the Sienese into frenzy, it was this mocking bravado. In the dusk they marched forth from their city to camp in the fields, and when the next day's sun arose, the clear, hot sun of Saturday, September 4, they streamed in a solid mass of cavalry and infantry across the Arbia, shallow with the summer's drouth, and rushed with maddened shouts upon the enemy. Of what followed the Sienese and Florentine chroniclers have left us widely different accounts.[5] Under the delirious excitement of a hand-to-hand combat the fancy of men is wont to blossom so exotically that it is doubtful if the true picture of any battle that was ever fought can be recovered twenty-four hours after it is over. Nor does it much matter except perhaps to men who follow war as a profession. In the case of

[5] For the Sienese version with its inflamed patriotism and manifestly legendary touches see Schevill, *Siena*, pp. 175 ff.

Montaperti an examination will show that, while the Florentine and Sienese versions emphasize each a particular set of determining circumstances, these are not necessarily contradictory. Granted that the victory won was not wholly, as the Sienese asserted, a matter of the impetuous charge by Count Giordano's German horse supported by the crushing momentum of the patriotically inflamed infantry; and granted that the contention of the Florentines that they lost solely through treason in their own ranks is equally one-sided, there is nothing to hinder us from holding that these factors operated together to produce the result. Let us frankly concede the possibility of treason in view of its extraordinary persistence in the political framework of the age; and since we are following the history, not of Siena but of Florence, let us see what the prudent but certainly not unprejudiced Villani has to say of an episode which the Sienese for their part consistently bury under silence.[6]

Before giving in his famous chronicle his version of Montaperti, Villani offers copious details touching the political maneuvers and military ruses during the campaign of 1260 of the Sienese and their Ghibelline guests from Florence. Much of this is doubtless mere gossip; on the other hand, we must never forget that the Florentine exiles were unscrupulous adventurers who plucked at every means calculated to put them back in power and who certainly maintained unbroken secret communications with their partisans at home. In this connection it must further be kept in mind that, while some Ghibellines had deserted Florence, very many more, reluctant to have their property confiscated, remained behind, paying a facile lip service to the triumphant commune. That these secret enemies were prepared to co-operate with the avowed traitors, who had gone to Siena and who under the leadership of Farinata degli Uberti were fighting the battles of the upland city, goes without saying. It is on this indubitable private understanding between the Ghibelline groups outside and inside the Florentine walls that Villani's story of the battle is founded; and if he makes somewhat more of it than it deserves, he is guilty of no worse misdemeanor than an exaggerated patriotism. For, aside from enabling him to pass lightly over the warrior reputation which accrued to the despised Sienese because of their victory, the treason theory held the distinct satisfaction for a man of Villani's colossal bias of proving that it was, after all, his own countrymen who defeated his countrymen and that nobody else could have turned the trick.

After declaring that the Sienese launched their attack unexpectedly and that their sudden appearance spread immediate confusion in the Florentine ranks, Villani continues:

And what caused particular alarm was that the Ghibellines in the Florentine camp, both mounted and on foot, when they saw the enemy approach took to flight, as had been agreed beforehand; and among them were members of the Pressa, Abbati, and other families. Moreover, they did not permit the Florentines and their allies to

---

[6] No one interested in the factual basis of Montaperti can afford to overlook what Davidsohn has assembled in *Forschungen*, Vol. IV, pp. 143-72. It is an amazing piece of scholarly detective work. However, when Davidsohn in his turn undertakes to describe the battle (Vol. II[1], p. 500), we are made aware that a pen strictly governed by a body of imperfect facts will never do justice to the vivacity of life.

form rank and join battle. And just as the squadron of Germans violently struck the troop of Florentine knights, whose banner-bearer was Messer Jacopo del Nacca of the family of the Pazzi and a man of great valor, that vile traitor, Messer Bocca degli Abbati, who rode close to his side, struck the said Jacopo with his sword, cutting off the hand which supported the banner. And immediately Bocca was set on and killed. Seeing the banner on the ground and themselves betrayed at the very moment when they were powerfully assaulted by the Germans, the knights and foot soldiers were in brief order put to rout. But because the horsemen of Florence were the first to learn of the treason, they had only thirty-six casualties distributed between dead and captive. A great butchery ensued, however, of the Florentine infantry as well as of the Lucchese and Orvietans, who had shut themselves up in the castle of Montaperti. And such as were not killed were taken. More than twenty-five hundred remained dead on the field and more than fifteen hundred of the best commoners of Florence, Lucca, and the other allies were led away into captivity.[7]

An apology if you will; certainly not the full story of that famous rout. Yet he would be rash indeed who, in the face of the corroborative touches supplied, not by the emotional chroniclers, but by impeccable contemporary documents, should set down Bocca degli Abbati's treason as a myth.[8] Nor may the evidence of Dante, one of the most candid souls that ever lived, be overlooked. On reaching the lower depths of hell, where men who have been guilty of treason suffer punishment by being imbedded in eternal ice, the poet, accidentally perhaps, but with deep inner satisfaction nonetheless, drove his foot into the traitor's face. Bocca and his misdeed were as real and indubitable to the Florentine wayfarer through the underworld as the beloved San Giovanni in which he had been baptized.

However, to concede Villani a respectful hearing is not to free him from the charge of attempting to belittle the Sienese triumph. His figures of the losses suffered by the Guelphs are preposterously low in view of the circumstance that a Tuscan, not just a Florentine, army of approximately seventy thousand men had been literally pulverized. True, the cavalry suffered comparatively few casualties for, as Villani explains, they spurred their horses from the field at the very beginning of the battle. But the infantry, more particularly the commoners of Lucca and Florence, who bravely stood their ground when the high-born gentlemen ran for their lives, were savagely broken. Instead of the modest losses reported by Villani, we must conclude that close to ten thousand dead covered the field and that no less than twenty thousand captives were jammed into the improvised hell-holes of Siena made to serve as prisons. In this connection authentic documents inform us that the prisoners languished for years in these noisome quarters, unfit habitations for dogs and even swine. Happy they who, overcome by black despair, swooned off into eternal sleep.

When all is said, the battle of Montaperti signified an overthrow which for completeness invites comparison with that of Frederick Barbarossa at Legnano. Whether its consequences would prove as durable was another matter and re-

---

[7] Villani, VI, 79.
[8] Davidsohn, *Forschungen*, Vol. IV, pp. 152-53.

mained for the future to disclose. Certainly for the time being King Manfred's vicar-general in Tuscany, Count Giordano, ruled the land, and with him triumphed Siena and the Ghibellines. Crushed and exhausted Florence did not have the strength to offer the slightest further resistance. Its fugitive Guelph knighthood rode into Florence only to ride out again. Confronted with the bottomless despair of the shattered remnant of the citizens, they saw they could not count on further support. On September 12 the victorious Ghibellines returned to their native city headed by Farinata degli Uberti and followed by Count Giordano with his German mercenaries. Not a protest was voiced when, in the name of King Manfred, they took over the government. The democratic interlude of 1250 had come to an abrupt end. Let us take leave of it with Villani's just and moving words: "And thus was broken and annulled the old democracy (*Il Popolo Vecchio*) of Florence which had won so many victories and boasted such power and grandeur for ten years."

X. The Fall of the Hohenstaufens and the Ghibelline Collapse in Tuscany (1260–70)

WHAT happened at Florence after Montaperti was promptly re-enacted throughout Tuscany: the Guelphs abandoned town after town, leaving the government in the hands of their Ghibelline rivals. Exactly as in the Arno city, the people as distinguished from the magnates belonged as yet neither to the one party nor to the other and could therefore readily enough accommodate themselves to the new situation. Besides, in this instance the success of the Ghibellines signified the end of Florentine control and the resumption of an independence which all alike eagerly craved. So great was the resentment against the former proud mistress now humbled to the dust that the demand even made itself heard in some quarters for her total destruction. At a Ghibelline congress held in the flush of victory at Empoli, Count Giordano, at the urgence of King Manfred himself and with the passionate support, we may be sure, of the Sienese, brought this extreme retributive measure to discussion. Then arose Farinata degli Uberti, who, having just regained his fatherland, was not minded to lose it again at the bidding of its enemies. In his immortal poem Dante has celebrated the deed of the gallant nobleman, who, laying his hand to his sword in that hostile parliament, covered his native city with his body and so saved it from destruction.[1]

As soon as it was decided that Florence should be spared, it became necessary to provide for its government. The simplest course was to ignore the recent democratic episode and to return to the earlier communal constitution. Accordingly, Manfred's vicar-general appointed Count Guido Novello as podestà, and Guido in conducting the affairs of his office consulted with the usual councils of the citizens. This gave the government a certain air of being independent, although it is clear that, with an appointee of Manfred in control, nothing could be undertaken that ran counter to the king's interest.

This Guido Novello belonged to the famous family which had for generations been one of the great landholders of Tuscany. Its fortunes, as we are aware, had begun to decline with the rise of Florence, but it still boasted numerous castles and estates, especially in the Casentino, the hill country of the upper Arno. In the course of time its possessions had become divided among several branches and, no longer held together by a single authoritative

---

[1] *Inferno*, X, 91-3. Dante has just told Farinata why he and his clan are held in such abhorrence at Florence. This draws the proud rejoinder: *ma fui io sol colà* (single-handed I saved her from destruction!).

chief, each branch followed the course best adapted to promote its particular fortunes. Thus there were now Guelph Guidi and Ghibelline Guidi; and these divided relatives had arrived at the inflamed state of mind which prompted them to regard their common blood less as a bond than an added grievance. While the new podestà of Florence, Count Guido Novello, was a passionate Ghibelline, his cousin, Count Guido Guerra, was the acknowledged leader of the Florentine Guelphs. On the occasion of the recent clash at Montaperti the cousins had fought on opposite sides, and Guido Guerra had led the defeated Guelphs back to Florence and thence into a resentful exile. The situation serves to illuminate the descending road which all the great Tuscan feudatories traveled in the thirteenth century. With domestic division added to the expansion of the towns their extinction would not be long delayed.

The most pressing concern of the returned Ghibellines was to revenge themselves on their Guelph enemies. The form of that revenge had by this time become so well established as to be automatic. Not only were the fugitives sentenced to death as rebels and their property confiscated, but their houses and towers, in town and country alike, were ruthlessly leveled with the ground. Within the walls of Florence alone about two hundred structures fell victim to this hateful folly. Since a large complex of Ghibelline dwellings had gone the same road a few years before on the occasion of the Ghibelline exodus of 1258, considerable sections of the town must by the end of 1260 have been in ruins. A chance visitor would have received the impression that he had come to a city erratically devastated by an earthquake.

The fugitive Guelphs congregated in Lucca, the only city of Tuscany which refused to bend its neck under the Ghibelline yoke. It followed therefore that Manfred's intrepid and victorious vicar-general could not rest content till he had driven the enemy from this last foothold and transferred Guelph Lucca to the Ghibelline column. This was the immediate political objective of the victors; and since it involved a struggle not with passive walls of stone but with determined human beings, it cost several campaigns before it was crowned with success. Count Giordano was after a while recalled by Manfred for service in the southern kingdom, and in his place Count Guido Novello was advanced to the Tuscan vicarate-general. It is a not uninteresting personal detail that, wed to an illegitimate daughter of Emperor Frederick II, he enjoyed the distinction of being the brother-in-law of the Sicilian monarch. To this connection rather than to his merits he must have owed his high appointment, for he was plagued with indecision and, first and last, made a very mediocre showing as captain of the Tuscan Ghibellines. In his military capacity his first care and duty was to hold the German mercenaries together, for they were the strong pillar on which the whole Ghibelline superstructure rested. Since their cost was apportioned among all the Tuscan towns enrolled in the Ghibelline league, their upkeep occasioned no insuperable difficulties. Exclusively a cavalry, they were not particularly effective against a walled town like Lucca. However, after a few campaigns, in which infantry contingents from the Ghibelline towns participated at the side of the German knights, Lucca was at last, in 1264, brought to terms. To save itself from threatened destruction the town agreed to banish the Guelph refugees from Florence and the other Tuscan localities and to take the oath of allegiance to Manfred and his vicar-general. As the sad train of his dejected enemies wound slowly up the Apennines to seek shelter among the Guelphs of the Romagna, Guido Novello may be imagined viewing that tragic exodus with partisan satisfaction. Tuscany had become a united province under his rule and from every city of the land waved the eagle banner of the empire.

While Manfred triumphed in this signal manner in Tuscany, difficulties which gathered volume like a swiftly descending avalanche arose in another quarter. The king's most implacable enemy was, as need hardly be said, the papacy. Stubbornly refusing to recognize him as sovereign in Sicily, Pope Alexander IV had made the vain effort to replace him with an English prince. Not long after the battle of Montaperti, which greatly strengthened the hated Manfred by putting Tuscany also in his control, the baffled Alexander died, to be succeeded first by Urban IV (1261–64), a Frenchman, and then by another Frenchman, Clement IV (1265–68). Intelligent and resourceful men, both these popes were inflexibly determined on ridding the papacy, once and for all, of the intolerable incubus of the house of Hohenstaufen. The English solution of their predecessor having failed, they evolved a French plan on which they did not scruple to stake every moral and material resource of their office.

The contemporary French king was the famous Louis IX, afterward raised to the honors of sainthood. He took an interest in the papal project to the extent of permitting his younger brother, the count of Anjou, to accept the proffer of the Sicilian crown and of putting no difficulties in the way of raising the funds necessary for the enterprise by papal levies on the ecclesiastical properties in his kingdom. The count of Anjou, Charles by name, was a man of unbounded political ambition, a good soldier, and, though without as much as a trace of his brother's saintliness, a correct and orthodox believer. A nose, bold as a hawk's beak, betrayed a fierce and impatient masculinity.[2] If the pope would provide him with the sinews of war, the count agreed to attend to the rest. The head of Christendom had therefore to put his financial mills to grinding; and as the measures which produced the desired golden grist were responsible for a vast expansion of Florentine banking, we are obliged to give them a strict attention.

With the intensification of the struggle between church and empire in the days of Frederick II, the financial operations of the papacy had become exceedingly important. Cruelly pressed for money, the popes sought to increase their revenues by levying on the various national churches on the ground that the war against the excommunicated emperor was equivalent to a crusade. In case of a crusade, let us recall, the pope was privileged to tithe the church. The important work of collecting the crusading tithes and forwarding them to Italy had been intrusted to the great trading companies of Siena and Florence, which through their permanent agents in France, England, and the

[2] Dante, who, as a youth, must have seen Charles during one of his visits to Florence, pictures him as "colui dal maschio naso." (Purg., VII, 113.) See also Villani's interesting characterization, VII, 1.

Netherlands were satisfactorily equipped for the service. It is hardly possible to overestimate the extent to which the ecclesiastical riches of Europe deflected into the papal treasury had contributed to the defeat of the great Hohenstaufen. However, the recent victory of Montaperti had made Tuscany Ghibelline; and although the bankers, after the accommodating manner of their kind, would have been pleased to serve both sides, the reigning pope, Urban IV, was unwilling to lean upon avowed enemies. Clever politician that he was and familiar with the nature of money-lenders, he saw in the situation an opportunity for driving a wedge into the Ghibelline solidarity of Tuscany. Hardly therefore had he assumed the keys of St. Peter, when he put Florence and Siena, now officially Ghibelline, under interdict. Not content with this measure, he excommunicated their merchants and ordered their debtors throughout the world to refuse to make payment on loans and goods on pain of being excommunicated in their turn. Only in case the merchants made formal submission to the pope and could show a letter of pardon from the curia or one of its authorized agents certifying the fact, was the satisfaction of the debt declared to be permissible. It followed that the Sienese and Florentine trading houses were condemned to bankruptcy unless they sought and obtained the pope's favor. Under this ecclesiastical pressure the big business men, though naturally as inconspicuously as possible, went over to the Guelph side. If we now remember that it was the Sienese and Florentine merchants who were the outstanding figures in papal banking, we can see that by the unscrupulous application of his power of excommunication the pope had gained the inestimable advantage over Manfred of marshalling the Tuscan money interests behind his cause.

The next measure carries us to France. Urban first, and Clement after him, having stipulated with King Louis IX that the French church was to bear the bulk of the expense of Charles of Anjou's armament, commanded the bishops and abbots of the realm to tithe themselves during three successive years. As in the earlier case of Frederick II, the tithing was based on the theory that the projected campaign against Manfred ranked as a crusade. Not able to raise the tax fast enough to suit the impatient pope, the French prelates were obliged to borrow from the Italian bankers. Money advanced under these pressing circumstances brought anywhere from 20 to 60 per cent annual interest, thus extending to the canny Tuscan traders an opportunity for enormous profits. No wonder we find them scurrying to secure the pope's pardon and falling on their knees before him at Rome or his deputies in France to protest that they were to all eternity his humble servants. Tuscany might be officially Ghibelline, but its business leaders, the bankers and merchants, were secretly or openly Guelph and enlisted their money power on the papal side.[3]

When, in the spring of 1265, the careful preparations in France of Charles of Anjou were approaching completion, he proceeded with an advance guard of five hundred knights and one thousand bowmen to Marseilles. Embarking in twenty ships, he sailed to the mouth of the Tiber and passed thence to Rome. The main army of some thirty thousand men did not get under way

[3] On the reckless financial activities of the pope and his Italian agents in France, see Davidsohn, Vol. II[1], pp. 566-69.

till the autumn, when it moved leisurely across Lombardy to proceed via the Romagna and the Marches of Ancona to its rendezvous with Charles at the papal capital. It remains a riddle why Manfred, who had exhibited a most energetic character in conquering his throne, showed a slackness in meeting the French attack which must have greatly discouraged his followers. The sea power of the Pisans, who were his allies, was more than sufficient to have scattered to the winds the small flotilla which had pushed out from the harbor of Marseilles with Charles himself on board. But the Pisans rested on their oars on account of a quarrel they had with Manfred's vicar-general in Tuscany, Count Guido Novello. When they had at last wrested from Guido the concessions they considered their due, it was too late to intercept the pretender. Again, with his numerous adherents in Lombardy, Manfred would seem to have been in an excellent position to harass the march of the main army; but here, too, no resistance worthy of the name was made against the invader.

Such hesitations and delays show conclusively that something had gone wrong in Manfred's camp. Perhaps the key to the secret is the strong oriental trait in Manfred which he shared with his famous father and which manifested itself in a capricious alternation of sensuous languor and feverish activity. In any case it is a fact that he did as good as nothing to hinder the junction of the main French army with the advance guard under Charles already at Rome. Heartened by the apparent paralysis of the enemy, the count of Anjou joyously celebrated his coronation as king of Sicily in the ancient capital on the Tiber and immediately afterward pushed south to seize the prize. On February 26, 1266, the eager pretender encountered King Manfred's forces not far from Beneventum. In the fierce fight that followed the Florentine Guelphs, who had been wanderers on the face of the earth since Montaperti, took a distinguished part; but, consistently sluggish under Guido Novello's inept leadership, the Florentine and Tuscan Ghibellines shone by their absence. The rest is too well known to require elaboration. Manfred's army was routed and himself killed. When after a close search of the battlefield the hacked and disfigured corpse was recovered and brought before Charles, he had the dead monarch's captive barons brought from their prison cells to identify the body. Full of fear, they hesitated to speak in that hostile company; but high-hearted Count Giordano, the gallant victor of Montaperti, at the first glimpse of his mutilated lord dropped his face into his hands and sobbed: "Omè, omè, signor mio." [4]

The effect of Beneventum on the political situation of Tuscany was not so sudden and overwhelming as might have been expected. Undeniably the pope's credit rose promptly to such a pitch that all the Tuscan towns expressed a desire to be reconciled with him. Willing to meet their pliant mood halfway, he offered to remove the interdict with which they had been smitten, in return for a vow of submission to himself. This conciliatory offer Florence accepted, without, however, exhibiting the least haste to meet the additional commands of the pope. What Clement wanted, above all, was the withdrawal from the city of the German mercenaries, who constituted the formidable standing army

[4] Villani, VII, 9.

of the still dominant league of Tuscan Ghibellines. The league had remained intact after Beneventum under its commander, Guido Novello, and was naturally looked on askance by victorious Charles and his eager papal mentor. If Guido maintained his German host at Florence, the strategic center of Tuscany, and resolutely stood his ground, Pope Clement could not get control of the province short of open war. Resolution, however, was the very quality Count Guido had always conspicuously lacked; and when on November 11, 1266, there occurred in Florence a rising of the people against the Germans engineered by papal partisans, rather than fight in the narrow streets unsuited to the style of mounted troops, the quaking Guido led his foreign cohorts out of the city.

It was a fatal act of pusillanimity. Even so, although the departure of the Germans gave the city back to its citizens, it did not hand it over to the pope and the Guelph faction. Promptly reasserting themselves on the disappearance of the foreign troops, the Florentine popolani returned to their normal policy of independence from all outside control coupled with internal peace. While the two noble factions, the Guelphs and the Ghibellines, had by this time acquired a certain following among the masses, the people in general were still of neither party and hoped in the common interest to bring the hostile magnates to an accommodation. Consequently the departure of the Germans was not followed by a move to drive out the Ghibellines. On the contrary, they were permitted to stay, while at the same time an invitation was issued to the exiled Guelphs to return to the city. To this policy of reconciliation the pope was strongly opposed, for he wanted Florence to be delivered exclusively into Guelph hands and no mercy to be shown to his Ghibelline enemies. Clement took the view that the Hohenstaufen snake, which had been scotched at Beneventum, was not killed as yet by any means because in Germany there lived the boy Conradin, who would only have to appear in Italy to bring the Ghibellines back to life. It naturally confirmed him in his set hostility to a Guelph-Ghibelline pacification to learn, early in the year 1267, that the prince, a spirited youth of fifteen, was about to embark on the attempt to recover his Sicilian kingdom.

As soon as the situation was complicated by this new factor, Clement IV with characteristic swiftness of decision gave his negotiations with the Florentines a different character. He would no longer attempt to persuade them to submit to his will, he would employ force. Having, however, no military power of his own, he was obliged to turn once again to his French champion, to Angevin Charles. He commissioned him to be his representative in Tuscany to the end of "pacifying" the province in the papal interest. The ambitious Sicilian king had been impatiently waiting for this very call. Already master of the south, he could now with the consent and at the behest of the pope advance his foot into the heart of Italy. He dispatched a troop of French knights northward, to whom the exiled Florentine Guelphs, who had fought at Beneventum, added their strength as they crossed the boundary of Tuscany. On *Sabbato Santo,* the day before Easter of the year 1267, and five months after the convulsion which had rid the town of its German occupation, the combined forces appeared unexpectedly before Florence.

The Ghibellines in the city, afflicted with the feebleness which had been their curse ever since Guido Novello had become their head, at once resolved to give up the city. Would it have been different with them if the fiery Farinata degli Uberti, who had died three years before (1264), had still been among the living? All that we know of him justifies the surmise that his indignation would have exploded against the craven slackness of his fellows. If we linger for a moment over the ignominious retreat, it is because, as the event proved, the Ghibellines lightly surrendered the last chance they ever had to make an exit from the Florentine stage in honorable accord with the traditions of a military caste. By their cowardly evacuation of the city at the coming of the French, they did indeed for the moment save their lives; but instead of falling like heroes in a gallant charge, they died in dispersion, munching as impecunious beggars the scant crumbs tossed them by a resentful charity. Once again in the long seesaw of Guelph-Ghibelline strife, as the Ghibellines rode out by one gate the Guelphs rode in by another. And just as the Ghibelline rule, now ended, had been built on German troopers, the new Guelph rule, which succeeded it, rested on King Charles and the horsemen of France. The bloodless revolution which made Florence Guelph (and kept her Guelph for as long as her independence lasted) took place on Easter Sunday, the fifty-first anniversary of the famous murder of Buondelmonte at the head of the Ponte Vecchio.[5]

Once more in accordance with the ruthless *vae victis* of Italian politics the Guelphs began their rule with a wholesale proscription of the departed Ghibellines and with a general confiscation of their goods; again, in lieu of the escaped individuals, their houses, which could not escape, were dedicated to destruction. As the Guelphs owed their triumph to the intervention in their behalf of King Charles, whatever reward he might demand would have to be conceded. Pope Clement promoted him to the vicarate-general of Tuscany, while the Florentine Guelphs elevated him to the podestàship of their city. However, since at the time of the Guelph revolution he was still in the south, and since at best he would be only occasionally in Tuscany, he filled these two important offices with trusted followers charged to carry out his policies. On taking over the rule of Florence, he instituted a system identical with that of Manfred's time with the single difference that the roles of Guelphs and Ghibellines were now reversed. The acting podestà, who was always Charles's personal appointee, duly observed the form of consulting the two councils traditionally attached to his office; but as only approved Guelphs from the upper and middle classes were permitted to sit in these bodies, the government presented the picture of a strictly partisan regime. The renewed organization of the people under the captain, a conspicuous democratic feature of the Primo Popolo, was prohibited. The people as such counted for no more in the new Guelph than in the late Ghibelline system. This deserves to be expressly said since the view propounded by Villani and echoed by all his imitators to the

---

[5] The political plans and intrigues that agitated Florence from the summer of 1266 to the Guelph triumph of Easter (April 17), 1267, have given rise to grave controversies. They are discussed with a grateful resultant clarification by Davidsohn, Vol. II¹, pp. 598-612; *Forschungen*, Vol. IV, pp. 174-97.

effect that the victorious Guelphs, as distinguished from the defeated Ghibellines, exhibited popular leanings still enjoys general acceptance. Every act of
the new rulers proves that they were fundamentally as anti-democratic as their
rivals and that they had a heart that beat as one with that of their energetic
patron, King Charles. This grand personage, who assumed the podestaship in
1267 and retained the office for an unbroken stretch of thirteen years, regarded
all commoners, whether in his native France or in Italy, the land of his adoption, as laborious clods whom God in his goodness had provided in order
that sovereigns and their barons, the true elect of the earth, might lead an
honorable and dignified existence. In short, he was a faithful exponent of his
class and age.

Untroubled by either urban-democratic or evangelical-Franciscan leanings,
Charles had a firmness of character and a political understanding which raised
him far above the average ruler of the day. It was largely to his own high
qualities that he owed his Sicilian throne; and now that that throne was
threatened by the descent into Italy of Conradin, in the eyes of strict legitimists
the lawful heir, he was resolved not to leave a stone unturned to repeat his
victory over Manfred. Therefore a month after his troops had occupied
Florence, he came in person to Tuscany with the purpose of organizing the
province as the first line of defense against the German claimant. Although
the Guelph league was now clearly dominant and boasted the support of the
majority of the Tuscan towns, the Ghibellines were still formidable since, besides the many castles of their noblemen, two considerable communes, Pisa
and Siena, and a number of smaller settlements, like Poggibonsi, obstinately
refused to recognize Charles as vicar-general. When in the summer of 1267 it
became known that Conradin with a small but well-equipped body of knights
was on the point of setting out from Germany, the resistance of the Tuscan
Ghibellines was naturally stiffened by this news; and when, in October, the
prince actually appeared in Verona, warmly acclaimed by his Lombard adherents, a hope was lighted in every Ghibelline breast in Tuscany that induced
the enemies of Charles to resist his authority more vigorously than ever.
Quick to see that under the prevailing circumstances the decision rested with
the sword, he resolved to bring the recalcitrants to terms before Conradin
should arrive upon the scene. But little Poggibonsi, his first object of attack,
heroically resisted him for five months; and when on its surrender he turned
against Pisa, his forces were too exhausted to take it by assault. Could he
have captured the great seaport, he might very probably have halted Conradin's advance, for it was through the territory of Pisa, habitually friendly
to his family, that the young prince planned to march southward into the
kingdom which he hoped to wrest from the usurper. No fault can be found
with Charles's strategy. It failed because of the resistance he encountered,
chiefly from Poggibonsi and from Pisa. Accommodating himself to the altered
situation, he determined to retire to his kingdom and settle the issue with his
rival on the soil they both claimed.

It was in the early spring of 1268 that Charles abandoned his central Italian
position as militarily untenable. Shortly after, young Conradin led his band
of German knights, strengthened by numerous Lombard partisans who had

eagerly flocked to his standards, across the Apennines above Pisa. On April 7 the inhabitants of the Ghibelline seaport gave him a welcome as clamorous as any they had ever offered to his imperial ancestors. He was a youth of sixteen, blond and of goodly figure, and his comeliness, added to his exalted birth, stirred the quick sympathies of the people wherever he appeared. His most intimate friend and adviser, Frederick, duke of Austria, was only three years older than himself. Launched without preparation upon the wild sea of Italian politics, the two inexperienced young men must at times have been utterly bewildered by the party passions which roared and grimaced about them in uncontrolled fury. Had they not known the goal toward which they were steering and had they not resolutely pointed their course southward, they would have lost their way as on an uncharted ocean. From Pisa the journey led onward to Siena, which tried to outdo Pisa with its acclamations; and from Siena the Ghibelline host, steadily increased by fresh volunteers, streamed southward and ever southward in search of the French rival. Charles's great patron and ally, Pope Clement IV, unable to hold Rome, had sought refuge in well-fortified Viterbo. From the battlements of his Viterban palace he saw on a hot summer's day the luminous cloud of dust some miles to the west which marked the passing of the hostile army. Not for a moment even did doubt assail the stout heart or flit across the features of the inflexible old man. "He will vanish like that golden dust," he prophesied of the young Hohenstaufen to the cardinals intently gazing westward; and after a pause, "They are leading him like a lamb to the slaughter." [6]

From Rome still pressing southward, the Ghibelline army entered the southern kingdom to be confronted at last, on August 23, by the Guelph champion in a valley not far from Tagliacozzo. Conradin's forces were more numerous, but Charles handled his army with greater skill, and victory, as sweeping as two and a half years before at Beneventum, again perched upon his banners. The Suabian lad attended by the duke of Austria and a handful of Italian lords, who remained faithful to the last, made his escape from the battlefield; but to no avail. Betrayed to the conqueror in the hope of gain, at the command of the resentful Charles, he, together with his devoted friend and a stalwart band of Italian Ghibellines, was beheaded on the market square of Naples. He was the last of the Hohenstaufens, a line of kings, who, as in a Greek tragedy, had been carried to the sun-lit summits only, because man may not vie with the gods, to be swallowed up in darkness and defeat.

Although the death of Conradin signified the fall of the strongest pillar of the Ghibelline cause, the Tuscan Ghibellines did not on that account at once give up the struggle. As King Charles was obliged to remain in the south in order to stamp out the rebellion which had here and there sporadically raised its head, he dispatched a representative at the head of a French force to Tuscany charged to resume the policy of reducing the province to a single Guelph mass. The preliminary step to this end would have to be to bring to terms Siena and Pisa, ever the enthusiastic champions of the Ghibelline cause. In spite of the bitter cup of Tagliacozzo the two towns were so little inclined to submission that they impertinently braved the Angevin sovereign.

[6] Davidsohn, Vol. II[2], p. 36.

Siena even had the audacity to lay siege to little nearby Colle, like Montalcino and Montepulciano always a thorn in the flesh of the larger town. At this provocation the French vicar attended by the Florentine host started for the scene of action and on June 17, 1269, under the walls of Colle, signally defeated the Sienese and their Ghibelline allies. It was the Red Lily's revenge for the rout at Montaperti some nine years earlier. Reluctant even now to accept its fate, Siena continued to offer resistance; but when, in the following year, Pisa, seeing no prospect of Ghibelline help from any quarter, entered the Guelph system, the upland town, in order to escape the grinding siege that threatened, also came to terms (August 4, 1270). Into the hands of Guido of Montfort, official representative of Charles, she swore fealty to the Guelph cause, agreed to take back her Guelph exiles, and, in conclusive token of submission, accepted a Guelph podestà. No sooner had the Sienese Guelphs re-entered the city in accordance with the treaty than they drove out the Ghibellines amidst retributive measures as familiar as they were revolting. In this manner did Siena become Guelph and bid farewell forever to its Ghibelline age, the period of its greatness. Continuing on its triumphant course, the Guelph league broke down the steadily weakening resistance of its remaining adversaries until only occasional castles in the inaccessible mountain areas floated the Ghibelline pennant. Approximately two years after Conradin met a felon's death at Naples, Tuscany had been welded into a Guelph dominion obedient to the pope and King Charles.

For Florence the Guelph triumph involved a number of such important social-political changes that we are obliged to give them close attention. Granting that the local Guelphs owed their success to Charles and his French knights, and granting further, that the Angevin exercised a more or less autocratic authority through his right to appoint the podestà, it was also true that he could not maintain himself in the town without the backing of the Guelphs, organized as the parte Guelfa, and that he was therefore constrained to accept their partnership. In sum, Charles and the parte Guelfa shared the government between them. Since Charles had numerous general interests up and down the Italian peninsula and was usually far away, while the parte Guelfa, as exclusively Florentine, was always on the ground, it followed also that the king and the party could co-operate without a perilous amount of friction. What rendered the partnership particularly harmonious was the fact that Charles was willing to hand over the entire domestic field to the Guelphs, provided he was permitted to retain control of Florentine foreign policy. The situation has been oversimplified by writers who are content to describe Florence as subjected to the king of Sicily. Undoubtedly it was; and yet the immensely important internal developments went forward under the impulsion, not of Charles, but of the parte Guelfa, resolved, first, to revenge itself on the defeated Ghibellines and, second, to maintain its new-won power at all costs. Revenge had been a feature of the Guelph-Ghibelline feud since its inception a half-century before, but organization for continued power, at least in the rigorous form now adopted, was a novelty.

We have learned that the Guelph and the Ghibelline parties came into being when the ancient society of the nobles, the societas militum, could no longer be maintained. All the evidence which has come down to us confirms the belief that the two parties were organized along identical lines. But as we know much more about the parte Guelfe than about the parte Ghibellina, and as the parte Guelfa played a much more conspicuous and continuous role in the history of Florence, we are justified in concentrating our attention on this truly extraordinary organization.[7] The executive or governing committee consisted of six captains, all of them members of magnate families. While this indicates an aristocratic association, rich popolani were by no means excluded from membership in the party, for the nobles may have remembered that their own ancestors had once to a large extent been popolani and that their present exalted station represented a relatively recent achievement. The parte Guelfa was frankly a union of birth and wealth. If the executive power represented by the captains was reserved to birth, wealth received recognition in the department in which it was certain to have the greatest interest, the treasury. This was intrusted to a committee of six, three of whom were required to be popolani. Final authority rested with the general assembly of the party, which elected the officials and voted on all important measures. In all matters pertaining to their office the six captains sought the advice of a small secret council of fourteen members, called *credentia*. Among the officials there stood out one with the ominous name of Accuser of the Ghibellines. He was in effect the head of the detective service with the whole party membership serving under him as volunteer informers. This officer alone should suffice to convince us that if the end sought by the party was power, the means adopted to achieve the end was a continued terror.

Although the repressive measures of the party were directed against the Ghibellines, the latter were not by any means all of one kind, for there were Ghibellines and Ghibellines. The most dangerous group of Ghibellines were the *ribelli* (rebels). This uncompromising designation was attached to all those who had voluntarily left the city. They were condemned to death, their houses were subject to destruction, and all their possessions, real and personal alike, were confiscated. By far the greater number of Ghibellines, however, did not go into exile but stayed on in Florence in the hope of somehow weathering the storm. In the eyes of their Guelph adversaries they constituted a body of the suspect and consequently were fair game for the Accuser of the Ghibellines and his following of patriotic spies. When such a resident Ghibelline was denounced to the captains of the party, he could at the discretion of these potentates be required to leave the city for a place assigned him as a residence, which would be near or far from Florence according to the degree of suspicion he had incurred. There was no trial and the sentence was indeterminate as to time. In distinction from voluntary exile, which rated as rebellion, imposed exile was called *confino* and its victims *confinati*. If the confinati abandoned their allotted residence, they automatically became rebels, subject to the rebel's lot of death and confiscation. Rebels and confinati, distinct legal

[7] Villani, VII, 17; Davidsohn, Vol. II¹, pp. 618-20. The earliest statute of the parte Guelfa which has reached us bears the date 1335. It was published by Bonaini in the *Giornale Storico degli Archivi Toscani*, Vol. I, pp. 4-41. A valuable contribution is by U. Dorini, *Notizie Storiche sull'Università di Parte Guelfa in Firenze*. Florence, 1902.

categories but hardly distinguishable in the misery of their lot, henceforth loom large in Florentine political history.

It remains to describe the feature by which the Guelphs completed the ruin of their adversaries. As the victors desired, above all, to make sure that their vanquished opponents should never again return to power, they were not satisfied with the death sentence *in absentia* and the sweeping sequestration of goods. These measures had in the past been imposed by the Ghibellines on the Guelphs and, notwithstanding, the Guelphs had come back and regained their position and their property. Plainly the fatal thing for the future of Ghibellinism would be to dispose of its wealth, first by turning it into money, and then by distributing the money beyond any chance of recovery. With the clairvoyance inspired by hate this radical measure was with some unavoidable exceptions put into execution and the resultant revenue divided into three parts: one part for the commune, one part for the party, and one part for individual Guelphs claiming indemnity for previous losses at the hand of Ghibellines. If the plutocratic element was well represented in the party from the first, we may assume that it was not weakened when the liquidation of the immense Ghibelline properties in town and country got under way and the money-changers were invited to seat themselves at a unique banquet of percentages and commissions. The one-third share diverted into the party treasury deserves particular attention; it had the effect of providing the party with ready money, while giving it besides the credit and authority of a great bank.

The political ruin of the Florentine Ghibellines resulted from many causes which the foregoing pages have illuminated. The main cause surely was that they aimed to perpetuate their rule in their native city with the help of the empire, which proved a broken reed. But their financial ruin, which made their political failure irretrievable, was brought about by a relentless economic persecution by which their victorious opponents undermined their existence and reduced them to the level of homeless beggars.

XI. The Second Democracy: The Priors and the Ordinances of Justice (1282–93)

HE developments in Florence following the sweeping Guelph victory cannot be grasped without a preliminary understanding of the effect of that victory on the papacy. The papal court was still celebrating the fall of the Hohenstaufens when it was visited by an uneasy foreboding that it had avoided Scylla only to be threatened by Charybdis. In order to escape the German and Hohenstaufen grip the popes had drawn France and the Angevins on the scene; and promptly, on the execution of Conradin, they learned that they were now hardly less dependent on King Charles than they had once been on his Suabian predecessors. Another development complicated the crisis. By leaning heavily through several decades on France and its royal house the papacy had been unable to escape the consequences of this association, and in both outlook and personnel had become markedly gallicized. To mention a single but significant item: in the college of cardinals the French representation had steadily increased; and this growth in numbers, abetted by the impalpable spread of French sentiments through the whole body of the Roman clergy, brought it about that candidates of French nationality tended with waxing frequency to emerge as popes from the papal conclaves. We have taken account of the decisive role played by the two French popes, Urban IV and Clement IV, in the last act of the Hohenstaufen tragedy. They were both of them men of sterling quality, unflinchingly devoted to the papal cause. But if they had not been Frenchmen we may doubt whether they would have committed themselves with the ardor that characterized their policy to the establishment of a French king in southern Italy. When the death of Conradin put the political destinies of Italy into the hands of King Charles, Pope Clement IV began to show signs of uneasiness and, had he lived longer, he might not improbably have become sufficiently fired by the formidable tradition behind his office to attempt to clip the wings of the protégé who had waxed too strong. But he died a month after the Suabian boy's execution while still exulting over the manifest intervention of the Lord of Hosts in his behalf.

When the cardinals met at Viterbo to elect Clement's successor, the hidden crisis within the papal institution burst irresistibly into the open, revealing itself to all the world. The college split disastrously into a French and an Italian faction; and so evenly matched were the opponents that the ensuing deadlock was not broken for almost three years. The prolonged contest signified that the French group of cardinals was under Angevin influence and wanted a pope friendly to the Angevin alliance, while the Italian group, alarmed at the growing French dominance, was determined to return to the Italian tradition and to raise to power a man of their own nationality who would bestir himself to ban the Angevin specter.

When an Italian, who took the title of Gregory X (1271–76), at length emerged as victor, Europe did not have long to wait in order to learn that the eminence achieved by King Charles was not to the papal taste. Gregory was not in Europe but at Acre in Syria at the time of his election. During his residence at that seaport he had been deeply distressed by the waning power of the Christians in the east. It was a particularly insufferable circumstance in his eyes that the infidels had been permitted again to possess themselves of the Holy Places of Jerusalem, which had been regained for the occident a generation before by Emperor Frederick II. No sooner therefore had Gregory been elected pope than he returned to Europe, single-mindedly resolved to initiate a new crusade. With a minimum of delay he issued a call for a General Council of Christendom at the city of Lyons to consider and prepare a united expedition. Having reached this decision, he saw that if his proposal was to enjoy the universal support at which he was aiming, a necessary preliminary would have to be the pacification of Italy, and that, as a first step to this end, a reconciliation must be effected between the Guelphs and Ghibellines of Tuscany. Although he was aware of the opposition to any such plan of the Guelphs and their ally, King Charles, who were unwilling to surrender any of the fruits of victory, he would not let himself be deterred and firmly informed these partisans, and the Ghibellines as well, that he was determined to act as peacemaker between them. While the beaten Ghibellines naturally welcomed the proposal, the Guelphs, although stiffly hostile, could not openly reject the initiative of the ecclesiastical ruler in whose name their league was concluded and for whose benefit it was supposed primarily to exist. When, on proceeding leisurely to the assembly to be held at Lyons, Gregory, in June, 1273, arrived on the Arno, he was permitted with sulking reluctance on the part of the ruling Guelphs to negotiate between them and their Ghibelline victims.

The presence of Gregory X in Florence is chiefly notable because it bore witness to his perception that, if he continued to identify himself with the Guelph faction, he was destined to remain a client of King Charles, while if he succeeded in strengthening the Ghibellines in Florence and throughout Italy, he might hope to raise himself to the level of an arbiter. Besides, the settlement of the Guelph-Ghibelline feud would greatly aid the crusade on which he had set his heart. Owing to the untiring zeal with which he pursued his project of reconciliation Gregory achieved the apparent miracle of bringing the rival factions to an agreement; and after its terms had been laid down in an elaborate document, the event was celebrated by one of those public spectacles in which the Florentines, like all medieval Italians, took a naïve delight. Its climax was reached when chosen representatives of the two venomously estranged groups exchanged, with what dark looks and private reservations may be left to the imagination, the conventional kiss of peace (July 12, 1273).

The plaudits of the spectators were still ringing in his ears, when Gregory began to suspect that he had been tricked. A man more versed in the ways of the world than he would never have committed himself to so futile an under-taking. Such a man would have known from the beginning that a party as vindictive as the Guelphs and exercising so unchallenged an ascendancy would never surrender its advantage save as a consequence of defeat on the field of battle. Even more than the Guelphs was the resolute, iron-nerved Charles opposed to letting the reins slip weakly from his hands. He had come in person to Florence in order that his Guelph friends might learn from his own mouth that, in spite of the lip service he paid his papal patron, he had not changed in his heart. Under these circumstances Gregory was so effectively baulked by his tricky antagonists that he was not able to give the treaty of reconciliation a really equitable character; and what few advantages it con-tained for the Ghibellines were quickly nullified when Gregory, on departing from the city, intrusted its execution to none other than his vicar-general in Tuscany, to Charles himself. We must conclude that this last partisan action was forced on the pope by his Guelph allies. When on leaving Florence he reviewed the recent events, he gradually convinced himself that he had been the victim of a cleverly spun plot. To this belated illumination the outraged Ghibellines contributed their share, for their complaints at the vindictive treat-ment accorded them followed him into the hills of the Mugello, whither he had retreated during the summer heat in order to restore his shattered health. In September, only two months after blessing a sham fraternization, he ex-hibited his irate state of mind at having been duped by the Guelph rulers of Florence by laying their city under an interdict.

In the light of the pope's Tuscan plans his interdict signified his strong disapproval of the local parte Guelfa; and although the anathema did not embrace Charles, it might well be taken to mean that all was not well between the pope and his secular advocate. Even before coming to Florence Gregory had taken another step not calculated to improve the relations between the two men. Deeply convinced that the most effective counterweight to the power of Charles would be the restoration of the fallen empire, he had opened negotiations with the German princes, pleading with them in fatherly tones to end the anarchy which had prevailed since the death of Frederick II by electing a successor. Pope Gregory had turned Ghibelline! At least that is what the disgusted Guelphs said, first in whispers and finally aloud to all the world. In their passionate partisanship they forgot that since the popes of the past had become Guelph for no other reason than to escape the control of the emperor, they might with impeccable consistency throw themselves on the Ghibelline side as soon as it became necessary to break the shackles of a Guelph master. Regardless of the confused happenings on the restless human stage, the unalterable lodestar of the papacy was and would remain complete independence from temporal control.

In response to unremitting papal pressure the German electors on Septem-ber 29, 1273, acclaimed an inconspicuous south German count, Rudolph of Hapsburg, as German king; and although the authority of the German king had in the course of recent decades declined beyond recovery, Gregory wholeheartedly rejoiced that there was now again someone in the world whom he might hope to play off against the overbearing Angevin. He went so far as to plan for Rudolph's early descent into Italy in order to invest him with the imperial crown; but first one event and then another intervened, causing repeated adjournment of the project. In the end Rudolph confined himself to Germany and never crossed the Alps. He was the first of the new, the diminished German kings, who were conscious of being so feeble in their homeland that the dangerous Italian adventure, although it never ceased to exercise a powerful fascination, persuaded only a few of them ever again to stake their lives and happiness upon it.

After presiding over the General Council held at Lyons and inaugurating numerous negotiations concerned with the prospective crusade, Gregory turned his face again toward Italy to undertake the final preparations for the event which, according to his devout intentions, was to make his pontificate forever memorable. During his absence the Florentine Guelphs had finally and completely sabotaged the treaty they had at his behest negotiated with the Ghibellines and held more exclusive sway than ever in their city. Toward the interdict with which they had been punished they maintained an attitude of stubborn insolence. Not even when, some two years after it had been imposed, Gregory again entered Tuscany on his way to Rome, did they condescend to seek the forgiveness of the offended pontiff. With Florence under his curse, Gregory planned, in sign of his displeasure, to give the city a wide berth and to cross the Arno on his southward journey by an upstream ford. But a sudden downpour—it was the month of the December rains—rendered his plan impracticable. Obliged for reasons of safety to use one of the Florentine bridges, he found himself under the necessity of lifting his ban, since it was improper for a pope to enter an excommunicated town. Accordingly he suspended the interdict for the limited period of his traverse. Thereupon, preceded and followed by a numerous suite, he entered the gate and moved as fast as his porters could carry his litter through the narrow streets, along which dense, kneeling crowds implored the blessing which the baffled pontiff, already stricken with a mortal disease, languidly accorded. When he had crossed the river and left the city by the eastern gate, he ordered his litter to be set down and the long procession halted. Then turning his face toward the town, with raised hand he solemnly renewed the suspended curse: a scene so medieval as to be not easily forgotten. The broken old man got no farther on his Romeward journey than Arezzo, where on January 10, 1276, his troubled earthly pilgrimage touched its final goal.

Three popes followed each other in rapid succession until on November 25, 1277, an Italian of the great Orsini family of Rome, who assumed the name of Nicholas III, mounted the chair of the chief of the apostles, and with far greater energy than the well-intentioned but feeble Gregory, but also with far greater lack of scruple, resumed his predecessor's policy. A handsome man of princely bearing and tradition, Nicholas was much more interested in pushing the fortunes of his family than in reviving the failing crusading fervor of his Christian flock. But, first and foremost, he wished to withdraw the papacy from under the mailed fist of the doughty Charles; and since in a reign that lasted less than three years he succeeded in doing the thing that Gregory had tried but failed to do, he invites our hesitant regard. One of his earliest acts was to renew the invitation to King Rudolph to come to Italy to assume the imperial crown; however, as a born bargainer, he was not minded to extend a favor without asking a favor in return. He let Rudolph know that he expected by way of payment for his support the cession of the great north-central province of Italy, commonly called the Romagna. A bold demand indeed, which would have made the eyes of the predecessors of the puny count of Hapsburg blaze with indignation! However, as the reduced aspirant to the empire could not maintain himself even in his German kingdom without the help of the pope, he yielded, and on June 30, 1278, issued the diploma which carried the temporal power of the papacy beyond the Apennines far into the Lombard plain. The thought which prompted Nicholas to insist on this expansion is perfectly transparent. It was, in final analysis, the grave temporal weakness of the papacy which had caused it during the recent decades to be tossed, like a ball, from Hohenstaufen to Anjou. The ruling pontiff, a man dominated exclusively by political considerations, held the opinion that, while an even balance between Rudolph and Charles might contribute to his independence, this desirable condition would not be definitely and finally secured until the papacy itself had come into possession of sufficient territory to serve as the basis of an adequate secular dominion.

No sooner had Pope Nicholas acquired title to this new and extensive territory than he sent thither his nephew, Cardinal Latino, as legate with full powers. He was to reduce the province to obedience by ironing out the cantankerous Guelph-Ghibelline feuds which it shared with Tuscany and the rest of Italy. Although the cardinal-legate achieved a clamorous success, it cannot be denied that it was hollow since it fell to pieces a few months after his departure. Latino heads the long line of papal legates destined to learn that the Romagnoles, regardless of a feigned submission to their new liege lord, were born to rebellion as the sparks fly upward. However, these unhappy developments were as yet hidden behind the veil of the future, when, with the aureole of his Romagna triumph about his head, the cardinal-legate turned his face to Tuscany, there to repeat his recent miracle of civic pacification.

In order to understand the activity unfolded in Tuscany by the papal nephew we must grasp that this province held a central position in the plan of Pope Nicholas to strengthen the papacy and to diminish the power of King Charles. Nicholas had therefore, even before dispatching Latino on his Romagna mission, terminated the Tuscan vicarate, on the strength of which the Sicilian monarch had dominated central Italy during the past decade. In place of the deposed Charles, Latino was to exercise the powers of a vicar-general for the pope, who by this means planned to bring Tuscany under the immediate control of the papacy. As a preparatory measure the papal representative was ordered once more to attack the thorny problem of persuading the Florentine Guelphs to an accommodation with their Ghibelline foes. The reign of a single faction was to be brought to an end to be succeeded by the peaceful rule of both factions under the guaranty and blessing of the pope. On October 8, 1279, the cardinal made his formal entry into Florence.

Cardinal Latino was a Dominican friar, a man of upright character, famous for his learning and eloquence. If he is, as is widely believed, the author of the *Dies Irae,* a medieval hymn of unrivaled majesty, we are obliged to acclaim him also as a great religious poet. To enable him to play his role of arbiter, that ancient democratic mechanism, the parlamentum, was brought from the municipal lumber-room, and in a great public assembly the papal emissary was by popular acclamation endowed with full political powers. Thus elevated above the battle, he made such good headway that after a few months he was able to announce a settlement. Its first feature was the reconciliation of Guelphs and Ghibellines in a public ceremony culminating in the exchange of oath and kiss between chosen representatives of the two embittered factions. The spectacular event, a close imitation of the scene staged by Pope Gregory X seven years before, took place on January 18, 1280. It was followed a month later by the publication of a new constitution, by the terms of which the two hostile factions were henceforth amicably to share the government of their native city between them.

There is no denying that, at least so far as the first, the pacificatory feature of his settlement is concerned, the cardinal achieved a certain measure of success. According to the treaty the exiled Ghibellines were to be repatriated after reasonable delays and by groups, carefully spaced, in order to avoid a too sudden and therefore dangerous influx; they were even to receive back their confiscated property insofar as it had not yet been sold and the proceeds distributed. It is this significant qualification to the amnesty accorded them which particularly invites our attention. Had not their spirit been broken by their long exile and its attendant misery, it is inconceivable that they would have accepted the loss and injury implied in this condition. For under its terms they cannot, in the main, have entered into possession of anything other than the heaps of stone and brick, to which their demolished houses had been systematically reduced. Deterred by the appalling prospect, a considerable number of Ghibellines, the proud Uberti among them, curtly declined to take advantage of the invitation to return. This unreconciled group continued therefore to constitute a nucleus of fuorusciti (exiles). They sought refuge in the more inaccessible parts of the Apennines, where, joined by the purely lawless elements to be found in all medieval societies, they remained a source of provincial disturbances for many decades to come. Undeniably, however, the majority of the Ghibellines came back to their native city, where, reduced in numbers and prestige and economically ruined, they gradually dropped out of sight. There is no reason for withdrawing or even modifying the statement made in the previous chapter that the Ghibellines signed their death warrant as a political party when, in 1267, they abandoned the city to the Guelphs without lifting a hand in their own defense.

Notwithstanding their having been ousted from exclusive control by the arbitral decision of the cardinal, the Guelphs remained an organization of practically undiminished might. In view of their wealth and their powerful connections at home and abroad, there was no reason at any time why they should despair; and no sooner had the hostile Pope Nicholas expired some six months after Latino had instituted the new political order, than their spirits, as well as those of their steadfast ally, King Charles, registered an immediate improvement. Not only had the late pontiff deprived the Angevin king of the vicarate-general of Tuscany, but as soon as the cardinal's new constitution was put into effect, the king had also been forced out of the podestàship of Florence. Doubtless Charles confidently looked forward to his early restoration to the two posts so necessary to the continuance of his Tuscan supremacy. All such hopes were blasted, however, by an unexpected succession of events. For one thing, Rudolph, the newly elected German king, came forward to demand the Tuscan vicarate for himself. It was a claim which, constitutionally, was incontrovertible. If, following the demise of Emperor Frederick II, the popes had asserted and exercised the right to appoint the representative of the empire in Tuscany, they did so on the assumption—a most questionable assumption, too, let it be said—that during an imperial vacancy they were empowered to act in the emperor's stead. While the feeble and distant Rudolph might not succeed in getting the Tuscans to recognize the vicar whom he dispatched to their province, no successor of Pope Nicholas could fail to acknowledge that, with a German king once more on the throne, the head of the church no longer possessed the slightest constitutional pretext for interfering politically in Tuscany.

A second event fell even more heavily into the scales against Charles and the resumption of his Tuscan hegemony. At the Easter festival of the year 1282 occurred the famous general massacre of the French occupying forces on the island of Sicily known as the Sicilian Vespers. Unexpectedly and over night, as it were, one half of his southern kingdom shook off the yoke of the Angevin tyrant. The rebels promptly offered the island to King Pedro of Aragon on the theory that, as husband of Constance, the daughter of former King Manfred, he was the legitimate heir to the Sicilian crown. Thus, after King Charles had so effectively laid the Hohenstaufen ghost that he had lost all fear of it, it made a vengeful reappearance in his declining years. Not even his enemies will say that he blenched at the sight. He took up the war against the usurping king of Aragon with the same vigor he had displayed against Manfred and Conradin, but in his old age Lady Luck, who, woman-like, favors the young, turned her back on him and he died in 1285 after having experienced a succession of grave disasters. His son and successor, Charles II, continued the struggle, but to no avail. The island of Sicily became an independent kingdom; and although the Angevin rulers succeeded in preserving the peninsular half of their monarchy for themselves, the title, king of Sicily, to which they clung, became a transparent mockery of the facts.

The blow administered to the power and prestige of Charles by the Sicilian revolt put an abrupt end to whatever dreams he and the Guelph party may have entertained to recover their lost Tuscan supremacy. But the fact stands out that Guelphism survived the elimination from municipal control of the original Guelph champions, for Florence now became Guelph by its own decision. No development in the town is more important than this, and none is more easy to grasp the moment we direct our attention to the economic situation. During the period of a little more than a decade of Guelph rule, Florence had experienced an economic boom involving an immense expansion of trade and population. By the year 1280, according to a conservative estimate, the town had come to embrace some 45,000 people,[1] a multitude so great that it could no longer be confined within the second circle of walls. Real estate values and shop rentals registered an uninterrupted advance. The prime cause of these encouraging, if socially disturbing, phenomena was the growing volume of trade, overwhelmingly due to the favors extended to Florence by the Guelph bloc of powers, consisting of the pope, King Charles of Sicily, and the king of France. It was Florentine houses which were intrusted with the immensely lucrative banking of the pope, and it was these same houses which, in their double capacity of bankers and merchants, enjoyed special trading privileges within the dominions of the two powerful Guelph sovereigns. Every citizen noted the mounting curve of prosperity and every citizen capable of reflection was aware that its continuing to mount depended on keeping the town politically aligned with the Guelph powers. To be sure, the profits of the economic expansion accrued chiefly to the enterprisers and capitalists, who became immensely wealthy, while the common people continued to wrestle with poverty, hunger, and squalor; but this unequal distribution of the commercial returns did not keep the unreflecting masses from sharing the Guelph sentiments of their superiors. With business flourishing on account of the Guelph connections of the town, Florence became instinctively and rabidly Guelph.

Matters standing thus, the time had come for the steadily expanding merchant element of the citizenry to take over the government. No violence was necessary and none occurred. In view of the fact that the rich traders were strongly represented in the parte Guelfa, this group, in spite of its nobiliary origin and tendencies, possibly even favored the movement. As for the Ghibellines, they were, even after the partial repatriation of 1280, too feeble either to promote or to hinder political change. All that was necessary to bring about merchant control was imperceptibly to supplant the shaky government which had been imposed by Cardinal Latino and which, an artificial creation excogitated by a learned divine, was laughably out of touch with the Florentine actualities. In the view of Latino the two dominant city groups were still as in the past the parte Guelfa and the parte Ghibellina, and the government he dictated divided the power between them as equitably as conditions permitted. As, owing to continued Guelph predominance, the new government never really operated along Latino's lines, we shall spare ourselves the effort of examining its extraordinarily complicated details. What the cardinal had failed to grasp was that the two parties between which he divided, or rather tried to divide, the power belonged essentially to another era, and that the present was dominated by the great traders, who, though Guelph in sentiment and therefore well disposed toward the Guelph party, had become sufficiently self-conscious to take the protection of their interests into their own hands. Now the traders were organized in gilds or arti. However, long before these associations began to make their power felt the merchants as individuals had exercised considerable influence. During the democratic interlude of 1250, for

---

[1] Davidsohn, Vol. II[2], p. 171, discusses the conflicting estimates. See also Caggese, Vol. I, p. 484, note 15.

example, it was they and not the gilds as such that had exercised political control. At that, economically speaking, still relatively backward period a substantial equality seems to have reigned among the gilds, and trade and handicraft associations, co-operating together, constituted a single and harmonious democratic mass. By 1280 the Guelph boom had taken place and the earlier harmony and equality had disappeared. The immensely expanded money power was now concentrated in the merchant gilds, against which the craft gilds, although they too had not stood still, were no longer able to hold their own. It is this situation which explains why, beginning in 1282 and directly under the nose of the feeble authorities created by Latino two years before, the merchant gilds were able to nominate representatives, called priors, who quietly began to appropriate the functions of government. Meeting no opposition, they became bolder, and in the course of the following year (1283) they liquidated Latino's absurd constitution completely by establishing their own government, which from its chief executive has received the name of the priors.

When we realize that with ups and downs and with certain subtractions and additions the new government of the priors lasted for two hundred years, that it lasted in fact as long as Florence remained a free commonwealth, we cannot escape a conclusion of absolutely central importance. It is that Florence owed its material greatness to its merchant gilds and that it achieved something as close to stable government as was possible under the complicated play of the municipal, provincial, and world-forces to which it was exposed, when in 1282 its merchant gilds seized the political power. The merchant gilds were locally not called merchant gilds but greater gilds (*arti maggiori*) and were seven in number. They were (1) the gild of judges and notaries; (2) the Calimala gild, comprising the dealers in and refiners of foreign cloth; (3) the Cambio or gild of money-changers; (4) the Lana or wool gild, which dealt in cloth of local manufacture; (5) the Por Santa Maria gild, in which the leading retailers of the shopping street, called Por or Porta Santa Maria, were joined with the silk merchants; (6) the gild of physicians and apothecaries (*speziali*), the latter including the dealers in oriental spices; (7) the gild of furriers, the importers of pelts and manufacturers of fur garments. While the gild of judges and notaries was manifestly not a gild of traders, it comprised the important legal group, which at Florence and everywhere else became so intimately associated with the rising bourgeoisie as to be inseparable from it. The other six gilds embraced the men of affairs and captains of industry, whose clever capture of the rapidly multiplying economic opportunities of the thirteenth century had succeeded in making Florence a leading focus of Italian and world-trade.

It was the seven arti maggiori which by instituting an executive of six priors to be chosen from its membership took over the government in 1282-83. However, they preferred to exhibit a certain moderation in respect to their victory. The little bourgeoisie of shopkeepers and artisans was organized at the time in certainly no fewer than twenty-five lesser gilds (*arti minori*) and probably in many more. The members had little or nothing in common with the great traders, who held them in contempt but feared them nonetheless because of their numbers. On this account the merchant gilds on seizing power resolved to hold out an olive branch to the artisan element by inviting five of their gilds to share the power with them. The gilds so honored were doubtless the strongest of the minor gilds and for this reason are frequently referred to as middle gilds (*arti medie*). They were (1) the butchers; (2) the shoemakers; (3) the blacksmiths; (4) the builders, including both carpenters and masons; (5) the *rigattieri,* the second-hand dealers, a much more respectable category in the Middle Ages than among ourselves, largely owing to the solid and durable character of medieval goods. As these five were accepted by the seven as co-rulers, we may with some justification speak, for the time being at least, of twelve greater gilds. But that the five middle gilds were never anything more than a decorative flourish on the system of merchant domination is proved by the fact that in the first decade (1282–92) of the existence of the priorate it was exercised exclusively, or all but exclusively, by members of the merchant oligarchy.[2]

Again as on previous occasions when the constitution had undergone a change in order to bring it abreast of the altered social situation, it was not reshaped from the bottom. The podestà, for instance, was not disturbed, nor were his two traditional councils modified in any way. The podestà was still to be a foreigner, appointed for a year to act as chief judge and to lead the army in war. However, he was now understood to be immediately responsible to the priors, who were the new executive charged with initiating legislation and directing the policy of the commonwealth. Six in number, the priors served for two months, during which time they lived together as a single family in a private house hired for the purpose, until a generation later when they moved into their own splendid palace, the Palazzo dei Signori, now the Palazzo Vecchio and still the most impressive reminder to native and visitor alike of the former greatness of the city. Toward the close of their term they elected their six successors in a session in which the heads of the twelve ruling gilds participated together with a number of wise men (*sapientes*) chosen at pleasure among the six wards (*sesti*) of the city. To fortify the control achieved by the twelve arti maggiori they were organized into a militia under a captain and defender of the gilds. This militia, purely political in character, must not be confused with the citizen militia, which from the early days of the commune had been and still was the Florentine population mobilized for war. The gild militia rendered a purely domestic service, which consisted in assembling at the call of its captain in order to protect the regime of the priors against the attack of its local enemies. Like the podestà, the captain, who was rated as one of the heads of the state, was provided with two councils completely dominated by gildsmen in good standing. In comparison with the aristocratic Guelph and Ghibelline governments that had preceded the priors, the new government may with some justification be called democratic; but as it was a democracy strictly

[2] N. Ottokar, *Il Comune di Firenze alla Fine del Dugento.* Florence, 1926. On p. 25, note, the author gives the figures revealing the gild connection of the priors in the decade 1282-92 and shows that the priors belonging to the middle gilds were so few as to be all but negligible. In this period, and in almost all the subsequent periods as well, the priorate was the prerogative of the great merchants.

HOUSES OF THE ALIGHIERI FAMILY AS RECONSTRUCTED EARLY IN THE TWENTIETH CENTURY AROUND AN AUTHENTIC CORE (ALINARI).

left: DANTE. FROM A MANUSCRIPT OF THE FOURTEENTH CENTURY IN THE RICCARDIAN LIBRARY AT FLORENCE (ALINARI). *right:* PETRARCH. FROM A MANUSCRIPT OF THE FOURTEENTH CENTURY IN THE MEDICEAN LIBRARY AT FLORENCE (ALINARI).

left: ANDREA PISANO. THE LABORS OF OUR FIRST ANCESTORS (ALINARI). *right:*
ANDREA PISANO. THE ART OF WEAVING (ALINARI).

left: PANEL (TREE OF LIFE) FROM THE PULPIT IN SAN LEONARDO IN ARCETRI
(ALINARI). *right:* ANDREA PISANO. BURIAL OF ST. JOHN. A PANEL OF THE FIRST
BRONZE DOOR OF THE BAPTISTRY (ALINARI).

limited by membership in twelve ruling gilds, it would seem to be more properly described as a gild democracy. Such was the only kind of democracy of which Florence was at this time capable, and such, as a matter of fact, was the only kind which, in spite of occasional movements to broaden its base, Florence ever attained.

Although we have no knowledge of any disturbances attending the establishment of the new constitution, it had hardly been set up when it encountered opposition from the nobles. Owing to the shrinkage in the Ghibelline ranks the most conspicuous members of the nobility were now Guelphs, who, associated together in the powerful Guelph party, were far from looking on themselves as representatives of a lost cause. Enriched by the Ghibelline confiscations, the parte Guelfa occupied extensive club quarters, from which as a center it exercised a vast social and financial influence. The day of the old tower associations was over; and although many of the towers, deprived by civic enactment of their dizzy upper stories, still stood and vendetta continued to be the unwritten law of the land, men now conducted their feuds on a smaller scale and with less disturbance of the public peace. We cannot doubt that the civic order was already in far better case than in the rude consular age.

Owing to the almost stealthy establishment of the new government, the nobility did not at once realize that they were no longer the ruling power in the state. Then, with the gild democracy firmly consolidated by means of an armed militia, all that remained for the aristocrats to do in order to signify their displeasure was to vent their spite on the people by manifestations of contempt and individual acts of violence. Undoubtedly they had treated their social inferiors in this way in the past and with entire impunity. But the people, or at least a part of the people, were now in power, and a cry went up that this insufferable conduct must cease and that the nobles should at last, if necessary by special legislation, be brought into the common civic frame. As early as 1281, during the short-lived government instituted by Cardinal Latino, an effort had been made toward this end by a law which required individuals designated as magnates to give surety for their good behavior to the amount of two thousand *librae*. The law was resented by the individuals so designated and only irregularly enforced. On being re-enacted in a much stiffer form in 1286 it again remained very largely a dead letter. This persistent nullification can be accounted for only by the wavering attitude of the new government of the priors. It was made up of merchants with material interests, to defend which the new system had been devised; but many merchants, indeed the richest and most influential of the town, were members also of the parte Guelfa and connected by marriage and business partnerships with the Guelph nobiliary families. Consequently they became involved in a moral ambiguity. While their membership in the merchant gilds pushed them to defend popular interests and to support legislation directed against the lawless nobility, their kinship with the former ruling group filled them with a secret sympathy for this order and impelled them to soften whatever blows might be aimed at its arrogance. In short, confronted in its first phase with the problem of an unruly upper class inherited from the past, the government of the priors blew hot and cold for the simple reason that the leading individuals in the seats of power stood avowedly in the popular, but secretly also in the aristocratic, camp.

The whole first decade of the new government is troubled with this confusion.[3] But while, with secret allies in the priorate, the magnates were able to nullify some of the measures taken against them, there were other measures, behind which there was such a pressure of an aroused public opinion that resistance was impossible. In a class struggle, such as in essence we are here confronted with even though the class lines were not yet clearly drawn, the economic weapon is as certain to be brought into play as the political weapon and may, if effectively wielded, do quite as much damage. It has been contended by Salvemini but denied by Ottokar that it is in this sense that we must interpret the tendency more frequently to levy the tax on real property, the common form of nobiliary wealth. Be that as it may, a measure much more indisputably aimed at the nobles was the law of August 6, 1289, which liberated the serfs on the estates throughout the Florentine dominion. But here, too, considerable caution is in place. Without doubt the liberation of the serfs had begun in Tuscany with the earliest appearance of the commune. The towns with their copious opportunities for getting on in the world exercised a subtle lure, to which so many serfs had responded that Dante, the scornful and aloof scholar and poet, was moved contemptuously to refer to the numerous additions to the Florentine population in his day as a vile peasant breed. To keep the agricultural laborers from abandoning the countryside in a solid mass, the lords themselves had been compelled to improve the lot of their dependents by conceding them a better tenure through a contractual relation. This usually took the form of owner and peasant sharing the wheat, wine, olive oil, and other products grown by the peasant at some agreed ratio. The arrangement, called *mezzeria,* is to this day the common form of agricultural production in Tuscany. To all intents and purposes it was gradually worked out in the age of the communes when the serfdom of the earlier, the feudal, age could no longer be maintained.

Conceding that the liberation of the serfs had been making headway from as far back as the eleventh century, especially in the areas close to the towns, we must not forget that in the less accessible upland regions there were still vast noble properties where serfdom was rigorously enforced. It was these more remote noblemen whom the liberation law of 1289 was intended to smite; but in order that no lord, near or far, should escape, the law in question was declared to apply to the whole Florentine jurisdiction. It may be that, since medieval enactments were rarely carried into prompt effect, there was still sporadic serfdom even after the new law was passed; but that serf-

---

[3] That the social-political situation during the crucial decade (1282-93) was very complicated is proved by the unusually divergent opinions regarding it of scholars and historians. Few periods of Florentine history have been more intensely studied. The fundamental archival publication is the work of A. Gherardi, *Le Consulte della Repubblica Fiorentina dell'anno 1280 al 1298.* 2 vols. Florence, 1898. The consulte are in effect the minutes of the various Florentine councils. See also: G. Salvemini, *Magnati e Popolani in Firenze dal 1280 al 1295.* Florence, 1899; Davidsohn, Vol. II[2], chaps. 9-10; Caggese, Vol. I, chaps. 6-7; N. Ottokar, *Il Comune di Firenze,* etc. This last work is a detailed study of the cross- and under-currents that churned the Florentine social and political waters in the period in question.

dom, already long before 1289 a moribund institution, moved thenceforward precipitately to its demise can no more be doubted than that its passing in Tuscany antedates by generations and even centuries its end in the countries north of the Alps.[4]

In this same critical decade (1282-92) the current of opinion did not always and in all respects run against the magnates. They were a warrior group who fought on horseback and made their value felt the moment the city became involved in active conflict. Since the end of the Suabian line, the whole land of Tuscany had, largely under Florentine guidance, become Guelph, and the peace of the province undoubtedly depended on maintaining the Guelph predominance. Notwithstanding that the once vigorous and enterprising Florentine Ghibellines had dwindled to a pale and innocuous remnant, there were still enough virile Ghibellines left in other Tuscan towns, such as Pisa and Arezzo, as well as among the upland nobility, to constitute a perpetual threat to the established Guelph ascendancy. This was made manifest when, in 1287, the Ghibelline group of Arezzo ejected their Guelph rivals from the city and appropriated the government. The Florentine Guelphs, desiring to help their Aretine brothers, immediately clamored for war; and the citizenry and the priors were sufficiently averse to seeing a Ghibelline outpost set up at the head of the Arno stream to be themselves infected with bellicose sentiments. War followed, during which, with the nobles enthusiastically serving their country, it would not have been a handsome procedure to enforce the special code enacted against them as though they were enemies. The Aretine war culminated in the battle of Campaldino, fought not far from Arezzo on June 11, 1289; and when the Florentines won a crushing victory, owing in large measure to the reckless charge of their cavalry, they could not hinder the nobles on their return from conducting themselves in the streets and public squares with a more brazen swagger than ever.

The war at the source of the Arno was followed by a war at its mouth against Pisa. Clinging more than any other town of Tuscany or even of Italy to its Ghibelline memories, Pisa needed only the example of Arezzo to persuade it to restore (1288) its Ghibelline government. At the same time it had the good sense to intrust its defense against the Guelphs, sure to resent this backsliding, to a great soldier, the Ghibelline nobleman, Guido of Montefeltro. The result was that when the Florentines, thinking to repeat their Aretine triumph, began a war against Pisa, they made no headway against the clever defensive tactics of their opponent. They returned to the assault in three successive campaigns and on the failure of the third campaign suffered the not unusual revulsion characteristic of democratic communities. They complained they had been drawn into an unnecessary war by their Guelph nobles, all sense of gratitude for the Campaldino victory disappeared, and the resentment they had so long been nursing against the arrogant brawlers in their midst erupted volcanically.

This is the plausible version rather than the documented certainty touching the fresh and decisive outburst against the magnates which occurred in the

---

[4] The interesting act of liberation is printed in Villari, *I Primi Due Secoli*, etc., Vol. I, pp. 268-70.

winter of 1292–93. Even now nothing might have been done, if the outraged people had not found a leader capable of giving effect to their angry sentiments. This was Giano della Bella, descendant of one of the most ancient families of the city and a member of the Calimala, the oldest and richest of the great trading gilds. Much has been conjectured about Giano, very little is securely known. As certain we may set down that, animated by hatred of his fellow-nobles, to many of whom he was bound by ties of blood, he resolved to spare no effort to put an end to their excesses. Recognizing that if his attack was to be successful, he would have to broaden the base of the democratic regime, he inaugurated his campaign by drawing the remaining gilds, which by a process of fusion were reduced to nine, into the existing system. These least important gilds, called arti minori, were, to name them by their leading members: (1) the retailers of wine; (2) the innkeepers; (3) the sellers of salt, oil, and cheese; (4) the tanners; (5) the armorers; (6) the ironworkers (other than blacksmiths); (7) the girdlemakers; (8) the woodworkers (other than carpenters); (9) the bakers. The nine were given a military organization, which was added to and incorporated in the already existent militia of the twelve greater gilds. Thus strengthened, the government launched a new attack upon the magnates of a far more uncompromising character than any that had yet taken place. It assumed the form of the promulgation on January 18, 1293, of the most famous act of Florentine constitutional history, the Ordinances of Justice.[5]

The early articles of the Ordinances of Justice are strictly constitutional in nature, for they are concerned with defining the outstanding features of the government, particularly the priors, the captain, their respective councils, and the political brotherhood of the twelve major gilds enlarged by the recent addition of the minor gilds to the number of nine. There follow the interesting regulations regarding the election of the priors and their fraternal living during their two months' term of office. An important addition to the six priors authorized by the Ordinances deserves particular attention. This addition was a seventh prior with the special designation of a gonfalonier or banner-bearer of Justice (*vexillifer justitiae, gonfaloniere della giustizia*). The function of the banner-bearer was to execute the sentences pronounced in the court of the podestà against the magnates and to this end he was assigned a force of one thousand men. This special force was required to assemble, properly armed, at the order of the gonfalonier and to follow his special banner of white silk conspicuously marked with a red cross whithersoever he carried it in execution of the podestà's judgment against an offending magnate.

By far the largest section of the Ordinances of Justice is concerned with the magnates (*magnati, grandi*), who furnished the immediate occasion for this sweeping constitutional document. It is notable and somewhat surprising that the older term "nobles" was in this law completely replaced by the newer word. The change may be taken to signify that by 1293 it had become well understood in Florence that the highest citizen group was no longer noble

[5] Published first by Bonaini, in *Arch. Stor. It.*, Nuova Serie, Vol. I, pp. 3 ff. A better edition, with the emendations of 1295, will be found in Salvemini, *Magnati e Popolani*, etc., pp. 384-432.

or feudal in the true sense of the word but merely a limited body of families whose wealth dated farther back than that of the growing mass of successful traders. In strict accord with human nature from the beginning of time the families of older wealth gave themselves feudal airs, cultivated horsemanship, practiced themselves in arms, and sought the honor of knighthood. It is this last-named distinction, knighthood, on which the law fastened when it came to drawing up the list of families who, designated as magnate, were to be put under special restraints and subjected to special penalties. We know, not from the Ordinances themselves but from another source, that on the strength of the knighthood provision not quite one hundred and fifty families of Florence and its county had the magnate or grande stigma put upon them. As each family was really a sum of related families, that is, a clan, it is difficult to estimate the number of individual males that may have been affected by the measure.[6] To put their number at a thousand would hardly seem to be an exaggeration.

Each male member of each family designated by the law as magnate was obliged to swear a special oath of obedience to the government of the priors and to give bond in the sum of two thousand librae that he would keep the peace. In case he failed to pay, his next of kin was liable, since the law laid down the principle of familial responsibility. If from the act of violence committed by the grande against the popolano death did not follow, the aggressor might be fined up to the total amount of the surety, depending on the gravity of the wound. In the case of death, however, the law knew no paltering. On the outrage being reported to the podestà, this official was obliged with the least possible delay to pronounce the death sentence against the offending magnate together with the confiscation of his goods and the destruction of his houses. At this point the banner-bearer of Justice and his special militia of one thousand men entered into action as executors of the sentence. Even more irksome to the magnates than these financial and social disabilities were the political disabilities imposed on them. They could not be elected to the priorate (Article III); they could not sit in the councils of the captain (Article XV); and, although they might continue to belong to a gild, they could not exercise authority within the gild by serving as consul or rector (Article XXXIV).

Although Giano della Bella did not sit in the priorate that passed the Ordinances of Justice, as the spiritual father and prime mover of the fuller democratic system with its special edge against the magnates, he was bound in honor to show his countrymen that the teeth he had put into this legislation were effective. He therefore had himself elected into the subsequent priorate which began its bimestrial term on February 15, 1293. As, in accordance with the requirements of the constitution, the six priors were distributed among the six wards or sesti in such a way that each sesto always boasted a prior from its territory, we learn on this occasion that Giano represented the sesto Porta San Piero, in which the houses of his family were located. A high-spirited, impulsive man, persuaded that it was his mission to bring jus-

---

[6] Salvemini, *Magnati e Popolani*, p. 376, gives the list of *town* magnates—seventy-two families in all.

tice to his city, he saw that the success of the reform hinged on making a good start; and when it was reported that a member of the Galli, a family inscribed under the requirements of the law on the roll of magnates, had murdered two Florentine commoners, he resolved on immediate action, even though the crime had taken place in distant France and the murderer himself could not be apprehended. The case was brought before the podestà who pronounced sentence according to the Ordinances. Thereupon, the new official, the gonfalonier of Justice, doubtless under pressure from the watchful Giano, had his bell sounded as the law prescribed, his guard of one thousand men streamed together before the residence of the priors, and with his banner of white silk marked with a red cross leading the way, the functionary specially appointed to deal with magnates marched upon the houses of the Galli. They lay along Por Santa Maria, one of the streets most densely crowded with the towers and houses of the old families. Under the direction of skilful masons the work of destruction was promptly taken in hand, while the banner-bearer and his militia maintained a sharp lookout against a possible diversion on the part of the outraged magnates, and the trumpeters of the commune added to the solemnity of the occasion by sounding their instruments as though the Day of Judgment had arrived.

The Day of Judgment for magnates. For thus had Giano della Bella and his following of commoners highly resolved. It remained to be seen whether the magnates took the same view of their impending doom and were prepared to give up the ghost without further struggle.

XII. A Tragic Interlude: The Blacks, the Whites, and Pope Boniface VIII

THE crisis precipitated in Florence by the Ordinances of Justice may, without doing violence to the facts, be dramatized as a duel between a tribune of the people and the order of patricians; but to understand the resolution of the crisis we must go beyond these simple terms. Giano della Bella's following consisted of the lesser gilds and the unorganized proletariat, an excitable mass which from the beginning of time has proved a most unreliable support. Undoubtedly, too, he had the backing of some of the upper gildsmen; but many members of this group openly, and even more of them secretly, took the view that the Ordinances bore too heavily on the magnates, who in their majority not only were merchants like themselves but were also actually associated with them in business. The leaders among Giano's merchant opponents were men of the soft-treading, vulpine type and, as masters of intrigue, were able to render invaluable assistance to their more forthright allies, the magnates, who, prompted by their feudal habits, were not averse to appealing to the sword. Finally, the character and role of Giano must not be overlooked. In the ungoverned pursuit of what was to him a great cause, he had become a demagogue; but he was not a wholehearted demagogue, for he had too many moral scruples and too much personal delicacy to identify himself with the mob in all its aspects and activities.

We are remarkably well informed about these hidden elements in the situation by one of the most spirited works of the whole range of Florentine historiography, the chronicle of Dino Compagni.[1] A member of one of the greater gilds, Dino was the type of the mounting trader instinctively hostile to merchants of an older date than himself who had the bad taste to play at being gentlemen of ancient lineage by the adoption of military customs. He could fairly regard himself as one of the founders of the new democratic government, for he had served as prior as early as 1282; and naturally when Providence deigned to give the plain people in Giano Della Bella a leader resolved to bridle the overbearing magnates, Dino, like the simple and honest soul he was, hailed him as a deliverer. In afteryears when, as a sequel to the Ordinances, Florence had gone through a painful agony and Dino himself had been politically snuffed out, he sat down to write his recollections. By that act he became the producer of a type of literature of which there were

[1] The standard edition is that of I. Del Lungo, *Dino Compagni e la sua Cronica.* 3 vols. Florence, 1879-80. For an evaluation of this work see Introduction.

as yet few, if any, examples. The unfamiliarity of the age with Dino's kind of document is proved by its having been passed on to us under the name of a chronicle, a traditional form to which it no longer bore any resemblance. Like all memoirs, those of Dino, owing to his reliance on the ever treacherous human memory, are crowded with innumerable errors of detail; nonetheless they disclose so many piquant and picturesque incidents that they constitute quite the most precious single source we have on the rise and fall of Giano della Bella and on the subsequent ferocious feud between the Blacks and the Whites. Present-day writers have been greatly encouraged to lean on Dino by the fact that the abundant documents recently brought to light have almost invariably confirmed the old merchant's veracity.

Having served as prior from February 15 to April 15, 1293, Giano della Bella became, in accordance with a requirement of his own Ordinances, ineligible for re-election to the priorate for two years. However, since he was now the head of the dominant party, his retirement from office did not interfere with his exercise of an indirect control. It was this continuing power that persuaded his enemies that the first step toward getting rid of the new system would be to get rid of him. Many of the magnates, as might be expected, favored an armed uprising. Apart, however, from its certain failure so long as the people presented a solid front, the upper class was so little united, owing to its interminable private feuds, that anything resembling a generally accepted plan of action was out of the question. It was therefore agreed to adopt a suggestion originating with a group of clever, intriguing lawyers. Associated from the start with the new regime as members of the gild of judges and notaries, the lawyers in the main had no patience with the recent democratic turn of events, and, like most of their kind throughout the ages, were animated with a strong conservative preference for inherited privileges and established wealth. As their chosen weapon was not the sword but the word as sharp as and sharper than the sword, they urged a whispering campaign against Giano which would picture him as a tyrant and fill one group after another with suspicion of his designs. It greatly helped their purpose that the tribune was an ardent spirit given to the habit of easing his mind by passionate outbursts against his opponents. By picking up these temperamental utterances and giving them a subterranean currency a definitely hostile atmosphere could be gradually created. All that would then be needed to explode the bomb was the spark supplied by some chance event.

Most appropriately, the needed happy accident was furnished by the most daring, picturesque, and uncompromising member of the class which the new fundamental law designated as magnates and enemies. Corso de' Donati had led the cavalry attack which smashed the Ghibellines at Campaldino in 1289. His consciousness of having deserved well of his country did not tend to reduce his class pretensions, which, deeply bred in the bone, had, even before Campaldino, brought him into repeated conflicts with the new social order. The average gildsman consistently regarded Corso as his enemy; the common people, on the other hand, were alternately for and against him. We owe to Dino a sharply etched vignette giving evidence that the lower orders were often carried away by the glamor emanating from Corso's ancient name and feudal bearing. For, says Dino, when, armed and mounted on his charger, Corso rode grandly through the streets, he was greeted on all hands with a spontaneous *Viva il Barone!*

Superfluously, one is tempted to say, but inevitably in view of his violent character, the head of the Donati family had involved himself in half a score of feuds with other magnate houses. It was these innumerable divisions among the grandi which hindered their effective union and greatly accelerated their decline. By this time, when the Ghibellines had practically vanished from the local scene, to avoid the threatening tedium of existence Guelphs had begun to quarrel with Guelphs and, not content with this new viciousness, a single Guelph family often fell into two implacable factions. Thus it was with the Donati. The swaggering Corso was not the man to regard a relative who had rebelled against his headship with a culpable leniency; and when, on a December day of the year 1294, he encountered his hostile cousin, Simone, in the streets, a fracas followed in which Corso wounded Simone and killed one of Simone's grooms. The case came under the Ordinances of Justice for the sole reason that the unfortunate groom was a popolano. At the hearing before the podestà, a foreigner and a knight as both law and custom demanded, the brazen Corso succeeded in presenting the incident in such a light that, although he was smitten with a money fine, it was not himself but his cousin who was condemned to loss of life and property as the guilty party. The sentence was pronounced on January 23, 1295; and no sooner did the report of it spread among the people whom the sensational trial had drawn in a dense mass to the gates of the podestà's palace than an outcry arose over this monstrous miscarriage of justice, ending in an uprising. By setting fire to the wooden doors of the grim stone fortress the mob forced an entrance into the interior. Only by swift and ignominious flight over the neighboring house roofs was the podestà able to save his life. The cheated victors vented their rage by plundering his residence from cellar to garret.

This orgy of popular lawlessness greatly shocked the instincts of the propertied classes and produced a sharp mental reaction. No sooner therefore was order restored than the priors were invited by the councils to institute an investigation in order to discover and punish the leading culprits. The inquiry disclosed that a brother of Giano della Bella's, Taldo by name, had taken a prominent part in inciting the people against the podestà. Giano himself had adopted exactly the opposite course. Mounting a horse, he had forced his way into the crowd to dissuade it from committing violence, but the maddened people had turned their spears against their erstwhile idol and had obliged him to desist. His spell had been broken and his enemies took heart. When, a few days later, the election of a new group of priors took place, his opponents dominated the situation and put in power a magistracy uncompromisingly hostile to his person and cause. On the very day (February 15, 1295) on which they took the oath of office, they ordered Giano's arrest on the impudently false charge that he had caused the recent public disorder. Dino Compagni, who loved his leader deeply but not uncritically, afterward declared that in his opinion the champion of the people should have met the challenge by one last effort to rally his followers about him. Giano was of another mind, perhaps because of disgust with the fickle populace he had so wholeheartedly served. He decided to leave the country, and the government, happy to bring the issue to a close without a trial of strength, threw no difficulties in his way. But as soon as he was well out of reach, in accordance with that bitter irony which has rung down the curtain on the career of so many public men, he was condemned under his own Ordinances of Justice to loss of life and goods. He retired to France, where he continued to live for more than a decade, a true Florentine to the end, for he attempted to recoup his shattered fortunes by a fresh trading venture.

On Giano's disappearance from the scene, Corso Donati and his magnate following imagined it would be an easy thing to dispose of the Ordinances. But they were mistaken. When in the summer of this same year they tried a sudden rising, they encountered so vigorous a resistance on the part of a united people that they were obliged to resort to negotiations. Undeniably, however, they prospered in these more than they had reason to expect because of their secret friends in the government. While they agreed once again to submit to the Ordinances, which thus triumphed as the law of the land, they were accorded a few mitigations, of which one at least was not unimportant. The original requirement regarding eligibility to the chief magistracy had been that the priors must be chosen from such gildsmen as actively exercised their profession (*de artificibus continue artem exercentibus*). After the revision of July 6, 1295, all persons carried on the gild rolls were eligible, regardless of whether they were actively engaged in the business of the gild or not. This opened a way for such members of the old families as chose to give up their feudal habits to be absorbed into full citizen fellowship. However, the central and essential article of the Ordinances, excluding from the priorate and the various institutions that had arisen with the priorate all families, any individual member of which had acquired the honor of knighthood, remained untouched by the revision.[2]

On the heel of the foiled magnate uprising of the summer of 1295 a new difference appeared among the great houses which, by spreading gradually to the other classes, ended in a rupture culminating in a fresh set of devastating calamities. Ever since Corso Donati had raised his head as a spokesman of the magnates a close neighbor of his of the Porta San Piero quarter, Vieri de' Cerchi, had put forth pretensions of his own to magnate leadership and had gained a considerable following. Vieri, too, was a knight who on the field of Campaldino had ridden furiously into action. However, his knighthood was only a garment for festival wear, for he was the richest and shrewdest banker of his day and the head of the most flourishing trading company of the city. This immersion in business invited the scorn of Corso Donati who, as the representative of an older, prouder, but impoverished family, was bent on presenting himself to view exclusively in the role of a great baron. The opposed interests and attitudes of the two men had produced nothing worse than back-biting and ridicule until the renewed acceptance of the Ordinances forced on the magnates in 1295. With that date a political divergence made its appearance over the policy by which the magnate interest would hence-

---

[2] Article III. Salvemini, *Magnati e Popolani*, p. 390.

forth be best served. Vieri, the banker, intimately linked with all the far-flung business of the town and exercising an indefinable influence among all the merchant gilds, made up his mind that the time had come to give up the struggle against the Ordinances. The people regarded them as their Bill of Rights and, fickle though they might be in other matters, flew to arms the moment this palladium of their liberty was threatened. Moreover, the movement within the government since the fall of Giano della Bella showed that, with the lower orders deprived of a leader, political authority had slipped back into the hands of the lawyers and merchants of the arti maggiori. Of these, the head of the great banking house of the Cerchi was the intimate associate, and among them he could hope, even though as a knight he was excluded from the priorate, to exercise a commanding influence. A not inconsiderable number of magnates, who, though magnates, were also business men, fell in with these views and, joining themselves to Vieri, created a Cerchi party. To the intransigent Corso such conciliatory action was no better than treason. When his fellow-irreconcilables gathered under his banner, he found himself at the head of a rival party of the Donati. True, the two parties were loose political rings rather than parties in a modern sense, but they represented a definite split among the magnates with ramifications reaching far down into the people. Above all, the split signified a division among the dominant Guelphs and this undoubtedly held a threat for the continued Guelph character of the city.

The invaluable Dino affords us vivid glimpses of how the Guelph feud developed amidst an atmosphere of constantly increasing tension. The following scene befell on December 16, 1296, although Dino does not say so, since, as a rambling memoirist, he has a mind elevated above dates.[3]

One day many citizens came together in the Piazza de' Frescobaldi to assist at the funeral of a woman, it being the custom of the country on such occasions for the men of title to sit on wooden benches, while the simple citizens sat on the ground on straw mats. [This was the usual form of mourning among well-to-do Florentines. While the men honored the dead acquaintance by solemnly gathering in the manner here described, the women, gathered around the corpse in an inner room, demonstrated their sorrow by loud weeping.] With the Cerchi partisans on one side and the Donati partisans on the other, someone stood up either to smooth out his garment or for some other reason. At once, from suspicion, those of the opposite party stood up and laid hand to their swords. Their opponents did the same and blows fell. The neutrals who were present interposed and stopped the fight. Notwithstanding, many people rushed to the houses of the Cerchi, demanding to be led against the Donati; but the Cerchi refused.[4]

Still further to enlighten us touching the charged atmosphere, Dino follows this episode with another, which probably befell in the ensuing year, although the careless author again vouchsafes us no date. The story introduces us to Guido Cavalcanti, poet and friend of Dante Alighieri. The Italian title "messer" is the equivalent of the Latin "dominus" and was reserved for the highest social order, the knights and judges.

[3] Davidsohn, Vol. III, p. 27, supplies the date from another source.
[4] This and the following episode in the Del Lungo edition, pp. 88-92.

There was a noble young knight, Guido by name, son of messer Cavalcante Caval-canti. He was courteous and brave but contemptuous of the common people and given to solitude and study. He was an enemy of messer Corso and had repeatedly attempted to do him an injury. Messer Corso feared him greatly because of his intrepid spirit; and once, while Guido was on pilgrimage to Santiago de Compostella, Corso plotted to have him assassinated. But the attempt failed. On which account, having on his return to Florence heard of the plot, he incited many youths against Corso, pledging them to come to his aid. And being one day in company with some youths of the house of Cerchi mounted and with javelin in hand, he spurred his horse against messer Corso, trusting he would be followed by the Cerchi. . . . And as he rode past Corso he threw his javelin and missed. With messer Corso at the time were Simone, his son, a brave and powerful youth, and Cecchino de' Bardi, and many others, all armed with swords. And they pursued Guido but, unable to reach him, threw stones at him. And from the windows stones were thrown so that Guido was wounded in the hand.

It must have been becoming harder and harder for the government of the priors to maintain the peace between the two inflamed factions. Secretly the rulers leaned toward the Cerchi because the Cerchi had accepted the situation; but this only made the Donati more implacable. Nor were these latter without weighty support of their own. As the temper of the official organization of the Guelphs, the parte Guelfa, was uncompromisingly aristocratic, it did not hesitate to throw its considerable influence into the scales on the Donati side. Besides, the resourceful, turbulent Corso was a host in himself. In the winter of 1298–99 he even managed by means that remain unrevealed to acquire a dominant influence in the government. At any rate the appearances favor this view, for he succeeded in having a podestà elected who, when he arrived in Florence, regarded himself as Corso's personal agent. He was messer Monfiorito da Coderta, a native of Treviso and of course a knight. Possibly it was his class feeling which explains his friendship with Corso and which led him to commit an act of outrageous malfeasance. In a civil suit brought by Corso against his mother-in-law the obliging podestà went the partisan length of condemning the defendant to the loss of all her property. So monstrous was the sentence and so general the indignation over it that messer Monfiorito was arrested, deprived of office, and assessed a fantastic fine. And, once aroused, the public wrath was not appeased till the insolent Corso, who had so manifestly tampered with the leading official of the state, was himself brought to justice. He was smitten with a heavy money penalty and sent into exile (May, 1299). The unscrupulous magnate had overplayed his hand and had lost.

The elimination of their leader so weakened the Donati that the Cerchi gained an unchallenged ascendancy in the town. The government continued as before to rest with the priors and the gilds, but the appointment to office fell more and more in accordance with the wishes of an inner ring made up of the Cerchi and their friends. While the mass of the Florentines accepted this turn of affairs, at least for the time being, the Donati, their banished leader, and the allied parte Guelfa had thoughts only of restitution and revenge and searched the sky in every direction for a helper. They found him in the pope, who in point of fact had already for so long a time been pondering interference that he did not have to be importuned to be induced to act.

The pope who now thrust himself as a leading character into the Florentine drama was Boniface VIII, one of the most eminent and problematical, though certainly not one of the worthiest, successors of the Apostle Peter. Boniface was elected to the papacy in December, 1294, after having gained a wide experience in the varied business of the church. Like so many of his greatest predecessors, he was by both temperament and education a canon lawyer and, thus equipped, became the exponent of the most extravagant claims of the ecclesiastical jurists. If, as was freely whispered among his countrymen, he did not believe in the immortality of the soul, it might be argued that, in rejecting this central tenet of Christianity, he had removed himself, in an ideal sense, from the Christian fold. On the other hand, we should not forget that the Christian fold had long ago been institutionalized as a church, and that for Pope Boniface to play his magnificent part it was much less important for him to be a true believer than a strict and energetic churchman. It was certainly as a churchman that he has established his place in history, for his name is forever associated with the culmination of the papal claims to world-control. The early medieval view that the rule of Christendom was to be shared equally between pope and emperor had gradually, under the strain of conflict, been replaced by the doctrine of papal supremacy. Certainly it is difficult to see how the position taken by such vigorous authoritarians as Gregory VII and Innocent III can be interpreted other than as outright abandonment of the original balanced dualism. When Boniface VIII in his turn faced the problem, he cannot be said to have done more than give the Gregorian theory of the relation of church and state a more precise and ringing formulation than it had yet received. His declarations were absolutely uncompromising and left not the least doubt that he regarded emperors, kings, and princes throughout the Christian world as holding their positions subject to his good pleasure. The pope derived his power from God, but the heads of states derived their power from the pope.

While it is not permissible even to mention Boniface VIII without indicating his eminence in the field of politico-ecclesiastical theory, his importance for Florence derives much less from his papal than from his personal ambitions. To be sure, he took toward the Florentine government the attitude imposed by his view of papal supremacy. That meant, as regards the ruling clique identified with the Cerchi, that they must do the papal bidding or suffer the consequences. However, he was principally moved in regard to the Cerchi by a consideration of a more personal sort, which was to subject Florence and, together with Florence, Tuscany to himself in order to hand them over to one of his relatives. For—and now we are touching on a side of his character hardly less important than his unswerving canonical dogmatism—Boniface VIII was a ferocious nepotist. In this respect, too, he cannot be said to have been an innovator. Almost from the earliest days of their great office, occasional incumbents of St. Peter's chair had yielded to the temptation of using their power to advance the fortunes of their families.

The great feudal clans of Rome, the Colonna, the Orsini, the Savelli, owed their vast wealth and historical status exclusively to this evil practice. If we now remind ourselves that Boniface VIII belonged to a lesser clan of the Roman Campagna, the Caetani, and that throughout his early life he had been exposed to the slights of the greater lords, we have no difficulty in understanding that from the moment he commanded the unbounded resources of the papacy he resolved to use them to raise the Caetani to a level with the oldest and most powerful barons of the capital.

The procedure most commonly followed by the popes to enrich their relatives was to endow them with manorial properties within the papal state. While Boniface adopted this measure, and that, too, with such characteristic legal thoroughness that the Caetani are to this day the lords of the largest aggregate of lands in central Italy, he followed also another course, which may have been suggested to him by Nicholas III. In this pope we meet another Roman magnate, a member of the Orsini clan. Animated with all the characteristic Roman ambitions, Nicholas, as has been noted in the previous chapter, had taken advantage of the enfeebled empire to induce Rudolph of Hapsburg to make over to him the province called the Romagna. The ultimate purpose of Nicholas had been to endow one of his nephews with the Romagna, and only his premature death had kept him from carrying out the plan. To Boniface VIII it seemed that Albert, son and successor of the accommodating Rudolph, might with equal ease be persuaded to repeat Rudolph's act of self-denial by surrendering to the head of Christendom another portion of his Italian kingdom, the province of Tuscany. He, Boniface, might then enfeoff with it some member of his family to help magnify the Caetani name.[5]

This analysis of Boniface's motives will serve to explain the disastrous role he came to play in Florentine affairs beginning with the assumption of power by the Cerchi faction. If this ruling junta had been willing to submit to his orders, it is quite unlikely that Boniface would ever have quarreled with it. But his orders, based on the view that the Donati were sound Guelphs and deeply devoted to his person, consistently ran to the effect that the Cerchi were to make peace with the Donati and share with them the offices and honors. And this the Cerchi refused to do, for selfish reasons in the first place, but also because they had become perfectly clear in their minds that the pope planned to use the Donati as his means of acquiring personal control of the city. In resisting the pope they were therefore following the policy which was as old as the Florentine commune, and which regarded independence as more precious than life. They twisted and turned, like the crafty democratic politicians they were; they protested their eternal devotion to his Holiness; but his bidding they would not do, conscious that in defending Florence against a planned papal encroachment they were doing their patriotic duty in accordance with the hopes and prayers of the vast majority of their fellow-citizens.

To a man of so autocratic a temper as Boniface the instinctive response to a rebuff is an appeal to force. And Boniface might have resorted to force at

---

[5] G. Levi, *Bonifazio VIII e le sue Relazioni col Comune di Firenze*. Rome, 1882. This author was the first to disclose Boniface's Tuscan ambitions. In their light the pope's resolve to subdue Florence, the capital of Tuscany, to his will becomes much more intelligible.

once, had it not been that when the Florentine deadlock occurred the Christian world had arrived at the turn of the century. For the year 1300 the pope had proclaimed a great Catholic Jubilee to be celebrated in the city of Rome; and if the capital of Christendom was to be visited by the expected masses of pilgrims on horse and on foot from all over the world, it was absolutely necessary that the highways of Italy should not ring with the shrill alarms of war. In order to further the Jubilee, Boniface was therefore willing to adjourn his reckoning with Florence. And when, amidst conditions of unusual peacefulness, the great festival occurred, it carried his self-esteem to its acme. It was estimated that 200,000 people visited Rome to pray at the shrines of the martyrs and to receive the papal blessing; and Boniface, a man in many respects more pagan than Christian, again and again presented himself to the pilgrim multitudes enthroned majestically above them and inhaling their adulation like a rich incense.

There was therefore peace between Florence and the pope in the year 1300. But at Florence itself it was a peace electrically charged. Aware that the pope was on their side, the Donati faction never ceased to annoy their antagonists in the seats of power. On May Day, when the city was in the habit of celebrating the return of spring with feasting in the homes and dancing and merry-making in the streets and public squares, a group of Donati youths wantonly attacked a company of the Cerchi assembled to watch a group of girls delicately treading a measure on the Piazza Santa Trinità. In a moment there was an uproar, but before the combatants could be separated the young Ricoverino de' Cerchi had suffered the shocking indignity of having his nose cut off by a Donati sword. Other similar clashes kept the city at a feverish temperature, informing all who were not deaf and blind that the Roman Jove had suspended but not cancelled his wrath. Indeed it was public knowledge that he was busily preparing a military expedition to break the stubborn Florentine resistance to his will.

In order to understand the new turn of the papal policy, we shall have to take note of still another of the varied activities of the restless pontiff. He had hardly been elevated to power when he spurred his Angevin protégé, King Charles II, to renew his efforts to conquer the island of Sicily; and to prove his sincerity he lavishly provided Charles with subsidies in support of naval and military forces assembled to drive out the Aragonese usurper. When these mighty efforts had proved vain, the undiscouraged Boniface evolved a fresh plan which looked to the king of France for help. This was Philip IV, called the Fair, the only man in the contemporary world who in bold self-esteem and frenzied ambition might be called a fit match for the pope. Their sharp tempers had already clashed over the king's attempt to tax the French clergy in the interest of the royal purse. Pope Boniface had promptly interposed his veto but, with so many other quarrels on his hands, he had adjourned the issue by agreeing to a provisional settlement. When, in the year 1299, he approached Philip with the project to lend a hand in the conquest of Sicily, he hoped the flattery of the invitation would not be lost on the king. Specifically, he requested that Philip send his brother, Charles of Valois, to Rome with a band of French knights to serve as the nucleus of an army to be recruited at the

expense of the pope and to be sent to Sicily to end at last the struggle which
had now been going on for twenty years. The bargain was struck and the coming of Charles of Valois fixed for the summer of the year after the peaceful
Jubilee. It was the subjugation of the Sicilians for which the French prince
was engaged; but by way of curtain-raiser Boniface planned, as soon as he
would have his agent under his hand at Rome, to send him to Florence to
settle the score with the recalcitrant Cerchi.

All this was so well known on the Arno that there was no doubt in the
minds of the ruling group that in the year 1301 they would have to fight for
their existence. It is this consciousness which accounts for the action the Cerchi
now took in regard to Pistoia. This nearby town had for many years been
riven with a local strife of so terrible a character that one is at a loss to account
for it except on the ancient Greek theory that whom the gods wish to destroy
they first make mad. The struggle had its origin in a division of the leading
local family, the Cancellieri, into two camps, the White Cancellieri and the
Black Cancellieri. By degrees the quarrel had spread like an insidious contagion to the whole population which, with every man's hand against his
brother, was threatened with extermination. In the year 1296 the government
of Florence interfered, assumed supreme control over Pistoia for five years
and, by dividing the offices equally between the Whites and the Blacks, and
at the same time by enforcing order, established a precarious truce. In the
spring of 1301 the Cerchi faction, peering anxiously into the future, became
alarmed by the thought that the expiration of the Florentine control over
Pistoia exactly synchronized with the prospective struggle for independence
with the pope. Should the Florentines surrender control over Pistoia, and
should this town then put itself under the protection of the curia, Florence
would, in a military sense, be greatly imperiled. On this account the Cerchi
staked their safety on a very dangerous plan. They conspired with the stronger,
or at least the better disposed faction of the Pistoiese, the Whites, and with the
aid of these allies and amidst a renewal of the horrible local atrocities, in
May, 1301, drove the leading Blacks from the city. It was this identification
of the Cerchi with the Pistoiese Whites which led to their having the label of
"Whites" now applied to themselves; and naturally with the betrayed Pistoiese
Blacks calling desperately to the Donati for help, this Florentine party came
soon to be known as "Blacks." Although it was never forgotten in Florence
that the new civil struggle with which the city was tormented originated in a
conflict of opinion between the families of the Donati and the Cerchi, beginning with the summer of the year 1301 the old party names were completely
superseded by the newer and more colorful designations borrowed from
Pistoia.

The only possible way in which the Cerchi could have justified their monstrous breach of faith toward Pistoia would have been to make it appear as
the inaugural act of an energetic struggle for independence against a power-
maddened pope. But that is precisely what they failed to do. After the wholly
isolated act of daring connected with Pistoia, the Cerchi or, as we shall call
them henceforward, the Whites, were smitten with complete paralysis. In the
late summer, in accordance with the bargain struck with Pope Boniface,

Charles of Valois reported at Rome with a small force of French knights, and again, exactly as had been planned and generally foreseen, the pope, before sending him off to conquer Sicily, dispatched him to Tuscany to bring the Whites to heel. Agreeing that the Whites, if they stood for anything, stood for the freedom of their city, we are bound to declare that they made as despicable a defense as any recorded in history of a cause which men have universally acclaimed as noble. The miserable truth is that the leading Whites were in the main prosperous merchants who had no stomach for the grinding realities of war. At their head was Vieri de' Cerchi, the great banker, and Vieri's financial interests made him pitifully tremulous for the safety of his investments. When, in moments of danger, feebleness sits at the helm, discouragement quickly masters passengers and crew, and Vieri's timidity was not long in communicating itself to the priors and the other governing bodies. They seized on the idea that the French wolf advancing against them was possibly no wolf at all. They even encouraged one another to view him as a lamb, and to fortify their willing credulity lent an eager ear to the prince's ambassadors who announced that their lord was coming with the single object of making peace among the citizens. Peace! In their terror they fastened on this fiction, although at the bottom of their hearts they knew with absolute certainty that the mission of the scion of the house of Valois was to depose the Whites and put the Blacks in power. Tremulously the priors receded from position after position, until on November 1, 1301, the papal forces of less than a thousand men rode through the southern gate without having flung at them so much as a hostile cry. The central figure of the military pageant of that fatal day was the contemptible French prince and executioner, whom the most famous of his Florentine victims did not fail duly to gibbet in his great poem. He pictured Charles of Valois riding into Florence not with the loyal weapons of a *preux chevalier,* but "armed with the lance that Judas swung." [6]

Solely because of this victim, the austere thinker and unrivaled poet, Dante Alighieri, the revolution precipitated by the coming of the French prince has induced so thoroughgoing an investigation of every scrap of the surviving evidence that we are exceptionally well informed about the tragic incidents following the occupation of the city by the Franco-papal army.[7] The poet was a member of an ancient Florentine family which, though noble, had never been particularly conspicuous and which in its recent representatives had consistently aligned itself with the Guelphs. Seventeen years old when the priorate was established in 1282, Dante enjoyed the advantage of having to adjust himself to the democratic victory while he was still undeveloped and flexible. There can be no doubt that the young man made his peace with the new system, for, in sign of his acceptance of it, he joined the gild of the *Medici e Speziali.* Membership in a gild, it will be remembered, was the prerequisite for the enjoyment of political rights. However, to be carried on a gild roll did not

---

[6] *Purgatorio,* XX, 74.

[7] The first modern presentation by Del Lungo (in Vol. I of his edition of Dino Compagni) was followed by numerous studies dealing with special aspects of the event and crowned by a searching recapitulation by Davidsohn, Vol. III, chap. I; *Forschungen,* Vol. III, p. 2 ("Die Schwarzen und die Weissen"); *Forschungen,* Vol. IV, pp. 259-68.

necessarily signify (after 1295) that the member actively exercised the occupation the gild in question denoted, and Dante of course has never been suspected by anyone of being either a physician or an apothecary.[8] He was a scholar, poet, and gentleman of leisure who, like his forebears, derived his living from a modest property. In spite of his eligibility to public office, he did no more than occasionally participate in politics till the independence of his beloved city was threatened by Pope Boniface. Then, with a quick decision, he took his stand with the Whites. By serving as a prior in the June 15 to August 15 period of the year 1300, when the Cerchi were in full control, he made himself forever hateful to the Blacks. His attitude in the following year to the pressing problem of how to meet the papal force advancing under Charles of Valois is not revealed by any document. If we strongly incline to free him from responsibility for the course pursued, it is first, because he did not sit in the inner ring of the ruling merchant group, and second, because his upright and energetic nature presents the strongest possible contrast to the cowardly evasion consistently practiced in that year by his party affiliates.

The story of the White disaster and the Black triumph is told by Dino, himself a leading White, with such strong feeling and such touches of vivid detail that in his pages the past again becomes alive for the moved reader. As it would be foolhardy to attempt to compete with the chronicler's simple and instinctive art, the present writer will content himself with an unadorned record of the catastrophe which overwhelmed the city. When, after prolonged parleys, Charles of Valois was permitted to enter the gates, he took a solemn engagement to assume the part of peacemaker (*paciarius*) and not forcibly to change the government. Of course he broke his word, thereby demonstrating not only to Dante but to the whole world that he boasted the name but not the honor of a knight. Four days after the French force had occupied the town and at nightfall of the very day on which the prince renewed in a particularly solemn form his oath to uphold the civil order, Corso Donati with a handful of followers appeared under the walls of Florence and in the early dawn forced an entrance at one of the gates. Sentenced to exile over two years before, he had by leaving his place of banishment, automatically become a rebel, condemned, as the phrase ran, in goods and person (*in avere e persona*). If the outlawed magnate now ventured violently to repossess himself of his native city, it was for the single reason that he enjoyed the special protection of the pope and had been privately assured of the support of the pope's Florentine representative. Nothing short of this assumption will explain the effrontery with which, once within the walls, he regarded the town as his prize. Rallying his Black intimates, he went the rounds seeking out his personal enemies and sacking their houses. To increase the confusion and terror he opened the prisons and incited the delivered criminals to make the most of their freedom. Next, he descended on and drove from their respective residences the priors and the podestà. And finally, to crown his iniquitous labors,

[8] He appears on the roster of the gild in 1297 in the following form: Dante d'Aldighieri degli Aldighieri, poeta Fiorentino. C. Fiorelli, "Dipintori a Firenze nell'Arte dei Medici, Speziali, e Merciai." *Arch. Stor. It.*, Vol. II, 1920, p. 7.

he set up a podestà obedient to his will and inducted into office a group of hand-picked priors of proved Black faith.

For five terrible days following Corso Donati's vengeful return the town was given over to plunder, arson, and violence. Unless the defeated Whites inhabited impregnable towers, they were made the helpless victims of every imaginable outrage. Their warehouses were looted, their women abused, their children captured and held to ransom. At last the papal peacemaker bestirred himself to put an end to the disorders. The pope, too, tried to make himself heard above the din in the interests of that accommodation between the two warring Guelph factions which he had always advocated. Far-seeing statesman that he was, he wanted a united Guelph Florence and not a Black Guelph ascendancy of so relentless a character that the White Guelphs would either leave the city of their own free will or else be driven out in a solid mass. In either event they would have no choice but to join the Ghibellines, thereby greatly raising the fortunes of this anti-papal party throughout Tuscany.

Under strict papal orders the Valois prince tried to temper the victory of the Blacks and to issue to the Whites the necessary guaranties of safety. It was too late. His plan, so often tried before, to appease the passions by a formal reconciliation of the leading families miscarried; and when the Blacks insisted that nothing short of their appropriating to themselves the undivided fruits of victory would assure the Guelph triumph, the Frenchman abandoned an opposition which had never been other than perfunctory. The new plan of Corso and his partisans was to resume the destruction of their enemies under the cloak of the law. In seizing the power after driving the Whites from office they had not changed the constitution; they had not even abrogated the Ordinances of Justice. With good Black Guelphs in all the leading positions it was not necessary to abolish this hated legislation, for the accommodating Black priors would see to it that it was not enforced. By summoning the Whites before a Florentine court manned by a Black podestà, the victors could demonstrate to the pope, and to all the world besides, that they were lovers and practicers of "justice," while at the same time they would resume the pleasant, momentarily interrupted game of annihilating their enemies.

The new plan was inaugurated on January 18, 1302, by a summons issued to a group of Whites to appear for trial. Fresh lists followed at short intervals and showed that it was the intention of the victors to let no leading enemy escape. As the defendants entertained no illusion as to what was in store for them, most of them saved their lives by flight. This served as an excuse to declare them in contumacy and to condemn them in a sweeping sentence to loss of life and property. An examination of the lists of the proscribed makes plain that the leaders of the Blacks vengefully resolved that no citizen who had served as a White prior or who in some other official capacity had identified himself with the White government should go unpunished. It was because of his priorate in the summer of 1300 that his fate now overtook Dante. Summoned to trial by an order of January 27, 1302, he left the city, whereupon a new decree of March 10 condemned him with a roster of thirteen other victims to death by fire. The sentence, which, if executed, would have extinguished as though he had been a common felon one of the most luminous spirits of all the ages, has prompted the hearts of later generations to deep indignation. The sentiment will be shared with particular vivacity by the readers and lovers of his great epic; and yet to this same group another thought is unescapable. Dante became a wanderer on the face of the earth and suffered every grief and hardship to which man is heir. Without this racking experience and the accompanying single-minded dedication of himself to the poetic mission in which he sought oblivion for his loss of ease, family, friends, and country, he would never have risen to the intense vision which endowed our western culture with the unique splendor of the Divine Comedy.[9]

Throughout the year 1302 an organized reign of terror, which reached its greatest intensity after the month of April, held Florence in its grip. It was in April that Charles of Valois finally took his departure, and his going marks an intensification of Black persecution because his presence had, after all, imposed a measure of restraint upon the victors. In the course of this year two successive podestàs pronounced five hundred and fifty-nine death sentences by either hanging, decapitation, or the fagot. If in their vast majority the verdicts were not executed, it was only because, like Dante, the intended victims had saved themselves by flight. The names of the condemned, preserved by the documents, summon before us no more than a long file of pallid ghosts. As we let our eye glance over the list of what must have been the leading citizens of Florence, our attention, if we except one immortal name, is likely to be caught by just one other, that of ser Petracco. The title "ser" indicates a notary, and the notary in question had made himself obnoxious by serving the White regime as a governmental secretary. Two years after his condemnation he was living as an exile at Arezzo, where he begot a son, Francesco, who afterward changed his family name to Petrarca as having a more pleasing sound. The linking through the medium of a common death sentence of the two men hailed as the supreme poets of the Italian people is an arresting caprice of blindly groping Chance.

In addition to the almost six hundred citizens sentenced to death, other hundreds were sent into confino throughout the length and breadth of the peninsula. As such exiles were usually ruined in health and fortune, their lot can hardly have been happier than that of those who, as rebels, had been smitten with the sterner verdict. In the eyes of the triumphant Blacks all White Guelphs alike had become Ghibellines, and it was by this argument that Corso and his followers justified their ferocious proceeding.

Designated and condemned as Ghibellines, the defeated Whites played into the hands of their enemies. For though it would be difficult to indicate any other course they might have followed, on being driven from Florence they made their way to such Ghibelline centers as Arezzo, Pisa, and Pistoia, which joyfully bade them welcome. There, uniting with their former enemies, they became before long completely fused with them. Like them they

[9] In connection with Dante's condemnation it is proper to point out that the house, hard by the little church of San Martino and commonly accepted as his birthplace, cannot have been his, since in virtue of the sentence pronounced against him his house was destroyed. Undeniably, however, the existing structure, erected in the fourteenth century, occupies the *site* of a house of the Alighieri family. See the impressive demonstration of Davidsohn, Vol. III, pp. 198-99.

spent their days dreaming of the revenge which would be theirs, should they ever return to power. The consequence for Tuscany of the White exodus was therefore a new war of Guelphs and Ghibellines, which owed much of its vigor to the initiative of the latest converts to Ghibellinism, the Whites. Fortune on the whole favored the Blacks; or, to resort to a more human judgment, the lack of manly resolution characteristic of the Whites continued to tell against them. They found their mainstay in the great Ghibelline families of the upper Arno, such as the Ubertini and the Pazzi—the latter not to be confused with the urban family of the same name—but these fine lords were naturally more interested in their own welfare than in that of their needy and often troublesome guests. More than once the new allies launched an attack which carried them to the very walls of Florence, but they were pursued by ill luck and at the last moment something regularly went wrong.

Throughout his first year of exile Dante, who, like his humble friend, ser Petracco, had taken refuge in Arezzo, abode with the militant Whites. Then, disgusted with the wrangling and incompetence served up to him as a daily spectacle, he withdrew from their company and, as he put it proudly in his poem, formed a party by himself (*averti fatta parte per te stesso. Paradiso,* XVII, 69). Thenceforward we may think of Dante as a convinced, theoretical Ghibelline, but divorced both in flesh and spirit from the many successive plots of the Whites and their Ghibelline allies to reconquer Florence by force of arms. To follow the activities of the group he deserted is to share in his contempt for their meager endowment with decisive gifts of heart and brain. We suffer no loss by dispensing ourselves from tracing their repeated futile assaults on this and that military position of the Blacks. Suffice it that the latter maintained the advantage they had won and continued to hold the City of the Red Lily in the hollow of their hand.

The unqualified supremacy of the Florentine Blacks—such was the net result of the interference of Pope Boniface. It was a conclusion far removed from his original purpose, for Boniface, as has been said repeatedly, schemed to bring the city under his own control, and when, on that November day of the year 1301, Charles of Valois, acting as his agent, entered the city gate, the pope must have thought that the game was won. In reality it was already lost, though no contemporary, however sharp-witted, would have ventured to assert as much on that day of the apparent papal triumph. Yet, before two more years had passed, the whole world reverberated not only with the relatively unimportant matter of Boniface's failure to acquire Florence and Tuscany, but with a papal overthrow so enormous that to his innumerable impassioned enemies at least it was comparable only to the fall of Lucifer.

Because the catastrophe of Boniface, though belonging to the general history of the occident, bears also directly on the fortunes of Florence, we are not permitted to neglect it. Its fated instrument was that self-willed Philip IV of France, with whom Pope Boniface, almost from the beginning of his reign, had developed differences of opinion regarding the royal claim to tax the clergy and whom, with a blind worship of his own superior acumen and authority, he imagined he need not fear. It must have been this sense of an inviolable security that moved him to solicit the aid of Philip's brother,

Charles, for the realization of his Italian plans, even while refusing to abate a jot or tittle of his assertions regarding the immunity of the church from secular control and the ultimate subjection of all civil sovereigns to himself. Thus it came about that the military activity in Italy, with which the Valois prince was charged, went on side by side with the development of the acrimonious ecclesiastical controversy between Boniface and the Valois prince's brother, and that at the precise moment when one member of the house of Capet triumphed at Florence, the conflict with another and greater Capet entered a final bitter phase. No more than a short month after the Arno city had been captured the pope issued the bull, *Ausculta Fili Carissime,* in which he affronted his royal opponent past every chance of reconciliation by categorically asserting his subjection to St. Peter's chair.

Here in its essence, if not in its details, was the issue back again which had rocked the occident to its foundations in the days of the Hohenstaufen emperors! But the world had moved on to new thoughts and sentiments since that time. A succession of venal and worldly popes had put Rome under a cloud; and the development of the royal authority in France had concentrated in a single hand the strength of a great people firmly resolved to be a nation. Philip did not hesitate therefore to defend his crown. He boldly burned the obnoxious bull and, on summoning the three estates of his realm, had the satisfaction of seeing them range themselves unanimously behind him. Popular support of such energy had never cheered the emperors in their earlier struggle with the papacy. Indeed it was because both their German and Italian subjects had preponderantly sided with the spiritual power that the sovereigns from Henry IV to Frederick II had practically without exception gone down in defeat. A nation united behind its monarch against the claim of priestly control of its secular concerns was a novelty on the European stage and provided the French ruler with an invulnerable armor.

Unconcerned with the details of the clamorous conflict between Philip and Boniface, we shall pay attention only to a few central and decisive circumstances. An almost immediate effect of the intensification of the struggle was that the pontiff dropped his ambitions with regard to Florence and Tuscany. For, overconfident though he was by temperament, he did not fail to recognize, as soon as Philip had committed the *Ausculta* bull to the flames, that he now had so crucial a controversy on his hands that for its sake he would have to sacrifice every minor interest he had been pursuing. He did not at once break with Philip's brother. With the Florentine mission brought to a conclusion, the papal impresario ordered the French prince to proceed with the Sicilian campaign, the original purpose of his descent into Italy. Accordingly, in the spring of 1302 Charles of Valois abandoned Florence and conducted an invasion of the contested island from which he reaped no honor. After a brief struggle with the Aragonese incumbent, against the express wishes of the pope he brought the war to a close with an ignominious treaty. Thereupon beating a hasty retreat to the mainland, he continued his northward march without interruption until, before the year was over, he had recrossed the Alps and stood again on French soil. Doubtless even Boniface was glad to see the last of this shifty and unimpressive champion of the papal interests in

Italy. Besides, he was a French prince and the whole French royal house by this time had, like the Hohenstaufens to Boniface's predecessors, become a race of vipers to be trodden under foot.

With the deliberate, measured tread of fate the struggle between Boniface and the French king now moved to its issue. In another famous bull, *Unam Sanctam,* the pontiff affirmed that he wielded both the spiritual and the temporal sword and, after a further interval, he put his antagonist formally to the ban of the church. Still closely supported by his people, Philip countered this thrust by declaring the pope a heretic and demanding an ecumenical council for his trial and deposition. As pontiff and king glared at each other across Europe, each equally firm and equally unwilling to yield an inch of his position, it became clear that one or the other would have to break. Against every medieval precedent it turned out to be the pope. But if the lordly Boniface was overtaken by a nemesis, which myriads of his contemporaries, with Dante at their head, hailed as proof that justice, though laggard, still endured, even these enemies were shocked by the unexampled combination of perfidy and treason which brought about his overthrow. A political agent of King Philip, Guillaume de Nogaret by name, conspired with the savage brother of a Colonna cardinal to seize the pope's person; and on September 7, 1303, their forces were, with the connivance of traitors in the papal inner circle, admitted to the fortress of Anagni, where Boniface as usual had set up his summer residence. After a brief resistance the armed horde burst into the chamber of the pope, and Nogaret, in the name of his master, summoned the head of Christendom to acknowledge the charges which had been preferred against him and resign. The Caetani was an old man of over seventy years. There is no denying that he had lived his life as a worldling with little thought given to his Nazarene exemplar. But it is also true that he had manifested a quality of Roman grandeur which on meeting his supreme crisis he did not betray. For three days Nogaret and the fierce Colonna brigand kept him closely imprisoned in his room without bending him to their will. Then a revulsion of feeling among the people of Anagni in favor of the defiant old man drove the conspirators from the town. Boniface was free. He promptly removed to Rome, where, on October 11, he died, doubtless of natural causes but in part no doubt too, consumed by a helpless rage over the unparalleled indignity of which he had been the victim.[10]

When the defeated Boniface VIII was buried, his extravagant papal claims were buried with him. In the eyes of all the world the French crown had emerged as victor from the conflict. Ever since the day a pope had called on a French ruler to help him against Emperor Frederick II the influence of France in the government of the church had been on the increase. Seen in historical perspective, the triumph of Philip IV therefore appears as the logical culmination of a movement long under way. The French king was not the man to miss the significance of his victory and on his adversary's death took steps to bring the papacy completely under his control. He was not at once

[10] Inside the cathedral of Florence between the two main doors there is a seated statue of Boniface VIII in the act of blessing. It once adorned the original façade of the edifice and is a worthy memorial of the great pope in the grave Gothic spirit.

successful, for a reaction against the perpetrators of the Anagni outrage prompted the conclave to elect a moderate adherent of the dead Boniface who took the title Benedict XI. After less than a year Benedict departed this life in his turn (July 7, 1304); and with King Philip using his influence with a devoted faction among the cardinals to hold out for a French candidate, the new conclave, in which the French and the Italian parties were well matched, did not elect a new pope till the following summer. Then it was a French prelate, the archbishop of Bordeaux, who carried off the victory. Taking the title Clement V, he never even gave himself the trouble to cross the Alps and quietly resigned himself to accept King Philip as his master. Before long he set up his residence at Avignon on the Rhone, thus inaugurating the chapter of papal history familiar as the Babylonian Captivity. It is a period of French domination during which the pope, estranged from Italy, played a diminished part, politically speaking, in Tuscan and Florentine affairs. But let us make no mistake. So ingrained in the western mind was the concept of a single church under a single head that the purely spiritual power of the pope over Christian believers either in Italy or elsewhere showed little impairment during the period of abasement when not Rome, but Avignon, served as the papal capital.

XIII. The Last Emperor

ON THE transfer of the papacy to Avignon, Florence was, at least for the time being, affected neither favorably nor unfavorably by an event which was fraught with so many grave consequences for the Catholic church. The Blacks were in power, and under their tutelage the city enjoyed, if no more, surely no less, security and freedom from outside control than under the many preceding governments. Since the Whites, on being violently hunted from the town, had joined forces with the Ghibellines, the law classified them as Ghibellines and did them all the injury to which a ferocious, time-honored custom lent an evil sanction. It sounds like a perverse dream, but is no more than the bare truth to say that almost over night these two colored factions had exchanged political principles. The Whites, who were driven into exile because they had dared to oppose the plot of Pope Boniface to bring the city under his yoke, became committed by the mere act of turning Ghibelline to the policy of subjecting Florence to imperialist, that is to say, to German, influence, while the Blacks, who had not scrupled to betray their country to Boniface, now ruled the city as the proud champions of its independence against their imperialist adversaries.

That the central purpose of the Ghibellines of Tuscany, like that of the Ghibellines of all the other provinces of Italy, was to revive the might of that power which had sunk into its grave with Frederick II, does not admit of the slightest doubt. To this end each Ghibelline provincial group maintained a fighting organization which carried the eagle of the empire on its banner. The Guelph provincial leagues were equally warlike and proclaimed as their point of union their common devotion to the church. Exactly like the Guelph leagues of Lombardy, Tuscany, Liguria, and the other provinces, the corresponding Ghibelline leagues kept in close touch with one another by exchanging information and rendering military aid. Party loyalty, however, did not go deep. The individual members of each league habitually put their selfish advantage above every other consideration and held themselves to be at liberty to desert the common cause without alleging a reason and even without first serving notice. In spite of such unprincipled practices there were always enough members left in a given organization or enough fresh recruits were won to its ranks for the various leagues to maintain a continuous political existence. Hence, from a general peninsular point of view, the substance of Italy's history during most of the fourteenth century continued to be, exactly as in the previous century, the struggle between the Guelph and the Ghibelline factions. While, generally speaking, the latter party supported the empire and the former the church, the single member of either faction sought in the main nothing but his own advancement and looked on the league of his adherence as the convenient ladder by which to raise himself above his fellows. In spite of the uncertain loyalty commanded by the Guelph and Ghibelline leagues and in spite of their consequent instability, it remains a fact that they provided the only existing principles of national coherence. The unceasing civil war between the rival groups was indeed devastating, but without the party bond extending from province to province, every commune would have been a separate center of anarchy and the peninsular chaos would have been unmitigated and complete.

Ever since the restoration of the German kingship in the person of Rudolph of Hapsburg the partisans of the empire in Italy had been in the habit of sending embassies across the Alps to urge the monarch to undertake the journey which would refurbish the tarnished imperial crown and bring aid and comfort to his Italian followers. But the successive German rulers had remained deaf to these siren calls, chiefly because they lacked the resources necessary for an expensive transalpine expedition. Before venturing to look abroad, they would have to fortify their enfeebled position in Germany. When Rudolph I died in 1291, he was followed by Adolph of Nassau, who, on meeting death in battle in 1298, was succeeded by Rudolph's son, Albert. It was this Albert of Hapsburg who occupied the German throne when the crisis occurred in Florence which substituted a Black for a White government. As soon as the banished Whites had joined the Tuscan Ghibellines, the two fused groups made Albert the target of renewed impetuous petitions. Together with the Ghibellines of Lombardy and the Romagna they implored him to rouse himself and come to the assistance of his Italian adherents. And when their humility failed to make the desired impression, they did not hesitate to sound stronger accents. We have already touched upon the conduct of him who, among the earliest of the White exiles, became the leading Ghibelline of his generation, nay, of the whole Middle Ages. In speaking of him in these superlative terms we assign him to the place to which he has been raised by the judgment of posterity but which the inconspicuous, powerless wanderer was far from enjoying in his own day. We have learned that after a brief experience in the fighting ranks of his party, he abandoned the heat and dust of battle in order to promote the cause he had at heart by his unaided effort and in his own way. Under the spur of a profound inspiration he became, as it were, the disembodied voice of Ghibelline idealism. Undoubtedly his utterances were at the time hardly heard amidst the clash of arms around him; but for a later age, when the profane clamor of his own day has long since been silenced, they ring out with a celestial clearness. In his immortal poem the Florentine exile apostrophizes the delinquent Albert of Hapsburg in a passage which he prefaces with an unforgettable picture of the political anarchy reigning in Italy during the first decade of the fourteenth century.

Ah, servile Italy, abode of woe!
Bark without pilot in a stormy sky!
Queen once of fair domains—now fallen low! . . .
For now thy living ones are constant foes,
And each one gnaws the other, even they
Whom the same moat, the self-same walls enclose.
Search, wretched one, thy sea-girt shores around,
Then inward turn to thine own breast and see
If any part in joyous peace be found. . . .
And ye,[1] who should to things divine be given,
And let Augustus in his saddle sit
(If ye had listened to the voice of Heaven),
Look how the beast, refusing all command,
For want of spurs obeyeth not the bit,
Since to the bridle ye have put the hand.[2]

There follows, without interruption, his apostrophe to the laggard German
sovereign:

O German Albert, who desertest her,
Ungovernable now and savage grown,
When most she needed pressing with the spur,
May on thy race Heaven's righteous judgment fall!
And be it signally and plainly shown,
With terror thy successor to appal,
Since by thy lust yon distant lands to gain,
Thou and thy sire have suffered wild to run
What is the garden of thy fair domain.

To gain lands in distant Germany Albert and his sire before him neglected
Italy, the paradise of their realm. Cannot Albert be persuaded to open his
eyes to the ferocious civil wars that are turning over every Italian province
as with a giant plough?

Come, see the Capulets and Montagues,[3]
Monaldi and Filippeschi, reckless one! . . .
Come, cruel man, behold what ills endure
Thy nobles and avenge their injuries. . . .
Come and behold thy Rome, how she doth mourn!
A lonely widow, day and night she cries,
"When will my Caesar to my arms return?"
Come and behold thy people, how they love!
And if no pity our distress inspire,
Let blushes for thyself thy pity move.

[1] Ye—the pope and his clergy who have usurped the temporal power.
[2] *Purgatorio*, VI, 76 ff. Translated by I. C. Wright.
[3] These are the two factions whose implacable hostility disturbed their native city of Verona and
furnished the plot for Shakespeare's tragedy of Romeo and Juliet. They and a second pair of opponents, the Monaldi and Filippeschi, serve as a reminder that every city of Italy was riven by the
same disastrous Guelph-Ghibelline feud.

If distant Albert was a potential factor in the Italian situation, he fell from this role on May 1, 1308, when he was assassinated by his nephew. In the following autumn the German electoral princes raised to the throne the count of Luxemburg, who figures in history as Emperor Henry VII. Viewed from the angle of personal resources and inherited lands, Henry was a sovereign as little impressive as his immediate predecessors; and exactly as in their case, his only chance to be something more than a feeble symbol of unity in a Germany which had fallen apart into many scores of all but independent principalities was to increase the territory under his immediate control. Owing to the fact that the ruling dynasty of Bohemia was at the moment of Henry's accession opportunely reduced to a single female heir, the newly elected king, by betrothing his son to this princess, acquired at a stroke a very considerable sovereignty for his house. Without this fortunate accession to his strength it is most unlikely that he would have been in a position to play an active part even in Germany; and for him to lead an expedition into Italy would have been entirely out of the question. Affirming this much does not mean that from the moment of his election Henry's heart was not set on the Italian venture. Nonetheless it is true that he could not have got his expedition under way without the lucky addition to his purse of the Bohemian revenues. It was also a help, and by no means a negligible feature of the general situation, that Germany happened just then to be enjoying an unwonted interval of peace and could be temporarily abandoned by its sovereign without the pressing fear of losing it.

The county, later the duchy, of Luxemburg, Henry's original possession, lay on the western border of Germany and embraced a population partly of French, partly of German language and culture. In the person of Henry both influences met to produce a happy mixture. While he was German in appearance, being blond, high-colored, and of vigorous frame, he had been brought up at the court of France and bore himself in speech and manners as a Frenchman. A fine product of the age of chivalry, he was a courteous, brave, and pious knight, who impressed whomsoever he met with his candor and sincerity. Nonetheless he belonged to a culture that was passing and by reason of his very merits was ill equipped to cope with the new culture only just dawning in his own north and already well established in the Mediterranean basin.

The mental estrangement between the new sovereign and his Italian subjects did not augur well for the success of his transalpine journey, for even if he should bring himself to a certain measure of accommodation to the novel social and intellectual conditions of the peninsula, he would not be willing to renounce his imperial rights. It is a central feature of Henry's outlook that he held as grand a conception of the place assigned to an emperor in God's inscrutable plan as any of his Saxon or Suabian predecessors. He was the heir of ancient Rome called to universal rule to the end of bringing peace and justice to all the peoples of the earth. Was there in the Europe of the fourteenth century still room for this conception? Could Italy with its free communes dedicated to trade and engaged in developing a specifically urban culture cancel its immediate past and reconfine itself within the legal frame of an agrarian feudal kingdom? Merely to put these questions is to answer them: Henry's courageous attempt to revive a glory for which the living generation had no longer any understanding was foredoomed. Happily for his own peace of mind he did not experience the full force of the failure which was in store for him, for he died of a fever contracted in the field before his defeat was clearly manifest. Even before attacking the details of his Italian intervention let us therefore admit that it represents a labor of Sisyphus and by sober, matter-of-fact standards deserves to be classified as romantic folly. But that is not the whole story, since it is always a question on this earth of ours not only of what it is that men do but also of how they do it. And of Henry it may fairly be said that he went his difficult way with such nobility of purpose and such unwavering courage that his defeat is transformed into a spiritual victory.

In support of this judgment we may appeal to the much more striking case of Henry's greatest contemporary. For even more convincingly than Henry the poet Dante brings home to us that outworn conceptions and crushing defeat are fully compatible with personal distinction and high moral integrity. At the mere rumor of the coming of the German king, the Florentine exile, in tones more like those of a prophet than of a political partisan, uttered his delirious joy at the approach of the divinely appointed universal judge and ruler. "Behold now the acceptable time which brings consolation and peace. For a new day is dawning which shall scatter our darkness," he declared in a letter issued like a royal proclamation to the princes and peoples of Italy. And in the same ecstatic vein, he added: "Rejoice, oh, Italy, . . . for thy bridegroom cometh, the hope of the world, the glory of thy people, the ever clement Henry, who is Caesar and Augustus." [4] The man who expressed himself in these extravagant terms was looking backward to a past that could not be recalled. However, by defending the civil power against the excessive claims of the church he was also looking forward to an Italy cured of its terrible divisions by the creation of a national sovereign standing firmly on his feet and freed in all respects of papal tutelage. It is this prophetic note disengaging itself from Dante's medieval message, it is the strong patriotic sentiment within the antiquated form that explains why the poet is enshrined in the hearts of the living generation of Italians not only as their greatest singer but also in hardly less degree because he was the champion and herald of their political unification.

Let it never be forgotten that if Henry erred, he erred with Dante and has linked his name forever with that greater name. But let it not be forgotten

---

[4] *Dantis Alagherii Epistolae*. With Introduction, Translation, Notes, and Indices by Paget Toynbee. Oxford, 1920. Epistola V, pp. 46-62. Three of these Dante letters bear on Henry's expedition and reveal the Ghibelline idealist.

Either at this time (1309-10) or somewhat later—the authorities are in disagreement—Dante composed his famous political treatise, *De Monarchia,* in which he championed the conception of an empire wholly independent of the church and, like the church, deriving its power directly from God. In the *De Monarchia* Dante returned to the dualistic position of an empire and a church, equal and independent each of the other, which was the commonly entertained medieval doctrine until supplanted by the theory of papal supremacy championed by the great popes from Gregory VII to Boniface VIII. While by his tract the Florentine poet strengthened Ghibellinism theoretically, it was of course too late to save the cause in fact and practice.

either that, in spite of the glamor with which these two, each in his own way, invested the king's coming, the venture was a hopeless anachronism. Nobody felt this more instinctively or deeply than those Florentine burghers, who, though infinitely beneath their exiled fellow-citizen in gifts of heart and mind, had the advantage over him of being, through their daily duties in the home and shop, in touch with the most immediate verities of existence. They looked from the start with cold distrust upon this first imperial expedition since the death of their great enemy, Frederick II. Before long their instinctive opposition hardened into so settled a hostility that Florence became the very nub and focus of the forces which were resolved not to be dominated by the ghosts of the past, even though those ghosts walked in clanking armor and spread a very actual terror. The farther Henry got on with his Italian expedition the more he became aware that it was Florence which he would have to overcome, Florence, which, refusing to be seduced by a mirage, clung obstinately to the benefits immediately in hand, such as an ever-widening trade, industrial enterprise, self-government, and the proud first-fruits of a new and vital urban culture. For us engaged on the task of tracing the development of the free commune of Florence, the main interest of the attempt of Henry to revive the feudal age lies in the circumstance that it culminated in a duel between himself and that same commune, which by Henry's time had become the foremost representative of the new Italian civilization.

For the first two years of his reign Henry was occupied with fortifying his position in Germany and in making preparations for his Italian expedition. He then crossed the Alps at the head of an army and in October, 1310, stood upon Lombard soil, the first monarch to take seriously the task of exercising rule in the peninsula since the fall of the Hohenstaufens. And at first his success was highly gratifying. He let it be known that he had come not as a partisan but as a kindly disposed judge; and for a time even the Guelphs were sufficiently impressed with his attitude to sheathe the sword and cheer him on his way. Moreover—a circumstance bound to count heavily with the Guelphs—he had arrived in Italy with the express indorsement and blessing of the pope. Clement V, the first of the Avignon popes, had chiefly his own feeble disposition to thank if he had sunk to the level of a mere chaplain of the French king. But since, after all, he was the Roman pontiff and head of Christendom, his subservience to a temporal sovereign was not wholly to his liking. He came to see that only through the restoration of the empire could he hope to regain control of the papal dominions in Italy and to recover even in part his lost independence. With a view to creating a counterweight to France, become too potent for his self-esteem, he had therefore, secretly at first and then more openly, encouraged Henry's plans. Finally, he went so far as solemnly to promise Henry to do everything within his power to promote his coronation as emperor at Rome. It was this novel solidarity of pope and German sovereign that took the wind out of the Guelph sails. We may adduce it as the leading explanation of the all but universal acclaim with which Henry was received by Guelph and Ghibelline towns alike, when he marched through Lombardy on his way to Milan, where on January 6, 1311, he assumed the iron crown of Italy.

Then, with the first item of his comprehensive program happily realized, difficulties sprang up like armed men in Henry's path and abruptly ended his Italian honeymoon. Cremona raised the banner of rebellion and had to be brought to obedience by a show of force. Undismayed by the harsh punishment meted out to the rebel commune, neighboring Brescia followed suit and made renewed submission only after a siege which detained the imperial army in Lombardy through the hot and disease-breeding months of an Italian summer. With much of the enthusiasm evaporated which his coming had aroused, Henry turned toward Genoa to pass the winter and refit his reduced forces for the crucial southward thrust toward Rome set for the coming spring. There, on the Tiber, his coronation would place a divine seal upon his labors. As the proposed march would take him through Tuscany and was likely to meet with the greatest obstacles if the leading Tuscan city proved unfriendly, the obligation arises at this juncture to examine at some length the contemporary Florentine situation. And being less interested in the details of municipal politics than in the outstanding social and political trends, we shall select such events of the period between Henry's election and his expected passage through Tuscany as are calculated to give us a better understanding of the temper of the citizens and their daily life within the walls.

At the very time the German princes were preparing to confer the German crown on Henry of Luxemburg, Corso Donati, the indomitable roysterer, met a characteristic end. It was Corso who had been chiefly responsible for driving out the Whites in order to put his own Black faction in control. By reason of the forceful leadership he had supplied, a large place in public affairs was his not unreasonable expectation. But he failed to take into account the jealous temper of his fellow-magnates. Afraid of his reckless courage and suspecting that he was planning to make himself the tyrant of the town after the usurping fashion already general in Lombardy, these heads of rival houses checked and hindered him at every point, and by the use of a cunning with which the forthright warrior could not cope succeeded in keeping his authority well within bounds. To be sure, only good Black Guelphs were permitted to fill the public offices, but they were the appointees, not of Corso, but of his envious partners. With developments so little in keeping with his expectations the indignant nobleman refused to be content. Perpetually revolving plots for his aggrandizement, he was regularly balked in their execution by the subterranean activities of his cleverer opponents. Sooner or later the protracted undercover conflict was bound to burst into the open and be brought to a decision.

In the autumn of 1308 Corso's personal finances, which had a way of getting out of hand not unusual in noblemen of his irregular habits and spendthrift disposition, gave his enemies the opportunity of threatening him with trial and imprisonment. Incensed beyond endurance by this indignity, he openly assembled men and arms. When the news of these preparations got abroad, the people became excited and armed themselves to fight, some for, others against, the stormy petrel who for almost two decades had been the chief disturber of the local peace. The issue was decided by the hired troops of the government. Controlled by the Black faction in power and vigorously supported by the armed forces of the gilds, they enveloped the cluster of Donati houses which fronted on the Piazza San Piero Maggiore in the eastern section of the town. The plan of the attackers was to secure Corso's person and execute him as a rebel. Although tortured by gout, he managed during the confusion of the struggle to mount a horse and make his escape by the Santa Croce gate. When a troop of fast-riding Catalan mercenaries overtook him, rather than be led back to Florence a captive for his enemies to mock at, he threw himself from his horse and, after being dragged a short distance, was dispatched by a thrust through the throat of a Catalan lance (October 6, 1308). By way of stating his opinion of the iniquities of the destroyer of the Whites, Dante in his poem assigned his adversary to the everlasting pains of hell; but the historian is moved to express a milder judgment. He recognizes in Corso Donati a not unimpressive representative of the warrior virtues and vices of the dying Middle Ages. In a city which, in the course of recent generations, had undergone so thorough a commercialization as had Florence, he had become impossible. In point of fact he was the last of his kind. Never after his exit from the scene did Florentines of other than the banker-merchant type play a conspicuous part in the politics of the town.

In the summer of 1310, the Guelphs in control of the city were for the first time obliged clearly to define their stand toward Henry of Luxemburg. About to cross the Alps, Henry had sent ambassadors ahead to announce his coming to the towns and princes of Italy and to ask for the appointment of commissioners to be dispatched to him to take the customary oath of fealty. In July these emissaries arrived at Florence. Since the pope was lending Henry his support, a friendly policy might have seemed an advisable preliminary flourish; but so much more Guelph than the Holy Father were the Florentines that the royal agents were given a prompt rebuff. A leading Black magnate, Betto de' Brunelleschi, charged by the priors to speak for the government, uttered the rude boast to the ambassadors that "his countrymen had never yet bowed their sharp horns to any master." [5] Joining deeds to words, the commune resumed the construction of the new, the third circle of walls, inaugurated some twenty years before; and so rapidly did the work progress that before many months had passed the main section, which gave protection to that part of the city lying upon the right bank of the Arno, was completed. While paeans of welcome were arising from every town and province to greet the arrival of Henry in his kingdom, the uncompromising Guelphs of Florence, and of Florence alone among Italian cities, refused to be deluded and, expecting war, looked to their defenses.

It is a tribute to the courage of the Florentine rulers that they tossed the gauntlet to the monarch in spite of immediate local difficulties that might well have whispered compromise. Already in 1308 the two great banks of the Mozzi and Franzesi had failed and badly shaken the whole business structure of the city. Two years later, before more than a partial recovery had been effected, the bank of the Cerchi, which notwithstanding its connection with the banished Whites had continued to operate from Florence as its center,

[5] Dino, *Libro Terzo*, 35.

ORCAGNA. DEATH AND ASSUMPTION OF THE VIRGIN. OR SAN MICHELE (ALINARI).

left: CIMABUE. ENTHRONED MADONNA. UFFIZI GALLERY (ALINARI). *right:* GIOTTO. ENTHRONED MADONNA. UFFIZI GALLERY (ALINARI).

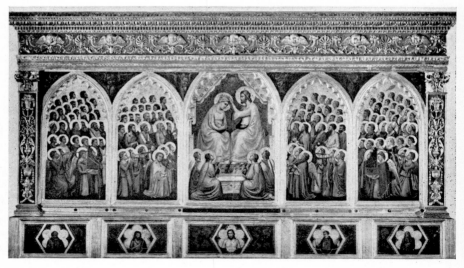

GIOTTO. CORONATION OF THE VIRGIN. ALTARPIECE. SANTA CROCE (ALINARI).

went the same road. As these and similar firms, which put the Arno city at the head of international banking, rested not only on the capital of the well-to-do but also on the savings of the small tradesmen, every bank crash brought loss and misery to many scores of families. In 1311, with the closer approach to Florence of the emperor, the local difficulties became even greater. A partial failure of the harvest doubled the price of wheat and obliged the government to alleviate the situation by making purchases in distant markets. Under these adverse circumstances it would have been prudent to reduce expenses by dismissing the mercenaries who formed the nucleus of the city's military establishment. The pusillanimous thought was not seriously entertained. Instead of being reduced, the army was on the contrary steadily increased, and to meet the heavy costs incurred by these open preparations for the coming struggle the property tax called *estimo* was repeatedly levied within a single year.[6]

In its swelling self-esteem and growing hatred of its adversary, the commune resolved to remove the last emblem in its midst of its former subjection to the empire. The symbol of the empire was the eagle. In earlier times it had been carved on the town gates or been painted or cut in stone on the house fronts by all citizens who desired to make a public avowal of their loyalty. A general order now went forth that all these imperial birds must be removed; and Dino, to whom we owe this interesting detail, adds that "a fine was assessed on whosoever refused to erase them."[7] But let it not be imagined for a moment that the prevailing burgher mood was just a senseless rage. Fully aware of the gravity of the impending struggle, the government recognized the advantage of reducing its very numerous local enemies in order to present as united a front as possible to the enemy. Only a prudent consideration of this sort will account for the relatively liberal amnesty for political offenses issued at this time (1311). It made possible the repatriation, on the payment of no more than a small money penalty, of those many hundreds of exiles who, though of White affiliation, had not figured conspicuously in the late civil war. The pardon, it need hardly be said, was not broad enough to include exiles who, like Dante, were considered to be White leaders and who had been condemned to death.

In spite of scarcity and bankruptcies, in spite of war preparations and multiplied taxes, the local feuds never rested. It would not have been Florence had it been otherwise. If it was chiefly the magnates to whom vendetta was a sacred obligation, the complete propriety of the ancient practice of retaliation was accepted without question by the whole citizen body. On Corso Donati's death it became incumbent on his family to avenge the spilling of his blood; and although he was actually killed by a Catalan soldier, it was known that some of his magnate rivals, and more particularly messer Betto de' Brunelleschi, were the instigators of the plot that culminated in his death. The surviving relatives of Corso maintained a close watch of the supposed guilty parties, but some years passed before they found an opportunity to strike. The eminent Betto, whom they particularly singled out as their victim,

[6] For these local problems and entanglements see Davidsohn, Vol. III, pp. 422-24.
[7] Dino, *Libro Terzo*, 35.

had reached still greater eminence by reason of Corso's disappearance. Owing to his local prominence and his merited reputation as an orator, it was he who was intrusted with the reply to Henry's ambassadors; and, as we have seen, he did not hesitate to give his words the brusque character of a declaration of war. Although a passionate patriot, he had the magnate's typical contempt for the common people, and when the food scarcity of the winter 1310-11 occasioned a wide suffering, he used his wealth to hoard grain and added insult to injury by openly mocking at the misery of the poor. In short, messer Betto was not an attractive type of magnate and no great public lamentation followed when two Donati youths made an end of him. On a day in February, 1311, when both the scarcity of grain and Betto's profits were at their height, the avengers burst upon him in his house while he was quietly playing at chess and dispatched him with their poniards. In this manner Corso, who in obedience to the local mores had in his day avenged many a murdered relative, was avenged in his turn. At the time the murder of his adversary occurred the popular hatred Corso had aroused in his lifetime was so far forgotten that he could at last be accorded the funeral honors which custom prescribed as his due. When, following his death at the hands of city troopers, his mutilated corpse was left lying in the dust of the road a mile beyond the eastern gate, it had been picked up by the monks of the nearby monastery of San Salvi and hurriedly put away within their precincts. Now since, with Betto's murder three years after Corso's death, the Donati honor was restored, the family removed Corso's remains from their temporary burial place and amidst pompous ceremonies, as if he had just died, laid the old warrior to rest in the family vaults in Florence.[8]

From this varied assortment of local items we may gather that, in spite of the vast reverberation caused by the emperor's presence in Italy, the daily life of the Florentines went on much as before. However, not for a moment did the ruling Guelph clique relax its watch on the movements of their imperial opponent or waver in their hostility to his person and undertaking. On Christmas Eve of the year 1311, Henry, while residing at Genoa, put an end to the negotiations he had been patiently conducting for over a year with the City of the Red Lily regarding the oath of allegiance to which he was legally entitled. By formal sentence rendered in his court he declared Florence outlawed, ordered the seizure of the goods of its citizens throughout the imperial dominions, and, for good measure, loaded the town with a fine amounting to no less than five thousand pounds of gold. When, some months later, the emperor proceeded from Genoa to Pisa, it was feared by the Florentines and expected by the rest of Italy that he would at once lead his army up the Arno Valley and make good his threats against the city. The Tuscan Ghibellines, who crowded to Pisa to honor their champion, outdid one another in urging this punitive measure upon him. We still possess the flaming epistle which Dante addressed to Henry recommending an immediate advance on guilty Florence. But the Luxemburger was of another mind. He had an eye only for the imperial crown which glowed mysteriously in the distance and

---

[8] Dino, *Libro Terzo*, 39, supplemented by Villani, IX, 12.

he was impatient to be invested with the magic round. Simple child of the medieval fancies which still ruled the north, he held to the belief that the effulgence with which he would be clothed at Rome would of itself suffice to bring rebellious Florence to obedience. Thus inspired, he pressed southward from Pisa by the Maremma route only to be shaken rudely from his dreams as he neared the goal of his ambition.

Such success as had thus far attended the Luxemburg sovereign was, as has been noted, primarily owing to the circumstance that his expedition enjoyed the backing of the pope. But in measure as Henry prospered, Clement V, who was far from being a free agent, turned cold, and under pressure from the royal court of France prepared to put obstacles in the German sovereign's path. When King Robert I of Naples, who had succeeded his father, Charles II, in 1309, sent his younger brother with an armed troop to occupy the Tiber city, the pope did not dare affront either the French king or that king's Neapolitan relative so far as to signify his displeasure with this act of war.[9] Here was the turning-point of Clement's policy, here the first unequivocal evidence of that papal opposition to Henry which Dante has branded as abominable treason against his *alto Arrigo,* the messenger from heaven. Under these altered auspices "high Harry" had to force his way into Rome under constant fighting and met with such formidable opposition from the Neapolitan troops that the crucial Vatican quarter containing St. Peter's church and the grave of the chief apostle remained unconquered. In the end Henry was obliged to content himself with holding the less distinguished eastern section of Rome, where lay the church of St. John Lateran; and there, contrary to tradition, he was crowned on June 29, 1312, by a committee of three cardinals, who had been delegated to this service by the pope before his French master had obliged him to change his mind.

Thoroughly aroused to the insecurity of his situation by this partial failure, Henry resolved to stake fame and fortune on the capture and punishment of that town which ever since his coming to Italy had been the head and front of the opposition. The most recent outrage of Florence had been to send all its available troops to Rome in order to co-operate with Robert of Naples in the plan to defeat the Luxemburger's coronation. On departing from Rome, Henry moved northward through Umbria and in September entered Tuscany by the valley of the upper Arno. Owing to losses in battle and, still more, to the ravages of disease, his forces had shrunk till his heavy cavalry, always regarded as the decisive branch of the service in those days, amounted to no more than two thousand knights, divided equally among Germans and Italians. As it was impossible with so limited a troop to lay siege to a town of the formidable circumference of Florence, Henry must have hoped that the Florentines would offer battle and bring their dispute with their lawful lord to that form of decision favored by the feudal world and celebrated as the Judgment of God. Or perhaps in his unconquerable romanticism he imagined his adversaries would think better of their recalcitrancy and abruptly change their evil course now that the Roman chrism sanctified his

[9] On the vehemence of the pressure brought to bear on Clement V by the French royal house, see the dispatch of the Aragonese ambassador quoted by Davidsohn, Vol. III, p. 469.

brow. He simply could not grasp that these solid, earth-rooted merchants and shopkeepers were forever done with the political flummery of the Middle Ages and thought only of their priceless communal freedom, determined to defend it by hook and by crook without the least regard for the frayed values of an outmoded ideology.

Buoyed by such sentiments, the Florentine rulers had, as soon as Henry's design against their town became clear, left no stone unturned to give him a reception that he would remember. They breathed new life into the league of Tuscan Guelphs, drawing into the fold every town within the province save those two impenitent hearths of Ghibellinism, Pisa and Arezzo. They established fruitful contact with the neighboring leagues of Lombardy and the Romagna and called on Robert of Naples to repay the aid so freely given in keeping Henry out of the sacred precinct of the Vatican. Finally, by ambassadors dispatched to France they assured themselves of the sympathy and, if the need arose, of the active help of King Philip and of Philip's obedient tool, the pope. As a result of this wide agitation and indefatigable energy it came about that when, on September 19, Henry appeared before the eastern gate of Santa Croce and established his headquarters at the Vallombrosan monastery of San Salvi, a composite Guelph army at least twice the size of his own was gathered at Florence to turn him from his prize.

Even with this preponderance in numbers the army of the Guelphs was discreetly kept behind the sheltering walls of the town in the assurance that lack of supplies, disease, and the inclement season would effect the ruin of the besieging host more quickly and decisively than the sword. And as they hoped and planned, so it befell. The imperial horsemen, though foraging far and wide, were soon without food; the autumn rains set in, turning the fields to swamps and raising the Arno to flood height; dysentery and similar camp diseases, against which the primitive medical science of the age afforded no protection, mowed down the harassed warriors by the score. When the emperor himself fell ill, his physicians gathered at his bedside to argue in their learned Latin the breathless question whether it was a quartan or a tertian fever which had laid him low. Henry had but lately turned forty and boasted an exceptionally vigorous constitution. While the savants were still disputing over the right name for his affliction, he mastered his weakness, rose from his sickbed, and, seeing the disastrous situation of his army, raised the siege, if siege it may be called.

Florence had stayed the imperial advance and turned the tide. Deliberately, with many pauses to show that they had not been routed, Henry's forces rolled down the Arno Valley toward faithful Pisa. Since the imperialists lived on the country, harrying it in their disappointment to the best of their ability, we may believe that the Florentine countryside for many miles around the capital was reduced to sorry desolation. The evidence which has come down to us proves overwhelmingly that the long campaign of attrition wrought burghers and peasants incalculable damage. But they remained stanch. And they had every right to rejoice for, without having risked the hazards of battle, they had been victorious.

When, once more safe within the walls of Pisa, Henry reviewed his present situation, he no longer underrated the difficulties connected with his purpose of raising the empire from its grave. Although in his unteachable simplicity he flatly refused to believe that his professed friend, the pope, had betrayed him, he at least ceased to count further on Clement's active support in carrying through his program. Henceforth he relied only on what was reasonably sure and that was the armed might of his willing vassals in Germany and Italy. With their reduced resources he was obliged to face a powerful bloc of enemies, whose concerted action had already proved too much for him at Rome and Florence and whom their recent successes had filled with soaring confidence. We cannot but think that throughout the winter spent at Pisa he must have been assailed with heavy doubts; but, if so, he kept them to himself. A pious and brave cavalier, he knew no other course than to go on with what he had begun till death should intervene; and therefore, instead of going back to Germany, which would have signified a public admission of defeat, he made extraordinary efforts to assemble a new army in order to deal his enemies a fresh blow. Pisa, the ever true, aided him with a liberal grant of funds, fresh troops came from across the Alps, and by the early summer of 1313 he was again the commander of an army, larger and better equipped than that with which he had assaulted Florence in the previous autumn.

Contemporaries have recorded the opinion that if Henry had again directed his spear against the Red Lily, he would not have been turned back a second time. When we reflect that the countryside had been laid waste and that the town itself had been drained of its resources, we must agree that the emperor's chances against the rebel city had considerably improved. But who will say that the dying Guelph fires would not once more have been fanned to flame at the enemy's approach? In any case the emperor, with that unsteadiness of objective so generally characteristic of feudal warfare, did not return upon his steps. He resolved instead to fling his new army on the king of Naples. In his guileless way of viewing politics, he saw, not the French pope, but Angevin Robert, with whom he had come to blows at Rome, as the villain of the piece, and desired to be revenged on him for his unchivalrous attempt to exclude a divinely called sovereign from his capital. Stirred to his depths by the Neapolitan's seizure of Rome in the previous year, Henry did not even desist from his plan when the double-tongued Clement now ventured into the open and forbade the expedition against Robert on pain of excommunication. With stern resolution he set his face to the south.

In August, 1313, the imperial host left Pisa, moving slowly up the Elsa Valley. Henry had never made a full recovery from the malarial attack which had prostrated him near Florence some ten months before. While cutting a circle around Siena, a stanch Ghibelline town in Hohenstaufen days turned Guelph these many years, he was again stricken. He had to be carried in a litter thenceforward, but did not get far. We are assured by the chroniclers that his mystified physicians, deeply alarmed by his condition, conscientiously purged and bled him, but on August 24, at the little hamlet of Buonconvento, he dispensed with their further services. He died as he had lived, an honorable Christian gentleman, consoled upon his deathbed by the last sacrament administered to him by his Dominican confessor. Although the monstrous charge that he was poisoned with the holy wafer laid upon his lips by this same friendly priest was widely credited at the time and is still repeated by uncritical historians, it may be dismissed as an invention wherewith the grief-stricken Ghibellines expressed their sense of the irrational manner in which fate interferes in the affairs of men.

The army, bearing the dead monarch in its midst, flowed sadly back to Pisa, and there the body was bestowed in the cathedral and a monument erected over it, the remnants of which may still be seen in the right transept of that famous edifice. The funeral over, the imperial forces dissolved like mist before the sun. They had been assembled to support the project of their liege lord, and as much time would have to pass before his successor could be elected in distant Germany, there was no authority in sight capable of holding the army together. Before many seasons rolled by the brief Italian adventure of Henry had become a memory which served to strengthen the already general impression that the Holy Roman empire had paled to a shadow and was extinct in all but name. An occasional German sovereign in the years ahead still showed that he was under the spell of the old imperial idea, and one or another of them even fared across the Alps in search of the imperial crown which only Rome could bestow. Henry VII was the last emperor who unquestioningly believed in the remarkable political institution which went back to Charlemagne and Otto and which in the general view had Julius Caesar as its founder. Because of this faith of his, Henry staked his all on forcing an antiquated order on a changed Italy and lost.

We cannot take leave of the defeated Henry laid to rest in his sepulcher in Pisa without returning to the much more arresting case of Dante, the last and greatest exponent of a universal order, of which Henry was but the political representative. Living at the close of the Middle Ages, when the thought of the period had been given a full and rounded formulation by the great schoolmen culminating in Aquinas, the poet and thinker made himself the mouthpiece of their view that the central concern of life was the problem of salvation. In Dante's solemn conception of our earth as the proving-ground of souls there was little, if any, place for the travel, commerce, experimentation, and other activities of a mundane kind which had transformed his native Florence from a nameless, sleepy hamlet to a lively metropolis with material and intellectual interests covering the known world. It was in substance these very innovations which Dante rejected when he declared for the coherent system by which the medieval philosophers had, or thought they had, provided for every legitimate aspiration of the sons of Adam by harmonizing faith and reason. Persuaded that the medieval way of life was prescribed by revelations vouchsafed the saints and prophets and supplemented by the ratiocinations of great thinkers, he had nothing but contempt for the novel political, social, and economic attitudes which were triumphantly asserting themselves among his fellow-citizens. The sum of these novelties came at a later time and with a somewhat misplaced emphasis to be called the Renaissance. We assign to Dante his distinctive place in the unfolding of European culture when we declare that, owing to his spiritual inheritance and tempera-

mental preferences, he identified himself with the theology and outlook of
the Middle Ages and indignantly rejected the rising secular philosophy inherent in the exploratory activities of his Florentine and Italian contemporaries. By this same judgment it becomes clear that they and not he were
in line with the fated forward movement of occidental civilization.

XIV. Florence Encounters the Problem
of the Despot (1313–43)

EVER since the rise of the towns their leading concern had been the growth of their power at home and abroad. Each had started existence with the plan of conquering its county and, as soon as that objective had been won, each with the characteristic unrestraint of youth had extended its operations into the county of its neighbors. We have seen that Lombardy, the Romagna, Umbria, and Tuscany were from the twelfth century on torn with this relentless strife. If the Hohenstaufen emperors had occasionally brought it to a halt, it had broken out again with elemental vehemence the moment the imperial overlord relaxed his vigilance. On the death of the high-spirited Frederick II the empire fell into such feebleness that it no longer counted in the Italian situation. When the attempt of Henry VII to revive the fallen empire failed, more emphatically than ever the towns were left to work out their territorial and other similar problems by their own strength.

The uninterrupted warfare among the towns throughout the flourishing town area lying between the Alps and the fringe of ancient Latium had a marked effect on their domestic constitution. Normally each town aspired to self-government, and in its first or consular stage of emancipation from feudal bondage had resorted to representative institutions as evidenced by an elected executive, consultative councils, and a parliament of the people. While this democratic machinery was overelaborate and the responsibilities under it too widely distributed, it might conceivably have worked had it not been for the martial and aggressive policy the towns saw fit to adopt. War calls for swift decisions and concentrated authority; and in measure as the struggle of each town against its neighbors assumed larger proportions and became a permanent feature of its foreign policy, the original constitution with its democratic elements was found to be inadequate and progressively broke down. As frequently before and after the Italian communal era, democracy was found to be hopelessly incompatible with war conceived as a legitimate and indispensable tool of policy.

A second consequence of the unceasing intercommunal struggle forces itself on our attention when we survey the general Italian scene. The democratically oriented communes had at first employed democratic armies, the organized forces utilized in their early enterprises being nothing other than the male population mobilized at the call to arms. Such a popular army sufficed for the work immediately in hand, which was to assault and break down the feudal castles in the contado and to encounter the onslaught of the similarly constituted army of a neighboring town. Moved by a passionate patriotism, it might even on occasion charge with irresistible abandon and overcome the proud chivalry of a Barbarossa. But undeniably there were defects in an army of this kind which in the long run would prove disastrous. There was always the likelihood, instanced by scores of actual cases, that the infantry or pedites, who were poorly equipped and inadequately trained, would at an unexpected turn of events disintegrate into a panicky mob, while a campaign unduly drawn out would be resented as an intolerable hardship, because it separated the citizen from his livelihood and exposed his family to suffering and starvation.

Much more dependable than the infantry was the cavalry made up of the milites and recruited from the well-to-do citizens, more particularly from the urban nobility. However, on social grounds the expanding democracy very generally turned against the quarrelsome and arrogant gentry and, after canceling its political rights, very often, for good measure, hounded it from its territory. The consequent reduction in numbers of the nobility did not necessarily signify a decline in the number of the urban horsemen. In the case of most towns, and certainly in the case of Florence, the duty of every man of means to maintain a horse for the commune and perform cavalry service in wartime remained an inalterable obligation. But when, with the accelerated expansion of Florence before and after the year 1300, many citizens, formerly poor, became well-to-do, they were found to have neither the desire nor the ability for effective equestrian service. The traditional obligation of the man of means to supply a horse in time of war was designated by the term *cavallata*. While the numerous new-rich admitted their liability to the cavallata, they often proposed and, in view of the sorry figure they cut on horseback, the authorities gladly accepted, a substitute rider. In this manner the cavallata already by the early fourteenth century commonly comprised two separate services, the one the maintenance of a horse in peace time, the other the riding or having it ridden into the field at the call to war. This bifurcation undermined the tradition of serving in person and brought about an indefinable loss of pride and patriotism. Where and whenever the old nobility, or even some part of it, survived, its fighting spirit was slow to be extinguished. However, the very opposite was true of the *popolani grassi,* the fat burghers, who came more and more to preponderate among the citizens subject to the cavallata. Taken up with money-making and personally averse to arms, they succeeded to a steadily increasing degree in being dispensed from the cavallata obligation by having it commuted into a pure money payment. The commutation came to be designated with a touch of wry humor as a *cavallata morta;* and it is with this supply of "a dead horse," already in full development by the early decades of the fourteenth century, that the once famous cavalry arm of the original municipal army came to an ignominious end.[1]

---

[1] As long ago as 1865, C. Paoli made a study of the *Cavallate Fiorentine* based largely on that inexhaustible source for all military matters pertaining to the republican army, the *Libro di Montaperti.* See *Arch. Stor. It.,* Serie 3, Vol. I, pp. 53-75.

In view of the steadily diminishing value of both branches of the popular army, it was inevitable that the town governments should begin to experiment with professional soldiers, with mercenaries. In this development the emperors had led the way. Disgusted with the self-will of the feudal levies which, as soon as the number of weeks' or months' service required by their feudal contract had expired, would turn their faces homeward without regard to military exigencies, they had formed a nucleus of hired troops calculated to stick with their commander at least as long as their wages were paid promptly. Such troops, well horsed, adequately armed and trained, and bound besides into an effective unit by an impalpable *esprit de corps,* came gradually to dominate the military situation.[2] Their leader or captain was at first regularly a nobleman born to the profession of arms. As such he would be disposed to comport himself with some regard for the conventional obligations of decency imposed by the theory and practice of knighthood. Inevitably, however, with war become an occupation in which soldiers were engaged for hire, the moral standards of the mercenary leaders declined until they and their following presented themselves to view as nothing more than profit-seeking, brutal adventurers serving whosoever offered the most pay and inaccessible to the appeal of honor and humanity. At first prevailingly of German nationality, the mercenaries we encounter in the Italian wars were before long recruited from the fighting stock of every country of Europe. A commune would hire a troop of men-at-arms for a particular campaign and turn them loose the moment the campaign was over. Or if, because the situation remained permanently critical, the troopers were retained on the municipal pay-roll, they assumed the character of a standing army and became an important factor in the local situation. In these circumstances it might easily happen that an unscrupulous political group within the town, or the ambitious head of such a political group, would try to manipulate them for selfish ends. In case the cunning plotter happened to be a nobleman practiced in feudal warfare, he might succeed in attaching the hired horsemen to his person; and by loosing them at a given moment on the city he could terrorize the community and hold it at his mercy. From such military bullying to the seizure of political power was but a step and the successful captain, native or foreign, would crown his career by becoming a despot or tyrant. The usual fourteenth-century Italian designation for such a usurper was *signore,* which is to say, lord or master.

We thus see that under the impact of many forces, political, military, and social, the free governments of the twelfth and thirteenth centuries tended to be replaced by a military chief with autocratic power. And just as the towns of the rich Lombard plain had been the ones to inaugurate the movement of communal liberty, so they were the first to exhibit the phenomenon of the signore. Throughout the second half of the thirteenth century the despotic movement continued to gather force in the Po Valley with the great Lombard metropolis, Milan, acting as pacemaker. And before the opening of the fourteenth century the development had begun to spread with the un-

---

[2] On the growing use of mercenaries by Florence, as well as on other military developments of the fourteenth century, see Davidsohn, Vol. IV[1], chap. 3. A lively account of Italian military history is by E. Ricotti. *Storia delle Compagnie di Ventura in Italia.* 3 vols. Milan, 1929.

reasoning authority of a new fashion to all the provinces bordering on Lombardy. We have already looked at the picture which, shortly after the year 1300, Dante painted of the distracted peninsula. While he is particularly distressed by the ruinous civil and provincial wars and their attendant misery and chaos, he does not fail to cry out also against the murder of the communal liberties by the rising despots.

> Che le città d'Italia tutte piene
> Son di tiranni ed un Marcel diventa
> Ogni villan che parteggiando viene.

> (For all the towns of Italy are full
> Of tyrants, and becometh a Marcellus
> Each peasant churl who plays the partisan.) [3]

If he called passionately on the absent emperor to come to Italy and exercise his sovereign rights, he certainly expected, among other benefits, to have an end made of the mad self-exaltation of Italy's countless military adventurers.

But when an emperor came in the person of Henry VII, he proved himself incapable of riding the storm and making himself master of the situation; and no sooner had he been buried with appropriate pomp at Pisa than Tuscany, which thus far had not been greatly influenced by the Lombard example, experienced the rise of so vigorous a succession of tyrants that the communal liberties of every town, including Florence, were gravely jeopardized. The story of tyranny in Tuscany starts with Pisa which, as the chief support of Henry's Ghibelline expedition, found itself exposed to a combined Guelph attack the moment Henry's army, following the death of its leader, began to disperse. The Guelph league embraced practically all the other towns of Tuscany with Florence at their head and was not likely to let the opportunity slip by to punish the impenitent Ghibelline nucleus of Pisa. Thoroughly alarmed for its safety, the maritime town invited one of Henry's trusted Italian lieutenants, the nobleman Uguccione della Faggiuola, to assume its defense. As his family estates lay in the highlands of the upper Arno, Uguccione was by tradition both a Ghibelline and an enemy of Florence. In a long and agitated military career he had proved himself a mighty warrior and carouser and, alert to the many possibilities of advancement offered by the political anarchy of the peninsula, had fixed his mind on carving out an urban signory for himself. At the same time that the Pisan commonwealth turned to him for help it persuaded a body of eight hundred German knights, who had lost their paymaster when they buried Emperor Henry, to enter its service. By this fortunate coincidence the energetic nobleman, who personally commanded no following, found himself at the head of an experienced troop of fighters.

Uguccione lost no time in launching his program. He declared war on Lucca, ever a popular measure with the Pisan populace owing to the immemorial feud between these close neighbors. When some Pisan merchants, anxious about their profits, protested against the unnecessary disturbance of

---

[3] *Purgatorio*, VI, 124-27. Marcellus is the Roman general, M. Claudius Marcellus, and serves here as the perennial military type.

the peace, he arrested and executed a number of their leaders. Thereupon, summoning a public parliament, he persuaded it to offer him the lordship of the city for ten years. The action signified the abolition of constitutional government and its replacement by Uguccione's despotism. Immediately after, on June 14, 1314, he justified his dictatorship to his Pisan partisans by capturing Lucca. The unhappy town was put to the sack for three interminable days. For many generations past the famous industrial specialty of Lucca had been the manufacture of fine silks, in which it stood foremost among all the towns of Italy. As a result of the havoc wrought by an unloosed horde of plundering mercenaries, hundreds of silk artisans emigrated, chiefly to Florence and Bologna, which welcomed them with open arms. When quiet was again restored the manufacture of silk was resumed by the Lucchese who had survived the recent crisis, and, before long, the town had again acquired a certain standing as a commercial and industrial center. But there can be no doubt that the disaster of 1314 administered a blow to the industrial prestige of the old Tuscan capital on the Serchio from which it never recovered.

With the combined resources of Pisa and Lucca at his disposal, Uguccione could assume the offensive against the Guelph league of Tuscany. And at once he directed his attention to Pistoia as the point from which the security of Florence itself, the fiery head of the league, could be most successfully threatened. The ever-watchful metropolis was not caught unawares. Already in the spring of 1313, at which time the Arno city was expecting a fresh attack from Emperor Henry, it had tightened the bonds which joined it to King Robert of Naples by granting him the *signoria* over it for a term of five years. The submission must be interpreted as an emergency measure, for it was carefully safeguarded by the citizens, resolved, as soon as the immediate danger had passed, to resume the reins. In exchange for his all-important military help, King Robert was to be allowed to appoint the Florentine podestà, without otherwise altering or setting aside the constitution. While the king was thus to be represented in the town by a leading official as well as by a body of Neapolitan troops, he was obliged to acknowledge that there were constitutional bounds which he must under no circumstances overstep. How far this was from the typical tyranny of the period is made clear by referring for comparison to the case of Uguccione, who, from the day of his seizure of power at Pisa, was its unquestioned sovereign. Nonetheless by its acceptance of King Robert as overlord the Arno city experienced its first taste of subjection to the rule of a master since the inauguration of the government of the priors. And this first taste was destined not to be the last. Although her historians have delighted in extolling Florence as the most stubborn center of self-government in Italy, and although the town fully deserves to be singled out in this respect, it is an exaggeration to repeat with some too fullsome admirers that Florence never felt the yoke of tyranny till it was fastened on her neck by the treachery of a family nursed in her own bosom.

The war begun by Uguccione against the league of Tuscan Guelphs reached a climax on August 29, 1315, in a great battle fought just west of Pistoia, near Montecatini. It was a signal victory for the Ghibellines who administered such a rout to the Guelphs as they had not suffered since Montaperti, half a century before. However, the lord of Pisa failed to squeeze all the expected advantages out of his victory, probably because of difficulties that had arisen in his own camp. His chief lieutenant was a young warrior, Castruccio Castracane by name. Castruccio belonged to a noble family of Lucca, the Antelminelli, the members of which had been banished, when Castruccio was a lad, because of their Ghibelline sympathies. The young exile had tried to retrieve his fortunes by the usual avenue of war, had joined the forces of Henry VII on the descent of that monarch into Italy, and, with an ambition that allowed no chance to slip by unused, had co-operated with Uguccione on the day when the Pisan signore took Castruccio's native town by storm.

Since that capital event Castruccio had secretly aspired to nothing less than to the independent rule of the city to which he belonged by birth and to which he had returned by force of arms. He was as capable a soldier as the much more experienced Uguccione and every whit as eager to achieve an independent sovereignty. At the same time he had the advantage over his much older chief of a cooler head and a wider political vision. By sheer military servicableness he made himself so indispensable that, although Uguccione watched him with the usual suspicion of the tyrant, he delayed action until it was too late. Then, on the day before Easter of the year 1316, the lord of Pisa suddenly ordered Castruccio, who was residing in dependent Lucca, under arrest. By accident or, much more probably, by Castruccio's secret machinations, a rebellion occurred on the same day in Pisa, which the young Antelminelli utilized so cleverly that he was able to bring down the whole edifice of Uguccione's power. It was one of those sudden upsets so characteristic of the period. Pisa promptly resumed its independence, while Lucca, to mark its gratitude for having been liberated from the yoke of its hated neighbor, gratefully conceded the scepter to the vigorous warrior who was its own beloved son. It does credit to Castruccio's moderation that he permitted the defeated and crestfallen Uguccione to pass safely out of the country.

Castruccio was thirty-five years old when he found himself the adored ruler of his Lucchese countrymen. Moving cautiously at first, he accepted the offer of the Guelphs to discuss the points of difference between them and him. As a result an agreement was reached which, in May, 1317, led to the pacification of Tuscany. Needless to say there were too many incurable animosities between the two ancient factions for the peace to prove lasting. Besides, the dominant Tuscan figure was now the young Lucchese despot, and he was animated by too unbridled an ambition to be content with the territory already won. In 1320 he became involved in a war against Genoa, which city the Guelphs had recently acquired and which the rasped and angry Ghibellines desired to bring back into their ranks. To help their friends, the Genoese Guelphs, the Florentines invaded the contado of Lucca and obliged Castruccio in self-protection to hurry home. Thereupon for a number of years Lucca and Florence with their respective allies cruelly harried each other's territory. At the same time they were quick to spring to the aid of friends beyond the limits of Tuscany. Avoiding the always tiresome details of these local conflicts, we should not fail to note that more and more the struggle between the Tuscan Guelphs and Ghibellines tended to enlarge its field of action. Each group entered on increasingly close relations with the related groups of Liguria, Lombardy, and Umbria with the result that when war broke out in one of these provinces, it quickly spread to all the others. With this widening of the political horizon no Tuscan government could any longer afford to shape its policy with sole reference to the local situation.

So little faith, and justifiably as the events just recounted prove, did the Florentines put in the Tuscan pacification of 1317 that when the five-year term of King Robert's signory expired, they renewed it for four years more. It was agreed that it should run till 1322. However, when that year rose upon the world, even though, as we shall presently see, the Ghibelline danger had again become acute, the men of Arno were so thoroughly tired of the Neapolitan guests in their midst that they refused further to extend King Robert's term and resumed control of their affairs. Florence was herself again! And to signalize her return to popular sovereignty, she reinstituted the capitano del popolo, the particular official whom the people regarded as their leading defender, and who for this very reason had been obliged to disappear from the political scene when the king of Naples with his anti-popular tendencies took hold. Being now newly appointed, he was, according to custom, supplied with a constitution drawn up to define his office and its obligations. The instrument of 1322 enjoys great honor among scholars because it is the earliest constitution of the capitano to come down to us. Three years later (1325), a periodic revision provided a new *statuto* also for the podestà; and this document, as being the oldest surviving record of an even more ancient and dignified office than that of the capitano, has very properly been accorded a position of honor at the side of the captain's document. The two documents together supply the solid basis for every serious inquiry into the constitutional history of Florence.[4] In this connection it may be well distinctly to point out what should be already apparent from the facts just recounted, that there is no single document which may be called *the* Florentine constitution. It was customary to provide a statuto for every official or set of officials, on which he or they took the oath of office and by which their respective duties were defined. We have just seen that such was the case with the podestà and the capitano del popolo. Since the leading governing body from the year 1282 consisted of the priors, the priors of course had a constitution of their own. It is in this light that we should regard the Ordinances of Justice (1293) with their prescriptive statements touching the manner of election of the priors, their term of office, their power of legislative initiative, and other similar matters. Under the ruling system of statutory regulation the officials charged with the indirect taxes (*gabelle*) and with the supervision of the grain market at Or San Michele (*I Sei del Biado*) also had their special constitutions. All

---

[4] The two constitutions have been published by Romolo Caggese in two volumes under the title *Statuti della Repubblica Fiorentina*. Vol. I, "Statuto del Capitano del Popolo degli anni 1322-25." Florence, 1910. Vol. II, "Statuto del Podestà dell'anno 1325." Florence, 1921. Failure to meet the requirements of an advanced scholarship has been charged by several authoritative critics. See a review of Caggese by G. Rondoni in *Arch. Stor. It.*, Series 5, Vol. XLVII, pp. 181-95; also a body article by R. Palmarocchi, "Contributi allo Studio delle Fonti Statuarie," in *Arch. Stor. It.*, dispensa 3 of 1930, pp. 56-107. Consult also Davidsohn; Vol. IV, *Anmerkungen zum Zweiten Theil*, pp. 1-4, "Die Aeltesten Statuten von Florenz."

these documents with the records of the council sessions, the *Provvisioni* and *Consulte,* thrown in for good measure, make up the fundamental constitutional material of the republic of Florence. They will have to be collected, analyzed, and interpreted, a work that has as yet been no more than begun, before we can reach a full understanding of the public law and private practices of the sons of the Red Lily in the period of their most vigorous self-expression.

It cannot be truthfully said that as soon as Florence in 1322 again took over its own affairs, it prospered more vigorously than had been the case under Neapolitan direction. If throughout the peninsula republican forms were giving way to despotism, the reason, as cannot be too often repeated, was that democracies are in their very nature ill adapted to the successful conduct of war. Again and again in the years ahead Florence was to have this truth brought home to it, but never more crushingly than in the pending struggle with the unusually capable lord of Lucca. Like Uguccione before him, Castruccio aimed to reduce Pistoia to obedience in the persuasion that the capture of this strategic post was the necessary preliminary to the overthrow of Florence and the subjection of Tuscany to his person. For nothing less than the conquest of the whole province had become the goal of his ambition; and Florence, he argued, though too strong to be directly attacked, would fall like ripe fruit into his lap as soon as he had made himself master of Pistoia and the many small supporting fortresses among the rolling hills of the Pistoiese contado. On May 5, 1325, Castruccio won the Pistoian prize by a sudden stroke, which would hardly have been successful had he not been helped by traitors within the walls. Traitors or no traitors, he had captured the city and news fell upon the ears of his Arno enemies like a peal of thunder. They realized that they were as game stalked by a cunning hunter and angrily resolved to bring the issue to a quick decision.

By this time it had already become the settled practice of Florence to hire foreign horsemen as soon as war hove in sight. Under the same impulsion it had become usual to name a special war captain (*capitano di guerra*), to whom rather than to the podestà, as had formerly been the case, the conduct of the campaign to be undertaken was intrusted. Accordingly, within a day after the capture of Pistoia, the government appointed the Spaniard, or rather Catalan, Raymond of Cardona, to the post of war captain and invited him to increase the mounted mercenaries already in hand as rapidly as possible by new enlistments. These preparations illustrate perfectly the military revolution which was sweeping Italy at this time and on which we enlarged at the beginning of this chapter. The core of the Florentine army, as that of every other town, was by now the body of heavily armored horsemen recruited on the open market at a wage determined by the law of supply and demand. When, after a month of hurried preparations, Raymond inaugurated the campaign, he commanded about twenty-five hundred knights representing a veritable Babel of tongues, for the recruits who had flocked to his banner hailed from France, Spain, Germany, Italy, and England. But note well: four hundred of this cavalry body were native Florentines, of whom some were rich popolani patriotically resolved to satisfy the ancient cavallata requirement, and the others survivors from the depressed and declining nobility who still fought in the wars of Florence as a matter of pride and pleasure. But how had the importance of the native cavalry diminished! By 1325, as the figures show, the local horsemen were completely overshadowed by the mercenaries. And with such giant footsteps did the decline of the old republican army proceed that in the course of the next few decades the native horsemen dropped altogether out of sight. Therewith the military revolution, a social revolution in its origin, had reached its logical goal. Machiavelli writing some two hundred years later, when Italy exhibited a painful helplessness before the assaults of France and Spain, ascribed the absence of a fighting spirit in his countrymen to the systematic uprooting of the nobility by such measures as the Ordinances of Justice. Had it not been for this legislation, he argued, the town cavalries would never have run to such sorry seed as they did. The great political thinker erred in this opinion because he did not consider all the factors of the situation. Without any doubt whatever, the main reason for the decline and extinction of the urban cavalry was not the Ordinances of Justice but the circumstance that, with the fourteenth century, war became the affair of professional soldiers. Compared with them the local milites, even when they had not abandoned the exercise of arms, looked and acted like an awkward squad. The Florentine army system of republican days fell by the wayside—and the statement holds for both infantry and cavalry— owing, in the main, to a feature invariably accompanying social change and increasingly in evidence through all the subsequent phases of occidental civilization. We may call it refinement of function or specialization.

In point of fact the infantry was even less capable of meeting the severer fighting standards of the new age than the horsemen. Nonetheless the democratic army did not die easily and at once; and just as we find Florentine milites still mobilized for the campaign of 1325, so also do we encounter Florentine pedites in the army led into the field by the Catalan captain. On a brilliant day of the month of June, when Raymond had completed his preparations, some fifteen thousand citizen foot-soldiers marched out of the western gate with the bells of all the churches ringing madly to speed them on their way.[5] Quite the most curious, because the most anachronistic feature of this host marching forth to battle for the honor and safety of Florence was that ancient emblem of the free commune, the caroccio. Drawn by white oxen swathed in crimson cloth and carrying a mast and bell—the famous *martinella*—upon its ample platform, it drew the reverent gaze of the populace strung out along the line of march. What Cardona's steel-clad mercenaries on their heavy barbs may have remarked on this gay carnival float would constitute an interesting comment on changing manners if someone had been sufficiently interested to preserve their words.

Throughout the summer the Florentines were occupied with the siege and capture of the numerous small castles held by the enemy in the region between Lucca and Pistoia. Offering no active opposition, Castruccio kept his

---

[5] Villani, IX, 300. The chronicler's burgher pride moves him to enter into picturesque details and statistical data regarding this great host which the interested reader will do well to look up.

army intact in a central position among the foothills above Altopascio, from where he could forestall an attack aimed at either Lucca to the west or at Pistoia to the east. Thus passed the hot summer days with Raymond's effectives steadily declining through disease and desertion. Nonetheless a number of small successes were chalked up for the City of the Baptist. These caused the Florentines to swell with such confidence that they insisted, before ending the campaign, on measuring swords with the Ghibelline lord, apparently grown timid in the face of the bold Guelph initiative. Under these circumstances the campaign was brought to a head with a battle fought on September 23, 1325, near Altopascio, in which Castruccio enjoyed the advantage of occupying higher ground and commanding a less exhausted army. In a very short time the Florentine resistance was broken and in the rout that followed many thousands of knights and foot-soldiers, together with the rich equipment of the camp, were captured by the enemy. Of course that lumbering relic of other days, the caroccio, also fell into the enemy's hands and without doubt filled the hearts of the people of Lucca with more pride than the sight of all the other trophies when, following his victory, Castruccio held a triumphal entry into his capital. In the seared hearts of the Florentines, on the other hand, Altopascio took its place beside those two other names of evil omen, Montecatini and Montaperti.

The vigorous Castruccio pursued the fleeing enemy to the very walls of Florence and during the subsequent weeks occupied himself with laying waste the fertile fields around the city. He did not undertake the siege of so vast a town for the excellent reason that he lacked the necessary forces to surround it. Moreover, in connection with the recent intensification of the war, the Florentine government had been spurred to complete the new circumvallation of the town, thereby rendering it impregnable to direct assault. We are aware that the third circle of walls had been begun more than a generation ago and that it had gone forward with often prolonged interruptions ever since. The year 1310, when Henry VII descended into Italy, had brought about a revival of activity; and so far had the work been pushed on that occasion that, when the mortal crisis connected with the name of Castruccio arose, the whole costly structure could between 1322 and 1325 be brought to completion. We are well informed on this crowning phase of the undertaking because our leading chronicler, Villani, acted as one of the municipal overseers and is happy to communicate the results of his labors to his readers.[6] Castruccio paid the new defenses a fine compliment in his way by declining to try them out.

That the dejected Florentines harbored the gravest anxieties, however, in regard to the Lucchese lord is proved by the renewed surrender of their liberties into the hands of a Guelph signore. Long accustomed to look for succor in periods of stress to the house of Anjou, they now (December, 1325) offered themselves to King Robert's son and heir, Charles, duke of Calabria. In the

<hr/>

[6] Villani, IX, 137. "Ed io scrittore, trovandomi per lo commune di Firenze uficiale con altri onorevoli cittadini sopra fare edificare le dette mura." . . . See also IX, 256, 257. For the fully documented record of the construction of the third circle beginning as far back as 1284, see Davidsohn, *Forschungen,* Vol. IV, pp. 447 ff.

agreement as ultimately ratified Charles was made regent and protector for ten years; he was to maintain a body of one thousand French knights and be paid an annual stipend of 200,000 gold florins; he was to nominate the podestà, the priors, and all other officials; and finally, he was to exercise that most sovereign of all rights, the right of peace and war. Comparing these sweeping terms with those of the very qualified submission of 1313 to Charles' father, we are forced to admit that they come close to abject surrender. In seeking safety from the attack of one tyrant the frightened republic had thrown itself into the arms of another. In July, 1326, Duke Charles arrived in person from the south at the head of a splendid cavalcade. It was not the least ominous feature of the new venture in despotism that on the duke's taking up his residence in the palace of the podestà, it was promptly re-christened Palazzo Ducale. In spite of this act of shoddy servility, the republican spirit was not so dead that it did not command many votaries who looked with barely concealed ill-will on the royal ruler in their midst and who prayed earnestly for the day when the city might again free itself from the noose into which it had thrust its head.[7]

Meanwhile an event was ripening in another quarter of the world which must have tended to confirm the Florentine merchants in the wisdom of their surrender to a master who was a tried and impassioned Guelph. Another German sovereign, Ludwig of Bavaria, was making ready to cross the Alps and hearten his Ghibelline following. Having traced in some detail the fortunes in Italy of Henry VII, we need not hesitate for a moment to declare that every imperial intervention after his time was foredoomed to failure. The coming of Ludwig was therefore no more than an empty gesture. However, that the Italians alive at that time should be disturbed by his arrival may be readily admitted. The Ghibellines would rejoice at the strength about to be added to their ranks, while the Guelphs would register a corresponding flutter of alarm. Especially in Tuscany, dominated by Ghibelline Castruccio, the depressed Guelphs would show concern and Guelph Florence would not unnaturally feel the need of nestling more closely than ever under the wing of its Angevin protector. While still beyond the barrier of the Alps, Ludwig had taken note of Castruccio's success and had rewarded him with the title of imperial vicar. His usurpations thus legitimized, the Antelminelli might entertain as not too extravagant the hope of making his lordship hereditary in his house. The potential strength added to their dangerous provincial enemy was the main reason for alarm on the part of the Florentines over the coming of the Bavarian. In every other respect the event left them entirely unmoved.

In the spring of 1327 Ludwig crossed the Brenner pass and came to Milan, where on the last day of May he was crowned in the church of Sant' Ambrogio with the iron crown of Italy. He owed this initial success to the Ghibellines of Lombardy, for he had brought with him only a small force of his own Germans. When, in the autumn, he proceeded into Tuscany, he passed from under the protection of the Lombard Ghibellines to that of the Ghibellines

---

[7] For a close study of the episode connected with the name of Charles of Naples see *Arch. Stor. It.*, Serie 5, Vol. XLII (1908), pp. 45 ff., 259 ff. The author, G. degli Azzi, has illustrated his study with many documents.

of Tuscany and was accordingly met and welcomed at the Tuscan border by Castruccio. Though playing ostensibly the part of his sovereign's obedient servant, the successful adventurer was in reality the guardian of his master; and when he now requested of that master to be made hereditary duke of Lucca, he could not be denied. This was a first step. Others would follow in due course until the lord of little Lucca had expanded into the duke of the great province of Tuscany. Tuscany was without doubt Castruccio's goal, although he was content for the present to keep the thought locked closely in his bosom.

The new duke's immediate purpose was to make himself indispensable to Ludwig by speeding him on his way to Rome, where the Bavarian desired to be crowned emperor. In this connection it will be necessary to set forth a literary controversy which arose at this time and which is just about the only feature of this Roman expedition with a real claim on our attention. The controversy in question had its origin in the renewal of the papal declaration that the church is superior to the empire and consequently can make and unmake emperors at its pleasure. The pope reigning in Ludwig's time was the Frenchman, John XXII (1316–34). He was disliked by many Italians, not necessarily Ghibellines, because he refused to give up his residence at Avignon and return to Rome; and he was looked at askance by pious Christians generally because of his gross financial exactions and his ferocious persecution of that faction of the followers of the Assisan saint called Spiritual Franciscans. These Spirituals had become the object of the papal wrath for no other reason than their fanatical devotion to the evangelical doctrine of poverty. John had opposed the election of Ludwig as German king and, when it took place in spite of him, promptly declared it null and void. In his counterblast to this thunder Ludwig enumerated the sins of his Avignonese enemy and, because of John's fanatical opposition to the doctrine of poverty preached by the Spirituals, roundly declared that his opponent was a heretic. As one defamation calls for another, pope and king continued to fire reverberating broadsides at each other until they had exhausted the objurgatory resources of the Latin language and destroyed every prospect of an amicable settlement of their differences. It will convey a sense of these rancorous amenities if we remark that the pope habitually referred to Ludwig not as king or emperor but as "the accursed Bavarian." He even corrected Ludwig's pedigree by confidently affirming that his real father was none other than Beelzebub.

Similar pleasantries having been exchanged between the two putative heads of Christendom for some centuries past, this latest version of an old controversy might be overlooked were it not for the fact that, when it was about two years old, it gave birth (1324) to something new, a book to wit, indicative of the dawn of a new era of political thought. It was written by Marsilius of Padua (with the probable assistance of the Frenchman, John of Jandun) and bore the intriguing title, *Defensor Pacis* (Defender of the Peace). It projected a philosophy which, though held as yet by few men, signified a lively response on the part of the author to such tremendous recent happenings as the growth of towns, the emergence of national monarchies, and the overthrow of Pope Boniface VIII by Philip IV of France. In view of the vast expansion of secular interests indicated by these events, Marsilius, who, besides being an Italian townsman, was a physician of a scientific bent, found it impossible further to subscribe to the opinion that the civil development of Europe must continue to be subjected to the direction of the church. He went back to the Aristotelian position that the state is a purely mundane institution created for the protection and happiness of its members; and from this premise he deduced that, instead of the state being the civil department of a church which might claim to be omnipotent because instituted by God, the very opposite was true and that the church was rather the religious department of an all-powerful state. He pushed his claim far beyond the Reformation leaders of the sixteenth century, and in effect anticipated a position which enjoyed no general support till the French Revolution. He was thus some centuries ahead of his time, and as the champion of a doctrine that would have dragged the clergy from its eminence aroused a furious resentment in ecclesiastical circles. Nor did he content himself with moving with academic caution in the tenuous realm of theory, for he climaxed his exposition with a vitriolic denunciation of the ignorance, avarice, and worldliness of priests and prelates and particularly of their head, the pope. Although the papal anathema fell promptly on the revolutionary agitator, his book continued to circulate widely for the excellent reason that it expressed a viewpoint which was in accord with some of the leading movements of the age. In short, the *Defensor Pacis* is a literary monument of the first order.

To save himself from clerical persecution Marsilius, who was living at Paris when he composed his great work, had been obliged to put himself under the immediate protection of Ludwig in Germany. He was a big factor in pushing the Bavarian into the Italian venture and, in complete accord with his secular doctrine, he took the position that it was not at all necessary for an emperor to be crowned by the pope. Such radicalism was not easy for any medieval person to accept, and we may take it as certain that Ludwig himself would not have accepted it, if he could have discovered any other way out of his difficulties. As long as Pope John XXII took the hostile stand he did, Ludwig could not hope to have the imperial crown set upon his head; and all that remained, if Ludwig clung to his Roman project, was to subscribe to the Marsilian teaching that the true and legitimate bestower of the imperial diadem was the purely civil group of the Roman people.

It was with the resolution to act on this idea that Ludwig, after receiving the Italian crown at Milan, pushed southward into Tuscany, where we have found him making the most of Castruccio's ascendancy. With the Tuscan's strong support he pressed onward to Rome, where on January 17, 1328, he received the coveted imperial diadem from Sciarra Colonna, acting as syndic of the historic populus Romanus. This Sciarra Colonna, we may note in passing, is the very dubious character who, a generation before, had managed the ambuscade of Anagni, to which the arrogant Boniface VIII had fallen victim. It is interesting to learn that a purely secular coronation did not, after all, satisfy Ludwig, as would have been the case had he been wholeheartedly converted by Marsilius, now in constant attendance on him as his personal physician. The medieval man was still strong in Ludwig and even stronger in his followers. Not content therefore with the civil act, he had himself consecrated at the same time by two bishops. True, they did not claim to represent the pope and the pope for his part did his best to discredit them by declaring them to be heretics; but they wore the robes appropriate to the occasion and applied what passed for holy chrism to the Bavarian's brow. Thereafter every good Ghibelline who cared to argue the point might affirm that Ludwig was emperor *both* by the grace of God and of the Roman people. The chronicler affords us a glimpse of Castruccio at the Roman ceremonies which is so precious that we may not pass it over. Castruccio knew, and everybody knew, that it was he, Castruccio, who had enabled Ludwig to win the imperial diadem. As there was no false modesty about the Lucchese lord, he presented himself to view during the coronation ceremonies in a flame-colored robe, which bore across the front in golden letters the inscription: He is what God ordains; and across the shoulders, also in letters of gold, ran the legend: And he shall be what God shall ordain.[8] He wished to tell the world that, while it had already seen wonders, it might expect still greater wonders in the future.

While Castruccio was at Rome, the Florentines resolved to take advantage of his absence from their neighborhood. They made a sudden night attack on Pistoia and captured the city. The loss drew the discomfited signore speedily back to Tuscany determined to retake the stronghold. The siege that followed did not yield its prize till early August, and in the hour of his triumph the conqueror was himself laid low. A fever contracted during the operations before Pistoia slowly undermined his strength and on September 3 brought his brilliant career to a close. On his deathbed he made provision to have his young sons succeed him, but they were not of his mettle and after only a few weeks were obliged to abandon Tuscany. Even Emperor Ludwig, forgetting what he owed their father, turned against them; had they, however, enjoyed his support instead of his enmity, they would not have gained greatly by the exchange. For the emperor had hardly left Rome when his opponents took over the city on the Tiber; and as, in the course of the summer and autumn, he slowly retreated northward to Pisa, the whole frail edifice of his might began to crack in all its joints. During the winter 1328–29 he did his best to hold Tuscany in submission but, with Castruccio gone, he found the Guelph tide flowing too strongly for him successfully to stem it. In the spring he withdrew to Lombardy, whence, with his partisans falling away from him in increasing numbers every day, he escaped, a sorely tried and beaten man, across the Alps. In February, 1330, he was back in his capital of Munich.

The jubilation of the Florentines at the passing of Castruccio shook the welkin. Death, as Machiavelli maliciously remarked at the sudden demise of another enemy, was ever his countrymen's best ally. Two months later the impersonal Reaper rendered them another egregious service, for on November 9, he mowed down the Florentine signore, Charles of Calabria. When,

---

[8] Villani, X, 59. The two inscriptions read: *E quello che Iddio vuole;* and *E si sarà quello che Iddio vorrà.*

in the previous winter, Ludwig had left Pisa for Rome, the duke had abandoned his Florentine residence in order to help defend his father's kingdom against a possible invasion. In the capital city of Naples he died, still a young man; and instead of being obliged to overthrow by force of arms the master whom they no longer needed now that Castruccio was no more, the Florentines had the good fortune of having their freedom returned to them as a pure gift. They at once resolved to revert to the old constitution, of which the emblem was the priorate, although not without adopting, in the restless manner pilloried in Dante's immortal verse,[9] a few supposed improvements. The revision of 1328 may not be overlooked because it added to the popular government inaugurated in 1282 a last characteristic feature. Not that other features were not excogitated and tried later on. Of some of them we shall be obliged to take at least passing notice. However, of all constitutional reforms after those of 1328 it may be safely said that either they proved ephemeral and promptly disappeared or else that they did not in any notable way modify the established machinery.

Since the priorate was based on the gild system, eligibility to office was reserved to the membership of the twenty-one gilds recognized by the constitution. Of the twenty-one, seven had been originally classified as arti maggiori, five as arti medie, and nine as arti minori. But the association of the middle with the greater gilds in the first stage of the revolution had brought it about that in the Ordinances of Justice these two classes had been grouped together as the twelve greater gilds. To a certain extent this was misleading since only the seven upper gilds were engaged in the export business, and since only among their members were to be found individuals possessed of considerable resources. In any case, regardless of whether we consider the greater gilds to have been seven or twelve in number, there were rich gildsmen and poor gildsmen, and, as might be expected in a period of commercial domination, it was the rich and not the poor who preponderantly served as priors and banner-bearers. While the greater gildsmen may have owed their preponderance to their greater ability and wider experience, it was also due to their secret and unscrupulous manipulation of the elections. The result was that from the very start the priorate showed a tendency to circulate among a relatively small number of families of the new-rich, designated by their less fortunate fellow-citizens with a mixture of admiration and contempt as *il popolo grasso,* the fat bourgeoisie.

Davidsohn has closely studied the prior lists for the years 1310 to 1313 and noticed the occurrence and recurrence of names belonging to families destined to dominate the next two centuries of Arno history.[10] He enumerates, among

[9] . . . . che fai tanti sottili
Provvedimenti, ch'a mezzo Novembre
Non giugne quel che tu d'Ottobre fili.
            Purgatorio, VI, 142-44.

(. . . . . who makest such fine-spun
Provisions, that to middle of November
Reacheth not what thou in October spinnest.)
[10] Davidsohn, Vol. III, p. 401.

others, such characteristic surnames as Soderini, Valori, Albizzi, Foresi, Strozzi, Machiavelli, Corsini, Acciaiuoli, Peruzzi, and Medici. The great families of the previous century were slowly sinking below the horizon, certainly not wholly because of the Ordinances of Justice. They had passed their meridian and were encountering that law of decline which rules all living organisms. The families which replaced them owed their wealth to exactly the same sources as their predecessors, that is, to money-lending and barter. However, they followed a different course from their predecessors since, owing to the taboo put upon knighthood in the Ordinances, they were in growing measure willing to forgo the use of arms and to concentrate on the two engrossing concerns of business and politics. In the generations to come the proudest boast of a good Florentine sprang not from the number of his ancestors who had ridden to battle or gone on crusade but from the number who had served as priors and banner-bearers. With this exaltation of the new republican magistracies it is intelligible that from their first appearance a small clique should have attempted to monopolize them. When criticism became disagreeably clamorous, a reform might be effected which for a time would carry a larger percentage of lesser gildsmen into the priorate. But before long the good resolutions would weaken, and the "fat" burghers, resuming control, would with their intelligence and persistence aided by their money bags successfully render null and void their theoretical equality with small shopkeepers and dependent craftsmen.

Even before the resumption of self-government on the death of the duke of Calabria the suggestion had been repeatedly made to reduce the predominance of the new-rich in office by replacing the existing method of election by a system of drawings by lot. Proposed again in 1328, the measure was so confidently recommended as a sure cure for past evils that it was enthusiastically adopted. Under the new enactment the names of those eligible for the various magistracies were selected by an extraordinarily complicated procedure, called the *scrutinio* or scrutiny, from the membership of the twenty-one gilds possessed of political rating, and put into *borse,* leather purses or bags. From these borse, at the expiration of the terms of the various officials in service, the names of the new officials were extracted by lot. The borse were to be periodically renewed by means of a new scrutinio and they were secured against fraudulent manipulation in their place of deposit with the same elaborate precautions as were used in their preparation.[11] In view of the fact that that will-o'-the-wisp, the democratic equality of all gildsmen, great and small, rich and poor, continued to elude its pursuers, it is impossible to avoid the conclusion that all these involved arrangements represent an enormous futility. Since there was no change in the Florentine social order, we may reasonably ask how the borse could be expected to produce an equalitarianism which did not exist. Not many months after the citizens had adopted the great ballot reform of scrutinio and borse, mutterings were heard to the effect that the same old clique was still on top. Instead of "guiding" the elections, as had been the case in the past, it now, by means best known to itself,

[11] The intricate safeguarding devices, absolutely unique in the history of democratic government, may be consulted in Villani, X, 108, and in Davidsohn, Vol. III, pp. 862 ff.

juggled the lists of the eligibles before and after they got into the borse. In sum, we may agree that from the inauguration of the priorate in 1282 there was in Florence so persistent a drift toward an oligarchy of a plutocratic type that we are obliged to conclude it constituted a reasonably correct expression of the city's social structure. However, neither the slighted members of the lesser gilds nor the steadily growing body of the unorganized and, let us never forget, wholly disfranchised workers were willing to accept the situation. By continuing to demand rights for themselves they projected an element of unrest into the play of politics which successfully kept Florence from hardening into such a comfortable, set oligarchy as already before the end of the thirteenth century had succeeded in monopolizing the government of that other great Italian republic, Venice. In spite of powerful oligarchial tendencies, democratic aspirations never ceased to stir among the common people. They were even vigorous enough to unseat the oligarchs from time to time and to oblige them at all times to be on their guard.

It should not be overlooked, although it was not exactly an epochal event, that in connection with the reform of 1328 the system of councils was genuinely simplified. Instead of the traditional two councils of the podestà there was to be henceforth but a single council of the podestà composed of two hundred and fifty members; and instead of the traditional two councils of the captain, there was to be a single council of the captain composed of three hundred members. Furthermore, in place of the council of One Hundred hitherto attached to the priors, this governing committee was held to be sufficiently advised by Twelve Good Men (*boni uomini*), to whom, a little later, were added the Sixteen Captains of the Military Companies. The Twelve Good Men and the Sixteen Captains (*gonfalonieri*) constituted what was called the college (*collegium*) of the priors. Following this reorganization, a bill, after having been approved by the priors and their collegium, was transmitted to the councils respectively of the captain and the podestà and, on being passed by them, became a law. Though it is not a novelty introduced by the revision here discussed, it deserves to be recorded that the priors and gonfalonier of Justice were by this time no longer housed in a private residence hired for the purpose, as had originally been the case. The palace of the priors, in our day still the proudest landmark of the city under its later designation of Palazzo Vecchio, was begun in 1299 and already in 1302 was far enough along for the new executive to take possession.[12] When we think intimately and humanly of the seven heads of the government, we may visualize them as living together during their two months' term of office in the quarters provided in the new municipal center. The constitution closely and elaborately regulated their lives. They ate together with some ceremony at the expense of the republic, which for purposes of pomp surrounded them with numerous servants. They were prohibited from leaving the palace on private business and no one of them was permitted to conduct official negotiations to the exclusion of his colleagues. The priorate was a commission form of

---

[12] It was in 1302 still far from its present appearance. The stages of its construction may be traced from the documents given by Davidsohn, *Forschungen*, Vol. IV, pp. 499 ff.

government and every conceivable difficulty was put in the way of any one prior exercising a greater authority than his fellows.

The decade following the resumption of Florentine self-government was a period of prosperity, indeed in Villani's eyes his beloved city reached a peak from which it greatly declined in the subsequent decade, the last of the chronicler's life. Between 1328 and 1338 trade and industry visibly advanced, the population grew by leaps and bounds, important public works were undertaken, and a life pulsed through the streets and squares which filled the solid burgher that Villani was with patriotic exultation. And since, as a trader who passed many hours each day bent over a ledger, nothing was more eloquent to his mind than figures, he resolved to take a census of his native town at the close of its most prosperous interval. It is not likely that any medieval man before him ever planned an undertaking so difficult and withall so modern. He had to assemble his material as best he could without authoritative help from any quarter. Admittedly his private researches cannot be accepted without important reservations; let it be said, however, that whenever modern investigators have discovered data enabling them to test Villani's statements, they have been moved to voice their admiration of the old chronicler's veracity and accuracy.

On the basis of the consumption of grain Villani arrived at a figure of ninety thousand men, women, and children within the walls.[13] There were usually about fifteen hundred strangers in Florence, a figure indicative as much of the commercial eminence of the city as of the medieval love of travel. This well-attested passion of our forefathers we moderns, who are inclined to associate travel with the conveniences resulting from steam and electricity, are wont to overlook. From eight to ten thousand children, boys and girls, attended the elementary schools which taught the rudiments of reading and writing, while some six hundred boys were enrolled in four schools of a higher grade which introduced them to the mysteries of grammar and logic. That means of course that they were made acquainted with Latin and dialectics, the recognized foundation of all medieval intellectual culture. There were one hundred and ten churches in the city and its suburbs, of which fifty-seven served as parish churches; the remainder belonged to the various religious orders. Thirty hospitals with a capacity of more than one thousand beds served the poor and the sick. Two hundred shops of the wool gild, giving work to about thirty thousand hands, turned out annually between seventy and eighty thousand bolts of cloth worth more than one million two hundred thousand gold florins. This bit of information alone suffices to show that it was the textile industry which gave Florence its economic eminence. But while once upon a time it had been the merchants of the Calimala gild, the importers of coarse

[13] Villani, XI, 94. He speaks picturesquely of *bocche* (mouths). Modern students, statistically trained, have indorsed Villani's figures. In view of the new suburbs, which had already grown up around the third circle of walls only recently completed, they favor a total population for 1339, including city and suburbs, of one hundred and fifteen to one hundred and twenty thousand. N. Rodolico, *La Democrazia Fiorentina nel suo Tramonto,* chap. I. Bologna, 1905. G. Pardi, "Disegno della Storia Demografica di Firenze," *Arch. Stor. It.,* Serie 5, Vol. I, pp. 3 ff., 185 ff. Rodolico discusses the population figures for the town through the Middle Ages and Renaissance; Pardi discusses them from the beginnings to the present time.

Flemish or French cloth for the purpose of refining it, who had been the leading manufacturers, shortly after the turn of the thirteenth century the merchants of the wool gild, who made an excellent native cloth, though generally from imported, more particularly from English, wool, acquired a supremacy over the Calimala merchants which they never again lost. In other words, the *arte di Lana* dominated the trecento much as the other woolen gild, the *arte di Calimala,* had dominated the dugento. In abstracting as our final items from this part of Villani's census that Florence was served by eighty banks, six hundred men of law, sixty physicians and surgeons, and one hundred apothecaries, we get a picture that obliges us to conclude that here on the middle Arno we encounter a society already so richly differentiated as to be no longer medieval.

It is when our annalist takes up the revenues and expenditures of his beloved town, that his bosom swells with a very special pride.[14] The form of tax favored and almost exclusively used by the city fathers was the indirect tax, the *gabella.* Most of the gabelle were collected at the town gates on merchandise, both as it entered and passed out of the city, and on the food of the people, grain, wine, salt, and meat. The total revenues, constituted overwhelmingly of gabelle, came to three hundred thousand gold florins, a sum, according to the enraptured statistician, which would be a magnificent income for a kingdom (*sarebbe gran cosa a un reame*). Indeed King Robert of Naples, whom the Florentines were pleased to think of as their protector, had no such sum as that to jingle in his pocket. As no more than fifty thousand florins were required to meet the ordinary costs of administration, the remainder, constituting about five-sixths of the annual budget, was swallowed up by war. It happened that in the years of which Villani has written most fully war had practically become chronic, for first, there were the defensive wars against Castruccio Castracane, and after Castruccio's death came the offensive wars (of which we shall presently hear) to acquire Castruccio's Lucca and to confirm the Florentine mastery of Tuscany. We receive ample evidence from Villani's data touching the military revolution, to which we have repeatedly referred in this chapter. While the chronicler speaks of the continued liability to service in the field of every son of Florence between the ages of fifteen and seventy, he makes it perfectly clear that the citizen militia was only rarely summoned and that at least in his declining years the wars of the Arno city were mainly fought by hireling troops. When the campaign was over, the mercenaries were, as a rule, discharged, but the responsibilities which Florence had assumed as an expanding power made it necessary to retain a portion of them on the pay-roll at all times to assure peace and order throughout the ever-widening dominion of the state. If we realize that the city kept even in time of peace a small standing army of from seven hundred to one thousand horsemen, we are prepared to admit that the republican system inherited from the consular days has been superseded. These changes, above all, the continuous wars with their inordinate cost, stirred humanitarian regrets in the historian's heart. He was a bourgeois of the moralizing type who approved the democratic system of the gilds but grieved that it tended to produce magistrates too fond of power and overprompt

[14] Villani, XI, 92, 93.

to make war. In fact so thoroughgoing was his humanitarianism that he reveals himself at times as a theoretic pacifist. This will explain why, in concluding his account of the disproportionate expenditures for military purposes, our
usually matter-of-fact trader and statistician was shaken by an emotional par-
oxysm. In a furious apostrophe addressed to the rulers of Florence, with whom,
let us not forget, he was closely tied up, he cries out: "O Signori Fiorentini,
what a perverse and wicked policy is this of yours to increase the revenues of
the commune from the substance of poor citizens by means of increased taxes
and to invest them in insane undertakings! . . . Moderate, most beloved, your
inordinate ambitions, for thus you will please God and will cease to burden
an innocent people."

Villani's presentation of the Florentine budget opens up the whole important matter of taxation. As a recent work [15] has at last presented the issue in its
historical perspective, we can now find our way through the intricate financial
labyrinth of the young commune, although many of the developments ante-
dating the triumph of the Blacks still remain obscure. As in the case of one and
all of the services and institutions created by the commune, the taxes have a
haphazard, accidental, and empirical beginning. Their origin must be sought
in certain feudal dues wrested from the empire, more particularly a hearth-tax
of twenty-six pennies (*denarii*), and in way-tolls collected at the town gates
and commonly called *pedaggi*. Since the hearth-tax was a direct tax and the
pedaggio an indirect tax, we observe that the two great categories of taxation
figure in the communal finances from the start. It was with an increase of the
returns from the indirect taxes that the young republic attempted to meet the
waxing burdens of government. Even in full feudal times the town had resorted to imposts on ovens, wine, grain, and similar consumption taxes, and
these dues, added to the tolls on goods in transit, increased automatically in
measure as commerce and population expanded. The generic name for indirect
taxes being gabelle, we may think of the growing commune as operating
largely with them. However, toward the middle of the thirteenth century a
new direct tax put in an appearance, the *estimo*. It represented an attempt to
graduate the tax burden according to the wealth of the individual and thereby
to moderate the injustice of the consumption taxes, which fell with crushing
severity on the common people. Commendable in intention, the estimo caused
unending complaints, in part because from the beginning of time men have
been averse to paying direct taxes, but also because the assessment, based on
both capital and income, varied so greatly from man to man and was so subject to fraud and favor that it developed monstrously inequitable features.
There was as yet no great body of statistical material on hand from which it
would have been possible to arrive at acceptable norms for a scientific income
tax, even if such an ideal had lain within the mental range of the taxing bodies
of that age. When the imperfect estimates, called estimo, were ready, the government, acting on resolutions passed by the councils, levied a tax called *libra*
based on the estimo and naming a rate of payment calculated to bring in the
sum of which the treasury stood in immediate need. Owing to the ever-widen-

[15] B. Barbadoro, *Le Finanze della Repubblica Fiorentina: Imposta Diretta e Debito Pubblico fino all'Istituzione del Monte*. Florence, 1929.

ing range of action of the commune and to the consequent growth of expenditures, chiefly for war, it might often happen that the owners of property
were *allibrati* several times within a year. In 1315, when Florence was obliged
to meet the danger which threatened her ascendancy owing to the sudden rise
of Uguccione della Faggiuola, a financial crisis was precipitated which enables
our authority, Barbadoro, to give us the first clear view of the principles and
practices underlying the taxation structure of the state.

By the year 1315 the Blacks had been in power for over a decade and the
rule of the Blacks had worked out as the triumph of the popolo grasso, the
"fat" bourgeoisie. It was these well-to-do rulers who had to submit to a disgusting inquisition into their possessions for the purposes of the estimo and
who had to arrange to pay the libra as often as it was voted in order to meet
an extraordinary expense. In 1315, in the very face of the peril threatening from
Pisa, they revolted, and with an apparent unanimity in all the councils sweepingly rejected the combination of estimo and libra as a means for balancing
the budget. Never did a possessive bourgeoisie more neatly than on this occasion reveal its intimate mind and heart. Far removed from giving up the policy
of an expanding control in Tuscany and Italy, the dominant merchants were
firmly resolved to continue the wars which their policy made unavoidable, but
they would no longer finance them by a method obliging their class to bear a
large portion of the tax burden. Their war finances—and Florentine taxation
throughout the Black period falls substantially under this head—were based on
a conception so typically bourgeois that it has reappeared ever since when and
wherever a bourgeoisie has exercised control. The men who dominated the
priorate and the councils determined to meet the war costs by spreading them
among the people through increased indirect taxes (*gabelle*) and among themselves through loans (*prestanze*) carrying an interest rate of 8 or more per
cent. Since the course adopted in 1315 was still followed twenty years later
when Villani took his census, we are not surprised to learn that the immense
regular revenues, amounting to three hundred thousand gold florins, were
almost exclusively raised by gabelle. The most considerable exception which he
lists is the estimo of the countryside. On abolishing the estimo for the city,
where they had their residence, the self-seeking burghers did not extend the
favor to the agricultural population. Apparently an impost based on possessions was a welcome source of revenue, provided it fell on magnates and country yokels and not on the urban lords of trade.

If we keep in mind the hardly ever interrupted wars of the decades immediately following the adoption of the new financial plan, we are prepared to
understand the crisis that slowly gathered around the policy of loans, the second string to the bow of taxation. The prestanze were numerous, they bore an
engaging rate of interest, and in order to effect their redemption they were
assigned on issue to one or another of the many gabelle. But when the wars
not only gave no sign of coming to an end but grew steadily more expensive,
the repayment of the loans had to be adjourned, while the interest they drew
was subjected to reduction or indefinite postponement. With the campaigns of
the late thirties and early forties connected with the attempt to capture Lucca
these unhappy effects made themselves violently felt. By considering them at

this point we are forging ahead of our story, but the procedure is justified by the need of bringing our financial argument to a logical conclusion. The point to keep in mind is that at the beginning of the forties there was an immense public debt, which was no longer being redeemed according to contract and on which even the interest payments were but irregularly made. The only way to save the whole device of the prestanze from collapse was by a consolidation of the old loans, together with a slash in the interest rate and by at least a partial abandonment of the feature of redemption. By a series of measures belonging to the period 1343–47 this reform was carried through [16] and an orderly administration of the public debt created, picturesquely called *Monte,* from the single heap or "mountain" to which the varied items of indebtedness had been reduced. Considered purely as a technical operation in public finance, the Florentine Monte represented a notable achievement. By means of it the system of loans was re-established in the public confidence, thereby enabling loans together with indirect taxes to remain the characteristic features of Florentine taxation for many years to come. The dark side of the successful consolidation of the national debt signified by the Monte was that it indefinitely adjourned the return to the estimo, the direct tax, by which individuals contributed to the support of their government in some reasonable proportion to their means.

Appropriating Villani's habitual way of marking a transition, we shall now leave the issue of taxes and resume our interrupted political narrative. As soon as, with the death of the duke of Calabria in 1328, the Florentine oligarchs had reacquired control, they took up again their plan of territorial expansion, which the successive, meteor-like appearances of Uguccione della Faggiuola and Castruccio Castracane had obliged them to abandon. Their instrument for extending their power over Tuscany had now for some two generations been the league of Tuscan Guelphs. While this was a useful device, it represented a very loose federation, and from the angle of a power aspiring to an unchallenged mastery, was much less satisfactory than direct control. From the first, therefore, Florence had not hesitated to impose its immediate rule whenever the opportunity offered, with the result that, in addition to the scores of castles seized and garrisoned by it at various strategic points, it had gradually acquired possession of most of the small markets and communes of its county and district. It tried to make its yoke as light as the circumstances permitted by contenting itself with sending an executive or podestà and a small troop of men-at-arms under a captain to the subjected town and by conceding, in return for this hegemony, a considerable measure of self-government.[17]

Another and a higher stage in the growth and consolidation of the Florentine state would be reached when the great towns, once the equals and still the jealous rivals of the Red Lily, should in their turn be brought beneath its sway. More than once in the past it had seemed that this stage had been reached, but always some unexpected event had intervened and saved the intended victim from Florentine dominion. However, when at the death of

---

[16] Barbadoro, chaps. VIII, IX.

[17] A typical case of submission is that of the small town of Colle. Its people agreed to receive "podestà e capitano di Firenze e la guardia della rocca alle loro spese." Villani, XI, 81.

Castruccio his loosely joined state fell apart, the desired day dawned at last. The chief object of contention between Castruccio and the Arno city had been Pistoia; and one of the first consequences of the collapse of the lord of Lucca's miniature empire had been the resumption of its independence by the cantankerous little neighbor of Florence which enjoyed the dubious honor of having given birth to the Black-White feud. But Pistoia was too utterly drained of its vitality by the frequent sieges it had recently undergone to be able to stand securely on its feet. On its own initiative it now accepted the supremacy of Florence, first by permitting its neighbor to appoint its chief official, and later by receiving a small Florentine garrison. The main effect of this welcome increment of power was to stimulate the Florentine appetite. So complete was the disintegration of Castruccio's state that Lucca itself, exhausted by its superlative effort, seemed ripe for subjection. For over a decade after this prospect dawned, the Florentines directed their gaze at the rival city on the Serchio with a kind of hypnotized intensity. Their waking and their sleeping thoughts were concerned with the capture of Lucca; and when in the end all their greedy plans miscarried, the political confusion and economic exhaustion caused by the long Lucchese effort led, as a similar crisis had already twice done in the past, to another signore or tyrant.

So amazingly tied up with the political upheaval throughout Italy was the long-drawn-out Florentine enterprise having Lucca as its object that it almost defies unraveling. The Visconti of Milan, the Scala of Verona, the astute oligarchs of Venice, and even King John of Bohemia, son of Emperor Henry VII (the same John, who, falling afterward at Crécy, left his three-plumed helmet on the ground for the Black Prince to pick up), play a role *pro* or *contra* Florence, while a score of minor city tyrants and feudal potentates, whom it would only add to the confusion to enumerate, make a sporadic appearance in the complicated plot. And yet the story in its essence is simple enough, for it turns on the helplessness of Lucca after Castruccio's fall and the greedy expectation of its neighbors, near and far, to appropriate the enfeebled state. It told against the Florentines that they were not the earliest bystanders to take advantage of the confusion produced in Lucca by the death of its signore. The first group of profiteers was a body of German mercenaries. Having deserted Ludwig of Bavaria when he was no longer able to pay them their wages, they occupied Lucca by force and set themselves up as its owners. Overwhelmed before long by the practical difficulties of government, they sold their possession for a lump sum to a rich Genoese banker. This gentleman, a member of the famous house of Spinola, transferred it for a consideration to the aforementioned son of Emperor Henry VII, who, a typical knight-errant, had come to Italy in the early thirties ready to try his hand at any adventure that might happen to come his way. After having met with a number of rebuffs that signally dampened his romantic ardor, John in his turn sold (1334) the Serchio city to the Rossi of Parma. The Rossi, too, did not hold it long, for under pressure from the powerful lord of Verona, Mastino della Scala, they handed it over to this leading Lombard signore; and when Mastino, owing to his frequent wars, stood in need of money, he entered into negotiations with the Florentines who all along had watched this succession of dizzy transfers of title with the liveliest anxiety. But the Veronese lord proved as slippery as an eel. While he craved the bills of exchange of the Arno merchants, he wanted just as eagerly to keep his new-won political foothold in Tuscany. He therefore blew alternately hot and cold in the Lucchese matter. Vastly indignant at this double-dealing, the Florentines in 1336 made an alliance with the republic of Venice in the hope of extracting Lucca from Mastino by military pressure from two sides, and once again they met with disappointment. For no sooner had the allied Venetians gained their own particular end than they made a separate peace with the Scala tyrant and obliged Florence to come to terms or meet the concentrated attack of the enemy (1338). Apparently regardless of whether they followed the course of bribery or war the Florentines were destined to be balked of the Lucchese prize.

Unwilling to concede themselves beaten, they now returned to their original plan of buying Lucca from Mastino with a chest of good gold florins and straightway ran into a new difficulty. The closest neighbor of the Serchio city was Pisa; and Pisa, indisposed to have Florence established at its gates, opened negotiations of its own with Mastino and followed them up with an attack on Lucca in the hope of capturing it. Thus matters stood in 1341. After the Florentines had wasted large sums in attempted bribery of the slippery Mastino and after they had lost even larger sums in levying war on him, the Pisans had the impertinence to come forward in order to reap where the Florentines had sown. In their desperation the Arno burghers suspended the constitution and intrusted a committee of twenty citizens (*I Venti*) with full powers for one year. To no avail; for when on October 2, 1341, the Twenty authorized an attack on the Pisan host besieging Lucca, the Florentine army suffered a capital rebuff. This accumulation of disasters prompted the lugubrious Villani to raise the theological issue as to why God was so hard on his native city; and, as a good, believing Christian, he found the answer in the heaped sins of his fellow-citizens.[18] But though the merchants might lament and beat their bosoms, they were not even yet prepared to abandon the prize on which their heart was set. In the spring of 1342 they made a new attempt to raise the siege of Lucca by the Pisans which ended in a new failure; and on July 6 Lucca surrendered to the Pisan commander. The coveted town was lost and all Florence groaned aloud. Half crazed with rage and disappointment, it resolved as a last desperate measure to try its luck with a military adventurer.

On August 1, 1342, immediately after the expiration of the power conceded to the Twenty, the Frenchman, Count Walter of Brienne, called duke of Athens, was put in charge of the war as *capitano di guerra*. This office had become a feature of the constitution some years before and was in no way irregular. Indeed it was the priors, the guardians of the democratic system, who appointed Count Walter to the command of the army. They chose him, it is true, less for his own sake than because of his relationship by marriage to that house of Anjou to which Florence had long ago contracted the habit of appealing in periods of stress. In this French nobleman we encounter another characteristic figure of that age of swift political flux. His father had actually

18 Villani, XI, 135.

been lord of the duchy of Athens, one of those curious states of the Byzantine east created by the combined prowess and treachery of the knights of the Fourth Crusade. But he had fallen in battle against a band of Catalan mercenaries, who, having seized the duchy, obliged his young son and heir to seek shelter under the wings of King Robert of Naples. Brought up at court and married to a royal princess, Count Walter employed the now empty title of duke of Athens as a stimulus to his ambition. With antecedents such as his it was inevitable that he should cast himself for the role of knight-errant in an Italy teeming with opportunities for *ogni villan che parteggiando viene.* In the passing of the years he had seen much military service, but, apart from his knowledge of war and a certain tenacity of purpose, he possessed no qualities whatever calculated to recommend him to his contemporaries. Villani, who, while detesting him, does not indulge in vilification, describes him as a dark-skinned, undersized man with a long, scraggy beard and a furtive eye completely incapable of arousing a generous enthusiasm.[19] Encouraged by a Florentine merchant group abroad to offer his sword to the Red Lily, he arrived at the precise moment when the city, disorganized and panicky, was looking about for a savior. Appointed as capitano di guerra, he was no sooner in office than some of the magnates with a following of rich popolani began to urge him not to rest content with his limited position but to make himself absolute lord of the city. While the leading contemporary chronicler insists on regarding the magnates as the main instigators of the intrigue, a recent investigator has adduced sufficient documentary material to oblige us to see the event in a somewhat different light.[20] However, to give due weight to this new evidence we must halt our narrative for a moment, while we examine the grave economic crisis which struck Florence at the very moment when it was receiving blow on blow in connection with its Lucchese enterprise.

The economic crisis of these years was in its origin a purely financial crisis and sprang from the reckless grant of loans on the part of the great Florentine trading and banking companies to various European governments for the unproductive purpose of waging war. The trading companies, great international concerns with branches in all the leading cities of the west, had made Florence the world's leading money center. If, toward the end of the dugento, such great houses as the Mozzi, the Scali, the Spini, and the Cerchi held the lead in supplying needy governments with funds, in the course of the first third of the trecento their places had been taken by the even larger and more flourishing establishments of the Frescobaldi, the Bardi, the Acciaiuoli, and the Peruzzi. Business was severely competitive, and while some firms had succeeded in making themselves particularly strong at the papal court or in the kingdom of Naples, others had gained a commanding position in Flanders, in England, and in France. In England, beginning with the reign of Edward I and reaching a climax under Edward III, the Bardi and Peruzzi had acquired a status that gave them a practical monopoly of the export of wool, the leading raw product of English origin figuring in the world-market. The two houses owed their eminence to the favor of the sovereign, to whom they made a return

[19] Villani, XII, 8.
[20] A. Sapori, *La Crisi delle Compagnie Mercantili dei Bardi e dei Peruzzi.* Florence, 1926.

GIOTTO. THE RAISING OF DRUSIANA. SCENE FROM THE LIFE OF ST. JOHN THE EVAN-GELIST. FRESCO. PERUZZI CHAPEL IN SANTA CROCE (ALINARI).

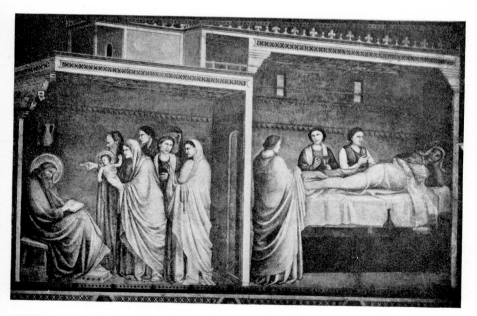

GIOTTO. TWO SCENES FROM THE LIFE OF ST. JOHN THE BAPTIST. FRESCO. PERUZZI CHAPEL IN SANTA CROCE (ALINARI).

ORCAGNA. ALTARPIECE IN THE STROZZI CHAPEL IN SANTA MARIA NOVELLA (ALINARI)

ORCAGNA. PARADISE. FRESCO IN THE STROZZI CHAPEL
IN SANTA MARIA NOVELLA (ALINARI).

by supplying his treasury with the cash whereof it was in perpetual need. When Edward III was seized with the ambition to conquer France, he proposed to meet the cost of the enterprise with loans from his Florentine servants; and although they knew that the investment was dangerous, they had by gradual stages become so involved in the royal finances that a retreat was impossible. After extending themselves to the limit in Edward's early campaigns, by 1339 they were completely exhausted; and when the king, drawing only inconsiderable revenues from his as yet poor and backward realm, was unable to pay his creditors either interest or principal, there was nothing for the English branches of the two houses to do but to go into bankruptcy.

When the news of this disaster reached Florence, it produced a run not only on the Bardi and the Peruzzi banks but on all the banks of the city, large and small. The general confidence was shaken, and it required a series of moratoria on the part of both government and depositors before the public became somewhat calmed and orderly business could be again resumed. But without any doubt whatever, owing to Edward III's default on his enormous war debt, the Florentine financial structure was in perilous case as early as 1339. Had the budget of the Florentine state been on a sound basis, there might presently have been a pick-up. But Florence, too, had just squandered vast sums on war, and what is more, it continued to squander them long after the crisis of 1339 had sounded a first warning. The government was in the hands of the popolo grasso, and there was nothing for the bankers to do, so long as they were an integral part of the system, but to support the Lucchese enterprise to which the whole city had become rapturously committed. When the hard-pressed authorities were forced by the state of the treasury increasingly to suspend payment on the city's obligations, a second and a final financial convulsion could not be long delayed. It was under these circumstances that the great trading companies, wishing to avoid the catastrophe that threatened them, turned to the plan of giving the city a tyrant of their own choosing. Having raised him to power, they hoped as their reward to be intrusted with the shaping of his foreign policy and with the exclusive control of his finances.

This, in substance, is Sapori's theory regarding the origin of the tyranny of the duke of Athens, and it differs from that of contemporary Villani in bringing the role of the bankers into greater relief. But it cannot be said to contradict Villani, for the alert eyewitness was fully aware that the magnates and bankers co-operated in foisting the French nobleman on the city. In offering his version of the event he was confronted with the ambiguity which we have repeatedly pointed out and which remains a source of confusion to this day: the magnate and rich popolani classes in Florence were largely indistinguishable. The Bardi and Frescobaldi, for instance, were magnates, while the Peruzzi and Acciaiuoli were popolani. Doubtless they and many other traders of both legal categories acted together in the great emergency of the summer of 1342 for the unexceptional reason that they had an identical interest to defend. In reporting the event Villani makes too much of the purely magnate element, on which account Sapori's correction may be welcomed since it shows that the conspirators were, economically, a single class induced to act together by the commonest of class motives, self-interest.

Thus oriented in regard to the hidden powers behind the duke of Athens, we arrive at a much clearer understanding regarding the events following his appointment as capitano di guerra. The plotters, magnates and rich traders as Villani truthfully states, in private audiences with the new commander-in-chief urged him to make himself signore. At the same time they prompted the common people, more ill-disposed than ever to the popolo grasso after the accumulated political failures of the foregoing decade and the accompanying economic crisis, to greet him with wild acclamations whenever he appeared in public. Fearing a revolutionary outbreak, the intimidated priors sought to save the situation by offering the war captain the signory of Florence for the duration of one year. But when on the day after this offer, on September 8, a parlamentum was called in the great public square before the palace of the priors (the present Piazza Signoria) in order to have the people confirm the bargain, the popolo minuto, instigated by the magnates, raised a deafening shout *a vita, a vita* (for life, for life); and suiting their action to their words, they lifted the duke to their shoulders and triumphantly carried him into the palace. It was an act emblematic of the acquisition of sovereignty. By the work of a packed and disorderly parliament Walter of Brienne had become the despot of the City of the Baptist for the length of his natural days.

Raised to power in this manner, the duke might be supposed to have adopted the policy of leaning heavily on the highest and the lowest classes of the population. And such indeed seemed at first to be the case. Owing to a desperate attempt on the part of two of the leading magnate-banker families, the Bardi and Frescobaldi, to seize the power two years before, in 1340, they had been banished from Florence. Of course they had not ceased to exercise influence, owing to their essential solidarity with the great mass of monied men left behind. Nonetheless they desired to have the ban against them canceled and this favor the new ruler promptly accorded. At the same time he made peace with Pisa in order to stop the heavy financial drain which had gone on for years and had in the main been met by forced loans from the Florentine banks. And finally, he protected the slipping trading companies from the molestations of their creditors by conceding them a moratorium for a period of three years. As for the popolo minuto, who looked upon him as their man and cheered him to the echo, he showed his sympathy for them by filling the priorate largely from their ranks. It was a feature of his tyranny that, while leaving the constitution intact, he operated it in his interest by appointing the officials. The priors having in this way become a purely ornamental feature of the government, there was no reason why he should not flatter the vanity of butchers, wineshopkeepers, and wool-carders by inviting them to serve as a mock executive. But while prepared to favor the groups to which he owed his signory, he had no mind to be ruled by them or to conduct his government on any counsel or in any interest save his own. Before long the noble plotters found the doors of the palace shut against them and themselves excluded from every exercise of power. And when, on November 20, the duke sanctioned the suspension of payment on all the city's war loans on the ground that the gabelle, from which the loans were to be paid, were needed for current expenditures, he straightway transformed his banker-supporters into his enemies. The proclaimed suspension of payments was really a veiled bankruptcy of the Florentine state. It would have been followed at once by the bankruptcy of the trading-houses, if the duke had not already conceded the three-year moratorium, which kept their creditors from flying at them like angry hornets. It is an interesting detail that the tyrant returned to the direct tax, the estimo, as a convenient means of raising revenue. In this he may have acted merely from avarice, as the good Villani claims; but the student of a later day will not fail to recall that despotism was the political form toward which all Italy was feeling its way, and that despotism, in spite of the evils inseparable from personal rule, usually bestirs itself to end the domination of a privileged class by reducing the whole population to a common level before the law.[21]

Without believing that the new despot was as malevolent and avaricious as his enemies afterward made out, we should find no difficulty in persuading ourselves that the Florentines, after the manner of fickle man, soon tired of their master, and that the group, particularly eager to get rid of him, were the heads of the trading-houses disappointed in their hope that he would be content to act as their tool. The group below the great traders, the broad middle class, had never looked on him with favor; and as for the lower orders who unquestionably had helped him seize the power, they too began to grow cool when they discovered that he could not master the economic crisis, which was deepening every day and spreading a disastrous unemployment. By the spring of 1343 three separate conspiracies against the tyrant were under way, hatched by rival groups of magnates and rich popolani. On the duke's somewhat belatedly getting wind of one of them and taking action by arresting its promoters, in self-defense the three movements coalesced, armed their followers, and on July 26, 1343, set them in motion against the palace. With such celerity was the rising effected that the duke was not able to assemble more than a fraction of his troops scattered over the Florentine dominion. Even the common people, whether from disillusionment, as already hinted, or from thoughtless abandonment to the excitement of the moment, rallied to the rebels. With the apparent hearty co-operation of all its social elements Florence laid siege to its ruler in the palazzo, which he occupied with four hundred soldiers hurriedly gathered together and scantily supplied with food and water.

As his precarious situation put victory out of the despot's reach, he was not long in opening negotiations with his besiegers. But the population, aroused to frenzy and thirsting like wolves for warm blood, would not hear of a surrender which permitted their ruler to withdraw with the honors of war and which cheated them of their vengeance. They called for victims, and on the sixth day of the siege the duke, broken in spirit and resolved at all costs to save his precious person, was obliged to sacrifice the man who had acted as his chief of police, and to push him, together with his eighteen-year-old son, through the palace gate into the arms of the waiting mob. Let Villani re-

[21] On these measures of the duke see Sapori, pp. 146-50. On the whole incident of the duke of Athens, the work of C. Paoli is still invaluable. See *Giornale Storico degli Archivi Toscani,* Vol. VI, pp. 79 ff., 169 ff.; also *Arch. Stor. It.,* Serie 3, Vol. XVI, pp. 22 ff.

count what followed: "In the presence of the father and for his greater sorrow they first dismembered the son, cutting him into small bits (*minuti pezzi*); and this done, they did the same to the father. And one planted a piece of flesh on a lance and another on a sword, and in this manner they made the rounds of the city. And some there were so cruel and possessed of such bestial fury that they ate of the raw flesh." [22] With its savagery placated by this revolting demonstration, the multitude began to disperse, permitting a Committee of Fourteen, to which full powers had been given by a parlamentum hurriedly assembled in the church of Santa Reparata, to make the final arrangements with the fallen signore. Accordingly, on August 6, under safe conduct from a body of Sienese, who had rushed from their hills to help their Florentine friends, the duke with his dependents made his departure from the palace and the city. It was the closing act of the third and most substantial experiment in despotism on the part of the republic since the beginning of the century.

The Fourteen, intrusted with the reorganization of the government, were made up half of magnates and half of leading burghers. This composition of the committee tells us without further argument that it was the trading-houses that overthrew the tyrant, as it had also been they who had installed him in the palace. In the sessions they held to discuss the composition of the new government their central concern must have been the continuation of their power. But as, for the moment, they had the whole city behind them, it was the part of wisdom to exhibit a certain moderation. They therefore re-enacted the old constitution of the priors with a few alterations. Some of these belong to the mere mechanics of administration, as, for instance, the article which replaced the old division of the city into sixths with a new division into quarters; and another article which raised the number of priors from six to twelve, three for each of the new units. What alone mattered to the victors was their own adequate representation in the priorate, and to bring this about they took the bold step of abolishing the Ordinances of Justice. With the magnates, after half a century of political ostracism, again made eligible to the chief executive, the Fourteen ordained that henceforth the priorate should be composed of four magnates (one for each quarter) and eight popolani (two for each quarter), selected from the membership of the twenty-one gilds.

Great as must have been the exultation of the magnate-bankers over the revamped constitution, they made the error common to the upper classes of every age of paying too little attention to the feelings of the people. Consequently, the priors of the new dispensation had been in office only a few days when, on September 22, a mob of immense dimensions gathered around the palace, declaring that it would storm the building unless the four sitting magnates were immediately ousted from the priorate. There was nothing to do but to yield, and thus the planned rehabilitation of the magnates came to naught. The lords of trade saw the last chance of saving their ailing firms slip from their hands and, as an extreme measure, resolved to resort to arms. Warned

[22] Villani, XII, 17.

by the open preparations of the magnates at several centers of the town but particularly on the left bank, the quarter of Oltrarno, the people were not taken by surprise and resolutely attacked their enemies wherever they found them (September 24). When the Bardi, easily the leading magnate clan and occupying with their clustered houses a dominant position along the steep hill of San Giorgio, found themselves entirely enveloped by a raging multitude, they gave up the struggle. The associated banking heads had been beaten all along the line and the people were free to carry through another reorganization.

The reform effected in the course of deliberations conducted by the victors during the month of October was much more moderate than might have been expected in view of the revolutionary character of the uprising against the magnates. The old priorate constitution was retained, together with some of the surface changes recently introduced, as, for instance, the division of the town into quarters instead of sixths. With the priorate again limited to popolani and with two priors assigned to each quarter, there resulted a college of eight priors, to whom the gonfalonier of Justice was added as a ninth member. Of course the Ordinances of Justice were re-enacted, not, however, without a mitigation of some of the features which the passing years had made imperative. A considerable number of families designated as magnates back in the days of Giano della Bella had become so greatly impoverished that it was ridiculous to regard them as still constituting a peril to the state. Accordingly, they were stricken from the magnate rolls and reintegrated with the Florentine citizenry. It throws an interesting light on the mad whirligig of Time to learn that in the countryside a number of individuals rightfully carrying the title of counts had so declined in the social scale that they made their living as agricultural laborers (*lavoratori di terra*). Far and away the most significant change brought about in connection with the reaffirmation of the traditional gild rule was that the seven greater gilds were deprived of their too exclusive control. In view of the fact that the political and economic system associated with the "fat" bourgeoisie had suffered shipwreck, no other result was to be expected. The five middle and nine lesser gilds insisted on being given an opportunity to pull the city out of the mire; and finding themselves on account of the revolution at the helm, they were able to carry their point. When the new borse were prepared for the various offices, the heads of the fourteen lesser gilds managed to get enough names of small artificers into the purses to assure this class a respectable representation in the future. To clinch the matter it was ordained that of the eight priors, two were to be henceforth members of the seven upper gilds, three of the arti medie, and three of the arte minori. While the popolo grasso was thus not completely shelved, small shopkeepers and craftsmen in the main took over the government. It was a dislocation of power within the established framework of the gilds. That it was but a mildly revolutionary change will appear the moment we reflect that the great body of workingmen, chiefly wool workers, remained as completely disfranchised after 1343 as before.[23]

---

[23] I have followed the usual interpretation of Villani's description of the new government given in XII, 22. Some recent students have favored an interpretation in accordance with which the control remained, after all, with the greater gilds.

Under a government responsive to the pressure of a petty bourgeoisie the fate of the trading-houses was soon sealed. They had been tottering ever since the crash of the London branches of the Bardi and Peruzzi in 1339 and had managed to keep afloat only by means of extensions granted by their creditors and of moratoria conceded by the government. Their desperate situation, growing worse with every year, was reflected in their numerous criminal designs to get possession of the Florentine government and treasury. But with the crushing of the September rising and the taking over of the government by their enemies they had arrived at the end of their tether and the bankruptcies, so long expected, could no longer be delayed. The series of failures was opened by the Peruzzi and Acciaiuoli and continued without interruption till practically all the houses, great and small alike, had gone the same road. It was an unexampled financial collapse.[24] As the house of the Buonaccorsi, of which our friend Villani was a member, crashed with the rest, we have an explanation of the note of bitterness which crept into his account of the new government. The new rulers were obliged to struggle with the evil heritage left on their hands by the popolo grasso and, as is not unusual in a conflict among envenomed political groups, were charged with the sins of their predecessors. That they were not unmindful of their responsibilities toward the sorely tried commonwealth intrusted to their care is proved by their liquidating the Lucchese fiasco by renewing the peace which the duke of Athens had concluded with Pisa and which left Lucca in Pisa's hands. At the same time, instead of repudiating the public debt, as the duke had done, they officially recognized it by carrying through those conversion and consolidation measures already described, which culminated (1347) in the establishment of the Monte. The last bank to fail was the greatest of all, the house of the Bardi. It managed to struggle along till 1346, when it at last surrendered its assets into the hands of its creditors. If Florence should ever rise again to play a part in international commerce and finance, it would have to be under the leadership of new men capable of making the very ruins by which they were surrounded serve as the foundations of daring new ventures.

The period following the tyranny of the duke of Athens was not a happy one either for Florence itself or for the new government. The terrible financial convulsion with its extinction of credit forced many small industrialists, chiefly manufacturers of woolen cloth, to go into bankruptcy, and the shutting down of so many shops was attended by widespread unemployment and starvation. To fill the cup of local woe to overflowing the Tuscan crops were frequently inadequate and the attendant undernourishment prepared the ground for a succession of death-dealing contagions. They reached their climax when, in 1348, there descended on the city, on Italy, and on all Europe the greatest pestilence known to history, the famous Black Death. Even if the number of victims in Florence did not reach one hundred thousand, as the novelist Boccaccio reports, and even if the dead, according to the more moderate figures of living scholars, did not come to more than two-thirds of the population, the toll exacted overwhelms the mind, especially if we take into

[24] The most convincing account of the long banking crisis of 1339-46 is still that of Villani, XII, 54, 56.

account that the havoc at Florence was repeated in every city of Italy and Europe. Among the leading victims of the pestilence in the Arno city was the historian, Giovanni Villani. Before taking final leave of one to whom every lover of Florence owes an inestimable debt of gratitude, let us turn again the pages of his book, this time not to hear him give his, on the whole, amazingly illuminating version of political events, but with the very human purpose of recovering the daily aspects of the town he loved and of catching the pulse beat of the citizens whose hopes and fears he shared and faithfully recorded.

XV. Seeing Florence with Giovanni Villani

BEFORE consulting Giovanni Villani's book in order to note some of the many familiar aspects which he records of his town and its inhabitants, it may be well to supply a biographical sketch of the man whom we have already learned to honor as an invaluable guide through the mazes of the commune's political fortunes. He was born at Florence around the year 1280. The date is exceedingly important because two years later, in 1282, there began that democratic revolution which led to the creation of the priorate and culminated in the Ordinances of Justice (1293). As his father, Villano di Stoldo, was a well-to-do merchant, the family belonged to the class which the revolution had made supreme in the state. In the household of the successful trader there abounded a vigorous burgher self-esteem, which became the very breath of young Giovanni's nostrils. By achieving a minor partnership in the great company of the Cerchi, Stoldo found himself incorporated in the political party of the Whites, and in 1300, the year of the Jubilee so critical for the Arno city, shared in the triumph of his group by sitting among the priors. In good Florentine fashion Giovanni followed in his father's footsteps. He was destined to be a merchant and normally would have become a White Guelph, if the great disaster of 1301 had not overtaken the party. With the responsible leaders of the Whites dispersed and persecuted, the young man found it convenient to disappear from view for a time by representing Florentine trading-houses in distant Flanders and afterward, nearer home, at Naples. On his return to the banks of the Arno, he quietly affiliated himself with the victorious Blacks and was established in the same world of trade as his father before him by a partnership in the firm of the Peruzzi, which he later gave up to join his fortunes with the Buonaccorsi. That he did not shirk the responsibilities of citizenship is proved by his serving, at one time, as an official of the mint and, on another occasion, as a member of the commission intrusted with completing the third circle of walls; but his high standing in the ruling merchant world and in his own gild of the Calimala is best attested by his appointment to the highest office of the state, the priorate. Indeed he was prior no less than three times. In his old age he was overtaken by misfortune, for he went down with his firm, the Buonaccorsi, in the great financial crash of the early forties. A relentless creditor even had him incarcerated for a while in the infamous prison, Le Stinche. Not long after his release, the terrible Black Death invaded the occident and on reaching Florence carried off the honorable burgher and industrious chronicler when he was not far from seventy years of age.[1]

While Giovanni, as the son of a well-to-do merchant, was doubtless sent to one of the several grammar schools that flourished at Florence and there made acquaintance with Latin and dialectics, his real education came to him from the wide practical experience growing out of his commercial contacts and his quickening travels through Italy and Europe. He had a natural gift of observation coupled with an insatiable curiosity about the world in which he lived. It is to this factual turn of his mind that we owe the abundance and variety of his information. But inevitably he colored whatever he saw and reported with a very personal point of view. He was a passionate patriot devoted to the honor and glory of Florence, and he believed that his country possessed in the gild constitution elaborated in his youth the precise government it needed. That under the practical working-out of this system the merchants of the arti maggiori largely monopolized the offices seemed to him to be wholly right and proper in view of their higher social station and broader knowledge of the world. Perhaps because of the sad fate of his father's friends, the Whites, who had had the audacity to oppose the pope and were punished by the loss of home and fortune, he became an unswerving papal partisan, who never ceased proclaiming that opposition to the church was a sin sure to be punished in both the Here and the Hereafter. With the same intellectual submissiveness he accepted the role which the Middle Ages ascribed to the movements of the stars and to the wiles and plots of an ever-watchful Satan. In short, on the reflective and speculative side of his mind he remained contentedly a medieval man. On the other hand, when it came to business and politics, in which he felt securely at home, he did not hesitate to use his personal judgment and to buttress it with rational analysis. In these related fields he has all the essential earmarks of one who has left the medieval outlook behind him. Whoever is inclined to contend that the social and economic revolution connected with the rise of the communes represents the first stage in the supersession of the Middle Ages, and that the second stage, which carried the revolution into the realm of abstract thought, is nothing other than a belated but inevitable development from the first stage, should find strong evidence supporting this view in so manifest a transition figure as that of Giovanni Villani.

Villani himself has told us how he came to be the historian of his city. When Pope Boniface VIII proclaimed the Great Jubilee of the year 1300 and the thought of all the world turned to the Roman pilgrimage, Giovanni, a young man of twenty, found his heart swelling with promptings mixed of devotion and adventure and, yielding to his inner voices, set out for the Eternal City. Let him tell us in his own words what happened to him in the papal capital.

And being on that blessed pilgrimage in the sacred city of Rome and seeing its great and ancient monuments and reading the great deeds of the Romans as de-

[1] Elogio di Giovanni Villani attached to Villani, IV, 189-207; Davidsohn, Vol. IV³, pp. 159-60.

scribed by Virgil, Sallust, Lucan, Livy, Valerius, Orosius, and other masters of history . . . I took my prompting from them although I am a disciple unworthy of such an undertaking. But in view of the fact that our city of Florence, daughter and offspring of Rome, was mounting and pursuing great purposes, while Rome was in its decline, I thought it proper to trace in this chronicle the origins of the city of Florence, so far as I have been able to recover them, and to relate the city's further development at greater length, and at the same time to give a brief account of events throughout the world as long as it please God, in the hope of whose favor I undertook the said enterprise rather than in reliance on my own poor wits. And thus in the year 1300, on my return from Rome, I began to compile this book in the name of God and the blessed John the Baptist and in honor of our city of Florence.[2]

This very personal statement with its strong patriotic note calls for no comment unless it be to say that Villani occupied himself during many years with the task of assembling his materials before he began the actual composition of his *Cronica*. In proceeding now to make selections from the work with a view to illustrating the life of Florence in the first half of the fourteenth century, occasional explanatory comment will be unavoidable, although our plan will be to yield the floor so far as possible to our guide. In preparation for the next excerpt it will be necessary to recall that in the very year following the Jubilee Charles of Valois rode into Florence as the military arm of the ambitious Boniface VIII and that in the wake of that invasion the Whites succumbed to their foes, the Blacks. As the Whites refused to accept their defeat, the city remained gravely convulsed for many years to come. Nonetheless life went on much as before: people went to church and market, and the customary festivals were punctually observed. Among them was May Day; and when the first of May of the year 1304 dawned, it was celebrated in the usual manner with dancing and merrymaking in the streets and public squares. However, on this particular occasion the residents of Borgo San Frediano resolved to provide a special entertainment of their own and sent a herald through the town to invite their fellow-citizens to a representation of hell on the waters and banks of Arno. Whoever was eager to have authentic news of the other world (*novelle dell'altro mondo*) was to betake himself to the Carraia bridge and its approaches for a good view of the spectacle.

And on barges and boats moored in the Arno they erected platforms and thereon pictured hell with its fires and punishments and sufferings; with men in the likeness of demons horrible to see; and with other men acting the part of naked souls. And the demons subjected their victims to various tortures amidst a hurly-burly of cries and shrieks hateful and terrible to see and hear. And many citizens crowded together to view the novel spectacle, and the Carraia bridge, which was constructed of wooden planks laid from pier to pier, became so burdened with people that it broke in several places and crashed into the river with its load. For which reason many people were drowned and many others suffered injuries so that play turned to earnest and, exactly as the public crier had announced, many went to get news of the other world. . . .[3]

2 Villani, VIII, 36.
3 VIII, 70.

Thus was the merry month of May ushered in *con grande pianto e dolore* and we may believe that the furious strife between the Blacks and Whites was temporarily forgotten. But only very temporarily, for five weeks later, on June 10, 1304, it flared up anew and led to a conflagration so disastrous that it threatened the whole city with destruction. The background for the event is supplied by the fact that on his death in October, 1303, Pope Boniface VIII had been succeeded by Benedict XI and that the new pope was resolved to heal the division caused by his predecessor by effecting a reconciliation between the two envenomed factions. To this end he dispatched a cardinal to Florence with full powers. Only a few families credited with Black sympathies, the powerful Cavalcanti among them, were willing to give ear to the proposal. In order to frustrate the cardinal's plan an intransigent group of Blacks began an attack on their enemies, who unexpectedly made so vigorous a defense that it seemed likely they would capture the city. In their acute alarm the Blacks commissioned a dissolute member of the Abati family, a priest by profession, to divert the attention of the victors by setting fire to the city at several places and particularly to the mass of the Cavalcanti houses on or about the Mercato Nuovo.

And so impetuous was the accursed fire fanned by a north wind, which blew hard on that day, that there burned the houses of the Abati and of the Macci and the whole loggia of Or San Michele and the houses of the Amieri, the Toschi, the Cipriani, the Lamberti, the Bachini, the Buiamonti and the whole street of Calimala. And then attacking the houses of the Cavalcanti, it traveled round the Mercato Nuovo and consumed the church of Saint Cecilia, whence it made its way down the street of Por Santa Maria as far as the Ponte Vecchio. . . . In sum, it destroyed the medulla and core (*midollo e tuorlo*) of the city of Florence, consuming a total of one thousand seven hundred palaces, towers, and houses. The loss in furniture, treasures, and goods of every kind was incalculable inasmuch as in this area were all the merchandise and valuables of the town. And what was not burnt up by the fire was carried off by robbers, who were aided by the circumstance that civil war continued to rage throughout the city. By reason of which fire and sack many trading companies and clans and families were reduced to misery.[4]

Dismayed by the fire which, partly by design and partly by the accident of the powerful wind, destroyed the extensive real estate holdings of the Cavalcanti, these magnates became excited and took refuge in the country. They fortified themselves, among other places, in their castle in the Greve Valley called Le Stinche. Thereupon in the month of September the government, again securely controlled by the uncompromising Guelphs, ordered an expedition against this stronghold and captured it—a success which produced a strange transference of the castle's name to one of the more sinister of the city's institutions.

And when the castle had been destroyed, the prisoners were brought to Florence and incarcerated in the new prison erected by the commune on ground formerly owned by the Uberti next to the church of San Simone. And because the prisoners

4 VIII, 71.

from Le Stinche castle were the first to be lodged in the new jail, the said jail received the name of Le Stinche.[5]

Le Stinche remained one of the notorious institutions of Florence for many centuries, although we have no reason to believe that the conditions in this particular prison were worse than elsewhere in Italy and Europe. In the fourteenth century and for generations afterward it never occurred to anyone to treat prisoners as other than social outcasts; and if we add that even the educated and well-to-do were ignorant of the simplest rules of private and public hygiene, we may leave the prison conditions obtaining in Florence and throughout the west to the imagination. The reader will not overlook another feature in the epithet popularly conferred on the new jail. The Cavalcanti castle in the valley of the Greve was a hated nobiliary stronghold, and it tickled the rising third estate to deride their enemies, the magnates, by attaching a high-sounding feudal title to a hideous domestic lockup. However, this defeat does not mark the exit of the Cavalcanti from Florentine history—far from it. A few years after their expulsion they became the beneficiaries of an amnesty, and such members of the great clan as were still alive again took up their residence in Florence. But they did not for that reason pardon their enemies. The blood feud was an aristocratic institution in good moral standing and, with murder begetting murder, largely accounts for the bewildering excesses which were commonplace incidents of every Florentine family history. Without any question their own bloody divisions were a big factor in the ultimate overthrow of the noble class. Let Villani tell us how in a manner possessed not even of a tincture of the boasted chivalry of the Middle Ages a returned Cavalcanti practiced vendetta upon a fellow-nobleman.

In the said year [1312], on January 11, it happened in Florence that messer Pazzino de' Pazzi, one of the small clique in control of the city [that is, he belonged to the ruling group of Black Guelphs], on going on a falcon hunt to the island of the Arno, without any guard other than his falconers and servants, was killed by Paffiero de' Cavalcanti with the aid of the Brunelleschi and certain mounted troopers in their pay. . . . It was an act of revenge in behalf of Masino de' Cavalcanti and messer Betto Brunelleschi, whose deaths were laid at the door of messer Pazzino. In order to bring the greater infamy on the Cavalcanti family, the body of the dead man was brought in state to the palace of the priors. Thereupon the whole city rose in arms and under the banner of the people rushed upon the houses of the Cavalcanti and, setting fire to them, once again drove their owners from the city.[6]

While our chronicler is chiefly interested in his own Florence, he does not fail to record striking events from all over Italy and Europe. Naturally the restless religious movements of the day do not escape his attention. Here is his account of one of those mass explosions of self-accusing penance which throughout the Middle Ages made a periodic appearance among all the European groups of the Christian family.

In the said year [1310] a great marvel made its appearance. It began in Piedmont, advanced through Lombardy and the Genoese littoral, and spread thence to Tus-

[5] VIII, 75.
[6] IX, 33.

cany and almost covered all Italy. Many people of the commoner sort, men and
women and children without number, left their occupations and their cares behind
them and, with the cross to point the way, went from place to place beating their
bodies and crying *misericordia* and turning people to penance by persuading them
to make peace with one another. The Florentines and the inhabitants of a few other
cities refused to let them enter their territory and drove them away saying that they
were an augury of evil to the land.[7]

On this and some other occasions as well the hard-headed merchant governors of the Arno town showed that they were proof against the current
religious excitement; but as the Florentines in the mass were undoubtedly true
sons of the Middle Ages, they too were frequently swept off their feet by
fervid, popular movements of an evangelical origin. Even at the height of the
Renaissance, it will be recalled, in the brilliant and pagan age of Lorenzo de'
Medici, a fanatic fervor seized the citizens at the call of Savonarola and, renouncing their worldliness in sackcloth and ashes, they offered a spectacle
at which the rest of Italy gazed in mute astonishment. In dealing with Florence it will be well regularly to distinguish between a small, much-traveled,
and relatively sophisticated merchant class and the stay-at-home conservative
masses. While the former gradually developed an intrepid skepticism which
became an important factor in shaping the new and modern European mentality, the latter, even far into the Renaissance, clung to the familiar attitudes
and conventions of the Middle Ages.

Our journalistic guide records the outbreak of fire in his overcrowded town
with monotonous frequency, although not many fires were so destructive as
that of the year 1304, at which we have glanced. Nor were they, like that
calamitous affair, started by incendiaries in the interest of a political group.
They may be ascribed in the main to the simple circumstance that a large
part of the city was, in Villani's day, still built of wood and highly inflammable. We are likely to overlook this detail by picturing Florence to ourselves
as made up of picturesque feudal towers and palaces formidably constructed
of masonry to withstand the assault of enemies. True, the nobiliary edifices
were both numerous and durably built, but around them clung the wooden
shops and miserable shelters of the common people, who contributed to the
swollen revenues of the fortress-owners by the payment of rent for quarters
which by our standards were unbelievably insubstantial, dark, and squalid.
Villani, as a reporter who permits no event, great or small, to escape his
attention, enumerates such a steady succession of fires that he furnishes ground
for the belief that the city must have been in large part renewed with every
generation. Opening the book almost at random, we get an alarming picture
of the fire risks to which the rapidly expanding Florence of the fourteenth
century was exposed.

In the said year [1331], on June 23, during the night of the vigil of Saint John,
a fire broke out on the Ponte Vecchio, toward the left bank, and all the shops on
the bridge to the number of twenty were burned with heavy loss to many craftsmen.
And two apprentices perished in the fire. . . . Further, on September 12, at dusk,

[7] VIII, 121.

a fire broke out at the house of the Soldanieri by the church of Santa Trinità in certain lowly structures housing some carpenters and a blacksmith. And six persons perished, who because of the furious blaze occasioned by the lumber and the horse-stalls were unable to escape. And again, on February 28 [1332], at oncoming night fire attacked the palace of the podestà and burned the roof of the old structure and two-thirds of the new palace from the first story up. On which account the government ordered both structures to be rebuilt in stone all the way to the roof. And a half year later, on July 16, the palace of the wool gild by Or San Michele took fire and everything was consumed from the first story up. . . . The wool gild thereupon ordered their palace to be reconstructed on a larger scale with stone vaults to the roof.[8]

All of which speaks so eloquently for itself that it requires no remark unless it be that even a great public structure, like the palace of the podestà, was long in assuming the all-stone, fire-proof guise in which it presents itself to view today. Villani's statement apprizes us that seventy-five years after the palazzo was begun—the foundation stone was laid in 1255—it still had a roof of wooden beams, and that the recent addition to the rear had only its first story built of stone and that the second and third stories had been hurriedly and provisionally raised of wood. Only after the alarm occasioned by the fire of 1332 did the residence of the podestà acquire that look of eternity which is perhaps its main distinction in the eyes of a present-day visitor of the Arno city.[9]

In a diary-like record of the external events of a lifetime there is bound to be frequent reference to tempests, hailstorms, drouths, floods, and other accidents of the weather. Villani brings home to us that in his day, as with all generations before and since, the natural phenomena engaged a large proportion of the thought and conversation of men. What is, however, peculiar to him and the medieval period to which he belonged is the explanation offered of the freakish and often disastrous behavior of the elements. Our simple friend shared all the views current in his age regarding the influence of the stars and planets on man and his multiple affairs. Just as we children of a later time have systematized our elaborate observations of the celestial bodies in the science of astronomy, so our medieval predecessors reduced their ignorance and superstition to a system in the pseudo-science of astrology. Of this highly elaborated body of misinformation Villani was more than a casual student, and he delights in consequence to weave its mysteries through the whole fabric of his chronicle. Over and over again he records eclipses of the sun and moon and the ever recurrent conjunction and opposition of planets and then very confidently ascribes a subsequent pestilence or flood or unexpected demise of a great personage to the celestial phenomenon. His theory of these supernatural influences is propounded in Book XI, 68, on the occasion of two comets which appeared in rapid succession in the year 1337. First he gives the view entertained of the wandering bodies by the *filosofi,* the students of nature, according to whom comets, being plainly un-

---

[8] X, 182.

[9] Even if, as Davidsohn contends (*Forschungen,* Vol. IV, p. 505), the fire of 1332 injured what is now the Palazzo Vecchio and not the earlier palace of the podestà, our comment loses none of its force.

classifiable as fixed stars, are of planetary origin, being "dry vapors . . . collected in the fiery atmosphere under the sky of the moon by reason of the dissolution [*corruzione*] of the celestial bodies called planets." Then he continues:

But whatever they may be, every comet is the sign of some event [*novità*] in the world and generally a malignant one; and sometimes it is the sign of the death of great lords or of revolution in kingdoms and among people more particularly in that planet which has given birth to the comet [by the above-mentioned process of *corruzione*]. And wheresoever the comet extends its mastery, it produces many evils, such as famine, pestilence, revolution, and other grave occurrences, as any man of good understanding may find out for himself by reading onward in this book.

By reading onward we encounter a general texture of happenings in the world wholly indistinguishable from what has gone before and, as "men of good understanding," are obliged to conclude that the deflection of human destiny from its appointed course owing to the two *stelle comete* of 1337 was precisely zero. But such modern skepticism should not hinder us from noting that Villani's faith in astrology considerably colors his narrative, as does in no less degree his and his age's opinion regarding the activity of God's ever busy and versatile adversary, Satan. The cloven-footed potentate and his myriad army of evil spirits are as tirelessly bent on the capture of human souls as are the shining battalions of their opponents, the saints and angels operating from heaven as their base. Our annalist, who, as a traveled, common-sense trader, is inclined to concede the dominion of the law of cause and effect in the fields of business and government, is nevertheless puzzled, as we unfortunately continue to be to this day, by the presence of a certain erratic and incalculable element in human events. This element, which we have decided non-committally to call chance or fate, Villani is prompted to refer to spirits, good and bad, who pull the strings behind the scenes. Of course he piously leaves the last word in the human drama to the commander of the good spirits, to Almighty God; but as innumerable undertakings manifestly go wrong in the world, he ascribes their deflection from their intended course to the devil, to whom he refers with genuine but superstitious respect as the enemy of the human race (*nemico della umana generazione*). In sum, Villani mixes with his often lucidly rational analysis of events, by virtue of which we recognize his closeness to ourselves, hidden causes, such as the stars, God, and Satan, with which the present-day historian with consequent severe loss of picturesqueness has been obliged to dispense.

On attacking the greatest flood disaster which ever visited Florence, Villani starts off in a very modern manner by ascribing the calamity to an extraordinary fall of rain over the whole watershed of the Arno. We learn that the rain began on November 1, 1333, and that it came down in cataracts without a break for four nights and days to the accompaniment of frightful lightning and thunder.

Wherefore everyone was filled with great fear and all the church bells throughout the city were rung continuously as an invocation to heaven that the water rise no farther. And in the houses they beat the kettles and brass basins raising loud cries to God of *misericordia, misericordia,* the while those in peril fled from roof to roof and house to house on improvised bridges. And so great was the human din and tumult that it almost drowned out the crash of the thunder.[10]

Although the whole chapter dealing with the flood is in one way or another remarkable, we shall have to be content with excerpts.

By Thursday noon, November 4, the Arno had swollen so vastly at Florence that it covered the whole plain of San Salvi to a depth of from ten to sixteen feet. [San Salvi lay to the east of the town and the water was dammed up on the plain by the stout city wall.] And at the first sleep of night the water washed away the city wall above the Corso de' Tintori . . . for a space of over two hundred feet. Thereupon the whole volume of the flood rushed into the city with such fury that it filled all Florence. It covered and drowned the streets, some more, some less, but it was worst in the sesti of San Piero Scheraggio and Porta San Piero and Porta del Duomo. . . . In the baptistery of St. John the water rose above the altar and reached to over half the height of the columns of porphyry before the entrance. [These were the columns presented by the Pisans over two hundred years before. They are to this day in the indicated place with a line scratched on them showing the level reached by the water in 1333.] And in the palace of the commune, where dwells the podestà, it rose in the courtyard, where he pronounces justice, to the height of ten feet. . . . And in Or San Michele and in the nearby Mercato Nuovo it rose to almost four feet. . . . And the Carraia bridge fell with the exception of two arches toward the right bank. And immediately after fell the Trinità bridge, save for one pier and one arch toward the church of Santa Trinità. It was now the turn of the Ponte Vecchio. When it was choked by the logs brought down by the Arno, the waters leaped over the arches and, rushing on the shops upon the bridge, swept everything away except the two central piers. And at the Rubaconte bridge the water washed over the top at one side and destroyed the parapet at several places. . . . And the statue of Mars, which stood on a pedestal on this side of the Ponte Vecchio, fell into the Arno. . . . And when Mars had fallen and all the houses between the Ponte Vecchio and the Carraia bridge had come down and all the streets on both banks were covered with ruins—to look at this scene was to stare at chaos.

By the afternoon of the next day the worst was over and the waters began rapidly to recede. Our conscientious chronicler follows the flood downstream and shows that, although it brought serious injury to every village and town as far as Pisa, it wreaked its chief spite on Florence. His bill of particulars for his native city includes three hundred dead, the loss of innumerable domestic animals, the ruin of uncounted houses, bridges, mills. He does not forget the many kinds of supplies which were carried off, such as the cloth of the weavers, the casks of wine, the stores of grain. He confesses his inability to state the total loss in money value, but he illustrates the damage by going to the municipal account books for the information that Florence paid out for the single item of repair of walls and bridges the sum of one hundred and fifty thousand gold florins. And he concludes his tale of woe with the statement "that not since its destruction by the Gothic king, Totila, the scourge of God, did Florence suffer *si grande avversità e dammaggio come fu questo.*"

10 Villani, XI, 1.

The great flood had a curious intellectual aftermath. A people so alert and inquisitive as the Florentines were stung to raise the issue of the why and wherefore of this disaster; and it characterizes the fourteenth century as an age of slowly advancing reason that the theologians, who categorically explained the flood as a judgment of God upon the wicked, no longer had it all their own way. We hear that a group of "philosophers" put up a stiff fight in favor of the view that the flood was just a natural event (*venuto per corso di natura*). The position signified a notable measure of rational enlightenment, although the arguments with which it was supported were borrowed from astrology and have an undiluted medieval character. Villani himself, as we have seen, a passionate amateur astrologer, patiently rehearses the "natural causes." "On May 14 there was an eclipse of the moon in the sign of Taurus . . . and then at the beginning of July there followed a conjunction of Saturn with Mars at the end of the sign of the Virgin. . . . And, added to all this, the planet Jupiter, which is sweet and kind and brings good luck, found itself in the sign of Aquarius so that its favorable action was eliminated," and so forth through a long, solemn section unrelieved by so much as a fugitive twinkle of the eye.[11] But with a single sweep of their mighty arms the theologians brushed aside both the naturalist hypothesis and the astrological cobwebs in which it was entangled. Corso di natura? Tut, tut! The corso di natura is a matter of God's will and pleasure. And very certainly the laws of nature and the actions of the elements and the demons as well are nothing other than divine scourges and hammers to punish men for their sins. We gather that the correct theological position is that the great concern of God is to punish the accursed seed of Adam for its innumerable derelictions, and that in pursuit of this high purpose he may act according to nature or above nature or even contrary to nature, exactly as he sees fit, since he is Lord Omnipotent. Of course the amateur theologian, who is even stronger in Villani than the amateur astrologer, gives the victory in the great debate between faith and reason to orthodoxy and the Catholic church. And in concluding his report of the controversy he adds his personal view: "I, the author, hold to this opinion on the flood, that by means of the laws of nature God pronounced judgment on us for our outrageous sins." A confession of faith, let us admit, of impeccable orthodoxy; but let us also take note that with his avowal of the existence of the laws of nature he has opened a crack in the conservative armor certain to prove dangerous in the future.

A grave concern of every medieval commune was its food supply. With its fast-growing population and limited territory Florence in particular was perpetually threatened with scarcity. A very intelligent grain-dealer, a contemporary of Villani's by name of Lenzi, calculated that the Florentine contado normally furnished about five-twelfths of the wheat annually required by the population.[12] The remainder had to be imported from the outlying districts of Tuscany; and when Tuscany, as frequently happened, failed to

---

[11] XI, 2.

[12] Davidsohn, *Forschungen*, Vol. IV, pp. 307-14, bases an interesting study of *Die Getreidepolitik der Kommune* on Lenzi's copious and reliable data. On the control of the food supply by the government see also Davidsohn, Vol. IV[1], pp. 130-33.

satisfy its considerable provincial needs, the Florentine market became dependent on shipments by land from the Romagna and by sea from southern Italy. Under these circumstances scarcity and its offspring, famine, always hovered on the horizon and the government was moved to intrust the very critical problem of the food supply to a standing committee of six men with extraordinary powers, *I Sei della Biada.* The grain market was located in Villani's time on the piazza of Or San Michele, and the specially constructed loggia, under which the dealers met and over which the Six had jurisdiction, was always a lively place, and in periods of scarcity, when the price shot up like a rocket, a veritable inferno. The standard measure for grain was the *staio,* which has been calculated as the equivalent of seventeen and two-thirds kilograms. Reduced to our standard, the staio would thus represent a weight of thirty-nine pounds. During the first half of the fourteenth century the normal price of the staio of wheat was about twelve soldi. At any rate both Lenzi, the professional grain-dealer, and Villani, the sharp merchant observer, agree that wheat is abundant if the price sinks below twelve soldi per staio and that a scarcity is in the wind if it tends to rise above that figure.

Now one of the most interesting aspects of Florentine life reflected by Villani's chronicle has to do with the recurrent scarcities. It has been argued by some modern economists, familiar with a free market of world-scope, that the medieval scarcities were primarily due to the prohibitions to export, by means of which the governments of the time, and Florence with the rest, attempted to safeguard their limited local supply. That these prohibitions wrought a certain mischief may be admitted, but to make them account for the permanent food shortage of Florence is absurd. That phenomenon must be referred, as already indicated, to the town's fast-growing population and the inability to feed it from the limited grainlands of Florence or of Tuscany as a whole. In seasons when the crop suffered either from too much or too little rain or sun, a crisis in a crowded center like the Arno city was inevitable. Owing to the prevailing primitive means of transportation, grain could not be brought from distant countries nor could the amounts drawn from relatively accessible points, such as the Romagna and Naples, be indefinitely increased. For one thing these provinces, to which Florence frequently resorted as granaries, might be afflicted with a scarcity of their own and, for another, the mules and ships which served as carriers moved very slowly and possessed a painfully small carrying capacity. If, in addition to all this, we allow for the hazards of the sea route due to piracy, and of the land route because of the innumerable wars, we must conclude that a sum of conditions prevailed in the fourteenth century which, rooted in the civilization of the time, made the Florentine nervousness over the bread question as perennial as it was incurable.

The situation is copiously illustrated by our faithful guide. Throughout the book we find him giving a hawklike attention to the fluctuations of the food prices chalked up at the local produce exchange of Or San Michele; and we gather from his statements that a scarcity of a more or less severe character put in an appearance on an average of about three times each decade. About once each decade the scarcity became so intense as to assume the proportions of a famine. When this pitiless, unbidden guest visited the city, he caused unspeakable misery and confusion. Not only was Florence a proletarian city, most of whose wage-earners dwelt habitually on the margin of starvation, but it was also crowded with beggars living upon the charity which medieval Christianity inculcated as a duty and which was habitually dispensed by well-to-do individuals and even more bounteously by numerous religious institutions founded in part for this very purpose. Famine prices at once tended to put the cost of bread beyond the reach of the workers and perforce checked, and in the end completely dried up, the stream of charity. Speaking of the year 1328, Villani reports a growing scarcity which became steadily more acute until by Easter, 1329, the staio of wheat cost forty-two soldi; and just before the new local crop was in, which would be toward the end of June, the price had reached sixty soldi and therewith the equivalent of a gold florin. This figure, the highest that was reached on the occasion of this particular famine, represented a 500 per cent advance on the normal price.

The famine was felt not only in Florence but throughout Tuscany and a large part of Italy. And so terrible was it that the Perugians, the Sienese, the Lucchese, the Pistolese, and many other townsmen drove forth from their territory all their beggars because they could not support them. Guided by wise counsel and divine pity, the commune of Florence did not do this; in fact it received and provided for a large fraction of the poor mendicants of all Tuscany. . . . It sent for grain to Sicily, ordering it to be brought to the port of Talamone in the Maremma and transporting it thence to Florence at great risk and expense. The government sent also to the Romagna and to the contado of Arezzo; and as long as the scarcity lasted, disregarding the heavy charge upon the public purse, it kept the price of the staio at half a gold florin [which would be two and a half times the normal figure] although to effect this reduction it permitted the wheat to be mixed to one-fourth its volume with coarser grain. In spite of all the government did, the agitation of the people at the market of Or San Michele was so great that it was necessary to protect the officials by means of guards fitted out with ax and block to punish rioters on the spot with the loss of hands or feet.

And in mitigation of this famine the commune of Florence spent in those two years more than sixty thousand gold florins. Finally, it was decided not to go on selling grain in the piazza but to requisition all the bakers' ovens for the baking of bread in order to sell it on the following morning in three or four shops in every sesto at four pennies for the loaf of six ounces. This arrangement successfully tamed the rage of the people since wage-earners with eight to twelve pennies a day could now buy bread on which to live, whereas formerly they had been unable to find the sum necessary to buy a whole staio of wheat.[13]

In the wake of a medieval famine there generally followed a pestilence, which attacked the enfeebled population and carried them off by the hundreds. It must not, however, be supposed that contagious diseases took root only when undernourishment had cleared the way for them. The sanitary conditions in a town like Florence can hardly be painted in sufficiently dark colors. Water was supplied first, from public fountains, of which there was one for each of the fifty-seven city parishes, and second, from numerous private wells

13 Villani, X, 118.

with a capricious action and of a very doubtful purity. Not only was there no underground sewage system but the government recognized no obligation to collect and dispose of the city refuse. Everybody tossed the household waste into the street, where it lay till it was eaten by wandering hogs or washed by the rain into the river. If on this score alone Florence would receive a very low rating from a modern health commission, it would be declared completely outside the pale by the way the people satisfied their private necessities. Only the houses of the well-to-do had cesspools, while the mass of the population, without causing the least scandal, utilized for their needs the less frequented streets, the plentiful ruins of the houses of magnates destroyed under the Ordinances of Justice, and the vast circle of the city walls. If we add that the very numerous poor were housed either in skimpy, wooden shacks or in damp cellars without light and air except from the open door, we shall understand that diseases like typhoid, tuberculosis, and influenza were endemic in the population. In fact it was in the Florence of the trecento that the name influenza was invented for the catarrhal affection which, then as now, periodically became epidemic and levied a heavy toll on all the communities it smote.

Wholly unconscious of the to us incredible deficiencies of the personal hygiene and public sanitation of his time, Villani innocently ignores them in his record. But he neither does nor can ignore the pestilences which periodically descended on his city and which the complete neglect of even the most rudimentary health provisions alone made possible. With his uncommon intelligence he suspects that the abundant filth has something to do with the recurrent plagues, but in the end he falls back for their explanation, exactly as he did in the case of the flood of 1333, on the will of an offended God supplemented by the astrological mysteries. His account of the *grande mortalità* of 1340 is typical.[14] He introduces it by reference to the comet, which in March of that year appeared in the eastern sky. Brief, we are told, was the stay of the celestial wanderer, but the ills which followed his visit lasted a long time.

For at once began a great pestilence, from which, if one fell ill, he but rarely escaped. And more than a sixth of the citizenry perished, among them the best and most beloved of our men and women. There was no family which did not lose one and even two and three of its members. And the pestilence lasted till the approach of winter. And in the city alone more than 15,000 corpses of men and women were buried. Wherefore the city was full of grief and lamentation and people hardly attended to anything other than burying the dead. . . . In the county the mortality was not so great but there too there died a plenty; and with this pestilence there came a new scarcity on top of that of the preceding year and, in spite of the decrease of the population, the staio of grain was sold at thirty soldi. And the price would have risen higher if the commune had not made provision by importing grain by sea. . . . And on account of this pestilence the bishop and the clergy advised the holding of a great procession. It took place on June 18 and almost the whole body of citizens, men and women, followed the relics of the body of Christ, which are

[14] XI, 114.

preserved at Sant' Ambrogio, and marched through the city till nones [3 P.M.] carrying more than one hundred and fifty lighted candles as large as torches.[15]

In spite of this fine demonstration of piety the pestilence persisted till the
November chill. Villani, now a man of sixty, was greatly depressed by the
calamity, in which he lost innumerable dear friends. Indeed at this juncture
disaster followed disaster both for him and his beloved city, enveloping his
closing days in deepening shadows. He grieved over the interminable war for
the possession of Lucca and the long string of disappointments the war
brought in its train. When the capture of Lucca by Pisa led to the Red Lily's
subjection to the debasing tyranny of the duke of Athens, he felt that the
bottom had been touched in public turpitude. His private fortunes, however,
did not reach their lowest depth till, with the casting off of the yoke of the
despot, the series of bank failures began which included his own firm of the
Buonaccorsi and lodged him for a period in the debtors' prison. He could
not have been long released when a new plague began to throw its shadow,
this time not only over Florence but over the whole world. The fresh affliction was the famous Black Death, the most widespread and sweepingly destructive pestilence in the annals of Europe. Villani, now greatly broken by the
continued buffets of adversity, watched its oncoming with undiminished curiosity, especially as it was an epidemic different in its nature from any with
which he was familiar. He gives the new disease no name but from the
symptoms he enumerates, supplemented by the report of other witnesses, of
whom the novelist, Boccaccio, is the most famous, we know it was the dread
bubonic plague, which on this occasion made its way for the first time from
its home in the orient into the west.

Villani reports that the disease put in an appearance at Florence in the
year 1347 but that its violence diminished with the winter season. As in this
preliminary visit it carried off only four thousand persons it did not impress
him at the time as deeply as the epidemic of 1340 had done which, according
to his figures, had mowed down some fifteen thousand people and which,
although he does not tell us clearly what it was, in no case was the bubonic
plague. But with the returning spring of the year 1348 the havoc began again.

The said plague was greater than among us in Pistoia and Prato . . . in Bologna
and in the Romagna. It was greater also at Avignon, where the pope keeps court,
and throughout the kingdom of France. But where it reaped the greatest harvest
was in Turkey and among the countries beyond the sea and among the Tartars. . . .
Having grown to vigor in Turkey and Greece and having spread thence over the
whole Levant and Mesopotamia and Syria and Chaldea and Cyprus and Crete and
Rhodes and all the islands of the Greek archipelago, the said pestilence leaped to
Sicily and Sardinia and Corsica and Elba, and from there soon reached all the shores
of the mainland. And of eight Genoese galleys which had gone to the Black Sea only
four returned, full of infected sailors, who were smitten one after the other on the
return journey. And all who arrived at Genoa died, and they corrupted the air to
such an extent that whoever came near the bodies died shortly after. And it was a
disease in which there appeared certain swellings in the groin and under the armpit,

and the victims spat blood, and in three days they were dead. And the priest who confessed the sick and those who nursed them so generally caught the infection that the victims were abandoned and deprived of confession, sacrament, medicine, and nursing. . . . And many lands and cities were made desolate. And this plague lasted till . . . . .[16]

So far did the diarist get in his tale of the ravages of the Black Death. He left a blank space after the word "till," planning to fill it in when the curse had been lifted from Florence and the world. But before that happy day dawned the old merchant himself had been carried off by the relentless pestilence. No particulars touching his demise have reached us. We know just this: the pen fell from his hand because together with thousands of his fellow-Florentines and hundreds of thousands of men and women throughout all the countries of the occident he perished in the *annus terribilis* of 1348.

However, we are not yet prepared to bid farewell to our crotchety and kindly cicerone. We have not tasted his most precious honey, the pages wherein he conveys to us the proud story of how Florence was rebuilt in his day. For it was within the span of Villani's life that the manifold activities, on which the Arno city had embarked since the revival of commerce in the eleventh century, began to flower in the spiritual culture, which is the occasion for the intense preoccupation of the world down to our time with this, quantitatively considered, fairly negligible state. To some of the more delicate aspects of this burgeoning, the plodding Villani, deeply entangled in business and politics, presented a tightly sealed mind. Accordingly he took no notice of them in his book. He failed, for instance, to give an account of the new school of poetry, though there stood at the head of it so tragic and dynamic a figure as Dante Alighieri. The chronicler's silence in this matter is particularly revealing as to his limitations, since we may assume that, although he was a somewhat younger man than the austere visionary, he knew him personally. The assumption seems reasonably safe not only because within the narrow bounds of Florence everybody knew everybody else, but more particularly because Giovanni's father, when Giovanni was a youth of twenty, was closely associated with the poet in the same political party of the White Guelphs. When Giovanni grew up and in due time himself joined the writing fraternity, he displayed, it is true, a certain patriotic pride in the fame acquired by his exiled fellow-countryman. On the occasion of the poet's death in 1321 he even devoted a chapter of his chronicle to a review of Dante's literary labors. It is the statement of a conscientious pedant, its even tone of respectful gravity being unruffled by as much as a flicker of imaginative understanding.[17] In short, Villani lacked the ear to catch the more delicate voices abroad in the trecento, but it would not on this account occur to us, who have looked somewhat into his mind, to charge him with rusticity. His undeniable refinement was of a social rather than an individual order and drew its strength from the root of the new burgher mentality. The aspirations to which he gave voice derived without exception from community living and culminated in the hope that Florence would express the wealth and power to which it was visibly

[16] XII, 84.
[17] IX, 136.

adding every day by an impressive outer garment of brick and stone. He wanted the Arno town not only to *be* the first in the world but also to *appear* as such. It is this patriotic passion which flutters his pulse with a subdued fever and envelops his pages with a much richer than merely a counting-house atmosphere. Had he been only the merchant absorbed in his balance sheet, he would have smothered his text under a leaden blanket of common sense.[18]

We remarked at the beginning that the great event of our annalist's youth was the seizure of political power by the twenty-one gilds. Spiritually this meant, if it meant anything, the coming of age of that civic spirit in which, as just stated, Villani's culture had its roots. However, just as the commercial expansion which culminated in the burgher victory of 1282 had gone on for many previous generations, so the civic spirit had begun to unfold long before the chronicler's birth. There therefore existed in Villani's boyhood concrete evidences of its long incubation and when, as a youth, he roamed through the city, he was brought face to face with them. Certain to arrest his attention would be the two walls encircling his native town. The inner wall, though largely removed in the interest of traffic, could still be traced without difficulty. Traditionally as well as by palpable evidence, it went back to Roman days and served to remind the thoughtful boy that his city was the authentic daughter of the great mother on the Tiber. But the first wall had been superseded by a second wall. Begun in 1172, in the days of Emperor Barbarossa, the new inclosure had trebled the original walled area of the city.[19] In his *Cronica* Villani for some undisclosed reason lets the second circle of walls be erected a hundred years earlier than was the case.[20] Perhaps he was led astray by older chroniclers from whom he drew his information. His error is unimportant for the purpose in hand, for at this point we are solely concerned with the civic impressions of Villani's boyhood and with the pride that swelled his bosom at the recognition that the city of his birth was a steadily expanding organism. And the evidence on this head continued to pile up, for the Florence under his youthful eye had already outgrown its second circle. Before each major city gate he saw stretching a populous *borgo* or suburb not without the alarming thought that all these people, their houses, and their possessions were exposed to destruction in case of an assault on the town. Over this situation grave burghers, such as Giovanni's father, would wag their heads when they met in the market-place and would declare, not without secret exultation, that the erection of a third and still more ample circle of walls could not be long adjourned. As we shall presently see it was in the son's lifetime and finally, under his supervision that the third circumvallation of Florence was carried to completion.

In addition to the walls there were only two public buildings in the Florence of Villani's boyhood likely to stir his civic imagination. They were the baptistry of St. John and the palace of the podestà, respectively the leading ecclesi-

---

[18] The private life of the Florentines, of which Villani affords us glimpses in this chapter, has been treated by two experts: G. Biagi, *Men and Manners of Old Florence*. London, 1909; A. Schiaparelli, *La Casa Fiorentina . . . nei Secoli XIV e XV*. Florence, 1908.

[19] Davidsohn, *Forschungen*, Vol. I, pp. 113 ff.

[20] Villani, IV, 8.

astical and the leading secular structure of the town. Around the history of the Florentine baptistery, which is to this day one of the most distinguished Christian monuments in Europe, a good deal of mystery gathers. Was it built in the period of declining Rome, or in the seventh century during the Lombard domination, or did it rise to view in the eleventh or twelfth century as the first fruits of the communal movement? The issue has released a heated debate among the experts into which it will not be necessary to enter. Suffice it that such slight *documentary* evidence as exists would seem to refer the structure to the Lombard period. On the other hand, the *artistic* evidence supplied by the building itself would make the fifth century the more probable period of origin.[21] Dante, Villani, and the local members of the writing tribe down to recent times have voiced the opinion that the baptistery went clear back to the pagan era and that it had originally been a temple of Mars, the god of war. Owing to the great age of the Mars legend, it continued to find stout champions until excavations conducted during the last generation established beyond a doubt that the baptistery was erected *ab origine* as a Christian house of worship and that it never had had a pagan predecessor. The excavations established also that the structure goes far back of the eleventh century. We would thus seem to be reduced to a choice between the fifth and the seventh centuries, between an early Christian and a Lombard origin. As in either case we have to predicate an architect who, steeped in the Roman tradition, produced an outstanding Roman-Christian monument, the question as to the preferable date is not particularly important. Moreover, in view of the fact that the unknown architect must have assembled his unusually fine columns, capitals, and architraves from abandoned pagan temples, we are, after all, obliged to ascribe much of the merit attaching to this manifestly classical structure to pagan Rome.

Over innumerable other issues, chiefly of construction and ornamentation, the controversy among the experts continues to rage unabated. It will serve our purpose if we take note that, like every other structure of venerable antiquity, the baptistery has experienced many changes. From an early time it had an administration called *opera,* and from at least the twelfth century on the opera, in evidence of the growing interest of the citizens in all the concerns of the town, was under lay management. As each new *operaio,* or head of the works, would be prompted to outdo the achievements of his predecessor, there were carried out with the advent of lay management numerous alterations and improvements which are rendered indubitable by surviving documents. Thus, for instance, the apse was given its present square form in place of the semi-circular form which it had had originally, and the incrustation of the interior in white and green marble was either renewed or brought to completion. As the incrustation, inside and outside, is the chief decorative feature of the baptistery, the question presents itself but cannot be answered whether on the occasion of the twelfth-century incrustation of the interior

---

[21] Davidsohn reviews the controversy and at the same time adduces the evidence for his opinion of a Lombard origin in the following passages: Vol. I, pp. 72, 736; Vol. IV, p. 3; *Forschungen,* Vol. I, p. 144; *Forschungen,* Vol. IV, p. 461. The case for the supporters of the fifth-century origin is persuasively put by E. W. Anthony, *Early Florentine Architecture and Decoration.* Cambridge (Mass.), 1927.

the original pattern was adhered to or whether a different pattern, more pleasing to the living generation, was adopted. Then, in the thirteenth century, it was resolved further to enrich the interior by giving it the incomparable glow of mosaics. In 1225—we have now reached the period of precise dates—the new apse with its triumphal arch received the fine mosaic envelope which it still boasts; and a half century later, in 1271, the resolution was taken to cover the lofty cupola with pictures in mosaic illustrative of striking scenes from the Old and the New Testament. Often interrupted, owing to lack of funds, the work on the cupola took some thirty years to bring to completion. The scaffolds on which the artists stood to do their work must have obstructed the interior during a large part of Villani's boyhood, and as often as he entered the door, he must have lifted his eyes to such scenes as, having just been completed, were disclosed to the public gaze and constituted the latest wonder of the town. We know for certain that a greater man than Villani gave the new work a most eager scrutiny. For when, an exile from his native city, Dante came to recount his epochal journey from hell to paradise, he wove numerous remembered details of the striking illustrations of the cupola into the imagery of his great poem.[22]

The mosaics of the cupola were not yet finished when the baptistery benefited from a new attention. The opera of San Giovanni had by this time been taken over by the wealthy merchant gild of the Calimala, which assumed all expenses both of maintenance and improvements. In 1293 the Calimala generously provided the means for removing the large tombs of stone and marble which, besides disfiguring the outer wall of the baptistery, constituted a hindrance to the growing traffic of the town. These tombs belonged to certain leading families, which, in accordance with an old Florentine custom, reserved them for the burial of their members. At the same time the Calimala supplied the funds for a new marble envelope of the exterior. Again we are in doubt as to how closely the new outer incrustation followed the original design. It is even possible that some parts of the exterior were now incrusted for the first time. Villani was perhaps thirteen years old when San Giovanni received its fine exterior garment of white and green marble slabs and bands, and when he came to write his chronicle he did not fail to mention the remembered splendor.[23]

A few hundred steps eastward of the baptistery of St. John rose the only other building in Florence in Villani's youth calculated to stimulate his local pride. This was the palace occupied at that time by the podestà, although it had originally been erected as the *palatium populi Florentini* to house the city's first democratic government. When, as far back as the middle of the thirteenth century, the people had for the first time ousted the nobility from control, they had resolved to celebrate the event by building a residence for their new rulers. Hardly was it ready for occupation when, in 1260, the disastrous battle of Montaperti put an end to the democratic interlude by redelivering the city, first into the hands of the Ghibelline, and later, into those of the Guelph nobility. At this recession of the democratic tide the fine new palace

[22] E. H. Wilkins, "Dante and the Mosaics of his Bel San Giovanni," *Speculum,* Vol. II, pp. 1 ff.
[23] Villani, VIII, 3.

of the people was assigned to the podestà as his residence, and as such it was still serving when Villani was growing to manhood. It was and remains to this day one of the most impressive piles reared anywhere in Italy in the age of the emerging third estate. The spirit of the time was still feudal and the main concern of the great landowners as well as of the rising communes was self-defense. The structure originally evolved for this purpose was the castle, and in one form or another it dotted all the hills of Tuscany and, for that matter, of all Europe with its rude piles of masonry. Although the burghers, struggling into existence against the will of the feudal class, were obliged to spend much of their fresh energy on the destruction of castles, when they faced the problem of their own safety they could find nothing better suited to their end than the stronghold of their enemies. In consequence they gave their towns something of the aspect of enlarged castles by equipping them with gates, moats, drawbridges, battlements, and every other engineering device developed by the feudality; and when they built their first town halls, again thinking primarily of defense, they repeated the castle pattern. The result for Florence of this outlook on the world was the massive structure, which, erected by the people, became identified with the podestà, and which since the sixteenth century has been called the Bargello from the police official whose residence it had meanwhile become. With its imposing walls of rough-hewn stone and its vigorous battlemented tower it seems prepared to defy a world of enemies. But its architects did not forget that primarily it was intended to serve certain novel communal purposes. Hence the handsome inner court with its columns supporting a spacious vaulted portico and with its ceremonial stairway leading to an impressive open loggia at the level of the first story. If this palace, planned as a house of the people, was still a feudal castle, it had felt a breath of that urbanity which it was one of the many functions of the communal revolution to bring into the world.

The two strong girdles of stone, the baptistery, the palace of the podestà—with these items we exhaust the monumental features of the Florence of Villani's boyhood. Parish and monastery churches, some of them of great age, were of course sown thickly through the town, but they were the handiwork of a poverty-stricken generation and, as a rule, were completely devoid of distinction. Even Santa Reparata, the cathedral church fronting the baptistery on the east side, was a modest, commonplace edifice, which so little met the new opinion the Florentines were beginning to entertain of their importance that they were eagerly discussing ways and means for replacing it with a more magnificent pile. As for the two great begging orders of St. Dominic and St. Francis, they too possessed as yet quite unimpressive churches assigned to them on their first establishing themselves on the Arno. With these humble structures also neither the friars nor the citizens were any longer contented, and the plans under way for their enlargement elicited enthusiastic popular support. Our living generation, looking into these matters, will be struck by the fact that the inhabitants of Florence, as well as of the other rising towns of Italy, made no distinction between the ecclesiastical and the civil buildings in their midst. They embraced them with an equal love, in part because all structures encompassed by the same wall were manifestly municipal and, above all, because medieval people experienced no difficulty whatever over the double allegiance owed by them to church and state. The two institutions might clash and clash vigorously by taking opposed positions in issues of politics and taxation. Florence, for instance, so frequently resisted the demands of the Roman curia of a political import that it lay sometimes for months and years together under the papal interdict. But such a conflict did not shake the confidence of the people in the soul-saving mission of the church nor diminish their devotion to the shining company of the saints and martyrs. They were convinced, rich and poor alike, that the blessed spirits dwelling in the shadow of God's throne would favor their worshipers both individually and as a nation, provided they were approached with a humble heart and honored with loaded altars and far-seen temples.

And now we are prepared to deal with the building era which was inaugurated in Florence with the democratic triumph of the decade 1282–93, and which in the course of the next half century gave the city a new aspect. Because this architectural transformation coincided almost exactly with Villani's lifetime, we are in the fortunate position to extract from his own minute record the story of how the City of the Baptist adorned itself with most of the monuments constituting its fame among the cities of the world. While making Villani our guide, so often as it is necessary to correct an error into which he has fallen or to round off a story which he has not completed, we shall draw on the many other authoritative sources which have become available.[24]

In the year 1296,[25] when the city of Florence was in very tranquil state after the revolution associated with the name of Giano della Bella, the citizens agreed to renew their leading church, which was a rude affair and small for such a municipality. They resolved to lengthen it by extending it eastward [di trarla addietro] and to make it of marble and sculptured figures. And the foundation was laid with great solemnity on the day of St. Mary of September [26] by the cardinal legate of the pope and many bishops. And there were present also the podestà and the captain and the priors and all the officials of Florence. And the church was consecrated to the honor of God and St. Mary and given the name of Santa Maria del Fiore, although the people continued to call it by its former name of Santa Reparata. And in aid of the construction of the said church the commune ordered a subsidy of four denari on each libra paid out of the city treasury and a head-tax of two soldi on every male. And the legate and bishops endowed the church with liberal indulgences and pardons to whosoever should aid with alms.

Let us admit that this is a disappointingly dry and colorless report of a great event, but we are by now aware that Villani was more of a chronicler and a statistician than an artist. Nonetheless the bare statement contains some interesting particulars, as, for instance, that church and state co-operated in the dedication and that the new cathedral, as the expression of the new burgher

[24] A remarkable compendium of all the established facts concerning the history of Florentine buildings is W. Limburger, *Die Gebäude von Florenz*. Leipzig, 1910. It is an indispensable vademecum for the student in this field.

[25] VIII, 9. Villani gives the date 1294 for this event but Davidsohn shows (*Forschungen*, Vol. IV, p. 457) that 1296 is correct.

[26] St. Mary of September would be September 8.

pride, was to be erected by the taxes and free-will offerings of the citizens. In this financing of the project we have the explanation why the work was so often interrupted and took so many generations to bring to completion. Owing to local disturbances and expensive wars civic resources were sometimes for protracted periods simply not available. The architect to whom the new cathedral was intrusted and whom Villani does not name was Arnolfo di Cambio, a native of the val d'Elsa and a Florentine by adoption. He was without question the most famous builder of his day. Taking advantage of the fresh enthusiasm of his fellow-citizens, he made rapid headway and in a comparatively short time had raised and vaulted a number of bays at the western end and provided them with a façade. In the early fourteenth century, owing to the disturbances occasioned by the civil war between the Blacks and the Whites, work ceased completely. Unfortunately Arnolfo's façade, which must have been one of his notable creations, no longer exists. A little more than half a century after its erection, in 1358, it fell victim to one of those changes in architectural taste which are always taking place. It was ordered to be destroyed in order to permit Francesco Talenti to erect a façade more in the ruling Gothic style. Over two hundred years later Talenti's façade was in its turn sacrificed to a new revolution in taste and was replaced (1587) by a wretched late-Renaissance makeshift. This was endured for three hundred years, till 1887, when the present front, the extravagant dream of an expert sugar-baker, was substituted, without any perceptible improvement, for its feeble predecessor.

From this recital of the vicissitudes of a single feature of the new cathedral we may divine how complicated is its total building history. Probably the earliest façade was the best of the four, and the whole church, had it been erected according to Arnolfo's original plan, would have had a unity which was lost by reason of the many hands and periods destined to leave their mark upon the pile. However, medieval cathedrals were never built in a single, uninterrupted effort, according to an inalterable plan, and, everything considered, they usually compensate for their lack of stylistic harmony by a flexibility and variety which are extremely ingratiating. Arnolfo died, certainly before 1310. Exactly how far eastward toward the choir he had succeeded in carrying the new Santa Reparata, no surviving document reveals. We know merely that, owing to the above-mentioned disturbances supplemented by lack of funds, all work on the structure had been discontinued some years before Arnolfo's death.

Construction was not resumed for a quarter of a century. Villani reports the advent of a new building period under the year 1330 and informs us that the commune, besides reviving the former tax levies in the cathedral's favor, put the opera in charge of the arte di Lana, the richest gild of the city, in the hope of expediting the work.[27] On this occasion a more ambitious plan was substituted for that of Arnolfo and a few bays of a more ample span than those already completed were constructed which carried the nave eastward to its point of junction with the choir. This, in the form of a vast octagon, was projected as the outstanding feature of the new edifice. As its construction and

<hr>

[27] Villani, X, 192.

that of the famous cupola over it is a story carrying us well into the Renaissance, we shall leave it to a later chapter.

Less than three years after the commune had committed itself to the formidable cathedral enterprise, it undertook another work of hardly inferior magnitude. Here is Villani's report of the transaction.

In the said year 1299 [28] the commune and people of Florence laid the foundation of the palace of the priors. They were moved to take this step because of the party divisions and the brawls resulting therefrom between the people and the magnates on the occasion of the renewal of the priors, which occurred every two months. And it did not seem that the priors, who ruled the people and the republic, were secure in the house they inhabited which belonged to the White Cerchi [29] and lay behind the church of San Brocolo. And there, where they laid the foundation of the said palace, had formerly stood the houses of the Uberti, rebels of Florence and Ghibellines. And the ground whereon the houses had stood was converted into a piazza to make sure that the houses would never be rebuilt. And the commune bought the houses of other citizens, as, for instance, those of the Foraboschi, and raised the said palace on the purchased ground. And for the tower of the palace of the priors they utilized the tower of the Foraboschi, which was almost one hundred feet high and was called La Vacca [the Cow]. And in order that the said palace be not built on the former land of the Uberti the committee in charge placed it askew [il puosono musso], which was a great imperfection inasmuch as the palace should have been given a square or rectangular shape and should not have been carried so close to the church of San Piero Scheraggio.[30]

The palace of the priors is the present Palazzo Vecchio, while the piazza created by clearing away the débris of the Uberti houses is, at least in considerable part, the present Piazza Signoria. It throws a curious light on the ferocity of the party spirit that these Uberti ruins had been permitted to encumber the city for a whole generation. As in this instance, too, Villani fails to name the architect intrusted with the new enterprise, we have to go to other authorities to learn that it was Arnolfo di Cambio. Plainly, after his success with the new cathedral, he was recognized as the master-builder of the city. Our chronicler offers the interesting information that the architect was obliged to submit to several serious limitations. Not only did he have to avoid utilizing as much as an inch of the accursed Uberti ground but he was required to incorporate the existent tower of the Foraboschi in his design. Villani, who like most simple souls was hypnotized by the regularities of geometry, was not particularly pleased with the result. But later ages, disagreeing with him, have given an enthusiastic approval to Arnolfo's solution of a difficult problem. Taking his inspiration from the earlier palazzo of the podestà, he erected a

---

[28] Villani, VIII, 26. The exact date of the foundation ceremony was February 24, 1299 (Davidsohn, Vol. IV³, pp. 3, 270). Villani gives the year 1298, but as by the Florentine calendar the year began on March 25, the day of the Annunciation, Villani's 1298 is 1299 by the common Christian calendar.

[29] The clan of the Cerchi was at the head of the political party called the Whites. They were composed of two branches, distinguished because of the color and complexion of their respective founders as White Cerchi and Black Cerchi. White Cerchi and Black Cerchi belonged alike to the political party of the Whites.

[30] San Piero Scheraggio hugged the south wall of the new palace. It was removed in the sixteenth century to make room for the Uffizi.

second civic edifice which, while it clung, like its prototype, to the fortress form and uttered brazen defiance to the enemies of the commonwealth, was an entirely independent creation. Above all, it was a more imposing, a more soaring mass; and instead of letting the tower of the Foraboschi become a handicap, Arnolfo so successfully mortised this ancient landmark into his design that, lengthened and battlement-crowned, it became the most distinctive feature of the edifice. In contrast to the cathedral, work on the communal residence proceeded so rapidly that after three years the building was far enough along for the priors to take possession (1302). But both it and the new piazza were still far from their present appearance. The records assembled by Davidsohn show that every year brought some innovation, though often slight and unimportant.[31] In 1306, for instance, the piazza was carefully paved, and in 1307 a bell was ordered to be cast to call the councils together and for similar official purposes. Because Arnolfo's tower was not yet ready at that date, we learn that the iron summoner was installed on a temporary platform in front of the structure. Indeed Arnolfo had departed this life long before the tower was completed; and completed, it was not complete because in its case, as in that of the whole edifice of which it was a part, the subsequent generations considered themselves privileged to make alterations according either to their taste or their changing necessities.

Immediately on their founding in the dugento, the two great begging orders of the Dominicans and the Franciscans had become the most alive and pushing elements in the Catholic church. They simply radiated energy; and since their vigor did not diminish in the trecento they were bound to be represented by great monastic establishments in all the growing communes of Italy. We have already noted that from an early time, and therefore long before Villani's birth, the Dominicans were settled at Santa Maria Novella and the Franciscans at the opposite, the eastern, end of the town in buildings which had been repeatedly enlarged. But with the great forward stride of the whole city coincident with the seizure of political power by the gilds, ideas of grandeur manifested themselves among both friars and citizens which refused to be content with anything less than the total reconstruction of the two monasteries on a magnificent scale.

The Dominicans led the way. In 1279, at about the time of Villani's birth and when the poet Dante was a lad of fourteen, they laid the foundation of a new monastery intended to replace the old one; and, a few years later, on February 2, 1283, they laid the foundations of the present imposing church of Santa Maria Novella. As Villani could not report these happenings from his own experience, he mentions them in a brief and confused statement not worth quoting.[32] However, as they mark the initiation of an enterprise which continued for many generations and gave Florence not only one of its most distinguished churches but also cloisters, a refectory, a library, a chapter house, and a bell tower constituting as imposing a monastic group as may be seen

[31] Davidsohn, *Forschungen*, Vol. IV, pp. 499 ff.

[32] Villani, VII, 56. Among the most important documents assembled by Davidsohn in regard to the architectural history of Florence are those bearing on Santa Maria Novella. See *Forschungen*, Vol. IV, pp. 466-82. He shows that the traditional attribution of the great temple to the two Dominican brothers, Fra Ristoro and Fra Sisto, is a pure invention.

anywhere in the world, we cannot afford to overlook the story. The individual structures were built, apparently without exception, by architects selected from among the brothers themselves. This need cause no surprise, for the order exercised a powerful attraction on men of the highest station and the most varied gifts, who, after their adoption of the cowl, were encouraged to put their talents at the service of the brotherhood. Much more remarkable is the consistently Gothic inspiration of the many friars busy at one time or another on this monastic monument. Within the circumference of Florence there is no ecclesiastical edifice which conveys more of the feeling of true, that is, of northern Gothic, than the church of Santa Maria Novella; and the features subsidiary to the church, such as the cloisters and the chapter-house, are in general keeping with the lines and feeling of the temple. In short, Santa Maria Novella constitutes one of the rare areas in Tuscany dedicated to the Gothic spirit.

We may remind ourselves in this connection that the Florentines were, architecturally, a very conservative people and persisted in cultivating the traditions native to their soil. So far as we are able to go back in history we encounter this trait. As soon as they began to outgrow the extreme poverty of the Middle Ages and were able to abandon wood in favor of stone, they developed a "style" representing a fusion of Roman traditions and current elements of taste. As the process was duplicated everywhere in Italy and western Europe there sprang into existence many distinct but interrelated styles, which, from the element common to them all, are distinguished as Romanesque. In northern Europe, more especially in France, the crude Romanesque was gradually sublimated into Gothic and brought to perfection in such magnificent cathedrals as Rheims and Chartres. In these marvelously harmonized monuments Gothic represents the conquest of a strikingly new world of architectural forms. As the story of how the Gothic style arose in northern France is not our concern, we may content ourselves with noting that with its highly developed elements of expression, such as the pointed arch, the massive buttress, the audacious flying buttress, and the soaring vault, it achieved a lightness and grace in the sharpest possible contrast with the ponderous gravity of the best examples of Romanesque.

Measured by the Gothic standards furnished by the great French cathedrals, the Florentine church of Santa Maria Novella is a very imperfect creation. Its nave—to concentrate on a single but significant feature—lacks the characteristic lift and flight of true Gothic by reason of the total suppression of the triforium and the employment of a merely rudimentary clerestory. But only pedants who are lost when their familiar categories fail them will refuse to enjoy this church of the Dominicans. Is it not enough that it has a noble spaciousness admirably suited for the worship of a united population? And if it must perforce be classified, let us call it a Tuscan variant of Gothic. Obviously the brother or brothers who devised it were under the influence of the graceful, yet vigorous northern style which in their time was making a triumphal march throughout the extent of western Christendom. But as they were also Tuscans, born and bred, they could not escape the native traditions which ruled their environment; and they did not hesitate to fuse them with the northern borrowings.

The Franciscan foundation of Santa Croce grew somewhat more deliberately than its Dominican rival. To be sure, Franciscans and Dominicans equally enjoyed both the favor of the citizens and the financial support of the government; but the injunction of poverty was so special a feature of the Little Brother of Assisi that a considerable section of his followers continued for a long time to protest against property of any kind and, particularly, against sumptuous houses of worship. They constituted an evangelical and puritan group called the Spiritual Franciscans, which with constantly diminishing success opposed the powerful worldly faction in their order until in the first half of the fourteenth century they completely lost the battle. The climax came when Pope John XXII of infamous memory denounced them as heretics and brought all the rigors of the Inquisition into play to effect their suppression. When some decades before this tragic event the Franciscans of Florence resolved to construct a new Santa Croce on a much larger scale than its inconspicuous predecessor, by thus committing themselves to a program of material expansion they gave proof of having effectively silenced the Spirituals in their midst. Although Villani does not expressly say so, we may be sure that so stout a burgher and defender of property as he sympathized with the victors.

In the year of Christ 1295, on the day of the Holy Cross of May, the foundation was laid of the new church of the Brothers Minor of Florence, called Santa Croce.[33] And at the consecration of the first stone there were present, amidst great pomp and solemnity, many bishops and prelates and priests and members of religious orders as well as the podestà and captain and all the good people of Florence, men and women alike. And work was begun at the chapels at the east end in order not to disturb the old church which the friars needed for religious services until the new chapels should be ready.

Santa Croce, too, though we do not get the information from Villani, was committed to the city's foremost architect, Arnolfo di Cambio. In fact it was the first of the three public enterprises associated with his name to be intrusted to his care, Santa Maria del Fiore following in the next year (1296), and the palace of the priors three years after the cathedral. But owing to the rather languid flow of funds, this earliest work progressed more slowly than the other two ventures and Arnolfo never lived to see more than the bare beginnings of Santa Croce. It is impossible to say whether, when at successive intervals work was renewed, his plans were adhered to, although it is usually assumed that such was the case. We know that the small, original church was not demolished till 1336, when it was at last removed to make room for the nave and aisles of the new structure. On these being added to the chapels of the choir, where, according to Villani, the work had begun, Santa Croce had been brought to substantial completion. In 1336, however, Arnolfo had been dead for over a quarter of a century, and we have no way of telling whether the nave and aisles followed his plans or not. That even after these sections had been completed there remained much to be done and that the church

---

[33] Villani, VIII, 7. Holy Cross of May would be May 3. The chronicler gives the date 1294, for which Davidsohn substitutes 1295. For documents bearing on the construction of Santa Croce see his *Forschungen*, Vol. IV, pp. 482 ff.

marched forward at the usual deliberate pace is proved by the fact that the nineteenth century arrived and still found Santa Croce without a façade. The tawdry front which was then erected in a burst of mistaken municipal patriotism will never cease to evoke a profound regret.

To enter Santa Croce is to find one's self in a very different world of form and feeling from that of Santa Maria Novella. On being intrusted with his task Arnolfo must have resolved to depart very substantially from the gloomy, if impressive, churches of the Florentine tradition and to raise a well-proportioned structure carried on slender piers and permitting the light from choir and clerestory agreeably to flood a spacious interior. It may well be that the artist, thoroughly Tuscan though he was, strove in this instance for a certain elegance characteristic of Gothic. In no case, however, was he fully committed to this imported style or particularly proficient in it. Had the northern architecture been a deep concern with him, he would not have surrendered the most characteristic Gothic feature, the vault, which in all sound Gothic examples soars high above the nave and majestically crowns it. In its stead he raised a roof of open beamwork, such as may be found in most of the older Tuscan churches. Owing perhaps to its inexpensiveness, he must have had this feature in mind from the first, for his piers were so slender that they could never have been intended to support a ponderous roof of stone. Because of these and other departures from the accepted norms, Gothic fanatics have not hesitated to scoff at Santa Croce, while sworn followers of the Romanesque have been hardly less disdainful. Both groups of critics make the mistake of approaching this building with a fixed preconception, instead of enjoying it directly for such merits as it has. These, as already indicated, lie in the direction of a warm, even light playing through the wide spaces of a nave and transept lightly floating on the slenderest possible supports.

Unless we somewhat hasten our steps we shall never have done with gazing at the fine new garment which Florence gave itself in Villani's time. The church of the Badia, the oldest and most honored monastery of the town, was totally rebuilt in the early years of the new government of the priors (around 1284); but four hundred years later an age of false refinement utterly destroyed what must have been a veritable treasure-house of early art in order to replace it with the existing structure, which so perfectly expresses the mental vacuity of its projectors. Fortunately the graceful hexagonal campanile, which belongs to the year 1330, was spared by the elegant vandals and still delights the visitor.[34] In this same year the Calimala gild, which, as we may recall, administered the opera of the baptistery, ordered of Andrea Pisano the first of the three magnificent bronze doors which still adorn that celebrated edifice. We shall return to this door when we take up the story of Florentine sculpture. Its quiet beauty prompted our pedestrian friend and guide to indulge in what for him is a burst of unrestrained enthusiasm. Nor does he forget to record the proud circumstance that it was none other than himself who represented the Calimala gild in connection with this enterprise.[35]

[34] The erection of the campanile is recorded by Villani, X, 174. Consult also on the campanile, Davidsohn, Vol IV[3], pp. 271-72.

[35] X, 174. For the official records covering the gate consult Davidsohn, *Forschungen*, Vol. IV, p. 464.

A little later, in 1337, an important measure was taken regarding Or San Michele.[36] But before discussing it, let us review the changes effected in the course of the centuries at this spot in order to remind ourselves how colorful is the history of every square foot of the city's area. Originally there stood on the site of what in Villani's day was the grain market, a small church dedicated to Saint Michael. It went all the way back to Lombard days, and because it stood in a garden, was called San Michele in Orto or Or San Michele for short. In 1239 it was destroyed, probably in connection with a civil outbreak occurring in that year. Thereupon the commune removed the débris and appropriated the open space thus acquired to various uses of its own. In 1284 the piazza was reserved as the market for the trade in grain and, in order to protect the dealers from the weather, a roofed loggia was erected to serve as shelter. Shortly after, a Madonna, which had been painted in fresco on one of the piers supporting the loggia, was declared to have operated a number of miraculous cures and at once leaped into such popularity that the candles and wax images dedicated to her by the faithful before long almost hid her Ladyship from view. The huge incendiary conflagration of 1304 started by the Blacks to save their regime completely destroyed the loggia and greatly damaged the fresco. Nonetheless it was incorporated in the new loggia which was promptly erected to replace its predecessor. This was so skimpily built that frequent repairs were necessary, and finally, in 1337, the priors resolved, as mentioned *ad annum* by Villani, to reconstruct the loggia in a more substantial manner and to crown it with two vaulted stories serviceable for storing grain. The original Madonna in fresco must by this time have faded out entirely, for in 1346 Bernardo Daddi was commissioned to paint on wood and in the most substantial manner a new picture of the Virgin. When this was ready it elicited such admiration that the leading Florentine sculptor, Orcagna, was ordered (1349) to provide for it the most beautiful shrine of which he was capable. It was not till the fifties, when Villani was already dead, that the combined loggia and storehouse for grain, decided on almost twenty years before, began to approach completion. When the structure, which is the present Or San Michele, was finished, an agitation was started to have the grain market with its vulgar hubbub removed to another piazza in order to provide an atmosphere more in keeping with the magnificent tabernacle on which Orcagna was engaged. In 1357 the transfer of the grain market was carried out and, two years later, when Orcagna had completed his shrine, the loggia was dedicated as a church. As soon as the loggia had been converted into a house of worship, it became urgent to give it a protective inclosure and accordingly, beginning in 1366, the open spaces between the loggia piers were walled up as we see them today.[37]

The most interesting communal undertaking of Villani's last decade was the rose-colored, marble-incrusted campanile, very generally regarded as the loveliest architectural monument of the town.

---

[36] Villani, XI, 67. Davidsohn, *Forschungen*, Vol. IV, p. 510.

[37] C. Schubert-Feder, "La Loggia di Or San Michele," *Arch. Stor. It.*, Serie 5, Vol. VII, pp. 67-88. Davidsohn, Vol. II¹, p. 244; Vol. II², pp. 191-92; Vol. IV³, pp. 265-70; *Forschungen*, Vol. IV, p. 510.

In the said year [1334], on July 18, was begun the new bell tower of Santa Reparata [we observe that Villani too, much like the common people, was slow in applying to the cathedral its newer, more pretentious name of Santa Maria del Fiore] close to the front of the church on the piazza of San Giovanni. And there were present for the blessing of the first stone the bishop of Florence with all his clergy as well as the priors and the other magistrates with many people and a great procession. And the foundation was made as solid as possible. And as superintendent and overseer of the opera of Santa Reparata the commune appointed our fellow-citizen, Giotto, the most sovereign master of painting in his time, who drew all his figures and their postures according to nature. And he was given a salary by the commune in virtue of his talent and excellence.[38]

Villani, who omitted to name the architect of Santa Croce, Santa Maria del Fiore, and the Palazzo Communale, an artist who stood at the head of his profession in his time, does not hesitate to distinguish Giotto as the builder of the campanile for the reason that his fame was so widespread that it could not be ignored. Giotto is correctly signalized as a great painter (*maestro in dipintura*), whom it may surprise us moderns to find appointed operaio of Santa Reparata and architect of Santa Reparata's new bell tower. That Villani finds nothing out of the way in the appointment is clear evidence that the arts had not yet become as specialized as they are with us and that in those days a man who called himself an artist was expected to be an all-around craftsman. Giotto's bell tower replaced an unimportant predecessor which stood at the northwest corner of Santa Reparata. Instead of remodeling this humble structure, an entirely new structure was planned and a site selected for it at the opposite or southwest corner of the cathedral front. The celebrated operaio died at the age of seventy, two and a half years after his appointment. He lived to carry his project no farther than just above the first row of sculptures; but so completely did he stamp his creation with his genius that although the work, interrupted by the usual delays, was not finished till half a century later, it was carried through with only unimportant deviations from his plans.

Undoubtedly the campanile employs Gothic elements of expression, as, for instance, in its engagingly varied fenestration, and yet it is as little a "correct" Gothic structure as Santa Croce, Santa Maria Novella, or any other Florentine monument of the trecento. Once again it brings home to us that the Florentines of this age clung stubbornly to their local tradition, modifying it with imported or freely invented features according to their pleasure. Granting that its racy, native style enables the campanile to fit harmoniously into the Florentine ensemble, nonetheless, like every other work of genius, it has the very individual touch of its creator. For this reason the bell tower, which rises with the ease and grace of a lily in the center of a city which has the lily for its emblem, has never been called other than Giotto's campanile.

As one more structure completes the list of the notable Florentine edifices of the medieval period, it must be added to the record at this point, although it was not erected in the life-span of our guide. When a new set of priors was inaugurated into office or when a foreign ambassador was to be formally received, the republic made a practice of conducting the exercises in public on

[38] Villani, XI, 12.

the platform or *ringhiera* in front of the palace. If it rained during the ceremony, the enthusiasm of the orators and, even more of the drenched listeners,
suffered a considerable diminution. This inconvenience had started an agitation
for a covered loggia, and although from a relatively early time the matter was
frequently discussed in the councils, nothing definite was done till 1376, when
a number of private houses close to the palace were bought and leveled with
the ground. Shortly after the task of building a public loggia was intrusted
to the opera del duomo and by 1382 the structure, called originally Loggia dei
Priori (or Signori) was completed. As in the sixteenth century, when the republic had perished, Duke Cosimo used the loggia as a station for his German
bodyguard called Lanzi (from the German *Landsknecht*), it came gradually
to be called Loggia dei Lanzi; and Loggia dei Lanzi it has remained to this
day. The Loggia dei Lanzi is an impressive open hall of three round arches
of bold leap and wide span. With its clustered piers, its stone vaults, and its
decorative motifs it fits perfectly into the picture of Gothic Florence with
which we have become acquainted. However, in applying the term Gothic to
our city let us always bear in mind an architectural system consisting of a
native Romanesque kernel, to which have been added a number of imported
Gothic features. The Loggia dei Lanzi is a perfect illustration of the fusion of
these two elements. While there is no lack of Gothic decorative features, the
three great arches with their all but spoken welcome to the visitor of the great
square have not been pointed as would have been the case if the architect had
possessed the true Gothic feeling; instead they are smoothly rounded, presenting themselves to view as the authentic descendants of the arch of triumph,
so congenial to the monumental feeling of the ancient Romans. In his great
history of the arts Vasari ventured the guess that the plans for the loggia were
drawn by the painter-sculptor Orcagna. He was wrong, but his speculation has
become a part of the impregnable Florentine legend. Modern investigators
have shown beyond dispute that the loggia was built by the contemporary
heads of the cathedral works, sound professional workers of good standing in
their day but enjoying no such reputation among the later generations as the
master of the tabernacle of Or San Michele.[39] Under these circumstances it is
easy to understand why the ever active legendary spirit, wishing to connect a
famous object with a famous name, should have hit upon Orcagna, although
in point of fact Orcagna had died eight years before even so much as the first
step toward the construction of the loggia had been taken.

We are aware that the four bridges of Florence were all severely injured,
if not totally ruined, by the historic flood of 1333. The oldest of these, which
belonged to the miniature Florence of the early Middle Ages and which went
back to Roman times, was the Ponte Vecchio. The other three had been added
in the first half of the dugento. The Carraia bridge bears the date 1220 and
was followed in 1237 by the bridge called Rubaconte, in honor of the podestà
of that year, under whose auspices the foundations had been laid. For the
designation Rubaconte there was afterward substituted that of delle Grazie
from the shrine of a much-visited Madonna, Santa Maria delle Grazie, who
by her perpetual presence bestowed her blessing on the structure. The fourth

39 C. Frey, *Die Loggia dei Lanzi zu Florenz*. Berlin, 1885.

and last bridge was erected in 1252 and named Santa Trinità after the church on the right bank, near which it terminated. The addition of three bridges to the original Ponte Vecchio within a stretch of some thirty years of the thirteenth century is excellent proof of the rapid and often insufficiently realized growth of Florence in that relatively early period. The impression of the degree of this expansion is deepened when we reflect that these four bridges satisfied the needs of the city through the subsequent flourishing periods of the fourteenth and fifteenth centuries. Following the catastrophe of the year 1333, the commune put in service provisional bridges of wood until sufficient resources had been accumulated to rebuild these invaluable links of traffic on a larger scale and with stronger foundations than their predecessors.

We may learn of the generous manner in which the destroyed bridges were reconstructed by looking into the single instance of the oldest and most celebrated of them, the Ponte Vecchio.

In the year 1345, on July 18, was completed the new bridge over the Arno which replaced the Ponte Vecchio. It consisted of two piers and three arches and cost . . . gold florins [space left vacant and never filled in]. And it was raised on solid foundations and had a width of thirty-two braccia with a roadway in the middle of sixteen braccia. It was too wide in my judgment since the width was the cause of the lowering of the arches by two braccia. [Villani evidently held that it would have been better to have the bridge high and narrow than low and wide.] And the shops at either end of the bridge were each eight braccia wide and eight braccia long and were raised of stone on the solid arches. There were forty-three of these shops, from which the commune drew an annual rental of eighty and more gold florins. Originally they had been constructed of wood and been extended out over the Arno on beams since the old bridge had been only twelve braccia wide.[40]

The shops were rebuilt in stone, instead of wood, in order to put an end to the fires which had repeatedly destroyed them in the past. To this day, as everybody knows, the Ponte Vecchio has retained the picturesque feature of a double line of *botteghe* at either bridge end. Particularly interesting in Villani's report is the evidence of the greater traffic capacity of the new bridge. If we reckon the braccio roughly at two feet—it was in reality somewhat less—the open roadway of the new bridge was eight feet wider than the whole earlier structure! With its forty-odd shops of stone, which rested firmly on the stone vaulting of the arches without any overhang, the new bridge must have struck Villani's contemporaries as a notable advance in size and dignity on the vanished structure.

By way of curiosity we may note that the equestrian figure of Mars, which had long stood at the head of the bridge on the right bank, was not fished out of the waters which swallowed it on the occasion of the great inundation of 1333. Already in an earlier flood of the year 1178 the statue, located at that time on the opposite or left bank of the Arno, had been washed away only to be salvaged and set up again on the right bank. That is where it stood when, on a certain Easter morning, the truculent Uberti and Amidei used it as an ambuscade, from behind which they leaped upon and brutally dispatched the

[40] Villani, XII, 46.

handsome Buondelmonte, that too casual lover. Neither Villani nor Dante nor any other Florentine of the Middle Ages doubted that the ruined and featureless rider, "quella pietra scema," [41] represented the Roman god. Did not Florence boast in the baptistery a former temple of Mars and, dedicated as the city was supposed to be to the pagan god of battles, was it not highly fitting to possess his statue? These old Mars legends, which constituted so living an element of the thought of the divine poet and his contemporaries, have been shown by modern criticism to have little or no basis in reality.[42] That is of course not very important since what chiefly counts in building up a national mentality is not the truth but the quality, high or low, of what is deeply held to be the truth. However, in view of the proved attachment of the Florentines to their disfigured, putative Mars, it remains perplexing that neither Villani nor any other writer has recorded any attempt to rescue the ancient horseman, become a patriotic emblem, from his watery grave. We are forced to conclude that his last plunge from his pedestal reduced him to such a dilapidated state that every hope of further restoration was rendered vain.

It would be ungracious if, after taking advantage of the services of our ancient guide, we should dismiss him before he had been permitted to show us the structural addition of his day which constituted perhaps the chief object of his civic pride. From the very beginning of its rise as a commune Florence had never for a moment been permitted to forget that it was confronted with a hostile world and that to relax its efforts against its environment was to fall behind in the race. Of this perilous situation the constant reminder was the city wall, which bound the inhabitants into a single sheepfold and made them secure against their enemies. In considering Villani's youth we have dealt with the two circles with which, as a boy, he became familiar, the first going back to Roman days, the second erected in the reign of Barbarossa and embracing about three times the area of the first. We are also aware that, long before Villani's birth, the continuously expanding town had burst beyond the bounds of the second girdle and that populous suburbs or borghi lay along every highway leading from the city. Owing to this situation, as soon as the victory of the gilds had energized the government, a plan was considered to create a third girdle; and in 1284 the project was initiated by four new gates on the right bank raised as barbicans or outposts at a considerable distance beyond the second circle. The four gates were joined provisionally by palisades of wood, which traced the line the walls would ultimately follow. However, owing to the expense of so immense an undertaking coupled with the momentary absence of danger, the work soon came to a standstill and was not resumed till fifteen years later, in 1299. An era of intense municipal construction had at that time been inaugurated, as Santa Croce, Santa Maria del Fiore, and the palace of the priors amply witness, and it was natural for the awakened civic enthusiasm of the citizens to turn again to the interrupted enterprise of the third circle. But again little was done, this time owing to the outbreak of the civil war between the Blacks and the Whites; and it was not till the descent into Italy of Emperor Henry VII coupled with the certain expectation of his enmity

---

[41] Dante, *Paradiso*, XVI, 145.
[42] Davidsohn, Vol. I, pp. 748-52.

that a new and feverish period of construction set in (1310). Florence counted on war with its sovereign and war came, the grimmest sort of war, culminating in the year 1312 in the city's siege by the imperial host. To Villani, reporting the event, it was only the improved eastern defenses toward San Salvi, where Henry spread his camp, that saved Florence from destruction.[43]

When Henry died in the following year (1313), the city heaved a sigh of relief and again discarded hammer and trowel not to resume them till another cloud rose on the horizon from which emerged the dread face and form of Castruccio Castracane. This threat stimulated the commune to renewed effort; and between 1322 and 1324 the walls of the right bank, which inclosed five of the six sesti of the town, were actually and finally brought to completion. It is a stroke of good fortune that our chronicler, on account of his having been one of the overseers of construction during this particular period, was prompted to furnish his readers with a detailed description of the finished work.[44]

In order that the memory of the greatness of the said city be always kept alive . . . we shall give an ordered account of the building of the said walls together with the measurements made by myself, the author, who, in behalf of the commune, served as official of the walls.

There follow details and figures so unusual in a work of this period, when men were notoriously indifferent to accuracy, that we would be tempted to challenge them if we had not by now accustomed ourselves to Villani's very modern factual sense. In closing his minute description he sums up as follows:

And thus we find that the new circle of walls measures, on the right bank of the Arno, seven thousand seven hundred braccia. And this section possesses nine gates, that is, four master gates and five posterns [postierle], each with a tower of sixty braccia and with a barbican in front of it. And along the wall rise forty-five towers, counting also those of the gates.

Turning thence to the wall of the left bank (which we may note was not completed till 1328) he follows the same precise procedure employed in treating the wall of the right bank. And in a final survey he informs us that the wall throughout its extent was three braccia, that is, almost six feet, thick and twenty braccia, that is, almost forty feet, high to the top of the battlements, and that the total circumference of this tremendous mass of brick, stone, and mortar was five miles. The picture in our minds becomes still more impressive on learning that there were fifteen gates in all (nine on the right, six on the left bank), seventy-three towers along the wall at four-hundred-foot intervals, and a broad circumambient moat. That provision was made for the future increase of the population appears from the statement that much garden and vegetable land (orti e giardini) was included within the new circuit.

Bristling with the imposing masonry of its third circle, Florence was for many generations regarded as the best fortified city of Italy. When, with the seventeenth century, artillery and high explosives gained an increasing ascendancy, the defenses declined in value, and by the nineteenth century they had

[43] Villani, IX, 10. "La qual cosa fu poi lo scampo della città."
[44] IX, 256, 257.

become completely useless. In the period of Italian unification it was therefore resolved that the wall on the right bank should be leveled with the ground except for the three gates of Al Prato, San Gallo, and Alla Croce. The site of the ancient girdle is at present marked by a wide, tree-lined boulevard. On the left bank, however, in Oltrarno, the wall was happily spared and to this day spills its red mass over the irregularly formed ground. Whoever wishes to recover the sentiment which made Florence a self-contained community set off against a hostile world and inspiring the citizens with an unconquerable resolution cannot do better than on some fresh spring or mellow autumn morning to climb the hill of San Giorgio and, issuing from the gate still expressively carved with the dragon-killer whose fame it celebrates, drop thence slowly along the path which follows the ancient wall to the bank of the Arno. His walk will take him by the side of quiet vineyards and silvery olive orchards, among which, losing the sense of time, he will be joined unawares by Giovanni Villani with the eager proffer of his services as guide, while not far behind will hover the gracious, more reticent ghosts of Arnolfo, Giotto, and Dante Alighieri.

left: THE MEDICI PALACE, WITH THE MEDICI COAT OF ARMS. MICHELOZZI (ALINARI).
right: THE COURT OF THE MEDICI PALACE. MICHELOZZI (ALINARI).

left: THE PITTI PALACE (ALINARI). *right:* THE STROZZI PALACE. BENEDETTO DA
MAIANO AND IL CRONACA (ALINARI).

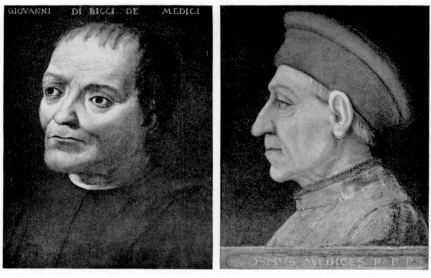

left: GIOVANNI DI BICCI DE' MEDICI. MEDICI PALACE (ALINARI). *right:* COSIMO
DE' MEDICI. MEDICI PALACE (ALINARI).

DEATH MASK IN PLASTER OF LORENZO THE MAGNIFI-
CENT. MEDICI PALACE (ALINARI).

XVI. Democracy versus Oligarchy: The Final Struggle (1343–82)

WHATEVER the system of gild rule seemed to promise at its inception, from the time of the defeat and exile in 1295 of the popular champion, Giano della Bella, it had worked out in effect as an oligarchy which recruited its members from the greater gilds. By their intelligence, their energy, and, let us not forget to add, their entire lack of scruple, the oligarchs had in the course of the first half of the fourteenth century succeeded in making their city the leading financial and industrial center of the contemporary world. When we reflect that Florence was an inland town on a small river, that it boasted neither an exceptionably favorable location nor an easy access to abundant and cheap supplies of raw material, we cannot deny these bold adventurers and enterprisers our frank admiration. However, in measure as their fortunes rose higher and higher, their activities became more and more speculative until they found themselves inextricably tied up with numerous governments to which they had advanced the funds required to conduct unprofitable wars of conquest. When, beginning with Edward III of England, one of these governments after another defaulted on its loans there followed the great crash and crisis of the forties. It is chiefly connected in the minds of men with the names of the Bardi and Peruzzi, but, in point of fact, it brought down every trading firm of any consequence, robbed hundreds of large and small investors of their savings, and plunged the town into the trough of a prolonged depression.

It need hardly be expressly said that the crisis of the forties struck a terrific blow at the prestige of the ruling oligarchy. Since the rapid expansion of Florentine business and political power following the establishment of the priorate had not improperly been attributed by the ruling merchants to their own energy and sagacity, it was inevitable that the common people, who were the chief sufferers from the collapse, should with equal propriety ascribe the unexampled crash to this same group. In a supreme effort to avoid bankruptcy the bankers had promoted the rule of the duke of Athens; and when, disappointed with his lack of subserviency to their interests, they drove him from the town, the last remaining chance to escape destruction lay in their own bold seizure of the state. But this intrigue was promptly defeated by the now fully aroused democratic masses; and when the series of revolutions inaugurated by the rising against the French adventurer was over, the old government of the priors had been reconstituted, but on so different a basis as to present a greatly altered appearance to the world.

We have agreed that ever since the overthrow of Giano della Bella the power in the state had rested with the seven greater gilds. This was a clear departure from the Ordinances of Justice which attributed the new executive, the priorate, to the twenty-one gilds, great, medium, and small, recognized by that famous constitutional document. But so great, owing to their wealth, was the authority of the seven greater gilds that their usurpation, modified by the occasional magnanimous admission of a lesser gildsman to office, was not challenged so long as the prosperity and, let us add, the territorial expansion of Florence moved forward in an unbroken line. Men are not given to worrying about constitutional orthodoxy so long as success smiles on the efforts of their rulers. So it was with the Florentines, until with alarming suddenness and with the cumulative effect of successive deadly blows came the disastrous Lucchese war, the crumbling of the town's financial foundations, the industrial stagnation with its attendant unemployment, the disappointing and disgraceful episode of the duke of Athens. When, as a sequel to all these calamities, the constitution of the priors was rehabilitated, no one should be surprised to hear that the common people were resolved to assert themselves. They took the stand that the undue authority so long exercised by the seven upper gilds must terminate in order to be replaced by the government of the whole body of the twenty-one gilds, exactly as the law prescribed. It was therefore decreed that of the eight priors two were henceforth to represent the seven greater gilds, three the five middle gilds, and three the nine lesser gilds. The ninth prior, the gonfalonier of Justice, was to be chosen from each of the three groups in turn. Although this arrangement did not punish the merchant gilds for the recent catastrophes by excluding them from office, it secured a definite preponderance to the small bourgeoisie and the organized craftsmen. As, on the other hand, the reorganization made no concession whatever to the great mass of the textile proletariat, it cannot possibly be said to have had a distinctly radical or revolutionary character.[1]

Nevertheless it remains a fact that the government inaugurated in the autumn of 1343 assumed a popular cast entirely unfamiliar to its oligarchic predecessor. We may even assert with regard to it that more or less consciously and consistently it indicated an attempt to move forward along democratic lines. Modest as was this tendency, it represented so wide a departure from past

---

[1] Even though our knowledge of Florentine history, which, originally derived exclusively from the chroniclers, has in recent years been greatly broadened by the use of documents, extensive periods remain in contention, and none has aroused livelier disputes than the period (1343-82) treated in this chapter. The disputes are in part due to the loose use by the men of the trecento of class terms such as magnates, popolo grasso, mezzana gente, popolo minuto, plebe, etc. Until present-day students agree upon these terms they will always be writing at cross-purposes. A valiant attempt not only to avoid weasel words but also accurately to define the classes making up Florentine society in the trecento has been made by G. Scaramella, *Firenze allo Scoppio del Tumulto dei Ciompi*. Pisa, 1914. According to Scaramella it is a mistake to interpret the chroniclers as conceding a preponderance to the arti minori after 1343; they did not win control till 1378 and only the next three years (1378-81) constitute a genuine democratic interlude. If this is true, the present chapter ascribes to the government between 1343 and 1378 more of a democratic character than it actually had. While this is not unimportant, it belongs to the always disputable realm of interpretation and does not impugn the correctness of the events themselves as here set forth.

practice that it elicited frequent and usually alarmed contemporary comment. To Giovanni Villani, for instance, identified through a long life with the fallen oligarchs, the new government was the occasion of ever-renewed carping. And when, after Giovanni's death during the great pestilence of 1348, Matteo Villani undertook to continue his brother's chronicle, Matteo, too, never ceased to ring the changes on the stock lament that "every vile craftsman of the city aspires to reach the priorate and the great offices of the commune." [2] As Matteo died in 1363, his work has not the importance for the period treated in this chapter as that of his younger contemporary, Stefani, which covers the whole democratic interval. Granting that Stefani is much better disposed toward the popolo minuto than the two Villanis, he is hardly less emphatic in his criticism of the doubtless often arrogant demeanor of the little folk, whose sudden rise to power went to their head with the explosive energy of new wine.[3] Boccaccio, too, he of the hundred spicy tales composed to tickle the palate of a jaded bourgeoisie, repeatedly flung out against the new democracy in the most cutting manner. In short, the writers of the age and spokesmen of the new culture were without exception, though with varying emphasis, on the conservative side. Since the well-to-do and the educated have always been outraged by the assumption of the honors of government by their social and intellectual inferiors, we need not feel any surprise at the discontent manifested by these groups at Florence when the middle and minor arts appropriated the lion's share of the offices. Our sole concern at this juncture is that, beginning with the autumn of 1343, shopkeepers and artisans actually sat in the seats of power and with varying fortune clung to them till 1382. This period of almost forty years therefore constitutes a democratic interlude inviting the closest scrutiny. When, owing to the mistakes of the small people and, far more than to measurable human shortcomings, to the operation of blind social forces beyond the control of feeble men, the democracy lost the battle, the oligarchs again resumed the reins, thenceforth to retain them in one guise or another as long as the republic lasted.

We may therefore very properly begin our story of the democratic episode with a general survey of the impersonal factors which explain why it was bound to end in failure. And here, first and foremost, belongs the circumstance revealed by all the preceding chapters of this book that from the earliest days the destiny of Florence had been shaped by its merchants prompt to take advantage of the economic opportunities springing from the revival of trade and industrial enterprise. By their matchless energy spread over many generations these undaunted adventurers had committed the Arno city to a policy of economic imperialism, the earliest object of which was the mastery of Tuscany. The most immediate and palpable evidence of the immense success of these endeavors was Florence itself in its purely physical aspect. Just before the devastation wrought by the Black Death (1348) the town had swollen to a population of approximately 120,000, if to the dwellers within the third cir-

---

[2] M. Villani, II, 2.

[3] ". . . They are arrogant without judgment, and because the offices had come into their hands each one thought he was a king [*parea loro essere ciascuno un re*]." Marchionne di Coppo Stefani, *Cronica Fiorentina*. Ed. by N. Rodolico. Muratori (new ed.), Vol. XXX, r. 616.

cumvallation we add the crowded suburbs.[4] The fivefold increase in the course of a single century was largely represented by the proletarian workers of the two wool gilds; and these former peasants, who had migrated to the city to serve as carders, spinners, dyers, and weavers, made a living by manufacturing or refining the cloth which the merchants undertook to distribute to all parts of the known world. Once assembled, the industrial population could not be maintained save by the perpetuation of the system which had brought it into being. Every society is the beneficiary or victim, as the case may be, of its own past and cannot, unless it wishes to make an entirely new start, abandon its foundations. Nor may the psychological implications of a body of inherited customs and activities be overlooked. To keep pace with the imperialist program of the merchants and government the whole Florentine population had developed a corresponding imperialist mentality. From the lowly beggars and day laborers up to the great merchant princes, the Arno dwellers were passionate patriots, committed to a man to a forward policy in Tuscany holding out the hope of an ever larger participation in peninsular and world-decisions.

This was the situation, these were the problems which faced the petty bourgeoisie when it took over the power in 1343. If, as a rule, the actions of men were determined by purely logical considerations, the renunciation of the far-ranging imperialism of the great merchants in favor of a narrow stay-at-home policy would now have been a not unreasonable expectation. But there, in their crowded, dingy quarters were the working masses, which could under no circumstances be ignored. For one thing, they had to be fed, a problem which had been one of the most troublesome concerns of the old government and which offered no prospect of becoming less pressing in the years to come. Furthermore, with the bread question was tied up the wages question, and, as matters stood, the wages necessary to buy the bread could be furnished from no other source than the capitalists in touch with the world-markets. But even assuming that the wheel of Time could have been turned back and the wool workers redistributed among the farms they had abandoned—which is of course absurd—the new rulers would have refused to carry out the measure since they, too, took pride in the recently won glories and were patriotically averse to a policy calculated to reduce Florence to its original parochial dimensions.

The net result was that the new government did not reverse the course but continued in the main along the path blazed by its predecessors. This is particularly true of the foreign field. In fact it is difficult, if not impossible, to detect any departure whatever from the territorial aims which had become traditional. For several generations Florence had been engaged in creating a state as nearly commensurate with Tuscany as possible; and if this purpose had never been quite attained, the Red Lily had at least become provincially dominant and, as a clear indication of its program, had brought all its smaller neighbors under its rule. However, during the despotism of the duke of Athens the various subject towns had seized the opportunity to renounce their allegiance. Consequently we must agree that when, after the duke's expulsion, Florence resumed its independence, it was in a singularly advantageous posi-

4 On these incurably uncertain figures the reader is referred to Rodolico, *La Democrazia Fiorentina,* chap. I.

tion to break with the policy of expansion once and for all. It flatly refused to do anything of the sort. To be sure, the priors exercised a wise restraint toward the rebellious subject communities; but never for a moment did they entertain the least doubt regarding the necessity of territorially reconstituting the Florentine state. And already after a few years their watchful waiting brought them a considerable success, for by a little past the middle of the century Colle di Val d'Elsa, San Gimignano, Prato, and Pistoia, either voluntarily or as the result of a tactfully applied pressure, again submitted to Florentine control. If it might be argued that the new government differed from its predecessor in being somewhat less prompt to appeal to arms, it was far from submitting humbly to the aggression of an arrogant neighbor. Thus when the archbishop of Milan, Giovanni Visconti, in pursuit of his ambitious design to create a strong north-Italian state, in 1351 invaded Tuscany, the government met the attack with energy, nor did it come off second best in the encounter.

That Archbishop Giovanni, who operated with hired mercenaries, had to be confronted with precisely the same kind of gentry was unfortunate but cannot be blamed on the artisan regime. The national army of the early days of the republic had gone to pieces during the rule of the greater gilds and, as we have seen, beginning with the early decades of the fourteenth century, Florence, yielding to a general Italian precedent, had wholeheartedly committed itself to the system of professional soldiers. When these professionals, organized in so-called companies of adventure, became aware that they were less the servants than the masters of the rich cities of Italy alike estranged from the use of arms, they flaunted their power through the length and breadth of the peninsula, levying ransom on every community in their path and, in case money was denied, stripping the country like a plague of locusts. We shall have frequent occasion to treat of these soldier or, more properly, robber bands, which constituted one of the major disasters of the peninsula during the second half of the fourteenth century. At this point we are content to note that the Florentines, too, were exposed to their insolence and repeatedly saved themselves from a threatened harrying of their territory by a lavish payment of blood money. Disgusting as this submission to blackmail was, it constituted no specialty of the Florentine democracy and, if contemptible, may be declared to have been unavoidable under the military conditions which had come to prevail in the Italy of that age.

Having touched on events in the foreign field, we may note that throughout the period here considered this field is of subordinate interest, and that no event following the Visconti aggression of 1351 arrests our attention till we come to 1362, when the ancient feud with Pisa flared up in a new war. It was precipitated by Florence and furnished the clearest possible evidence that the inland town was as attached as ever to its imperialist dream. In a sudden access of fury against Pisa, which, contrary to treaty, undertook to lay a small tax on Florentine goods in transit through its port, the injured city revived the project of a former generation to develop the hopelessly embogged Talamone on the Maremma coast as a Florentine harbor. Of course Pisa resisted this move, war followed, a cruel war of rival mercenary hosts, and the struggle continued for over two years till both sides were financially and economically exhausted. In the end Florence gave up the Talamone delusion and Pisa accepted the long-established Florentine immunity from transit dues. The episode bears an exasperating character of futility and was not very different in this respect from the innumerable earlier conflicts between the two towns. But it has historical significance nonetheless, inasmuch as it proves that under the little tradesmen, precisely as under the great merchants, the leading territorial aim of Florence continued to be the control of the Tuscan coast, and that attachment to this purpose meant a struggle with Pisa which would not terminate till Pisa had been conquered. In fine, we can but repeat that the Florentine foreign policy underwent no change of principle during the democratic interlude, and that the priorate dominated by the minor gilds was not perceptibly less expansionist than the priorate of the merchant period.

But it is by its domestic policy that the democratic character of a government is best gauged. And as the local happenings are peculiarly interesting, and as at the same time they are better documented than at any earlier period, they hold out the promise of a most profitable investigation. Indeed so revealing regarding the structure of Florentine society and the various pressures to which it was subject are the internal events of the four decades under consideration that the historian may under no circumstances overlook them. As our point of departure let us take the three main social-economic groups of which the population was at this time composed: the merchants of the seven greater gilds, the shopkeepers and artisans of the fourteen lesser gilds, and the proletarian masses which constituted the unorganized popolo minuto. The most important single feature of a very complex situation may without hesitation be declared to have been the desire and resolution of the last-named group, the industrial workers, to improve their lot through imitating the two superior classes by acquiring the advantages of organization. This was an entirely novel tendency, since during the long-continued advance of Florentine industry the workers had in the main been so thoroughly quiescent that they had come to be looked on by their employers as no better than dumb animals.

It was the misery inflicted by repeatedly experienced major and minor depressions that gradually convinced the lowly wage-earners of the need of action. Notwithstanding, it was not till 1342, when the duke of Athens had become master of the city, that they made their first appeal to the government for relief from conditions that threatened to crush them. In view of the fact that their complaint was directed against the popolo grasso, whom the tyrant, too, regarded as his special enemies, he was pleased not only to lend the petitioners a gracious ear but actually to authorize them to form a gild of their own. This was a first success; but it promptly went by the boards on the duke's expulsion. While the fourteen lesser gilds, which on the tyrant's disappearance secured a preponderant authority, were also in more or less declared opposition to the greater gilds, they had unfortunately no sympathy for the industrial proletariat, from which they felt themselves separated as by a wide chasm. They were concerned with keeping the workers fed, thereby forestalling hunger riots and social revolution, but they had no inclination whatever to raise the despised mass of carders, spinners, and dyers to their own level. This selfish interest of the lesser gilds in their own predominance defines the character of their democracy. In respect of their superiors, the merchant oligarchs, they present themselves to view as the democracy of the gild system, but in respect of their inferiors, the workingmen, they constituted a privileged class as averse to relinquishing their privileges as the privileged have ever been. The democratic or popular issue of the period under review has therefore a twofold aspect: there is first the struggle of the lesser gilds to hold fast to the concessions recently wrested from the burgher oligarchs; and second, there is the effort of the proletarians to win the right to organize in order to overcome the worst evils of their lot. Owing to the class tension between the petty bourgeoisie and the workers, the two democratic movements unfolded side by side in all but complete isolation until, after some thirty years, they were drawn into a single comprehensive action in the great revolution of 1378.

Taking up the second and more radical democratic movement first, we are obliged to begin by defining the legal status of the former peasants who had drifted into Florence and become the industrial workers of the merchant gilds of the Lana and the Calimala. The gilds in question, and the other greater gilds as well, were associations of masters, and the workers employed by them were their subordinates or *sottoposti*. The masters alone determined the wages of the workers and, in order to keep them at a minimum level and the workers themselves in secure subjection, declared every attempt of their subordinates to form a gild of their own a punishable crime. If we turn for confirmation of this statement to the statutes of the wool gild bearing the date 1338, we learn not only that they prohibited every organization of the sottoposti but that, in order to close every possible avenue to proletarian action, they went the length of declaring unlawful any meeting of more than ten workers for any purpose whatever.[5] Every least breach of these injunctions was subject to action by the court of the gild enjoying a sweeping jurisdiction over masters and sottoposti alike, and was punished by the *divieto,* that is, the exclusion of the transgressor from the list of approved workers for one or more years. Tantamount to a sentence of death by starvation, the mere threat of the divieto was like a sword perpetually suspended over the worker's head. We cannot get away from the conclusion that in the view of the masters of the Lana as revealed in their own statutes, the wool workers were no better than human chattels required to subsist on a submarginal wage and forbidden under the severest penalties to attempt to increase their pittance of a salary by collective bargaining. As all the labor-employing gilds boasted similarly repressive legislation, and as the government of Florence lay entirely in gild hands, we should feel no surprise to learn that the gild enactments against every sort of association or collegium of workers had been incorporated in the public law of the land. Both the constitution of the podestà and that of the captain contained articles which obliged these political officials to defend the economic privileges of the masters by alertly detecting and promptly punishing every attempt at association on the part of the sottoposti.[6]

[5] Rodolico, *La Democrazia Fiorentina*, p. 114. The author cites the relevant restrictions as given in the Statuti dell'Arte della Lana of 1338 preserved in the Archivio di Stato.

[6] Rodolico, *La Democrazia,* etc., p. 116. The author reproduces the relevant rubrics of both the statute of the podestà and that of the captain.

Here, if ever, was regulative legislation with teeth in it. However, stronger than any law is necessity. Immediately after the overthrow of the duke of Athens it gripped the workers in the form of the crisis precipitated by the bank failures of 1343-46 and the attendant unemployment and starvation. The indefinitely prolonged agony could not fail to produce repercussions among a group, which by its recent brief enjoyment under the duke of Athens of gild autonomy had seen a faint ray of light flash across its somber sky. To illustrate the kind of outbreak which following the economic crisis became common among the proletarians, a single instance will suffice. In the year 1345 a certain Ciuto Brandini, a wool-carder, tried to reconstitute the shattered gild of his fellow-workers. Seized one night in his bed, he was haled before the capitano del popolo and promptly sentenced to be hanged.[7] The arrest and condemnation carried out by a public official strikingly bring home to us the extent to which the state was the obedient tool of the masters of the gilds. In spite of Ciuto's cruel fate, irregular outbreaks against the ruling system continued until the Black Death of 1348 swung its giant scythe among both masters and men and temporarily weighted the scales in favor of the latter. The catastrophic mortality, especially in the crowded quarters of the poor, produced a deficiency of hands and a consequent increase of wages. But immediately on the cessation of the pestilence the peasants, tempted by the higher pay, poured into the town in such numbers that before long the proletarian ranks were again filled, inviting a return to the old wage scale. Whatever economic achievements the Black Death may be credited with in other respects, it brought only a very ephemeral advantage to the harassed wage slaves of Florence.

In the legislation of the fifties there is noticeable an occasional attempt to attract immigrants to Florence by the relaxation of some of the laws dealing with citizenship; but all enactments of this nature were sporadic and sprang solely from the desire to strengthen the lesser gilds. These were the people in power, and except insofar as a measure planned to advance their own cause may incidentally have helped the workers, they did not so much as lift a finger in behalf of their oppressed fellow-citizens. During the whole period here considered the scarcity of food continued to be felt throughout Tuscany and large sections of Italy; and again and again, in the wake of a famine, came the inevitable pestilence. Whipped by this double scourge, the tormented workers might have burst through every restraint, if the situation had not carried with it its own ironical alleviation. When there were more workers than there was food to go round and hunger lashed the starved masses till they were ready to rebel, a pestilence would providentially appear out of nowhere, kill enough workers to ease the pressure on the bread supply, and enable the quaking government to congratulate itself on having escaped a violent overturn. That even, under this appalling system, movements of protest were not unusual may be

[7] Rodolico, *Il Popolo Minuto* (*1343-78*). Bologna, 1899. The official record of Ciuto's trial is printed as Document 14. This particular book of Rodolico represents the first attempt ever made to investigate the movements among the exploited workers of the greater arts. On the class struggle as well as on the numerous other problems of the democratic interlude the histories of Capponi, Perrens, and Caggese make suggestive contributions. Capponi offers a valuable Appendix of Documents. The contemporary diaries and chronicles are numerous. The most important after Stefani is the *Diario d'Anonimo Fiorentino dall'Anno 1358 al 1389* (*Documenti di Storia Italiana*, Tomo VI).

confirmed by recounting certain events of the year 1368.[8] On an August day of that year a famished and ragged crowd invaded the grain market to the cry of "Viva il Popolo" and seized and carried off twenty sacks of wheat. The action was no more than a riot induced by the not unusual scarcity, and the demonstrators were quickly dispersed. But immediately after, and due to the same incurable deficiency of bread, there occurred something so novel and ominous that it may be set up as a landmark: a strike on the part of the very important group of the sottoposti, the dyers. Although the dyers did not on this occasion quite go the length of forming a gild, they did by calling a strike indicate that they were engaged in what the law called a collegium or conspiracy and automatically drew on themselves the dreaded divieto or lockout. Under the application of this penalty the dyers' strike was quickly broken up. However, a new method of threatening the employers had been discovered and was not likely to be again forgotten. While the material which has come down to us bearing on the labor situation during this period is casual and incomplete, it yet suffices to attest so continuous a restlessness among the proletarians that the view of the older historians, who held that the revolution of 1378 fell like a bolt from the blue, must be abandoned. It is a fact, however, that the upheaval of that year, famous under the name of the rebellion of the Ciompi, was not originally instigated by the working masses but that it developed from an intensification of the struggle for power between the greater and the lesser gilds. This, a conflict among legally constituted groups, supplies the masterthread of the domestic history of the period. We shall now follow this conflict from its inception in the year 1343 to the outbreak of 1378, when it was reenforced and for a time completely overshadowed by an irresistible general rising of the proletariat.

The increased political power of the lesser gilds after the overthrow of the duke of Athens was an intolerable offense to the great merchants, which to remove as soon as possible they were prepared to leave no stone unturned. Nor was it long before they discovered an instrument admirably suited to their purpose. This was the parte Guelfa, which had risen to power in the days of Charles I of Anjou and which in the name of Charles had actually governed the city till the reorganization of 1280 dictated by Cardinal Latino. But, though forced thenceforward somewhat into the background, the party had by no means lost its grip. Owing to its having acquired title to immense Ghibelline properties, it had vast revenues at its disposal requiring a permanent administration. The party was accordingly housed in an imposing palazzo [9] not far from the Mercato Nuovo; and since the Guelphs were an organization with governors and councils and with many kinds of political and economic interests, there were larger and smaller rooms adapted to these several purposes. Although the party had originally been a society of magnates, from the first it had not hesitated to open its doors also to rich popolani. When Florence in the first half of the trecento became a world-center, the merchant element, which had raised it to that eminence, did not fail to win increased recognition.

[8] Caggese, Vol. II, pp. 224-26. The pertinent documents in Rodolico, *Il Popolo Minuto* (Nos. 11, 26).

[9] The great Gothic palace, recently restored, is admirably suited to convey an impression of the power of the party.

It thus came about that while, according to the original constitution of the party, the governors, called captains, had been six in number and had all to be of the noble class, in 1323 it was ordained that three of the captains were thenceforward to be popolani. By that time the distinction between nobles and wealthy commoners had become so artificial as to have all but lost its meaning and, for all practical purposes, the party membership may be regarded as a singularly coherent group of individuals of established means who, swayed by strictly conservative sentiments, regarded the state as the indispensable tool for the protection of their interests. Throughout the period of oligarchic control ending with the usurpation of the duke of Athens we may think of the government of the arti maggiori as effectively identified with the parte Guelfa.

When, on the expulsion of the duke, the merchants and bankers had been obliged to concede a preponderant political power to shopkeepers and artisans, the vanquished groups did not have to despair chiefly for the reason that their natural ally, the parte Guelfa, was still intact. The merchants and bankers, or at least their leading representatives, were members of the party in good standing and, as such, could freely air their grievances in its sessions. In point of fact there was no need whatever of impressing the desirability of action on the captains of the party since the vigorous tradition behind these powerful officials prompted them to an impassioned opposition to any government even faintly redolent of democracy. True, as a private association, the party could not, at least at once, step into the open and carry on the political struggle in behalf of the greater gilds. The proprieties had to be respected. But it could and did without delay make itself the secret rallying-point of the conservative influences in the city until such a time as it would feel strong enough to cast off the mask and in its own name to inaugurate the movement to drive the usurping little folk back to their shops and alleys.

As it took some years for the party's action to get under way it was not till 1346 that the first success was achieved. In that year the priors and councils were persuaded to pass a bill which declared that no citizen could hold office unless he and his father before him had been born in Florence. The act was a blow aimed at the small gildsmen, whose ranks were being uninterruptedly swollen by immigration from the country. As the malice of the measure was a trifle too apparent, it was almost immediately resolved to substitute a more subtle procedure, and by a supplementary act passed a few months later (1347), not recent immigration but Ghibellinism was defined as the blot punishable by exclusion from office. By this time Ghibellinism per se was undoubtedly a dead issue. Neither in Florence nor in its contado did any Ghibelline any longer venture to raise his head, so complete had been the house-cleaning effected by the Guelphs in the course of three and more generations. But during the prolonged Guelph-Ghibelline feud, originally purely a concern of the upper class, the whole Florentine population had become so imbued with guelfismo that even after the city had no further reason to fear the empire—and dread of the empire was the meat and kernel of Guelph sentiment—the Ghibelline bogey, as ancient bogies have the habit of doing, lived on in the hearts of the citizens. Consequently no more serious charge could be presented against a fellow-townsman than to allege that he was openly or secretly an imperial partisan; and so spontaneous was the heat engendered by the mere imputation of Ghibellinism that guilt was at once assumed without the tedious formality of legal proofs. Without this emotional background the role played by the parte Guelfa, which before long carried it to an all but complete domination of the state, cannot possibly be understood. The party was the dragon which for almost a century had guarded the treasure of guelfismo, the spiritual food of the Florentine population. Surely no one knew better than the lords of the party what constituted a genuine Guelph; and therefore should the captains render a decision, averring that this or that other citizen did not measure up to proper Guelph standards, it was as if judgment had fallen on him from on high. It was this immense moral prestige enjoyed by the party that it now resolved to exploit in the interest of big business, which was also its own interest. There were no indubitable, hall-marked Ghibellines left, or as good as none; the existing enemies of the party were the gildsmen of the lesser arts who by no reasonable procedure could be classified as either Guelph or Ghibelline. But if a small inn-keeper or waggoner recently arrived from the countryside should on the strength of the law of 1347 have the Ghibelline label clapped on him, he would not be permitted to take public office, even if his name should be regularly drawn from the borse. By claiming and exercising the right to detect Ghibellines and by their detection to exclude them from office the parte Guelfa completely dominated the elections and filled the ruling artisans with a vague fear.

Then something happened which nullified the victory. After a law was passed its execution rested with the authorities, and if the authorities declined to apply the law, the new statute, being still-born, was quietly buried. It was the peculiarity of the Florentine republic, and of all the other Italian republics as well, that they passed laws in such profusion and precipitation that it was a physical impossibility to have them all enforced, especially if it happened that they encountered opposition within the government.[10] Besides, before the parte Guelfa could take its next step in pursuit of its plans of indirect control, the Black Death intervened (1348) and for a time forced the issue between the greater and the lesser gilds into the background. But no sooner had recovery from the pestilence begun than the conflict again reared its head, and in the year 1354 the party renewed its offensive by sponsoring the revival, in a far more rigorous form than before, of the law forbidding Ghibellines to hold public office. But again the difficulty of applying the law put in an appearance, for the arti minori, more acutely aware by now of what was concealed under the Ghibelline legislation, utilized every political trick in their repertory to block the execution of the act. The issue was tossed to and fro until in high dudgeon the party put an end to continued subterfuge by proposing and carrying (1358) under loud threats and violent intimidation of the government a law which gave the determining of who was and who was not a Ghibelline exclusively into the hands of the party executive. Thus become a supplementary government outside the frame of the constitution, the party adopted a procedure which was simplicity itself. Whenever there was drawn

---

[10] Stefani, r. 728, joins the long list of witnesses who complain of the abundant and often contradictory enactments which were not enforced.

for office the name of an artisan who had invited the enmity of the party, or whenever there was drawn the name of a member of a greater gild even remotely tainted with democratic sympathies, he was handed a warning (*ammonizione*) by the captains of the party to the effect that he was a Ghibelline and could not serve. In case he should pay no attention to the remonstrance, the captains were prepared to summon him before the podestà on the charge of treason, for which offense the penalty was death or exile. As no one was willing to run this risk, the curious device of the ammonizione sufficed to give to the party the control to which it aspired. In connection with each successive election to the magistracies a number of citizens, whose names were regularly drawn from the borse but who were distasteful to the all-powerful captains, were served warning to keep off the premises with the result that in the course of a few years the "warned" or *ammoniti* were a body, and a very angry body as can be readily imagined, of several hundred persons. Turn and twist as the government would, it found no way of casting off the Guelph incubus. For eight unbroken years it suffered an intolerable infringement of its normal powers and might have suffered it longer, had it not been for a conflict which developed in the ranks of the arrogant Guelphs themselves.

The parte Guelfa was an oligarchy and it is the nature of an oligarchy, while united by a common interest, to be divided by personal ambitions. Oligarchies have regularly split upon this rock, as the case of Florence itself convincingly demonstrated by such earlier conflicts as those between the Uberti and the Buondelmonti and between the Cerchi and the Donati. And now history repeated itself, for hardly had the parte Guelfe acquired the mastery of Florence,[11] when the conflict within the party began over the question who was to be the party's master. The two leading claimants to the honor were a Ricci and an Albizzi, behind whom gathered their large and powerful respective clans. When Piero degli Albizzi, although rated a popolano, sought the support of the conservatives of the strictest observation, who were papalists and magnates, Uguccione de' Ricci inevitably was driven to establish contact with the moderates. Indeed in the manner of men who play for the stakes of power he did not hesitate to go for help to the enemy himself, to the arti minori. In the year 1366, when serving as one of the priors, he seized the occasion to trip his rival Piero by having a law passed which put certain obstacles in the way of finding a citizen guilty of Ghibellinism, chiefly by a reorganization of the executive of the parte Guelfa. On the strength of this law representatives of the lesser gilds were given seats among the all-powerful captains, who by this unwelcome association found themselves greatly hampered in the pleasant game of knocking down their enemies like so many tenpins. For a few years the practice of ammonizione signally declined until the two rival oligarchs, patching up their quarrel, arranged for a new law which invalidated its predecessor, and by re-establishing harmony within the parte Guelfa enabled it to resume its reign of terror. It is unnecessary and would be extremely tedious to trace the new moves by which the harassed government tried to

11 Stefani's phrase, r. 778, is memorable in this connection. He says: "Chi era signore della parte era signore di Firenze."

escape the reknotted Guelph noose. Suffice it to say, and it goes without saying, that larger and ever larger groups of citizens lost patience with a situation that made mock of constitutional forms and hung a pall of fear over the whole city. The resentment against the overbearing tyrants who dared set up a subsidiary government in their private palace grew till, bursting all bounds, it led to an act as spontaneous as it was irrational: a war against the pope.

It is true that there were other causes besides the inflammatory domestic issue which contributed to this conflict. To understand them we must lift ourselves above the Tuscan scene to a height affording a survey of the contemporary situation of the papacy. Although planted since the first decade of the fourteenth century at Avignon, the papacy had never ceased to affirm that its appointed seat was Rome, whither it planned to return as soon as the time was ripe. But either conditions matured slowly or Avignon proved a too seductive garden, for it was not till past the middle of the century that a pope, the unusually enterprising Innocent VI, took the first step necessary to clear the way for a return. He intrusted a Spanish cardinal, Albornoz, who had been bred a soldier, with the task of bringing back to papal obedience the State of the Church, commonly designated by clerics as the *patrimonium Petri*. This undertaking Albornoz carried out with such a judicious mixture of military might and conciliatory diplomacy that by 1357 he could publish a constitution for the central Italian territories which for the first time since their acquisition by the papacy gave them something like a coherent political organization. With that achievement the papacy was at last prepared to assume the character of an Italian state capable on the strength of its own resources of entering the game of Italian politics. Moreover, with the patrimonium pacified the last excuse for clinging to the haven of Avignon was removed, and hesitantly and regretfully a new pope, Urban V, made ready to resume the abandoned Roman seat. In 1367 he came to Italy and, urged onward by most of the European sovereigns, including the emperor, triumphantly entered the Eternal City.

The reigning emperor, Charles IV, was of so different a stripe from all his predecessors that we are obliged at this point to bring him into historical focus. If we have long ago agreed that the empire, as a power capable of struggling with the church for world-supremacy, perished with Emperor Frederick II in 1250, we have not failed to note that its theoretical claims lived on and that they were not unworthily represented by such Hohenstaufen princes as Manfred and Conradin and by such a blameless knight as Henry VII. Even Ludwig the Bavarian, although suffering personal shipwreck in Italy, had clung tenaciously to the traditional luster of his office. But when Charles IV was elevated to the German kingship (and to remember that he was the grandson of Dante's *alto Arrigo* gives the measure of the immense reversal), he made a clean break with the past. From a purely common-sense angle the course which he adopted might well be called judicious and prudent, for it was based on recognition of the fact that he lived in a changed world, that the universal empire could not be revived, and that even to acquire the bare title of emperor, he would have to seek and retain the favor of the pope. In line with this political realism Charles openly avowed himself a Guelph and was rewarded by being formally invited by his triumphant rival to cross the Alps to have himself crowned emperor. The event occurred in 1355, and it characterizes the submissiveness of this strange Caesar that he left the Tiber city on the evening of the very day of his coronation. His purpose was scrupulously to avoid giving the impression that he any longer regarded Rome as his or the empire's capital.

When, twelve years after Charles coronation, Pope Urban V plucked up courage for the long-delayed return to Italy, in expectation of difficulties with which he might be confronted, he called on Charles for support, and the humble papalist actually crossed the Alps a second time to add his mite toward making the pope secure in the regained patrimonium. On this occasion, exactly as during his former visit, Charles lingered for some months in northern and central Italy, where the Saxon and Hohenstaufen emperors had chiefly unfolded their might. Even here, where the empire still enjoyed a considerable following, he was content to adopt a purely practical attitude toward a society which had visibly slipped its medieval moorings. The usurping tyrants in person and the city-republics through representatives visited his court in crowds in order to have their new political status confirmed by an imperial charter. In this situation the calculating merchant-monarch detected remarkable opportunities for profit, offered documents of the most liberal scope to all comers, and in 1368, as he had already done in 1355, returned to Germany laden with Italian gold but totally shorn of respect for himself and for his diadem.[12] When, following his second journey, he disappeared behind the Alps, the empire may be said to have vanished with him: *exit imperium*. We shall encounter an occasional emperor after Charles coming almost stealthily to Italy lured by the bauble of the imperial crown; but as even the theory of the empire now began to evaporate from the minds of men, that institution lost its last shred of meaning and all but ceased to figure in the busy interplay of peninsular political forces.

However, the other universal power, the papacy, vigorously lived on, although not without a certain loss of prestige, owing to its abandonment of Rome and to its concomitant subjection to French national interests. When Albornoz for the first time fused the papal provinces in Italy into a political unit, he may well be said to have inaugurated a new phase of papal history. The long, world-shaking struggle between the popes and the emperors had been conducted, on the part of the popes, with their vast spiritual and financial resources and with as good as no help from the dominions immediately subject to their rule. Of course, in the future as in the past, the pope would continue to owe his authority, in the main, to his lordship over the church; but in consequence of the statesmanlike services of Cardinal Albornoz, he would, from the second half of the fourteenth century on, have also a not inconsiderable civil state on which to lean. To be sure, even after the labors of Albornoz the papal state long continued to rest on insecure foundations and

---

12 "Colla borsa piena di danari, ma con assai vergogna in abbassamento dell'imperiale maestà." Thus Matteo Villani, V, 54, had already commented in 1355. On the occasion of this same earlier visit Charles sold a charter to Florence for one hundred thousand gold florins. The tranaction has received detailed treatment from F. Baldasseroni, "Relazioni tra Firenze, la Chiesa, e Carlo IV (1353-55)," in *Arch. Stor. It.*, Serie 5, Vol. XXXVII, pp. 2 ff.

was beset by many difficulties. One of them of particular weight at this time was the French nationality of the Avignon popes. While Urban V had again established his seat at Rome, he never felt happy in Italy, and after a two years' residence on the Tiber, succumbed to an overmastering nostalgia and returned to his seat on the Rhone. His successor, another Frenchman, who took the title Gregory XI, pledged himself on his elevation to office in 1370 to realize the plan that Urban had abandoned, but such was the pressure brought to bear on him by his French college of cardinals that years passed before he could summon the energy to redeem his pledge.

Meanwhile the State of the Church, as we shall henceforth call Albornoz' creation, had to be governed and, as might be expected, a French pope intrusted the task to French agents. To win the obedience of the local powers accustomed for generations to an anarchic independence was no light matter, and the foreign rectors, high prelates to a man, were frequently obliged to resort to harsh measures to enforce their rule. It is the essentially upstart papal state governed or, as its subjects claimed, misgoverned by French ecclesiastics in the name of an absentee pope, which is the first fact to hold in mind as we now return to the apparently so irrational war that Guelph Florence declared against the church.

To the republic of Florence, accustomed to regard itself as the leading central Italian state, the creation of a State of the Church was a disturbing phenomenon. Enveloping Florence on the north, east, and south, it threatened the republic's freedom of movement and might under certain conditions even endanger its independence. Without any doubt the Florentines preferred the former anarchy, for it had enabled them to deal individually with such cities as Perugia and Bologna and with the innumerable little Romagnese tyrants, such as the Ordelaffi of Forlì, the Montefeltri of Urbino, and the Malatesti of Rimini. Consequently, when with the enforcement of the new system the local powers raised their voices in clamorous complaint against the French ecclesiastics, the Arno republicans were lavish with their sympathy. A number of other incidents contributed to irritate the Florentines. When in the winter of 1374-75 they were overtaken by a food scarcity of famine proportions and turned, as their habit was, to the Romagna for relief, they learned with indignation that the papal legate at Bologna had put an embargo on the exportation of grain. Apparently there was a scarcity in the Romagna, too, and the legate felt that his first duty was toward his own subjects. While the Florentines were still fretting over what was to them an unfriendly act, behold in June, 1375, an invasion of their territory by John Hawkwood and his band of foreign devils. Hawkwood, who had been in the service of the legate, was dismissed when no longer needed and turned his steps toward Florence in the hope either of plunder or of ransom money. That was the familiar alternative with which the companies of adventure confronted their victims, and we do not need to believe that the ruffian Englishman required any prompting from the Bolognese governor to undertake his incursion. But the Florentines would not have it other than that the soldiers had burst into Tuscany at the instance of the legate. They bought off the unwelcome guests with a painfully high tribute and then proceeded to revenge themselves by making war upon the church.

The daughter against the mother, the consistent champion of the Guelph idea against the institution which embodied that idea! It seemed incredible. Without any doubt Florence had frequently in the past resisted demands made on it by the popes to the point of inviting excommunication and inter-dict. But it had never drawn the sword against the representative of Christ, and the orthodox Guelph doctrine as expounded on the Arno by the hiero-phants of the parte Guelfa regarded the mere suggestion as utterly wicked and blasphemous. If we now recall that with its "warnings" and its indirect control of the government, the parte Guelfa had by 1375 made itself the object of a livid hatred on the part of the vast majority of the citizens, we shall put ourselves in possession of the master-key to the astonishing event. So closely allied with the party as to be identified with it, the church together with the party had insensibly become the target of Florentine animosity. However, the resentment against the church had developed by such gradual stages that it remained hidden under the threshold of consciousness until the incidents just reported, no one of which was particularly significant in itself, brought it to the surface with an irresistible momentum. On an overmastering wave of anti-clerical sentiment the Florentines plunged into war with the pope, partly no doubt to express their ill-will toward the papal state in process of forma-tion, but chiefly in the hope of shaking off the intolerable yoke of the papalist parte Guelfa.[13]

Considered as war, the conflict between Florence and the pope is completely uninteresting. It was fought on both sides by hireling companies of adventure, which saw no reason for the spilling of blood, considering that, if they dis-creetly survived the campaign, they could count on an easy existence at the expense of their unarmed employers. Aside from the occasional brutal excesses of a soldiery that could not always be kept under control, there are really no military events for the historian to chronicle. Moreover, in view of the unreliable character of their troops, the Florentines were prudent enough to count on winning the war not so much by fighting as by diplomacy. Their plan was to incite the innumerable local powers of the State of the Church, cities and tyrants, to rebellion, to aid the rebels against the pope with money and men, and by the eloquence at the command of their diplomatic secretary, the celebrated humanist, Coluccio Salutati, to present the struggle to the world as the insurrection of oppressed subjects against an overbearing master. In hundreds of communications to the states of Europe, great and small, Salutati affirmed that the single issue involved was Liberty, for which his fellow-citizens were represented as unselfishly sacrificing themselves to the sole end that the brave little communities of central Italy might not perish under the heel of an inhuman tyrant. So successful was the Florentine agitation among the subjects of the pope that by the spring of 1376 the whole papal state was in convulsions and the pope's hold on it reduced to a few scattered strong-

[13] The most thorough study of the war is by A. Gherardi, "La Guerra dei Fiorentini con Papa Gregorio XI," in *Arch. Stor. It.*, Serie 3, Vol. V, Parte II, pp. 35-131. The supporting documents in *Arch. Stor. It.*, Serie 3, Vols. VI, VII, VIII.

THE CLOISTER OF SAN MARCO. MICHELOZZI (ALINARI).

THE LOGGIA DEGLI INNOCENTI. BRUNELLESCHI (ALINARI).

left: THE CHURCH OF SAN LORENZO. BRUNELLESCHI (ALINARI). *right:* THE SACRISTY
OF SAN LORENZO. BRUNELLESCHI AND DONATELLO (ALINARI).

THE CATHEDRAL OF SANTA MARIA DEL FIORE AFTER THE COMPLETION OF BRUNELLESCHI'S CUPOLA (ALINARI).

holds. But that the hard-pressed pontiff still commanded the spiritual weapons with which he had once brought great emperors to their knees, the sons of the Red Lily were now regretfully to learn. Not only did Gregory XI place the city under interdict, but he invited all and sundry peoples of the earth at their pleasure to appropriate the goods and seize the persons of Florentines when and wherever they might lay hands on them.

It might be supposed that the papal reprisals would have quickly dampened the ardor of the self-appointed champions of Liberty. This was so far from being the case that the enthusiasm which the war elicited on the Arno is its most amazing feature. Its conduct was from the first assigned to a special committee of Eight, *I Otto della Guerra,* and when this committee became the object of the deadly hatred of the papal partisans within the gates, it gained from a war-crazed population the extravagant designation of the Eight Saints, *I Otto Santi.* Supported by the suffrages and prayers of the vast majority of the population, the government was able to go to incredible lengths in answering the violence of the pope with appropriate counterviolence. Hard pressed for cash in the long-drawn-out struggle, it ordered the seizure and progressive sale of ecclesiastical property; and, as a crowning measure of resistance to ecclesiastical authority, it made mock of the papal interdict by ordering the local clergy under heavy penalties to unveil the altars and celebrate the divine offices. That such extraordinary measures of religious revolt could be proposed and carried through is the best possible evidence of the popularity of the war and of the continuing support by the people of the Eight Saints and the rest of the government. In the autumn of 1376 Pope Gregory XI at last left Avignon and in January of the following year entered Rome amidst the acclamations of the inhabitants. It is well known that the fiery exhortations of the saintly Catherine of Siena were a factor in the papal decision to restore Rome to its ancient primacy in the Christian world. But it is more than probable that, as much as by St. Catherine's magnetic appeal, Gregory XI was brought to the sticking-point by purely political considerations. Among these figured prominently his desire to end the rebellion of the patrimonium and bring the dangerous war with Florence to a close.

That for its part the Arno town could not go on indefinitely with the struggle was becoming apparent to even its most intransigent supporters. Not only had the expenses reached a fantastic figure but the merchants, who were each day returning from abroad with stories of the brutal confiscation of their goods under the blanket order of the pope, filled the town with their laments. Naturally the parte Guelfa made all the capital possible out of the accumulated public and private calamities. Although opposed to the war from the start, it had been silenced by the spontaneous nature of the outbreak; but no sooner had the inevitable revulsion set in than the party made itself the rallying-point of the various groups of critics. When it at length felt encouraged experimentally to resume the ammonizioni, which the war had obliged it to abandon, the government became sufficiently alarmed to open negotiations with the pope. They might have quickly led to peace, had not the death of Gregory in March, 1378, caused them to be broken off. Nonetheless fighting was not resumed, although the formal treaty ending the conflict had to wait on the pleasure of a new pope and was not signed till July.

Throughout the last and dying phase of the passionately waged war with the pope the domestic situation had been becoming more and more tense. Encouraged by the failing popularity of the conflict and the manifest strengthening of the ranks in favor of peace, the leaders of the parte Guelfa concluded that their hour had struck and resolved to overthrow their enemies by violence. Since their indirect control of the government was no longer effective, they fastened on direct control as alone calculated to assure their ascendancy and set June 24 for the bold stroke. That was St. John's day, the Florentine national holiday. But the secret, shared by too many initiates, leaked out and prompted the enemies of the party to strike first. We are aware that from the earliest showing of the party's hand the opposition to its tactics centered in the lesser gilds. To them there had gravitated by slow degrees a not unimpressive percentage of the members of the greater gilds. It was the capricious ammonizioni of the parte Guelfa that had given offense to these elements of the popolo grasso till in their alarm they made ready to stand shoulder to shoulder with the lesser gilds to defeat the projected *coup d'état*. But how to proceed? Fortunately, a merchant of proved hostility to the party held the crucial office of gonfalonier of Justice. He was Salvestro de' Medici, and at the mere mention of his name something somber and ominous seems to inject itself into the plot about to unfold. That is because the historians, aware of the subsequent role of the family to which Salvestro belonged, have ascribed to this fourteenth-century figure the subtle intelligence and sly intrigue displayed by later Medici representatives in bringing Florence under their yoke. For this reading of Salvestro's character there is entirely insufficient justification in the few facts which have come down to us. He belonged to a family which, beginning with the thirteenth century, had been steadily coming to the front by the usual avenue of trade and which by the fourteenth century had gained a secure position among the popolo grasso by its merchant enterprise coupled with its strict adherence to Guelph principles. While there were many Florentine families both richer and more prominent, the Medici by Salvestro's time were already an "old" clan in the sense that for several generations their representatives had been admitted to all the offices of the republic. It was therefore a man of established reputation that served as gonfalonier of Justice in the May-June period of 1378. While in the main it was the accident of the parte Guelfa resolving to seize the power during his official headship of the state that brought him to the front, we cannot but agree that to have profited from this circumstance as he did testifies that he was a man of swift intelligence and virile resolution.

Salvestro delayed launching his counterstroke until the close approach of the critical St. John's day had filled the city with waxing apprehension over the coming events. Then on June 18 with the support of some merchant leaders of the same stripe he made an appeal which brought the people into the piazza. To the cry, "Viva il Popolo," they rallied around the government until a few days later, their fury bursting every bound, they took the offensive and plundered and set fire to the houses of all the plotting leaders of the parte

Guelfa. Only by precipitate flight did the leaders themselves escape destruction. Under pressure from the exultant mob the defeated plotters were exiled from the city, the laws which had enabled them to play their sinister part were canceled, and their victims, the ammoniti, were formally absolved of their public taint. The parte Guelfa had succumbed to the might of the lesser gilds under the leadership of an allied faction of the great merchants. So far as Salvestro and his political associates were concerned the revolution had done its work and was over.

But it was not over, by reason of the feature so common to revolutions through the ages: it got out of hand. The June commotions leading to the discomfiture of the conservative parte Guelfa turned out to be only a first revolutionary stage, followed a month later, in July, by the second stage, in which the June victors had little or no share, since the leading part was taken by the hitherto disfranchised popolo minuto. Made up of the workers and sottoposti of the greater gilds, the starved and oppressed multitude had during the preceding decades given so many evidences of restless discontent that its seizure of an opportunity so favorable for a rising as the disturbed state of the city in the summer of 1378 should cause no surprise. It will be recalled that the sottoposti had owed a first, though very ephemeral, recognition as an independent gild to the favor of the duke of Athens. The memory of that triumph still lingered, spurring the successors of the earlier leaders to renewed action. Another memory of the famous French episode was preserved in the curious name of *ciompi,* which dated from 1343 and was loosely used to designate the popolo minuto. We hear that the French soldiers of the duke had in the manner of their country addressed the man encountered in the street and wineshop as *compère.* Of this the Florentine tongue by some strange philological alchemy had made ciompo; and owing to some quality of humor in the hybrid term, it had quickly acquired universal currency.[14] While the word seems to have covered the whole mass of the common people, this mass consisted so largely of the workers of the woolen industry that they have been sometimes singled out as the only genuine and indubitable ciompi. That is an unimportant subtlety. Our excuse for this etymological digression is that it explains how it came about that the famous workers' rising of 1378 figures in Florentine history as the revolt of the ciompi.

In accordance with usage, on July 1 Salvestro de' Medici had been replaced as banner-bearer of Justice by Luigi Guicciardini, and together with the latter a fresh body of priors had taken office. But the new government did not enjoy a single day of peace, for the public agitation begun on June 18, instead of abating, grew more intense, especially when it became known that conferences were taking place among the workers which pointed to their early descent upon the Palazzo Pubblico. At length on July 21 the ciompi in an irresistible wave swept into the piazza carrying a petition boldly demanding the right of association and of consequent participation in the government as an acknowledged gild. While the frightened signori tried to gain time, the mob got out of hand and, scattering through the town, engaged in plunder and arson. On

[14] This is the explanation given by Stefani, r. 575, which most modern historians have not hesitated to accept.

the following day the wild demonstration was repeated, and this time its leaders resolved to make a clean sweep by driving the government from the palace. One after another the overawed officials beat a retreat at the demand of the roaring mob until at last the building had been vacated and the shouting, sweating, and triumphant ciompi took possession. At the head of the dense column which, ascending the stone stairway, burst into the deserted council chamber was a young wool-comber, Michele di Lando by name. Dressed in a ragged shirt and bare-legged except for a pair of sandals, he carried the abandoned banner of the gonfalonier of Justice and dramatically came to a halt under it in the captured hall. Immediately his followers proclaimed him gonfalonier, thus making him, in view of the collapse of the legal government, the master of the city. The next day a parliament was called and gave to Michele and the sindics of the gilds authority (*balìa*) to exercise rule till the end of August with the special prerogative to reform the government.

As the old government before dissolving had accepted the petition of July 21, the interim government with the humble wool-carder, Michele di Lando, at its head, at once set about realizing the main demands of the victors. It was a single gild of all the workers which had been asked for and conceded during the most recent convulsion. On the balìa's canvassing the situation, it resolved, probably because of the vast number of the workers, to organize them not in one but in three gilds, the *Tintori* or dyers, the *Farsettai* or shirt-makers, and a gild of the *Popolo Minuto,* which was by far the largest of the three and which, because it embraced most of the wool workers, was commonly called the gild of the ciompi. As the three new gilds, which swelled the total of the constitutionally recognized gilds to twenty-four, were at the same time conceded an appropriate share of the offices, it looked as if the workers had at last reached port and might rest comfortably on their oars.

But the hubbub and excitement had become so great that the revolution could not be arrested. For the greater gilds the July developments, permitting the legally dependent workingmen to escape the control of their masters, signified a defeat certain to bring financial ruin in its train. Though ousted for the moment from the seats of power, they still had at their disposal an economic weapon of the highest efficacy. They closed their shops and, as the keys creaked in the locks, hollow-eyed starvation entered the dwelling of every workingman, lashing him to renewed fury at the sight of the suffering of his wife and children. Instantly the disenchanted proletarians resolved on a fresh revolt, the third in the agitated series of this topsyturvy summer. Like simple people of our own and every period, they had an unshakable faith in the magic power of politics and never doubted that their employers could be brought to terms by resolute pressure on the government. Once more therefore, toward the end of August, they made a succession of maddened demonstrations before the Palazzo Pubblico. Finally, an ultra-radical group took a decisive step and, setting up a rival government in the broad piazza before the church of Santa Maria Novella, on August 31 sent two messengers to the interim rulers at the palace insolently demanding that the rebels be admitted to a share in the state. It was too much for the former wool-carder, Michele di Lando, temporarily the leading official of the city and intoxicated with a naïve pride of place. Seizing a sword, he drove the two emissaries of the insurgents from the chamber and down the stone stairway. Then mounting a horse, he bade all those who loved their city to join him in routing the enemy. The larger portion of the bystanders enthusiastically followed his lead and, throwing themselves on the radical rebels encamped on the Piazza Santa Maria Novella, pursued them through the streets and out of the gates until they lost track of them among the vineyards and olive orchards of the rolling countryside. By the resolute action of a single individual clothed with visible authority the radicals had been overwhelmed. When with the day's work done Banner-bearer Michele returned to the Palazzo Pubblico, he was hailed on all hands as the man who had saved his country.[15]

On the next day (September 1) the balìa presided over by Michele came to an end and a new group of priors, taking office, undertook such a house-cleaning as the sweeping character of the victory over the rebels seemed to authorize. The insurgents had been largely made up of the ciompi of the woolen industry aggregated in the newly created gild of the Popolo Minuto. The other two workers' gilds, the Tintori and Farsettai, had at the critical moment detached themselves from the ciompi and thrown in their lot with the government. In consequence a distinction was made; and while the insurrectionary gild of the Popolo Minuto was abolished, the gilds of the Tintori and Farsettai received renewed approval as arti minori in good standing. There were therefore now sixteen lesser gilds against the unchanged number of seven greater gilds. The eternally contested issue of power between the two groups was met by decreeing a substantial equality of representatives in the various magistracies with, however, a slight preponderance of the lesser gilds in most of them. The salient feature of the settlement was that, although the defeat of the radicals without doubt benefited the major arts, these did not at once achieve an ascendancy. On the contrary, the minor arts resumed the place in the state which they had held ever since the great overturn of 1343. Indeed it might be contended that, as the net result of the revolutionary summer just passed, they had even somewhat improved their position, since two new arts, representing certain groups of formerly disfranchised workers, had been added to their number. Unquestionably class jealousy continued as before to dig a chasm between the petty bourgeoisie of the original body of the lesser gilds and the wage-workers of the two recent additions. This was admittedly a difficulty and a weakness. Nonetheless the common people and

---

[15] It need hardly be said that the most diverse opinions have been voiced on the disturbances of 1378, on the roles and characters of Salvestro de' Medici and Michele di Lando, and on the causes and objectives of the third and most radical revolt. I have preferred not to pronounce on the motives of Salvestro and Michele since, owing to the slightness of the contemporary material dealing with them, every statement is no better than conjecture. It is amusing to note that when in the course of his history that incurable romantic, Machiavelli, got to the ambiguous Michele di Lando, he had him play a role that wins him a niche in the author's pantheon of heroes not much below those occupied by Castruccio Castracane and Caesar Borgia. To the authorities already cited the following, particularly concerned with the events of 1378, should be added: C. Falletti-Fossati, *Il Tumulto dei Ciompi*. Rome, 1882. G. Corazzini, *I Ciompi: Cronache e Documenti con Notizie intorno alla Vita di Michele di Lando*. Florence, 1888. *Il Tumulto dei Ciompi: Cronache e Memorie*. Muratori (New Ed.), Tomo XVIII, Parte 3.

not the great merchants were in the saddle, and the democratic experiment, inaugurated in 1343 and subjected to terrific strain in the summer of 1378, was found to have been salvaged when the storm was over. It continued to stamp its peculiar imprint on Florentine history for the next three years.

In some respects this last phase of the Florentine democracy is its most interesting period, largely because the strengthened people were somewhat more free to give effect to their peculiar purposes. No longer as before the revolution of 1378 was the parte Guelfa able to nullify the democratic policy of the rulers, for the party had had its teeth drawn and was at least temporarily innocuous. The elimination of this ultra-conservative club was perhaps the outstanding achievement of the disturbances through which the city had just passed. For the present resistance to the new government was centered in the great gilds, which, although they were still strong enough in law and tenacious enough in character to make the passage of democratic legislation extremely difficult, had to concede something to their opponents in order to have something conceded to themselves in return. With this constitutional balance in mind we can profitably pass in review the events of the next few years to the moment when a combination of circumstances drove the minor gilds from the helm, thereby once more giving over the ship of state to the exclusive control of the merchants of the arti maggiori.

The first concern of the government that issued from the third and final revolution and that began its rule on September 1 was to defend itself against its many enemies. At the head of the list were the exiled magnates of the parte Guelfa. Without exception men of consequence, they were so passionately bent on effecting their return that they never ceased stirring up the enemies of Florence against their native city. The same animosity characterized the beaten and fugitive ciompi. Regardless of whether he was of high or low degree, no Florentine ever meekly accepted the verdict that made him an outcast from his place of birth. Dangerous as were these two groups of enemies outside the city, the enemies within the walls constituted an even graver problem. They consisted of all those who for one reason or another held a political grudge against the government or nursed a personal ambition. While such ciompi as, driven by hunger, had returned to Florence in search of employment were the most numerous internal enemy group, the magnates and merchants of an uncompromising conservative outlook constituted a more immediate danger. No doubt, however, the greatest of all the perils to which the democratic regime was exposed, sprang from its false friends, ambitious ex-magnates, like Giorgio Scali, and ambitious popolani, like Tommaso Strozzi, who assumed the role of demagogue and flattered the people in the selfish hope of being carried by some lucky turn to the lordship of the city. The sheer endless succession of plots and crises that followed from the activities of both the inner and the outer enemies of the regime fills many a wearisome page in such contemporary records as that of Stefani. Ever on its guard, the republic usually seized and ruthlessly executed its opponents before their plot was ready to be touched off; sooner or later, however, somewhere, somehow a cog would be sure to slip and a combination of accidents bring down the precariously established democratic government.

In no single political field did the government succeed in giving more unambiguous evidence of its democratic character than in that of finance. In an earlier chapter [16] we took occasion to look into the revenue policy imposed on Florence by the triumphant merchant oligarchy. In last analysis we found it reduced itself to a simple scheme of endlessly multiplied consumption taxes (gabelle), supplemented by forced loans (prestanze) bearing a high rate of interest. When at length in 1343 the lesser gilds gained a greater weight in affairs, they attempted, with very little success it must be conceded, to break with a system so favorable to the rich and so injurious to the already heavily burdened masses. The only really important reform they carried through was a consolidation of the prestanze into a unified national debt (Il Monte), carrying a modest interest rate of 5 per cent, which it was decreed was never again to be exceeded. The Monte was an achievement of the first years (1343-47) of the new regime and with this one act the whole financial reform movement had come to a halt. In point of fact, owing to budgetary difficulties that reared their head on the occasion of the war with Pisa in 1362, even this single reform had suffered impairment. With the government sorely needing a loan and the well-to-do unwilling to furnish it for the niggardly 5 per cent fixed by law, a cunning notary, ser Piero di ser Grifo, found a way out. He suggested that every lender be entered in the books of a new Monte for three times the amount of his actual subscription; he would then receive a handsome 15 per cent without the government appearing to pay more than the 5 per cent fixed by the law. The Monte thus created became known as *dell'uno tre* (three for one), and the fraud was so generally acceptable that on the occasion of a later war there was created a more modest Monte—one wonders why more modest—yielding but 10 per cent and commonly called *dell'uno due* (two for one). Should we ask how under a popular regime it was possible to introduce financial practices so unfavorable to the lesser gilds in power, the answer is supplied by the persistent vigor of the conservatives amply attested for the years when these new Monti came into existence by the directive activities of the parte Guelfa.

But the parte Guelfa fell in 1378, the lesser gilds were strengthened by being increased from fourteen to sixteen in number, and with a refreshed spirit the critics of oligarchic finance attacked the problem of reform. It is gratifying to note that in and out of season these critics brought the question of how to relieve the poor of the burdens under which they groaned before the various councils. Granted that the measures which became law did not go very far and that, besides, they were usually but partially enforced, nonetheless a spirit manifested itself presenting such a lively contrast to the notions hitherto in vogue that it claims our respectful attention. Of course the recent fraudulent circumvention of the original Monte was the financial crime that aroused the most furious discussion. Indignant artisans did not mince words in denouncing the scandalous subterfuge connected with the name of ser Piero; and at length in December, 1380, a law was passed which suppressed the falsely inflated existing Monti and substituted for them a single Monte yielding an inalterable 5 per cent on the actual, not on the supposititious, sums loaned to

[16] Chap. XIV, pp. 214-15.

the government.[17] As a result of this adjustment of a monstrous wrong the state saved annually an item of sixty thousand gold florins, of itself an emphatic justification of the measure. It was inevitable that the lesser gilds should attempt to pass on from this success to a correction of the unjust and greatly overworked system of indirect taxation. The memory of the direct tax, the estimo, current in the early years of the century, had not perished and an effort was made again to re-establish it in order to oblige the well-to-do to contribute to the support of the state in some adequate proportion to their wealth. And actually an estimo was voted and put in force; but it encountered so much secret and open opposition that it failed of its purpose and, in the face of insurmountable difficulties, had to be abandoned. Perhaps the most important deduction to be drawn from these rather timid and certainly sketchy achievements in the realm of financial reform is that, while the minor arts may have enjoyed a small preponderance of votes in the colleges and councils, the major arts through their unbroken economic power commanded the hidden resources enabling them substantially to nullify the reform measures of their opponents.

In the perpetually disturbed domestic situation of the Florentine republic the three years constituting the last phase of the rule of the lesser gilds represent an apex. Plots, denunciations, executions, sentences of exile, repatriations followed each other in unbroken, frenzied succession. With these agitations drawing the attention of the citizens the members of the sixteen lesser gilds often forgot or at least were not steadily mindful of the fact that the great merchants were sleeplessly on the watch to restore their political power and to bring the two remaining gilds of workers, the Tintori and Farsettai, back into the dependence to which the gild of the ciompi had already been obliged to return. In January, 1382, a violent uprising against the capitano del popolo headed by Giorgio Scali, the magnate demagogue who had imposed himself on the people as their leader, was the occasion of a new domestic crisis. The determined co-operation of all the authorities with the threatened capitano led to the quick seizure and execution of the unlamented Giorgio. The event filled the leaders of the greater gilds with rejoicing. As in their eyes the popular leader had fallen and the people were moved by divided counsels, the long-awaited hour for merchant action had come. Making the most of the favorable moment, the employers of labor, above all the employers of the great woolen gild, organized an armed assault on the shops and dwellings of the Tintori and Farsettai. They followed this by the measure which had become conventional whenever a change was to be effected in the government: they induced the priors to summon a parliament which gave the power (balìa) to reform the government to a handpicked committee.

As the balìa was voted on January 21, 1382, we may accept this date as marking the formal demise of the Florentine democracy. Of course the commission impeccably did its duty as defined by the victors. It canceled the charters of the two workers' gilds, thereby once more reducing the minor arts to

<hr>

[17] For detailed information on this and all the other financial reforms see Rodolico, *La Democrazia Fiorentina,* chap. VI (Parte Seconda). Our authority for the trick of ser Piero is Stefani, r. 883.

fourteen in number. In the hope of amicably persuading the fourteen minor gilds to detach their fortunes from the proletarians, once more degraded to the level of sottoposti of the greater gilds, these latter, though victors, exercised a certain measure of restraint. They accepted an arrangement of the governing commission whereby, although the preponderance of power recently exercised by the lesser gilds was shifted to the greater gilds, the former were still conceded a relatively liberal participation in the government. There was no denying, however, that the oligarchy had triumphed. In the next few years it steadily added to its strength until its victory became sweeping and complete. Without doing violence to the truth a funeral orator of the defunct Florentine democracy might point out that it had made a firmer and more prolonged stand than that of any other Italian town. While it went down to defeat because of its lack of intelligence, leadership, and organization, much more, after all, than to its own defects, its overthrow must be attributed to the numerous economic and political forces which co-operated to favor the oligarchs and which in their sum were irresistible.

We end as we began by calling the episode of 1343 to 1382 a democratic interlude. It owed its origin to a temporary setback of the triumphant oligarchy which had reared its might on the gild system as formulated by the Ordinances of Justice. As soon as the setback was overcome the underlying forces, once more surging to the top, re-established the oligarchic system. Under these circumstances we are justified in accepting that system as a reasonably accurate expression of the distribution of power among the social classes making up the Florentine state.

XVII. Aspects and Problems of the New Urban Economy

THUS far in this book we have been concerned in the main with Florence as a political organism and, beginning with its origin, we have traced the stages of its development till the final victory in 1382 of the oligarchic principle. We have been at pains to point out that, like every other commune, Florence owed its existence to the revival of commerce around the year 1000, and that it grew to strength and achieved a virile dignity by adopting an urban way of life which brought it into violent conflict with the dominant agrarian forms identified with the feudal age. The unfolding of this epochal struggle obliged us to take account of trade routes, goods exchanged, money, merchant companies, and a score of similar economic items entering into the situation; we have dealt with the Florentine woolen industry as the leading source of the national prosperity; and, above all, we have taken account of those primal economic cells, the gilds, which so completely dictated the pattern of the city's material activity that they were enabled to take over the government. Should anyone ever be tempted to forget that Florence owed its greatness in the first place to the vigorous economic forces of which it was the focus, let him remember that throughout the two leading centuries of its history it was, at least in form, nothing other than a democracy of twenty-one constitutive gild units. Nonetheless we have thus far regularly subordinated the economic factors to our main problem, which was the consolidation of the Florentine state and the part it succeeded in playing between the two world-powers of the church and the empire. The time has now come to examine the economic activities systematically and for their own sake in order that we may arrive at as clear a picture as possible of the forces and institutions which contributed, each in its degree, to raise the city to its commercial and industrial eminence.

The communal movement which ended the long stagnation of the early Middle Ages was chiefly prompted by the renewal of the broken ties between the backward European west and the more advanced countries strung along the coast of the eastern Mediterranean. The Arab conquest, inaugurated by the Prophet Mohammed in the seventh century, had driven the already feeble Christian commerce from the Mediterranean and converted that sea into a Moslem lake; and, although the Arab empire had in the course of the eighth and ninth centuries lost some of its energy by falling into many separate emirates, these Arab succession states were alike interested in keeping Christian shipping from a sea which they regarded as the special preserve of the children of Allah. Some of the Moslem political units, especially in the western region of the Mediterranean, in Africa and Spain, were no better than pirate federations and, in addition to preying on such commerce as the Christians still ventured to conduct, they periodically descended on the Christian coasts to kill and plunder the inhabitants. We have learned in an early chapter [1] how Pisa on the Tuscan and Genoa on the Ligurian littoral about the year 1000 A.D. summoned the courage not only to resist the invaders but also to pay them home with raids so successfully conducted that after a few generations the Christians were permitted to regard the western Mediterranean as again at least in part their own.

At the same time Amalfi and Naples, cities of the southern coast, and, more energetically still, Venice, at the head of the Adriatic, took advantage of their never wholly interrupted association with the Byzantine empire to intensify their commerce with Constantinople. It was the Byzantine connection which enabled them to act as the distributors of the luxury articles of the orient among the rude peoples of the west. These articles consisted, besides the much-prized spices for the flavoring of the extremely simple and monotonous diet of the occident, of products indicative of a highly developed civilization, such as jewelry, silks, ivory, and ornaments of gold and silver. It was these precious articles which gave birth among the western barbarians to the idea of the fabulous wealth of the orient and which were, though certainly not the main cause, a contributory element in those stirring and perplexing invasions of the near east called the Crusades. Taken purely at their face value, the Crusades were an attempt to free by force of arms the Holy Land of Palestine from its Mohammedan masters and give it back to Christendom. We are aware that, apart from occasional successes of relatively short duration, the movement conspicuously failed, and that the vast crusading effort, many times renewed in a period of something less than two hundred years, would have to be enumerated among the major fiascos of history, had not consequences in other than the military field made the successive penetrations of the Levant something like a turning-point in western civilization. For one thing, to the western half of the Mediterranean, which the Genoese and Pisans had by their unaided effort reclaimed as a field of enterprise for Christendom, the eastern half was now added. This is not to say that the Crusades made the great middle sea a Christian instead of a Mohammedan lake, but merely that thenceforward the Mohammedans were sufficiently held in check no longer to be able to hinder the Christians from sailing the Mediterranean from one end to the other. From this extension of the physical range of the Christian mariners it gradually followed that the backward and self-repressed west, confronted with what its imagination pictured as the "gorgeous east," surrendered many of its narrow provincial customs and achieved a new mental and moral perspective. And since cause and effect in the realm of both mind and nature constitute an endless chain of energy, the communal movement, which was in its first infancy when the Crusades began, received a stimulus from them enabling it

[1] Chap. V.

steadily to wax in vigor till it was at last strong enough to overthrow the reigning feudal order.

The invaluable unity of occidental civilization attributable to a common faith and church, far from being disrupted by the commercial movement, was actually confirmed and fortified by it. This would not have been the case had not the awakening reached all the western lands without distinction. Since, however, the movement originated in the Mediterranean, the southern countries responded to it somewhat earlier than those bordering on the North and Baltic Seas; and among the Mediterranean areas the peninsula of Italy, owing to its central location, became the predestined clearing-house for an east-west exchange of goods. On this advantage, conferred by an accident of geography, the alert Italian towns seized without delay, thereby converting the very profitable trade in eastern spices and luxury articles into an Italian monopoly. Adriatic Venice, as first in the field, led the way but, even before the launching of the First Crusade (1096), it had already to reckon with the competition of such energetic upstarts from the west-Italian coast as Genoa and Pisa. Engaged chiefly in the importation of the much-esteemed eastern goods, the three leading seaports were spurred to develop appropriate organizations for their distribution through France, Germany, and England; and in measure as these western, as yet preponderantly agrarian countries in their turn acquired a taste for luxury and display, the Italian merchants increased the volume of both their business and their profits. It was accordingly the seaports which first waxed powerful in Italy as well as, for that matter, in the rest of Europe. But inasmuch as the commercial movement spread until it became general, inland towns favorably located on navigable rivers or on important cross-roads began before long to prosper in their turn.

We learned in an earlier section of this book that Tuscany, the province inviting our particular regard, experienced the gradual vitalization of a considerable group of inland towns intent each one on making the most of the novel opportunities. An identical situation developed in Lombardy, Liguria, Umbria, and the Romagna. The amazingly large number of communes between Verona at the foot of the Alps and Perugia in the heart of the Apennines that sprang to life and made a bid for power and wealth is a tribute to the magnificent animation of the period. They recognized, subconsciously probably rather than consciously, that if they wished to advance their fortunes by trade they would have to have something to trade with, and this perception led to the stimulation of the local crafts. Presently it came about that the towns which were most energetic in developing a manufacturing specialty, or which had an advantage in the matter of certain desirable raw products, or which enjoyed a supply of water sufficient to turn a mill wheel, or which commanded a system of convenient roads, forged ahead of their neighbors and ended by dominating them. In this way Bologna became the commercial metropolis of the Romagna, Genoa of Liguria, Milan of Lombardy; and rather surprisingly, in view of Pisa's earlier start and more favorable position on the coast, Florence slowly forged ahead and became the metropolis of Tuscany.[2]

---

[2] For the economic history of the whole of Italy there is now available an excellent survey by A. Doren, *Italienische Wirtschaftsgeschichte*. Jena, 1934.

That Florence for some generations after the communal movement had begun was economically inferior to Pisa and even to Pisa's near neighbor, Lucca, is undeniable. Indeed it cannot be asserted that in that early time it counted for more than any of its fellows of the Tuscan inland such as Pistoia, Siena, and Arezzo. Lucca, as the capital of Tuscany during the Lombard period, enjoyed a prestige within the province which continued well into the new period of urban self-assertion. Among other ways, this primacy expressed itself in the prerogative to mint the silver penny (*denarius*), the common medium of exchange for all Tuscany. Moreover, the presence within its walls during several centuries of a powerful duke or margrave attended by a numerous court had stimulated the crafts, which got well under way in Lucca some generations before they came to the front in the other Tuscan towns. True, as soon as Pisa roused itself to cast off the incubus of Moslem piracy, its development, though more along commercial than industrial lines, carried it well beyond Lucca in economic power. As commanding the sea route to Rome and southern Italy, it acquired a very special significance for the emperors of the Franconian and Hohenstaufen lines and was able to sell its assistance to its imperial masters in return for extensive privileges of an economic-political nature. Among these was the right conceded by Barbarossa in 1155 to issue a silver penny of its own and by this means to terminate the monopoly hitherto enjoyed by the Lucchese mint.[3] Naturally this thrust at the already shaken Lucchese supremacy only added fresh fuel to the fierce rivalry of the two close neighbors dating from their birth as self-conscious political organisms.

For lagging Florence the unquenchable feud between the two leading Tuscan communities constituted a brilliant opportunity. Coolly examining the situation with an eye to the main chance, the as yet inconsiderable commune dedicated to St. John and Santa Reparata resolved to align itself with Pisa. The reader will recall that when Pisa, fighting for its life against the Moslem corsairs, issued a general appeal for help, Florence made wholehearted response and shared in the famous expedition, which in 1115 captured the island of Majorca. The two porphyry columns, still guarding the main portal of the baptistery, serve as a perpetual reminder of the early sworn brotherhood of the two Arno towns.

Felicitous as the twelfth-century association of Florence and Pisa was, let us not close our eyes to the fact that it rested on a solid basis of interest. Pisa was naturally willing to accept aid against its pirate enemies from any quarter that offered, while land-locked Florence had a clear perception of the advantage for her trade of an outlet to the sea. In the years following the Majorcan campaign of 1115 the inland town with few exceptions clung fast to its Pisan friend and doubtless to a considerable extent owed its steady advance to this association. The reward for its continued devotion reached a peak in a famous treaty signed in 1171. This is so important as an economic milestone that the privileges Pisa therein conceded to Florence must be enumerated with some detail. The first of them touches the silver penny coined by Pisa under the imperial concession obtained sixteen years before. In order to

[3] Davidsohn, Vol. I, p. 467.

persuade Florence to put and keep its influence behind that coin the Pisans conceded to the Florentines one half the profits of their mint. Next, in order to remove every obstacle in the way of the maritime trade of Florence, Pisa promised to carry Florentine citizens and their goods across the water on the same terms as those offered to Pisans. Finally, to make the measure of Pisan good-will full and overflowing the Florentines were in the matter of the shore tolls in Pisa to be treated even better than the Pisans themselves, since the guests were to be charged only half the dues levied on natives.[4]

Of this treaty with its amazing favors the unescapable interpretation is that, while the Pisans were as yet too far in front to reckon with the Florentines as rivals, the inland town was already formidable enough to be courted and won with favors. In view of the fact that Florence enjoyed the concessions embodied in the treaty for half a century without a break, the opinion may be ventured that the alliance of 1171 was a significant factor in the steady rise of its fortunes. During those fifty years constantly increasing numbers of Florentines with their goods made their way to Pisa and from Pisa to the Pisan settlements across the sea in Africa and the Levant. Even more important for Florence, however, was the continuous movement of rough woolen cloth from France which, after subjecting to certain refining processes, the enterprising merchants of the Calimala with expert salesmanship distributed over half of Europe. This cloth trade was the earliest source of Florentine prosperity. It swelled to such proportions that the traders, waxing proud, after a while no longer willingly accepted the traditional Pisan supremacy. To their rising resentment the Pisans responded in kind, and a brief reign of these dangerous emotions sufficed to undermine the ancient friendship between the two towns. In the year 1220 occurred the first overt act indicative of the new state of feeling. The Florentine and Pisan delegations dispatched by their respective communes to Rome to attend the coronation ceremonies of Emperor Frederick II indulged in an exchange of taunts while encamped before the Eternal City which culminated in blows and bloodshed. Two years later (1222) war broke out; and although this first serious quarrel was after some years patched up, the old partners had come to the parting of the ways and were henceforth irreconcilable enemies. This dramatic revulsion in their relations admits of but one interpretation: having grown in strength till it was able to challenge the ascendancy which Pisa had exercised in Tuscany for two hundred years, Florence resolved not to rest until it had forced the maritime town into a dependence which would oblige it to become the serviceable instrument of Florentine commercial expansion.

The political history of Florence as traced in this book has revealed a sum of moral qualities on the part of the merchant leaders which the economic history, constituting our present concern, will be found to confirm at every point. More clearly than any other Italian commune the Florentine burghers recognized that they were bringing a new social order into the world and that, as a consequence of their revolutionary activity, the emperor, who stood at the head of the traditional feudal system, was their inalterable enemy. In this enlightened perception much more than in any sentimental devotion to the

---

[4] Davidsohn, Vol. I, pp. 518-19. For exact details see Santini, *Documenti,* etc., No. IV.

pope lies the explanation of their consistent Guelph partisanship. They became the obstinate and aggressive opponents of the imperial power, not, however, without resorting to a flexibility of judgment and action which, especially in the early days, was absolutely necessary in the face of the possession by the emperor of an irresistible army. With the death in 1250 of Frederick II, the last emperor to command respect by reason of his military might, the Florentine opposition to the wielder of the imperial scepter became fixed and immutable. On the passing of the great Hohenstaufen the commune felt encouraged to treat the empire as though it had itself expired and at once seized all the prerogatives it needed to round out its sovereignty. This was less a novel than a culminating act since, as our exposition has made clear, having begun its usurpations of authority at its birth, the Arno town had never failed to appropriate a new imperial right whenever the favorable moment beckoned. It is therefore certain that if Florence may be said to have achieved its independence in the year 1250, it had been steadily moving toward that goal for almost two hundred years before that time.

All this is recalled at this point because the daring, the elasticity, and the vigorous grasp of the actualities which Florence exhibited in the political field characterized the citizens also in the realm of business. Not that the two departments can be strictly kept apart. It is rare indeed that a political action does not imply economic considerations or that economic considerations do not inspire political action. But as in the present chapter we are putting economic matters to the fore, it will be permissible and proper to emphasize the economic aspect of events which, viewed from another angle, may be considered as possessing also a political, a juridicial, or a social import. In the light of this opinion we desire to draw attention to two usurpations of sovereign rights on the part of Florence which befell, one a little before, the other a little after, the demise of the second Frederick, and which, though highly political, greatly affected the business world and therefore call for an evaluation on their economic side.

In discussing the coinage situation we observed that the silver penny of Lucca, an inheritance from the long-vanished ducal regime, ruled the realm of Tuscan business till Pisa in 1155 obtained from Frederick I the right to issue a silver penny of its own. Presently a number of other towns, such as Siena, Arezzo, and Volterra, gained by imperial diploma the same privilege as Pisa and the Tuscan monetary situation fell into confusion. This was owing not so much to the great number of legal pennies in circulation as to the circumstance that each town, as soon as it found itself in financial straits, took the immediately convenient course of relieving its treasury by debasing the currency. With a variable silver content in the competitive municipal pennies expert money-changers had to come to the rescue to determine their intrinsic worth and this intervention of a third party hampered traffic, besides afflicting it with a burdensome service charge. The Florentines bore the situation for a time with great patience. They minted no penny of their own for the simple reason that they had never been willing to kneel at the throne of the emperor as humble petitioners. In their characteristically cautious way they waited for a favorable opportunity and in the period 1234-1237 (the exact moment has thus far escaped detection) resolutely took action. The reigning emperor at the time was that Frederick II who figured so prominently in Italian and Tuscan affairs in his day. In the year 1235 he was obliged to hurry to Germany in order to crush a dangerous rebellion led by his own son. The imperial overlord entangled in perilous civil strife far from the Italian scene—that was a situation than which Florence could not imagine anything more auspicious. In the light of what has already been said touching Tuscan coinage we are aware that the mint was un unchallenged imperial prerogative: only the emperor issued money or those lords and towns to whom he had conceded the right by formal patent. The Florentines knew this as well as everybody else but, fiercely opposed to the emperor, they preferred to filch his rights from him rather than to get them by meek submission and money paid in hand. In this frame of mind they watched his disappearance behind the Alps with quiet glee and in the spirit of reckless bravado issued their first coin, the silver solidus.[5]

Not only was the silver solidus, politically considered, a revolutionary act but economically it was a startling innovation. From the early Middle Ages the common circulating medium not only in Italy but throughout Europe had been the thin silver penny (denarius), of which twelve made a solidus (called soldo in Italian). Twenty solidi or two hundred and forty denarii made a libra (called lira in Italian). As both solidus and libra were merely reckoning units and were not minted, it must be understood that only the penny was in actual circulation. The penny met every need so long as the commercial movement, which set in around the year 1000, was in its infancy and trade was conducted on a relatively small scale. However, by the thirteenth century trade had assumed considerable proportions and a larger unit than the silver penny, which, small of value in itself, had been still further reduced by admixture with baser metals, had become imperative. The Florentine solution of the difficulty was the silver solidus, a creative act! Confronted with the new coin, worth twelve of the old pennies, the Lucchese, Pisans, and Sienese must have wondered why they had not thought of it themselves, for they immediately paid it the flattery of imitation. The sudden plethora of solidi did not alter the impression that the Florentines had proved themselves to be the most original thinkers along financial lines in Tuscany.

Not much more than a decade later, in 1252, they took a step which carried their name far beyond the limits of Tuscany and, in connection with the whole capitalist movement to be presently discussed, made them the financial leaders of the western world. They issued a gold coin, the florin, which showed their patron saint, St. John the Baptist, on one side and their coat of arms, the lily, on the other.[6] It must be granted that they had been preceded in the issuance of a gold coin by Emperor Frederick II with his famous augustales. His were the first gold coins put out by any western sovereign

[5] Although Villani, VI, 53, casually mentions the issue of this coin, it remained for Davidsohn to clear up the details (Vol. II¹, p. 213; *Forschungen*, Vol. IV, pp. 316-22).
[6] Villani, VI, 53; Davidsohn, Vol. II¹, pp. 411-12.

since the passing of the Roman empire. But Frederick's mint was closed at his death, and again we receive confirmation of the mental alertness of the Arno merchants in that they at once filled the gap with their own gold coin, the *fiorino d'oro*. It was issued as the equivalent of twenty solidi or of one libra.[7] Thenceforward the commune regarded it a matter of pride as well as of sound business to maintain the full gold value of the new coin to the intent of thus creating a stable unit of exchange. Its success in this respect is attested by the rapidity and completeness with which the florin conquered the markets of Italy, the Mediterranean, and even the European north. It became and remained for several generations the most prized of the many scores of gold and silver coins put into circulation in competition with the florin. For in an attempt to keep abreast of the Florentines numerous towns and sovereigns put forth gold coins of their own and, in witness of the success of the piece bearing the lily and the Baptist, many of the rival issues were nothing other than impudent counterfeits of the revolutionary florin. According to David-sohn no less than forty-eight European mints were guilty of this barefaced fraud.

By serving themselves in pertinent and intelligent fashion the Florentines had served the whole contemporary world, and their prestige rose enormously. The name of Florence was whispered and finally shouted through all the lands until fifty years after the issuance of the gold florin Pope Boniface VIII, on the occasion of the reception in 1300, the year of the Great Jubilee, of a number of special ambassadors, who, although representing different com-munities, were all Florentines by birth, was moved to greet them with the smiling compliment: "You Florentines are the fifth element." In Boniface's opinion, as in that of all his contemporaries, the world was made up of four substances called elements: water, fire, earth, and air. These had constituted the universe until the Florentines came along and manifestly enriched the mixture with the fifth element of their fine ingenuity. Of this the florin, invented half a century earlier, was for most Italians of Boniface's time the outstanding instance.

Since the new coin made its influence felt to the ends of the earth, it natu-rally became a factor also in the local Tuscan struggle for supremacy between Florence and Pisa which had begun around 1220. On this particular situation Villani throws light with such a sparkling tale that, although his *novelletta*, as he calls it, may not be strictly true, it cannot be passed over because it illustrates the waxing Florentine reputation more effectively than a volume of statistics.[8]

---

[7] "E contavasi l'uno soldi venti" (Villani, VI, 53). However, the fiorino d'oro steadily appre-ciated. By the early fourteenth century it was usually worth more than thirty solidi; and a hundred years after its appearance frequently rose to the value of sixty silver solidi or three librae of silver pennies. The appreciation was chiefly due to the continuation of the evil practices of the Tuscan and European mints in general of debasing the silver penny by increasing the ratio of cop-per. With the process continuing indefinitely the penny was bound in the long run to reach the state when, with its silver content gone, it would be wholly a copper coin. Undoubtedly a second factor in the gradual appreciation of the florin was the burden put upon gold in supporting the world's business. With the demand for gold constantly increasing the metal naturally rose in value.

[8] VI, 53.

When the said new florins had begun to travel through the world some of them reached Tunis in Barbary and, brought to the attention of the king of Tunis, a wise and valiant lord, they pleased him greatly. And he ordered that they be assayed and, on learning that they were of fine gold, praised them much and bade his interpreters explain the imprint, which showed John the Baptist on one side, and on the other, the lily with the word Fiorenza. Seeing that it was money of Christians, he sent for the Pisan merchants, who, as privileged traders, stood high in the king's esteem [even the Florentines in Tunis passed as Pisans] [9] and asked them what sort of a city among Christians this Fiorenza might be that made the said fiorini. Out of envy the Pisans answered contemptuously saying: "They are the Arabs of our hinterland," by which they meant to signify the equivalent of our own [Florentine] mountaineers. Thereupon the king responded wisely: "This does not look to me like the money of Arabs; and you Pisans, what gold coin do you issue?" On this they were confused and gave no answer, and he next asked if there was not someone from Florence in their midst. And such an one was found, a wide-awake fellow from Oltrarno by the name of Pera Balducci. Him the king asked concerning these Florentines, who, according to the Pisans, were their Arabs. And Pera answered wisely, exhibiting the power and magnificence of Florence and that Pisa in strength and population did not amount to half of Florence; and that Pisa had no gold coin; and that the florin was the result of the many victories won by Florence over Pisa. By which statements the Pisans were shamed and the king on account of the florin . . . issued a charter to the Florentines which gave them the same privileges as those enjoyed by Pisa. And by virtue of them the Florentines were to have at Tunis a warehouse [*fondaco*], dwellings, and a church.

Granting that the gold florin was a factor in the mounting commercial importance of Florence, an even greater factor was the merchant company; and as this institution, far from being a Florentine specialty, sprang from the complex phenomenon called the rise of capitalism, we shall have to give this larger issue our close consideration. Among the most prominent analysts and historians of capitalism is Sombart, who has made himself the champion of the view that the most common source of the earliest accumulations of capital in medieval times were the surplus ground rents of the great feudal landowners. Sombart argues that the magnates were obliged to put their excess returns to work, thereby instituting a new system. In his view capitalist production differs from manorial production, which preceded it, by being conducted with free funds to the sole end of profit. Conceding that he makes out a good case for his ground-rent theory for many parts of medieval Europe, we are obliged to insist that its application to Florentine conditions is much less convincing. The leading Florentine authority, Davidsohn, does not hesitate to declare that Sombart has so patently misinterpreted the Florentine evidence that what he alleges about capitalist beginnings on the Arno is completely erroneous. Davidsohn thereupon advances a theory of his own, which he buttresses with such a wealth of documents that it is difficult to see how it can be successfully attacked. Let us see how, according to him, it came about that Florence rose to be the foremost center of the new and

[9] This identification of Florentines as Pisans in Tunis and other ports, where the Pisans enjoyed special privileges, was a consequence of the treaty of 1171. For details of this fusion of Florentines and Pisans abroad see Davidsohn, Vol. IV[2], pp. 2, 256.

revolutionary system of production and exchange that passes under the name of capitalism.[10]

In the early Middle Ages wealth took the form of land and was concentrated in the hands of great prelates, such as bishops and abbots, and of secular lords. Our interest in what happened to this wealth on the coming of the communal revolution is limited to Tuscany, which constitutes no more than a particular instance within the general situation. Far from accumulating pecuniary reserves, from the time of the earliest records which have come down to us the landlords of this province are found to be in the most serious financial straits. While commanding ample returns from their vassals and serfs in the form of services and supplies, they received little or no ready money. Consequently when, by the intensified distribution of oriental goods, commerce and the crusades had raised the western standard of living, the feudal masters found it difficult to satisfy their newly acquired tastes.

While the new time called for expensive amusements in the form of feasts, hunts, and tournaments, there were, besides, campaigns to be conducted and periodic journeys to be undertaken to the court of pope or emperor. As these various activities signified for the ruling lords the need of providing costly apparel and elaborate armament for themselves and their train, it became incumbent on them to borrow money from the *mercatores,* the new class of traders born of the urban movement. We must remember that we are dealing with a small upper stratum of society as improvident as it was pleasure-loving. A great nobleman would ride into the nearest town, tap at the door of a trader with his spear, and putting his cross, in lieu of his name which he could not write, to a mysterious Latin document, would vanish as soon as a few pounds of pennies had been delivered into his hands. Likely enough he did not actually handle the cash, for the money-lender was also a merchant and cunningly supplied the goods the money was intended to buy from his own stock. When after a few months the debt had to be repaid, the improvident borrower, incapable of making restitution, grasped eagerly at an extension offered him at a higher rate of interest and registered no objection against throwing in an additional field or vineyard as security for his loan. The process, begun in the eleventh century, was accelerated in the twelfth and carried to a climax in the thirteenth century. The documents tell a clear and entirely unambiguous story.[11] They show, for instance, how the Florentine family of the Gianfigliazzi began its career by lending money in a small way to the bishop of Fiesole. Once begun, the movement continued until the Gianfigliazzi and other families associated with them had stripped his lordship of all of his possessions and left him a pauper. In the same way the Cerchi battened on the abbot of the Badia, the Cavalcanti on the nuns of Santa Felicità on the left bank of the Arno near the Ponte Vecchio. And the bloodsucking of the bish-

[10] In his work, *Der Moderne Kapitalismus,* in addition to accumulated ground rents, Sombart operates with two other sources of early capitalism, mining and colonial enterprises. Of these, however, he does not affirm that they apply to Florence. Davidsohn's position is most fully stated in his study, "Uber die Entstehung des Kapitalismus," *Forschungen,* Vol. IV, pp. 268-94. See also Vol. I, pp. 796 ff.; Vol. II², pp. 402 ff.

[11] Davidsohn, *Forschungen,* Vol. IV, pp. 281-94. For the detailed record of the impoverishment through continued borrowing of a great prelate, the bishop of Volterra, see F. Schneider, *Bistum und Geldwirtschaft.* Vols. VIII and IX of *Quellen und Forschungen aus Ital. Archiven.*

oprics and monasteries was strictly paralleled by what happened to the temporal lords. The Guidi, the Ubertini, and the other great barons of the Tuscan countryside found that, once in the clutches of the money-lenders, they could not again extricate themselves and had to suffer the gradual transfer of their houses and lands to the Spini, the Mozzi, the Frescobaldi, the Peruzzi, and other similar urban residents. By the thirteenth century each of the families named, and many others besides, had risen from a level akin to that of small pawnshop dealers to the status of great bankers and, forgetting their plebeian origin, looked upon themselves in comparison with their poorer fellow-townsmen as born to the purple. Like the new-rich from the beginning of time, they aped the old-rich whom they supplanted and ordered their existence as far as possible according to the military standards of their victims. Within a span of perhaps two centuries the whole landed wealth of the Florentine contado and of a large part of Tuscany as well had passed from the original feudal owners into the possession of townsmen who, regardless of their social pretensions, were, or at least had begun their existence, as traders and bankers.

Traders and bankers, yes; but in unvarnished speech they were nothing but usurers. Far from this being an unfair modern judgment, it was shared by their contemporaries, as we can still learn from a document of the year 1294 which referred to the Gianfigliazzi as "mercatores, immo usurarii," merchants, nay rather, usurers.[12] It is of course well known that usury, meaning interest on a money loan, high or low, fair or unfair, interest of any sort, was forbidden by the church; and it is or should be equally well known that no one, including the highest dignitaries of the church up to and including the popes themselves, paid any attention to the prohibition in their daily affairs. Doctrinally, however, the church never budged from its traditional position. Whenever the issue of usury was brought before a church council or whenever the pope pronounced on it *ex cathedra,* the declaration against the lending of money at interest was solemnly renewed and usury was denounced as a deadly sin. Accordingly, Dante was doing no more than giving expression to sound Catholic doctrine when he reserved one of the least comfortable compartments of hell for usurers, although we may agree that when he could not restrain his satisfaction at finding so large a Florentine contingent there, he was voicing a purely personal animosity.[13] The chasm yawning between profession and practice has been a feature of every society since Priam was king in Troy, but in no age was it wider and deeper than in medieval Europe. That a usurer on his deathbed was often obliged by the priest, before he would administer extreme unction, to restore to his victims some of his ill-gotten gains or, as a substitute measure, to leave a lump sum to the church to distribute in charity as it saw fit, cannot alter our view of the shocking hypocrisy of the whole business. High as interest would normally have been in the Middle Ages, owing to the scarcity of money and to the general public insecurity, the official sinfulness of usury, perpetually exposing the usurer to seizure and condemnation as a heretic, added to his risk and helped make money dear to the purchaser. In any case the usual interest rate was appallingly high, 30 and 40 per

[12] Davidsohn, *Forschungen,* Vol. III, document 221.
[13] *Inferno,* XVII, 34-75.

cent per annum being not unusual during the infancy of commerce.[14] In the course of the fourteenth century, by which time the volume of trade had greatly increased, the original opinion regarding usury underwent a modification and the Florentine merchant world developed the distinction between interest and usury familiar to our own business practice. Exactly as with us a reasonable charge came to be considered legitimate and the word usury experienced a restriction in scope, being limited to excessive percentages. However, as a rate up to 20 per cent lay within the fourteenth-century criterion of reasonableness, we may agree that the returns from money-lending of even the respectable sort enjoying the support of the municipal law courts remained very high; and from this continued height we may draw the further conclusion that the huge profits of the banking business were an expression of its heavy risks and of the undiminished scarcity of money.[15]

The dizzy rate of interest had to be injected into the argument at this point because it helps explain the ease and completeness with which many or most of the original feudal lords lost their property to the money-lenders graciously prepared to relieve their necessity with a loan. It was only after the money-lenders had in their turn become the proprietors of houses and farms and had utilized them to broaden their credit structure that they achieved the dignity of bankers. But their great reputation rests on their next step, which was to rise from the level of local bankers to world-bankers; and in order to make this advance they had to be helped by a world-event. This was the struggle between the church and the empire which in the last years of the reign of Frederick II developed into a fight to the finish. Pope Gregory IX took the view that in order to win the victory he might levy on the ecclesiastical property of all Christendom, while his successor, Innocent IV, went a step farther and by rating the struggle against Frederick as a crusade in behalf of the Cross claimed and exercised the right to collect the crusading tithe. There is no occasion to retell at this point the ferocious combat of Frederick's last years nor the dramatic crises associated with the Guelph-Ghibelline wars of the second half of the thirteenth century. It will suffice if we recall that the church in the end won the day; but particularly pertinent to the economic matter treated in this chapter is the fact that the Guelph victory resulted to a very large extent from the superior resources of the pope. Neither Gregory IX nor Innocent IV nor any of their successors failed to strain every nerve to assemble in their hands subsidies and tithes levied on abbots and bishops throughout the west with which to equip the armies required to stamp out the accursed seed of the Hohenstaufens. To collect these dues the popes used the Italian merchants and bankers, whose business enterprise had scattered them over the western world. While their profits merely as papal collectors

[14] These are the figures of Davidsohn (Vol. I, p. 795; *Forschungen*, Vol. I, p. 158) based on an examination of thirty Florentine loans covering the years 1016 to 1210.

[15] In an excellent article by A. Sapori, "L'Interesse del Denaro a Firenze nel Trecento," in *Arch. Stor. It.*, Serie 7, Vol. X, pp. 161-86, the distinction gradually made between legitimate and usurious interest is discussed as well as the height of each toward the end of the fourteenth century. The author also shows how the doctors of both the civil and the canon law were gradually moved to descend from their ivory towers and to exercise their ingenuity to accommodate the original stark theory regarding usury to current business practice. Divine law beat a strategic retreat before common utility.

must have been considerable, they enjoyed even greater rewards from advancing the papal assessment to the bishops and abbots at a variable but regularly stiff rate of interest. In other words, they performed a variety of offices which, ranking as war services, were urgent in character and yielded an inordinate return; and although the popes at first used Italian bankers indiscriminately and, if they showed a preference at all, may be said to have favored the Sienese, the battle of Montaperti (1260) produced a crisis which revolutionized the situation.

As Montaperti was a Ghibelline success, and as no more sweeping victory had ever been won in Tuscany, it followed that all the Tuscan towns, with or against their will, were brought under the Ghibelline banner. Therewith the only effective means left in the pope's hands for undermining the hated Ghibelline hegemony was his so-called spiritual power. Accordingly, he laid every Ghibelline commune under interdict and ordered the debtors of merchants of these communes in every country of Europe to refuse to pay their debts under pain of excommunication. At the same time he let it be known that he would individually readmit to the Christian communion all merchant-bankers prepared to desert the Ghibelline cause, and that he would favor the reconciled firms by intrusting the papal business to their care. Almost precipitately the Florentines, especially those who, as confirmed Guelphs, had fled from their native city after Montaperti, accepted the papal offer. Since Siena was too closely and officially tied up with the Ghibelline ascendancy, the Sienese could not to anything like the same extent come to terms with the pope, and as a result the men of Arno gradually replaced their rivals of the City of the Virgin at the papal court. When, a few years after Montaperti, the pope resolved to draw Charles of Anjou across the Alps in order to oust Manfred from southern Italy, he committed the financial preliminaries of the campaign chiefly, if not exclusively, to good Florentine Guelphs. And before another decade had passed so great an intimacy had been established between Florence, now become passionately and uncompromisingly Guelph, and the venerable and unchanging head of the Guelph cause that the Arno merchants crowded out all rivals and came into a virtual monopoly of the vast and lucrative papal business.[16]

The bankers, whom the world-struggle between pope and emperor had made an international power, were organized in partnerships or merchant companies, and the characteristic feature of the merchant company was that it engaged not only in banking but also in trade. Representatives of the Florentine firms appeared at all the great European fairs, particularly at the fairs of Champagne in eastern France, which were the largest trade gatherings of the thirteenth century, while with the expansion of international commerce in the following century agents of the Florentine houses settled permanently in France, England, Flanders, Sicily, Catalonia, Tunis, and every town and country affording commercial opportunities. It was the Italians and, among them of course our Florentines, who chiefly profited from the commercial movement because, as the earliest European people in the field, they possessed special information about goods, markets, and costs, besides commanding all the new technical

[16] Davidsohn, Vol. II, chap. 7, pp. 532, 546, 551-54.

devices, such as the bill of exchange. The way in which a Florentine company would utilize its position as financial agent of the papacy in order to extend its trade may be illustrated by reference to England. When the pope laid a tax on the English monasteries, a Florentine agent residing in England would present the bill. Since in all probability the abbots could not immediately pay, the ingratiating stranger, in his capacity of banker, advanced the assessment as a loan secured by the wool which the English monasteries produced in great quantities; or, in case a loan was not necessary, the Arno visitor, in his capacity of merchant, offered to buy the wool outright in order to ship it to the continent, where it was in demand for the manufacture of cloth. While the wool at first went generally to the cities of Flanders, toward the end of the thirteenth century the dealers widened their range and diverted the English wool in ever larger quantities to the banks of the Arno as an aid to the further development of the native woolen industry.

By this measure the merchant company added to banking and trade a third department, industrial promotion, and in the course of the fourteenth century fairly outstripped with this activity the other two. It has already been stated that when industry in Florence first transcended a purely local scale, it rested exclusively on the refining and dyeing of a very rough kind of cloth imported from the markets of Champagne in eastern France. These were the so-called *panni franceschi*. Merchant companies, the members of which belonged overwhelmingly to the gild of the Calimala, undertook both the import and re-export of the French cloths. However, at the side of this purely processing industry there existed from an early time a modest manufacture of cloth from native wool. Owing to the poor quality of the home-grown article this industry remained insignificant till the merchants bethought themselves to bring in better foreign wool, first from Spain and finally from England. The latter long-stapled product was considered to be the best wool grown; and when the Florentine merchants, having in their capacity of papal agents become acquainted with the English article, resolved to direct it to their native city, Florentine industrial development entered on a new phase. By taking advantage of the skill and taste which had been developed by the native workmen, above all, in the selection and use of dyes, the merchants calculated that they could produce from imported wool a cloth which would be without a rival. If only the necessary capital was supplied, manufacture might be started on a large scale and all accessible markets be captured with the prospect of very handsome profits. The enterprisers who went in for this particular venture gradually congregated in a second wool gild, the Lana; and as shortly after the turn of the century, in the early days of the victory of the Blacks, the volume of business done by the Lana began to outstrip that of the older Calimala gild, we have evidence of the quick success of the plan to intensify the city's industry. Before the middle of the trecento, the production of woolen cloth, according to Villani, furnished a livelihood for thirty thousand people and completely dominated the local economic situation. However, the industry continued to be ruled as from the first by traders, who, apart from financing by the putting-out method the various operations of spinning, dyeing, and weaving, were content to assemble the finished cloth in order to distribute it over Europe.

This will explain why, although Florence owed its rapid fourteenth-century expansion to manufacture, the leading men of the town always present themselves to view not as industrialists but as merchants. It follows that the organization through which they operated continued to be the merchant company. These associations were of all sizes, great and small, with much or little capital, with many or few partners, and the goods they most commonly bought and sold were raw wool and finished cloth together with the various materials necessary for textile manufacture, such as alum and dyestuffs. But they dealt also in leather, weapons, salt, spices, wheat, wine, linen, in fact in every article that sought a market and from the buying and selling of which there was likely to result a profit.[17] Since in the course of the fourteenth century banking became a more highly specialized occupation than had been the case in the preceding centuries and required more ample resources for its successful conduct, only the larger merchant companies, such as the Bardi, the Peruzzi, and the Acciaiuoli, continued to act as banks. The smaller trading firms felt more and more constrained to limit their scope to purely commercial transactions. However, so closely did their interests remain tied up with the great houses that, when a financial crisis befell they were sympathetically affected; and in case the big companies crashed to the ground, there was every likelihood that the smaller companies, inextricably entangled with the leading firms, would also go down.

The fourteenth century repeatedly supplies the proof of this statement and in no instance more convincingly than in the famous crisis of the forties. We heard in an earlier chapter how this was precipitated, at least in its first phase, by the circumstance that the two great companies of the Bardi and Peruzzi had overextended themselves by continued and excessive loans to Edward III of England in support of his madly ambitious project to conquer France. When the king defaulted on both interest and principal, not only the two firms directly involved but the whole business structure of Florence was shaken to its foundations. The threatened interests made a desperate effort to save the situation, but when the republic of Florence in its turn was obliged to cease payment on its huge war debt piled up in connection with the attempt to conquer Lucca there was no further staving off the avalanche of bankruptcies (1343–46).

It is a tribute to the undaunted energy of the Florentine merchants that they would not admit defeat in spite of this unparalleled disaster. They formed new companies which manifested no less zeal and resolution than their predecessors and which operated with such success that Florence was enabled to retain the same dominating place in the European business world during the second half of the fourteenth century as it had held in the first half. Among the great houses of the new period of prosperity were the Alberti, the Albizzi,

---

[17] The recent spurt of interest in economic history has produced many valuable studies dealing with the innumerable economic and juridical problems connected with the merchant, such as contracts of partnership, the draft, the fondaco, transportation, insurance, etc. Such are: E. Bensa, *Francesco di Marco da Prato. Notizie e Documenti sulla Mercatura Italiana del Secolo XIV.* Milan, 1928. A. Sapori, *Una Compagnia di Calimala ai Primi del Trecento.* Florence, 1932.

the Strozzi, and the Medici. Let the fresh set of upstarts remind us that there had been in Florence from the earliest days a constant rise and fall of merchant companies. It should serve to bring home to us that the opportunities which offered of inordinate gain were matched by the risks which were equally inordinate, and that only the happy concomitance of business acumen and good fortune would secure to a merchant company an even relative permanence of existence. In point of fact it was the exception and not the rule for a merchant company to continue in business for the length of more than a human generation.[18]

If we turn now to examine the field of operation of the merchant companies, let us begin with France where we have encountered them as active from an early date and from where they radiated toward Flanders, on the one hand, and toward England, on the other. All three of these northern areas continued throughout the fourteenth century to receive the attention of the Florentines; but it was France which, as from the first, exercised the greatest attraction and with which the business ties became most numerous and intimate. After the decline of the Fairs of Champagne, a movement already well advanced before the year 1300, the city of Paris became the great emporium of the kingdom, and at Paris and the nearby towns to the north and east innumerable young Florentines served their business apprenticeship in representation of the trading houses which had their seat on the Arno. Already by Villani's time it was a business commonplace that the exploitation of the French market was the main source of Florentine prosperity. It has been repeatedly pointed out in these pages that the obstinate guelphism of the City of the Baptist has one of its leading roots in this dependence of Florentine business on the protection and good-will of the kings of France. In a natural effort to sentimentalize the hard reality, the Florentines were at pains to represent themselves as standing shoulder to shoulder with the house of Capet, its Angevin offshoot in southern Italy, and the popes in an idealistic undertaking to advance the cause of Holy church. As final and conclusive proof of the spontaneous and preordained nature of the association between themselves and the French kingdom the Arno folk were wont to point to the circumstance that both states boasted the lily as their emblem. This was of course a mere accident, but it helped to strengthen the pro-French enthusiasm and contributed its share toward introducing into Florence French customs, fashions, and epics of chivalry, which in their turn operated as a by no means negligible factor in shaping the local social and literary developments. However, let us make no mistake. The decisive reason for the historical intimacy between the Kingdom of the White and the City of the Red Lily was the very substantial advantage Florence enjoyed during many generations in France through its domination of the French markets due to the commercial acumen and the superior organizing skill of its merchants.

While northern France was undoubtedly the chief magnet of the Florentine merchant-adventurers, they were to be encountered also in practically every

---

[18] O. Meltzing, *Das Bankhaus der Medici und seine Vorläufer*. Jena, 1906. This is still the most serviceable history of the leading Florentine trading companies, disclosing, as it does, their organization, their activities, their wealth, and their swift decline.

Christian land and in many Mohammedan realms besides. It goes therefore without saying that they were to be found in such leading contemporary emporia as Bruges, London, Barcelona, Avignon, Marseilles, Naples, Genoa, Venice, Constantinople, and Tunis; but even inconspicuous communities, provided they were strategically located along the great trade routes, were favored with their presence. Wherever they went, and whether in small or large numbers, they settled among their hosts in a tight little native group, which constituted a solid phalanx for the defense of common interests and which enjoyed considerable rights of self-government. We shall not find our merchants in great numbers in Germany because Germany belonged to the area of Venetian exploitation. However, in spite of the near east, too, having been from the earliest days of the commercial awakening the special preserve of Venice and such other seaports as Genoa and Pisa, so alluring were the prospects of profit in this opulent field that the Florentines refused to be excluded from it. The earliest Florentine merchants came to the Levant by taking advantage of the treaty with Pisa of 1171, which, as we have noted, secured to them all the rights enjoyed by the Pisans themselves. When war with Pisa closed this easy avenue and dried up the eastern profits, the Florentines, in revenge, nursed the resentful design of bringing Pisa under their rule. Since this was not effected till 1406, it was only after that time that Florence was enabled to send out merchant fleets under its own flag and to aspire to a much larger share than before in the Levantine trade. That in the fifteenth century the town succeeded in postponing the already threatening decline of its prosperity by finding a partial substitute for its shrinking western business in the east is a not unimportant economic detail; but that Florence, even after acquiring Pisa, ever became a great maritime power, able to take its place at the side of Genoa and Venice, must be emphatically denied.

Of all the countries invaded by Florentine enterprise none experienced a more thorough and heartless exploitation than the allied Angevin kingdom of Naples. Under the Norman kings and their Hohenstaufen successors this kingdom in its earlier and larger form of a kingdom of Sicily had been in many ways the most advanced region of the occident. A disastrous turning dates from the resolution of the popes to replace the hostile Hohenstaufens with the more subservient house of Anjou. In order to effect the overthrow of the older line the successors of St. Peter determined to mobilize every possible resource at their command and turned for help to their Italian financial agents, among whom the Florentines soon gained the lead. The Arno bankers and usurers may be said to have arrived at Naples and Palermo simultaneously with the victorious Charles and, like their parasitic kind before and since, never again left his side. Toward the end of Charles's reign the island of Sicily revolted (1282) and could not be again subdued, although the attempt was constantly renewed during a span of fifty years. The prolonged struggle signified an increasing dependence of the Neapolitan court on the Florentine money-lenders, who, as a reward for their advances, demanded trade concessions which in the end and in their sum became an all-inclusive and crushing monopoly.

The southern kingdom was then and still is the granary of Italy. Pisa and Venice, as sea cities, had been the first to become aware of the value of the

Neapolitan grain trade. They succeeded in dividing it between them, Pisa acting as distributor of the grain of the west coast, Venice of that of the east coast. Although they arrived late, the Florentines, when they came, labored so thoroughly and systematically that they gradually drove out both rivals and won the whole grain trade for themselves. As at the same time they secured their money loans to the sovereign by an assignment on the taxes, and as they brought into the kingdom all the manufactured goods which the inhabitants required, we may speak of an exploitation than which it is impossible to imagine anything more complete. The Bardi and Peruzzi, who played so large a financial role in England, were the leaders among the many Florentine companies which in the days of King Robert of Naples (1309–43) took possession of this lucrative field. When they failed and vanished from the scene, other Florentine houses succeeded them and squeezed fresh fortunes out of their hapless victim. It was the Acciaiuoli, who, although they had co-operated with the Bardi and Peruzzi and had failed with them, brought the game to an unexampled climax. A certain Niccolò Acciaiuoli rose to be the greatest man of the kingdom, virtually exercised the royal power under the title of grand seneschal, and became the possessor of one of the great fortunes of his age. Never, in spite of his lofty state and years of absence, forgetting that he was a Florentine, he founded the Certosa outside of Porta Romana, where he was buried when he died in 1365 and where a monument by a follower of the great sculptor Orcagna still recites his honors and merits.[19]

Nothing brings us humanly so close to these hard-headed traders and unscrupulous profiteers as the dangers to which they were exposed and the courage they exhibited and had to possess in inexhaustible abundance if their labors were to be crowned with success. The goods that went by land were loaded in bales or rolls on pack animals, which for better protection traveled over Europe in long, well-guarded caravans. The roads were in pitiful case, generally not surfaced roads at all but rutted paths churned into knee-deep mud in the rainy season and in hot summer weather heaped high with choking dust. The streams and rivers had usually to be forded, for bridges were few, and at these few some lord invariably exacted the payment of a toll. But not only at bridges but at scores of points along the road feudal noblemen, who dominated the local situation, collected dues allegedly to meet the cost of maintenance. Without even alleging a reason other than their good swords, other nobles, indistinguishable from common highwaymen, exacted a payment for safe conduct through their territory, and if refused, attacked and plundered the caravan. If romance is born of chances defying calculation, there has surely never been a time when it is more fitting to speak of business as romance than in the days of the merchant companies.

But we are only at the beginning of the long tale of merchant hazards. In the earliest phase of the commercial movement a visiting merchant was a foreigner without rights, who was admitted into an alien community purely on sufferance and at his own risk. If he defaulted on a payment and fled, the local judge allowed the creditor to indemnify himself by seizing the goods of any

---

[19] For the details of the ruthless Florentine exploitation of Il Regno see Davidsohn, Vol. IV², chap. VIII. See also L. Tanfani, *Nicola Acciaiuoli*. Florence, 1863.

of the defaulter's fellow-citizens who happened to be at hand. On or even before the delivery of the sentence the implicated innocent strangers gathered together what they could of their possessions and ran for their lives. On arriving breathless in their own commune they lodged a complaint with their government, which promptly avenged the insult to its subjects by ordering the wholesale confiscation of such goods in its midst as pertained to the citizens of the offending commonwealth. This frenzied exchange of injuries went by the name of reprisals and was a universal concomitant of commercial intercourse in its earliest and still barbarous phase. It was inevitable that, in measure as trade became more intensive, all traders alike should become interested in abolishing the monstrous system worthy of Bushmen and Mohawks. The reasonable solution was to concede a foreigner legal protection by the local court and to declare the contracting individual alone responsible for his debt according to the principle *a cui dato a colui richiesto* (payment is to be exacted solely from him who received the goods). By slow degrees this saner system won recognition, largely because it met the interest of all alike, but also because it accorded with the principles of Roman law, the revival and growing empire of which was a significant feature of the waxing communal movement. By the twelfth and, more commonly still, by the thirteenth century the Italian municipalities adopted the practice of negotiating commercial treaties with each other in which they took steps, first to mitigate, and finally to abolish reprisals altogether. In connection with this more humane and rational procedure the merchants themselves of a given town would set up a commercial court capable of receiving suits from both native and foreign traders and prepared to pronounce sentence according to generally accepted principles of justice and without regard to nationality. This type of trade court culminated in the case of Florence in the *mercanzia,* established in 1308. It was created by the united action of all the trade gilds, the arti maggiori, and acquired a great and merited reputation among the commercial classes of all Italy. Finally, in sweeping evidence of the advance made by rational procedure during the thirteenth century let it be said that by the time the Florentine mercanzia was established reprisals in their original raw, collective form had already become the exception and were no longer the rule of Italian commerce.[20]

However, in some countries not subject to Italian inter-communal regulations, reprisals long continued. France was such a land. From time to time the French government, yielding to the clamor of the debtors among its subjects unwilling or unable to pay the foreign merchants doing business under its aegis, liberated its subjects from their obligation to pay; and to make the measure of the punishment full and overflowing the government might go farther and authorize the seizure of both goods and persons of the foreign traders. If it seemed desirable to justify these violent procedures, this could be done by referring to the allegedly usurious practices of the visitors. Royal decrees illustrative of this exercise of retributive justice were issued by Louis

[20] On reprisals and the long fight to overcome them see Del Vecchio and Casanova, *Le Rappresaglie nei Comuni Medievali e specialmente in Firenze.* Bologna, 1894. G. Arias, *I Trattati Commerciali della Repubblica Fiorentina.* Florence, 1901. On the mercanzia see pp. 745-51 of A. Doren, *Das Florentiner Zunftwesen.* Stuttgart, 1908. G. Bonolis, *La Giurisdizione della Mercanzia in Firenze nel Secolo XIV.* Florence, 1901.

IX in 1269, by Philip III in 1274 and 1277, and by all their successors well through the fourteenth century. The frequency of the confiscations arouses the suspicion that they were not thoroughly carried out and that in launching their thunderbolt the sovereigns had their eye much more on their own advantage than on that of their subjects. Surviving documents make it perfectly clear that on satisfactory payment to the royal agents the Italians, among whom the Florentines easily preponderated, were considered to have compounded their felonies. While the original decree of the king's chancellery gave eloquent and moving utterance to the moral indignation of the monarch over the sinful usury practiced by the foreigners, the subsequent action of the royal officials induces us to believe that the whole upflare was nothing other than a financial maneuver to fill the royal treasury, since such traders as promptly paid tribute were not further molested.[21] Agreeing that the confiscations of the French and of occasional other sovereigns were not so disastrous to the Italian merchants as would appear on the surface, they nevertheless constituted a serious risk and should not be overlooked in an estimate of the extremely aleatory character of the activities of the great merchant companies.

Of all the continued reprisals uncured and incurable by treaty, the most generally injurious were those imposed by the pope. Let it be said at once that the two most deadly weapons of the supreme pontiff, excommunication and interdict, do not in and by themselves belong to an economic discussion. They were of a spiritual nature and visited spiritual penalties on the evil-doers at whom they were aimed. Over and over again since the first emergence of self-government, Florence had been put under interdict by the pope in connection with some ecclesiastical transgression, such, for example, as subjecting the clergy within its jurisdiction to a municipal tax. This, as threatening the independence of the clergy, was denounced at Rome as an infringement on the liberty of the church. Undoubtedly the pope was on sound canonical ground when he held it to be his right and duty to defend the supremacy of the institution of which he was the head and in that defense to employ as legitimate, if extreme, measures the interdict and excommunication. But become a leading political power, the pontiff had fallen into the habit of using his spiritual prerogatives to punish a purely political opposition; and on the on the whole rare occasions when Florence deserted the Guelph banner, interdict and excommunication were brought into play to smite the citizens exactly as if they had made themselves guilty of an ecclesiastical transgression. Thus in 1261 when, following the battle of Montaperti, Florence was compelled to become Ghibelline, Pope Urban IV not only punished the city with the interdict but added the invitation to the governments of the whole world to seize Florentine goods and imprison Florentine traders when and wherever encountered. It has already been told how quickly this threat induced the bankers at all costs to seek an accommodation with the pontiff. If the companies of the Arno town did not on this particular occasion suffer heavy losses, those of many other Ghibelline communities visited by the same anathema did; and in any case the power which the pope arrogated to himself in his interest and at his pleasure to level a destructive blow at trade deserves to be set down in every catalogue of the special disadvan-

---

[21] Davidsohn, Vol. IV[2], pp. 211-14.

tages under which merchants labored in the communal age. While reaffirming that Florence, as the most devoted Guelph government of Italy, was not often in political opposition to the pope and that it was therefore relatively untouched by the pope's political wrath, let us not forget that its business had always to be conducted with an eye to reprisals which it lay within the pope's power to impose. As late as 1376, on occasion of the war between Florence and the State of the Church, the so-called War of the Eight Saints, Pope Gregory XI attempted to break Florentine resistance by coupling with his interdict the order to good Christians throughout the west to throw Florentine merchants into prison and to appropriate their goods.[22] Since the war lasted till 1378 the losses suffered by Florence under the papal enactments ran into the hundreds of thousands of gold florins. In short, the hazards under which Florentine and medieval commerce in general labored were extraordinary. They helped to account for such characteristic features of contemporary business as the high rate of interest, the sudden enrichment of a trading company by a bold, successful stroke, and the early collapse of every company practically without exception.

We have learned that, beginning with the awakening of commerce, the great feudal properties of Tuscany, whether belonging to bishops, abbots, or temporal lords, began to pass into the possession of the merchants of the towns. Not improbably these merchants were at the same time themselves landowners, though on a small scale. Become by their acquisitions landowners on a large scale, they not only achieved a more elevated social status but also gained a valuable credit basis for their expanding commercial transactions. There followed a notable agricultural expansion from this amassing of land by urban families. In the main the great manorial properties of the past had been cultivated by the labor of serfs, although surviving records prove that even in the deep feudal age land was frequently cultivated under a lease, by the terms of which the worker or peasant paid the owner an agreed portion of the crop. The ratio at which the harvest was shared varied greatly, but the trend from an early time was toward an equal division between the two contracting parties. This is substantially the *mezzeria* system, which afterward became and which remains to this day the characteristic form of land tenure throughout Tuscany. As the specialists assure us, the first faint beginnings of the mezzeria reach so far back that they may even antedate the Germanic invasions. With the downfall of feudalism and the taking over of the fields and orchards by burgher interests, the disappearance of serfdom, a system suited to resident landlords, was accelerated and the partnership of the mezzeria which, while raising the status of the peasant, freed the city owner from the necessity of immediate superintendence became more and more common. When in the year 1289 a decree of the new government of the priors abolished serfdom throughout the Florentine jurisdiction, this characteristic institution of feudalism had already declined to such an extent that there was but little of it left. We may therefore think of the often cited act of liberation of 1289 as crowning a development which had been inaugurated many generations before and which was an inseparable feature of the whole communal movement. Owing

[22] See chap. XVI, p. 275.

to the radical character of that movement even the Tuscan land, the stronghold of the feudal classes, passed into possession of the burghers, who favored the mezzeria and gradually made it all but universal in the province. Thus we see that it was a sum of historical conditions and not the hypothetical generosity of the ruling merchants which brought about the abolition of serfdom.

Nonetheless the merchant successors of the nobles, far from being just a passive landlord group, made an important contribution to the practice of agriculture. They poured capital into the farms they took over in order to increase the return, and as skilled business men they contributed to the enlarged venture a valuable element of management. In Florence, a rapidly expanding industrial town, they had close at hand a market capable of absorbing all the foodstuffs they could possibly grow. No wonder that Tuscan farmland became a much-prized form of investment, and if it did not yield as high a return on capital as trade, the latter, as much more speculative, suffered recurrent severe losses unknown to the former. On the whole, the advancing fourteenth century showed a distinct tendency on the part of merchants to give up trade as carrying too many risks and to be content with the smaller but safer return from farms worked by free peasants on the mezzeria plan.

The foregoing condensed history of the Florentine adventurers and their characteristic organization, the merchant company, will have served its purpose if it has made clear that the town of the Red Lily owed its rise and importance to this enterprising class. Fully conscious of their value, the merchants undertook from a very early time to safeguard their interests at home by joining forces in an association or gild. That there was a gild of merchants in Florence as early as the beginning of the twelfth century is as good as certain, although it is true that the oldest existing document referring to such a gild belongs to the year 1182. As the leading merchants of that period were the importers of foreign cloth, and as they were installed in shops (*botteghe*) along a narrow street near the Mercato Vecchio, they came to be known from this street as the merchants of the Calimala. Not long afterward we hear of other merchant associations. In 1202 there is reference to a gild of cambiatores or money-changers and ten years later we first hear of a wool gild (arte di Lana). The merchants of the Por Santa Maria gild are mentioned for the first time in 1218. With the spirit of association abroad in the land and with the gild offering itself to the individual as the most suitable means of self-protection, it was natural for the humble craftsmen to follow the example set by the wealthy traders. A document of the year 1193, according to which in a political crisis an unnamed number of craft gilds acted together in order to make their weight felt with the government, makes it clear that organization had by that time reached down into the artisan strata of society.[23] Again, as in the case of the merchant gild, let it be said that the craft gilds go far back of their earliest documentary mention, but the only authority for the statement is reasonable conjecture.

Although the thirteenth century constitutes a period of rapid economic de-

[23] A. Doren, *Entwicklung und Organisation der Florentiner Zünfte im 13. und 14. Jahrhundert* (Schmoller's *Forschungen,* Vol. XV). Two further works conclude Doren's invaluable studies of the Florentine gilds. They are: *Die Florentiner Wollentuchindustrie* (Stuttgart, 1901) and *Das Florentiner Zunftwesen* (Stuttgart, 1908).

velopment, very little information touching the gilds is available till we reach the political revolution of 1282. Aware as we are that the considerable expansion of Florence, which had occurred during the period prior to 1282, was primarily the work of the merchants, we have no occasion to register surprise at learning that it was they who made the above-mentioned revolution and, what is more, that they made it for the express purpose of taking over the government. By 1282 the merchants were organized in seven gilds representing a vast economic power. Quite possibly the seven could have appropriated the government by their own strength alone; but as their action was not without certain risks, they resolved to move cautiously and invited the five strongest craft gilds to join them in their undertaking. The result was the successful setting up of a government of twelve gilds, from the membership of which the new executive of the priors had to be chosen. When, ten years later, the twelve undertook to crown their revolution by that famous blow at the magnates familiar under the name of the Ordinances of Justice, they prudently resolved still further to strengthen their hand by drawing nine additional craft gilds to their side. There thus came into being the government of the twenty-one gilds, of which, seven qualified as arti maggiori, five as arti medie, and nine as arti minori.[24] However, the distinction between the middle and minor gilds is artificial and did not long survive. Compared with the seven merchant gilds, the middle and minor gilds alike were so plainly the organizations of artisans and shopkeepers, and furthermore, so wide an economic chasm yawned between the merchants on the one hand, and the artisans and shopkeepers on the other, that common parlance soon grouped all the craft associations together as the fourteen minor gilds. Nor did it take long for the distinction between what was major and minor economically to achieve political expression. While the theoretical participation in the government of the fourteen craft gilds was not disputed, the priors, especially after the fall of Giano della Bella (1295), were so generally chosen from the membership of the greater gilds that we may without fear of contradiction speak of the priorate as a merchant government. To be sure, owing to circumstances considered in the previous chapter, the merchant ascendancy was challenged during the period 1343–82; but when the popular movement failed, the merchant oligarchy resumed and thenceforward retained control until the development out of its midst of the principate of the Medici. Most of what has been said about Florentine democracy by historians, and especially by literary essayists, savors of exaggeration or sentimentality. In spite of Florence being an industrial city populated by shopkeepers and workers, it was dominated by its merchants who, distributed among seven major gilds, constituted a privileged political body.

The twenty-one gilds which gained political recognition by the constitution of 1293 were, generally speaking, not single but composite gilds. A constituent unit was called a *membrum,* and as new units continued to be added, especially during the early decades of the fourteenth century, the gilds tended to become compounded of more and more membra. To illustrate by reference to the gild of the *medici* and *speziali,* usually listed sixth in order among the

---

[24] See chap. XI where the gilds are listed under their historical names.

seven arti maggiori: to the medici (physicians) and speziali (apothecaries) there were gradually added the *merciai* (retail merchants), *sellai* (saddlers), *borsai* (purse-makers), and *dipintori* (painters). An examination of this rather artisan-like list of membra makes the claim of this gild to be a great merchant gild appear rather doubtful.[25] Skepticism also assails us in the case of the seventh of the greater gilds, the *pellicciai* or furriers, although this gild undoubtedly imported pelts from the Black Sea and elsewhere and made them up into garments for distribution. While the furriers indisputably had the character of a merchant gild, the volume of their business cannot have been very large. The fact is there were gradations of importance among the greater gilds just as there were gradations among the lesser gilds; and the deeper we penetrate into Florentine economic history the more we are persuaded that its ruling element was not the seven great gilds as such, but rather the two wool gilds (Calimala, Lana), the Cambio (bankers), and later, when the silk industry developed, the Por Santa Maria. It was substantially in these four gilds that were concentrated the wealth and influence of the merchants who guided the fortunes of the city.

But we have drifted away from the issue of the many occupations united in a single gild. On the whole the lesser gilds were more likely to be constituted of many members than the powerful gilds, whose very power derived in part from their more perfect unification. The *pizzicagnoli* had four membra, generally small retailers like the pizzicagnoli themselves. The *fabri* (smiths) had six membra, while the *albergatori* (inn-keepers), the *rigattieri* (second-hand dealers), and the other lesser gilds regularly embraced several constituent groups, although, owing to frequent changes, the exact number is not always easy to determine.[26] The conclusion to be drawn from these data is that, while there were only twenty-one gilds recognized by the law, three and four times this number of occupational groups were associated together within the gilds, thereby enabling these societies to embrace a larger membership and develop a richer existence than the conventional figure of twenty-one gilds would lead us to believe.

But while a considerable body of local craftsmen and small shopkeepers enjoyed organization and the political rights which organization alone conferred, the much larger mass of the workers of the two woolen gilds, and later of the silk gild (Por Santa Maria), could claim none of these benefits. Technically incorporated in one or another of the textile gilds, the workers were subjected to sharp regulations and prohibitions without any corresponding benefits. The textile gilds were gilds exclusively of masters, while the textile workers were industrial serfs or sottoposti required to subsist on starvation wages and forbidden under heavy penalties to form gilds of their own. In the previous chapter we have dealt with the attempt the sottoposti made in the period 1343–82 to improve their lot. Their main effort was directed to getting from under the heel of their masters by the formation of independent gilds. In the

[25] The character of this gild is treated in detail by R. Ciasca, *L'Arte dei Medici e Speziali nella Storia e nel Commercio dal Secolo XII al XV*. Florence, 1927.

[26] The frequent shifts in membership are treated in detail by Doren, *Entwickelung und Organisation*, etc., chap. III.

great rising of 1378 they realized their dream by the creation of three gilds of workers, thus raising the official list of gilds endowed with political rights to twenty-four. But what was medicine for the workers was poison for the masters, who neither slumbered nor slept till they had destroyed the three workers' gilds and again reduced their employees to mere sottoposti of their own organizations. The defeat of 1382 must have broken the spirit of the proletarians, for they gave up the fight and never again, as long as the republic lasted, challenged the control of their superiors. The struggle of the fourteenth century constitutes an early chapter in the very modern conflict between capital and labor, and in the relatively easy victory won by capital reveals the difficulties which then and ever since have confronted capital's opponent.

The inner organization of the gilds is disclosed by their statutes, innumerable manuscripts of which are still preserved in the Florentine Archives.[27] The oldest existing statutes are those of the rigattieri of the year 1295; immediately after them come the Calimala statutes of 1301. The vast majority of the manuscripts belong to the fourteenth century, the period when the gilds were most active and vigorous. They show that, though there was considerable difference in detail in the organization of the different gilds, they all had so much in common that a generalized description is not impossible. The gild was governed by a college of consuls, who held office for half a year and who were obliged in all important matters to seek the advice of a council. Since, to satisfy its self-respect, the gild owned a house (casa)—only the great woolen gild, the Lana, boasted a palazzo—collected dues and fines, paid out money for salaries, festivals, and benefactions, it had to have a treasurer and a budget. Moreover, as is indicated by the innumerable prescriptions and prohibitions imposed by the statutes touching production and distribution, the gild claimed police power over its members. This was exercised by bailiffs, who on receiving a denunciation haled the offender before the gild court for trial and punishment. While the statutes cannot be said to have aimed at destroying the initiative of the individual member, they so rigorously provided for a just price and a high standard of excellence in the article produced that the gildsman was never able to forget that he labored not only for himself but also for the community. In spite of the worldly temper induced by the general character of the urban movement, the medieval religious spirit was still strong and gave each gild something of the character of a fraternal organization. In daily practice the social and religious implications of the gild may not always have successfully imposed themselves, but they were subtly intermingled with the system and account for much of its strength.

It admits of no dispute that the economic, social, and political life of Florence during the two hundred years following the establishment of the government of the priors received its characteristic imprint from the gilds. Not only were most of the officials beginning with the highest executive, the priors, chosen from the gild membership, but the consuls of the gilds (capitudines artium) had a seat in the council of the captain and were, besides, called into consulta-

---

[27] The manuscripts are described by Doren, *Das Florentiner Zunftwesen*, Anhang I. Doren's work rests firmly on this original material. The first step toward a systematic publication of these manuscripts has been taken by the issuance of the *Statuti dell'Arte dei Medici e Speziali . . . per cura di R. Ciasca*. Florence, 1922.

tion by the priors in all issues affecting the welfare of the state. While there were gilds in all the Italian communes without exception, and while in many communes they acquired a measure of political importance, they did not anywhere else so completely take over the government as in Florence. And in spite of difficulties, risings, and disastrous lapses, the gild-controlled government of Florence developed a greater measure of effectiveness than that of any other commune with the single exception of Venice. Our analysis cannot fail to have made clear that at the core of the system was the compact oligarchy of the upper gilds. For better and for worse the gild system of Florence operated strictly as a class regime. And since the governing class were the merchants, who, beginning with the twelfth century, had been engaged in opening new paths to adventure and wealth, we may instance Florence as a community in which the political responsibilities very accurately reflected the distribution of economic power.

XVIII. Intellectual Change: The Coming of Humanism

I N THIS chapter it is proposed to show how in the fourteenth century
Florence and Italy provided themselves if not with a new, at least with
the beginnings of a new, mentality. Before making a start, however, it
will be necessary to engage in a brief discussion of a general nature. In the
Introduction, in which the author passed in review the movement through the
centuries of Florentine historiography, he explained how the concept of history
has so greatly broadened during recent generations that a work calling itself
a history will no longer meet present-day requirements unless, in addition to
politics, it gives attention to various other aspects of society so intimately
interwoven with politics that politics remains incomprehensible without them.
Inevitably therefore a modern history will have something of the character of
a history of civilization. Although the author continues to uphold this contention, he has now arrived at a point in his own history when he feels urged
to elaborate his position. Above all, he wishes to guard against possible mis-
conceptions to which his statement in its bare, overgeneralized form is exposed.

If it is agreed that history, so long limited to affairs of state, has recently
widened its outlook, it must not be understood that the new procedure imposed on the historian obliges him simply to enlarge his scope and that his
revised task consists in adding to a history of the traditional political type an
indefinite number of other histories dealing respectively with the economic,
social, intellectual, artistic, and other similar developments. Apart from the
circumstance that such a production, lacking the unity characteristic of a work
of art, would be an encyclopedia rather than a history, the fact is that no single
individual can in our day hope even remotely to master the various techniques
and bodies of information which such an undertaking would require. Let us
therefore agree at once that it will be wise to let the specialists in political
economy, philosophy, literature, and art, in the future as in the past, write
the histories for which they alone possess the indispensable preparation and
training. The enlarged task of the traditional historian, who has burst the
too narrow bounds of his subject, is neither to enter into competition with all
the other kinds of existing historians nor to attempt the impossible enterprise
of occupying the whole field of human knowledge. His concern is still with
politics, the state must continue to be the core of the subject matter inviting his
investigation. But having learned from the developments in his field since the
middle of the nineteenth century that the state may no longer be regarded as

an isolated, self-contained unit, and that without any doubt whatever the nature and undertakings of the state are determined by the activities unfolded in the economic, social, philosophic, and other related fields, he will have to take account of these other matters, not so much for their own sake as in the interest of his primary, his political preoccupations. Moreover, as he will not be expected to be an expert save in his immediate department, he will have to content himself with the results furnished by the experts in the departments that neighbor on his own, and he will have to present their findings in summary form and in due subordination to his main, his political theme.

It is this conception of the enlarged requirements of a present-day history which the author has attempted to apply in the work in hand. While making the formation and development of the Florentine state his main concern, he has been at pains to discard the political blinders, which were so integral a part of the authoritative classical tradition, and to see the Arno commune from its first appearance amidst the chaos of the feudal system as a social-economic entity. What, in contrast to or, more accurately, in supplementation of, the political emphasis, may be called the social-economic viewpoint has dominated his narrative throughout its course. But, beginning with the preceding chapter, the moment seemed to have come for a separate and more concentrated presentation of some of the special agencies that figured in the shaping of the state and society under review. That chapter therefore was devoted to a cursory sketch of the economic activities in which the Florentines succeeded in peculiarly distinguishing themselves. While it is hoped that it makes an appreciable contribution to the understanding of the general Florentine situation, not for a moment does it pretend to be a reasoned economic history of the Arno town during the period in question. For this the reader especially interested in economic matters is invited to consult the economic historians. The same statement applies to the intellectual and artistic material which will be offered respectively in the present and in the succeeding chapter. The two chapters together markedly contribute, in the author's view, to the understanding of Florentine social and political conditions and accordingly serve the central purpose of this book; but they present data for which the author has been obliged to go to the specialists in these particular fields, and which he hopes to succeed in fusing with his main matter into an intelligible and vital whole.

The intellectual background of the Middle Ages is relatively simple and incomparably unified. This is due to the fact that when the new or western civilization came into existence, it was dominated by Christianity in the organized form of the Roman Catholic church. The clergy inculcated the Christian doctrines of the Fall of Adam, the Atonement through Christ Jesus, and the Last Judgment, which were the central features of a magnificently elaborated system defining the relations between God and man; and far from encouraging, they deprecated any intellectual curiosity in excess of the official matter, which, as divinely revealed, possessed the character of final and incontrovertible truth. Faith exercised exclusive rule, and the intelligence, with which man is endowed by nature and which a deep-seated instinct urges him to employ in order to increase his knowledge, was for several centuries treated with suspicion and systematically restrained. But when after the year 1000 the urban development set in, producing a stimulating and greatly multiplied movement of men and goods, it occasioned also a spontaneous generation of ideas until the clergy found themselves unable to hold the Christian flock to the original static norm of thought. In fact the clergy, as the most cultivated members of society, were themselves the first to raise their voices in behalf of a more liberal use of the intellect; but as at the same time they remained convinced Christian believers, they finally, but only after lively and at times perilous disputes, agreed on the exercise of mind, or of *ratio* (reason) as they called mind in the terminology of the period, provided always that reason would keep within bounds and would modestly refrain from invading the hallowed ground of Christian dogma.

It was in the eleventh and twelfth centuries that the struggle in behalf of reason began, and so eager was the interest in the issue that it gave birth to a special institution, the university. In the course of still another century, the thirteenth, not only did the intellectual turmoil at the new university centers reach its height, but in the person of Thomas of Aquinas (1225–74) it brought forth its most eminent representative. In his famous work, the *Summa Theologica,* Thomas harmonized faith and reason in so just a manner that the church gave his exposition its formal indorsement. According to the position adopted by him there need be no quarrel between faith and reason, since each of them could lay claim to a special function and dominion. However, harnessed together though the two were henceforth to be, they were not to be considered equals, for, should a dispute arise between them, it was reason and not faith that must give way since the continued primacy of faith was undebatable and axiomatic. It follows that, while it is unexceptional to speak of the early Middle Ages up to about 1000 as an age of faith, the statement holds good of the later Middle Ages only with a certain reservation. For characteristic of the period coming after the year 1000 is the fact that it cultivated and even exalted reason, provided always that reason would agree to respect as inviolable the special dominion of faith. It will not escape the reader's attention that the true age of faith coincides in the main with the backward agrarian period dominated by feudalism, whereas the successful, if limited, assertion of reason is a concomitant and result of the disturbance introduced into the conservative agrarian mentality by the communal revolution.

Now our town of Florence had no part in shaping either the earlier or the later medieval mentality. Both outlooks derived from the only existing learned class, the clergy, with the interesting difference that the members of the order who effected the recognition of reason expounded their views not from ecclesiastical pulpits but from the lecture platforms of universities at which they served as professors. As such they were often denominated *doctores scholastici* or schoolmen, while the philosophy they propounded was commonly designated as scholasticism. By the thirteenth century scholasticism had become the possession of the whole body of European intellectuals, who in the expanding towns, especially of Italy, came gradually to include, besides priests, monks, and friars, considerable numbers of the laity. In that age of increasing intercourse among the nations of the west as well as between the opposed oriental and occidental worlds, many laymen by reading books and attending the universities had acquired the same learning as their clerical contemporaries. The time therefore came when a layman might feel as free as a clergyman to expound the newer Christian system in which faith had made a pact with reason and reason had become faith's ally. It was only when this particular development had been reached that Florence projected itself into the intellectual history of Europe. And the layman who by thus stepping forward indicated that the exclusive rule of the clergy in the realm of thought was passing was the city's greatest son, the greatest not only of his own but of every age, Dante Alighieri.

We have already dealt with Dante as a poet, who at the call of patriotism plunged into politics, found himself on the losing side, and was driven into exile. There is no need of entering again into his story, for at this point we are concerned exclusively with the intellectual significance of his great poem, the *Divine Comedy*. In that work Dante planned to set forth the Christian scheme of salvation, as he himself had learned it from the writings of the Fathers and, in greater detail still, from the recent great scholastics with the saintly Thomas at their head. Disinclined to elaborate his theme heavily and argumentatively like a theologian and impelled by his peculiar genius to body it forth in the pictorial fashion appropriate to the artist, he represented himself as taking a journey through the world-to-come beginning in the depths of hell and ending in high heaven in order by this device to inform his readers through the evidence of an eye-witness of the rewards and punishments meted out to souls for their conduct while inhabiting the house of flesh on earth. There is no question at this point of our evaluing the *Divine Comedy* as poetry. Let it suffice to refer to the chorus of approbation which, sounded by critics through the ages, places it among the masterpieces of world-literature. It is the intellectual significance of the poem that here alone concerns us; and on this score it is not too bold an affirmation to declare that Dante, a Florentine layman writing in the first quarter of the trecento, crowned the labors of the scholastic philosophers by setting forth the Christian order of the universe with such understanding, faith, and fullness that later generations have not hesitated to regard him, if not as the most authoritative, certainly as the most exalted, voice that made itself heard in the whole course of the Middle Ages.

Thus belatedly did Florence make a richly imaginative contribution to the intellectual development of medieval Europe. But instead of a starting-point it proved to be an ending: the *Divine Comedy* was the swan song of the Middle Ages. For even as Dante was writing his passionate verses, the communal revolution, entering a new phase, began to respond to other forces than medieval Christianity and to give shape to other human purposes. For the communal revolution, uninterruptedly continuing, signified uninterrupted change, with the result that no sooner would a foreshadowed goal be approached than another more distant goal would be descried and the strenuous onward march resumed. Closely studied, the scholastic movement itself was no more than a manifestation in the realm of thought of the social-economic changes brought about in the twelfth and thirteenth centuries. While the scholastic doctors declared and honestly believed that they had projected a philosophy which would serve as a frame for human thinking to the end of time, after the manner of ephemeral men they deluded themselves by ascribing to a purely temporary system the quality of eternity. The very next university generation after that of the great Aquinas began to gnaw at his structure. At the same time something far more ominous than academic criticism put in an appearance by reason of the circumstance that increasing numbers of the intelligentsia frankly and definitely turned their backs on the issues that had been involved in the scholastic movement. Apparently these issues ceased to interest the new generation, which threw itself on a new set of problems more immediately relevant to the altered aspects of society. In the intellectual history of Europe scholasticism was succeeded by humanism, and humanism is so largely an Italian and even a distinctly Florentine product that we shall have to give it our close attention.

The early Middle Ages, the true age of faith, had a markedly transcendental character, for they inculcated the vanity of the brief and imperfect Here and exalted the eternity of the Hereafter as alone worthy of the regard of a true Christian. Even though the later Middle Ages made a concession to our mortal state by authorizing the pursuit of mundane knowledge through the exercise of reason, the transcendental emphasis was not greatly modified. While the thirteenth-century intellectuals, overwhelmingly members of the clergy confined within the barriers of their class, wrestled with the difficult abstractions of philosophy, the great body of the laity, composed of merchants, lawyers, physicians, and artisans, continued to occupy themselves with the pressing practical problems of living. They struggled to rise in the world by the successful exercise of their craft or profession; they traveled and became acquainted with other peoples, other countries, other customs; and, as citizens of an expanding town, they tried to contribute to its expansion and to win the right to participate in the conduct of its affairs. For these men constituting the urban laity, the transcendental message of the clergy imperceptibly began to lose its lure. Passionately concerned with the earth and with their human kind, they gradually, so gradually that it long escaped their own notice, set up for themselves a new scale of values. Inevitably the heaven of the teachers and preachers faded from view in measure as the urban laymen became increasingly absorbed with the engrossing concerns of everyday life. In brief, there took place a switch of attention, a mental re-orientation, which in the course of time received the name of humanism. Humanism is derived from the Latin *humanitas* (and ultimately from *homo,* that is, man), and its becoming a banner and a watch cry signified that the intellectual revolution produced by the urban movement had reached the stage when the Hereafter with its remote, presumptive glories would be gradually dethroned to be replaced by the Here with its pungent, ever-present, life-giving realities.

It was in the fourteenth century that humanism came clearly into view under its first great champion, Petrarch. But since it was, as we have been insisting, a consequence of the earth-directed communal movement, it had been in obscure gestation for several generations before, in the person of Petrarch, it presented itself to the eyes of men. From our own town of Florence we may learn by a particular instance how the movement was prepared in the womb of time. A leading lay intellectual of the generation before

Dante was Dante's teacher, Brunetto Latini (d. 1294?). As he was at the same time the first permanent chancellor of the Florentine republic, he was in his day one of the outstanding personages of the town. Latini became so absorbed in the fresh secular knowledge which was being slowly accumulated in consequence of the unwonted contemporary curiosity that he wrote a kind of encyclopedia under the name of *Il Tesoro* (the Treasure).[1] It contained very simple matter, indeed so incredibly simple that nothing short of a perusal of its offerings in the way of physiology, zoölogy, and astronomy will serve to convey an idea of what in Latini's time was able to pass for knowledge. Nonetheless the work denotes a mental tendency which was bound to gain strength with every fresh generation. In proof of this assertion we may adduce the case of Latini's great pupil, Dante. For Dante was moved to undertake a secular encyclopedia of his own, *Il Convivio,* though it is true that he never brought it to completion. Perhaps he tired of the effort because, absorbed as a visionary poet in the religious idealism of the Middle Ages, he found an imperfect satisfaction in a prolonged occupation with purely mundane matter. The fact remains, however, that he was extraordinarily responsive to the colorful and palpable sense-world about him, as every reader of his great poem will readily recall. There is certainly no occasion to entertain a doubt as to his strong attachment to the earth on which he stood and from which he drew the solid substance of his verse. Only because he was stirred to his depths by the inexhaustible moods of nature and the striking aspects of men in their characteristic activities did he succeed in incorporating them in his poem with a vivacity and power that have never been surpassed.

And so we come to Francesco Petrarca, the conscious herald of a new day. As his father, a notary and man of law, had been banished from Florence in 1302 along with Dante and the other leading Whites, it happened that when, two years later, Francesco was born, the event took place not in Florence but at Arezzo on the upper Arno. Eagerly seeking employment in order to win a living for himself and his family, the father settled finally at Avignon, which as the new papal capital had become the busiest legal center of Europe. When Francesco was approaching early manhood, he was sent to the University of Bologna to study law and make ready to follow in his father's footsteps. But the youth revolted against the intricate and tedious matter of the civil code and boldly decided to devote his life to literature.[2] Let the immense fame he acquired in his day with the sonnet sequence dedicated to Madonna Laura stand as proof that he persisted in his purpose.

[1] As Latini composed his encyclopedia while living as an exile in France during the brief period of Ghibelline ascendancy in Florence (1260-66), he actually wrote his book in the French tongue under the French equivalent of the Treasure, *Le Trésor*. It was later translated and circulated, not in Latin, let it be observed, but in Italian. The literary use of the vulgar tongue was a feature of the advancing secularization.

[2] In accordance with the procedure followed thus far no attempt will be made to list the immense literature dealing with Petrarch. Absolutely essential to an understanding of his historical service are his Italian poems and his Latin letters. The poems under the collective title of *Il Canzoniere* (The Book of Songs) are accessible in scores of editions. The most convenient edition of the Letters, sometimes with, sometimes without, an Italian translation, has been issued by Fracassetti. A handy selection from Petrarch's correspondence translated into English from the original Latin has been issued by J. H. Robinson and H. W. Rolfe under the title *Petrarch, The First Modern Scholar and Man of Letters*. New York, 1898.

In the opinion of some of his contemporaries he had with the plaintive music of his *Canzoniere* proved himself an even greater poet than his predecessor, Dante, but that is a view which no longer enjoys the support of discerning readers. In fact Petrarch is one of those poets who in the course of the most recent generations have experienced a notable deflation. For the historians as distinct from the critics of literature, however, he continues to be the second figure in the great Italian trinity of Dante, Petrarch, and Boccaccio, and properly enough from their viewpoint they make much of the enormous influence exercised by him upon the subsequent literature not only of Italy but also of all the other countries of Europe.[3]

Engaged in this chapter in tracing the development of Italian thought, we willingly abandon Petrarch, the poet, to give our attention to Petrarch, the humanist. While the secular tendencies, which had for many generations been gathering strength, came to a head in him, they took a form which requires a word of explanation. Contrary to an opinion which still stubbornly maintains its hold, the literature of classical antiquity never ceased to be admired during the Middle Ages, especially in Italy, which always felt itself to be the legitimate heir of Rome in both blood and institutions. Nor was the authority and expressiveness of the Latin language questioned, since it completely ruled the intellectual world by its position at the very center of the medieval curriculum. But there were countervailing influences which tended to nullify this great heritage of speech and letters. For one thing, the content of the pagan authors was so far removed from the ruling norms of medieval thought that it was seen as through a veil and was often grossly misinterpreted; and for another thing, the ascendancy of scholasticism had recently given an additional impulse to the barbarization to which the Latin language had been exposed for centuries by adapting it to the purposes and needs of the scholastic dialectic. If we once more instance Dante, his extraordinary eminence must serve as the excuse for our frequent use of him as a point of reference. Not only was the Florentine poet familiar with the Latin language as the indispensable medium of the dominant scholastic philosophy, but he also had a wide acquaintance with Latin literature. In thinking of the Divine Comedy we immediately recall his boundless admiration for Virgil; however, as the Dante specialists have been at pains to point out, he was familiar not only with the Mantuan bard but with the whole extant body of the Latin authors. And yet, diligently as he read the classics, he read them through Christian medieval glasses and gave them an interpretation far removed from their original meaning.

It was by casting aside the medieval glasses and facing the world with so direct a gaze that he has been called the First Modern Man that Petrarch was able to render both the language and literature of Rome a revolutionary service. A circumstance absolutely determinative of his outlook was that, although educated under the scholastic curriculum, he reacted violently against its dialectical exercises and the domination of the crabbed, abused Latin to which the needs of dialectics had reduced the once proud speech of the former rulers of the world. He wanted the original beauty of the language to be re-

---

[3] For the most recent exposition of Petrarch's wide literary empire see J. B. Fletcher, *Literature of the Italian Renaissance*. New York, 1934.

stored and the ancient authors to be studied for their value as literature. Not content to preach, he set an example by teaching himself to write Latin in at least an approach to the older manner and by probing the Latin authors to their stylistic core. An outstanding feature of the literature of Rome was that it represented an urban civilization which, having freed itself from religious tutelage, faced the world relying on no other support than our five frail senses and our imperfect reason. In the fourteenth century a new urban civilization was arising, and to it, still groping in the dark, the older civilization, as disclosed by its literary remains, became a light and an inspiration. In short, the time was ripe and Petrarch's message found an extraordinary response throughout the length and breadth of Italy. In measure as ever larger bodies of men discarded the old scholastic in favor of the new classical learning, there arose a demand for copies of the Latin writings, which Petrarch was extolling as the fountainhead of wisdom. While the existing works were rapidly multiplied by copyists, a feverish search began for missing works which ancient or recent neglect had permitted to drop from sight. In case the preserved or rediscovered texts of a given work showed different readings these had to be carefully compared in the hope of restoring as far as possible the exact words and turns of phrase the classical master had used. Such labor called for scholarly diligence and critical acumen and laid the foundations of classical philology, an entirely new field of study. Finally, in measure as the enthusiasm elicited by the reglimpsed world of antiquity continued to grow, the Latin literary monuments figured more and more prominently in the education of the young, thereby preparing the way for a revised curriculum which should no longer be dominated by the logical exercises and philosophic teachings of the schoolman.

From its practitioners beginning with Petrarch himself the new literary interests received the name of *studia humaniora,* for which the approximate English equivalent is humanism. Later generations, however, adopted a different emphasis and brought other terms into vogue, such as the revival of learning (or antiquity) and the Renaissance. As they still figure with humanism in all discussions of the period, we have three vaguely synonymous terms which have been subjected to a distressingly loose usage by many generations of writers. Under the circumstances every new writer should feel obliged to make clear the meaning he proposes to attach to each expression. To begin with humanism, after what has just gone before there should not be any doubt as to how it is here employed. We hold it to be a movement of the human mind which began when, following the rise of the towns, the urban intelligentsia slowly turned away from the transcendental values imposed by religion to the more immediately perceptible values of nature and of man. Inaugurated timidly in the twelfth and thirteenth centuries, humanism first arrived at consciousness of itself in the fourteenth century and, holding the scene ever since, has, apart from an occasional setback, steadily widened its empire. For reasons heretofore set forth it happened that, beginning with Petrarch, the mounting secular interests were deflected toward classical literature and led to an eager revival of antiquity. Consequently, since humanism did not become an active force till Petrarch's time, there has been a tendency to equate it with the revival of learning. But that is an ill-advised procedure as the part can never be equal to the whole. In other words, the revival of learning was the particular turn taken under Petrarch's direction by the great secularizing movement which had set in with the communal revolution and which in one form or another has gone on uninterruptedly to our own day. It is therefore the writer's contention that humanism is a force which has been a factor in the civilization of the occident ever since the communal revolution, while the revival of learning is no more than the first conscious phase of humanism dating from the fourteenth century and owing its special character to an inspired leader. It helps to maintain the distinction between the two terms to think of the revival of learning as a literary movement of limited duration and of humanism as a far more inclusive and continuous social and intellectual phenomenon. Accepting this relation to each other of humanism and the revival of learning (or antiquity), we should not find it difficult to differentiate them both from a term of much later origin, the Renaissance. When this gained a foothold in the sixteenth century, it signified exactly what it etymologically denotes, rebirth, and had reference to the rebirth of that antiquity in which everybody gloried. However, in recent generations the word has been assigned a somewhat different use and the practice has come into vogue, to which the present writer wholeheartedly subscribes, of applying the term Renaissance, without the aesthetic and moral connotation it originally carried, to the particular period or phase of western civilization which, beginning with the fourteenth century, marks the close of the Middle Ages and continues for some two or three hundred years. In this book the Renaissance signifies an European epoch with an indeterminate beginning and end.[4]

It might be argued that when humanism, which was developing normally and naturally through the steadily widening experiences of an adventurous society, submitted to the direction of the dead world of antiquity it did itself an injury rather than a service. On the other hand, it is undeniable that for the Italians, who held the lead over the rest of Europe, the submitting, on the widening of their mundane knowledge, to classical leadership had a perfectly logical character, for they had never ceased to consider themselves as the direct descendants of Rome. To them to revive antiquity appeared as nothing other than to re-establish connection with their past, from which they had been unhappily divorced by the Germanic conquest. And by enthusiastically entering under Petrarch's captaincy into the possession of a highly finished and substantially unified body of secular thought, they undoubtedly greatly accelerated their emancipation from the medieval way of life. We have only to throw a glance at the following, the fifteenth, century to discover that Frenchmen, Englishmen, and Germans are still substantially and contentedly medieval, whereas the Italians already possess a strikingly modern appearance. The

---

[4] By far the largest number of books dealing with humanism regard it as identical with the revival of learning and therefore as purely or at least overwhelmingly literary. Such are G. Voigt, *Die Wiederbelebung des Classischen Alterthums*. 3d ed. Berlin, 1893. P. Le Monnier, *Le Quattrocento*. 2 vols. Paris, 1901. J. A. Symonds, *The Revival of Learning* (Vol. II of his *The Renaissance in Italy*). The larger social point of view is taken by J. Burckhardt, *Die Kultur der Renaissance in Italien*. The original edition republished by Kroener, Leipzig, 1922. Two excellent Italian works are: G. Volpi, *Il Trecento*. Milan; V. Rossi, *Il Quattrocento*. Milan.

Italians were therefore greatly transformed by the revival of learning; but what may under no circumstances be overlooked, they also suffered a heavy loss in exchange for whatever it was they gained. To bring this out it will suffice to consider what happened in the single field of Italian letters. So persuaded were the humanists that the Latin language was the only worthy vehicle of literature and so withering was the scorn they entertained for the youthful Italian idiom that its employment for literary purposes was almost completely abandoned. The result was that the light which had risen over Italy in the work of Dante, and to the diffusion of which Petrarch and Boccaccio made each a significant contribution, practically went out with Boccaccio's death not to be rekindled for a hundred years. For this calamity, a calamity of national scope, the Latin literature produced by the humanists could by no stretch of the imagination be called a compensation. While they conscientiously tried their hand at every literary category known to the older tongue, at poetry, philosophy, oratory, and history, their productions proved so feeble a progeny that they but rarely outlived their begetters. By reducing themselves in both form and language to slavish imitators of their great exemplars they sacrificed the freshness and originality, without which no work of art is ever other than a tinkling cymbal.

While there is thus a humanistic debit account which may not be overlooked, we should have no difficulty in agreeing that it is the positive achievement of the humanists which is our real concern. We have already seen that with Petrarch pointing the way their labors took the form of discovering lost classical works, of collecting and editing texts, and of transfusing their minds with the wisdom of the ancients in order to free themselves from the bonds of medieval thought and to widen and enrich their lives. When Petrarch died in 1374, his cause had already made such headway that it was not at all likely that the conservative opposition of the clergy and the schoolmen, active and virulent though it was, would succeed in blocking its advance. The great poet and scholar had been a tireless traveler, and in every community of Italy he visited he left behind him a body of disciples. In our town of Florence his leading spokesman was Giovanni Boccaccio (1313–75). Only a little younger than Petrarch, Boccaccio did not till middle life experience the Petrarcan influence. In his early period he accordingly followed his native bent and became a poet and writer. In his poetry he followed the current romantic and chivalrous tradition not without developing in the shepherd idyll an important literary form of his own; but his great vogue came to him when, on abandoning poetry, he turned to prose and composed the collection of one hundred tales known as the *Decameron*. While some of the tales are indefensibly slippery and immoral, not only are they in their majority free from these taints but they underscore and pointedly commend the sentiments which hold and have ever held society together. Taken as a whole the *Decameron* is an amazingly colorful reproduction of the aspirations, plots, accidents, disasters, and triumphs which have made up human destiny from the beginning of time and well deserves its reputation as an animated, pictorial presentation of the eternal human comedy.

But Boccaccio, too, could not escape the impact of antiquity, especially when, after having already passed the summit of existence, he became personally acquainted with Petrarch and fell completely under his spell. From that moment his mind, which had never aimed at a higher goal than to provide entertainment for his contemporaries, turned away from literature and became absorbed with classical research. From insufficient training as well as from lack of natural aptitude Boccaccio did not succeed in achieving distinction as a humanist; but that he took his new interest seriously is indicated by his compiling two dictionaries dealing respectively with classical geography and classical mythology. To his credit in our eyes, he never, like Petrarch, developed an active hostility toward his native Italian tongue; and, again in honorable distinction from his revered leader, to the end of his days he worshiped the memory of Dante, regarding his famous fellow-townsman as quite the equal of the very best of the fabulous ancients.

By the time of the death of Boccaccio Florence was so well won over to the new learning that the movement continued to rise like a flood through the next three or four generations. And although, as already said, the movement embraced all Italy, it found particular favor and touched its highest mark in the Arno city. The most prominent humanist of the generation following Boccaccio was Coluccio Salutati. He was the type of the pure scholar destined to become more and more common in the years ahead, who regarded philological pursuits as sufficient by themselves and having no need to be justified by parallel literary production. As he had to make a living, he became a notary and in middle life was appointed as head of the Florentine chancellery. This was one of the few permanent positions in the service of the Florentine state, which, as we are aware, was headed by an executive of eight priors and a gonfalonier with a term of office lasting only two months. The chancellor's permanence in the midst of so much flux made him a leading political figure. Among other duties Salutati had charge of the foreign correspondence and made a point of conducting it with the rhetorical elegance of a proud and culture-conscious humanist. It is proof of the spread to the governing circles of all Italy of the new literary mode that the Milanese tyrant, Gian Galeazzo Visconti, once let drop the remark that a state paper composed by Salutati fell into the political scales with the weight of a thousand horsemen.

Salutati lived into the fifteenth century—he died in 1406—and had the pleasure before his end of contributing to an immense extension of the field of learning. Owing to the break during the Middle Ages of the Latin west with the Greek world, the Greek language and literature had completely dropped from view in the countries west of the Adriatic Sea. No less a person than Petrarch had sensed the gravity of this misfortune, but his efforts to remedy it were rendered vain by his inability to find more than a very bungling preceptor of the lost language. Petrarch was hardly dead when a world-event played into the hands of his successors. By their steady pressure on the Byzantine empire and their successful encroachment, beginning with the fourteenth century, on its European territory the Ottoman Turks induced an intermittent migration of scholarly Greeks to Italy, where they were eagerly welcomed. In the year 1396 the Florentines invited one of these refugees, Manuel Chrysoloras, to give public instruction in Greek in their city, and the example set was so generally imitated that before long the Greek language and literature were expounded from academic platforms throughout the land. With the opening of this door such a fresh wave of fervor passed over the whole brotherhood of the humanists that not only did they in a surprisingly short time master the new tongue but before fifty years had passed they had, either through importation by fugitive Greeks or by their own voyages of discovery to Constantinople, possessed themselves of the whole extant body of Greek literature.

Only when the conquest of Greek had been effected was the foundation laid for a really solid structure of classical learning. For Latin literature was, after all, no more than a limited supply of neatly dressed stones compared with the inexhaustible Greek quarry from which it derived. Many quattrocento scholars, without deserting the Latin tradition to which they were patriotically attached, fell strongly under the spell of the older and richer literature. Two such scholars were Leonardo Bruni of Arezzo (1369–1444) and Poggio Bracciolini (1380–1459). Both of them served for a time as Florentine chancellors and both of them acquired an immense reputation through writing histories of Florence by which, because they employed the Latin tongue and slavishly imitated the ancient masters, they were supposed to have revived the glory of Rome. But that is an estimate which has long ago ceased to enlist support. Without the least hesitation we may assert sweepingly of the whole tribe of humanists that as creative artists they are, in spite of their fine passion for letters, a quite negligible quantity. We give them their full due when we declare first, that by rediscovering antiquity they disclosed new horizons for mankind; second, that by wrestling with the details of their discovery they gave birth to an important branch of learning, namely, classical philology; and third, that they discredited the medieval curriculum and gradually replaced it by one which had the classics as its core. The many other claims which enthusiasts have made in their behalf may be regarded as completely lacking in foundation.

Generally speaking, the humanists did not settle in a particular town but preferred to live their lives as wanderers seeking a precarious existence in the houses of sympathetic burghers or at the courts of princes. In spite of this characteristic unsteadiness there was always an assembly of greater and lesser members of the genus at Florence with the result that not merely a small upper class of the studious but a broad section of the well-to-do citizen element became thoroughly indoctrinated with the new learning. To its many other claims to greatness the city in the quattrocento added the distinction of serving as the leading center of the new scholarship.

If we now turn to examine the various factors that co-operated to bring about the primacy of Florence as an intellectual center we may begin with the university. A university, called *studio* by the Italians, was so simple an affair compared with our present-day institutions for advanced studies that a word of explanation is not out of place. All that was needed in the thirteenth and fourteenth centuries to call a university into being was for a government to appropriate an amount of money for a staff of teachers qualified to offer instruction in the recognized professional studies of theology, law, and medicine. For good measure it might also provide a chair of logic or philosophy; and by the fifteenth century it could hardly avoid endowing a professorship dedicated to the new studia humaniora. Till far into this same century libraries were non-existent and even a book, which was a hand-produced and costly object, was a considerable rarity. It is hardly an exaggeration to say that it was his fortunate possession of a few books pertaining to his professional field that raised a man above his fellows and enabled him to qualify as a professor. Under these circumstances the present-day problem of providing an expensive equipment of libraries and laboratories in connection with a university caused no concern. Nor did stately lecture halls have to be erected since the modest classroom facilities demanded by that simple society could be secured by hiring a private house and repartitioning its interior according to immediate needs.

It was not till 1321, by which time universities had become established in many towns throughout Italy, that the Florentine republic first voted to create a university of its own. But the execution was delayed, and when at length a few lecturers had been engaged, owing to heavy pressure on the public purse their appointments were before long permitted again to lapse. Consequently the studio remained a feeble plant for many decades, although it deserves to be remembered that it was during this drab period, in 1373 to be exact, that Giovanni Boccaccio was appointed to a lectureship and that his contract invited him to honor the city's greatest son by expounding the *Divine Comedy*. Not till 1387 did the government resolve to end its trifling with the university idea and make a consistent effort to call an institution into being which might presume to vie with such ancient and celebrated universities as those of Bologna, Padua, and Pavia. While, as might be expected, attention was chiefly directed to providing teachers of reputation for the students of the two practical professions, law and medicine, one or more chairs were reserved for the apostles of the new humanistic learning. By being the first university, which by engaging Manuel Chrysoloras (1396) introduced Greek into the curriculum, the Florentine studio revealed a leaning toward the literary innovators. Never at any time in the past had the Arno town been a stronghold of scholasticism. In the course of the first half of the fifteenth century such elements of learning as the medieval system may have deposited among its citizens were all but completely swept away before the advancing tide of humanistic enlightenment.[5]

It will not be supposed that the university, chiefly concerned with supplying the Florentine state with lawyers, administrators, and physicians, was more than one of many factors in the unusually busy intellectual life of Florence at the end of the fourteenth and the beginning of the fifteenth century. Unquestionably the fires of local thought were mainly fed by the private activities of leading citizens either directly as scholars or indirectly as patrons. If we take the case of Chancellor Salutati, we learn that it was his pleasure to gather about him an eager circle of old and young for the discussion of the educational and philological problems precipitated by the humanistic

[5] Whatever is worth knowing about the studio can be learned from the *Statuti della Università e Studio Fiorentino . . .* pubblicati da A. Gherardi. Vol. VII of *Documenti di Storia Italiana*.

left: GHIBERTI. SACRIFICE OF ABRAHAM FOR THE COMPETITION OF 1401 (ALINARI).
right: BRUNELLESCHI. SACRIFICE OF ABRAHAM FOR THE COMPETITION OF 1401 (ALINARI).

left: DONATELLO. ST. GEORGE. MARBLE. MUSEO NAZIONALE. FORMERLY IN AN OUTER NICHE OF OR SAN MICHELE (ALINARI). *right:* DONATELLO. NICCOLÒ DA UZZANO. COLORED TERRA COTTA. MUSEO NAZIONALE (ALINARI).

DONATELLO. ORGAN LOFT. MUSEO DELL' OPERA DEL DUOMO (ALINARI).

LUCA DELLA ROBBIA. ORGAN LOFT. MUSEO DELL' OPERA DEL DUOMO (ALINARI).

movement. By his resounding success in his office he created such a prejudice among the citizens in favor of the intellectual tendency represented by him that he was followed by a long row of chancellors imbued with the same humanistic doctrine and alike eager to give it currency. Effective propagandist centers as the successive chancellors proved themselves to be, they did not by any means stand alone. While Salutati was still alive and active a cultivated friar of an ancient Florentine family made the Augustinian monastery of Santo Spirito on the left bank of the Arno an unofficial academy of learning. His name was Luigi Marsigli, and although he opened his mind freely to the knowledge propagated by the humanists, he did not let himself be seduced from the Christian faith. In the pleasant cloisters of Santo Spirito Marsigli and a large body of friends and disciples met daily to discourse upon the delights of classical literature, while at the same time they attempted to reconcile the ancient secular wisdom with the inspired declarations of the Fathers. Marsigli died in 1394 but his academy continued to assemble far into the next century, spreading a stimulus that was widely felt and gratefully acknowledged.

By the early quattrocento Florence had become the seat of a veritable republic of letters and to its perpetuation and enlargement the merchants who acted as patrons contributed no less than the scholars. The greatest single service of the patrons was their activity as book-collectors. Books, let us again remind ourselves, still meant manuscripts, and the absence of great libraries of manuscripts had been bemoaned by Petrarch, the brilliant innovator, as the most damaging handicap of scholarship. Accordingly, he employed much of his time and all of his limited resources to assemble as large a library as possible. When he died he left this treasure to the city of Venice on the understanding that it should be made freely accessible to scholars, but the neglect of his heirs permitted the bequest to be dispersed. Boccaccio, too, acquired a modest library which on his death he gave to the monastery of Santo Spirito, but we do not hear that it became the nucleus of a serviceable public collection. Without doubt the most tireless and successful early collector of books was the Florentine merchant, Niccolò Niccoli (d. 1437). He was not a leading merchant, and when he retired from business in order to devote himself exclusively to his literary hobby, he commanded no more than a modest competence. Had he not been at pains to acquire a fine handwriting with which to produce his own books, he would never have been able to assemble the eight hundred volumes in his possession on his demise. Even so, he died a bankrupt, and his collection would have been scattered to pay his debts, had not a great merchant-prince come to the rescue. Niccoli belonged to the circle of the much younger Cosimo de' Medici, who already at Niccoli's death had become the secret ruler of Florence. Cosimo is deservedly celebrated as the greatest patron not only of letters but also of the Fine Arts of his age. By satisfying his friend Niccoli's debts he acquired title to his books and by depositing them in a beautiful building, incorporated in the monastery of San Marco and erected at his expense, he created what was probably the first broadly serviceable public library of modern times. Besides steadily increasing the San Marco collection by judicious purchases, the lordly Cosimo assembled another, a second, library which he lodged in the monastery under Fiesole known as La Badia.[6] When Pope Nicholas V (1447–55) who, although not a citizen of Florence, had spent many years of his life on the Arno, mounted the papal throne, he at once leapt to the front as a patron and collector. Not only did he employ the most eminent humanists to translate the Greek masters into Latin and pay them lavishly for their services but he also brought together what was easily the largest library of medieval and classical authors of the contemporary world. Although Nicholas did not live to carry out his plan of housing his collection in an appropriate structure, he did not labor in vain as his cherished manuscripts constitute the nucleus of the present great Vatican library.[7] Stimulated by the example of Cosimo and Nicholas many princes of Italy, both secular and ecclesiastical, collected libraries according to their means. In the story of the advance of scholarship the beginning made in the quattrocento toward the creation of great repositories of books holds a place of hardly to be exaggerated importance.

As the Florentine humanism of the second half of the fifteenth century will be treated in a later chapter, we shall close this brief sketch of early humanism by referring to a significant change very generally noticeable in humanist mentality by, let us say, the year 1450. It is characteristic of men's thoughts that they take their color from the element in which they are steeped. The enthusiasts of antiquity are no exception to the rule; and after they had for several generations saturated themselves in classical paganism it was inevitable that they should be shaken in their devotion to the Christian faith. When Petrarch launched the new learning he was not visited by any suspicion of this possibility. In spite of his classical enthusiasm, he was and remained an earnest Christian believer and an obedient son of Mother church. In fact there persisted in him a strong medieval vein and he was consequently often visited by compunctions touching the worldly implications of his beloved literary studies. The incident of his ascent of Mont Ventoux, related in one of his own letters,[8] is well known. He made the ascent for the very unmedieval reason of mere pleasure and, arrived at the top, he indulged himself in an ecstasy of classical memories by recalling Livy's description of Hannibal's crossing of the Alps. Then suddenly his exultation died, as he bethought himself of the vanity of his undertaking, and drawing St. Augustine's *Confessions* from his pocket, he gave not another glance to the vast and glorious prospect under his feet as he pored over the dark warnings of his ghostly companion. Boccaccio, too, in spite of the very worldly matter of his *Decameron* became not less, but actually more, devoted to the faith of his fathers with his advancing years. By the early fifteenth century, however, we encounter evidence of the spread of religious indifference which in the course of another genera-

---

[6] Counting the collection Cosimo made for his private residence, we may even think of him as the founder of three libraries.

[7] According to the book-dealer Vespasiano da Bisticci, the library of Pope Nicholas reached the extraordinary figure of five thousand volumes. This same well-informed and garrulous old gentleman has left us in his *Vite di Uomini Illustri del Secolo XV* a very precious record of the fun, envy, and excitement experienced by such men as Niccolò Niccoli, Cosimo de' Medici, and Nicholas V in connection with the game of book-collection at a time when a book was a hand-written treasure.

[8] Robinson and Rolfe, *Petrarch*, pp. 307 ff.

tion frequently took the form of an active skepticism. At its peak it manifested itself as a rejection of the truth of revelation in favor of a truth to
be attained by our unaided natural endowment of sense and intellect. It would
be an exaggeration to charge the whole body of humanists with turning
skeptic in the course of the fifteenth century. Some people always managed
to make Petrarch's compromise and to live in two worlds at once, in the
world of revelation and the world of private judgment. But there is no denying that the tendency toward skepticism gained ground and that in a few
extreme instances it ended in outright agnosticism.

In Petrarch's day the Inquisition would have had a word, and a loaded
word, to say about so sharp a departure from the beaten path. However, in
the course of the fifteenth century this grim institution lost both its vigor and
its teeth. That, too, was an effect of the new learning, for classical antiquity
had succeeded in enlisting the favor of a large section of the clergy, especially
of the great prelates, including a generous number of cardinals and popes.
We have heard of the activity of Pope Nicholas V which was so little of an
exceptional order that a number of ecclesiastical princes competed with him
as patrons of letters and collectors of classical manuscripts. It followed from
these secular pursuits that Rome became a nursery of humanistic scholarship,
which after Nicholas's time yielded in no respect to Florence. Who under
these circumstances will wonder that the Inquisition fell into general disuse
and that the right of free opinion exercised by the neo-pagans remained un-
rebuked by the institution which during the previous two hundred years
had regarded the defense of orthodoxy as its real reason for existence? To
turn from the trecento to the quattrocento is to face an entirely different
intellectual landscape. For, at least as far as the upper classes of the Italian
peninsula are concerned, the Middle Ages have passed away and we are
gazing at the modern world.

XIX. The Fine Arts: The First or Medieval Phase

AS THE purely ancillary character of the chapters of this book dealing with Florentine culture has already been set forth, it will not be necessary to preface the following story of the Fine Arts with another declaration of purpose. Since what by long-established usage passes under the name of the Fine Arts are the three sister-skills of architecture, sculpture, and painting, we would begin our presentation of the field of art with architecture, were it not that we had found it convenient to recount the building history of medieval Florence in the chapter in which we accepted the guidance of that most excellent of ciceroni, Giovanni Villani.[1] Villani was the kind of intelligent and patriotic burgher who in his capacity of chronicler and diarist would not fail to take proud note of every new fine structure that arose in his day. On the other hand, he would be much less attentive to the more concealed and intimate work of the sculptor and painter, and accordingly we find that he made very little mention of it in his book. It is therefore sculpture and painting that will be treated in this chapter, and we shall trace the development of each in turn through the Middle Ages to the threshold of the great change marked by the coming of humanism and the revival of antiquity.

Just as Florence, a backward inland town during the early generations of the communal movement, lagged behind maritime Pisa in political and economic development, so also it was outstripped by its neighbor on the lower Arno in the practice of the arts. True, the church of San Miniato, begun in 1018, points to an early artistic activity at Florence; but unfortunately San Miniato remained an isolated achievement and cannot in regard to the influence it exercised remotely vie with the great cathedral of which the Pisans laid the foundation stone in the year 1062. With this structure they created an ecclesiastical type which was admired and imitated over a large area of Tuscany. In the following century they raised the neighboring structure of the baptistery, and with these two handsome buildings completed or approaching completion, the desire made itself felt to enrich them with ornament and figure work. Thus was supplied the impulse which led to a local, a Pisan, school of sculpture. While the earliest work of the native artists, examples of which still adorn the cathedral façade, was very crude, a gradual improvement may be observed in the later work on the façade till suddenly, a little past the middle of the thirteenth century, a giant forward step was taken by

[1] Chap. XV.

326

a man of genius, Niccolò Pisano. It was in the year 1260 that Niccolò completed his famous pulpit for the Pisan baptistery. In the six scenes in relief which constitute the sides of the hexagonal structure he returned to the forms and costumes of antiquity, as he had become acquainted with them on certain late Roman sarcophagi which had outlived the storms of the migrations and which may still be seen at Pisa at the present day. With his pulpit Niccolò proclaimed the greatness of classical art, of a very inferior and decadent classical art it is true, because the inferior and decadent phase was the only one to which through the above-mentioned sarcophagi he had access. Nonetheless he turned his face resolutely to the past, and if his enthusiasm had taken general hold the rinascimento might have captured the Fine Arts a century and more before it did. But the time was not ripe and Niccolò's own son, Giovanni (1250?–1328), reacted violently against his father's tendencies. The period was, after all, the Middle Ages, when men were swayed by strong religious emotion and were not likely to be deeply impressed with a purely imitative classic calm. Giovanni Pisano therefore developed an animated subjective art, which derived its inspiration from contemporary French rather than from ancient Roman models, and which was essentially Gothic in spirit. So greatly did this Gothic art of Giovanni's appeal to his age that through him and his numerous followers it established its empire over a large part of Tuscany and Lombardy.

It was the vogue given to sculpture by the Pisan school that first called sculpture to life in Florence. Although the Florentines possessed in their baptistery of San Giovanni a noble monument of essentially classical design, even if it cannot be indisputably proved to have been erected in the classical period, and although as early as the eleventh century they had with San Miniato revived ecclesiastical construction of the Christian basilican type, they had gone no farther on the road of decoration than to supply the façade of these two buildings with a marble incrustation of interesting, if simple, pattern. Figure work, manifestly a higher form of sculptural invention than abstract ornament, remained for a long time outside the range of their ambition. Not till the first quarter of the thirteenth century do we come upon a considerable piece of figured sculpture of distinctly Florentine provenience. It is the pulpit which once adorned the vanished temple of San Piero Scheraggio and which is now set up in the small suburban church of San Leonardo in Arcetri outside Porta San Giorgio. The pulpit is inclosed by a number of panels in high relief, the human figures of which, though of extremely crude workmanship, are occasionally assembled into a naïvely effective composition. Granting that here was a promising beginning, the fact remains that the art continued to languish for another hundred years, when at last the Pisan torch lit a native fire and Florentine sculpture came not alone to life but arrived immediately at manhood with the magnificent bronze doors which between 1330 and 1336 Andrea Pisano fashioned for the baptistery.[2]

While the name of this artist serves to recall his Pisan origin, he developed

---

[2] On the beginnings of sculpture in Tuscany (and of architecture as well) see E. W. Anthony, *Early Florentine Architecture and Decoration.* Cambridge (Mass.), 1927.

a sculptural language which is so different from that of his master, Giovanni Pisano, that we may accept him as marking the advent of a genuine Florentine style. The most reasonable explanation of the very individual manner developed by Andrea Pisano is that, summoned to Florence to undertake a monumental work, he fell under the influence of Giotto, one of the greatest innovators of all time and predominantly, although by no means exclusively, active as a painter. By his noble types of men and women, his simple and dramatic compositions, and his unpaltering honesty of spirit, Giotto had acquired an authority in the art world of the first third of the trecento which established him as its unquestioned leader. By the best of all evidence, the evidence of his work, it is clear that Andrea passed under Giotto's spell. In addition to eight single figures, representative of the theological and moral virtues, the baptistery gate exhibits in relief twenty scenes from the life of St. John. The simplicity and directness of both figures and scenes point unerringly to Giotto, although the compositions would never have attained their high measure of expressiveness if Andrea had not been a master in his own right. In the free movement of the human body in much of this work the artist even scored an advance over the art of Giotto, who, pursuing an ideal of static dignity, only rarely strove to impress movement on his figures.

Andrea was also employed in Florence in connection with the sculptures that adorn the base of Giotto's campanile. He worked on them in such intimate collaboration with the great master that the exact share of each in the completed work will never be determined. From evidences of style it would seem probable that the seven panels on the west face of the campanile are mainly by the hand of Giotto. The series begins with the creation of Adam and continues with the creation of Eve and with the Fall; in this, the third panel, Adam and Eve are delving and spinning according to the curse they have drawn on their heads. On this strictly Christian and orthodox introduction to human history there succeeds in a continuous band inclosing the four sides of the tower a fascinating record of the inventions and occupations by which the descendants of our first parents forced the stubborn earth to yield them a satisfying living. However, as only three sides were finished in Giotto's and Andrea's time, the panels of the fourth, which is the northern, face remained blank until filled in a hundred years later by Luca della Robbia, an artist of an entirely different inspiration.

Together with the three introductory panels, but without those of Luca della Robbia, the reliefs are twenty-one in number and tell with extraordinary skill the heartening tale of how man, who for his disobedience had been cast forth from paradise into a hostile world, rose to a new and self-earned dignity by his restless energy and amazing ingenuity. What is here offered is in sum a picture-book of civilization, and not only is it the earliest work of its kind but as a statement of man's achievements in the language of a graphic art it has perhaps not been excelled down to our time. We can hardly go astray if we attribute this broad and eminently pictorial vision of man's upward journey to the master artist, Giotto. But if he was responsible for the plan, it is more than likely that he left the execution of the individual panels, with the possible exception of the first six or seven, to the younger craftsman who with his baptistery gate had proved himself a worthy associate.[3]

Following this first creative burst of energy there was a lull. Not that sculpture failed to receive due recognition from the church, the state, and occasional private patrons, or that there was a dearth of plastic workers desirous of winning honor by following the path blazed by the two great masterpieces, the bronze gate of the baptistery and the marble story-book strung about the base of Giotto's campanile. The cathedral, Santa Croce, Santa Maria Novella, and the smaller houses of worship which abounded in the town were at this time still far from that state of adornment in which they presented themselves to view at a later age. Consequently their façades and portals required statues commemorative of the saints, while the bare interiors needed to be furnished with carved stone altars, pulpits, and holy water fountains. In the decades following Andrea Pisano, work of this kind was produced in considerable quantity, to which should be added a funeral monument characteristic of the time, consisting of a marble sarcophagus adorned with figures of the saints and presenting, amidst a wealth of Gothic ornament, the image of the deceased asleep upon the tomb. Serving in most instances as the coffin of some great ecclesiastical dignitary, such a monument was usually placed high above the ground along the wall of aisle or transept. Examples of all these kinds of work can still be seen in the Florentine churches and the names of their makers can in practically every case be identified. But almost without exception they suffer from a mortal flaw in that they are the uninspired handiwork of mere craftsmen. The decades immediately following Giotto and Andrea might be dismissed by us without another word, were it not that one sculptor, deserting the common herd, proved that he was a man and artist.

This exceptional individual was Andrea Orcagna (active 1344–68). Like the other artists of his time he by no means limited himself to sculpture, but it is as a sculptor that we involuntarily think of him by reason of his famous tabernacle of Or San Michele. Wrought as a shrine for an exquisite panel painting of the Madonna by Bernardo Daddi, it engrossed Orcagna's heart and soul to such an extent and for so many years that it became in his hands one of the most unusual combinations of jewel-like inlay and decoration with sculpture in the round and in relief within the whole range of Italian art. It could not be more unfortunately placed than it is at present, for, owing to the walling up of the windows of Or San Michele, it is now practically invisible except with the aid of artificial illumination. In its plan and proportions as well as in its details the tabernacle is a thoroughly Gothic monument and proves that Orcagna was in sympathy with the tradition of northern art as represented by Giovanni Pisano and his successors. But like all Florentines from the first moment that Gothic gained a foothold in their territory, he took of the importation only what he could use without injury to the genius

---

[3] The fundamental history of Italian art is still Vasari's *Lives,* accessible in many English translations. The standard Italian edition is by Gaetano Milanesi. The main facts of the medieval phase of Italian art, and of the subsequent phases as well, are obtainable in innumerable handbooks, which need not be listed here. We shall limit ourselves in the footnotes to the mention of an occasional special work of outstanding worth.

of his race. To this he remained inalterably attached, for his love of fine ornament patterned in many colors goes back to the baptistery and San Miniato,
while in his figure work he is the faithful follower of that most pungent and
solid of Florentines, Giotto. By their gravity and poise the prophets and
apostles, who either as full or half-figures adorn the shrine, proclaim their
relationship to that master; but as they have also a novel flavor of realism
and are more carefully individualized than is usually the case with Giotto's
more generalized men and women, they announce that Orcagna was an independent artist, who without denying his indebtedness to his forerunners
stood firmly on his own feet. The sculptor reached his highest level in some
of the scenes in relief from the life of the Virgin, and in the last and crowning
episode he fairly surpassed himself. This is in two related sections. Below we
have the death of Mary surrounded by the mourning apostles, while above
she is seen already floating in the sky, lifted upward by attending angels. By
reason of its movement, its unity, and fine reserve this composition takes rank
as one of the great achievements of the trecento.

The single figure of Orcagna cannot alter the impression that Florentine
sculpture was becoming enfeebled in the latter half of the fourteenth century
and that it was doomed unless it managed to tap a fresh source of inspiration.
And this is the very thing it succeeded in doing, thereby inaugurating its second
or quattrocento phase. The event is closely tied up with the contemporary
revolution which we have agreed to call humanism, and which actually and
simply was humanism until Petrarch and his followers gave it the narrower
significance of a revival of ancient learning. As, toward the close of the trecento, the outlook of the upper and learned classes was being rapidly transformed, it was inevitable that the artists should be caught by the prevailing
thought currents and be revolutionized in their turn. Thus it happened that,
beginning about 1400, the architects, sculptors, and painters shed their old
and acquired a new, or at least a partially new, mentality. The man who was
chiefly instrumental in mediating the change so far as sculpture is concerned
was Donatello (1386–1466). Than this nothing more fortunate could have
happened, for while Donatello became fascinated by the art of the ancients
and to develop his skill diligently copied the classical remains still relatively
rare in his day because buried in the ground, even more than to the ancients
he was drawn to nature itself. Seeking renewal for his art by every available
path, by some profound instinct which defies analysis he turned most avidly
to the earth and its inhabitants. In this way, instead of leading sculpture up
the blind alley of antiquity, he conducted it into fresh pastures and made its
quattrocento phase one of the glories of his town and country.

In turning, next, to painting we approach the art which the Florentines
found peculiarly suited to their genius and in which their contribution was
so significant that it has largely determined the whole subsequent course of
European expression in design and color. Their starting-point was the later
Greek or Byzantine practice of the art. In the eleventh and twelfth centuries
there had been a revival of painting at Constantinople, and the religious altar
pieces which issued from this movement had in many instances found their
way to Italy. Occasionally a Greek artist had even established direct touch

with his western patrons by setting up his shop at Rome or Venice or some other rising commune. In the course of time native-born Italians took up the Greek practice, thereby giving birth to a considerable number of local schools dominated in varying degree by the Byzantine manner. One such school arose in Florence and one of its earliest adepts was a certain Cimabue. A veritable man of flesh and blood in his time, he has for us dwindled to a rather ghostly figure since hardly a single work exists in which present-day experts agree in recognizing his hand. However, the Cimabue problem does not greatly concern the general student, since the real fountainhead of Florentine painting was Cimabue's pupil, Giotto. Of Giotto we luckily still possess a large body of authentic works enabling us to detect exactly what the elements were he introduced into the art and which his contemporaries hailed as novel and quickening beyond compare.[4]

In spite of there having come down to us much work by Giotto's hand, and in spite of the positively bewildering amount of painting by his trecento successors still extant in churches and museums, we are met with a difficulty in attempting to enjoy and understand the master and his followers which it is well to face at once. With very few exceptions the handiwork of all this group of artists has suffered and continues to suffer such grave impairment that we may speak of it as a body of remains slowly crumbling to complete ruin. While the accidents of time coupled with human neglect and maltreatment are largely responsible for this lamentable state of affairs, it has been brought about also by the technical processes under which the work was produced. These are materially and aesthetically so important that without a measure of acquaintance with them the fourteenth-century artists and their works will always remain outside our comprehension. Like everything else about early painting the technical processes go back to the Byzantines and fall under the two heads of wall (or fresco) and panel painting. In either case the colors were carried in a medium of yolk of egg mixed with water, that is, as the saying went, they were "tempered" by these ingredients to the desired consistency. Commonly called tempera, the indicated method of color preparation was usual for both techniques. In every other respect, however, wall painting and panel painting were very different, although the same artist would and usually did practice both methods.

On being assigned to the wall of a church or a convent the wall painter encountered as his immediate task the preparation of the surface with the best and smoothest kind of plaster available. At the same time he set about drawing his designs in bare outline on large sheets of paper and in charcoal, making careful measurements in order that they might fit exactly into the space at his disposal. When he had transferred his outlined designs to the wall by tracing, and then, as his first step in color, had underpainted all the figures in shaded monochrome, he was ready for the crucial operation which was to cover with a fresh coat of thin lime plaster just so much of his design

[4] Berenson, The Florentine Painters of the Renaissance. 3d ed. New York, 1909. C. Carra, Giotto: 192 Riproduzioni in Fototipia. Rome, 1924. F. J. Mather, A History of Italian Painting. New York, 1923.

Attention should be called to a monumental work on Florentine painting now in course of preparation. R. Offner, A Corpus of Florentine Painting. Planned in 30 volumes.

as he thought he could finish coloring in a single day. The fresh paint fusing with the wet lime dried before the next morning, when the artist would repeat the process with the adjoining section. It was this application of paint to a fresh coat of lime which gave the method its name of fresco or, more correctly, of *al fresco* painting. Fresco called for good drawing, clear color, and a resolute attack, and, whenever it was successfully employed, resulted in a strikingly monumental style of work. Michelangelo, who was among the last Florentine painters successfully to practice fresco and who, putting aside the oil method popular in his day, chose it as his medium for the famous ceiling of the Sistine Chapel, expressed his admiration for it by saying that it made possible the kind of painting alone worthy of men.

Panel painting was painting on a wooden board overlaid with an absorptive ground of plaster of Paris and was on a smaller scale than fresco and much more delicate. It was concerned largely with altar pieces, which were to be made as luminous as possible by presenting a saint or a group of saints with stamped gold aureoles and in raiments of various colors projected against a background of shining gold. The first step following the tracing of the design upon the panel consisted in underpainting the figures in a greenish monotone. Next, the draperies were brought to the desired color key and, last of all, the heads and hands were delicately enameled by means of a succession of thin coats of white and red. As it was the heads and hands that were intended particularly to draw the eyes of the spectators, all other features were treated as subordinate. The artist entertained no desire to be realistic in any sense whatever of that very elastic term. It sufficed him that the panel should exhibit one or more of the accredited inhabitants of heaven and that it should shine with the color and light of a jewel. So painstaking and delicate was panel painting that it had many of the qualities of miniature.[5]

Now while both these techniques yielded paintings of a high degree of durability, they were not proof against all the vicissitudes of nature and of chance. As for wall paintings, they will begin to flake when exposed to humidity, while the fine enamel finish, the glory of the altar pieces, will vanish under gradually accumulating dust and grime. As soon as in the past ages such physical deterioration manifested itself in either kind of work, the question arose as to how it was to be met. The issue presented itself to men, who, belonging to a later period, had little or no just appreciation of the work of the earlier generation. Whatever they might do under the altered standards of taste was therefore almost certain to be wrong. Let what happened to the Giotto frescos of the Bardi and Peruzzi chapels at Santa Croce, frescos probably as great as any in the world, serve for illustration. Having through persistent flaking lost much of what constituted pictorial beauty according to the canons of eighteenth-century art, they were in that century quietly and unceremoniously buried under an obliterating coat of whitewash. On being rediscovered toward the middle of the nineteenth century, an almost worse barbarism was committed, for they were "restored" by two daubers who

---

[5] For the technical processes the great authority is the painter Cennino Cennini, who lived at the end of the trecento and the beginning of the quattrocento. His work is available in English under the title: *The Book of the Art of Cennino Cennini*. Translated from the Italian with notes on Medieval Art Methods by Christiana J. Herringham. London, 1922.

wantonly repainted large sections, and especially the faces, according to their private pitiful standards of what constitutes good painting. As for the delicate panels, most of them now torn from the altars for which they were intended and herded in cold, uncongenial museums, they have so often had the dirt and soot scraped off them by insensitive hands that not only has the fine surface enamel very generally disappeared but in many instances hardly more is left than the original green underpainting turned black by time and human abuse.

With these vicissitudes in mind we are prepared to understand why it is that the novice taking up Giotto for the first time is likely to be disappointed. However, he will reveal himself as impervious to the message of painting or of any other art, should he not, by repeatedly returning to what, after all, still are radiant and inspiring remains, discover for himself the superb merits of this genius. Coming, as he did, at the beginning of the development of painting, Giotto (1270?–1337) lacked much of the purely technical ability that was afterward acquired by those who trod in his footsteps. He knew nothing of anatomy or perspective and very little of movement. Deprived of these valuable resources, he undertook to communicate what he had to say by the exclusive means of the draped human figure. It was by reason of this all-important decision of its founder that Florentine painting became essentially a figure art. Moreover, as the subject matter presented by Giotto was exclusively religious, he may at least in part be charged with having brought it about that Florentine painting became and for a long time to come remained a figure art with an essentially religious import. Giotto's world is a world of very humanly conceived saints, who possess an unmatched dignity and go with the greatest gravity about their saintly concerns. In depicting them in a particular attitude or engaged in a particular act he aimed to give the essence of the situation stripped of all useless side issues and accessories. This is the reason why we never cease to be impressed with his simplicity and sincerity, as it also explains the dramatic concentration of his compositions. With such unerring judgment did he seize upon the significant elements of the event to be depicted that we are convinced that precisely as he presented it and in no other conceivable manner must it have taken place.

Giotto's fame was so great that he had many patrons, at whose orders he worked in widely separated sections of Italy. His chief fresco series are to be found in certain churches at Padua, Assisi, and Florence. As any one work of his, carefully examined, will serve as a concrete instance of his qualities, we may turn for illumination touching his manner to the Peruzzi chapel at Santa Croce, where at the summit of his powers he painted on one wall scenes from the life of St. John the Baptist and on the opposite wall scenes from the life of the Baptist's namesake, the Evangelist. It is these frescos to which we referred as having experienced so miraculous a resurrection almost a century ago. In spite of the damage done by the unsympathetic restorer, the outlines of the figures are unimpaired and patches of the original color are still intact. If we turn to the wall at the right hand dedicated to St. John the Evangelist, we have two scenes, one above the other, showing respectively the raising by John of Drusiana and John's death and ascension to heaven. They are both magnificent compositions giving the essence of the event so directly and succinctly that there is nothing to be added. Attempted explanation becomes prattle and impertinence. John and the other dramatis personae are intensely human. But while they have unmistakably the quality of earthborn folk, they at the same time breathe an earnestness and solemnity that leaves no doubt in our mind that we have entered the realm of the religious sanctities. If Giotto was an artist with a definite aesthetic endowment placing him in the front rank of the artists of all ages, he never permits us to forget that he lived by the light of faith and that he was not a secular but a religious painter.

Giotto so overwhelmed his Florentine contemporaries that with few exceptions they all flocked to his banner and tried to work in his style; and when his contemporaries had passed from the scene, a second and a third generation of artists continued to copy his types and rethink his thoughts. Being so manifestly his followers, the painters of the later trecento have been grouped together under the name of Giotteschi; and if there is a touch of contempt in the designation, it is not unmerited. On the other hand, it is a mistake to conceive of the Giotteschi as a completely unindividualized mass of lifeless imitators. There were men of talent among them, like Giotto's favorite pupil, Taddeo Gaddi; and as one decade after another of the trecento slipped away, certain novel features began to appear among the men who to the casual eye seem to constitute just a docile following. To mention but a single matter: the austere, idealistic human types of Giotto began to recede in favor of figures closer to actual life. In itself such realism was neither good nor bad, but insofar as it indicated emancipation from blind authoritarianism, it may be regarded as the promise of a richer productivity. However, on the whole, the Giotteschi cannot be thought of other than as copyists. Undoubtedly they have all the weaknesses of copyists, of which by far the worst is that they do not understand what they copy. His followers picked up the externals of Giotto's art without comprehending its spirit with the result that their work falls unescapably under the curse of mediocrity.

But, as already said, these were exceptions to the rule, and one at least of the exceptional men must come in for a word, especially as we have already had occasion to note his contribution to sculpture. As a matter of fact Andrea Orcagna (d. 1368) was chiefly a painter, although, according to the custom of his age, he practiced many of the sister-arts of painting whenever the occasion arose to do so. We see him at his best as a painter in the Strozzi chapel at Santa Maria Novella. All the work here is by his hand, not only the altar piece in the middle exhibiting Christ with a number of saints, but also the two frescos of hell and heaven on the right and left wall respectively. While, owing to ruthless cleaning, the altar piece has lost much of its original luster, it is still a beautiful panel nobly and religiously conceived. The hell we will pass over as something which, however frequently attempted, has always defied pictorial presentation. But turn to the heaven and you will encounter a great, a breath-taking revelation! Its injury through restoration is immense, especially by reason of the modern artist's attempt to sweeten the faces of the women and to smooth out the wrinkles of the men. Notwithstanding this corruption, in its energy, its rhythmic balance, and its monumental proportions the composition is one of the exultant visions left us by the Middle Ages.

Lacking new impulses, Florentine painting would have perished of inanition if, a little past the year 1400, it had not responded to the new energy radiated by the humanistic movement. What happened to the art of painting constitutes a close parallel to the contemporary renovation of sculpture even to the point of the leadership furnished by a surpassing genius. Admitting that there was a blind groping on the part of many painters to find a new means of expression, not till Masaccio did his Carmine frescos around 1426 was the path to be taken indicated in clear and unambiguous terms. Masaccio turned for inspiration to the fresh life and knowledge of his time and thereby inaugurated the quattrocento phase of painting. As no classical painting had survived to be admired and imitated, he was influenced by antiquity even less than the sculptor Donatello. No lover of originality will doubt that this was a fortunate circumstance since it obliged the quattrocento painters to carry their art forward by the exercise of their own strength.

With a new day dawning for sculpture and painting it was impossible for architecture not to feel in its turn the call for renewal. Between 1255, when the palace of the people, now called the Bargello, was projected, and 1389, when the city celebrated the completion of the loggia of the priors, Florence had acquired those churches and public buildings which to a very large extent determine its physical character to this day. They possess stylistically so strong a kinship and reveal so great a unity of spirit that we are justified to speak of them as a distinctly native product. However, even a superficial analysis will at once show that their underlying principles, far from being indigenous to Florence, were widely distributed over Italy and all western Europe. The historic fact is that the earliest builders of the city drew upon the general body of architectural information that passed under the name of Romanesque, and that their successors from about the time of Arnolfo di Cambio (active around 1300) cautiously took over some of the features of the northern art, commonly called Gothic. Their attachment to Gothic or, we should perhaps say, their understanding of it was so incomplete that every structure they erected in what passes as the Gothic manner exhibits a substantial Romanesque core. In this often overlooked circumstance we have the explanation of how it came about that, whether they are early or late, the medieval structures of the town, fundamentally considered, carry an identical imprint.

As soon as the revival of antiquity became the passion of the Florentine learned and professional classes, the very feeble dominion that the foreign importation called Gothic had exercised in the town came to an abrupt end. The new generation reverted to the older, never quite forgotten Romanesque until, carried farther and farther back by its classical enthusiasm, it directed its attention to the remains of Roman architecture, of which Romanesque was, after all, no more than a barbarous corruption. By the early fifteenth century it was only necessary for a born leader to appear to establish architecture on a new and classical foundation. This leader was Filippo Brunelleschi (1379–1446), and from him dates the quattrocento phase of Florentine building. In Brunelleschi, Donatello, and Masaccio we have the three men under whose inspiration the Fine Arts were born again and came to a second and astonishing flowering.

XX. The Triumphant Oligarchy (1382–1434)

W E LEARNED in the chapter dealing with Florentine political developments in the decades leading up to 1382 how the democratic movement was defeated by uncompromising oligarchical hostility, by paralyzing cross-currents among its own supporters, and by the absence of anything even remotely resembling honest, courageous, and authoritative leadership. But even had the democracy which went down to defeat in 1382 been more compact and unified, it could not have survived for long in the Italy which was taking shape in the fourteenth century, for the anarchy of the innumerable small tyrants, which already in the last years of Dante's life had stood out as the leading aspect of the peninsula, was being gradually replaced by the absolutism of a few large states, which based their power on the successful absorption of their weaker neighbors. The outstanding development of this character was the Milan of the Visconti family. The mounting power of the Milanese state moved the sea city, Venice, to seek protection against a possible attack from the west by means of a line of outposts on the mainland. Become thus a contender for land power, the Venetian commonwealth, which under the name of a republic was organized into one of the tightest oligarchies recorded in history, had projected itself as an important and permanent factor into the Italian political system. The oldest large-scale polity of the peninsula was the kingdom of Naples. Following the death of King Robert I in 1343, it was frequently threatened with dissolution owing to fatal divisions among the members of the ruling dynasty. Grave difficulties notwithstanding, the southern kingdom never ceased to figure prominently in the Italian parallelogram of forces. Although the papal dominion had presented itself to view during the medieval period as a mere mass of *disjecta membra,* a little past the middle of the fourteenth century the political genius of Cardinal Albornoz had shown that the scattered elements could be fused into a unified structure; and while we must admit that almost as soon as that able churchman's hand had been removed from his creation it had again collapsed, the proof had been furnished that a great papal state in the heart of the peninsula was a political feasibility and would henceforth have to be reckoned with.

It was in the midst of a chaos from which the above-mentioned four states, Milan, Venice, Naples, and the State of the Church, were slowly disengaging themselves that Florence raised its head with the plan of reaching the approximate level of these neighbors by making Tuscany the basis of its power. It was a program every whit as expansionist as that of the rival states, two of which lay to the north of Florence and two to the south. But that to carry out a program requiring the application of an unwavering resolution was an enterprise particularly suited to the nature of a democracy was very doubtful. For a democracy, driven as it invariably is by opposing winds of opinion, generally follows an impulsive, zigzag course. Frequently canceling today what it enacted yesterday, it exhibits a capriciousness hopelessly incompatible with the steady pursuit of a policy of conquest. On conquest, however, all Florentine classes alike had set their hearts, although the merchant class with its far-flung commercial interests may be considered to have originated the program. The merchants were probably right in thinking that with their greater compactness they could carry the town to its goal much more surely than the ignorant, disputatious masses. This explains why it was that, as soon as by the victory of 1382 they had re-established their power, they prosecuted with a much greater energy than their democratic predecessors had shown the territorial policy, which with a somewhat different emphasis the whole population, regardless of economic status, eagerly indorsed.

In the military conditions of the age lay another reason for conceding a higher probability of successful conquest to an oligarchic than to a democratic system. War was conducted by mercenary troops which by the second half of the trecento had greatly improved their organization. The mercenaries, held permanently together under condottieri enjoying their confidence, were willing to serve any employer capable of meeting their wage bill. Nonetheless it was natural that they should put more trust in the spokesmen of a system possessed of a certain promise of permanence than in the representatives of an ever-shifting democratic ruling group. A recent experience through which Florence had gone will confirm the argument. During the War of the Eight Saints the most famous condottiere of his day, the Englishman John Hawkwood, had not hesitated to sell his services to the democratic government then in power; but that he had no sympathy for his employers' system is proved by the support he gave the oligarchic plotters in connection with their successful revolution. In the critical month of January of the year 1382 this Giovanni Acuto, as the Italians called him, was present in Florence in the pay of the government. However, when the rising occurred, instead of putting himself behind the democracy to which he was under contract, he backed the opposition and was a factor in its victory. From that day onward Hawkwood served the oligarchy with such unusual devotion that there was established a bond of peculiar intimacy between it and him.[1] In sign thereof he was accorded the rare favor of Florentine citizenship together with a pension for life and exemption from taxation; and when he died in 1394 the grateful government not only honored him with a splendid funeral at public expense, but also commemorated his services by having him painted on the wall of the inner façade of the cathedral mounted on horseback in full panoply of war. Half a century later the same honor was accorded to another condottiere, Niccolò da Tolentino. To this day these two hireling soldiers proudly sit their war steeds on the entrance wall of the great central temple of the city, recalling to the reflective visitor one of the

[1] J. Temple-Leader and G. Marcotti, *Sir John Hawkwood: Story of a Condottiere*. London, 1889.

most curious perversions of the sentiment of patriotism recorded in history.

A much-remarked feature of this period regarding the condottieri and their troops must not be overlooked, although we may agree that it possesses no intrinsic importance. Hawkwood concludes the long line of foreign condottieri who operated in Italy preponderantly with foreign men-at-arms. After him Italian condottieri, preferably employing troopers of their own nationality, took over the lucrative business of mercenary warfare. More especially in the following, the fifteenth, century these native adventurers rose to great fame, and some of them became so powerful that they were able to appropriate the government they were supposed to serve and to found a dynasty. The outstanding example of this sort is Francesco Sforza, who became duke of Milan. But other heads of military companies, such as Jacopo del Verme, Niccolò Fortebraccio, and Niccolò Piccinino hardly made less stir in their day. Our concern with them at this point goes no farther than to bring out that it was by them and their likes that Florence got its fighting done in the oligarchic, and in the subsequent Medicean, period as well. It need hardly be expressly said that on taking the field the mercenaries failed to show conspicuous zeal for their employer and that not infrequently their conduct during a campaign was dictated by directly treasonable considerations. On the whole, however, the oligarchy during this, its last lease of power, may be judged to have received a fair return for its money, for, although frequently involved in extremely perilous wars, it managed to conclude them with reasonably satisfactory terms of peace. Indeed in view of its having made so many territorial gains that by the time it was superseded by the rule of Cosimo de' Medici it had brought under its control all Tuscany with the exception of Lucca and Siena, we may credit it with having put forth more power—and that means essentially military power—than any government with which Florence had been thus far provided. We shall be obliged to examine the foreign policy of the oligarchy and the wars in which it engaged with some detail, but before doing so it will be well to turn to the domestic story and trace the line of internal development taken by the government in the half-century between its birth and its demise.

From the moment the oligarchy had regained the preponderant influence in the government its main concern was not again to lose control. It had been moderate in the hour of victory and had conceded to the lesser gilds a share in the offices just short of that attributed to itself. However, democratic rule was too recent an experience not to be the cause of constant alarm to the new rulers. The moment there were mutterings among the discomfited proletarians or vague movements of protest among the members of the lesser gilds, such inevitable discontent was promptly exaggerated into a conspiracy against the regime and made to serve as an excuse for severe repressive action. And since repression looks less draconic when disguised under a harmless name, it was designated euphemistically as a "reform." The first such reform occurred in 1387 and laid down the procedure for a number of others that followed in due course. It had long been customary to suspend the constitution from time to time by calling a general assembly or parlamentum and by having it vote special power (balìa) to a commission to sweep existing difficulties out of the way before once more putting the constitution into force. Such a balìa created

left: LUCA DELLA ROBBIA. MADONNA IN ADORATION. COLORED GLAZED TERRA COTTA (ALINARI). *right:* GHIBERTI. PANEL FROM HIS SECOND BRONZE GATE WITH EPISODES FROM THE LIFE OF ABRAHAM (ALINARI).

left: DONATELLO. KING DAVID CALLED LO ZUCCONE. NICHE OF THE CAMPANILE (ALINARI). *right:* DONATELLO. BRONZE EQUESTRIAN STATUE OF GATTAMELATA. PADUA (ALINARI).

GHIBERTI. HIS SECOND BRONZE GATE COMMONLY CALLED THE GATE OF PARADISE
(ALINARI).

by a carefully manipulated parliament in 1387 cut down the participation of the arti minori in the public offices to one-fourth the total, and to make the measure effective ordered the old purses (borse) burned and a new scrutiny (scrutinio) to be carried through conducted on the plan of admitting to the new borse the names of none but accredited supporters of the regime and of rigorously excluding the names of known opponents.

Ever since the adoption of the system of filling the offices by lot the sure way of controlling the government was to control the borse. In the reform of 1387 the oligarchy showed clearly how this could effectively be done. It would seem that the borse thus manipulated might be held to offer a sufficient guaranty against an unpleasant surprise at the recurrent drawings. This was not the view of the anxious oligarchs; and further to guard against an unfavorable signory the balìa charged with correcting the constitution authorized the creation of what came to be called the *borsellino*. Borsellino means little borsa (or purse) and into it were dropped the names of the most devoted and ardent adherents of the oligarchy with the provision that henceforth two of the eight priors must be regularly drawn from this preferred list. While after all these precautions there were still two priors (two being the required one-fourth) hailing from the lesser gilds, these two small tradesmen could be reduced to effective nullity by their six colleagues of the greater gilds headed by a gonfalonier of the same social stratum.

With the oligarchic balìa of 1387 set on clearing obstacles of every sort out of the way it took occasion to banish Benedetto degli Alberti together with some of the members of his family. Benedetto was the richest Florentine of his time and therefore closely bound up with the interests of the ruling clique. But inclined to take an independent stand, he had come under the suspicion of his fellows, who seized the occasion afforded by the balìa to rid themselves of an unreliable and possibly dangerous associate. Besides, a feud existed between the Alberti and the family of that man whose talents had enabled him to become the effective head of the ruling faction. This was the merchant Maso degli Albizzi. Maso was a sane, vigorous, and relatively moderate party leader, but in one respect, in the sacred matter of vendetta, he was as extravagant as every other self-respecting Florentine. It was his opinion that a former head of the house, his uncle Piero degli Albizzi, had been put to death during the democratic period because of an intrigue spun by Benedetto degli Alberti; and when the chance came to even the score, Maso made the most of it without hesitation. Neither at this nor at any other period of Florentine history did motives of a purely personal character fail to play their part in the revolutions and reforms that followed one another in unbroken succession.

A second reform was instituted six years later, in 1393. As soon as it began to take shape it was clear that it was to have the same character as its predecessor, for its instigator was Maso degli Albizzi, who happened at the time to be gonfalonier of Justice. Accordingly, we meet with an exact repetition of the just-recited measures: creation of a balìa, exclusion of opponents from office by a new scrutinio authorized to make new borse, strengthening the party in power by a revised borsellino, and reissue in a more sweeping form of the decree of condemnation and exile against the clan of the Alberti. The new

measures signified a further tightening of oligarchic rule, to which same end
there was adopted an additional provision of a peculiarly revealing nature.
The reigning merchants were rich popolani who by developing the outlook of
a privileged class effectively closed the chasm which had opened a century before between them and an upper group of feudalized families designated by
the law as magnates or grandi. While under the Ordinances of Justice the magnates were still excluded from office, they had in the course of the trecento,
when war became the province of the companies of adventure, completely lost
their military character and were now, insofar as they had not through poverty
and concomitant social decline sunk to the level of the common people, nothing
other than dyed-in-the-wool conservatives. Judging that here was a body of
natural allies, the ruling oligarchs resolved to strengthen their cause by drawing these congenital tories to their side. In consequence the ancient clans of
the Frescobaldi, Cavalcanti, Ricasoli, Bardi, Rossi, Adimari, and many others
besides, constituting in their sum the hated magnates of the trecento, were
cleared of their magnate stigma and, by being declared popolani, again became
eligible for office. The conversion of status could of course also be made to
work the other way. If it was possible to win support from magnates by giving
them back their political rights, it was just as easy to get rid of undesirable
popolani by stigmatizing them as magnates. This is precisely what happened
in the case of the Alberti. Already exiled and therefore financially ruined, they
were for good measure and as a final gesture of aversion raised to the magnate
dignity.

Engaged in such multiple sleight-of-hand, which, although carried to a very
high technical perfection at this time, was by no means new since in one form
or another it had been practiced in the city from the earliest days of the republic, the oligarchy was not likely to overlook the device of ammonizione or
warning. Invented by the parte Guelfa to serve its attempted control of the
government, it had in the revolution of 1378 been struck from the hands of its
supporters. But that was no reason why it should not be taken over by the new
rulers. They were men without scruple, ready to employ every available means
to suppress their antagonists, whether these antagonists were simple folk of
the shops or too ambitious members of their own group. The ammonizione
was therefore cannily added to the weapons wherewith the government smote
its adversaries. Under no circumstances, however, did the new rulers intend to
share the resumption of this sharp implement with its inventors of the parte
Guelfa. By confirming the act of 1378, which forebade the use of the ammonizione to the party, they let it be known that they were not minded to
permit a rival government to function at their side. The once powerful organization obediently accepted the decision; and although it continued its
existence for many generations as a distinguished social club housed in a fine
palace, from the time of its defeat in 1378 it ceased to figure in any conspicuous
way in the political life of the town.

The many secret and open manipulations here indicated made the so-called
free republic of Florence a good deal of a travesty. Operating nominally as a
democracy of twenty-one gilds, it was in reality a government conducted by,
and in the interest of, a small class of the well-to-do. In actual practice, how-

ever, even a class government is not run by all its members but rather by a few capable and ambitious individuals prepared, according to their temperamental endowment, to share or to dispute the control among themselves. We have just learned that Maso degli Albizzi had early acquired a leading influence and that, among other ways, he used it to rid himself of the rivalry of the hated Alberti family. When after the fall of the wealthy and personally distinguished Benedetto Alberti, Gino Capponi and Niccolò da Uzzano rose more and more into public view, Maso got along fairly well with these vigorous representatives of the oligarchy and even took them into a kind of political partnership. Like himself, they were both hard-headed business men deeply and sincerely concerned with promoting the welfare of the state according to their light. Besides, all three were so genuinely possessed of the true optimate outlook that, while aspiring to stand in the front rank of the citizens, they entertained no pretensions to exclusive rule. Under these circumstances cooperation was possible among them and in point of fact all important decisions in domestic and foreign affairs alike were taken by them in consultation with such other merchants and friends as from motives of prudence they chose to draw into their counsels. Over each freshly arising issue they would hold an informal session in the mansion of one of the leaders, and as the fiasco of good red Tuscan wine made the rounds, they came to a conclusion which they would then convey by suitable channels to the constituted authorities. The control of the borse had made them the effective masters of the priors and of all the other governing bodies of the state as well. This extra-constitutional procedure could not be kept concealed from a people so alert as the Florentines, and grumbling complaints made themselves heard against a rule exercised "fuori del palazzo" (outside the palace), instead of by the priors within their appointed residence. To be effective a protest would have to swell to the dimensions of a revolution, and a revolution was difficult in the face of the sleepless watch maintained by the masters. In sum, Florence had become an undercover oligarchy which, while secretly asserting its preeminence, found it advantageous to flatter the traditional democratic pretensions of the citizens by an apparent deference to the constituted authorities.

The lively but splenetic contemporary, Cavalcanti, tells a story which illustrates so strikingly how the concealed control worked that it deserves to be quoted. By way of introduction it will be well to remind ourselves that the republic, moved from its inception by fear of individuals likely to become too powerful, had invented a system of checks and balances consisting chiefly of a number of councils, in which opinions might be freely voiced before a final decision was taken. There, for instance, was the council (usually called the collegium or college) constituted by the priors assisted by the Twelve Good Men and the Sixteen Captains of the Companies, thirty-seven individuals in all; and, again, there were the two much larger councils respectively of the captain and the podestà. To most republican societies, no matter how jealous of their liberty, three councils would have seemed sufficient and more than sufficient for the end in view, but not so to the Florentines. They had gradually brought into existence an additional council, which consisted of leading citizens summoned at the pleasure of the priors to advise them in a pressing issue.

Such a council, very informal in character, was called a *pratica,* and the pratica came more and more into vogue in the oligarchic period because it was found to lend itself admirably to the purposes of the ruling group. It would be entirely proper for the priors in seeking counsel to invite the secret party heads to attend the pratica, and it would be equally proper for the party heads to give their opinion. Their opinion would in reality, however, be a command and would be understood as such by their puppets in the seats of authority.

Cavalcanti's story introduces us to a pratica called to discuss a question involving nothing less than peace and war. During the very lively and long-drawn-out debate Niccolò da Uzzano, an outstanding member of the governing junta, did not utter a single word, in fact he paid his respects to the debaters by dropping into a deep sleep (*fortemente dormiva*). Aroused at last by a neighbor to give his opinion, he managed with difficulty to shake himself awake and, ascending the platform, briefly pronounced for war. No sooner had he sat down than his view was unanimously approved.[2] Is any other judgment possible than that the priors may have reigned but that the junta governed?

If in the light of these developments it will have to be agreed that the eclipse of the old and proud executive, the priors, had begun, we should not fail to see that their decline was not solely due to their having become the stalking-horse of a secret governing group. In spite of apparent stability the Florentine constitution was and had ever been in flux, and already during the recent democratic period changes had been introduced which, continuing under the oligarchy, gradually transferred to other bodies some of the powers originally reserved to the priors. There, for instance, were the Eight, the *Otto di Guardia.* It had long been the custom to appoint this committee in time of special peril and to intrust it with the task of ferreting out the local enemies of the government, but in the period under consideration the Eight acquired a character of permanence. Constituted as a secret police, they undoubtedly signified a measurable reduction of the sovereignty of the priors. A much more serious diminution, however, flowed from the Ten, the *Dieci di Balìa.* Whenever a war threatened it became customary to appoint a war committee, the above-mentioned Ten, and to put the complete management of the war into their hands. That meant the withdrawal of what had once been a leading interest of the priors from their control. While the Otto and the Dieci, far from signifying a loss in government efficiency, were probably an improvement on what had gone before, they establish the contention that the impairment of the city's celebrated chief executive, the priors, had begun, and that it was in part brought about by the desire to give the services of the state a greater measure of efficiency. A parallel decline may be observed in other characteristic features of the old constitution. In the great days of the past the vitality of the Arno city had found its most vigorous expression in the two large councils associated with the podestà and captain. They continued to be called together as before and their formal acceptance of a measure was still required ere it could become a law; but as these councils with their widely representative membership were viewed with suspicion by the oligarchy, which found it easier to operate with the informal pratica, the councils of podestà and captain imperceptibly lost credit

---

[2] Cavalcanti, *Istorie Fiorentine,* Book II, chap. I. 2 vols. Florence, 1838-39.

and showed it by a diminishing attendance. When, later, under the Medici this single family replaced the power of the oligarchic junta with its own, the enfeeblement of the constitution became so manifest that no one pretended any longer not to see it. But those writers who lay the collapse to the sole charge of the Medici are manifestly in error, since after the developments just detailed it cannot be denied that already under the oligarchy the hollowing-out of the constitution had made considerable headway.[3]

The very capable Maso degli Albizzi, around whom the governing group had chiefly cohered since its seizure of power, died in 1417. He was followed to the grave a few years later (1421) by Gino Capponi, who, another tower of merchant strength, was generally credited with the most popular single achievement of the period, the capture of Pisa, to be treated later on. With the death of Maso and Gino the burden of responsibility came to rest chiefly on the shoulders of Niccolò da Uzzano, one of the most widely respected and cultivated Italians of his generation. A colored terra cotta bust of him by Donatello is one of the great portrait busts of all time and reveals a man of alert and powerful intelligence. As Niccolò, on the passing from the scene of his two leading associates, was no longer young, he had no objection to sharing control with Rinaldo degli Albizzi, son of his former colleague, Maso. Rinaldo was endowed with high spirits, bore himself proudly, and possessed a ready and fiery eloquence. From among the practical, hard-headed products of the counting-house who made up the bulk of his party he stood out with the graces of a born gentleman and cavalier. His personal distinction recommended him as the elegant representative oligarch, suitable to be dispatched on embassies to the princes and governments of Italy. Accordingly, from early manhood Rinaldo had been employed on missions that sent him over the length and breadth of the peninsula. His many gifts coupled with his undoubted services tended to make him arrogant and to practice an aristocratic aloofness, than which it would be impossible to imagine a quality less in keeping with the solidity and earthiness of the typical Florentine business man. The brilliant Rinaldo was admired but not loved and his coming more and more to the front after the death of his father did not augur well for his party.[4]

So thoroughly, however, had the reforms carried through by the ruling

---

[3] The chronicler Dati in Book IX of his *Istoria di Firenze* gives an interesting review of all the public offices in his time. Amazing, however, is the circumstance that he never so much as mentions the secret control of the oligarchs and that he ascribes to the institutions he enumerates the free exercise of the functions with which they are endowed by law. It is an excellent example of the common human difficulty of distinguishing between shadow and reality.

[4] This is as good a place as any for a bibliographical note covering the material of this chapter. The most important source publication is *Commissioni di Rinaldo degli Albizzi per il Comune di Firenze dal 1399 al 1433* (Vols. I, II, III of the *Documenti di Storia Italiana*). Of the numerous chroniclers the most important are Morelli (Florence, 1785), Buonaccorso Pitti (Florence, 1720), Gregorio Dati (Florence, 1735), Domenico Boninsegni (Florence, 1637), Giovanni Cavalcanti (Florence, 1838-39). Machiavelli, who in his *History of Florence* treats the oligarchic episode with his unfailing liveliness and piquancy, should be employed with care, as he was content to take his facts without subjecting them to a critical re-examination from the above-mentioned chroniclers, chiefly from Cavalcanti. Ammirato was the first Florentine historian to offer a study of the period not exclusively based on the chroniclers, and his work is therefore still valuable. The general histories of Capponi, Perrens, and Caggese present much new material and are worth consulting not only for their facts but also for their astonishingly divergent estimates of the men and the issues of the period.

group—the great purges of 1387 and 1393 had been followed by further, somewhat less vigorous cures—crushed their antagonists that, as we approach the
period of Rinaldo's dominance, there was no longer so much as a trace of an
organized opposition. But that did not signify that the regime was without
enemies. Among the poor and the oppressed the ancient discontent lived on in
undiminished energy. It prompted them to hope for a deliverer, and from the
beginning of the fifteenth century they began to see in that light a man who
was coming more and more to the front as the leading banker of the town.
This was Giovanni di Bicci de' Medici. A generation before a Medici, Salvestro
by name, for reasons that can no longer be clearly disentangled, had sounded
the tocsin that started the famous revolution of 1378; and since that time the
common people would not have it other than that Salvestro and his whole
clan were warmly enlisted on their side. Giovanni, who was not a descendant
of the prosperous Salvestro, belonged to a branch of the family which had
only recently in the person of Giovanni's father, Bicci, risen from obscurity.
Relying on the gifts with which nature had endowed him, Giovanni had devoted himself wholeheartedly to business, which still meant, as had always
been the case in Florence, the union of money-lending with the purchase and
sale of goods. By slow degrees he succeeded in piling up a fortune, which as
he entered the middle period of his life equaled and possibly overtopped that
of any of his fellow-citizens. Although thus economically identified with the
ruling oligarchs, he had so recently risen from the ranks and was so patently
a *novus homo* that men of older wealth looked down upon him as an upstart.
As he was greatly absorbed by his private affairs and gave no hint of entertaining any political ambitions, he apparently did not much mind his exclusion from the inner circle of the optimates. Added to his being a Medici, a
family supposed to nurse democratic sentiments, his marked exclusion from
the councils of the mighty confirmed the inclination of the people to look up to
him as their leader. On making their attitude known to him, however, they
met with no encouragement. We have only to look at Giovanni's picture in the
family portrait gallery recently arranged in the palace built by his son Cosimo
to have an adequate explanation of his course. We are confronted with the
homely visage of a shrewd, unimaginative trader as far removed as possible
from the traditional conception of a merchant prince. The most conspicuous
feature is the set jaw, the hard effect of which is softened by a general expression of troubled kindliness. We can imagine this commonplace individual
moving among the people without the least display of condescension; but we
cannot conceive his letting himself be persuaded to stake his hard-won fortune
in a hazardous gamble for political power.[5]

The political quietism of Giovanni di Bicci explains why the oligarchs took
no protective measures against him. Perhaps as a gesture of appeasement
toward his supporters they even admitted him to the honors of office, for he
served repeatedly as prior; in 1414 he was a member of the important war
committee, the Dieci; and in 1421 he was promoted to the highest office of the
state, the gonfalonierat of Justice. When his son Cosimo reached manhood he

[5] A reproduction of this portrait will be found in G. Pieraccini, *La Stirpe dei Medici di Caffa-
giolo*. 3 vols. Florence, 1925. This is perhaps the most important single work on the Medici.

was treated with the same consideration. Suspicion no doubt spun its spider web between Giovanni and the ruling junta, a suspicion inseparable from the conditions of his rise to prominence, but that there existed an incurable enmity is a postulate based on developments belonging to the period after Giovanni's death. Nothing proves the absence of an inalterable hostility better than the great issue of taxation which arose toward the end of Giovanni's life in consequence of a fresh and peculiarly grinding war with Milan. By continuing for years the war swallowed up enormous sums and laid a burden of taxation on the people under which they threatened to succumb. We are aware that from the early fourteenth century a financial system was in use which favored the wealthy by raising the ordinary revenues of the state through a mass of indirect taxes called gabelle. On pressing occasions, like war, forced loans or prestanze were voted which were so irregularly and capriciously levied on the propertied classes that they caused the greatest bitterness and indignation. The clamor for a direct tax based on an exact estimate of the wealth of every citizen had never ceased to make itself heard, but the well-to-do had always succeeded in averting the measure.[6]

Thus matters stood when there arose the financial crisis of the twenties caused by a war with Milan, of which we shall presently hear more. After hot and prolonged debates in the various councils the long-desired reform was at last adopted. It was based on what were probably the broadest and most equitable principles of taxation which thus far had been evolved by any European state. Known from the register of the assessments as the *catasto,* the new tax became a law in 1427. Because direct taxation is always associated with democratic tendencies, it will never cease to cause surprise that the catasto was adopted by an oligarchy. For Machiavelli, who loved to reduce history to weighty precepts and epigrams but was averse to the time-robbing occupation of investigating the facts, the problem had little difficulty. He declared that the catasto was favored by Giovanni de' Medici and was carried by pressure from him and his popular following. It was so plausible an explanation that it early became an outstanding item of the accepted Florentine tradition. And it would still be accepted had it not occurred to a nineteenth-century scholar to verify the statement by turning to the record of the original debates.[7] These revealed to him that plausibility was a poor substitute for the facts, for to his amazement he learned that the catasto enjoyed the support of most of the oligarchs themselves and notably of Rinaldo degli Albizzi and Niccolò da Uzzano, whereas the attitude toward it of Giovanni di Bicci was often negative and never better than lukewarm. We cannot get around crediting the catasto in the main to the ruling junta, but we need not be at a loss for an explanation. The Milanese war was their war, the revenues had inescapably to be raised, and in the existing emergency there was no course open but for every man of means to dip into his pocket. Another circumstance may have had a certain weight. Although the new system put an end to many special favors hitherto enjoyed by the well-to-do, it retained a feature of the prestanze

[6] See chap. XVI.
[7] The scholar is P. Berti. See "Nuovi Documenti intorno al Catasto Fiorentino," *Giornale Storico degli Archivi Toscani,* Vol. IV, pp. 32-62.

which in the past had accounted for such favor as this levy enjoyed with the upper classes. Exactly as in the case of the prestanze the money paid under the catasto was declared to have the character of a repayable, interest-bearing loan. It was, in the current phrase, "written on the Monte," that is, it was regularly entered in the registers of the National Debt.

According to the law of 1427 every citizen was obliged to make a declaration of his possessions of every kind, gold, silver, jewels, houses, farms, animals, rents, mortgages, and capital employed in commerce. The declaration was subject to review by a tax commission, which after correcting the figures and permitting deductions for debts, house rent, and family maintenance, regarded the remainder as interest-bearing capital. On the assumption that the capital would yield 5 per cent, or five florins for every hundred florins, there was imposed a levy of one-tenth of every five florins of calculated income. Accordingly, while the system was called the catasto, the levy itself was known as the Tenth or *decima*. Precisely like the earlier prestanza, the decima was supposed to be raised only in cases of emergency such as war. While in time of peace it might not be demanded for years, on the other hand with the state engaged in an expensive conflict it might be levied repeatedly within the course of a few months.[8] To sum up: the decima was an income tax marking a vast advance in social justice since it fell substantially on the well-to-do, passed the poor by entirely, and exacted from those whose legitimate expenses were approximately equal to their earnings no more than a nominal sum imposed by the assessors.

Since the catasto was imposed by the oligarchy we cannot escape the view that it must have added to the prestige enjoyed by the rulers among the people. If, notwithstanding, the oligarchy fell only a few years afterward, it was for the commonest reason known for the collapse of governments: it engaged in an unsuccessful war. Therewith we are back in the realm of foreign policy, into the general character of which during the merchant supremacy we looked at the beginning of the chapter. We there learned that great states were taking shape all over Italy, and that Florence itself was aspiring to be a great state founded on the undisputed control of Tuscany. For all these governments alike, war was an accepted tool of policy. In the case of Florence it might be resorted to either for offense in Tuscany or for defense against any other state attempting to get a foothold in that province.

The first war of the oligarchic period was of a defensive order and was directed against Gian Galeazzo Visconti. This astonishing lord of Milan had seized the power in the northern metropolis by an act of unconscionable treachery against members of his own family, and, following up this measure by alternately playing the fox and the lion, he had made himself master of Lombardy up to the barrier of the Apennines. When he next revolved a plan to burst across this impediment into Umbria and Tuscany, Florence became alarmed and challenged his advance. The ensuing war began in the year 1390 and lasted, with trucelike interruptions of often considerable length, for

---

[8] The law regulating the catasto was published by G. F. Pagnini in Vol. I, pp. 214-31, of his work *Della Decima e di Varie 'Altre Gravezze Imposte dal Comune di Firenze.* 4 vols. Lisbon-Lucca, 1765-66. The author gives a good summary of the law on p. 17.

twelve years. Although frequently checked, Gian Galeazzo, a man of the most stubborn determination, would not be denied. Having at last acquired Perugia, Siena, and Pisa, he drew a ring of iron around Florence which threatened to throttle it into submission. In June, 1402, the Milanese tyrant completely closed the ring by the capture of the city of Bologna. In the face of this situation even the most sanguine citizens hardly dared hope that they would succeed in maintaining their independence. But before the expected disaster occurred Florence was saved by the sudden taking-off of Gian Galeazzo by the pest. At the news of the event the conqueror's vast dominion, held together solely by force, fell violently apart. Gian Galeazzo had left behind him as his heirs two boys who, when the precipitate defections were at last arrested, found their possessions reduced to the original kernel of the Visconti dominion.

The sudden relaxation of Milanese pressure gave Florence the opportunity to resume the construction of its Tuscan empire. Ever since their return to power in 1382 the greater gilds, the original exponents of territorial expansion, had been on the lookout to strengthen their position in the Arno Valley. They had at once directed their attention to Arezzo which, because of irreconcilable local strife, had become the prey of a succession of military adventurers. In the year 1384 the soldier in temporary possession, a Frenchman, De Coucy by name, let himself be persuaded to sell his prize to Florence for 40,000 gold florins. Although repeatedly before this time in Florentine control, Arezzo had always managed to wrest itself free again. On taking renewed possession of the key position on the upper Arno the Florentines turned their eyes more hungrily than ever toward Pisa occupying a corresponding position on the lower Arno. The long crisis connected with Gian Galeazzo had obliged them to control their appetite; but when on Gian Galeazzo's demise Pisa, which he had brought under his scepter, was awarded as a sort of consolation prize to a third son, the illegitimate Gabriele Maria, they thought the opportunity had come to satisfy their desire.

The new lord of Pisa was a young, ill-governed foreigner, who lost the favor of his subjects almost at once by burdening them with exorbitant taxes. When the Florentines judged that his position was becoming precarious, they drew him into secret negotiations with a view to relieving him of his troublesome signory for money paid in hand. On the Pisans getting wind of the treacherous action of their ruler they rose against him as one man and drove him from the city. The old love of independence still burned in their hearts and the blackest fate that could befall them in their eyes was to fall a prey to that town which had been sleeplessly plotting their destruction for two hundred years. But Florence was no less determined than its intended victim. It brought its negotiations with the deposed Gabriele Maria to a close by paying him 200,000 florins for his title, which, on thus being transferred to them, somewhat naïvely for such old hands at the imperialist game they expected the Pisans to honor. The spontaneous rising of the Pisans against Gabriele Maria and the acceptance by the deposed lord of the Florentine bribe belong to the summer of 1405. When the Florentines now sent commissioners to take possession of their purchase, the Pisans naturally refused to receive them; and just as inevitably the truculent imperialists from the middle Arno declared war to enforce what they were pleased stubbornly to call their rights. They began a siege of Pisa which drew so impenetrable a hedge around the city that a terrible famine gripped the population. When it could no longer be borne it brought the exhausted city to its knees. On October 9, 1406, Pisa and its very considerable territory passed into Florentine control. Perrens and other historians of Florence before and after him have indignantly denounced the Pisan war as an immoral enterprise. On the other hand, they have not hesitated to ascribe a sound moral basis to the wars fought against Gian Galeazzo and other ambitious princes. To anyone who lifts himself to a height above the murky atmosphere of Italian statecraft it becomes difficult to classify the wars of the Italian states as either moral or immoral, for none of them were waged on any discoverable ethical principle or for any consideration whatever other than that of power. It must certainly be conceded that Florence at all times shaped its policy with a view to playing an ever larger and larger part in the Italian world. The reception it gave the news that Pisa had passed under its yoke was therefore exactly suited to its power outlook. All the chroniclers are agreed that the much-divided population of greater gilds, lesser gilds, magnates, proletariat, and beggars was converted into a single happy family which literally went mad with joy.

There can be no doubt that the acquisition of Pisa added greatly to the reputation and resources of the Florentine state. The city now enjoyed the long-desired unhampered access to the sea. Enabled to appropriate the ancient Levantine connections of the Pisans, it rose to a distinguished position in many a Mediterranean port and notably at Constantinople. But Pisa itself sickened and shriveled. While its decline was partly owing to the hostile measures of the victors, who had no desire to see the vanquished town recover its strength, it followed partly also from natural causes largely beyond human control. Because of the continued silting of the mouth of the Arno, Pisa was already at the time of its capture some five miles from the coast. The Pisans themselves had attempted to remedy the situation by constructing a harbor farther down stream called Porto Pisano. But Porto Pisano, too, was an unsatisfactory location compared with Livorno directly on the coast a few miles south of the river and therefore safe from the river's vagaries. While the advantages of Livorno were not fully recognized for another hundred years and while therefore Pisa and its harbor remained the chief objective of Florentine ambition, it was already clear that Livorno must under no circumstances be overlooked. However, owing to a succession of accidents too involved to follow here, at the time of Pisa's capture by Florence Livorno was in Genoese hands. In their watchful way the Florentines awaited the auspicious moment and in 1421 acquired Livorno by purchase, the route for which they, as merchants and not warriors, had a natural predilection. Then only did they come into the unconditional possession of the main Tuscan coast.

Our growing town had enjoyed its Pisan laurels only a few years when it was again obliged to defend itself against attack from without. This time the blow threatened not from the north, as had thus far been usually the case, but from the south. A young and vigorous king of Naples, Ladislaus by name, was seized with the desire to imitate Duke Gian Galeazzo and bring as much of Italy as possible under his scepter. His initial advance was relatively easy, for the first opposition to a northward thrust on his part would be offered by the State of the Church. As this was the time of the Great Schism, the church was divided between two popes, one of whom made his capital at Rome, the other at Avignon. It was the Roman pontiff with whom Ladislaus was obliged to deal, and this ruler's position was so feeble that he could offer Ladislaus no serious resistance. It will confirm our view of the papal weakness if we note at this point that the state forged by Cardinal Albornoz a little past the middle of the fourteenth century had again fallen apart into a score of practically independent towns and principalities. King Ladislaus began his aggressions in the year 1408 by occupying the papal capital. From Rome as his base he gradually extended the range of his enterprise until it looked as if the whole of Peter's patrimony was destined to fall into his hands. At this turn Florence, bristling with alarm, bestirred itself to organize a league against the conqueror. The plan cleverly concocted by the league was to support the claim of a rival family to the Neapolitan throne. This family was headed by the duke of Anjou, a Frenchman, and he was put forward in the hope of creating difficulties for Ladislaus which would keep him in the south fighting Anjou and Anjou's partisans.

We shall not follow the Neapolitan war, which, as usual, was made up of a thousand and one confusing minor incidents. As usual, too, it was waged to the accompaniment of treacherous secret negotiations on the part of all the participants. One of these reprehensible arrangements, however, needs to be mentioned, for it led to Florence abandoning its allies and being rewarded for its treachery by the cession of the town of Cortona, which Ladislaus had seized. It was in January, 1411, that Florence was enabled to add Cortona to its dominion; nonetheless the bribe did not stick, since before many months had passed the City of the Red Lily was again in the field against the king. It could hardly do otherwise if it desired to survive as an independent commonwealth, for Ladislaus was a capable soldier and subtle diplomat who had set his heart on dominating Italy. The renewed war exposed Florence to a peril hardly inferior to that which had threatened a decade before from Duke Gian Galeazzo of Milan, and again, as in the earlier case, the city was saved by what patriots of the devouter sort hailed as an act of divine interference. On August 6, 1414, after a brief illness, Ladislaus died in the full flower of manhood.

On this rescue from extreme jeopardy there followed a rare and blessed interval of peace which lasted for eight years and was not terminated until Gian Galeazzo's heir, Duke Filippo Maria, having got his Milanese dominion well in hand, with much of his father's persistence but with little of his skill, resumed his father's policy of conquest. By 1422 his aggressions in the neighboring Romagna had become so dangerous that Florence, no longer able to ignore them, resorted to war. The struggle, which continued for years, went cruelly against the Arno city until in 1426 it succeeded in gaining Venice as an ally. Straightway the theater of war was shifted to the north, where the forces of Venice won such a succession of victories that in April, 1428, Filippo Maria was obliged to come to terms with both his adversaries. By this peace

Florence got no more than the restitution of the strongholds which had been taken away from her, but victorious Venice was enabled to push its boundary westward beyond Brescia, thus giving it control of the whole northeastern section of the peninsula. By far the most memorable incident of the war was the domestic event already recorded, for the prolonged struggle occasioned a financial crisis which in the year 1427 led to the adoption of the famous reform measure of the catasto.

It might be thought that, after the strain and agony of the grinding conflict with Duke Filippo Maria, Florence would have been glad to enjoy a long repose. It was not so. In the very next year, in 1429, without either provocation or excuse the city deliberately set out to conquer Lucca and its territory. Although the oligarchy directed the struggle and must accept responsibility for it, there is no denying that the whole population, eager to round off its Tuscan dominion, clamored for war with such unanimity that there was no resisting the general madness. Shortly before the Lucchese issue arose, on February 20, 1429, death carried off Giovanni di Bicci de' Medici, and his son Cosimo became the head of the house. As he had inherited his father's solid burgher qualities, coupling with them a much more lively interest in politics, he continued to be regarded by the common people as their spokesman. When the question of the Lucchese enterprise arose, Cosimo, perhaps from natural caution, was disinclined to support the war party, but he accepted the war wholeheartedly as soon as he saw the uselessness of standing out against so general a demand. That other prominent Florentines, however, from the very first vehemently egged the citizenry on to war is undeniable. Among them on the Medicean side was Cosimo's influential cousin, Averardo de' Medici, on the side of the oligarchy, Rinaldo degli Albizzi and Neri Capponi, the brilliant son of Gino Capponi, to whom the acquisition of Pisa had been mainly due. With frank admiration we learn, however, that the fine old merchant and statesman, Niccolò da Uzzano, employed all his authority and eloquence to turn his fellow-citizens from their purpose. While he labored to no avail, his courageous stand makes it forever impossible to represent the Lucchese war as an enterprise of the united oligarchs.

The war against Lucca got off to a bad start and was pursued by the most exasperating ill fortune. As happens everywhere and always, the people blamed the failure of the campaign on the government and the government in last analysis meant the oligarchic junta. And without any doubt the successive thrusts against Lucca were attended by a degree of mismanagement which even in Florence, accustomed to mismanaged wars, was unique. However, the maladministration cannot be fairly laid to the exclusive charge of Rinaldo degli Albizzi and his immediate following, for on the Dieci, the Ten, intrusted according to custom with the conduct of the war, oligarchs and Mediceans sat side by side. The capital mistake effectively accounting for all the subsequent ills was made at the outset and was of a political and diplomatic rather than of a military order. It consisted in the assumption that Lucca was weak and small, had no friends, and would fall at the first assault. But owing to the Italian power situation with which we have made ample acquaintance, every neighbor of Florence begrudged it its prospective increase in territory.

The doctrine on this head was (and for that matter still is) that no state entangled with a group of rivals in a struggle for eminence may add as much as a frog pond to its territory without first offering an equivalent frog pond to its competitors. Therefore, no sooner had Florence launched its attack on Lucca than neighboring Siena came to Lucca's aid, although not openly at first in order not unnecessarily to expose itself. Should Lucca fall a prey to Florence, Siena would be the only remaining free town of Tuscany, and it took no prophet to foresee what in that event would happen to the small upland state. In case any Sienese doubters needed to be convinced of what was in store for their city, the street urchins of Florence might have enlightened them, for they went about the city singing: *ave Maria, grazia piena; avuto Lucca, avremo Siena.*[9] They travestied the common prayer to the Virgin to serve notice that with Lucca conquered Siena was next on the list. In its justified alarm Siena communicated with Duke Filippo Maria of Milan, who was nothing loath to make trouble for the hated Red Lily. In short, by wantonly attacking Lucca Florence brought on itself another Milanese war as expensive and far-reaching as the one it had just terminated. It hired unreliable condottieri, although probably as good as any in the market, was defeated before Lucca by an army sent by the Milanese duke to Lucca's relief, had its territory brutally ravaged by the troops of the northern tyrant, and in the end was glad to make peace on the promise faithfully to respect the independence of its little neighbor on the Serchio.

The treaty concluding the Lucchese war was signed on May 10, 1433. While the negotiators were still haggling over its terms, the most respected and authoritative of the oligarchs, Niccolò da Uzzano, had passed from among the living. The event left Rinaldo degli Albizzi to defend the regime against the flood of criticism set in motion by the Lucchese disaster. There would of course be much talk of a change of government, and the opponents of the ruling sect, who had grown vastly in number and daring, would not hesitate to put forward as their candidate Cosimo de' Medici. Apparently Cosimo was not overpleased with the ardor of his followers, for when in June the term of the war committee, the Dieci, of whom he was one, came to an end, he abandoned the turmoil of the city and retired to his country place in the distant Mugello. But Rinaldo's suspicions against his rival were kept alive by the murmurs of the citizens, and he could not but feel the ground quaking under his feet. When the new priors, who entered on office on September 1, were found in their majority to be friendly to him and to have at their head as gonfalonier of Justice a man completely devoted to his interest, he resolved to act. Cosimo was recalled to Florence by a message, equivalent to an order, from the signory, and on being summoned to the palace on September 7 was put under arrest. He was confined in a small stone chamber high in the palace tower, whence through a tiny window he could look down on the central piazza and watch the constitutional comedy which his enemies now proceeded to stage. For with their victim in their hands Rinaldo and his friends took the step which had

[9] Cavalcanti, Libro VI, chap. 18.

long ago become the measure preliminary to every act of juridical violence or governmental change. On September 9 they summoned a parliament of the usual packed order and had it vote supreme power to a balìa of two hundred men. Then the balìa sat down to determine Cosimo's fate.

While some voices were heard that demanded the death of the prisoner, there were others which, in view of his great popularity and the excited state of the public mind, counseled moderation. A few soft-treading politicians, after the nature of their kind through all the ages of the world, were in favor of putting him secretly away. That Cosimo, who may be supposed to have known his countrymen, suspected that this would be the course adopted and that he was about to be removed quietly by poison is proved by the circumstance that he refused to eat the food supplied to him in his cell. Only after his keeper declared his readiness to share his meals with him was he reassured. Meanwhile the debate over his fate went on in the balìa and gradually opinion swung toward exile (confino) as, after all, the more usual sentence following political defeat. The story that Cosimo strengthened the sentiment for moderation by a bribe of money secretly conveyed to the hostile gonfalonier, although only a story, may well be true. In any case when at last on September 29 the verdict was reached, it was to the effect that Cosimo, his brother Lorenzo, and a few of the more outstanding Medicean partisans were to be banished to various cities of Italy. A few days later Cosimo was taken under guard to the frontier. He made his way to Venice which received him more in the manner of a great prince upon his travels than of a discredited and exiled commoner.

On Cosimo's departure it became apparent that the impulsive Rinaldo had not gained very much, since the opposition to him waxed rather than waned in strength. Henceforth his power hinged on the chance of his having a favorable signory; and since the signory was renewed every two months he could never be really at peace. When a year after Cosimo's fall, on September 1, 1434, a body of priors entered office who in their majority were hostile to him, his power collapsed overnight. The new government took steps at once to recall the banished Cosimo. In his desperation Rinaldo resolved to drive his enemies out of the palace and take the government into his own hands. He assembled an armed following, but the signory, warned of his action, occupied the piazza with troops. When the temperamental oligarch, checkmated, permitted himself to be drawn into negotiations, he showed that he lacked the unshaken resolution of the born leader of men. It happened that Pope Eugene IV had taken refuge in Florence at this time and was residing at the Dominican monastery of Santa Maria Novella. Eugene offered to mediate between the factions in order to make peace and at the pope's request Rinaldo paid him a visit in his chambers. At this exhibition of pusillanimity his disgusted followers dispersed to their homes and his cause was lost. Thereupon the scene was re-enacted with which we are familiar to the point of weariness as the customary accompaniment of every political crisis: a parliament was called, the constitution was suspended, and a balìa of three hundred Medicean partisans was empowered to reform the government. On September 29 the balìa decreed Cosimo's recall and in the course of the next few days visited banishment on Rinaldo and his most compromised adherents. In exactly one year to the day the wheel of fortune had come full circle round. On October 5 Cosimo re-entered Florentine territory and was welcomed by his fellow-citizens like a conqueror returning from the wars. The government was in his hands and for the present at least he was free to do with it as he saw fit.

XXI. The Government of Cosimo de' Medici

IMPORTANT a landmark as is the return of Cosimo de' Medici from exile in 1434, it has not quite the significance which has been assigned to it by many, especially of the older historians of Florence. For them, instead of a landmark, the event was rather in the nature of a chasm by which the history of Florence falls sharply into two periods labeled respectively Before and After the Medici. For this clean-cut dichotomy there would be some justification if, as indeed these same historians generally maintain, Florence before the Medici had been a free republic and immediately on the appearance of the Medici had passed under the yoke of a tyrant. Nothing, however, would be less well founded than such a contention. We have seen that at no time of its history had Florence made a conspicuous success of the democratic tendencies which it undoubtedly nourished; and when in the fourteenth century the lesser gilds had set up the closest approximation to a democratic government Florence ever achieved, the experiment broke down in 1382 before the attack of the greater gilds. These thereupon resumed control; or rather, under cover of the authority belonging constitutionally to the body of twenty-one gilds, a group of associated merchant families created an alert and jealous oligarchy. So ruthlessly did the oligarchic junta, to which the family of the Albizzi has lent its name, manipulate the constitution that for the half-century the junta lasted the constitution functioned not with its own energy but with that supplied by a sect or party. And if the Albizzeschi had remained united under firm and, above all, elastic leadership, it is very doubtful that they would have been overthrown when they were.

The governing group of the Albizzi yielded its place in 1434 to Cosimo de' Medici, who as much under the pressure of circumstances as by reason of his political ambition had become the head of a group of rival families. These had in the main only recently acquired their wealth and were for this very reason more daring and ruthless than the older families which gathered around the Albizzi. To all appearances it was they, much more than Cosimo, who were responsible for the orgy of vengeance in which they indulgèd against their defeated predecessors on beginning their rule. While the earliest victims of the Medicean revolution, among them Rinaldo degli Albizzi himself, got off with the usual sentence of exile, the animosity of the victors grew as they realized the completeness of their triumph. Thereupon not only did they multiply the banishments far beyond recent Florentine practice but they gave themselves the added satisfaction of spilling the blood of a considerable number of their enemies by sending them to the block. The forceful suppression of opponents had been a feature of every successful Florentine revolution and the indispensable concomitant measure was the adoption of constitutional "reforms" calculated to give the victory a desirable permanence. It is when we examine the alterations in the constitution effected by the victors that the chasm reputed to yawn between pre- and post-Medicean history should become visible. But no one has ever succeeded in detecting it nor has any objective observer ever come to any other conclusion than that the new government was the old government operated by a different set of beneficiaries. We must conclude that the Mediceans saw no reason for changing the system of control elaborated by their predecessors; and it is a fact that they took it over and made it their own with but a single important change.

The single change, however, so patly rounded out the inherited system that it must be given close attention. The control which had been elaborated by the oligarchs had, as its central feature, the periodical revision of the borse by means of a new scrutiny. As a new scrutiny was impossible without authorization, this was obtained from a commission or balìa to which a packed assembly of the people held in the public square voted full powers. It looked like an air-tight system and was air-tight, except for the fact that the men whose names went into the purses on the supposition that they could be depended on were liable, especially during a political crisis, to change their opinion. That was what on the occasion of the September drawings of the year 1434 had ruined Rinaldo degli Albizzi, for he found himself confronted with, and helpless before, a signory of Medicean complexion. On Cosimo and his friends taking over the power they were resolved not to be hoist by the same petard. They therefore had the balìa, authorized by the parliament called by them, appoint a subcommittee of ten *accoppiatori* who were to serve for five years with the power to choose the new priorate every two months from among the names in the purses. This process of election, which won the appropriate designation *a mano* (by hand), completely removed the danger inseparable from an election by lot. By the simple device of reappointing the accoppiatori at the expiration of their term for another five-year period, a handpicked signory was or seemed to be assured for an indefinite time.

To repeat: while the accoppiatori represent the finishing touch applied to an older system of control, it is absurd to maintain that only with their appointment was the Florentine constitution denatured. It had been more or less flagrantly manhandled practically from its birth and indisputably from the time of the adoption of the practice of choosing the signory by lot. From the very start of this system an evil inseparable from a resort to chance as a method of appointing magistrates had made itself felt. This was the elevation to office of a high percentage of the flagrantly incompetent. If to this evil we add the perilous flux imposed on the executive department by the brief two months' term of office, we shall be disposed to agree that anything approaching a considered and consistent governmental policy had become impossible. The plain truth is the constitution did not work; and Florence would have suffered incalculable harm if a group of men of substantially the same outlook and loosely formed into a party had not by variously devised subterfuges brought the recurrent drawings from the purses under control. The surprising thing is not that these practices, already old before the Medici came to power and merely perfected by them, should have been in vogue, but that commentators on Florentine affairs down to our time should have bewailed the trickery employed as an unpardonable crime. From the strict point of view of law it undoubtedly was a crime; but we follow a much more fruitful line of reflection when we take note that a political system, so offensive to the most rudimentary demands of common sense as this of Florence, cannot be maintained and that, if it cannot by legal means be adjusted to the most immediate needs of society, a way will unfailingly be found to circumvent it.

Among the most immediate needs of the Florentine state we can distinguish between a domestic and a foreign need and agree that in regard to either a much greater stability was desirable than the constitution afforded. The ten accoppiatori represent the Medicean contribution to stability in the domestic field. The importance attached to this contribution by its sponsors is made clear when we observe that the leading Mediceans, such men as Agnolo Acciaiuoli, Neri Capponi, and Diotisalvi Neroni, served regularly as accoppiatori. But what is surprising at first blush, Cosimo de' Medici himself was not on this decisive committee. The sufficient reason for this self-effacement was that, although leader of the victorious party, he was regarded by his jealous fellow-oligarchs as their equal and was obliged to tread warily; above all, he had to share the power with them and scrupulously to guard against the impression of being, or even of wanting to be, a tyrant of the type that had come to the top everywhere else in Italy. He therefore left the accoppiatori, the priorate, and most of the other honors of state as their due spoils to his associates. Except for his having been gonfalonier of Justice three times, in 1435, in 1439, and in 1445, thereby serving a total of six months as chief executive during a control of thirty years, he never held a high state office. However, if he was at pains to conciliate his followers, he had not the least intention to surrender control to them or to let them get out of hand and run amuck. First and foremost he was resolved that they should not harden into too close a corporation. It was this congealing into a narrow-minded caste that had been the undoing of the Albizzeschi. In measure as members of the lower ranks of society endowed with intelligence and energy amassed new fortunes they were to be admitted to the ruling circle. While government was to continue to be an affair of the few, it was Cosimo's intention that the reigning body of optimates should be constantly refreshed with new blood. As a result he had the ambitious, and the ambitious meant the alert and dangerous, rising young men of the common people on his side, for he placed no obstacle in the way of their aspiration to join the ruling junta and achieve the honors of office.

If by his readiness to welcome talent into the governing set Cosimo acquired something of the reputation of a democrat, he added to this report in other, still more effective ways. For, wisely, he never forgot that he owed much of his success to his and his family's popularity with the lower orders and that these orders, although their direct share in the government had by now become unimportant, still counted considerably in the general political equation.

Like the typical Florentine burgher he was, Cosimo had always practiced an easy familiarity with his fellow-citizens of high and low degree alike. A manner more removed from social snobbery than that of this most eminent banker of his day could not be imagined. Following his accession to power, he continued to dress, talk, and show himself in street and square exactly as before. Aware of the awed regard in which he was held owing to his great wealth, he had the intelligence to recognize that money by itself does not offer assurance of continued respect, and that in order to win abiding honor with his opulence he would have to spend it generously on enterprises of a public character. Accordingly he devoted immense sums to the building of churches and the founding of monasteries and libraries; and since by these creations he added to the beauty and fame of Florence among Italian cities, the people, to whom the glory of their town meant much, rewarded him with a lively affection. Floated into power on a wave of popular approval, the Medicean party steadily strengthened its hold on the people, and for this invaluable backing by the masses it was exclusively indebted to its calculating, intelligent head.

In view of the influence of Cosimo both over the Florentine masses and his own oligarchical party we will readily concede that his person was a large factor in the domestic stability of Florence after 1434, even though he himself avoided rather than sought office. But when it came to foreign policy he did not dare trust to a system of indirect control to achieve the stability absolutely indispensable in this field; for, since the state of Florence had by Cosimo's time become involved in a perilous power situation, its very existence was momently at stake. So difficult, complicated, and dangerous had its relations with its Italian neighbors become that they could no longer, save at the greatest risk, be intrusted to an ever-changing plural executive like the Florentine signory. Cosimo therefore quietly but unhesitatingly appropriated this all important department for himself. Of course he preserved appearances as much as possible and did nothing calculated unnecessarily to offend the dignity of the official heads of the state, the priors. But, in effect, he assumed the office of minister of foreign affairs, and his fine new palace in the Via Larga became the unofficial foreign office of the state. It was a delicate situation, for while it was he who shaped the foreign policy of Florence, the policy had to have the support of the constituted authorities, the priors with the gonfalonier of Justice at their head and the numerous councils. The signory, wholly composed of party nominees, was generally easy to manage, but the councils, in which public opinion continued to make itself heard, were frequently a source of embarrassment to the self-appointed foreign minister. In the end the deft and affable but steady and persistent Cosimo always imposed his will and, as long as he lived, both projected and steered the course which Florence followed among the Italian states.

Further to insure the control of the state under his hand Cosimo could not afford to overlook the public finances. They were to an eminent degree centered in the Monte, the administration of the National Debt. Cosimo insisted on serving in person on the board of directors, and as often as his term expired had himself reappointed. This was, therefore, in sharp distinction from his management of foreign policy, a service performed in the open. That Cosimo, whose position in regard to Florence and whose conduct in reference to his party have frequently invited a comparison between him and a modern American city boss, should, in the matter of the Monte, have departed from the secrecy which was his element and still is that of his American successor, proves the great importance he attached to an immediate influence over the public monies. Naturally his enemies made his connection with the Monte, the one point at which his carefully concealed association with the state machinery became visible, the main object of their attack. They tried repeatedly to eliminate him from the board, but, never quite succeeding, took revenge by circulating every conceivable slander against his integrity. Cavalcanti reports that they went so far as to spread the whisper that Cosimo treated not only the monies of the Monte but even the ordinary revenues of the state as his personal property, and that he had the gabelle, that is, the receipts from the consumption taxes levied at the gates, deposited every night at his house.[1] While the gossip purveyed by Cavalcanti should not be taken too literally, it has the merit of disclosing the malignant quality of the underground opposition which Cosimo had to face throughout his days.

The foreign policy of Cosimo was determined by considerations, first, of the safety and, second, of the possible enlargement of the Florentine state and was elastically adjusted to the ever-shifting situation within the Italian peninsula. It would be as tedious as it is unnecessary to trace the innumerable oscillations of his policy, especially as, in view of its set central purpose, it can without practicing any violence be reduced to a relatively simple pattern. On Cosimo's taking over the department of foreign affairs the outstanding feature of the Italian situation was the fixed resolution of Duke Filippo Maria of Milan to enlarge his dominions. To meet the threat from Milan Cosimo's predecessors, the Albizzeschi, had allied themselves with Venice, and to this alliance the new ruler gave a ready adherence as it was the only available means for holding the Lombard ruler in check. The duke was a savage and restless tyrant who, served by the most famous condottieri of the age, continually renewed his thrust, on the one hand into Tuscany, and on the other into the Romagna, the exposed northern province of the State of the Church. In consequence, even though the alliance between the two city-republics proved strong enough to repel his aggressions, the peace of Italy was permanently disturbed. The papacy was too weak to contribute greatly to the defense of its territory, which was at the mercy not only of the enterprising duke but also of every impudent leader of mercenaries disposed to invade the patrimony of Peter with the intention of carving out a dominion for himself. Shortly before Cosimo's return from exile Pope Eugene IV, unable any longer to maintain himself in his own capital, had taken up his residence at Florence as the city's guest. Under these painful circumstances the papacy did not, for the time being at least, count for much in the Italian situation. The kingdom of Naples, too, had been temporarily eliminated, owing to the fact that on the death, on February 2, 1435, of the childless Queen Joan the succession to the throne precipitated a contest between King Alfonso of Aragon and the French

[1] Cavalcanti, Vol. II, chap. 33.

duke of Anjou, the dead queen's distant relative. War followed between the two claimants which after many years was decided in favor of Alfonso; however, while the civil struggle lasted, the southern kingdom did not and could not make its power felt in the general situation.

Under these circumstances easily the most important event of peninsular scope during the early years of Medicean control was the struggle of the duke of Milan to penetrate the powerful defensive ring drawn about him by Florence and Venice. Battles were won and lost, the hireling condottieri frequently changed sides on the offer of better pay, treaties among the combatants were signed only to be broken—in the agitated succession of trivial events in field and council chamber there is no happening calculated to impress itself on our mind till we come to 1440. In that year Duke Filippo Maria at last lent an ear to the repeated representations made to him by Rinaldo degli Albizzi and the other Florentine exiles and dispatched an army under the famous general Piccinino directly against the Arno city. According to the exiles this army would only have to appear before the walls for the Florentines to rise in a spontaneous movement of rebellion against the hated Medicean tyranny. It was indeed a critical moment for Cosimo when the Milanese host, bursting through the barriers of the Apennines, sifted down the valleys of the Mugello range and appeared on the heights of Fiesole directly over the city. Nonetheless, contrary to the confident boast of Rinaldo and his band, the Florentine population did not so much as lift a finger against its reputed tyrant, and Piccinino, incapable of conducting the siege of so large a town, was compelled to withdraw to the Casentino. In this upper Arno area the Florentine forces caught up with him and on June 29, at Anghiari, beat him roundly. The invaders were obliged to abandon Tuscany and with them went the self-deceived and disconsolate Florentine exiles. When the spirited Rinaldo died two years later, the old oligarchy may be said to have been buried with him, for the Medicean rule was never again challenged from that quarter.

The sweeping victory brought certain territorial advantages in its wake, as it enabled Florence to strengthen its hold on the upper valley of its river. This mountain region had originally been and long remained a typical feudal area. In the course of time, however, most of the castle-owners had been ousted and their possessions taken over by the expanding republic. Up to the Milanese invasion the greatest of all the feudal lords, the counts of Poppi, had escaped this fate, owing to their having sought and obtained the friendship of the republic by formal acknowledgment of Florentine supremacy. Unfortunately for himself the reigning count joined forces with the commander of the invading host, with Piccinino, and when this general was defeated at Anghiari and abandoned the country, the overbold ally had to pay the penalty for his hardihood. The castle of Poppi, which, happily spared by the ravages of time, still overwhelms the visitor with its feudal grandeur, was appropriated by Florence together with its dependent territory and the count himself driven into exile. He was the last representative of the great Guidi family who had inscribed their names on many a page of Tuscan history during the preceding four centuries. The Guidi had now reached the end of their journey. The count Francesco's exit from the scene and descent into an engulfing oblivion is therefore not without the pathos that clings to every completed human destiny. During the Casentino campaign Florence had possessed itself of the mountain town of Borgo San Sepolcro and, in spite of its belonging to the State of the Church, was not minded to give it up again. As the homeless Pope Eugene was in no position to insist on his rights, he finally agreed to leave it in the republic's hands for a cash consideration. Borgo San Sepolcro and the Poppi lands gave Florence the unchallenged command of the upper Arno. They had the additional significance of enabling the Medicean regime to boast that it, too, had met the patriotic obligation laid upon every government, no matter what its nature, to enlarge the Florentine dominion.

By the time of the crisis so happily resolved by the victory of Anghiari a new factor had crept into the general Italian situation which materially changed its aspect. The greatest of all the freebooters of this era of mercenary soldiers was Francesco Sforza. Already before Cosimo's advent to power Sforza had taken advantage of the continued feebleness of the papacy to seize some of its territory and proclaim himself its lord, of course under the nominal suzerainty of the pope, whose ultimate authority was not disputed. But this success did not satisfy his ambition, which gradually directed its aim at nothing less than Filippo Maria Visconti's duchy of Milan. As the leading condottiere of Italy, Sforza had made himself so indispensable to the duke that this ruler could not prosecute his far-reaching military designs without taking Sforza into account. A strong bond therefore tied the duke to the hireling soldier. Now it happened that the Visconti ruler had no children save an illegitimate daughter, Bianca. As the prospective heir of Milan, Bianca was in her day the greatest match in Italy, and to this exalted lady the audacious, low-born Sforza ventured to lift his eyes with a view to acquiring her hand and throne. Although the duke, her father, at first angrily rejected his condottiere's proposal as nothing less than an insult to his birth and grandeur, so long as he persisted in his policy of conquest he remained in an unescapable dependence on the good-will of the powerful freebooter. In order to secure his continued attachment to the ducal cause, gradually and with what inner reluctance may be left to the imagination the Milanese tyrant was obliged to come around to Sforza's view; and, after first tentatively affiancing the general to his daughter, he at last consented to their marriage. The startling event took place in November, 1441. Thenceforward, as the duke's son-in-law, the condottiere might seem to have had smooth sailing, but such was not the case. The duke, who had yielded only to the pressure of necessity, remained instinctively hostile to his daughter's husband, while Venice, desiring to end the ancient quarrel with neighboring Milan once for all, laid its plans to utilize the confusion sure to ensue on the duke's death by seizing Milan for itself.

As soon as the Milanese succession question moved into the focus of political attention, Cosimo resolved to back Francesco Sforza on the ground that the alternative to Sforza was Venice and that Venice enlarged by Milan would completely dominate the peninsula. It was an attitude inspired by intelligible patriotic considerations, but it did not please the Florentines, chiefly because through the long years of waiting for the duke's death they were called upon to finance the Sforza claim to the Milanese succession. In spite of a grumbling, all but universal opposition, Cosimo clung to his purpose and by his unwavering support of Sforza more than by any other single episode connected with his rule, showed that when it came to a crucial issue he was resolved to do what the situation demanded even at the risk of losing his popularity. At last, on August 13, 1447, occurred the long-awaited death of the crafty and unprincipled Filippo Maria. The first effect of the event was that the Milanese in an access of democratic enthusiasm re-established their republic. But no longer possessed of the virtues required for this form of government, they made a miserable showing in their struggle against the two enterprising claimants to the duke's heritage, Venice and Francesco Sforza. In the end the condottiere carried off the honors and in February, 1450, was acclaimed by his new subjects as their duke.

The support, chiefly of a financial order, which Florence had for years uninterruptedly given Francesco Sforza was a big factor in his success, and when he now blossomed forth as the duke of Milan there followed a new alignment of the Italian powers. Deeply resenting the help given the hardy adventurer, Venice indignantly abandoned its long-standing alliance with Florence and sought the friendship of King Alfonso, who, having at length driven the Anjou claimant out of the Neapolitan realm, was now in secure possession of the southern throne. The revised political orientation produced a war, in which Milan and Florence were obliged to meet the attack of Venice and Naples. The new conflict, as wasteful and purposeless as its numerous predecessors, continued until there fell upon the ears of Europe with a sound like the crack of doom the news of the capture of Constantinople by the Turks (1453). The moving event prompted the successor of Eugene IV, Pope Nicholas V, to plead with all the combatants to compose their petty differences and present a united Italian front to the dangerous Moslem enemy. Although the appeal for union under the pope fell on deaf ears, the urgent self-interest of Venice obliged it to seek an accommodation. In order to have its hands free to deal with the situation in the east, a situation so grave that it threatened a complete catastrophe, the republic opened negotiations with Milan at the town of Lodi which on April 11, 1454, were successfully concluded. To the peace of Lodi, Naples, the ally of Venice, and Florence, the ally of Milan, ended by giving their adherence, thereby making it effective for the whole peninsula. In point of fact the treaty, through its acceptance by practically every state of Italy, great or small, assumed something of the character of an Italian confederation, since all the signatories agreed to support the cause of peace and to stand together against any member state that would thereafter commit an unmistakably aggressive act. While it is true that Lodi did not achieve its federative mission and that Italy continued to be torn with rivalries and war, it is undeniable that the political situation registered an improvement, at least for the time being. Florence perhaps benefited more and for a longer time than any other state. The policy incorporated in the Lodi document was an expression of the mature view, to which Cosimo had come after an experience of twenty years as foreign minister of the Arno city. That view was that Florence, a commercial republic, was not constituted so as to be able successfully to carry on a policy of aggression and that its best hope was a mutual guaranty of peace among the Italian powers on the basis of existing boundaries. To be sure, Florence did not, because of Lodi, give up its recently established intimacy with Milan. The union was even strengthened when, before long, King Alfonso of Naples joined it as a third member. The maintenance of a ring within a ring was naturally displeasing to the outsiders, to the pope and Venice. It clearly indicated that all was not well within the league of Lodi and that the old jealousies continued to smoulder under the surface. Nonetheless Florence achieved a peace which lasted for the remainder of Cosimo's life, while the system, of which the peace was an expression, was adopted by his son and, after some fluctuation, by his grandson and was accepted as a basic principle of government guaranteeing the Medici rule. The peace of Lodi was a triumph which constituted a new bright feather in Cosimo's cap and helps explain the ease with which he overcame the revolt in his own ranks—to be presently related.

Having with the peace of Lodi brought Florence to an arrangement with its Italian rivals and neighbors which Cosimo considered, and which probably was, the best attainable under prevailing circumstances, we shall turn to consider the domestic developments in his time, not without once more expressing regret that, in the interest of continuity, we are constrained to present foreign and domestic occurrences as two distinct series of events. Nothing could be farther from the truth than such an assumption; and before we have concluded our renewed domestic survey we shall be provided with at least one excellent opportunity to illustrate the always busy interaction between the happenings outside and inside the Florentine walls. And since events promoting our acquaintance with the tang and quality of Florentine life are no less important to us than strictly political movements, we shall begin our domestic record with the consecration of the cathedral of Santa Maria del Fiore on March 25, 1436. The occasion for the ceremony was the completion by the architect Brunelleschi of the great cupola over the octagonal east end. As Pope Eugene was a resident of the city at the time, he could be utilized as the leading figure in the spectacle and a magnificence could be unfolded in which the citizens, young and old, rich and poor, always took a childlike pleasure. The chroniclers vie with one another in describing the raised board walk which was constructed all the way from Santa Maria Novella, where the pope resided, to the cathedral, and along which, hung with carpets and gay with banners and garlands, Eugene IV attended by seven cardinals, thirty-seven archbishops and bishops, and the nine members of the Florentine signory moved in solemn procession to perform the act of consecration at the altar erected under the newly finished dome.

Three years later Florence became the seat of a General Council of the church, and during a period of six months its citizens enjoyed the spectacle of innumerable ecclesiastical ceremonies as well as the frequent formal entry and departure of exalted personages. Pope Eugene had issued a call for a Council in the hope of bringing about the union of the eastern and the western, the Greek Orthodox and the Roman Catholic churches, which, owing to doctrinal differences defying compromise, had parted company over six hundred years before. He had originally selected Ferrara as the place of meeting for the representatives of the two faiths; but Cosimo by bringing his great financial reserves into play had maneuvered so cleverly that in January, 1439, the assembly was transferred from Ferrara to Florence. In addition to the heads of the two churches, the pope and the patriarch, each attended by a cloud of bishops and learned doctors, a great secular prince, the Greek emperor, graced the Council with his presence. In fact it was really because of him that the Council was held, for, hard pressed by the advancing Turks and fearing the loss of his ancient capital, Constantinople, the emperor had come to the west to ask for help in his desperate struggle. Solely because the Turks were pressing a dagger to his throat, he and his clergy offered the theological concessions which made it possible for the breach between the two churches to be closed. On July 5, 1439, in a final ceremonial session held in the cathedral of Santa Maria del Fiore the union of Christianity was declared to have been happily restored. So important did the event appear to be to the contemporaries that it was resolved to perpetuate its memory by an inscription on one of the vast stone piers supporting Brunelleschi's soaring cupola. There, at the side of the door leading into the sacristy, it may still be read not without ironical amusement in view of the fugitive character of the triumph it celebrated. Hardly had the Greek prelates reached home when they repudiated the agreement; the emperor never received the political support from the west, to obtain which he had bent his knee before the pope; and not much over a decade after the Florentine gathering Constantinople met the tragic fate which the Turks had been preparing for it for more than a generation. The General Council of Florence lingers in the memory as one of the minor futilities of history; but with the coming and going through many months of a pope, a patriarch, an emperor, and innumerable gorgeously costumed prelates, the Council brought to the streets and squares of Florence an unwonted and long-remembered gayety, color, and excitement. A cultural by-product of the assembly should not be overlooked, especially as it shows Cosimo de' Medici in another than the political role with which we have become familiar. The most learned as well as the most venerable of the visiting Greeks was George Gemistos Plethon. A passionate champion of the philosophy of Plato, not only did he attract the attention of the numerous Florentine humanists but he won the special regard of the untitled lord of Florence. It was his contact with Plethon that moved Cosimo to consider the idea of a Platonic academy on the Arno, and as a preparatory measure to its creation to give the alert and promising youth, Marsilio Ficino, the son of his physician, a thoroughgoing education at his expense in the Greek language.

Following the peace of Lodi there occurred a movement within the Medicean party which furnishes a clear indication of the repeatedly asserted interaction between events in the foreign and domestic fields. With the long wars brought to a close and all danger from ambitious neighbors at least temporarily removed, certain associates of Cosimo within the ruling group believed that the time had come to reduce his swollen power and proportionately to increase their own. They hoped, on what grounds it is difficult to understand, to achieve their purpose by giving up the accoppiatori and returning to the older system of electing the priors by lot. Cosimo thought it prudent to let them have their way; and accordingly by successive steps in the latter half of the year 1454 the control exercised for twenty years was surrendered and the signory again drawn from the borse as chance determined. The leaders of the revolt were Luca Pitti, Agnolo Acciauoli, and Diotisalvi Neroni, all three of them men who had filled the highest offices of state. The Florentines, enamored of their "liberty," greeted with delight the elimination of the ten accoppiatori, stigmatized in private conversation as the ten tyrants, and praised to the skies the rebels who had freed them from an abominable yoke. But the satisfaction of the conspirators was of short duration. Before many months had passed they were made aware that if the removal of the accoppiatori weakened Cosimo's control, it weakened also their own. The signories that emerged from the unsupervised purses assumed a more and more independent attitude, and early in the year 1458 the then ruling government roused to indignation the whole body of wealthy Mediceans by resolving to draw up a new catasto. This meant nothing less than a radical reform of the taxation practices identified with the ruling group. The rivals of Cosimo responsible for the return to the older system of electing officials were without exception typical, well-to-do oligarchs. Exactly how they had profited from the taxation they had hitherto imposed must now be told.

Our last contact with Florentine taxation was on the occasion of the adoption in 1427 of the law of the catasto. Again affirming that this legislation was an improvement on everything that had gone before, we have now to note that, notwithstanding its fair appearance, it could be more or less completely nullified by being dishonestly administered. Unfortunately, in the matter of taxation, Florence suffered from an evil tradition, for the ruling groups of the past had never scrupled to levy the municipal imposts as they saw fit, and that means capriciously and without fixed principle. While it may therefore be said that, when the Mediceans on assuming power manipulated the taxes in their own interest, they merely followed a long-established custom, it is also true that they went beyond any of their predecessors by more effectively systematizing their outrageous partisanship. We have already insisted that Cosimo's party, far from inventing political control, merely perfected the inherited regime by adding the accoppiatori feature. To this main string of the bow of Medicean rule a second alternate string of equal strength was joined when it was resolved to manage taxation in such a way that the wealthy Mediceans would be favored and the wealthy opponents mulcted and crushed. From the point of view of the Medicean opposition the accoppiatori were bad enough, but the brutal oppression represented by an arbitrary system of taxation was several times worse, since he whom it selected as its victim was irretrievably ruined.

The falsifying of the provisions of the catasto began with the failure to renew the assessment at regular three-year intervals, as the law in its original form required. Since the leading followers of Cosimo were the new-rich whose wealth was steadily increasing, it was to their advantage to be taxed according to the register in operation on their arrival at power, which was the register of 1431. By refusing to consent to its renewal they escaped the heavier tax to which they were liable on account of their mounting fortunes. Even more profitable to them was the protection they enjoyed at the hands of the purely Medicean commissioners of taxation (*sgravatori*), for these officials had the power to name at their good pleasure the sum each citizen was obliged to pay on the basis of his supposed income. In the forties, owing to the growing need of revenue in order to meet the costs of the uninterrupted wars, the income tax was made progressive. In the light of modern opinion this must be considered an advance, since the low incomes escaped with a low assessment, while the rate increased for the higher brackets until all returns over fifteen hundred florins were subjected, depending on the needs of the public purse, to a rate ranging from 25 to 50 per cent of the taxable total. It constitutes an interesting comment on changing points of view to observe that with practical unanimity the contemporary chroniclers voiced their horror of the new graduated feature. Seeing that they were without exception members of the bourgeoisie, we need not take their outcry too seriously, since every bourgeoisie from the beginning of time has emitted similar moans. We should not fail to note, however, that the small tradesmen, whose favor Cosimo wisely never ceased to court, were pleased with the relief afforded them. Gladly conceding that the revision of the forties, usually referred to as the *scala,* was not without merit, we should not forget that it wrought no change in the intolerable central principle, according to which the taxes were so manipulated that they were a buckler for the friends and a poniard for the enemies of the regime.

It was natural for the signory, as soon as it was free of the accoppiatori control, to try to break the other chain, the chain of taxation, by which the city was held in Medicean bondage. Plainly the way to bring this about was to draw up a new catasto without fear or favor; and no sooner was this proposal broached (January, 1458) than the disgusted conspirators ran to Cosimo for aid. Sadder but wiser men, they now regretted the abolition of the accoppiatori and implored their leader to help them re-establish the lost control. This could not be done without the familiar trick of the parliament, and Cosimo, willing to teach his slippery friends a lesson, kept them whining at his threshold for over half a year. At length in the month of August he gave his consent to proceed. The gonfalonier of Justice of the July-August period was Luca Pitti, and Cosimo may have felt a particular satisfaction in having a leading rival and ex-conspirator assume responsibility for the parliament, thus offering himself as the target for the hatred that the use of this loathsome instrument invariably released. To what a monstrous abuse the so-called assembly of the people had by this time degenerated is handsomely demonstrated by a description of its action some days *before* the projected parliament was held. In 1458 Florence was closely allied with Milan, and in sign of this intimacy a certain Nicodemo resided in the Arno city as the ambassador of Duke Francesco Sforza. Living in the closest intimacy with Cosimo, Nicodemo dispatched to his master a succession of reports which constitute one of the most important sources for our knowledge of the period. The parliament, planned to bring back the system of the ten tyrants, was to be held on August 11. Three days before, on August 8, Nicodemo wrote to his duke as follows:

The lord of Faenza [a condottiere employed by Florence] will arrive tomorrow with three hundred cavalry and fifty footmen; there will also be the troops of Simonetta [another condottiere]. . . . On the morning of the day fixed for the parliament the troops will draw up in battle array on the piazza. The people will arrive without arms. Then the priors will read a list of the citizens to whom balìa shall be given to reform the town and will ask the people whether they agree. The partisans planted in the square will shout "Yes! Yes!" and the common people will join in the cry according to custom.[2]

The comedy of August 11 was acted out exactly as forecast by Cosimo's intimate: the people shouted their approval and the balìa was instituted. There followed the making of new purses and the intrusting of the nomination of the signory to a commission of ten accoppiatori. The brief interlude of the free purses was over. As Luca Pitti, in the capacity of gonfalonier of Justice, had been the visible impresario of the spectacle of August 11 he was regarded by the mass of the Medicean party as the hero of the occasion. This was also his own view and his self-importance expanded proportionately. He was a vain, affable, and vivacious man who held the view that his great wealth entitled him to a larger share of power than Cosimo had seen fit to accord him. With Agnolo Acciaiuoli, Diotisalvi Neroni, and many similar birds of fine feather he was of the opinion, traditional among the leading merchants of Florence, that the rule of the city belonged of right to the optimates. But while detesting the government of the many, these men of means were as little disposed to accept the domination of a tyrant. The signore was to them that intolerable thing: *il governo d'un solo*. It is a fact that, following the successful revolution of 1458, Luca Pitti came to be regarded by many observers as the most important figure in Florence. Cosimo was waxing old and, owing to his growing infirmities, showed himself more and more rarely in public. Under the circumstances it is perhaps not so strange that the whisper should have gone around that Luca had succeeded in wresting the scepter from Cosimo's hands. How superficial and mistaken this judgment was is amply attested by Ambassador Nicodemo's reports to Milan. Not for a moment did this intelligent diplomat, whose business it was to remain in touch with the true source of Florentine authority, turn from Cosimo to Luca. One of the old Medicean fox's most valuable gifts was his ability to read character. We cannot doubt that he saw to the very bottom of Luca Pitti and had arrived at the opinion that he had nothing to fear from this agitated and colorful but inconstant butterfly. When Luca presently undertook to feed his vanity by commencing on the slope of the hill of San Giorgio the construction of a palace twice as large as that of the Medici, we can imagine Cosimo's face wreathing itself in its familiar enigmatic smile. This rival of his was about to spend his energy in idle display. That he estimated Luca correctly is indicated by the fact that Luca did not live to finish the famous Pitti palace and that in due course of time it became the official residence of the dukes of the house of Medici.

It was a very different Florence from that he had known as a boy that Cosimo faced in his old age. Many of the shibboleths and battle-cries of his

[2] Perrens, *Histoire de Florence depuis la domination*, etc. Vol. I, pp. 187-88.

youth had lost their significance. Truth to tell, even at that early time many of them had already been long on the wane. What around the year 1400, when Cosimo was a vigorous adolescent, did the terms Guelph and Ghibelline still mean? Was not the empire, the hope of the Ghibellines, a withered plant and the papacy, the protecting arm of the Guelphs, paralyzed by the Great Schism? What was the significance of the Ordinances of Justice, when there were no longer any magnates whose excesses needed to be repressed? True, the oligarchs who preceded Cosimo had found the Ordinances useful as a device to exclude their enemies from the government by stigmatizing them as magnates, but this trickery only helped to bring it home to even the simplest minds that the original magnate class had disappeared. More important even than changes such as these was the fact that the gild system, so closely identified with the city's rise to greatness, was also no longer what it had been. The trecento was without question the great age of the gilds. In the quattrocento they were weakening, and the downward movement may undoubtedly be ascribed to the victory in 1382 of the greater over the lesser gilds and to the subsequent all but complete eclipse of the latter. Ever since their victory the greater gilds, and that, when all is said, meant the great merchants individually, enjoyed an unchallenged ascendancy. More and more they became pure enterprisers of the "putting-out" type, whose function it was to "put out" to the working people the tools and the raw products they needed for the various manufacturing processes. We shall have to conclude that, as soon as its democratic vigor was squeezed out of the gild system by the crushing defeat of the arti minori, the capitalists discovered that they no longer needed the gilds, especially as with their intricate restrictions and regulations they had become a good deal of a nuisance. Not to exaggerate, let us agree that while the gilds retained their full formal importance throughout the quattrocento, their sun was beginning to set. The new economic factor was the enterpriser, pure and simple, who aspired to liberate himself from shackles of every kind and to rule unhampered over a free labor market.

Hesitant as Cosimo was to change political appearances and desirous to give the impression that the inherited institutions operated exactly as before his advent, he could not keep changes from creeping also into the political segment of Florentine existence. Particularly marked was the decline of the podestà. While it is certain that already the generations before Cosimo had busied themselves to clip the wings of this one-time ruler of the commonwealth, not till the Medicean era was he deposed from the formal headship of the state and this honor assigned to the chief of the priors, the gonfalonier of Justice. At the same time the podestà's judicial powers, constituting his very life-blood, were sensibly diminished. Having already under the Albizzeschi suffered a loss of jurisdiction in favor of the police committee, the Otto di Guardia, he was now obliged to transfer to the Otto all cases involving the issue of politics. A judge to deal justly with political offenders was no longer wanted and the Eight were accordingly exalted over the podestà. From them, as strictly partisan nominees, the regime might expect the unqualified condemnations it demanded. It is worth while to call attention to these relatively unimportant changes to remind the reader that, like everything else in Florence, the apparently frozen forms of the constitution were undergoing alterations and that time never stands still.

Taken up with Cosimo's political activity, we have thus far hardly touched an interest of his which in the eyes of some observers still constitutes his greatest distinction. He lived in the quattrocento, a period of the rapidly expanding Renaissance, and took an eager part in its intellectual and artistic manifestations. There have been schools of historiography in the past which, aesthetically oriented and disposed to regard the Renaissance as one of the summits of human development, have celebrated Cosimo, because of his association with art and literature, as a hero of the world-cause of culture. Occasional encomiasts have even gone so far as to make it appear that he was the magician, by the waving of whose wand the Renaissance rose as a finished product from the void. The opinion is so absurd that it hardly needs to be expressly refuted. All serious students agree that the Renaissance is an epoch of European history which unfolded slowly under the action of innumerable forces and that it constitutes a definite link in the chain of western civilization. The idea that Cosimo or any other individual could have produced this era is simply laughable. Far from being the creator, Cosimo was the creature of the Renaissance. And because undeniably he was from his birth steeped in its spirit, he presents himself to view, exactly like the whole upper stratum of his Florentine fellow-citizens, as a Renaissance man: as a man of the *early* Renaissance, let it be observed, for the Middle Ages had not yet spent their vigor, and in the first half of the fifteenth century the medieval influences still counted greatly in the outlook of even such individuals as may have thought they had cast them off.

Since Cosimo was brought up as a banker and throughout his life gave his time and attention chiefly to business and politics, he was not, and could not be, in a professional sense either a humanist or an artist. However, endowed with a keen mind, he interested himself in all that the humanists and artists were doing and, possessed of vast means, he was pleased to encourage their activities by his patronage. This defines his historic role in the field of culture: he was a patron, a Maecenas. What this signified in respect to humanism, although already touched upon elsewhere,[3] may be briefly summarized at this point for the sake of the complete picture of the man. Apart from his assembling three libraries, on which he expended immense sums, he cultivated the acquaintance of a large number of leading humanists such as Leonardo Bruni, Carlo Marsuppini, and Poggio Bracciolini, all of them chancellors of Florence in Cosimo's day. When as the result of his contact with Platonic philosophy at the General Council of 1439 he resolved to bring up at his expense the promising youth, Marsilio Ficino, as the western interpreter of the great Athenian's message, he made what may perhaps be called his most important single contribution to Renaissance thought. For from this resolution emerged the Platonic academy, center of one of several movements by which philosophy attempted to steer its course among the uncharted speculative seas which confronted it as soon as it had abandoned the safe medieval moorings.

Much more widely noticed, because affecting a larger human circle, was Cosimo's patronage of the arts. Besides building himself the great palace, which

[3] Chap. XIX.

still stands and which in our own day has again very properly been given the Medicean name, he erected a villa at Careggi, another at Fiesole, and still another at Cafaggiolo in the Mugello, the original home of his race. For the city palace as well as for the convent buildings of San Marco, which he presented to the Dominican order, he employed the architect Michelozzo. But he by no means overlooked Brunelleschi, the most famous architect of his day. To Brunelleschi he intrusted the two very notable structures, the church of San Lorenzo and the Badia (abbey) of San Domenico below Fiesole. In sculpture Cosimo linked his name with that of Donatello, who became and remained his devoted friend. Among the painters he was particularly close to Fra Filippo Lippi, Fra Angelico, and Benozzo Gozzoli. The question so often discussed whether he practiced his lavish patronage of scholars and artists out of love of learning and the creative skills or from a selfish desire to increase his reputation is idle and unfruitful. His enemies said one thing, his friends another. To anyone raising himself above the battle of partisan opinion it is clear that Cosimo shared the tastes of his time and social class and easily and naturally slipped into the patronage, which was an all but universally recognized obligation of the rich and powerful men of the age.

Like every man whose character unfolded in the storm and stress of circumstance Cosimo exhibited many contradictory traits. In the main he was moderate, disciplined, and magnanimous; and if it is possible to charge him with occasional cruel and vindictive acts, he was nonetheless essentially humane and forgiving. Most characteristic of him was the hard, practical outlook of the Florentine man of affairs and, like this well-established type, he was not given to unnecessary words. Deficient in natural eloquence and avoiding speech-making as much as possible, he owed his authority in the state preeminently to his tact and skill as a party leader and to his great and unusual administrative talents. His habitual reticence did not keep him, however, from manifesting a remarkable power of terse comment, of which it is very much worth while to take note, as it permits us to penetrate to the very core of his being. His compact utterances, much cited in his own and still remembered in our day, have been used by his opponents to prove his cold and calculating cynicism. Cynical they no doubt are, but they have a pungency and bite that makes them entirely admirable on their level. States are not maintained by pater nosters; two yards of red cloth suffice to make an honorable citizen; envy is a plant that should not be watered; better a city ruined than a city lost: such are some of his sayings that went the rounds among his half-resentful, half-admiring countrymen. They have an epigrammatic edge which explains why they were incorporated in the local folk-lore and have persisted through the ages.[4] His personal appearance accorded perfectly with his words and actions. He was of medium height, spare of figure, of olive complexion with large rude features. His carriage as he moved about the city was dignified, his aspect benign. He spoke familiarly with merchant and market woman and

[4] A full collection of the sayings attributed to Cosimo will be found in Note 136 of A. Fabroni, *Vita Magni Cosmi Medicei.* Pisa, 1789. This is still the fundamental biography. See also Cosimo's life in Vespasiano da Bisticci, *Vite di Uomini Illustri del Secolo XV.* An English translation by William George and Emily Waters was published at London in 1926. The best biography of Cosimo in English is by K. D. Ewart, *Cosimo de' Medici.* London, 1889.

declined to underscore his position with such trappings of lordship as palace guards and a lavish household. His piety, as evidenced by his many ecclesiastical endowments, was represented by his enemies as pure hypocrisy. They adduced his patronage of humanism in proof of his religious skepticism, but the point cannot be said to have been well taken, for in his case, as in that of most of the leading spirits of the age, the old and the new managed somehow to lie down together without a disturbing inner conflict. In the monastery of St. Mark may still be seen a cell which he reserved for himself as an occasional quiet retreat from the clamor of the world. There is no reason to assume that he engaged in periodic prayer and penance except to satisfy a genuine need of his heart.

Cosimo was spared neither the cruel private losses nor the gradual impairment of health which are the common human lot. His son Giovanni died without offspring in 1463; his only other son, Piero, was afflicted with gout to such a degree that he had to keep to his bed often for prolonged periods. Piero had two promising boys, Lorenzo and Giuliano, but it would be some years before they could be charged with any public or private responsibility. To leave behind a large and prosperous family was the outstanding ambition of every true son of Florence: how much more then of a man like Cosimo who had carried his family to the headship of the city. After Giovanni's death he had himself, already bedridden, carried through the empty rooms of his city residence. We catch the intimate sorrow in his muttered words: "Too large a house for so small a family." Following the passing of this beloved second son, he sank rapidly. On August 1, 1464, at the age of seventy-five, he died at his villa of Careggi. He was buried without special pomp amidst a vast concourse of his fellow-citizens before the high altar of the church of San Lorenzo, which owed its existence to his munificence. The plain slab over his tomb carries his name and under it the simple legend *Pater Patriae*. This was the honorable title which, under the sharp impression of the loss they had suffered, his sorrowing countrymen united in officially bestowing on him.

XXII. The Government of Piero de' Medici and of Lorenzo the Magnificent to the End of the War with the Pope and Naples (1480)

WHEN Cosimo died on August 1, 1464, the question that sprang spontaneously to every tongue was whether the dominant position acquired by the dead statesman could be maintained by his heir and only surviving son, Piero. For, towering as Cosimo's authority was, it was a cloaked and extra-constitutional authority and would in all probability collapse if exercised by a political talent conspicuously inferior to his own. Now that Piero was the son but not the spiritual replica of his father was manifest to all observers, and particularly to Cosimo's jealous intimates who shared with him the control of the Medicean party. Already during the last years of their chief they had indicated in no uncertain manner that they refused any longer to be regarded as subordinates. In this connection it is proper once again to remind ourselves that it is the incurable weakness of every regime of optimates that, in measure as it becomes secure against outsiders, it is threatened by revolt within its ranks. We have had occasion in the previous chapter to touch upon the subterranean activity of three prominent Mediceans who, on being brought face to face with the ruinous consequences of their revolt, humbled themselves to petition Cosimo to have its effects undone, but who did not on this account abandon their secret hostility to their leader. These three rivals, thenceforth gnawed by an inner rage, were Luca Pitti, Diotisalvi Neroni, and Agnolo Acciaiuoli. Each had his own particular list of grievances against Cosimo, but private complaints, no matter how huge the mass of them may be on being heaped together, are not easily converted into a viable program of common action.

It is evidence of the decline of political principle among the oligarchs that only a single member of the ruling ring, Niccolò Soderini, was opposed to Cosimo on other than purely selfish grounds. This Niccolò was an idealist of the childlike, ingenuous kind that, instead of doing himself or anyone else any good by his agitation, gets no farther than to deepen the existing confusion by his failure to grasp the simple actualities staring him and everyone else in the face. We thus have a sum of four disgruntled Medicean subleaders, each one of whom was minded not to let slip by unused the opportunity afforded by the assumption of the shrewd Cosimo's succession by his feebler son, but who, prompted by diverse motives, found it difficult to agree on a plan of attack. When after some months an action was at length inaugurated, it was on the sole responsibility of the impetuous Niccolò, honestly but fatuously resolved to rouse the people in an effort by legal means to restore the constitution—the miraculous original constitution, which had made an impressive show on paper for almost two hundred years but which had always been manipulated by shrewd cliques in their own interest. Planning a return to the lost "liberty" of the Florentines, Niccolò could not under the most favorable circumstances have done more than overthrow the Medici in order to replace them with another tyranny, probably his own.

The first hurdle encountered by Niccolò Soderini on beginning action against the ruling system was taken without any difficulty. On September 6, 1465, a proposal was made and carried to return to the system of choosing the signory by lot; and when the first group of priors under the new dispensation issued from the supposedly unmanipulated borse, lo and behold, the name drawn for banner-bearer of Justice was none other than that of Niccolò, the impassioned champion of free elections. It was an excellent example of the "liberty" habitual to the Florentine system. On entering the palace for the term beginning November 1, the new gonfalonier was attended on the way by a wildly cheering multitude, whose acclamations reached a climax when an olive wreath was placed upon the hero's brow. This first was also the last of poor, sap-headed Niccolò's triumphs. Before large assemblies of his fellow-citizens called together by him, he delivered ringing addresses, which everybody agreed were magnificent but in which intelligent observers regretfully remarked the absence of anything that by any stretch of the imagination could be called a coherent program. Whenever the noble orator and patriot came forward with something even a trifle definite, it was buried in the councils under an avalanche of contrary votes cast by the followers of Piero de' Medici and the other leading merchants. For, as soon as the oligarchic system as such was threatened, Piero and most of his enemies within the optimate group stood together as one man. When at the end of his two months' service Soderini again abandoned the palace, he presented the usual sorry spectacle of the deflated reformer. His deep chagrin made him an embittered man prepared henceforth to employ almost any method which might rid the city of the Medici. Disappointed by the meager results attained by constitutional methods, he no longer scrupled to travel the path of violence. This altered attitude drove him into the arms of the three fellow-oligarchs, whose discontent was of an older date than his and who, on being strengthened by the accession of Soderini, felt encouraged to resort to direct action to unseat the hated Piero.

The new revolt against the Medici was favored by an event at Milan: on March 8, 1466, Duke Francesco Sforza passed away. His successor was his son, Galeazzo Maria, a young man of twenty without a particle of either the military or the governing talents of his rude, self-made father. It was uncertain whether the youthful heir would succeed in imposing his authority; and in the most favorable case it was probable that he would for a long time to come be so much concerned with affairs close at home that he would not be in a position to lend his distant Medicean ally support. The Sforza alliance, we must always keep in mind, had been made by Cosimo the very fulcrum of his policy; and just as Francesco Sforza had counted at every turn on the instant help of the Medici, so the Medici had been strong in their confidence of the ever ready succor of the Milanese duke. But now the duke was dead, the stability of his state to all appearances threatened, and Piero de' Medici deprived of the foreign support which was an important factor of his strength. The plot promptly hatched by the four conspirators was to induce the enemies of Florence, such as the duke of Ferrara and the republic of Venice, to lend them a body of troops on the understanding that their crossing of the border would serve as the signal for the domestic rising having as its goal the overthrow and attendant murder of Piero.

The plot, perfected in the course of the summer following the change of ruler at Milan, was brought to a sudden head by the threatened Piero's taking the offensive. This took his enemies by surprise, for they were persuaded that Cosimo's son, for whom they had nothing but contempt, would weakly suffer himself to be crushed. Physically incapacitated by gout, Piero was familiarly known as *Il Gottoso,* and perhaps because of his infirmity had developed the habit of avoiding open, uncompromising conflict as much as he possibly could. Nevertheless, on his becoming aware that his rule and life were jeopardized by the conspiracy hatched by his rivals, a hidden fire burst into flame and caused him to act with unfaltering resolution. While staying at his villa at Careggi, he was warned in a letter from the friendly ruler of Bologna that Ferrarese troops were being moved toward the Florentine border. The fuse was therefore about to be lighted. Without delay and bedridden as he was, he had himself carried in a litter to the city in order to inform the signory of the threatened invasion and to rouse them to defensive action. It was on August 27, 1466, that he made his unexpected appearance in the town and challenged the conspirators to strike the first blow. Whether it was the consternation caused by the premature revelation of the plot, or the small agreement among the four principals, or the settled Florentine burgher preference for political rather than for military action, the conspirators permitted the favorable moment to slip by. Their cardinal mistake no doubt was to let themselves be drawn into negotiations. These were proposed by the signory, and Piero, the avowed defender of the country's peace, was of course more than willing to engage in them. A few days passed amidst excitement and severe tension until with the elections for the September signory, which proved favorable to the Medici, the attack was beaten off, leaving control securely with Piero.

The upshot of the August commotion was the familiar parliament, which, called on September 2, conferred extraordinary power on the familiar commission or balìa. The balìa in its turn authorized the renewed abandonment of election by lot in favor of officials hand-picked by a committee of accoppiatori, the constitutional device identified with Medicean rule since the return of Cosimo from exile. Thus lifted to the saddle, Piero rode roughshod over his enemies. Niccolò Soderini, Agnolo Acciaiuoli, and Diotisalvi Neroni were banished from the city and its territory. To his greater shame Luca Pitti, the fourth head of the conspirators and generally considered their biggest figure, was suffered to remain. At the height of the crisis he had betrayed his associates and by visiting the stricken Piero in his sickroom had effected a reconciliation with that mild-tempered chief. Whether it was Luca s natural flightiness, or his enfeebled mind (he was over seventy years old), or his great riches which he was reluctant to jeopardize, or the vast Pitti palace, which, still incomplete, he wished to leave behind as his enduring monument, his courage failed him at the crucial moment and, renouncing the risk of war, like a panicky animal at the approach of danger, he ran to cover. He passed the few remaining years of his existence in the deepening obscurity that overtakes a man who has become morally discredited and universally despised.

Unfortunately there was an aftermath of foreign war. The exiled conspirators gathered at Venice and tirelessly spurred on to action against Florence the republic of St. Mark and certain minor states of the Romagna, which had been in guilty collusion with them from the start. They engaged as their commander-in-chief the Venetian condottiere, Bartolommeo Colleone. This is the same Colleone whose equestrian statue, wrought by Verrocchio's masterhand, still dominates one of the minor squares of the City of the Lagoons. Colleone was at the head of the wretched Italian mercenary business at this time, and the deluded Florentine exiles nursed the hope that he would lead them back to their lost paradise. The hireling soldier received enough support from the states openly or secretly hostile to Florence to threaten Tuscany with invasion from his base in the Romagna, but as Florence remained firmly joined with Milan and Naples, constituting with them the well-proved triple alliance, the danger passed and in April, 1468, the rather trifling struggle, usually called the Colleonic war but more readily identified if labeled the war of the exiles against the Medici, came to an end. The peace, which still further raised Piero's steadily mounting prestige, buried his opponents in oblivion.

The chief support of Piero in these trials was his young son Lorenzo. Indeed so constantly was Lorenzo at his father's side and so conspicuous was his part in all the negotiations conducted within and without the city that there were many who believed that he already was the head of the state. While this was an exaggeration, as Piero without doubt kept the threads of policy in his hands and Lorenzo never fell from the role of the dutiful son, it is true that Lorenzo was pushed into an early acquaintance with affairs of state which made him a master of all their intricacies by the time his father's mantle fell upon his shoulders. As Lorenzo was born on January 1, 1449, he was but fifteen years old at the death of his grandfather Cosimo; and he had not yet celebrated his twenty-first birthday when the long-expected death of the sorely stricken Piero put the full responsibility for the Florentine state into his hands. The character and career of this most brilliant ruler of the house have elicited the admiration of the succeeding generations of men down to our own time. Without any doubt the Medicean family tradition was the animating core of his being. Throughout the European world the family was still a more authoritative institution than the state, and all the movement and change imported into Florence by the vast network of its commercial relations had proved unable to weaken the grip of the family on its members. Even when the gild system had been at its height in the fourteenth century, the family had continued to count for more than the gild; and the gild system had no sooner been enfeebled by the rise of the enterpriser than the family completely overshadowed the gild as a social and political determinant. The obligation impressed on the youthful Lorenzo until it became the mainspring of his being was his duty to uphold and strengthen the position achieved by his forebears. An influence different in kind and yet of a like emotional pull can be ascribed without hesitation to his mother. She was Lucrezia Tornabuoni, a member of one of the oldest and most distinguished families of the city. While her sterling intelligence made her a valuable helpmeet of her husband Piero in all his concerns, her significance for Lorenzo, and for her other children as well, lay chiefly in her being a well-nigh perfect example of the woman type formed by many centuries of Florentine teaching and experience. On the one hand, she was the embodiment of common sense and a busy practicality, like the woman commended in the Bible arising betimes and looking well after the ways of her household; on the other hand, she was the robed priestess charged with the preservation of the ancient pieties of the hearth and altar. From his childhood she so steeped Lorenzo in the practices and folkways of Catholicism that, in spite of the overwhelming pagan influences to which he was afterward exposed, he never quite broke away from his Christian moorings. Together with the forceful family inheritance the never resolved residuum of faith at the bottom of his heart constituted the invaluable steadying element in his often stormy career.

After the home came the school, and the school for Lorenzo, as for every Florentine boy of his class and period, signified a prolonged bath in the Pierian spring. In the second half of the fifteenth century the last conservative resistance to the mounting tide of humanistic enthusiasm had broken down, and the curriculum of the new age took the form of the transmission to the young of the wisdom of the ancients as embodied in Greek and Latin literature. Accordingly, Lorenzo was given the best available tutors in Latin and Greek, and by the gracious Marsilio Ficino, central figure of the Platonic academy, he was inducted into the noble mysteries of Ficino's revered master of ancient philosophic thought. From the prolonged feast of alien learning many of Lorenzo's contemporaries arose as insufferable prigs, a fate that might also have befallen the young Medici had it not been for certain rival influences which enabled him to bring his manhood to a rich and natural maturity. In spite of the inculcated preference for the dead languages and literatures, Lorenzo had an unconquerable natural predilection for the living Tuscan speech and its great literary monuments and at a very early age developed the habit of setting forth his thoughts and feelings in the many available forms of native verse. To such eminence did he attain in the field of poetry that, short as his life was destined to be and incessantly concerned with the public interest, he is now generally held to rank as the leading Tuscan singer of his day. A second influence corrective of the excessive scholarly emphasis of humanism was his devotion to physical exercise and sport. He became an expert at football and at the vigorous form of handball known locally as *pallone;* he had an enthusiasm for horses, dogs, and falcons which converted him into a passionate follower of the hunt. In short, spiritual, intellectual, and physical elements of training were brought to bear on him in such perfect balance that in an age abounding in eminent personalities he stands forth as perhaps its best-rounded product. His personal appearance, however, was far from pre-possessing. He had a vigorous frame of more than average height, but his face was almost repulsively ugly with its sallow complexion, its strained, myopic eyes, its flat and spreading nose. Nor was Nature, which had so opulently endowed him in heart and mind, content to balance the account with these facial liabilities. It is strange to reflect that this man so conspicuous for inner harmony should have had a harsh and croaking voice and should have been almost completely lacking in the sense of smell.

The other children of Piero and Lucrezia de' Medici were a boy, Giuliano, five years younger than Lorenzo, and two sisters, Bianca and Nannina. We have a letter of their mother which affirms that her two daughters were extremely beautiful. In the absence of any other opinion on the subject, we may cautiously write her evidence into the record. According to Florentine custom the two girls were given in marriage at an early age to members of distinguished local families, Bianca being wed to Guglielmo Pazzi and Nannina to Bernardo Rucellai. Marriage as the life-blood of the institution of the family was of course the undisputed province of the head of the house. Although in successive brilliant ceremonies Bianca was married to her Guglielmo and Nannina to her Bernardo, the four principals had nothing to do with the preliminary arrangements, since these were the result of negotiations among the respective family heads, each exclusively concerned with advancing the fortunes of his particular group. In the case of Lorenzo's brother, Giuliano, the evidence regarding his good looks is so abundant and comes to us from so many sources that we may say without any reservation that he grew up to be an extremely handsome young man. As strong and tall as his brother, he had a greater natural grace of body and a far more harmonious assortment of features. He did not yield to Lorenzo in his addiction to games and pageants, but, while gladly consorting with scholars and artists, he had none of his brother's literary gifts. Nor did he boast Lorenzo's clear intelligence and swift energy but, modest, lively, and gentle, he was singularly cherished by all the town. His ingenuous spirit led him to subordinate himself with spontaneous deference to Lorenzo's authoritative leadership.

Long before Lorenzo reached his twentieth birthday his marriage had become the engrossing concern of his parents. After a careful survey of the scene they decided to negotiate for the hand of a daughter of the great Roman baronial house of Orsini. This was a startling departure from tradition, for hitherto the Medici had regularly contracted marriage among the other burgher families of their native town. But they were now virtually a reigning dynasty, and a family connection capable of strengthening their general position in Italy was undoubtedly desirable. No greater uncrowned house than the Orsini was to be found in the peninsula, innumerable members having for many generations past figured in the country's politics and wars. What particularly impressed the close observer was that the house had proved itself a veritable nursery of those two specialties of the Italian climate—cardinals and condottieri. By tieing themselves to a great feudal race the Medici ran some risk of offending Florentine republican sentiment; but the advantages were considered to outweigh the disadvantages, and on June 4, 1469, the wedding of the

Medici heir with Clarice Orsini was celebrated amidst a great burst of pomp. The splendor which was unfolded expressed the more firmly established Medicean rule quite as much as the exuberant disposition of the young bridegroom. Gone was the cautious self-concealment of old Cosimo for which there was no longer any need. For by this time the common people, if not yet the representatives of the substantial burgherdom, had come round to viewing the Medici as the native dynasty from which, somewhat in the manner of the public games offered to the Romans by their emperors, they had a right to expect a steady succession of free entertainments. Already in 1468 Lorenzo with his ailing father's consent had given a tournament in the Piazza Santa Croce in honor of the reigning local beauty, Lucrezia Donati. Doubtless he was prompted to stage this spectacle, the fame of which made its way to the four corners of Italy, by the still lingering ideals of medieval chivalry as well as by his own inborn zest for pleasure; but it is not improbable that even at that early age he was not inaccessible to the purely political consideration that splendor was an attribute of royalty and that nothing has delighted the multitude of every age so much as a good show. A year after the tournament offered to Lucrezia Donati, Lorenzo's union with the handsome copper-haired Clarice Orsini served as another occasion for dining friends and entertaining the masses on a lavish scale; and what was probably the climax in a long train of public pageants was touched in 1475 when Giuliano followed his brother's example by giving a tournament, again on the Piazza Santa Croce well suited to this kind of exhibition, which dazzled all beholders with its unnrivaled display of brocaded costumes strewn with pearls and precious stones. It was characteristic of the unwarlike, spectacle-loving Italy of the Renaissance that these Florentine tournaments no longer bore any resemblance to their medieval exemplars with their hard knocks, their abundant blood and dirt; they were more in the nature of ably directed theatrical shows, in which make-believe knights tried to outdo one another not so much in skill of arms as in picturesqueness of holiday costume and in the size and splendor of their retinues of squires, pages, and musicians. Tournaments or not in the true sense, these displays aroused keen delight, and the young brothers who presided at them with such unaffected gusto rose higher and higher in the public favor.

Six months after the wedding gayeties of Lorenzo and Clarice, Piero de' Medici at last made good his oft-repeated threat and departed this world in earnest (December 2, 1469). He was laid to rest in the sacristy of San Lorenzo, where a magnificent porphyry sarcophagus fashioned by Verrocchio received his mortal remains together with those of his younger brother Giovanni, who had preceded him in death by six years. And now Lorenzo ruled in his father's stead in nominal partnership with Giuliano, although the latter's youth and willing self-effacement left the power exclusively in the older brother's hands. The ease with which Lorenzo succeeded to the still unofficial Medicean rule of Florence measures the extent to which life had gone out of the old republican constitution. The leader of the Medicean party under Piero had been Tommaso Soderini. It is well to consider him for a moment, for, although a brother of Niccolò Soderini, he had not lost his credit with Piero when Niccolò had lent his strength to the revolt of 1466. The case of the brothers

Soderini shows that, despite the customary familial solidarity, there were instances, and some of them take us as far back as the early Middle Ages, when individuals of the same clan attached themselves to the fortunes of opposed factions. As Tommaso Soderini's loyalty was above suspicion, he was not molested by Piero after Niccolò's exile, and immediately after Piero's death he rewarded the trust put in him by assembling some six hundred leading citizens, whom he persuaded to petition Lorenzo to assume the place vacated by his father. In a diary-like record from Lorenzo's hand which has come down to us, Lorenzo voices a certain reluctance, which he declares he felt when the citizen committee headed by Tommaso Soderini requested him to take over the invisible Medicean scepter. The many historians of the city who have written as convinced and often embittered republicans unanimously cry out at this example of the familiar Medicean hypocrisy. But why the young Lorenzo with his strong attachment to literature and sport should not have felt a passing regret at irretrievably sentencing himself to the galley-slavery of politics is not clear. However, one of the reasons given by the young man for his acceptance of the position offered him is so revealing touching the character of Florentine politics that it must not be passed over. "In Florence," says Lorenzo, "one can ill live in the possession of wealth without control of the government." [1] For many generations past the party in power had been in the habit of oppressing its opponents with excessive taxation, and this ancient practice the Medici, as we are aware, had brought to an iniquitous perfection. From Lorenzo's frank avowal we learn that for him and his partisans the local issue reduced itself to the question of rule or ruin.

Everything considered, in no long established monarchy could the heir apparent have mounted the throne much more easily and securely than Lorenzo succeeded Piero on the latter's demise. It was probably on this account that he made no immediate move to trim the constitution still further to suit his figure. Its operations had been adequately controlled by his father and grandfather by means of the election supervisors called accoppiatori, and for the present this device sufficed also for Lorenzo. As the new ruler no more than his father and grandfather held an office by which he could be designated in public, it became customary to refer to him as *Il Magnifico* (The Magnificent). It was a purely honorary title never expressly authorized by a constitutional enactment. However, some slight constitutional tinkering in the manner sanctioned by long custom did take place at Lorenzo's accession. It effected no change demanding attention. We may therefore, following Virgil's excellent advice to Dante in the matter of merely bewildering details, be content to look and pass on (*guarda e passa*). [2]

Lorenzo's early familiarity with the government had made him aware that the Medici rule owed much of its vigor to the close association it maintained with Milan and Naples, and he took over this policy without change. Follow-

---

[1] "A Firenze si può mal viver ricco senza lo stato." Fabroni, Vol. II, *Adnotationes*, 21. The full title is: A. Fabroni, *Laurentii Magnifici Vita*. 2 vols. Pisa, 1784. Other biographies worth consulting are: W. Roscoe, *The Life of Lorenzo de' Medici*. 10th ed. London, 1895. A. Reumont, *Lorenzo de' Medici*. 2 vols. 2d ed. Leipzig, 1883. E. Armstrong, *Lorenzo de' Medici*. London, 1927. E. L. S. Horsburgh, *Lorenzo the Magnificent and Florence in Her Golden Age*. London, 1909.

[2] *Inferno*, III, 51.

left: DESIDERIO DA SETTIGNANO. PORTRAIT BUST IN MARBLE OF AN UNKNOWN WOMAN. MUSEO NAZIONALE (ALINARI). *right:* VERROCCHIO. PORTRAIT BUST IN MARBLE OF AN UNKNOWN WOMAN. MUSEO NAZIONALE (ALINARI).

VERROCCHIO. BRONZE EQUESTRIAN STATUE OF BARTOLOMMEO COLLEONI. VENICE (ALINARI).

left: VERROCCHIO. DAVID. BRONZE. MUSEO NAZIONALE (ALINARI). *right:* POLLAIUOLO. HERCULES SUFFOCATES ANTAEUS. BRONZE. MUSEO NAZIONALE (ALINARI).

ROSSELLINO. TOMB OF THE HUMANIST LEONARDO BRUNI OF AREZZO. SANTA CROCE (ALINARI).

ing the Colleonic war the peace of Tuscany remained undisturbed for almost a decade, and peace brought a welcome renewal of prosperity. The only disturbing event of Lorenzo's early years was the revolt of Volterra and, as it was quickly suppressed, it cannot be said to have struck the country a heavy blow. That the revolt nonetheless was a disaster in both a physical and a moral sense cannot be denied. Nor is it possible to free Lorenzo from blame, because, owing no doubt to the newness of his rule, he championed the use of strong measures against Volterra in order to impress the whole body of Florentine subject towns with his unshaken resolution.

Like every other subject town, Volterra accepted from Florence its two leading officials, the podestà, who acted as chief executive, and the capitano, who commanded a small occupying force. Under these two agents of the suzerain power the old local government retained considerable authority over both the town itself and the surrounding territory. In the year 1471 there arose a dispute between the local government and a private company organized to exploit the limited and relatively worthless alum mines within the Volterran dominion. Alum, we should remember, was an astringent mineral indispensable for dyeing; however, into the contest between town and company we need not go farther than to say that each party to the controversy was convinced that the law was on its side. When Florence interfered in behalf of the company, there was a popular upflare in Volterra which developed into a tumultuous demonstration against the Florentine representative on the ground, the podestà. The Arno citizens had always been nervous about their subject towns, all of which continued to nurse dreams of liberty; and spurred on to precipitate measures by Lorenzo de' Medici, the signory levied war on its rebellious dependency without first offering to negotiate. That, besides on the patent political ground, Lorenzo was inclined to take action also for private financial reasons is impossible to prove and very difficult to believe. As he was the sole lessee of the immensely more profitable alum mines at Tolfa in the State of the Church, he cannot very well be charged with acting in his selfish interest when he lent his support to a rival company operating at Volterra. A mercenary army was assembled and the recalcitrant town besieged until, recognizing the futility of further resistance, it signed an agreement with the Florentine commissioners accompanying the troops to surrender on the assurance that the inhabitants were to be secure in life and goods. But when on June 17, 1472, the Florentine condottiere, Federigo of Montefeltro, rode into the town at the head of his bands a terrible thing happened. Once within the walls the mercenaries broke rank, threw themselves on the inhabitants and their possessions, and could not be brought under control until they had put the ancient stronghold to a devastating sack. It is impossible to exaggerate the misery and despair into which the hideous excesses perpetrated by the troops plunged the poor people of Volterra. The sack supplied evidence, although additional evidence on this head was certainly not needed, that the mercenary armies of the day, always eager to avoid shedding each other's blood on the field of battle, were no better than organized robber bands. Conceding that the monstrous event is referable, in the main, to the revolting military system which prevailed throughout the peninsula, we cannot wholly free Lorenzo from responsibility. While he cannot be charged with the sack, as his enemies have clamorously done ever since the event, he was the author of the needlessly aggressive policy, which, getting out of hand, subjected the old Etruscan hill town to an unspeakable degradation.

Apart from the, after all, local character of the Volterran siege and sack, peace continued to prevail and the sky over Tuscany remained blue and hopeful until dark clouds began to rear their thunderheads along the Romagna border. Therewith we are obliged to turn to the papacy, to the honors of which, in the year 1471, the cardinals elevated a Franciscan friar, who took the title of Sixtus IV. As soon as the Great Schism had been healed over half a century before, a main object of the popes had come to be to establish themselves as the unchallenged civil rulers of their considerable dominions embracing a large part of central and north-central Italy. In measure as the four great states of Venice, Milan, Florence, and Naples emerged out of the Italian chaos, it became desirable and even necessary for the papacy to acquire a commensurate political power if it was not to fall into galling dependence on its stronger neighbors. However, the post-schism popes up to the accession of Sixtus IV had not made much headway with this program. In the country around Rome the great feudal families, such as the Orsini and the Colonna, exercised an undiminished authority, while in Umbria, the Marches of Ancona, and the Romagna a vast number of petty tyrants had established themselves in the various towns, who, in return for the formal acknowledgment of the papal suzerainty and the payment of a small tribute, expected to be left in undisturbed possession of the territory they had illegally appropriated. On his first mounting the papal throne Sixtus IV did not depart from the policy of his predecessors, for he accepted the situation as he found it. Then a savage energy, native to his rude blood, made him revolt against the merely decorative power which he found himself exercising and persuaded him to undertake measures calculated to bring at least Umbria and the Romagna under his more direct control. With this policy went hand in hand an illicit but ungovernable passion to push his family into prominence by endowing individual members thereof with papal lands in order to establish them as hereditary rulers at the side of the many other dynasts who were lording it over a divided Italy. Sixtus had many nephews, some belonging to his own, the della Rovere family, others, the sons of his sister, bearing the husband's name of Riario. In his early years the pope directed the main stream of his favors to Pietro Riario, who, being like himself a Franciscan friar, had benefice on benefice bestowed on him until it looked as if all the riches of the church were to be dropped bit by bit into his lap. But Pietro died in the year 1473, the victim of his own excesses, whereupon the pope picked as the new object of his extravagant family affection Pietro's brother, Girolamo. Before the papal favor drew the obscure Girolamo into the light of history, he had been either a small customs' clerk or an equally unimportant grocer's assistant. The momentous question never having been authoritatively settled must remain undecided. What is certain and alone matters is that the pope resolved to transform the customs' clerk (or grocer's assistant) into an Italian princeling by making the most of an opportunity afforded in 1474 of establishing him as lord of the Romagnole town of Imola.

That move completely reversed the friendly relations which had hitherto obtained between Sixtus IV and Lorenzo de' Medici. Lorenzo had inherited one of the great states of Italy, which his father and grandfather had labored to consolidate within and without. The state of Florence was enveloped on the south, east, and north by the State of the Church, than which moreover it was much smaller in extent. The political weakness of its papal neighbor was therefore an advantage for Florence, and this was so instinctively recognized that when, a hundred years before, the papacy had for the first time in its history been territorially consolidated by Cardinal Albornoz, the Florentines felt so deeply aggrieved that they waged the famous War of the Eight Saints against the Supreme Pontiff. However, the work of Albornoz proved ephemeral, the papal state again fell into scores of substantially independent principalities, and Florence breathed more easily on being freed from the nightmare of a powerful, enveloping neighbor. Since, owing to its dominantly commercial character, Florence found it impossible to engage in an undisguised career of conquest, it was content to perpetuate the chaos at its border and provide the needed security against the frequent Umbrian and Romagnole disturbances spilling over into Tuscany by a cordon of petty border states under Florentine influence. Communities of this kind were Bologna, Faenza, Città di Castello, and Perugia. Nominally papal, they hovered under the Florentine wing. Among these dependencies figured also Imola, the little city which in 1474 the pope determined to acquire for his nephew, Girolamo Riario.

In this first political clash between Lorenzo and Sixtus IV the latter was victorious and Imola, lying in the plain of the Romagna at the foot of the Tuscan Apennines, became the prize of Girolamo. Aware that this was but a first step, the alarmed Lorenzo cast about for means to hinder the extension of Girolamo's power over Faenza and Forlì, to which nearby towns it was known his ambition was directed. As Venice and Milan were as much interested as himself in keeping the pope from becoming too firmly established in the Romagna, the Magnificent entered into negotiations with them, and in November, 1474, perfected a new triple alliance dedicated, according to the dishonest verbiage of such documents, to the safeguarding of the peninsula's peace. To calm the alarm which the pope and the king of Naples might be expected to feel, an article was added inviting their participation in the new arrangements. Notwithstanding, these two powers took offense and answered the provocation with an alliance of their own. It can hardly be doubted, and later, after the disastrous outcome, Lorenzo himself did not doubt that it had been a grave error on his part to arouse the wrath of the pope by spinning an intrigue against him, especially as the new turn of Florentine diplomacy involved an abandonment of the old triple alliance, Milan-Florence-Naples, which had served as the solid rock of the city's foreign policy since the days of his grandfather. And once committed to a false program, Lorenzo got himself more and more entangled. When at about the time of the Imola affair the pope had trouble with the Vitelli family, which had usurped the power over Città di Castello, he discovered that Lorenzo was giving support to the enemy, and Lorenzo's disingenuous denial of the fact did not make his case any better. Despite these serious clashes over fundamental matters of policy, the differences between the two rulers might have been ironed out had it not been for the pope's inflammable temper and his brutal resolve to have his undisputed way. To his mind Lorenzo had become an implacable enemy, whom it was his business to injure in any and every manner he could. It was in this spirit that he seized the opportunity to appoint a Florentine enemy of Lorenzo's, Francesco Salviati, to the archbishopric of Pisa. What made the papal action worse, it occurred in the face of a solemn undertaking by Sixtus not to nominate any bishops or archbishops of Tuscany without previous consultation with the Florentine government. Deeply offended in his turn, Lorenzo revenged himself by forcibly preventing Salviati from taking possession of his see for three years. This enraged the archbishop, who was a member of a powerful Florentine clan, as much as the pope, and did not exactly strengthen the Magnificent's hold on the city.

The unfortunate conflict failing to be brought to a settlement tended in the manner of such personal issues to be exacerbated by every passing incident. How much more, then, by such a capital event as took place at Milan on December 26, 1476. On that day three Milanese youths, incited to their deed by the encomiums lavished by the classical authors on tyrannicide, murdered the Duke Galeazzo Maria as he was entering the church of St. Stephen. He was one of the most infamous representatives of the current political type of the despot, on whose bier it is not likely that there fell so much as a single tear. However, politically his disappearance had disastrous consequences not only for Milan and Italy but also for Florence. His heir was a three-year-old boy, for whom his mother assumed the regency. As her rule was challenged by the four restless and ambitious brothers of the deceased duke, Milan was threatened with a long period of disturbances, during which it would not count for much in the Italian parallelogram of forces. For Lorenzo this signified the enfeeblement and possible collapse of his leading ally and the consequent weakening of his own position. It followed from this blow to his prestige that his many enemies were encouraged to assume the offensive; and since they were desperate men, who had lost their moral scruples in an Italy which, cut loose from its medieval anchorage, had become the scene of every form of violence, they resolved to resort to murder and, after the manner of the Milanese assassins, to exalt their crime by representing it to themselves and to the world as an instance of the honorable practice of tyrannicide.

Therewith we have arrived at the Pazzi plot, which merits a close scrutiny, not only because it is the outstanding event of Lorenzo's political career, but also because it affords an unequaled opportunity for familiarizing ourselves with some of the less admirable manners of Renaissance Italy. The origin of the plot takes us to Rome, where, in the shadow of the papacy, most of Lorenzo's envenomed personal enemies were in the habit of congregating for the exchange of views. The plan to murder Lorenzo and his brother Giuliano, coupled with the design to seize the Florentine government, was in the first instance hatched by two equally unprincipled young men, Girolamo Riario and Francesco Pazzi. The ex-customs' clerk was inspired by a hatred of

Lorenzo as uncontrolled as that of his uncle, the pope, to which was added the ever-present fear that he would be dispossessed of his precious Imola by the resentful Florentine ruler as soon as the protecting hand of his aged uncle should have been withdrawn by death. A much more important figure, considered by himself, was Francesco Pazzi, member of the great Florentine clan which has given to the conspiracy its historical name. The Pazzi were a more ancient family than the Medici and had accordingly been stigmatized as nobles or, more properly, as magnates, by the Ordinances of Justice. In Cosimo's day they had, as a special favor, been stricken off the magnate list, thereby becoming eligible once more for all the offices of state. A certain intimacy between Medici and Pazzi had followed, of which one bit of evidence was that Lorenzo's sister, Bianca, had been married to young Guglielmo Pazzi, brother of the above-mentioned Francesco. But the spirit of family rivalry persisted, intensified by the circumstance that the bank representing the leading business enterprise of the Pazzi was in sharp competition with the bank of the Medici. Moreover, owing to the rift between Lorenzo and the pope, the Pazzi bank had recently scored a great victory over its Medici competitor. Following the example of his immediate predecessors, Sixtus IV on his accession continued to deposit the papal monies in the Roman branch of the Medicean firm until, angered by the conflict over Imola, he transferred his account to the Roman branch of the Pazzi. Now of that prospering Roman branch young Francesco Pazzi was the resident head, and by becoming the leading financial adviser of the pope and the pope's nephew was thrown into intimate personal relations with them. He is described as a small, thin, restless man, who had persuaded himself that the Medici had usurped a position in Florence which properly belonged to the more ancient and distinguished Pazzi and, kindling his enmity to Lorenzo at the wrathful fires of the upstart lord of Imola, he gradually prepared his mind for extreme measures to rid himself of his foe and the city of Florence of its tyrant.

To these two violent young men was added the sinister figure of Francesco Salviati, archbishop of Pisa, savagely averse to Lorenzo ever since the latter had attempted to block his appointment to the Pisan prelacy. The active participation in the plot by one of the most exalted officials of the Catholic church is a Renaissance touch one would not care to miss from the resulting blood-curdling drama. Better than anything else it helps us to realize how far the corruption of morals had gone under the dissolution of medieval culture and the reign of a fashionable paganism. And the murder charge, from which for the archbishop there is no escape, at least brushes the figure of none other than the vicar of Christ, the pope himself. When, after the plot had been well advanced by its three main promoters, Girolamo Riario, Francesco Pazzi, and the archbishop Salviati, Sixtus IV was informed of its character and objectives, he approved heartily insofar as the overthrow of the Medici brothers was concerned, but at the same time he salved his conscience by insisting that there must be no bloodshed. He might as well have ordered the brothers drowned but not in water! Giving the pope the benefit of every doubt, we cannot, unless we wish deliberately to bury our heads in the sand, exonerate him from the charge of having been at least an accessory before the fact. In spite of the papal warning, the conspirators went on with their murder plans exactly as if the pope had not spoken, and presently picked a daring captain in the lord of Imola's employ, a certain Gian Batista da Montesecco (a name any grand opera brigand might envy) as the man to do the deed. Montesecco accepted the invitation and, making all the necessary arrangements, carried them to the very threshold of fulfilment, when he withdrew on learning that it had been arranged for him to dispatch Lorenzo in church during the celebration of the mass. Owing to his superstitious reluctance to shed blood in a Christian temple, Montesecco had almost at the last minute to be replaced by less scrupulous assassins, but as he did not leave town, he was captured after the event. This is distinctly important, since before he was executed as an accomplice he wrote out a full confession, which is our main source for the plot.[3]

After many changes of program due to the difficulty of putting both the intended victims simultaneously, in modern gangland language, "on the spot," it was agreed that the murder was to take place in the great cathedral of Florence during the celebration of High Mass on Sunday, April 26, 1478. Because of Montesecco's default, substitutes had to be found without delay, and the dispatch with which this was done indicates that the Medici were surrounded by a host of deadly enemies. Two disaffected priests volunteered to replace Montesecco and to account for Lorenzo, while Francesco Pazzi and another oligarch with a personal grievance against the Magnificent, Baroncelli by name, agreed without hesitation to attend to Giuliano. The role which the archbishop Salviati assigned to himself was to occupy the palace and take over the government. In this undertaking he was to be aided by old Jacopo Pazzi, the head of the house and uncle of Francesco. Jacopo had at first refused to be drawn into the conspiracy, but as soon as he became persuaded that it could not fail, he joined the others, accepting as his particular task the rousing of the masses in support of the archbishop's action at the Palazzo Pubblico. Owing to the many interlocking divisions of the plot, so large a number of people had to be drawn into the secret that it will always remain a marvel that it was not prematurely divulged. Girolamo Riario, in all probability the original deviser of the conspiracy, chose not to endanger his precious life by direct participation, but he magnanimously conceded the honor of representing the Riario name to a young nephew of his and grand-nephew of the pope. Although this papal grand-nephew was only seventeen years old and was still attending classes at the university, he had already been named a cardinal, and his coming to Florence to pay the Medici rulers a visit was arranged in the expectation that they would be obliged to honor him with a succession of public entertainments. One of these occasions was the mass of April 26, which it is not likely the brothers would have attended, except to show respect for the city's guest. While young Cardinal Riario thus took an important part in the day's proceedings, his was almost certainly the role of the innocent decoy, since his elders considered him too young to be initiated into the bloody business about to be launched.

The signal agreed on for the simultaneous assassination of the brothers was

[3] Montesecco's confession will be found among the documents printed by Capponi, *Storia di Firenze*, at the end of his second volume.

that most solemn moment of the Catholic service, the elevation of the host; and no sooner, to the tinkling of the mass bell, was the host elevated by the officiating priest standing before the high altar under Brunelleschi's majestic cupola than the murderers leaped upon their victims. Francesco Pazzi and Baroncelli quickly dispatched the young and handsome Giuliano. When he was later laid out for burial, it was discovered that he had poured out his life's blood by nineteen gaping wounds. In such blind rage did Francesco Pazzi continue to hack at the prostrate form of his enemy that he wounded himself in the thigh so severely that it was only with the greatest difficulty that he made his escape from the scene. The two priests allotted to Lorenzo proved themselves less expert in the art of murder than the two civilians, and Lorenzo, alertly turning on his assailants, was able with drawn sword to hold them at bay until with the help of some friends he could take refuge in the sacristy. The vast concourse of worshipers, unable to grasp what was going on, filled the echoing vaults of the great cathedral with a clamor of confused cries and sped away in every direction. When after some moments of breathless waiting behind the doors of the sacristy (the north sacristy with the fine bronze doors of Luca della Robbia), loud knocking was heard to the accompaniment of voices assuring the group within that the newcomers were friends, the slender stripling, Sigismondo della Stufa, one of the devoted band who had helped Lorenzo make his escape, climbed agilely to the organ gallery over the sacristy door, from where he had a view of the whole spacious interior of the great edifice. It had been completely emptied by the panic of its worshipers, the men demanding admission at the sacristy doors were recognized as friends come to carry Lorenzo in safety to his house, and in the aisle just beyond the great octagon of the choir the startled eyes of young Sigismondo saw what they remembered till their light went out: the crumpled figure of Giuliano lying in a pool of blood.

While this only half-successful man-hunt was being conducted around the principal altar of one of the great temples of Christendom, the archbishop Salviati and old Jacopo Pazzi attempted to fulfil their part of the plot by seizing the government and inciting the masses to revolt against the lordship of the Medici. They failed miserably for the reason that the government and citizens sided with practical unanimity with their reputed tyrants. On invading the palace the archbishop and his troop of thirty helpers were promptly arrested; and when the pale and haggard figure of old Jacopo, armed and mounted on his war horse, passed through the streets hoarsely shouting *Popolo* and *Libertà,* the ancient rallying-cry of the Florentine masses, the people answered with a lusty, *Palle, Palle,* to signify their devotion to their present rulers. The shout referred to the six red pellets or balls constituting the Medicean coat of arms. Meanwhile the news of the assault in the cathedral had spread with the rapidity of lightning through the town, drawing the whole excited population into the streets and squares. Before the hostility of the constantly waxing crowds the routed Jacopo retreated to his palace and fled thence without delay into the mountains. And now there was no longer any possibility of restraining the maddened people. They became that murderous thing, a mob, which clamored for revenge and blood and would not be denied. Obedient to its raucous summons, the officials of the Palazzo Pubblico tossed one after the other of the archbishop's captured attendants through the windows to the pavement, much as a keeper might toss meat into a pit of hunger-crazed bears; and finally they followed up this gesture of appeasement by swinging the archbishop himself, with a rope tied around his neck, out of one of the Gothic windows, there to hang clad in his ornate vestments till he was dead. In another part of the town the crowd invaded the Pazzi residence and, dragging the murderer Francesco from the bed where he lay writhing with his self-inflicted wound, insisted on rushing him to the palace in order that, suspended by the neck from a mullioned window, he might serve as a companion piece to that arch traitor, the archbishop. Not till every individual even remotely connected with the plot had been captured and been either murdered outright by the mob or executed by the authorities in a manner indistinguishable from murder was, and then only after many days, an approximate tranquillity restored to the tumultuous town. Young and innocent Cardinal Riario was fortunately spared by the government's taking him into its safekeeping. Even the hate-blinded multitude seemed to have sensed that he was no more than the dupe of his criminal elders and desisted from its original intention to have his blood. If among so many gruesome acts of vengeance, there is an act of superlative gruesomeness, it befell old Jacopo, head of his house. Captured by peasants while he was threading his way through the hills of the Mugello, he was brought back to Florence to be tortured and hanged. Servants then laid him to rest in the beautiful chapel of his family at Santa Croce. But the populace was unwilling that he should enjoy so honorable an interment. Once and then again his body was dragged from its grave. On the second occasion it was a company of street urchins who took the matter in hand. The horrible mockery to which these children of the Florentine slums subjected the half-decayed corpse is too repulsive to relate. Suffice it that they at last tossed the mangled remains into the Arno and that they slowly floated down the stream until, after many days, they cleared the bridge at Pisa and passed out into the sea.

Thus amidst an orgy of violence and bloodshed expired the Pazzi conspiracy. Although the assassins had disposed of Giuliano, the far more important Lorenzo had made his escape and drew from an outraged people such extravagant expressions of loyalty that his rule, instead of being shaken, was more firmly established than before. But the threat to his life and state was by no means ended. In a sense it may even be said to have only begun. For the pope who, baulked of his prey, refused to consider any feature of the terrible Florentine drama save the enforced detention of his grand-nephew and the indignities heaped upon the sacred person of an archbishop, excommunicated Lorenzo and threatened to put the city and all Tuscany under interdict if the malefactor was not delivered into his hands to be punished as he deserved. As Florence steadfastly refused to do the papal bidding, the interdict was duly pronounced and immediately after was followed by war. Shoulder to shoulder with the pope stood his ally, the king of Naples; and when these two powers took the field against Lorenzo, the Florentine allies, Milan and Venice, automatically armed in Lorenzo's support. By the summer of 1478 all

Italy in the Age of
Lorenzo the Magnificent

Scale of Miles

0 20 40 60 80 100

D stands for Duchy
M stands for Marquisate
REP. stands for Republic
R stands for River

ITALY IN THE AGE OF LORENZO THE MAGNIFICENT

Italy was in arms, as most of the numerous small states joined one or the other of the two major combinations. However, the turmoil was not quite so devastating as the wide extent of the struggle would suggest. The wretched Italian military system made swift and vigorous action in the field impossible. To be sure, the evil worked both ways, but in the end it favored Florence since, if the enemy had commanded a more effective system, the Red Lily could hardly have escaped destruction. Never since the city had turned to the use of mercenaries had it had luck with them, and the new occasion proved no exception to the rule. What made a bad situation worse was that the help Florence expected to get from its two allies was insufficiently furnished. Venice was involved in a war with the Turks which called for the expenditure of all its strength, and Milan was so disturbed by the interminable struggle between the duchess regent and her intriguing brothers-in-law that the government was often completely paralyzed.

Under these circumstances King Ferrante of Naples and Sixtus IV, who assumed the offensive and invaded Tuscany on a common plan from the south and southeast, might have swiftly overwhelmed Lorenzo if their warfare had not been under the same curse as that of their opponents. Even so, in the course of the second campaign, fought in 1479, they came within a hair of achieving their purpose. At Poggio Imperiale, near Poggibonsi, the Florentines had constructed a fortified camp in order to block the advance of the enemy into the Arno Valley. On September 7, King Ferrante's son, Alfonso, duke of Calabria, made a surprise attack on the Florentine camp, captured it, and drove the enemy in headlong flight toward Florence. Not till the panic-stricken fugitives had reached San Casciano, some eight miles from the Tuscan capital, could they be regathered into even the semblance of a fighting force. It is probable that if Calabria had pushed gallantly on, he might have driven right through San Casciano to the gates of the city. But such determination was not in the military style of the day. Instead of pursuing his advantage, the duke returned on his track to lay siege to the little town of Colle; and on November 24, on the approach of winter, he proposed the usual seasonal truce, which the Florentines eagerly accepted.

When, on the signing of the truce, the clear-sighted Lorenzo reviewed his situation, he had to admit it was desperate. True, the Florentines had made their ruler's cause their own to a degree almost unparalleled in the history of Italy. But how much longer would they resist the grinding pressure of circumstance? To the heavy taxation necessitated by the war was added a wide destruction of crops, for the conflict had been waged largely on Tuscan soil. The diminished supplies brought famine and famine brought pestilence, famine's hideous twin brother. Finally, there was the interdict, which for the mass of the still deeply religious population was a very heavy trial. From the ever-deepening gloom suspended over Florence and its ruler there was no possible escape except through peace and the only avenue to peace was surrender. In measure as the pope, who had started the war in the spirit and with the aim of revenge, was cheered with the prospect of victory, he became increasingly implacable. It was impossible to surrender to him till every other resource had failed. Luckily for Lorenzo the king of Naples was not equally adamant.

For his own part the Magnificent was firmly persuaded that it was directly against the interest of Naples to weaken Florence and tip the always precarious balance of Italy in the pope's favor, If only he could present his arguments to King Ferrante in person, he might yet win his case. Distractedly revolving these thoughts, he resolved to appeal to his Milanese ally to intervene at Naples in his behalf. In that Lombard state the situation had recently achieved a certain clarification through the definite replacement of the duchess regent by one of her brothers-in-law, Lodovico. This is the complex, typically Renaissance personage, who, called from his dark complexion *Il Moro* (the Moor), was destined hereafter to play a sinister part in unbarring the gates of Italy to the foreigner who had long been waiting for the opportunity to enter. In spite of the traitor he became, Lodovico was a man of distinct gifts and from 1479 on the government of Milan rested exclusively in his hands as regent for his young nephew, the duke. His answer to Lorenzo's appeal was to assure him of Milanese support at Naples if he would frankly put his destiny into the hands of King Ferrante. When, following the Moor's advice, Lorenzo was unofficially assured that he would be honorably received by the Neapolitan court, he no longer hesitated. Early in December he secretly left Florence for the Tuscan coast, took ship at a small Maremma port, and set sail for the southern capital. It was a dramatic step which once more fanned to a blaze the waning devotion of his fellow-countrymen. In their eyes he was risking his person to obtain the peace, for the lack of which they were slowly perishing; and a feature that may have appealed to their volatile nature even more than his patriotism was that he boldly took the gambler's chance of staking his all on a single throw.

While the diplomatic correspondence in our possession[4] proves that Lorenzo's famous voyage was carefully prepared by him and was not the sudden improvisation he wished to have it appear, it nonetheless had about it an element of risk and sacrifice which could not but enthrall the imagination. There was always the chance that he might not be released if he did not sign the treaty which the victor dictated or that the treaty he finally accepted would be so ignominious that his angered fellow-citizens would reject the document and the negotiator along with it. Arrived at Naples, Lorenzo, although handsomely welcomed, trod anything but a path of roses. King Ferrante, and more especially his son, the duke of Calabria, had no idea of letting Florence escape without paying at least some of the usual penalties of defeat. For three months the Magnificent with cogent eloquence and ever-gracious manners argued the terms of peace with his victorious hosts until in February, 1480, the document was at last perfected. That the Florentines were mulcted in considerable sums of money and had to make some slight cessions of territory goes without saying; but only an intemperate enemy would have the effrontery to affirm that Lorenzo, on re-entering his city, had not brought back peace with honor. The vast majority of the Florentines accordingly overflowed with gratitude and greeted as their deliverer the man who had terminated the war which had pushed them to the edge of the abyss.

Even with Naples pacified the war was not terminated altogether. There

4 Fabroni, Vol. II, *Adnotationes*, 99, 104.

was still the pope to be placated, and the pope was not converted to a kindlier attitude by what to him was the base desertion of their common cause by his ally of Naples. At this point the hidden rulers of the universe came to Lorenzo's aid; at least what happened must have seemed to him like a divine intervention, even though its human instrument was the hated infidel Turk. On a hot August day of the year 1480 a Turkish flotilla made a sudden descent on the Neapolitan coast town of Otranto and captured it. The Moslem enemy had established a foothold in Italy and an apprehensive tremor passed through the length of the peninsula. The duke of Calabria, who had lingered on in Sienese territory unwilling, in spite of the peace treaty, to surrender the Florentine fortresses he had taken in the war, was obliged to return to the south with all possible speed. In the following year he recaptured Otranto from the Turks, certainly the most notable achievement of his undistinguished career. The enforced withdrawal of the Neapolitan garrisons from the Florentine towns they had hesitated to evacuate was a pure windfall for the Red Lily, but it was not the only advantage accruing to it from the Turkish menace. In the face of the Moslem invasion Sixtus IV was prompted to remember his responsibilities as shepherd of the Christian flock and, moved to proclaim the need of common action on the part of all Italians, he could no longer with any show of decency prosecute his private grudge against Lorenzo. He let himself be drawn into negotiations, which on December 3, 1480, were concluded with a remarkable act of reconciliation. Before the middle door of St. Peter's church a body of Florentine commissioners were received by him wearing the triple crown and seated on his chair of state upholstered in purple silk, and with the magnanimity becoming a supreme pontiff he granted the penitents his pardon for having attacked them. The commissioners, grave, elderly men, played the role of submission assigned to them with the same high regard for the proprieties; and after the pope had touched each in turn with his staff, thus cleansing them of their taint, they humbly kissed his foot and, in sign of their readmission to the Christian flock, followed him into the church to participate in a solemn mass of thanksgiving. Thus closed the dark chapter of the Pazzi conspiracy. Rescued as by a miracle from an infinity of perils, Lorenzo was henceforth regarded as fortune's darling and became the leading figure of the Italian political world.

XXIII. The Magnificent Lorenzo (1480–92)

ATROCIOUS as was the plot from which Lorenzo had barely escaped with his life and hardly less atrocious as was the subsequent war, he was too prudent and level-headed a man not to recognize that in a political sense he was himself not free from blame for the recent events. For, in order to create difficulties for the pope in his attempt to establish his relatives in the Romagna, he had abandoned the proved alliance with Naples and Milan, substituting therefor a union with Milan and Venice. But when the war waged against him by Sixtus IV and King Ferrante threatened him with ruin, he had been obliged by means of his hazardous voyage to Naples to find his way back to the earlier combination, from which, in sign that he had learned his lesson, he never again departed. For the remainder of his life he regarded the triple alliance of Milan-Florence-Naples as the anchor of his foreign policy and the best guaranty of the peace of the peninsula. At the same time he very substantially altered his attitude toward the papacy. If he continued to believe that it was to the interest of Florence that the State of the Church should not become consolidated at the expense of the many semi-independent lordlings established on its soil, he was no longer prepared to block every papal move in the direction of better control but rather to concede something to the pope in the hope of not again falling into that ruler's disfavor. For Lorenzo had been made aware of the enormous reserve strength of the papacy and was resolved, so far as lay in his power, not again to enter the lists against it. Without therefore wavering in his attachment to the triple alliance, he used his best skill to draw the pope within its orbit. That was difficult, however, as long as Sixtus IV lived, since Sixtus, having attacked the problem of the temporal power, neither would nor could recede from a course which kept his neighbors in a perpetual state of alarm. Even when the virile Sixtus was followed by the weakly vacillating Innocent VIII (1484–92), the situation was not materially changed, for the conversion of the loose dominion of the church into an effective civil state had by now become a papal obligation which no successor of Sixtus, whether bold or faint-hearted, could avoid assuming.

The policy of Lorenzo in the second and concluding period of his rule has been correctly described as the attempt to preserve the peace of Italy by maintaining a judicious equilibrium among the five leading states of the peninsula. Entirely contrary to the facts however, he is often credited with having achieved his purpose; and to clinch the argument it is pointed out that he had hardly disappeared from the scene when the whole delicate system of balance, which none but his extraordinary skill could operate, collapsed like a house of cards. Now while it is true that the invasion of the French of 1494, which totally disrupted the Italian state system and inaugurated the enslavement of the peninsula, did not take place till two years after Lorenzo's death, a French intervention had periodically threatened ever since the days of Lorenzo's grandfather, Cosimo. In fact, Cosimo and his ally, Francesco Sforza, as early as 1452 had signed an alliance with the then king of France, Charles VII, by which that sovereign agreed to aid them in their struggle against Naples and Venice. While the treaty did not on that occasion result in direct French action, Florence and Milan had threatened their Italian enemies with a foreign sovereign, and the example thus set was certain to be imitated. In the course of the following decades ambassadors from every Italian state at one time or another found their way to Paris to curry favor with the French king and invite his participation in peninsular affairs; and if Charles VII and his successor, Louis XI (1461–83), had, in spite of repeatedly renewed temptation, never crossed the Alps, it was solely because, deeply involved in domestic troubles, they were unable to embark on a perilous venture beyond their border. However, as this condition was not likely to last forever, the descent of the French was for many decades suspended like a portent over the peninsula, filling all its states, large and small alike, with alarm, but at the same time exercising a curious, hypnotic fascination. To appreciate the full significance of the half-dreaded, half-desired event, we must not forget that the ancient claim of the house of Anjou to the kingdom of Naples had by the recent extinction of the Angevin line (1481) passed to the French crown, and that therefore Louis XI's successor, Charles VIII, might readily persuade himself that in attacking King Ferrante he was doing no more than making an honorable effort to recover stolen goods. Moreover, in addition to the Neapolitan claim, there was the claim of another branch of the royal line, the house of Orléans, to the duchy of Milan based on its descent from a princess of the former ruling family of the Visconti; and with this claim the king, as head of his house, could also identify himself if he so desired. Every discussion of Italian politics in Lorenzo's time that does not assign a central position to the continued French threat of intervention based on either the Neapolitan or the Milanese claim is beside the mark. Indeed to understand Lorenzo's policy at all, it is necessary to see that it was governed by the aim to omit no measure calculated to cut off military action from beyond the Alps. That he had only a limited success is undeniable, since he had hardly departed this life when the long-threatened invasion took place, drawing down unspeakable calamities on Florence and all Italy. While we must admit that Lorenzo did not succeed in staving off the French avalanche, we may confidently assert that of all the Italian rulers he was the least guilty in connection with that dire event.

Only in case the French threat is conceded its due weight can it be clearly understood what is meant by describing Lorenzo's Italian endeavors as dedicated to the maintenance of peace. It required no particular insight on his part to arrive at the view which was the substance of his policy. This core and kernel was that if the five Italian powers continued their traditional quarrels, they would sooner or later with mathematical certainty draw the French into their conflicts, and that the measure alone capable of keeping the northern monarch from crossing the Alps was the solid peace front of Milan, Naples, Florence, Venice, and the pope. Toward this end the triple alliance of the first three, which, with interruptions, had been in existence since the days of Cosimo, was regarded by Lorenzo as a happy, preparatory measure; and after his one lapse, productive of the war of 1478–80, which had brought him to the verge of extinction, Lorenzo, as already said, faithfully based his Italian policy on this league. Furthermore, he attempted to extend its action by drawing the pope within its fold; and he would not have been averse to having it include also the Venetians, had it not been a matter of common knowledge that these islanders so doggedly pursued their exclusive advantage that they could never be trusted to follow a policy that took account of any other interest than their own. Had Lorenzo been able to expand the triple into a quintuple alliance, it would have been an achievement of absolutely capital import, as a sincerely conceived quintuple alliance would have been, in effect, an Italian confederation. In the light of subsequent events it is easy to see that nothing less than the unbroken front presented by such a confederation would have saved the peninsula from the French invasion of 1494 and from all the subsequent invasions, for which that first action served as precedent. But so impossible of fulfilment was the confederation program that, even in its most soaring flight, Lorenzo's thought no more than casually brushed the idea. For an effective federation the one indispensable pre-requisite was the sentiment of nationality. Unfortunately for Italy this senti-ment had not yet been born among the residents of the land or else was cherished by such small and scattered numbers that it possessed no collective vigor. The mainspring of the competitive Italian states was naked self-interest, and every government, having for generations pursued as its leading concern the widening of its boundaries at the expense of its neighbors, looked upon every contiguous government as an obstacle in its path and viewed it, if not always openly, at least secretly, with envy, suspicion, fear, and hatred.

Such was the monstrous situation to which Lorenzo, a realistic statesman, as he had to be, and not an empty daydreamer, was obliged to accommodate his policy. He therefore set himself no higher goal than peace, knowing full well that even peace was so considerable an innovation in war-torn Italy that he could do no more than strive with all his might to create a sentiment in its favor. The simplest measure to secure peace would have been the renun-ciation on the part of one and all of the states of their hitherto hotly pursued policy of expansion, but Lorenzo entertained no illusions regarding the possi-bility of having such a course adopted. The best and only pressure he could bring to bear in behalf of his cherished measure was perpetually to remind the Italian governments that a foreign power once admitted to the peninsula would enslave them all in turn, and that the very self-interest which each gov-ernment accepted as its law dictated the avoidance of upheavals calculated to convey the impression that divided Italy would fall an easy prey to an enterprising invader.

It does not impugn Lorenzo's statesmanship to declare that he was unable to impose on his fellow-rulers the peace policy in which he believed. He plied them with his powers of persuasion and they, hardening their minds against his arguments, with a stupid and criminal blindness persisted in the traditional pursuit of a narrowly selfish advantage. The peace of Italy was therefore as uninterruptedly disturbed after 1480 as had been the case before that date. Let the facts speak for themselves. In 1482 Pope Sixtus IV, still bent on improving his personal control in the Romagna, made an alliance with Venice for the purpose of partitioning Ferrara, thereby plunging Italy into a general war, since the triple alliance rushed promptly to Ferrara's aid. Although the Ferrarese war came to very little—what Italian war ever came to much?—it created disturbances that were not quieted for two years and freshly embittered the relations among the Italian powers. Besides, it revived the interest of France in the situation since France was urged by several reckless participants in the struggle to lend help and take sides. Hardly had this conflict been terminated when another war broke out (1485), this time between Naples and the pope. Each state thought it had good reasons to resort to arms, but it could easily be shown that the reasons were trivial and that essentially the outbreak was caused by nothing other than the savage ill feeling with which the Italian governments periodically overflowed. Again the other states were sucked into the vortex and again France began to loom, a shadowy giant clad in steel, across the summit of the Alps. Even after an accommodation had been arranged (1486) between Pope Innocent VIII and King Ferrante, a real pacification did not follow since the Neapolitan sovereign failed to comply with the terms of peace and the pope, filling the ears of all Europe with his protests, threatened every moment to renew the struggle. Lorenzo never ceased to pour water on the dangerous embers and to plead for a definitive settlement, but it was not till January, 1492, that the cantankerous recriminations between Rome and Naples, which an intriguing foreign power like France made it its business to keep alive, were brought to a mutually satisfactory adjustment.

Without taking the time to enumerate the countless minor disturbances of the Italian peace, chiefly in the ever-volcanic province of Romagna, the facts just recorded serve to show that, contrary to some encomiasts, who assign to Lorenzo the role of pacifier of his country, there was no peace in his day in passion-riven Italy. And again let it be said that his failure single-handedly to impose a policy, for which the other governments had neither sympathy nor understanding, draws no discredit on his head. It cannot even be fairly reckoned as an inconsistency on his part that, with the political competition continuing about him unabated, he should have utilized an occasional opportunity to strengthen himself territorially. As the head of the Florentine state he had a plain duty to improve its security, provided he could do so without turning the peninsula topsyturvy. This attitude will explain his action in regard to Sarzana. The important fortress of that name, which commanded the coast road leading southward from Liguria, had been acquired through purchase (1468) by his father Piero and ten years later had been seized by the original owners, the

Genoese, on the occasion of the threatening collapse of Florence toward the close of the war of the Pazzi conspiracy. The indignant Lorenzo was resolved to have Sarzana back as soon as the auspices were favorable. In 1484 he believed the moment had come, but he succeeded only in capturing Pietrasanta, some fifteen miles to the south of Sarzana and almost equally important as a defense against an enemy advancing on Tuscany from the north. Not till 1487 did Lorenzo retake Sarzana, and that the capture was effected under his personal direction and without precipitating a general war added greatly to his satisfaction. The Florentine people were no less narrowly patriotic than the inhabitants of the other Italian states and would not have given continued support to a ruler who did not make it a leading point of his policy to strain every nerve to maintain the integrity of their territory.

Nonetheless there was an ambiguous element in Lorenzo's pursuit of peace, of which he was himself well aware but which he was incapable of remedying. The Magnificent had made himself the advocate of peace largely in the hope of thus thwarting any ambition France might entertain to invade the peninsula. At the same time he maintained closer relations with the French court than any other Italian ruler and in and out of season protested that he was the devoted servant of the king. A number of pressing reasons imposed this course on him as unavoidable. For so many generations had the Florentines looked to the kings of France as the guardians of the sacred Guelph tradition that an attachment had sprung up, shared on the Arno by high and low alike and heartily reciprocated on the Seine. By Lorenzo's time the sentiment had acquired an independent life and, like the fabled chameleon, lived apparently on air. Notwithstanding, a close examination will reveal that it sucked its uninterrupted nourishment from the material advantages accruing to Florence from its commercial activities in the French kingdom. As far back as the thirteenth century it had been the French market which yielded the great mercantile companies of the Arno town their handsomest profits, and two hundred years later, in Lorenzo's time, the situation was still substantially unchanged. Moreover, the Florentines had ever been and still were in a highly vulnerable position, for their presence across the Alps was resented by the native traders and could be terminated at a moment's notice by the withdrawal of the special protection of the monarch. With Arno merchant prosperity hanging on the thread of the king's favor no Florentine government had ever been able to maintain any other attitude toward the Parisian court than one of a rather abject humility. To this general submission consecrated by long custom should be added the particular subjection into which the banking house of the Medici had slipped. Having already under Cosimo extended its operations into France, the firm had on the usual business score fallen into the royal dependence. Louis XI, to whom both Cosimo and his son Piero had shown themselves consistently devoted, in 1465 rewarded their zeal by an unusual concession. He permitted the Medici to stamp the lilies of France on one of the balls or *palle* of their coat-of-arms. Since that day a blue ball carrying three golden lilies stood out from the other five unadorned red balls in perpetual testimony of the grace conferred by a French king. As the heir of so honorable a royal friendship Lorenzo could do nothing but nurse it, especially as in his day the

Lyons branch of his bank rose to great eminence and served as the depository of the funds of innumerable French courtiers and noblemen.

The elements constituting Lorenzo's French problem were many and complicated but they are perfectly intelligible. While his political insight warned him of the peril threatening his own and every other Italian state from across the Alps, proper regard for the Gallic sentiments of his fellow-countrymen and important considerations involving their commercial interests as well as his own obliged him to cultivate an intimacy with the French court which caused the Arno republic to be regarded at Paris as a French protégé ready, whenever the call went forth, to smooth the king's way into the Promised Land beyond the Alps. Lorenzo was obliged to be deftly double-faced not to be found out at the Valois court as its secret antagonist. That he succeeded is clearly indicated by the unbroken good relations between himself and Paris to the end of his days. However, when two years after his death the French at length made their long-expected appearance on the scene and Lorenzo's son, Piero, came out into the open against them, their indignation flamed to heaven over what was to them his abominable treachery. This is not the place to enlarge on the incapable Piero's mistakes and puerilities; unquestionably they contributed to the disaster which overtook him and his state. Nonetheless, it is impossible to subscribe to the opinion voiced by many writers on Florentine history that, had Lorenzo been still alive, the catastrophe might have been averted. We may go so far as to grant that the resourceful Lorenzo would have found a way to avoid some of the worst consequences of the French invasion, but that he could have hindered the event and the many evils that flowed therefrom is a wholly unjustified assumption. It is to speak darkly and cryptically to declare that the invasion of 1494 was writ in the stars. However, the statement becomes defensible and even irrefutable if it intends to convey no more than that the grave event resulted from forces which were prepared in the womb of time and which no individual, not even one of such unusual talents as the lord of Florence, could have annulled. On the other hand, whoever is wont to weigh historical events in purely human scales will be disinclined to free Lorenzo from blame, in spite of his having been the only Italian who had a correct understanding of what foreign intervention signified. To such an interpreter of history Lorenzo's intimacy with and silent encouragement of France will constitute his tragic guilt, which, though dooming him to ultimate defeat, involved him in a heroic conflict with forces which he helped release and which proved stronger than himself.[1]

The domestic policy of Lorenzo was the product of the same subtle mind that conceived his foreign policy and it suffered, though not in the same degree, from a similar weakness. This was that, although dictated by essentially sound considerations, it did not enjoy the support of those immediately concerned and was imposed on unwilling citizens by a mixture of authority and sleight of hand. On succeeding his father he had, as we have seen, taken over the system of veiled control which had been in force since 1434. While it left

[1] For Lorenzo's relations to France see Buser, *Die Beziehungen der Mediceer zu Frankreich*, etc. Zweiter Abschnitt. For a recent appreciation of his peace policy see R. Palmarocchi, *La Politica Italiana di Lorenzo de' Medici*. Florence, 1933.

the old constitution of the priors apparently intact, it brought it under Medicean management by abolishing election by lot in favor of a hand-picked system operated by a board of accoppiatori. The constitution thus manipulated had, to put it moderately, at the very least worked as well as during any earlier period. Better control had, above all, greatly reduced the amount of domestic disturbance. Nonetheless, no sooner did the state become involved in war with its unescapable reverses and heavy costs, than the opposition, which normally remained in hiding, took heart and voiced its criticism in the councils. Not only were the councils still, as they had ever been, the outstanding popular feature of the Florentine system, but they were also composed of so many members that many individuals had found a seat in them who were not proved and tested Mediceans. During the disastrous war of the Pazzi conspiracy largely waged on Tuscan soil, a certain amount of opposition sprang to life in the councils, reasonably responsive as they would be to the trends of popular opinion. The repeated manifestations filled Lorenzo with alarm, and as soon as he had overcome the immediate crisis in his affairs by his surprise visit to Naples, he resolved on constitutional changes which would further weaken the popular elements still imbedded in the system.

If the Magnificent had not been a Florentine faced with a republican tradition of long standing, he might have considered that the time at length had come to replace the patchwork constitution inherited from the past with his open and confessed tyranny. All around him tyrants flourished, not because, though the thought must have occurred to many an indignant and suffering contemporary, that the time, long foretold, of Antichrist and the Day of Judgment had arrived, but because tyrants were the unattractive but solely available instruments for the reorganization of society following its medieval collapse. However, the powerful sentiments of his fellow-townsmen and doubtless, to a certain extent, his own sentiments forbade him openly to adopt the tyrannical solution. He would have to continue to respect republican appearances, while at the same time reducing the surviving liberal elements of the constitution and concentrating the power more effectively in his own hands. Only a few weeks after his return from Naples, on April 8, 1480, he attacked the problem by the measure which in Florence regularly initiated a "reform," a balìa endowed with sweeping powers. Without delay this balìa began its conventional, elaborate legerdemain, which we will deliberately ignore in order to fasten our attention on the rabbit it finally drew from its magical hat. This surprise animal was a new council, the council of Seventy, intended to supersede all the existing councils without, however, definitely and finally replacing them. In constitutionally conservative Florence nothing old was ever replaced, even though it no longer functioned in any effective sense.

Undeniably the council of Seventy was meant to become and became the core of the government. Its members sat for life, they filled vacancies in their ranks by co-optation, and all power in the state was concentrated in their hands. Moreover, as even seventy men more or less devoted to the Medicean interest were too many-headed a government to act efficiently and speedily, the Seventy delegated their most essential powers to two permanent committees. One of these was the *Otto di Pratica,* the Eight, intrusted with foreign and military matters; the other was a group of twelve set over finance, credit, and trade. The Otto di Pratica are not to be confused with the Otto di Guardia, a committee for police and criminal matters dating from the Albizzi era and left undisturbed by the latest reorganization. It is permissible to think of the Seventy as a self-perpetuating senate served by two working committees appointed from its membership. As already stated, the old councils continued to meet in order to approve the measures prepared by the Seventy, while the priors and gonfalonier of Justice, henceforth nominated by the Seventy acting as accoppiatori, continued their existence with no other significance than that of an ornamental figurehead of the still nominally republican ship of state. Lorenzo himself sat among the Seventy and was directly or indirectly represented on the two committees charged with the most important functions of government. In the gradual breakdown of the old constitution as well as in the complementary emergence of a Medicean monarchy the Seventy may be taken to mark a decisive step. There can be no doubt that the government became more responsive to a single guiding will; but the fact that the old forms, as hollowed out as a forest of dead oaks, were nonetheless left standing, testifies to a public state of mind which obliged the cautious Lorenzo substantially to continue the inherited Medicean anonymity and to refrain from too visibly playing the signore.

Probably it was the shaky public finances more than any other single governmental difficulty that prompted Lorenzo to strengthen his personal control. The finances were the feeblest feature of the Florentine and every other contemporary state; and the income tax of 1427, called the catasto, had not proved the cure-all that was hoped. Lorenzo clung to the commendable progressive feature added to the original system by Cosimo, while to his credit, be it said, he largely abandoned his grandfather's hateful practice of ruining his opponents by an excessive assessment. In spite of the complaints the income tax continued to elicit in Lorenzo's day, a modern student will find it difficult to disagree with its central principle. Still, the catasto was far from perfect since, for one thing, it was often levied many times in a single year, and again, because, though carried on the books of the Monte as an interest-bearing loan, the Monte, in periods of financial stress, arbitrarily reduced the interest or defaulted altogether. Deeply considered, the root of the trouble was that Florence wanted to play its part in the human drama as a great state but had no stomach for the increased costs which wars, frequent embassies, and a regulated administration of affairs entailed. Lorenzo could under no circumstances give up the income tax, but he could make concessions in regard to it to his main supporters, the merchants, who, like their kind through all the ages, were stiffly opposed to an examination of their ledgers to determine their profits. Besides, by various tricks of bookkeeping best known to themselves, the merchants could easily lead the tax authorities by the nose. In view of these circumstances, Lorenzo consented on the occasion of the reforms of 1480 to a bifurcation of the income tax. Henceforth the main burden of direct taxation fell on the returns from land and houses, while commercial profits, without being exactly made tax-exempt, escaped close governmental scrutiny by the imposition on the citizens of a progressive poll-tax.

While these changes in applying the income tax may from a purely administrative angle have been an improvement, they did not put an end to the irregularities which had always characterized the Florentine financial department. Indeed these irregularities increased through Lorenzo's direct interference and particularly owing to his permitting his personal finances to become inextricably tied up with those of the state. The beginning of this confusion went back to the days of Cosimo, to the possible advantage at that time of the public treasury, as Cosimo frequently came to its relief with advances from his private purse. This Lorenzo was no longer able to do, since, lacking the time and inclination to attend to business, he was penalized for his neglect with a shrinking income. At the same time his living expenses experienced a considerable increase, in large part no doubt owing to the obligations resting upon him as head of the state. He entertained visiting princes and their suites in the great palace in the Via Larga often for many days, and the display characteristic of this age of upstarts required him to practice a prodigal hospitality. Neither for this nor for the embassies he dispatched to the courts of his fellow-rulers nor for any other of the public services he rendered did he receive compensation; and if, on discovering that the inherited Fortunatus purse no longer automatically dropped gold florins into his palm, he argued that he had impoverished himself for the good of the state, he was not entirely in the wrong. His difficulty was that since his tyranny was unofficial, there could be no regular accounting between him and the government, and that if he dipped his hand into the public treasury, he was, regardless of his private convictions, formally guilty of theft. How far he went in the appropriation of public funds, especially to stave off the crises, which repeatedly threatened his bank with shipwreck and of which we shall presently hear, will never be known, but that there were irregularities is, to put it as mildly as possible, not improbable. On the other hand, it is fair to remember that the allegations against him emanate from disgruntled and hostile contemporaries who in no single instance have adduced the proof of their charges. When these same whispering opponents refer to the disorder, already mentioned, in the management of the National Debt (*Il Monte*) or to the scandalous manipulations of the dower fund for girls called *Il Monte delle Doti,* they do not hesitate, again without supplying any evidence, to lay the alleged malfeasance at Lorenzo's door. This must make us hesitate to put too much faith in their accusations, especially if we recall that there never was a time when the Florentine finances were not at loose ends and that at the bottom of the trouble, in Lorenzo's day as in the past, was the power politics of the Florentine republic. While it is possible and even probable that Lorenzo made a bad situation worse by diverting public funds to his private use, his enemies defeat themselves in ascribing all the financial embarrassments of an over-ambitious state to his personal wrongdoing.[2]

As it was the troubles of the Medici bank which gave rise to the rumors of Lorenzo's dishonesty, this is the place to review the fortunes of that institu-

[2] Reumont, Vol. II, pp. 405 ff., lists the charges of such contemporaries and near-contemporaries as Rinuccini, Cambi, Guicciardini, and Nardi, and apparently believes every one of them to be true. A much more judicial attitude is adopted by Armstrong, pp. 267-69.

tion in his day. It is often stated that the bank had passed its meridian even before Lorenzo assumed control.[3] Conclusive figures are not available and the matter must remain undecided. The bank still did business in every country of Europe and the Levant, it still received deposits and made loans, it still dealt in every known article of merchandise, more particularly in wool, cloth, silk, dyes, alum, spices, and furs. If it had got its start under Giovanni di Bicci through his connection with the papacy, it continued to profit from this association under the direction of all of Giovanni's successors. Even the mortal feud between Lorenzo and Pope Sixtus IV caused no enduring breach, since a year before he died Sixtus, who needed the bank as much as the bank needed him, received it back into favor. Nor was the value of the connection for the Medici family limited to the role of the pope as a leading depositor and borrower. Shortly after the middle of the fifteenth century great beds of alum were discovered at Tolfa in the papal state and presently their exploitation was intrusted by the pontiff to a company organized by the Medici interests. Alum, a mineral indispensable in the dyeing process, had hitherto been supplied chiefly from Asia Minor and other countries of the east. With the discovery of the Tolfa deposits not only did the importation of alum from abroad become unnecessary, but the Medici company acquired a practical monopoly in the Italian market, netting it considerable profits.

Failure of the papal favor cannot therefore be alleged as even a contributory cause of Lorenzo's business difficulties. The most plausible explanation of the decline of the bank lies in Lorenzo's insufficient training in trade and the necessity he was under, owing to his absorption in matters he held to be more important, of intrusting his material interests to agents whose choice was often extremely unfortunate. Another evil was the merging of business with politics. This practice had already begun under Cosimo and followed inevitably from the head of the firm becoming also the head of the state. However, both Cosimo and Piero after him, as trained, professional traders, employed a restraint which Lorenzo no longer observed. An examination of some of the worst crises of Lorenzo's time will show these various influences at work. It was the London house which first sent up signals of distress. The London and every other branch of the great Medici bank was in effect a separate firm which reported to Florence for orders but which was conducted with a large measure of independence by the partners on the ground. When the London house advanced the huge sum of 120,000 gold florins to Edward IV, and the king was obliged (1470) to flee from his realm, the investment had to be written to profit and loss. The blame attached to the London agents looking for speculative profits from a political gamble, but, in spite of warnings issued from Florence, the practice continued to flourish. A leading Medici branch was that of Bruges, where Tommaso Portinari, member of a family already highly regarded at Florence in Dante's day, was in control. The thirteenth-century ancestor of Tommaso was the father of Dante's Beatrice and founder of the great hospital of Santa Maria Nuova, expanded in our day to a vast and flourishing medical center. Tommaso, ill advised by his hunger for gain and under lax restraint on the part of Lorenzo, backed Charles the Bold of Burgundy,

[3] Meltzing, *Das Bankhaus der Mediceer*, etc., Part II.

and when in 1477 Charles perished in battle and his extravagant adventures came to an abrupt end, the Bruges office could be saved from disaster only by Lorenzo's coming to its aid. It was on this occasion that the rumors first became insistent that Lorenzo had abused his position as head of the state by diverting its funds into his pocket. The Lyons branch, which reached a high eminence through the intimacy between Lorenzo and King Louis XI, repeated the story of London and Bruges, for, when the death of Louis in 1483 occasioned a run of the French depositors, the bank had to suspend payments and did not become liquid till Lorenzo replenished its coffers. His liberality of course occasioned renewed whispers that he had saved himself at the expense of the state. Luckily not all of the Medici ventures were equally unfortunate and, so far as known, the banks at Rome, Milan, Naples, and Constantinople never gave Lorenzo any anxiety. Nevertheless it is clear that his enterprises owed their continued existence in his day less to his business acumen than to his political standing and prestige. As soon therefore as his son Piero lost his authority by being driven out of Florence (1494), the great bank with its network of connections throughout the known world collapsed over night. The history of the Medici as bankers had come to an end.

It is the more reasonable to ascribe the decline of the Medici bank to bad management of one sort or another, as Florentine business in general flourished and a prosperity reigned suggesting that, in commercial enterprise and industrial activity, Florence in the quattrocento did not fall below the trecento level. However, certain changes in the town's economic life had taken place which are interesting in themselves and merit attention. The manufacture of woolen cloth, on which throughout the fourteenth century the prosperity of the town had largely rested, with the beginning of the fifteenth century entered on a decline which became more marked with every decade. Nations, such as the French and the English, which had hitherto absorbed great quantities of the excellent Florentine product, undertook, often by importing Florentine artisans, to manufacture an approximately equivalent cloth, and then, by means of protective tariffs, to shut out the foreign supply. As Florence was at a disadvantage in the matter of raw wool, which it had to import to a large extent from Spain and England, there was no reason why its cloth should continue to command the world-markets as soon as the artisans of the other countries had taken over the taste, skill, and technical processes of their Florentine rivals. That the energy which had carried the Arno town to its great eminence was not yet spent was proved by the citizens promptly finding a substitute for the waning wool trade. This was the trade in silk which rose in measure as the trade in wool declined.

At the time of the revival of commerce in the eleventh century, silk fabrics were eastern luxuries imported by the Italian coastal cities, and only very slowly did the manufacture of these gorgeous stuffs, much desired by the clergy and nobility, acquire a foothold in the west. So far as Tuscany is concerned the earliest center of the silk industry was Lucca, and the Lucchese looms long retained their reputation even after other Tuscan towns, and Florence among them, had inaugurated a silk trade of their own. It is certain that an *arte di seta* was in existence by the middle of the dugento, at which time, or immediately afterward, it was incorporated as a membrum in the Por Santa Maria gild.[4] When in 1314 Lucca suffered an inhuman sack at the hands of its Pisan enemies, Florence by offering prompt, if not wholly disinterested, hospitality to the distressed weavers of the pillaged neighbor was enabled greatly to boost its production. While the advance of the industry continued steadily through the fourteenth century, it was not till the fifteenth century that it equaled and finally outstripped in importance the older textile craft. Exactly as had once been the case with its woolen cloth, Florence owed the vogue of its silk stuffs to the special skills developed by its artisans. They turned out light and heavy silks, taffetas, velvets, damasks, brocades, all without exception of outstanding excellence. The enriching of brocades with interwoven threads of gold and silver was a technique not mastered till around 1420, but was quickly carried to such a pitch of perfection that these costly, shimmering stuffs were in demand by the upper classes throughout Europe. When we learn that the Arno merchants disposed of their silk goods not only in all the countries of the west but also in the Levant, where the art had been practiced for centuries before it had spread to the occident, we find it easy to agree that the Florentine silk merchant uttered no idle boast who declared that his countrymen's *panni serici* surpassed those of all the countries of the world.[5]

It was in the fifteenth century, too, that the Florentines gradually overcame the disadvantage of being dependent on the orient for the raw product required by their looms. The mulberry tree was planted among the vineyards and wheat fields to a constantly increasing extent and by their yield of good silk fiber the imported silkworms intimated their satisfaction with the Tuscan climate. However, throughout the fifteenth century importation from the east of raw silk and dyestuffs continued, greatly facilitated by the development of Florence as a sea power. This event, a result of the conquest of Pisa, was the proudest achievement of the Albizzi period. Florence at once set vigorously about reviving the long-failing Pisan trade and met, on the whole, with considerable success. On the capture of Constantinople by the Turks (1453), representatives of the Arno government signed a favorable trade treaty with the sultan, who, out of enmity toward his maritime rivals, the Venetians, was pleased to favor their Italian competitors. Even before being made welcome at the Turkish capital the Florentines had established contact with the Moslem ruler of Egypt and in the course of time proved as much of a thorn in the Venetian flesh at Alexandria as on the Bosporus.

The expanding Levantine trade probably counted no whit less than the prosperous silk industry in keeping Florence to the fore among the leading cities of the world. Commercial statistics of the full and accurate modern type are of course not available, but we learn from a well-informed trader that in 1469 fifty-one Florentine firms did business in the Constantinopolitan area. As at the same time thirty-seven Florentine merchant companies were represented at Naples and twenty-four in France, we seem to be justified in concluding that by the second half of the fifteenth century the Levantine connection had

[4] Davidsohn, Vol. IV², pp. 71 ff.
[5] Davidsohn, Vol. IV², p. 73.

acquired a greater importance than belonged to either of the two markets which, during the two previous centuries, had stood out as the leading sources of Florentine wealth. We owe the above-quoted figures to a certain Benedetto Dei, who, early in Lorenzo's reign, was moved to discharge a thunderous broadside against *cierti Vinitiani gentilomini* who had had the impudence to speak slightingly of the economic position of his beloved fatherland.[6] To crush them utterly he added a number of other data illustrative of the material grandeur of Florence around the year 1470. He mentions eighty-three *botteghe d'arte di seta* and lists the markets from Turkey to Antwerp and London to which the finished goods were dispatched. Florence had thirty-three banks, in which connection we must remember that by Dei's time the smaller trading firms no longer dealt in money and therefore were not listed as banks. That there still were two hundred and seventy woolen shops (*botteghe di arte di lana*) would indicate that woolen goods were still being manufactured in considerable quantity, although, since nothing is said of the size of the shops, we have no way of telling what their actual output may have been. Further items declaring the splendor of *Florentia bella* are sixty-six apothecary shops, fifty-four establishments of stone-cutters who practice both *intaglio* and *rilievo,* forty-four master-goldsmiths and jewelers, and so on for two bewildering quarto pages. It is clear that to Benedetto Dei, a typical Florentine burgher, who spent his life circulating among all the countries of the Mediterranean in pursuit of gain, the thought never occurred that his city had begun to decline or had ceased to be what to his mind it had been for generations past, the hub of the universe.

No more than the bourgeois trader was the Medicean ruler of this busy community persuaded that its path had begun to slope downhill, nor did he believe, in spite of the heavy seas which his own business venture had encountered, that the twilight of Florence, even as one of the world's financial centers, was at hand. In addition to having a sufficiently open mind to ascribe his commercial difficulties to his own mistakes, Lorenzo was blessed with the optimism which permitted him to look upon every gathering of clouds as a passing event. His most conspicuous and attractive trait, his special gift from the gods, was his immense zest for life. A large section of his fellow-citizens must have been animated with an identical vitality or they would not have been so sympathetically affected by his activities. The Renaissance movement, fast mounting to its climax, was engaged in releasing enormous energies directed upon every conceivable form of human endeavor. There was a joyousness abroad which is the natural accompaniment of creative effort in a community untouched, or at least as yet not greatly disturbed, by paralyzing doubt. So far were the upper classes from distrusting the secular outlook championed by humanism that, in taking it over, neither were they agitated by any moral scruples nor did it occur to them that they had sharply divorced themselves from their religious past. As for the Florentine masses they had hardly so much as been brushed by the semi-paganism that had taken possession of the ruling group. This fact the episode carrying the name of Savonarola and only just be-

---

[6] Benedetto Dei's "Lettera per Difesa della Mercatura dei Fiorentini" was incorporated by Pagnini, *Della Decima,* etc., Vol. II, pp. 235 ff., in his still valuable essay, "Sul Commercio dei Fiorentini."

ginning to show its face during Lorenzo's last years was destined before long to bring to the startled attention of Italy and the western world. The life-span of the Magnificent, however, was not darkened by this shadow and owes its special flavor to the hopes and dreams, the attitudes and achievements of the poets, artists, and scholars who were lifted up as on wings by the spirit of their age and who, gathering around Lorenzo, hailed him as the captain of their band.

It was this precious zest of Piero's son that explains the many interests to which he gave himself with all his might from early manhood. Brought up by humanist scholars, he continued to live in their company on easy give-and-take terms to the end of his days. His most constant attendant and most intimate friend was Poliziano, the foremost classical scholar of his age and also its foremost poet, unless we confer this latter distinction on Lorenzo himself. His early and sincere devotion to Italian letters was followed up, in what could not have been other than rare moments of relaxation, with many kinds of poetic composition. Not particularly regarded in the writer's day, they have evoked a steadily increasing admiration with the passing of the years. While Lorenzo's verses were in the main addressed to the cultivated circle of his equals, in his Carnival songs he presented himself as purveyor to the ribald fun with which the common people in their traditional pre-lenten processions and masquerades sought compensation for the rigors of the coming season of penitence. It is characteristic of the age and also of the unchecked exuberance of the poet that many of his Carnival pieces are of a shocking indecency. He associated freely with painters, sculptors, and architects and helped them with commissions, although, owing to his straitened finances, he was far from practicing the lavish patronage of his grandfather. It is a tribute to his fastidious taste that among the sculptors he chiefly favored Verrocchio, among the painters, Botticelli. Nor should it be forgotten that he was the first to recognize the talent of Michelangelo, whom he befriended in his impecunious youth by generously assigning to him a room in his palace and a place at his table. Throughout his life he tirelessly enlarged the famous family collection of manuscripts, gems, cameos, and medals. In the immediately succeeding chapters, devoted to the intellectual and aesthetic developments during the quattrocento, Lorenzo's activity as a humanist, poet, and patron will receive further attention. Our purpose at this point is attained if we succeed in conveying an impression of the unrivaled versatility which enabled him actively and fruitfully to share in all the mental movements of the day. He had the happy gift, more characteristic of the fleet southern races than of the heavier northern breeds, to give himself, with entire surrender of his mind and senses and in swift succession, to the dictation of instructions to an ambassador departing on an important mission, to the examination of a newly discovered manuscript, to a discussion among experts of a mooted doctrine of Greek philosophy, and to the arrangements for a happy hunting expedition with a group of friends. Like his countrymen generally, he was not inhibited by an awkward self-consciousness but was of an open nature, courteous, and accessible to everyone he met. Thus easily and graciously identified with all that his fellow-citizens dreamt, thought, and did, he well deserves, much more by reason of his radiant personality than of his authority and position as a statesman, to have his period called the Laurentian age.

Lorenzo had hardly reached early manhood when he began to suffer from the inroads of a disease hereditary in his family and identified by the medical science of his age as gout. Probably it was something much more devastating than what we understand by that name; but whatever it was, it obliged him frequently to seek relief at one of the many warm baths dotting the neighborhood of Siena and Volterra. Before he was forty years old his illness had got to the point of obliging him to withdraw from public view for prolonged periods. The alarming condition of his health unescapably turned his thoughts to the future and the problem of transmitting his authority to his heir. Although no one was more anxiously aware than himself that his oldest son, Piero, whom he was bringing up as his successor, could maintain himself as lord of Florence only by that sum of gifts, for which the Italians of the Renaissance employed the word *virtù,* nonetheless as the head of the house, he considered it his duty to take every precaution to leave to Piero as solid as possible an edifice of power. There being no more effective means at hand to buttress the Medicean position than the tried device of matrimonial alliances, Lorenzo was on the lookout for the most valuable available consorts for his children as soon as they should reach the age of puberty. He married his oldest daughter, Lucrezia, to Giacopo Salviati, a relative of the infamous archbishop who had figured in so prominent a manner among the Pazzi conspirators. He wanted by-gones to be by-gones and the breach which had opened between him and another great Florentine clan to be closed. With a like view to multiplying his local adherents another daughter, Contessina, was wed to Piero Ridolfi. When the question was posed of the family connection most advantageous to his prospective heir, the Magnificent adopted the course which had been followed in his own case and arranged a union with Alfonsina, member of the great Roman clan of the Orsini. The marriage took place by proxy in March, 1487, and a year later, when the bridegroom was seventeen years old, the bride took up her residence in Florence. For his third and last daughter, Maddalena, Lorenzo developed a very ambitious plan. Ever since his disastrous quarrel with Sixtus IV he had been brought to an appreciation of the value of a close papal connection; and when, on surrounding Sixtus's successor, Innocent VIII, with flattering attentions, he found his regard reciprocated, he resolved to confirm the intimacy by means of a family tie. The result was that Maddalena was married (1488) to Francesco Cibò, a son whom the pope, with a candor exceptional in the succession of Roman pontiffs, frankly acknowledged as his offspring.

Much more important, however, in Lorenzo's eyes and so important historically for the Medici family as to prove decisive for its later fortunes, was the advantage Lorenzo was able to take of his intimate association with Pope Innocent to propose his second son, Giovanni (known afterward as Pope Leo X), for the college of cardinals. There was a third and last son, Giuliano, who was still so young that the father did not live to form any plans for his worldly advancement. We may therefore conclude our tale of the political bargains the Magnificent struck for his children with the memorable case of Giovanni. As his second son was a prudent, studious youth, Lorenzo may have felt a normal paternal pride in directing him toward an ecclesiastical career; however, his primary purpose in so doing was to promote him to a position of influence enabling him to be of service to what Lorenzo, already employing the royal manner, proudly called *la casa nostra*. Since nothing less than a cardinalate would meet this end, it was a cardinalate to which Lorenzo aspired. Rendered anxious by the increasing severity of his illness, he began to work on Innocent's sympathies while Giovanni was still a boy, and so stubbornly did he press the matter that finally, in 1489, when Giovanni was fourteen years old, the pope yielded. Giovanni was promised a cardinal's hat on the understanding that he was not to be endowed with the authority it conferred till three years later. Accordingly, in March, 1492, amidst festivities of an unexampled splendor, all Florence joined in acclaiming the newest prince of the church, whose youth, although it gave no offense in that callous age, constituted a scandal of the first order. The father of the seventeen-year-old cardinal was already too far stricken to take part in the celebration. On setting out for Rome to assume his exalted seat Giovanni bade the bedridden Lorenzo an affectionate farewell and, shortly after his arrival in the Eternal City, received from him a remarkable letter of instructions.[7] It has been extravagantly praised in some quarters as a model of its kind. While it may be a model, it is so far from being fresh and original that it differs in no respect from what solicitous fathers have counseled their sons from the beginning of time with a view to holding them to a line of conduct calculated to secure their worldly success. The most impressive feature of the letter for whoever is interested in the quality of Lorenzo's mind is its uncompromising realism. This reveals itself in the writer's exact knowledge of the contemporary Roman cesspool and in his careful prescriptions to his young son for escaping its contamination.

A few weeks after Giovanni's departure from Florence Lorenzo, in expectation of the end, had himself carried to his country seat at Careggi. He wished to die where his father and grandfather had died before him. So rapidly, as the ecstatic Tuscan spring once again took possession of the land, did his strength wane that, early in April, his sister Bianca was obliged to inform him that his last hour was drawing near. Owing to the death of Clarice Orsini some four years before, the household was without a competent head and this favorite sister had come to Careggi to assume control. On a priest being summoned the dying man confessed, was shriven, and received the Holy Sacrament. His closest friend, Poliziano, was in constant attendance, the young and handsome scholar, Pico della Mirandola, paid him a moving visit of farewell. There was a constant coming and going of friends and weeping members of the family, from all of whom in the manner becoming a great gentleman he took courteous leave. With his son and heir, Piero, he had a long last interview conducted without witnesses. Suddenly the Dominican friar, Savonarola, appeared and was ushered into the chamber. According to Poliziano, a bystander and eye-witness, the visitor summoned Lorenzo to repentance, and before taking his departure, at the dying man's request, with raised hand gave him his bless-

[7] Fabroni, Vol. II, *Adnotationes*, 178. An English translation in Roscoe, pp. 285-88.

ing. Poliziano's account of his friend and patron's last days was written in Latin six weeks after the event, and there is no reason to challenge its facts, unless it be to say that they received a certain artificial inflation by reason of the detestable practice of the contemporary humanists never to set pen to paper save with the intention to produce "literature."

If Savonarola had left his own account of the death-bed scene, in view of his impeccable character it would have to be given a much weightier consideration than that of the poet-scholar who was also a Medicean dependent and courtier. Unfortunately Savonarola did nothing of the sort; but when in the years following his tragic death, his sorrowing disciples began to assemble the materials suited to making a cult of his memory, they gave currency to a version of the meeting at Careggi which sharply contradicts that of Poliziano at every point. Their story took the form of drama, of drama moreover of the traditional religious kind, for it presented the trembling but insufficiently repentant sinner faced in the person of Savonarola with the personified Divine Wrath. With the instinctive preference mankind has always felt for irreconcilable opposites to be brought to an open breach, writers were persuaded before long to declare for the Savonarolist version, until by sheer force of repetition through the ages Poliziano, the eye-witness, has been discredited in favor of the visionaries and miracle-mongers who strove to honor their martyred leader by exhibiting him as a towering Old Testament prophet, through whom God delivers his judgments. Like every great religious teacher before or since, Savonarola was by his devoted adherents built up into a myth, and of this myth the death-bed episode at Careggi became an inseparable part. Its culmination has passed into every history of Florence, into every book dealing with either Savonarola or Lorenzo. That culmination came when, after Lorenzo had conceded two of the demands made upon him by the friar, his stern inquisitor confronted him with the third and crowning demand to restore the liberty of Florence. How this miracle was to be effected with Lorenzo lying at the point of death the story prudently refrains from telling. It contents itself with recounting the tyrant's refusal which he signified by turning his face to the wall. Here ended the tale; but the reader or hearer, familiar with the literature of edification, was invited to supply the conclusion, which could only be that, when the friar on his rebuff took his departure, the soul of the wicked tyrant went straight to its reward in Everlasting Fire. If history is to be constructed from the critical examination of documents, it cannot, in the matter of this much-mooted incident, do other than accept Poliziano's version even while freely admitting that the poet may have altered the facts in one or another particular in the interest of friendship. It cannot, however, under any circumstances reject Poliziano's for the Savonarolist version, for the latter, first circulated as hearsay at two or three removes from its source, did not make an appearance in print till after many years of incubation on the part of a group of honest but mentally unbalanced enthusiasts.[8]

Lorenzo died in the early night hours of April 8, 1492, and after simple ceremonies was buried in the ancestral church of San Lorenzo. If life is reck-

[8] Poliziano's testimony, in the form of a letter to a friend, is printed by Fabroni, Vol. I, pp. 199-212. For a temperate review of the evidence see Reumont, Vol. II, pp. 556 ff., 590-92.

oned by fulness of experience and not by length of days, he must, in spite of his death at the early age of forty-three, be considered to have had an enviable existence. As to the affection and admiration of his fellow-citizens throughout his life there can be no doubt, although a stubborn opposition never ceased to gnaw at his regime, intrusting to its secret journals the facts and comments which have ever since served as the chief ammunition of his detractors. Only rarely, however, has the favorable opinion of the contemporary generation been dissipated more rapidly. When Piero was driven out of Florence two years after his father's death, the new republican rulers knew not Lorenzo, and never afterward did his reputation experience a sufficient revival for his country-men to have felt moved to raise a monument to him adequately expressive of his worth.

XXIV. Intellectual Change: The Humanism of the Laurentian Age

IN AGAIN picking up the thread of Florentine intellectual development it will be a help to recall the outstanding features which humanism had presented to view up to approximately the middle of the fifteenth century. Enamored with classical antiquity, the early humanists inaugurated a group of attitudes and activities which may be summarized under four heads. (1) They founded classical philology and undertook by a critical sifting of the manuscripts to make available, in as correct a form as possible, the whole corpus of ancient literature both Greek and Latin. (2) By imposing this material on the curriculum of the schools they attempted to transform the educational system of the Middle Ages with its emphasis on dialectics into a humanistic education based on classical literature. (3) They favored the multiplication of books and the creation of libraries for the advancement of learning. (4) By immersing themselves in pagan thought they became more or less consciously divorced from Christianity and more or less openly converted to a religious attitude definable as neo-paganism.

In the second half of the fifteenth century dominated, so far as our town of Florence is concerned, by the name of the Medici and, more particularly, by that of the family's most brilliant representative, Lorenzo the Magnificent, all of the above-listed features experienced a steady, uninterrupted development. However, a full and ordered presentation of this expansion is not the function of this book, since by the fifteenth century humanism had extended its empire over the intelligentsia of all Italy. Boasting everywhere the same confident energy, it was everywhere the same movement with just those minor variations from town to town inevitable in so diversified a mental atmosphere as that of the peninsula. We have not pretended that humanism even at the beginning was an exclusively Florentine product, although it is undoubtedly true that the Tuscan capital contributed so largely to humanistic origins that its historian is in a position to do justice to its early phases without particularly encroaching on neighboring Italian territory. In measure as the quattrocento unrolls its scroll this becomes more and more impossible, and the Florentine historian is obliged to recognize that much or most of the material lies beyond his reach. In view of this situation the most feasible plan for presenting the leading elements of later humanism without bursting through the framework of this book would seem to be, first, to indicate the changes effected at Florence in the above-listed four outstanding features of early humanism, and second and far more important, to trace whatever new tendencies made their appearance within the range of the city which take rank as fresh and original growths.

Although the early humanists aspired to be Latin authors and turned out copious works belonging to every literary category known to the revered ancients, they were so greatly inhibited by the use of a dead language that they produced a progeny either stillborn or destined for an early demise by a fatal lack of vitality. All the energy of the imitators went into the effort to be "correct" in diction, grammar, form, and meter, and to stick so closely to their models that they would be able at need to justify every slightest turn of phrase by reference to a classical source. This lamentable literary mode underwent no change in the Laurentian age unless it be for the worse; for the worse in the case of such soulless counterfeiting would be the apparent better, when success has at last crowned the long effort to make the copy in every purely external respect so like the model as to be indistinguishable from it. All the rhetorical fluency and the finally achieved "correctness" of form and speech would merely serve to make more painfully evident the tragic hollowness of the reproduction.

To proceed at once to the humanist who represents the apex of this slavish development, let us glance at Poliziano, the housemate of Lorenzo the Magnificent and tutor of his children. His life-span is practically identical with that of his patron, for, a little younger than Lorenzo, he died two years after him at the early age of forty. Poliziano was admired during his life as being, and is still frequently declared to have been, the greatest poet the humanistic movement produced on the ground that he was the most perfect ape of antiquity. An amazing memory added to tireless industry enabled him to write Latin with a mastery no humanist before him had ever attained, to write it indeed almost as though it were his mother-tongue. The result, as manifested in a succession of odes, elegies, and epigrams, constitutes a surface of polish, glitter, dexterity, and charm, behind which there stirs not so much as a trace of individual thought and sentiment, the invariable substance of all true poetry. But this facile and, because facile, negligible poet was also a scholar, and as a scholar he moved on a high and constructive level. In moments when he manifested the clearest perception of his powers, he modestly called himself a grammarian. To this expert philologist Lorenzo assigned the professorship of Greek and Latin eloquence at the university; and Poliziano could not have been better employed than in putting his vast erudition, covering texts, medals, and inscriptions, at the service of ambitious students. In his lectures, his translations from the Greek (of course into Latin), and his editions of classical authors he maintained a critical standard that put philology on a definitely scientific basis. While Poliziano is but a single instance taken at the topmost level of achievement, he serves to bring out the fact that Laurentian humanism still closely resembled early humanism in that, while failing to produce an original literature, it registered an uninterrupted advance in learning and scholarly method.

On turning to the innovations the quattrocento introduced into the second of the above-listed fields, the field of education, we are obliged to begin by admitting that the most incisive experiments originated outside of Florence. Without any doubt the two schools for boys, organized respectively by Guarino at Ferrara and by Vittorino da Feltre at Mantua, went farther toward putting the training of the young on a new foundation than any attempt made anywhere else in Italy. While both of these great educators anchored their curriculum in the classics, they did not for that reason toss overboard the ethical and spiritual values of Christianity but attempted rather to fuse them with the rediscovered wisdom of the ancients. Their program was to utilize the classical authors for the enrichment of the mind without sacrificing the invaluable tradition of Christian conduct. We may think of the two schoolmasters as conservative innovators who did not believe, as did so many of their fellow-humanists, that to profit adequately from the ancients it was necessary to revert to paganism. If it is added that both Guarino and Vittorino placed great faith in games and bodily exercise, and that they upheld and put in practice the principle enshrined in the old apothegm, *mens sana in corpore sano,* we arrive at some notion of the extent of their departure from the ascetic ideal of the monastery school, against which their bright and gallant venture represented a reaction. It deserves at least passing notice that the influence of the two schools at Mantua and Ferrara spread far over Europe, and that they supplied the inspiration for the most notable foundations for boys called to life in the immediately following generations in France, England, and Germany.

In Florence no humanist arose to launch an educational experiment of equal scope, but that does not signify that Florence developed no interest in this particular aspect of humanism. In the hope of retaining for his city the intellectual primacy it had held for a hundred years, Lorenzo was at pains to have the professorships allotted to the new studia humaniora at the local university filled by the best scholars to be found in Italy. We have already heard that the most brilliant luminary of the humanist sky, Poliziano, was appointed to the chair of Greek and Latin eloquence. Cristoforo Landino, one of Lorenzo's tutors, had from as far back as 1457 lectured on rhetoric and poetry; other professors of equal caliber were the Platonist, Marsilio Ficino, and the Hellenist, Demetrius Chalcondylas. While with representatives such as these the university remained an authoritative center for classical studies, Lorenzo weakened it in other respects from very valid considerations of a political nature. Ever since its capture in the early years of the fifteenth century Pisa had been a moribund city, whose dwindling inhabitants looked upon their conquerors with a fixed and unalterable aversion. This situation perturbed the statesman in Lorenzo and very early in his reign he undertook to remedy it. He began by buying a house in Pisa and sought to win the favor of the citizens by going to dwell for extended periods in their midst; above all, somewhat to heal their wounded self-respect he resolved to revive their ancient university. At the same time, because two universities would be one too many for so small a state as his, the Magnificent worked out a division of the existing university at Florence in such a manner that, while Florence would retain its humanistic endowments, the faculties of law, medicine, and theology should be established at Pisa. This signified an enfeeblement of Florence for the benefit of Pisa, but the wisdom of the measure was so manifest that it was accepted without notable protest. By the last decade of Lorenzo's life the university of Pisa had become a flourishing institution drawing its matriculants not only from Tus-

FRA ANGELICO. ANNUNCIATION. FRESCO. SAN MARCO (ALINARI).

FRA ANGELICO. CORONATION OF THE VIRGIN. ALTARPIECE NOW
IN THE MUSEO DI SAN MARCO (ALINARI).

MASACCIO. THE TRIBUTE MONEY. FRESCO IN THE BRANCACCI CHAPEL OF THE CHURCH OF THE CARMINE (ALINARI).

left: FRA FILIPPO LIPPI. MADONNA. UFFIZI GALLERY (ALINARI). *right:* MASACCIO. ADAM AND EVE DRIVEN FROM PARADISE. BRANCACCI CHAPEL (ALINARI).

cany but also from many sections of Italy and even from foreign parts. They were in the main students of the professions and prospective careerists, while the devotees of philology and philosophy continued to congregate at Florence, thus maintaining the city's long-established eminence as a humanist center. In no case, however, must the university be regarded as exhausting the Florentine contribution to the advance of contemporary thought. At its side there flourished an institution destined to exercise a novel and even revolutionary influence in the mental realm. Of this we shall presently hear with some detail: it is the Platonic academy.

The library problem which had given such deep concern to Petrarch and his immediate followers, a little past the middle of the quattrocento met with a solution that struck contemporaries, and with the help of a little imagination on our part might still strike us, as hardly short of miraculous. Printing with movable types, invented in the Rhine Valley at the mid-century, spread rapidly over all Europe, and almost overnight put an end to the long-lamented scarcity and costliness of books. It was in 1465 that the first book printed in Italy made its appearance. It dropped from the press at Subiaco near Rome, the handiwork of two German journeymen. Native Italians quickly acquired the art, and before the close of the century practically every Italian city of any importance boasted a press of its own. The first book printed at Florence bore the date 1471 and was, characteristically enough for this hearth of classical scholarship, a commentary on Virgil. However, Florence never acquired the standing of certain other publishing centers and was notably outstripped by its ancient commercial rival, Venice. In the cutting and founding of type the Italians throughout the peninsula displayed such skill and taste that their first editions, largely of the writers of antiquity, take rank to this day among the most precious products of the new art. The impulse given to humanism by the revolutionary invention can hardly be exaggerated. Obviously the multiplication and cheapening of books made possible their acquisition by people of relatively restricted means, while the well-to-do were stimulated to add them in large numbers to their stock of manuscripts and either to found public libraries for the convenience of their fellow-citizens or else to enrich the libraries already in existence with liberal donations. From the narrow viewpoint of scholarship the printed texts represented a vast improvement over the written copies with their innumerable and unavoidable errors of transcription. Nor should it be overlooked that the publishers in the interest of accuracy were obliged to employ trained editors and proofreaders, and that editing and proofreading became professions by which scores of humanists, hitherto dependent on the bounty of princes, were enabled to earn an honest livelihood by their individual effort.

Contrary to a still too prevalent opinion, the humanists did not all slip into paganism, although it is undeniable that they inclined to adopt a skeptical attitude toward Christianity and in some extreme cases became, even if they did not openly profess themselves to be, outright agnostics. In a general way it may be said that those followers of antiquity who most completely withdrew from their fellow-men and lived as a scholarly coterie in the rarefied upper air were most disposed to adopt the pagan outlook. If their separation from the *vulgus,* the common herd, became the strength of their erudition, it was also the cause of their failure to achieve distinction as poets. Neither in the fifteenth nor in any other century have erudition and poetry lived harmoniously together. A group in touch with, but also distinct from, the scholars pure and simple were those humanists who specialized in philosophy and ethics. Generally speaking, they were not moved to divorce themselves from the society in which they lived nor did they deny the traditions on which that society rested. Members of this very important group were the projectors of fresh adventures in education already mentioned, Guarino and Vittorino da Feltre; and to this group belonged the two Florentines, Cristoforo Landino and Marsilio Ficino. With them may be collocated also Pico della Mirandola, for, although not a Florentine by birth, he settled in Florence and with Landino and Ficino made up the strength of the Platonic academy. Not offering any formal instruction and not concerned with developing a following, the academy nonetheless radiated an influence over Italy greater than that of any established school or university. It represents by far the most important contribution made by Florence to Laurentian humanism and must needs come in for a close examination.

The first thing to get in mind about the Platonic academy is that it bore no resemblance whatever to what we moderns understand by the term, for neither did it have an organization, officers, and revenues, nor did it give instruction or issue an official literature. It was nothing other than an occasional, informal gathering of men with a common interest in the Greek philosopher, Plato, and with a common faith in the guidance of a scholar who had been devoted to Plato from his youth, Marsilio Ficino. A further bond among the members was their attachment to Lorenzo de' Medici, who, besides revering Ficino as his teacher, shared the current curiosity which Plato, overshadowed throughout the Middle Ages by his foremost pupil and critic, Aristotle, had recently aroused. The devotees of Plato at Florence were Lorenzo's most intimate associates, and to be invited to hear Ficino expound a Platonic dialogue was to become a hall-marked member of the Medicean social circle.

It was not, however, Lorenzo but his grandfather, Cosimo, to whom the Platonic academy owed its inception. When on the occasion of the General Council of the church held at Florence in 1439 Cosimo met the philosopher, Gemistos Plethon, he was so deeply moved by the fiery enthusiasm of the venerable Greek for the great Athenian that he discussed with Plethon the creation of an academy dedicated to Platonic studies. Nothing came of the plan at the time and Cosimo might have dismissed it entirely from his mind, had he not learned some years later that the young son of his physician had been seized with a passion for the ancient sage like unto that of Plethon, but that he could only partially satisfy it, owing to his ignorance of Greek. The young man was Marsilio Ficino, whose modesty, lovable disposition, and rare zeal for learning quickly won Cosimo's favor. Accordingly, he resolved to supply Marsilio with the means necessary to complete his education on the understanding that his client would devote himself not only to making Plato accessible to the curious in Latin dress, but also to serving faithfully throughout his days as the master's apostle to the occident. Shortly before his death in

1464 Cosimo had the pleasure of receiving from the hands of Ficino the first-fruits of his labors; and under Piero, his son, and Lorenzo, his grandson, the work of translation continued without interruption until by 1477 or there-abouts the whole majestic roll call of the Platonic dialogues had been rendered into the recovered Latin of the humanists. Some fourteen years later, in 1491, advantage was taken of the new mechanical process of bookmaking to offer Plato's complete works in translation to the public. As an indication that Florence had missed the opportunity to put itself at the head of the publishing business we may note the circumstance that Ficino intrusted his monumental edition to a Venetian printer. However, old Cosimo's faith had been justified, for at last Italy and Europe had at their command the information enabling them to travel with assurance a philosophic path other than that traced by Aristotle and the scholastics.

In giving their philosophy its characteristic development the schoolmen of the Middle Ages had had recourse to Aristotle, and in order to put the intellectual system they elaborated beyond the reach of attack they had ascribed to the Stagirite an unassailable authority. Consequently, not the least important task of the humanists, who saw in scholasticism their chief enemy, was somehow to undermine Aristotle; and when Plato was rediscovered, first by the mediation of his occasional admirers among the Latin classical writers, the opportunity seemed to have come to hand. While the humanistic enthusiasm for Plato, which continued to make headway throughout the quattrocento, may be largely explained on this ground, there was no lack of other reasons for the Athenian's growing vogue. Plato propounded a transcendental philosophy; at least on the strength of his central doctrine, the doctrine of ideas, he could be called a transcendentalist who affirmed the most clean-cut separation imaginable between soul and flesh, spirit and matter. Long after his time, at Alexandria in Egypt, this sharp dualism of his was, with the aid of oriental mysticism, elaborated into one of the most fantastic systems of philosophy that have ever been spun by mortal mind. It was this revised Platonism, usually called Neoplatonism, which had captured the imagination of the Christian Fathers and had greatly influenced the shaping of Christian doctrine. In the course of the Middle Ages the early nexus between Christianity and Platonism or, more properly, Neoplatonism, had been gradually forgotten; and when Aristotle was adopted as the philosopher of scholasticism, as the one and only philosopher and its authoritative guide, Platonism inevitably fell into neglect and ultimately even into disrepute. However, when with the help of fifteenth-century humanism Plato rose once more into view, the close kinship of his dualism with Christianity was at once revealed. In ever-growing numbers the humanists gave him their allegiance because with him as their leader not only might they succeed in destroying the hated tyranny of Aristotle and the scholastics but also, persistently Christian beneath a mere veneer of paganism, they would be free to indulge the hope of bringing religion and philosophy into a new and stimulating harmony.

Under these circumstances Marsilio Ficino (1433-99) becomes a completely intelligible phenomenon. He occupied himself for many decades with translating Plato, and in the explanatory commentaries issued by him doubtless thought he was expounding the Hellenic master. However, as he approached Plato, on the one hand, through Christianity and, on the other, through the perverted doctrines of his Alexandrian followers, he saw him through an interpretative haze and read him in the colorful terms of expositors born hundreds of years after the great age of Greece. As Ficino's fellow-members of the academy and, later, his readers throughout Italy adopted exactly the same approach, he was not challenged from any quarter, and during his lifetime and for some generations afterward was regarded with as much reverence as though he were himself the ancient Athenian come again to life. His friend Lorenzo had presented him with an antique marble bust of Plato which, installed in Ficino's study, majestically presided over his labors. Let the setting up of this grave and uncompromising *genius loci* convince us of the utter sincerity of his Florentine disciple. Nonetheless, instead of a strict Platonist, he was an Alexandrian eclectic and expounded a philosophy which, although not unrelated to Plato, stemmed in the main from Neoplatonic mysticism.

What the high priest of the Platonic academy offered his friends under the name of Platonism will in its most succinct form be found in his Italian treatise *Sopra lo Amore* and reduces itself to what became current at the height of the Renaissance under the name of Platonic Love. This doctrine teaches that Love is the sustaining and ordering principle of the universe, and that it is identical with Beauty since Beauty is its visible emanation. The function of the individual soul, temporarily estranged from the Good by being imbedded in matter, which is Evil, is by laddered stages to find its way back to its source and to end, as it began, in the ecstatic contemplation of God. Unhappily there is a false, a lower love, the love of the flesh, which plagues us in our mortal span and which it is our duty to repress and overcome. The higher love is spiritual: it is the force that holds the universe together. The choice the individual soul caught in the web of flesh has to make is between animal and spiritual love and, as it chooses, it is lost or saved. It is clear that this exaltation of Love and Beauty was bound to appeal most strongly to the sensitive souls of artists and writers. In the case of the impressionable Botticelli we may see its effect in the two well-known allegorical presentations of Love, called respectively the Birth of Venus and the Realm of Venus, although the latter passes under the popular misnomer of Spring.[1] Platonic Love is the sustaining fire of Michelangelo's sonnets, as it is the peroration and climax of Castiglione's treatise on the gentleman, the famous *Il Cortigiano*. In brief, much of the painting, sculpture, and letters of the first half of the sixteenth century carries as its core and marrow the love doctrine of the Platonic academy.

A hardly less exalted philosophic figure than Ficino was Pico della Mirandola, who died in 1494 at the early age of thirty-one. He departed this life in the same year as Poliziano, whose close friend he was, although Poliziano, a grammarian steeped in letters, never pretended to be either a real philosopher or a real Platonist. In general outlook Pico was much closer to his other friend, Ficino, whose doctrine of Platonic Love he shared, carrying it, if possible, to

---

[1] On this matter see A. Warburg, *Sandro Botticelli's Geburt der Venus und Frühling*. Hamburg, 1893.

still more mystical and unscalable heights. If we add Lorenzo de' Medici as fourth to this inmost circle of the academy, it is not because he was either primarily a scholar like Poliziano, or a philosopher like Ficino and Pico. He was as, in spite of his many sympathies, we must never forget, primarily a statesman; but with his elastic nature he responded in turn to all the aspects of humanism and without any doubt satisfied some need of his complex soul by his intimacy with the chosen spirits of the academy. Next after his statesmanship his most important achievement lies in the realm of poetry; and since by his verses he rendered Tuscany and Italy the incomparable service of ending the learned boycott conducted by the humanists against the Italian language, we may fittingly close this brief sketch of the mental changes in his day by defining the literary contribution of the man, whose name is for many the sum and essence of his age.

Lorenzo was so frankly a follower of the Italian and not of the Latin muse that he never expressed himself except in his native tongue in all the many forms of poetry at which he tried his hand. That does not mean, however, that he sounded an original note throughout the body of his verse. As was the case with his contemporaries without exception the past possessed such authority for him that, whether it was a question of the metrical practice of his Tuscan predecessors, Dante and Petrarch, or of the literary forms sanctioned by the ancient writers, he felt constrained humbly to bow down before the dead. Thus it came about that, when he sang of love, as he did in many sonnets and in a much-admired work called *Selve d'Amore*,[2] he adopted the attitude and imitated the manner of Dante and Petrarch; and if he added anything not traceable to them, it was likely to be a borrowing from still another source, most probably from the modish and equally authoritative Platonism of his day. His love poetry is conventional, fictive, and unreal, as to its misfortune Italian love poetry continued to be to the very threshold of the nineteenth century. Not till Lorenzo turned to nature, did he succeed in shaking off the deadweight of the past and feel encouraged to express immediate experiences unmistakably involving his own lively senses and imagination. In his *Caccia col Falcone,* which is not easy to classify but which may be called a country idyll, he tells of a day spent at hawking and is so charged with the impressions of a happy outing, with the first flush of dawn, with the baying of the hounds assembled for the hunt, with the bold flight of the birds, that he thoroughly succeeds in transmitting his own animation to his reader. The realistic vein here revealed received its happiest expression in his *Nencia da Barberino*. In this rustic poem a young peasant tells of his love for a village girl, describing her charms and singing his woes with such simplicity and truth to nature that all the old hampering conventionalities drop away like broken fetters. The fact is that the attitudes imposed by Dante, Petrarch, and the Platonic mysteries were pure literary poses for this man of alert senses and active mind. His most constant purpose was to enjoy life to the full, for the night was coming followed by no morning of which he could be sure. By reason of this immediacy of sentiment he is particularly fresh and most emphatically himself in many of the *ballate*

---

[2] The standard edition of Lorenzo's works is by Attilio Simioni. Of Lorenzo's English biographers Roscoe and Horsburgh are most enlightening on his poetry.

and carnival songs which he composed, without an eye to literature, to be sung in their spontaneous merrymakings by the common folk of the town. Often as the most celebrated quatrain of his carnival literature has been quoted, it has such an infectious lilt that it can stand reprinting in this place:

> Quant' è bella giovinezza,
> Che si fugge tuttavia!
> Chi vuol esser lieto, sia:
> Di doman non c'è certezza.

> (Fair is youth and free of sorrow,
> Yet how soon its joys we bury!
> Let who would be now be merry:
> Sure is no one of tomorrow.) [3]

In these tripping lines we have the expression of a fleeting, but true and ever-renewed mood of the poet. And into their small compass he has packed so much of the spirit of the age that they have appealed to all the following generations as a kind of marching song of the Renaissance.

It cannot be doubted that the fifteenth-century Florentines of the upper social stratum confidently believed that they were living in a great cultural epoch and that the future held the promise of still greater achievements. "I wish to thank God," wrote Giovanni Rucellai, "for permitting me to live in the present age, which those competent to judge of such matters call the greatest age our city has ever experienced." And Marsilio Ficino sounded the following paean: "This is an age of gold, which has brought back to life the almost extinguished liberal disciplines of poetry, eloquence, painting, architecture, sculpture, music, and singing to the Orphic lyre. And all this at Florence!" [4] Notwithstanding this acclaim, scarcely two years after Lorenzo's death in 1492, a shock that was like an earthquake overtook this high-piled and splendid cultural structure, damaging it so radically that all the subsequent patching could never quite put it together again. For this sudden catastrophe, connected with the name of Savonarola and not even remotely divined by the self-centered champions of humanism, many explanations have been offered. As is always the case with significant social movements the Florentine crisis resulted from a vast complex of circumstances and defies the simplified explanation to which our mind is prone. However, a factor of peculiar pertinence to this chapter figured powerfully in the anti-intellectual rising championed by the Dominican friar. The new mental world, projected by the humanists and inhabited by writers and scholars and, fortunately for their own and their city's fame, to a much smaller extent by painters and sculptors, was the walled-off garden of a small upper class which prided itself on its clean separation from the untutored mass of the population. Under Savonarola's leadership this despised mass asserted its viewpoint and power, and the consequent despoiling of the garden was the penalty paid by an intellectual aristocracy for having lost contact with its humbler fellow-men.

[3] Translation by Fletcher, *Literature of the Italian Renaissance*, p. 132.
[4] Monnier, *Le Quattrocento*, Vol. II, pp. 52-53.

XXV. The Fine Arts: The Second or Quattrocento Phase

THE term Fine Arts invites so much misunderstanding that, before taking it up once more, a few words of explanation will be in order. The expression did not gain currency till some two or three hundred years ago, when architects, sculptors, and painters were, to their own grave misfortune, considered to be a race apart and designated as artists, while the practitioners of the humbler crafts, such as goldsmiths, carvers of wood and ivory, furniture-makers, and makers of other articles of common use, were classified as artificers or craftsmen. During the Middle Ages no such distinction was recognized in any country of Europe. In that period all shapers of any object whatever requiring the mastery of a special skill were indistinguishably called craftsmen, and while they were considered to have the character of artists, the term artist, at least as we employ it today, had not come into use. Consequently the arts in the medieval period were closely interrelated and the individual artificer often practiced two or three arts without any sense of exceeding either his rights or his powers. Instead of an attempt to set up a hierarchy among the arts, the only issue that counted was that of good or bad workmanship. This healthy attitude gave a noble unity to the whole range of artistic expression and explains why textiles, manuscripts, wood-carving, and metal-work are as much a part of the aesthetic inheritance of the Middle Ages as churches, statuary, and painted altar pieces.

It would have been well for both artists and craftsmen if their early intimacy had never been interrupted and the custom had persisted of applying an identical standard of perfection to every kind of handiwork. Genuine as such regrets are, they do not alter the historical fact that in the later Renaissance centuries, but not yet in the quattrocento to be treated in this chapter, a distinction came gradually to be made among artificers and also among their creations. And however deplorable, in view of the consequences, the distinction may be considered to be, it was not, let us admit, without a certain justification. For we do not have to do violence to our judgment to concede that since architecture, sculpture, and painting require for their practice a lifetime of preparation as well as high personal endowment, they are not misnamed when we classify them as Major or Fine Arts. By the same tests the other artistic practices may without impropriety be called Minor Arts or handicrafts. While such a division recommends itself on the ground of convenience, what we must strictly avoid is the assumption that ideally the arts are ever other than one and that with the passing of the Middle Ages they ceased being referable to a single unifying principle of excellence.

In turning in this chapter to the quattrocento phase of expression the reader is urged to keep in mind that there was as yet no sharply drawn line either between artists and craftsmen or between Major and Minor Arts. It follows that every thoroughly conducted review of the artistic activity of this age should cover the whole field. If this course will not be followed in the present instance, our excuse is the purely illustrative character of this book in the several sections ancillary to our main theme of political history. Deliberately omitting the Minor Arts in order to save space, we shall concentrate attention on the Major or Fine Arts on the ground that, exhibiting, as they undoubtedly do, a higher measure of training and imagination, they adequately meet our limited purpose of opening an avenue to the aesthetic world of the quattrocento Florentines.

When during the communal revolution the rapidly multiplying contacts of men with the world and one another led to that gradual change of mental attitude which we have agreed to call humanism, the immediate effect of this shift of attention on the intellectual élite of the Italian towns was to inspire them not only to cultivate classical literature but also, as far as possible, to revive the whole ancient world. Having in the previous chapter dealing with the fifteenth century looked into the consequences of this devotion for scholarship and letters, we shall now examine them for the same period in the field of the Fine Arts. As the artificers were uneducated in the pedagogical sense of that term and only in rare instances knew more than the rudiments of Latin, the enthusiasm for antiquity was rather slow in reaching them. However, they could not escape it, since, if themselves unlettered, they lived among the lettered and shared the view generally current that the Romans were their ancestors and had set a mark in every field of thought and action which it was desirable to reach again, even though the hope was bold to the point of folly. But in no case would mere enthusiasm suffice to effect a return to antiquity in the arts. For, handed down from the Middle Ages, a solid body of theory and practice held sway in every *bottega* of the city, and this mass of honorable tradition was certain not to give up the ghost without stubborn resistance.

No sooner therefore had the champions of antiquity sounded their trumpets than the battle was engaged all along the line with consequences of great but varying importance in each of the three fields claiming our attention. In architecture the innovators won a sweeping victory, although it was by no means so complete as some historians would have us believe. In sculpture the classical preachment exercised an important effect without depriving the art of its native impulses or impairing its essential autonomy. Finally, in painting, in which field, fortunately for the independence of the painters, there existed no ancient remains inviting imitation, the influence of the propagandists of antiquity was almost negligible. In all three fields the quattrocento endowed Florence with such an abundance of notable works that the period will always rank as one of the greatest epochs not alone of Florentine but of European art in general. However, discerning critics have never failed to insist that the products of the several arts do not stand on the same level of merit. It is their

BENOZZO GOZZOLI. SECTION FROM THE PROCESSION OF THE KINGS. FRESCO. CHAPEL OF
THE MEDICI PALACE (ALINARI).

DOMENICO GHIRLANDAIO. BIRTH OF THE VIRGIN. FRESCO. TORNABUONI CHAPEL. SANTA
MARIA NOVELLA (ALINARI).

BOTTICELLI. BIRTH OF VENUS. UFFIZI GALLERY (ALINARI).

opinion that the Florentines attained the greatest vigor and refinement of expression in painting; that after painting, and not very far behind it, came sculpture; and that architecture, because practiced with much less originality than the two sister-arts, brought up the rear. It will not escape the attention of the reader that this order of importance is in each instance in inverse proportion to the domination exercised by the classical fetish. But let each art rehearse its own facts and tell its own story.

The pathfinder in architecture was Filippo Brunelleschi (1377–1446). In the manner usual among gifted apprentices he began to practice several arts without distinction and might have ended by devoting himself primarily to sculpture if he had not been defeated in a public competition of the year 1401 for a bronze gate of the baptistery projected as the northern counterpart to the famous South Gate created by Andrea Pisano almost a hundred years before. When the prize in this competition was attributed to Lorenzo Ghiberti, Brunelleschi, a high-spirited artist content with nothing less than supremacy in everything he undertook, resolved to devote himself to architecture, and, setting out for Rome in company with a younger friend, Donatello by name, spent a number of years studying the still plentiful remains of buildings to be found within the compass of the City of the Seven Hills. So little at that time did anybody at Rome grasp the purport of the intensive sketching and measuring among the ruins conducted by the two strangers that for the perplexed natives they became the treasure-hunters (*quelli del tesoro*).[1] After a long apprenticeship involving the most severe self-discipline, Brunelleschi repossessed himself of the columnar principle of classical construction varied according to the three established orders of Doric, Ionian, and Corinthian. He also mastered the elements of classical decoration with its stylized motives of egg and dart, bead and reel, meander, and honeysuckle. However, on his return to his native city he did not become the spokesman of an architecture based exclusively on his recovered knowledge of antiquity. Even if he had been inclined to such stark dogmatism, he could not do other than graft the new learning on the medieval stem, for the moment he undertook the practice of his art, he had to reckon not with temples, baths, theaters, and aqueducts, but with churches, chapels, town halls, and private residences, and for these modern structures the classical tradition offered no precedent. The circumstance that behind the still dominant Gothic lay the older Romanesque, and that Romanesque was nothing other than a barbarized offspring of classicism, considerably eased Brunelleschi's problem. By abolishing Gothicism as a northern intrusion, which it was, he came face to face with the Romanesque, which he found it reasonably simple to yoke with the more elegant parent forms of which he was the rediscoverer. It is not improper to think of the changes effected by him as being essentially a return to the national tradition. Nonetheless his work so distinctly marks a departure from what went immediately before that we need not hesitate to regard him as the inventor of a new manner identified ever since as the Renaissance style.

It is not our purpose to name more than a few of the structures which serve to describe Brunelleschi's pioneership. In the Loggia degli Innocenti (Found-

[1] Vasari's *Lives* under Brunelleschi.

lings' Hospital) he employed a row of classic columns of such slenderness joined by round arches of such bold leap that we receive an impression of energy combined with elegance for which there is nothing in the Florentine record to prepare us. That his contemporaries were similarly impressed is proved by the fact that the loggias and cloisters built after this achievement invariably follow the Innocenti pattern. Brunelleschi did much work for Cosimo de' Medici, the most outstanding being the church and sacristy of San Lorenzo. Employing and ingeniously varying in the two buildings the structural elements of column (or pilaster) and round arch, which he again made basic, he achieved in each instance an attractive whole of harmonious proportions and balanced parts heightened by the application of perfectly executed ornament. The massive strength and towering majesty characteristic of good Gothic have been banished in favor of the lost ideal of urbanity, the goal of which is the avoidance of excess and the satisfaction of a cultivated taste.

By far the most famous of Brunelleschi's achievements is the cupola of Santa Maria del Fiore, with which he at last brought to completion an edifice begun one hundred and fifty years before by Arnolfo di Cambio.[2] It is probable that the octagon, into which the nave expands to the east and which was to be crowned with a dome, was a part of Arnolfo's original plan. When, toward the end of the fourteenth century, the nave and aisles had been at length completed as we see them today, the building commission, called the opera del duomo, attacked the problem of the east end and found itself for a time completely baffled. For, although innumerable consulting architects presented plans for the key feature, the cupola, none offered a solution which was adequate either from an engineering or an aesthetic angle. The single exception was Filippo Brunelleschi, whose project was so daring and brought so many novel structural features into play that it encountered even more vigorous objections than the rival projects assailable on the ground of calculable error. Only gradually did Filippo manage to infuse the commission with his own never-failing confidence and, hesitatingly installed as chief architect, between 1420 and 1434 he raised the magnificent cupola which, with Giotto's campanile, is still the far-seen landmark of the city.

By nothing which he did more than by this cupola did Brunelleschi prove that, if he drew his inspiration from the ancients, he still maintained his independence as an artistic personality. The only comparable cupola the Romans had erected was the Pantheon, which still stands, and on the score of scale the Pantheon is not really comparable since in neither elevation nor width of span does it approach the cupola of the Florentine cathedral. Besides, the Roman cupola was projected with sole regard to interior effect, while the cathedral dome was planned to make its chief impression from the outside and to dominate the urban unit, illustrious Florence, and proclaim its greatness to the enfolding hills. An examination of the soaring structure will reveal the leading steps by which the architect solved his problem. The octagonal substructure was heavily buttressed by means of a ring of apse chapels crowned by half-domes. From them the eye travels easily to the drum, which is

[2] See chap. XV.

penetrated on each of its eight sides with a circular opening to provide the interior with light. Eight powerful ribs of stone leap upward from the drum in curves of great power and beauty. They constitute the bony framework of the cupola and at their point of convergence are crowned by a magnificent lantern. This last feature Brunelleschi did not live to complete, although it was added (1462) in accordance with his plans. That all the domes built afterward in Europe were made possible by Brunelleschi's masterpiece, and that with the single exception of St. Peter's at Rome, the work of Michelangelo, another Florentine, no subsequent cupola ever achieved the majesty and power of Santa Maria del Fiore should serve to inscribe Brunelleschi's name high on the tablets of his art.

At least two young contemporaries of Brunelleschi require notice, Michelozzo Michelozzi (1396–1472) and Leon Battista Alberti (1404–72). The degree in which Michelozzi derived his inspiration from Brunelleschi can be readily divined by throwing a glance at the charming cloister of San Marco. Its graceful arches resting on slender columns were raised at the orders of Cosimo de' Medici but owe their finished artistry to the example furnished by the older master in the Loggia degli Innocenti. Also at Cosimo's command, but this time in complete independence from Brunelleschi, Michelozzi erected the great Medici palace in the Via Larga. It rises directly from the street in three stories, of which the first story bristles with rough-trimmed blocks of stone, while the other two, indicated by their smooth surfaces as the living quarters, are set with round-arched windows at regular intervals and terminate in a heavily accented cornice. By its rectangular massiveness and air of defiance the structure asserts its kinship with the medieval towers, the earliest residences of the town nobility. On passing through the portal, which reiterates the round-arch motive of the windows, we enter a handsome inner court where the more civil spirit of the new age disclosed itself in an open arcade supported on rows of vigorous columns. The Medici palace furnished the model for numerous mansions with which the prosperous merchants attempted to emulate their rulers. Such later and even more imposing structures as the Pitti and the Strozzi palaces make no secret of their affinity with the great house Michelozzi reared for Cosimo.

Alberti gained a vast reputation in his day because of his eminence in a great variety of fields. He is esteemed by many as the first of the universal personalities or supermen, whose genius lent a special luster to the Renaissance. In addition to winning renown as an athlete, a mathematician, a writer on the arts, a musician, and a painter, Alberti was acclaimed as an architect. However, a temperate modern judgment will not concede him a high place in this field. He permitted himself to be overwhelmed to such a degree by the accomplishments of antiquity that, in distinction from the more balanced Brunelleschi and Michelozzi, he tried to effect a complete breach with the medieval past. The result may be seen in two contributions made at the order of his patrons, the Rucellai family. One is the façade of the Rucellai palace, in which he abandoned without qualification the medieval fortress conception and gave his frontispiece a classical articulation by means of rows of superimposed pilasters. His other fabric is the façade of Santa Maria Novella, where his particular problem was to complete the front elevation of a great Gothic house of worship. A weakness from which Florentine churches of all ages suffer is that their façades, if provided at all, were added as an afterthought. When Alberti was requested to supply the missing front for Santa Maria Novella, he drew a design that had no relation to the structure behind it. The pedants of the Renaissance, an innumerable tribe, have rapturously eulogized both the church and the palace façade of Alberti's devising. Whosoever conceives of architecture primarily as structure and demands that every structure be a unified composition, will find it difficult to give to Alberti any other rating than that of a clever draughtsman. Since he indicates a trend in favor of unconditional surrender to antiquity, a trend which in the following generations completely gained the upper hand, he cannot be omitted from even the most compressed quattrocento record of the art of architecture.

When Lorenzo Ghiberti (1378–1455) won the competition of the year 1401 for the North Doors of the baptistery, he established himself as the leading sculptor of Florence. Not till twenty years had passed did he complete his design, which, patterned so far as its external form is concerned, on the older South Doors of Andrea Pisano, told in thirty-two panels the story of the life of Christ. In this impressive work Ghiberti reveals himself as an artist stemming from the Middle Ages, but also as alertly aware that a new day has dawned upon the world. While he has been affected by classical examples, he feels no strong naturalistic urge and achieves his attractive compositions by ordering each panel in flowing lines which fall into a pleasant pattern of animated movement. When, following this success, the third or East Doors of the baptistery were also committed to him, he was an older man who had not remained unaffected by the technical conquests recently achieved by the graphic arts, such as perspective, landscape, and anatomy. His new assignment obliged him to present scenes from the Old Testament; and in order to exhibit his freshly acquired professional powers he abandoned the Gothic frame employed by Andrea Pisano and followed in his own earlier gate, and divided his space into ten large square panels. Into each of these he crowded so many figures arranged in a deepening perspective that, as against a certain pictorial vivacity duly achieved, the monumental effect we normally demand of sculpture is completely lost. The easy graceful line, the essence of Ghiberti's genius, again dominates, providing Ghiberti's second gate, like his first, with a subtle witchery; but both gates alike declare that the artist was a gracious feminine spirit and not a virile innovator.

Virile innovation was the part reserved to Donatello (1386–1466), the indisputable fountainhead of all that is truly significant in fifteenth-century sculpture. As we are aware, Donatello was a close friend of Brunelleschi and, sharing the latter's enthusiasm for classical remains, went with him on his treasure hunt to Rome. From ancient coins and cameos, for the ancient statues were still largely buried in the earth, Donatello acquired an acquaintance with the spirit of antiquity, for which he ever afterward exhibited the most sincere admiration. Nonetheless he never permitted his zeal to divert him from the medieval tradition, from which he sprang, and from his instinctive love for the forms of nature, among which he was placed. Without fear of contradiction it may be asserted that, except for his taking over into his work occasional classical motives, he was not a classicist at all, but a product of the tradition native to his city revitalized by absorption in, and study of, the creature world about him. To bring the sculpture of the quattrocento into juxtaposition with that of antiquity is to be made startlingly aware of their wide divergence and to be readily persuaded of the complete spiritual independence of the later school.[3]

The unusually prolific art of Donatello covers so many varieties of work that it will not be possible to illustrate each category even by description of a single instance. His finest early work and one of the finest works of the whole range of sculpture is the St. George, hewn of marble for an exterior niche of Or San Michele but now withdrawn for safekeeping to the Museo Nazionale (Bargello). The St. George constitutes an excellent starting-point for any consideration of Donatello, as it reveals the master's rootedness in the Christian idealism of the Middle Ages to which he has communicated the incomparable vivacity of his freshened senses. The erect body of the young soldier of the Lord is aglow with life, and the head, an amazing realization of gracious youth, rises from the slim neck like a tulip from its stem. In many of his works both in the round and in relief Donatello gave himself with such passion to the exact rendering of the human figure that, in respect of these creations, we might be moved to set him down as an uncompromising naturalist. Such a realistic work is the Magdalen carved in wood in the baptistery, another, the *Zuccone* (meaning the pumpkin head) of marble high in a niche of Giotto's campanile. Purporting to be an Old Testament prophet, the Zuccone is nothing other than a close portrait study of a Florentine contemporary with a bald head, a dragging walk, and a dozen other details indicative of advancing decrepitude. That Donatello when he thought of himself as having a mission preached nature in the raw is indicated by the fact that his favorite oath was: "By the faith I put in my Zuccone." [4] Less headstrong and consequently more genial realism is encountered in his many portrait busts. Of these perhaps the foremost example is the representation in colored terra cotta of the sharp-featured pre-Medicean oligarch, Niccolò da Uzzano. It is difficult to conceive how the unfathomable complex we call personality could be more unerringly rendered.

It is Donatello's zest for life that explains his many works presenting children laughing and at play. To illustrate this particular class the *cantorìa* (or organ loft) he did for the cathedral will serve, especially as it embodies also his unflagging interest in movement. A procession of children have joined a dance, weaving in and out as they raise their voices and toss their limbs about in riotous abandon to the spirit of the moment. The artist's last great work is in a class by itself since it is a bronze equestrian statue and bronze equestrian statues had not been attempted in Italy since the fall of Rome. The rider he was asked to immortalize was a condottiere familiar under the nickname of Gattamelata, and the completed work was set up in the cathedral square of Padua. It will at once strike the beholder that the condottiere wears ancient

---

[3] W. Bode, *Florentine Sculpture of the Renaissance.* New York, 1909.
[4] See Vasari's *Lives* under Donatello.

armor and that the horse is not unrelated to the sculptured horses of antiquity. These are touches in which it would be a mistake to see more than a superficial concession to a fashion from which it was impossible wholly to escape. The horse is a massive war steed, which moves deliberately forward as the general with bared head and an authoritative sweep of the truncheon held in his right hand makes the necessary dispositions for the coming battle. Horse and rider are molded into a compact unit of controlled power. They remain with us as the expression of a genius who, though deriving from the near past and borrowing at his pleasure from the far past, received his main impulses from life itself, and who by directing his successors to this ever-bubbling fountain of renewal inaugurated the first great age of modern sculpture.

It is a tribute to the greatness of the age that, indebted to Donatello as were all who took up sculpture after him, they present themselves to view as highly individual artists. An effect, on the one hand, of the breakdown of medieval society, and, on the other, of the secular outlook we have called humanism, was for men to become more and more differentiated and for each one to develop his personality to its greatest potentiality. In the artists this bent becomes particularly marked, as a roll call of the sculptors will clearly bring to light. Luca della Robbia (1400–1482) was molded by the new realism, but he mixed it with something so uniquely his own that it is impossible ever to confuse his work with that of the realist Donatello. Look at the cathedral organ loft which he did (1437) as a counterpart to that of Donatello: it consists of ten panels exhibiting groups of children praising the Lord with dance and song. Some are in motion, others at rest, and all alike tell us with a startling immediacy that life in its Maytime is fresh and fragrant. But, although this is precisely what Donatello said in his organ loft and in a score of other pieces as well, he said it with an intonation which can never be confused with that of Luca. A sculptor of more narrow range was Desiderio da Settignano (1428–64), who in his portraits of the women of the upper social stratum achieved a delicacy and refinement which have never been surpassed. A girl's bust conveniently placed for comparison in the Donatello room of the Museo Nazionale shows an exquisite finish, which the older master never attained and to which, let us add, he did not aspire. A vigorous and restless experimenter in movement was Antonio Pollaiuolo (1429–98). His small bronze group of Hercules wrestling with Antaeus could not more superlatively convey an impression of energy, were it of heroic size.

In concluding our sculptural review let us throw a glance at Andrea Verrocchio (1435–88), than whom no quattrocentist of them all had a more personal savor. A boyish David (bronze) with drawn sword and the head of Goliath at his feet breathes the freshness with which everything the age produced is touched and at the same time renders charmingly the embarrassment of the young hero before the evidence of his own heroism. In a marble bust of a young woman, who with her left hand clasps a spray of daisies to her bosom, Verrocchio has combined the vitality of Donatello with the delicacy of Desiderio into a work which one need not hesitate to proclaim a supreme achievement in its field. The individually treated features and hands, which never belonged to any but to a single woman among all those that have ever lived, are rescued from every suggestion of the commonplace by the almost religious hush of the pose, the elegant lines of the closely clinging garment, and the elaborately stylized hair with its soft parallel waves broken at the temples into a storm of curls framing the tranquil face. Compared with this triumph of restraint, the sculptor's most celebrated work, the equestrian statue of Bartolommeo Colleone at Venice, is but an empty boast. Or let us call it an expression, perfect of its kind, of the frenzied energy that was a characteristic of the age. The alert and rigidly erect rider sits his proudly pacing steed as though he were the very god of war. It is absurd to suppose that we have here a portrait of the insignificant condottiere, whose name the figure bears and who died some twenty years before the work was undertaken. Rather than on any narrowly representative ground the monumental horse and rider have won the world's acclaim as a symbol of the glamorous Italian Renaissance.

A peril connected with periodization, be it of history, civilization, or art, is that the periods will be taken literally and the unbroken continuity of all human unfolding be forgotten. Often as a *caveat* has already been entered against this danger, it may profitably be repeated on turning to quattrocento painting. At the very outset we encounter a number of figures whom the official record of their life classifies as quattrocentist, but who by the evidence of their work occupy the border line between two ages and who should therefore be classified as men of the transition. Quite the most important member of this group is Fra Angelico (1387–1455). He sprang of peasant stock in the Mugello, became a Dominican friar at the age of twenty, and specialized, as many monks and friars had done before him, as a painter. After practicing his art in the Dominican monastery under Fiesole, he was transferred to San Marco shortly after the architect Michelozzi had begun to make headway with the reconstruction of that dilapidated foundation ordered by Cosimo de' Medici. At San Marco Fra Angelico painted in fresco in the cloister, the chapter house, and the cells of the brothers some fifty pictures which, well preserved on the whole, tell us of him today as directly as though he were still alive. And what they tell us is that, more important than his being a painter, Fra Angelico was a dedicated soul of such simplicity and candor that every work of his hand becomes a hymn addressed to God, giver of life and joy. Broadly speaking, we may call him a belated son of the Middle Ages, but on better acquaintance with his particular religious quality we will be struck with his failing to follow the beaten highway of the medieval Doctors of the church in order to take the less traveled path traced by St. Francis of Assisi. The argument that his membership in the rival order of St. Dominic makes such a spiritual relationship improbable is unconvincing. St. Francis distributed his inheritance among all men of a like disposition, and it is a fact that it became a calculable element of general medieval culture after his time. Now the essence of the faith of the *poverello* of Assisi was the goodness of God and the goodness of his creation. It was of course a mystic faith unrelated to the searching processes of the human reason, and its rewards for the believer were that he was flooded with joy and uplifted with ecstatic visions. Fra Angelico affects us like St. Francis come again to manifest his spirit in another field. Such an avatar is in itself less surprising than that it should have occurred at Florence, which more than any other city of Italy was hard, sharp-witted, disciplined, and earthy. Certainly Fra Angelico has no forerunner among Florentine painters, and though the mystic Botticelli is among his successors, Botticelli's mysticism is of so different an order that it constitutes an entirely separate world.

While Fra Angelico is a mystic and has endeared himself to the world as a rapturous visionary, he is professionally a painter who took over the practices of his predecessors and, with a vigor proving that he was after all a Florentine, added much of the new Renaissance knowledge to his medieval stock. To praise Fra Angelico's soul and belittle his hand, as is not uncommon, is to be blind to his honorable, uninterrupted striving as a craftsman. At San Marco at the head of the dormitory stairs leading to the double row of monastic cubicles is an Annunciation which shows Mary under a carefully drawn quattrocento portico in a smiling garden which deceptively recedes in exact accordance with the recently demonstrated laws of perspective. The Annunciation should scatter every doubt that the painter was not moving forward with his time. Of course these fashionable novelties of landscape and architecture do not make the picture. They remain subordinate elements so manipulated that they serve no other purpose than to heighten the hush and gladness of the central theme, which is the meek, surprised Madonna receiving the salutation of the Angel. One of the friar's leading resources in this and all his pictures is the use of transparent, high-keyed color. Than his bright palette nothing was better calculated to enforce the element of joy in which all his renderings of the acts of Christ and of Christ's soldiery are steeped. Nor should we overlook that the remarkable state of preservation of his frescos is convincing evidence of his high technical proficiency.

Equally capable in panel painting, Fra Angelico has endowed us with numerous altar pieces scattered at present through all the museums of the world. A large number have been brought together recently in a special room within the San Marco compound, where they may be studied in happy fellowship with their fresco kin. The Coronation of the Virgin, which is in no way exceptional, may be selected from the mass to illustrate the wonders of his brush. What we behold reveals itself at once as pure vision, wherein the subject matter is much less important than the emotion of the artist. And yet the ineffable scene is marvelously realized. Christ and his Mother are seated upon a cloud, the rapturous angels gather close, singing and sounding trumpets, and beyond them reaching to the very edge of the frame stands or floats the company of the saints in marshaled row on row. It is by these rows organized as concentric circles meeting in the heads of the Virgin and her Son that the picture gets its unity and pattern. Each saintly face is beautiful with a celestial beauty, and the pinks, blues, violets, and greens spread a veil of delicate hue that ravishes the eye. If this is not Giotto's art, which, like Florence itself, is concerned with subduing and possessing the world, still it is art, which in rendering our insubstantial dreams directs us from the necessary earth to the equally necessary sky.

That it was Giotto who was the true father of Florentine painting was made plain by a younger contemporary of Fra Angelico. Unseduced by the friar's blissful raptures, this man took Giotto for his teacher and with little more than his own genius as a guide discovered a new continent. In Masaccio, who was born in 1401 and died at the age of twenty-seven, we encounter one of the most vital and transforming agencies ever manifested in the field of art. We cannot imagine him other than as a youth aglow with energy and resolved, like his leading contemporaries in every field, on excellence and mastery. His development began with the very moment he was apprenticed to a painter; but as painting was slow to shake off the medieval lethargy and was lagging behind the more adventurous sister-skills of architecture and sculpture, it was by these latter rather than by his immediate master that he was introduced to the new spirit and the new knowledge. It was the sculptor, Donatello, who referred him to nature as the inexhaustible mother of forms, and it was the architect, Brunelleschi, who showed him the possibilities of the new science of perspective. All else he owed solely to himself. It is one of the many amazements connected with Masaccio that he lived to complete only a single important work, the frescos of the Brancacci chapel in the church of the Carmine. And not even all of these are by his hand. Nonetheless shortly after his death the modest chapel became a shrine of pilgrimage for his followers, and among his followers it is not an exaggeration to reckon the whole body of Florentine painters after his time. As for the historians and critics of art, beginning with Vasari they have set themselves to analyze Masaccio's revolutionary contribution and have not yet arrived at the end of the tale.

We shall have to rest content with the examination of a single picture of the Brancacci group. It is called the Tribute Money and presents Christ among his disciples confronted by the publican who has come to collect the head-tax levied by Caesar. At the left Peter is seen stooping to extract the coin from the mouth of the fish, and at the right he appears again, this time handing the penny to the tax collector. The great central group has in its single figures the fine dignity of Giotto, while the way the figures are brought together to tell their story suggests the older master's clarity and calculated order. The mind travels easily from Masaccio's Tribute Money to Giotto's Raising of Drusiana in the Peruzzi chapel at Santa Croce and back from Drusiana to the Tribute Money. Nonetheless, while the descent of the younger from the older man is undeniable, how much he has added to his inheritance! His figures have acquired a depth giving the illusion of being truly three-dimensional. At the same time each body underneath its robe has gained an articulation such as no merely painted body ever had before. Although this particular picture shows only clothed figures, there are nudes in some of the other frescos of the Carmine group which prove that Masaccio has dared to ignore the ecclesiastical tabu against nakedness and in his ardent pursuit of reality has arrived at the undraped human form. Had he not taken this forward step, he could not have given us the solidly constructed figures of the apostles and, above all, he could not have achieved the vivacious movement of the athletic young publican. Added to real bodies with dignified or lively carriage according to the character of their owner, we have besides and for the first time a background which is a real landscape of plain and mountain with the gradual recession that only the command of aerial perspective is able to supply. Finally, there is an abandonment of the old linear draughtsmanship and, in place of it, such a distribution of dark and light tones touched with color as to give a much more faithful representation of mass and distance than was possible with the traditional means of expression. Technically this chiaroscuro, as we may call it, was the discovery of Masaccio which was fraught with the greatest consequences for Italy and Europe. For, when his tonal invention was at last comprehended by his puzzled followers, it was so generally accepted as valid that it became the basis of all modern painting down to the threshold of the twentieth century.

It took the successors of Masaccio almost the remainder of the century before they had mastered his novel contributions. These successors fall in the main under two heads, the experimenters or scientists who tried to gain command of some new element of technical expressiveness considered by them to be important, and the traditionalists, who took over from Masaccio what they could understand and employed it in pictorial story-telling in the guileless manner of the age. Among the scientists, an unpopular but interesting group, belong such men as Paolo Uccello (1397–1475), Andrea del Castagno (1396–1457), and Domenico Veneziano (1400–1461). Not particularly regarded in their day, each made an important contribution to the mass of technical knowledge on which Florentine painting at its culmination came to rest. Paolo Uccello occupied himself tirelessly with the mysteries of perspective, Andrea del Castagno struggled as passionately with anatomy, and Domenico Veneziano, who was a Florentine by adoption only, exhibited for the first time the new richness that resulted from supplementing, but not yet supplanting, the old tempera technique with the use of oil.

Although the traditionalists made a much greater stir in the world, we are obliged to dismiss them, too, with a bare mention. Their leader is Fra Filippo Lippi (1400–1465). He was the first painter to tell the gospel stories in terms of Florentine everyday life. This gave his work a familiar and homely quality which would quickly have degenerated to vulgarity, had he not been saved by his ingenuous acceptance of the belief, common to that age of hope, that spring had come to the world and that in spring the earth was a goodly habitation. Certainly not a great artist in the sense of Giotto and Masaccio, he should not be grudged the popularity he owed to his love of existence on the plane familiar to himself and the commoner sort of his fellow-citizens. Benozzo Gozzoli (1420–98) lived equally close to the pulse beat of his time, but instead of picturing the men of the shops and the children of the streets, he took his cue from the pageants that featured the frequent Florentine holidays. An example of his work capable of affording the rarest pleasure, in part owing to its remarkable state of preservation, is the Procession of the Three Kings to the Christ Child's Manger in the chapel of the Medici palace. It is packed with details from the actual pageants of which Gozzoli had been the delighted witness. You see a procession winding around three walls of the rectangular chapel over hillsides, through forests, in leisurely haste to reach the Mother kneeling before her Son over the altar constituting the fourth wall. Eternal summer rules in the world disclosed by Gozzoli, a world of children untroubled by reflection and persuaded that the spectacle of today will be followed by a no less engaging show tomorrow.

The painter representing the culmination of this school of broad and genial narrative is Domenico Ghirlandaio (1449–94). In him Fra Filippo Lippi's honest love of commonplace sentiment joins hands with Benozzo Gozzoli's exquisite feeling for fine people in fine clothes making an appropriate display. Ghirlandaio must have found that life in his native city during the rule of Lorenzo the Magnificent, with whom his own years almost exactly tallied, fell little short of perfection. He became the household painter of families like the Sassetti and the Tornabuoni, who, adherents of the Medici and leading beneficiaries of their sway, accepted the painter's cheerful optimism as a delicate personal tribute. At the command of Francesco Sassetti, one of Lorenzo's numerous business agents, the artist decorated the family chapel at Santa Trinità with pictures from the life of St. Francis; and some years later, on order from Giovanni Tornabuoni, head of the Roman branch of the Medici bank, he covered the choir of Santa Maria Novella with scenes, on one wall, from the life of Mary and, on the opposite wall, from the life of St. John the Baptist. These frescos enjoy an immense reputation, which they fully deserve if taken on their own superficial terms. That means that we must not expect, for Ghirlandaio does not offer, representations in which there survives as much as a trace of the old religious feeling, wherein Florentine and all European art whatever had had its origin. We have here a completely mundane attitude toward the ancient stories of the Christian faith, which did not consider it an offense to transform the sacred personages into contemporary prosperous burghers dressed in their best finery, paying each other ceremonious visits in their houses, or meeting with mannerly exchange of greetings on city square or amidst pastoral delights. As Ghirlandaio was a minutely realistic observer of the house furnishings and clothes characteristic of every class of citizens but particularly of the well-to-do, his frescos constitute a uniquely valuable volume on the private life of the Florentines of quality. Since he was also a portraitist with an instinctive feeling for the elements constituting individuality, he utilized for his scenes the figures of the leading citizens, both men and women, thus making his unique treatise on manners an equally unique contemporary portrait gallery.

In view of the flashy accessories, which completely mask the essence, it can be readily understood that many sincerely religious people regard these elegant versions of sacred history as a blasphemous mockery. However, such critics constitute a vanishing minority, and in our time, as on the day when the frescos were first uncovered, they have enjoyed the unstinted admiration of the general public. In the light of this uninterrupted popularity two deductions may be safely ventured. They are, first, that, in spite of continued lip service in the churches, the secular attitude, which had been pushing to the front in Florence for several hundred years, in Lorenzo's day ruled the hearts and minds; and, second, that this secular attitude has maintained an unbroken domination to the present day.

In the very years in which Ghirlandaio was giving inimitable expression to the material well-being and naïve self-satisfaction of the ruling classes Sandro

Botticelli (1444–1510) produced work which mirrored very different facets of the age. As we are already aware that Botticelli was in touch with the inmost circle of Lorenzo's friends, we should from the outset be inclined to expect from him a much more specialized communication regarding Laurentian Florence than the rather generalized version offered by the creator of the choir pictures of Santa Maria Novella. Not only is this expectation realized, but Botticelli's work further tells us that its creator, who began his career with characteristic Florentine strenuosity, in his young manhood aspired to nothing less than to the conquest of all the technical means and styles of expression which painting had amassed since the dawn of a new day in the Brancacci chapel. His first master was Fra Filippo Lippi. Having learned all the genial friar had to offer, he roamed at will among his fellow-craftsmen, gathering a little here, a little there, and a great deal from such particularly vigorous con-temporaries as Verrocchio and Pollaiuolo. It seemed reasonable to expect that the broad and systematic training the young painter gave himself would culminate in a fulfilment associating his name with the starry names of Giotto and Masaccio, when something happened and the bubble burst.

This puzzling event figures in the history of painting as the Botticelli prob-lem. It has given rise to a stream of conjecture which, beginning with Walter Pater half a century ago, has gathered volume with each new decade.[5] Who-ever is interested in the issue will have to turn to the considerable literature on the subject. For the general student it will suffice to note that Botticelli was from his birth the victim of an exaggerated sensitiveness. His naturally vigorous physique and his normal Florentine appetite for power kept it for a long time under control. To this healthy, balanced period covering his youth and early manhood belong the works indicative of his triumphant assimila-tion of the skills distributed through all the *botteghe* of the town. An Adora-tion of the Magi in the Uffizi with a costumed display of the members of the house of Medici in the role of worshiping kings supplies evidence that, in his zeal to absorb the lesson of every school, he even fell into the pretentious vein of Domenico Ghirlandaio. However, try as he might, against his inner voices, which became more imperious with every advancing year, he could not persist in his course. It is likely the first break occurred when, through contact with the humanistic circle of Lorenzo, he became acquainted with the world of antiquity and had disclosed before his amazed eyes the Love doctrine of Neoplatonism. To this phase of intense self-realization belong the Birth of Venus and the so-called Spring, more properly the Realm of Venus, the serene kingdom over which Love rules. Later, nourished undoubtedly by the esoteric doctrines spread by Ficino and Pico, a vein of Christian mysticism gained an increasing empire over him; and somewhat later still, he was so overwhelmed by the visions and prophecies of Savonarola that they ended by taking complete possession of his being. It is well known that Botticelli in his last period became a devoted *Piagnone* and that, following Savonarola's mar-tyrdom, he gradually ceased to practice painting, dropping completely from the sight of men many years before he died.

Heaven forbid that any reader should take this telescoped analysis of a com-

[5] Essay on Botticelli by W. Pater in his volume, *The Renaissance*.

plicated destiny literally and conclude that Botticelli lived in three or four or six successive phases as in so many air-tight compartments. The thought suggested is rather that he was subject to many moods and worked in many manners, all of which persisted even when one happened temporarily to predominate, and that the year in which a picture can be proved to have been completed is not an infallible index of its ruling character. One point, however, is capital and must be reiterated. After following for years a line of development normal for a healthy Florentine and giving rise to the hope that painting would be carried to a new culmination, Botticelli abandoned the broad highway he had been traveling for a tortuous by-path, of which no one had knowledge save himself and which had been calling to him in seductive whispers since his boyhood. Yielding to an inner urge, which until he entered middle life he had managed to keep in subjugation, he became an eccentric, gave up the traditional Florentine view that art was a social function, and thereafter painted to no other end than to please himself alone. Had he been more resolute and less sensitive and fragile, he might have reached the heights to which Leonardo afterward mounted. He made another choice, leaving behind a range of works which proclaim him as one of the most individual and fascinatingly elusive artists of all time.

As it is impossible to pursue Botticelli through the wide gamut of his moods, and as it is equally impossible to take no account whatever of his individual works, we shall make the very halting compromise of examining two pictures, which derive from the later, the eccentric artist and which, although very different in subject matter, carry the same haunting message. The Birth of Venus belongs to what may be called his classicizing period, but perhaps never has there been produced a work farther removed from the true classical spirit. Indeed except that the subject is Venus, there is nothing whatever in the picture having the slightest bearing on antiquity. This Venus is love, the prime mover of the universe, and she comes in her cockleshell driven by the Winds (two male figures at the left) across the sea to the garlanded Earth (female figure at the right) aflutter with welcome on the shore. The Venus, a nude figure of indescribable loveliness, instead of expressing delight and joy, is enveloped in mute tragedy. She seems profoundly conscious that in bringing life to the generation of men she must needs bring also sorrow and heartbreak. This is no more than a feebly approximate statement of her import which, like all mystic communications, defies formulation in insubstantial words. It is much easier and critically sounder to speak of the technical means by which the coming of the sea-born goddess is impressed on the mind and senses. The magnificent swirling movement beginning in the agitated Winds on the left is moderated in the undulating body and blown hair of Venus, to be taken up once more with its original vehemence in the gesture and garments of the welcoming Earth. The tremulous motion is at last gratifyingly arrested by the three stiffly vertical trees at the extreme right. In analyzing Botticelli's command of movement Berenson declares him to be a lineal symphonist of a refinement of harmony beyond the achievement of any European artist before or since.

The other picture to which attention is invited is an altar piece in the

Uffizi showing the Madonna and the Divine Child surrounded by six angels. It is in the round, a shape for which Botticelli had a peculiar liking. It would be pleasant to linger over the reappearance in this picture of the artist's singing line, but we shall limit ourselves to the most immediately arresting feature. It is that this Holy Virgin is the identical Venus we have just seen wafted across the sea. In the altar piece she is of course not nude but amply garmented, and her sad face shows a certain softening through the veil fastened in her hair. But called the Virgin, she is none other than the Venus of the allegory and carries the same burden of unfathomable grief. Let who will unravel the mystery that troubled Botticelli's soul. Certain it is that as he grew older and dared to be, cost what it might, his sensitive and individual self, he had a very different communication to make from Benozzo Gozzoli and the pleasant narrative painters, Botticelli's predecessors and contemporaries, to whom life was a perpetual holiday.

When Botticelli by choosing the solitary path made the great refusal, it was as good as certain that someone else would undertake the task of gathering together the diverse knowledge and experience of the quattrocento into a magnificent synthesis. This man was Leonardo da Vinci. With him we reach the culminating, the cinquecento phase of Florentine art.

XXVI. The Savonarola Episode (1494–98)

I N THE year 1494, two years after the death of Lorenzo the Magnificent, King Charles VIII carried out the long-threatened French invasion of Italy. It completely shattered the delicately balanced peninsular relations with which we are familiar and inaugurated a new period of Italian history. In its further consequences it revolutionized the whole European situation by inaugurating that ferocious rivalry among nationally organized states which is a leading characteristic of Modern as distinct from Medieval History. Owing to these effects, many historians are inclined to accept 1494 as a convenient date for the beginning of Modern History; and if periodization is to be determined in the main by changes in the realm of politics, there is much to be said for this decision. It is clear, however, that to historians of religion or art or economics other dates will present themselves associated with happenings of greater significance in the field in which they are interested. We do not conceive ourselves as quarreling with these other historians, if, concerned in this book with a political unit, the republic of Florence, we accept the absolutely determining character of the great event of 1494. We have followed the successive stages by which Florence disengaged itself from the octopus embrace of feudalism and, becoming an independent city-state, developed into a commonwealth of notable political power and unique cultural creativeness. That age of struggle, the great age of the Red Lily, covering almost five hundred years, was now drawing to a close. Toward the end of the fifteenth century the peoples of Europe overcoming in their turn the conditions of the Middle Ages, which in their altered frame of mind they came to regard as barriers to their free development, had come to assemble their strength in great national monarchies; or rather, to state the case with greater historical sweep, they had gropingly inaugurated a movement of enlargement and unification which has continued uninterruptedly down to our day.

In this enormously significant development three peoples took the lead, bringing about at approximately the same time the rise of the national monarchies of France, Spain, and England. Acquiring a power hitherto unknown over taxes, the army, and the administration, the sovereigns of these three countries gained an immense advantage over their neighbors, whether republics or principalities, which for one reason or another had failed to bring themselves to the same size and concentrated might. This was the case of each and every one of the Italian states. It was therefore also the case of the republic of Florence, which, constrained from 1494 onward, to deal first with France and then with France and Spain, found itself completely outclassed by these great monarchies, a pigmy among giants. As will become presently apparent, from the moment the French set foot in the peninsula the republic was no longer free to formulate its own policy. It fell into a dependence on France, and afterward on France and Spain alternately, from which it struggled desperately to escape. The struggle went on without respite till 1530, when, having summoned its remaining strength and having clasped to itself its noblest traditions, it went down in final defeat. In the remainder of this work we shall treat this last phase of the republic covering some thirty-six years. Already shadowed by an implacably advancing doom, they constitute a not unworthy conclusion to the story of human ingenuity and heroism unfolded in this book.

Although the French invasion came as a surprise to most Italians, an occasional statesman had woven it into his calculations and had correctly estimated its absolutely fatal consequences. Such a statesman was Lorenzo de' Medici, who, as we have seen, had directed his main effort in the latter part of his life to the maintenance of peace among the Italian states as the surest available means for persuading the French not to embark on their transalpine adventure. Regardless of all that Lorenzo could do, the direct claim of the French crown to Naples and its indirect claim, through the younger or Orléans branch, to Milan kept the monarch interested in Italy at all times and on occasion aroused his cupidity to the danger point. In shaping their policy the rulers of Italy took no account of patriotism, which was a sentiment as yet unknown in the peninsula, and did not scruple about intriguing at Paris in the hope of scoring some petty advantage close at home with the aid of the distant but powerful king of France. Lorenzo himself had played at this dangerous game until, ripened by experience, he came to regard the French intervention as an event incapable of bringing its local abettors more than a temporary advantage and sure to end by putting the whole peninsula under a foreign yoke. His policy was therefore to close every break in the peace front of the Italian states as fast as it appeared; and he may be credited with having maintained a hazardous amity among the contentious peninsular neighbors sufficient to discourage the French from taking the offensive in his day.

Hardly had Lorenzo died in the spring of 1492, when the delicate Italian balance he had made it his business to maintain began to show signs of violent agitation. A leading culprit was none other than his own son and heir, Piero. A handsome, arrogant young man of twenty-two, Piero spurned his father's cautious policy in favor of bolder measures suggested by nothing more valid than his foolish, juvenile preferences. For some time an issue had existed between the king of Naples and the *de facto* ruler of Milan, which, owing mainly to the efforts of Lorenzo the Magnificent, had been kept under fair control. The *de facto* ruler of Milan was Lodovico, called the Moor, and he had acquired his authority as guardian of the titular duke, his nephew and a minor. At the death of Lorenzo the young duke had reached the age of twenty and was considered by his partisans to be ripe for rule. Sickly and docile, he made no personal disturbance, but his beautiful wife, who was a granddaughter of Ferrante, king of Naples, was a spirited creature resolved

BOTTICELLI. ADORATION OF THE MAGI. UFFIZI GALLERY (ALINARI).

BOTTICELLI. VIRGIN WITH CHRIST-CHILD AND SIX ANGELS.
UFFIZI GALLERY (ALINARI).

left: POPE LEO X. RAPHAEL. PITTI GALLERY (ALINARI). *right:* POPE CLEMENT VII. BRONZINO. MEDICI PALACE (ALINARI).

left: SAVONAROLA. PORTRAIT BY FRA BARTOLOMMEO. SAN MARCO (ALINARI). *right:* MACHIAVELLI. BUST IN TERRA COTTA BY AN UNKNOWN ARTIST. PROPERTY OF THE SOCIETÀ COLOMBARIA OF FLORENCE (ALINARI).

to have her rights. Accordingly, she stormed at her southern relatives to bring pressure to bear on the Moor with a view to having him put an end to his long regency. Lodovico, pricked by ambition and utterly unscrupulous, was greatly chagrined by the representations of the court of Naples. In his heart he had long ago decided never to yield his place, and to secure himself against a sudden stroke by the aggrieved husband and wife kept them under close watch.

Murder, as the confidential agent of every Italian tyrant, would doubtless have been brought into the situation at this juncture if the Moor had not been obliged to reckon with an immediate declaration of war on the part of the king of Naples. Carefully pondering the problem, Lodovico came to the conclusion that his own safety demanded the overthrow of the interfering dynasty. This was not so difficult as it might seem, since all it required was to induce the king of France to undertake the long-threatened campaign to vindicate his right to the Neapolitan crown. Of course Lodovico himself, through such an invasion, would be running a certain risk, for there was no assurance that the northern sovereign, once in the peninsula, would not recall that, in addition to a Neapolitan, his house had also a Milanese claim. Persuaded, as oversubtle plotters often are, that he could make a clown of another man by using him as a tool, the Milanese regent began to play upon the ambition of the French king by offering him help in the Italian undertaking and by teasing him with the prospect that, thus seconded, the conquest of Naples would cease to be much of a hazard. It was in connection with the growing friction between Naples and Milan that Piero de' Medici abandoned his father's mediatory role. Instead of insisting on an adjudication, he put himself unreservedly on the side of the king of Naples, thereby filling the Moor with the panic fear of peninsular isolation and prompting him to redouble his effort to bring the French across the Alps.[1] The French king was a young man, Charles VIII by name, who lent a fascinated ear to Lodovico's siren call. Deformed and feeble physically, and mentally in no better case, the royal youth was the very antipodes of his cunning father, Louis XI. He had a pathetic passion for old tales of derring-do and under the flattery of his courtiers readily persuaded himself that he was called to renew the glory of his medieval namesake, the half-fabulous Charlemagne. Of the five states reckoned as Italian powers, Venice as usual stood to one side, Naples, Florence, and the pope leagued themselves together to resist the French invasion, and only Milan offered active help. Nevertheless, in the spring of 1494 Charles assembled an army at Lyons near the passes of the Alps, and after much uncertainty due to the battering effect on his weak mind of the opposed opinions of his councillors, in the late summer he led his army unmolested over the mountains and emerged upon Italian soil.

[1] The relations of Piero with Charles VIII, as well as those of the republic after him, are revealed by the documents published by A. Desjardins and G. Canestrini, *Négociations Diplomatiques de la France avec la Toscane*. Paris, 1859. Invaluable sidelights on Franco-Tuscan relations are offered by the Memoirs of the French courtier and statesman, Philippe de Commines. A conspicuous place among the innumerable presentations of the Italian invasions, beginning with that of 1494, must still be conceded to the earliest of them all by F. Guicciardini, *La Storia d'Italia* (on which see Introduction).

At Asti the young sovereign was met by his ally, the treacherous Lodovico the Moor. There were the usual receptions and parades, but only after another attack of indecision had been overcome did the king give the order to resume the march. The army at the head of which he proceeded southward in the direction of the Apennines was of a size and efficiency whereof the peninsula, accustomed to the trifling and treacherous warfare conducted by relatively small bands of hireling condottieri, had absolutely no experience. Not only did the French forces amount to sixty thousand men, but they were armed and disciplined to a degree far beyond the Italian standard. Furthermore, at the side of the panoplied cavalry, constituting the arm on which the Italians exclusively relied for success in the field, there operated an effective infantry, among which figured a select body of Swiss mercenaries capable of withstanding the most determined charge of horse and just then at the height of their reputation. Finally, the French had developed the artillery service far beyond any other European nation, and with an abundance of light, mobile cannons discharging iron instead of stone balls were able to work havoc among the dense enemy lines before they could be brought into action. Under these circumstances it is not surprising that the campaign of the three Italian allies collapsed before it began. To begin with, the usual jealousies kept them from joining their forces into a single unit; and when, in addition, Alfonso, king of Naples, who had just succeeded his father Ferrante and who alone among Italian leaders commanded a halfway impressive body of troops, withdrew them from central Italy resolved to confine his defense to his own kingdom, Tuscany and the State of the Church were at the mercy of the invader. When the hesitating Charles at length crossed the Apennines and prepared in his march through Tuscany to treat it as enemy territory, the stupidly proud Piero de' Medici, who, firmly committed to the house of Aragon, had rejected the numerous friendly advances of the French court, suddenly and pitifully lost heart. Stealthily departing from Florence on a late October day, he made his way in a panic to the camp of the French king, and without waiting to give his fears a chance to subside signed a treaty by which he completely reversed himself. Not only did he go over to the side of the invader, but in sign of good faith he delivered over to the French the fortresses of Sarzana, Sarzanella, Pietrasanta, Pisa, and Livorno, constituting in their sum the key positions of his state.

When this precipitate and disgraceful surrender became known in Florence, a fierce resentment took possession of the whole population. Traditionally attached to France, the Florentines had never viewed with other than antipathy Piero's alliance with the house of Aragon; but they failed just as completely to understand why it was necessary to mollify the angered French king by terms so injurious to the power and dignity of the state. Ominous murmurs among all classes required only the return of the discredited Piero from the French camp to occasion a general uprising. When, on the morning of November 9, the unhappy young man presented himself at the palace to report on his visit to the French king, he was refused admission. Boiling with indignation at the rebuff, he returned to his residence to assemble his partisans and take the

Palazzo Pubblico by storm, but before he could carry out his plans, the rebellious signory had rung the great bell accustomed to summon the citizens to the piazza. Recognizing that he could not make headway against the aroused masses, Piero pusillanimously gave up the struggle, made his way to the Porta San Gallo, and, attended by his brothers Giovanni (the later Pope Leo X) and Giuliano, rode hurriedly across the Apennines into safety. After exactly sixty years of an unusually secure rule the domination of the Medici had come to an end and the Florentines once again took their destiny into their own hands. Aside from plundering from cellar to garret the great Medicean palace with its invaluable treasures and doing the same mischief to the houses of a few of Piero's favored henchmen, no grave excesses were committed. In the face of the perilous crisis confronting the city the signory was moved to maintain as united a front as possible and resolutely suppressed all further public disorder.

What chiefly troubled and perplexed the government was that Tuscany had passed into the hands of a foreign power, which, although no longer officially at war with Florence, was the unquestioned master of the situation. On November 9, the very day on which Piero had been expelled from the city, the French, pushing southward, had entered Pisa. This was all the encouragement the Pisans needed to rise in revolt against Florence and to appeal for the protection of their recovered liberty to Charles VIII. More from lack of understanding than from political malice the king accepted the honor conferred on him, thus giving his royal support to an act which deprived the Florentines of a possession hardly less dear to them than life itself. When Charles next moved up the Arno Valley toward Florence the hectic situation reached a climax. Did he come as a friend or as an enemy? To the anxious commissioners sent by the signory to his camp to press for an immediate agreement he returned the stock answer that he would negotiate when once inside what in his muddled Italian he called the *gran villa*. On November 17, amidst feverish excitement, he entered the city in triumph at the head of his army. On that day the Florentines witnessed the greatest military spectacle of their history. They greeted the finely disciplined and magnificently appareled troops with cordial shouts of *Francia, Francia,* but the leading actor of the show proved a strangely disconcerting sight. For what met their eyes was a little solemn-faced monkey of a man, who, clad in steel and bestriding a great war horse, sat impassively holding his lance at rest, the conventional gesture of conquest.

Making his entry in this fashion, the king divulged that in his view he had captured the city and could dictate whatever conditions he pleased. When he had taken his residence in the Medici palace, lately sacked by the mob but lavishly refurnished for the occasion by the government, negotiations began that did not get far in the face of the lively protest of the Florentine representatives. Refusing to accede to the king's opinion that theirs was a captured town, they indignantly rejected the treaty submitted by the putative conqueror. On Charles insisting on his document, Piero Capponi, the boldest of the commissioners and the worthy scion of one of the city's greatest families, snatched it from the king's hands and, tearing it to bits, tossed the pieces on the floor.

"We shall sound our trumpets," threatened the miffed little man. At which Piero, rising to the occasion, thundered: "And we our bells!" The dramatic exchange deservedly became famous among the Florentines, for it was the king and not the spokesman of the citizens that gave way. The narrow winding streets of a populous town were not suited for the unfolding of the might of a great army; and Charles thought twice before exposing himself to the risk of having his Neapolitan venture die prematurely on the banks of the Arno. In a chastened state of mind he agreed to return the fortresses surrendered by Piero de' Medici as soon as the war was over and to be content with a subsidy of 120,000 gold florins. The crucial Pisan matter was wrapped up in a bundle of inconclusive phrases. Plainly if the Florentines wanted Pisa back, they would have to send an army and conquer it.

The citizens heaved a sigh of relief when, ten days after their entrance, the French at length evacuated the town. It is not our business to follow the army on its southward march further than to note its amazing triumph. Rome, like Florence, was occupied without resistance and the pope obliged to abandon King Alfonso of Naples and to enrol himself on the side of the invader. The pontiff whom the French thus humiliated was Alexander VI, a Spaniard with the family name of Borgia. Elevated to the papal throne in 1492, he inaugurated a reign of ten years which constitutes one of the most amazing chapters of Christian history and which, owing to its impact on our city of Florence, will hereafter repeatedly invite our attention. Moving ever southward, the French army entered the city of Naples on February 22, 1495, without striking a single blow. Before the wind raised by the tremendous reputation of the Ultramontanes the cowardly Neapolitan forces scattered like dry autumn leaves. The despairing Alfonso resigned his crown to enter a monastery, and his youthful successor, Ferrante II, threw away his sword and fled for his life. By crowning himself king of Naples victorious Charles certified to the world that he had attained his goal. Almost before the cheering was over, he was fated to learn that he had made the frailest of conquests.

As soon as the French king had evacuated Florence, the citizens set about the business, adjourned by them in the presence of danger, of providing themselves with a new constitution. In this process the first traditional step was to call a parliament. On December 2 it assembled in the usual manner on the piazza and unanimously acclaimed the proposal of the signory to give power to a body of twenty accoppiatori to appoint the magistracies for the length of a year. With the most pressing necessities thus provided for the deliberations touching the new form of the constitution might proceed with some measure of security. In view of the excitement attending the fall of the Medici it was inevitable that the whole population should wish to share in the argument. The opinion most commonly heard when men gathered at street-corners was that the old constitution must under no circumstances be re-enacted without change, since it was with the aid of that instrument that the Medici had succeeded in imposing their tyranny. The exiled and active Piero still had numerous followers within the town, and for the anti-Medicean majority the main issue was to close every possible avenue to the deposed family's return.

It was this frame of mind that caused the general attention to swing to Venice. Here was a republic which had suffered no major change for two hundred years, and which, besides, had never been tyrant-ridden. Before long the general discussion concentrated more and more on two features of the Venetian republic, which, it was argued, not only explained its extraordinary stability but which also might, with no more than a few slight changes, be taken over by Florence. The first feature was the Grand Council, which in its Florentine version it was proposed to make up of a large body of citizens empowered to elect the leading officials and to vote the laws; the second feature was a smaller council or senate to be consulted by the executive on all matters of policy whatever. With these two stabilizing importations was to be combined the traditional system of a rapidly revolving signory of nine members (eight priors and a gonfalonier of Justice) with their advisory colleges of sixteen gonfaloniers of companies and twelve Buoni Uomini. The affection felt for this familiar executive, amounting almost to obsession, sprang in part from the fact that it was native, in larger part still from its enabling over a hundred citizens to achieve the much-prized honors of office in a single year. It did not escape the intelligent inquisition of the Florentines that whatever the Venetian Grand Council may have been in the beginning, it had long ago congealed into an hereditary chamber of nobles. As there no longer were any nobles in Florence and the very concept of nobility was unpopular, the necessity made itself felt of adjusting the Venetian borrowing to Florentine conditions. Accordingly, it was proposed that the Grand Council should be made up of all those who boasted among their ancestors for three generations back as much as a single occupant of one of the three major magistracies, that is, signory, gonfaloniers of companies, and Buoni Uomini. As it presently appeared that there were over three thousand citizens who on these terms might qualify for the Grand Council, and as so large a body was more in the nature of a mob than of a deliberative assembly, it was further proposed to divide the eligibles into three groups, each called to serve in turn for a period of three months.

Once again the relativity of all political concepts is startlingly brought home to us by the conflict of opinion that arose in the late autumn of the year 1494 over the Grand Council. The Florentines who favored an institution establishing a body of three thousand electors in a population close to one hundred thousand people were considered to be extremely democratic and were opposed by the great merchant families which, having traditionally exercised the power, were stubbornly averse to giving it up. Compared with these favorers of oligarchy, the supporters of the Grand Council were unquestionably democratic, regardless of their inability to qualify as democrats under a twentieth-century definition of the term. The clash of opinion over the Grand Council filled the town and, long continued, might have led to civil war, if a democratic champion had not put in an appearance who brought the issue to a quick and generally satisfactory close.

The democratic champion was Girolamo Savonarola, but before we consider his intervention in the Grand Council debate we must briefly sketch his career as it had unfolded up to the moment of his plunge into politics.

Girolamo was born at Ferrara on September 21, 1452.[2] His people were respectable middle-class folk loosely attached to the court of the ancient ruling family of Este. There is nothing in the known circumstances of Girolamo's family and upbringing that accounts for the preference he showed from his early years for solitude and prayer. We have to conclude that here was that phenomenon, much less common in our time than was once the case, of a soul naturally religious, for which life had no other purpose than earnestly to look for and, after finding, to hold fast to the road to heaven. Under the direction of his father he occupied himself with scholastic philosophy and its most eminent exponent, St. Thomas Aquinas, until at the age of twenty-three, unable any longer to support the burden of living in the world, he abandoned home and family and knocked for admission at the gate of the great Dominican monastery at Bologna. There followed a probationary period of privations, prayer, and ardent study, during which he strove with all his mind and will to make himself a worthy follower of the great founder of his order. By calling themselves Preaching Friars the Dominicans had indicated from the start that they regarded the preaching of the faith as their highest function. Not till he was sent to Florence in 1482 was Fra Girolamo put to the test in regard to this central feature of his training. However, on this first exhibition of his powers he scored an unqualified fiasco. He had taken his residence in the convent of San Marco, of which the Medici were patrons and where, some decades earlier, Michelozzo had built the fine cloister and library and Fra Angelico had painted his ecstatic visions. To the entrancing memories which to this day hang like a luminous halo above the place, Fra Girolamo was destined to make a notable contribution; but nothing that he did during his first residence of some four years figures in the record. The elegant Florentine humanists set the tone for platform and pulpit oratory alike, and with their purely rhetorical standards the rude sincerity of the Ferrarese visitor was in hopeless disaccord. He must have felt relieved on being recalled to Lombardy, where the humanist influence was much more feeble. Sent on a preaching round to many towns, he gradually got his magnificent resources of heart and mind so effectively in hand that the memory of his Tuscan failure was forgotten as his reputation mounted till its echoes filled the most remote corners of the peninsula. At the instance of Lorenzo de' Medici himself he was in the summer of 1490 recalled to San Marco, and on this second occasion, beginning with his very first pulpit address, he fairly brought the town to his feet.

It was now seen that the aping of ancient literature and the adoption of pagan manners were fashions which flourished among a limited upper class and that the Florentine masses still retained their medieval attachment to religion and the church. To be sure, the spontaneous sentiments associated with worship had been largely buried under the dead weight of elaborate,

---

[2] There are two outstanding biographies of Savonarola: P. Villari, *La Storia di Girolamo Savonarola*. 2 vols. Florence, 1859 (2d ed. 1887; latest ed. 1926). English translation published by Scribner's, New York, 1893. The other biography is by J. Schnitzer, *Savonarola: Ein Kulturbild aus der Zeit der Renaissance*. 2 vols. Munich, 1924. Both Villari and Schnitzer offer an illuminating and exhaustive discussion of the sources. In recent years Savonarola's *ipsissima verba* have been made accessible in excellent editions. His *Prediche Italiane ai Fiorentini* appeared in three volumes in the years 1930-33 under the editorship of F. Cognasso; and his *Lettere* appeared in a single volume in 1933 edited by R. Ridolfi.

multiplied ceremonies, but under the impact of the convictions which poured from Savonarola's mouth like molten metal, the superimposed forms were consumed like tinder and the fountains of faith again unsealed. The friar preached nothing new, for what he offered his crowded congregation was the gospel of Life Eternal to be won by wholehearted surrender to God and his commandments. He based his sermons strictly on the Bible, especially on the Old Testament and the exhortations and warnings of the prophets. Macerated by fasting and other privations, he became, as is not unusual with the progress of physical enfeeblement, subject to hallucinations and heavenly visions. Although he himself long doubted their validity, they ended by persuading him that he was the latest member in the long succession of the Lord's chosen vessels and that he had the double mission from on high to free men of their evil habits and to reform the church. As his self-confidence increased, the promises and threats he uttered from the pulpit become more definite and culminated at last in three ever-repeated declarations. The first was that the church will be scourged; the second, that it will be renewed; and the third, that the time was at hand. There had been no prophets, his awed followers whispered to one another, since the far days of John the Baptist, and now after hundreds of years God in his goodness had been moved again to send an inspired messenger to his erring children. When San Marco proved too small to hold the crowd of listeners, Savonarola uttered his warnings and prophecies to dense gatherings in the duomo, and to all these reawakened Christians his fiery eloquence and reiterated affirmation of what the future had in store certified him as the veritable man of God.

Even before Lorenzo the Magnificent's death the friar had acquired so large a following in Florence that the suspicious tyrant became filled with misgivings. Nor was his state of mind improved by the obstinate aloofness of the Dominican. In 1491 the brothers of San Marco elected Girolamo prior, and custom required that the new head pay a visit of respect to Lorenzo as patron of the establishment. This the new prior firmly refused to do on the ground that he owed his elevation to no one but to God. Like the great gentleman he was, Lorenzo overlooked the social lapse. In fact in his heart he could not help being deeply impressed with so much sterling independence; and when, in the very next year, death knocked at his door calling on him to prepare his soul for its uncertain journey, he summoned the prior of San Marco to his bedside. While the story that Savonarola's disciples afterward circulated as to what passed between the two men must be dismissed as apocryphal,[3] the fact that Lorenzo, the pagan-minded, pleasure-loving tyrant in the last hours of his earthly sojourn felt impelled to consult the unbending champion of the Christian way of living fixes a moment in the life of both these great men and of their contentious age as well which must remain forever memorable.

In the two years intervening between Lorenzo's death and Piero's expulsion from the city Savonarola's influence grew steadily until a large portion of the population looked to him for guidance in all matters pertaining to morals and religion. And when on the liberation of the city from the Medicean yoke

[3] See chap. XXIII, pp. 405-06.

the debate began to rage about the political system to be adopted, it was inevitable that his followers should turn for direction also in this matter to their celestially illuminated guide. A sharp struggle followed in Savonarola's own breast, for he never doubted that he was sent to labor in the vineyards of the Lord and not in order to waste himself in the petty quarrels of the market place. However, on recognizing the danger to the newly won civil freedom of an indefinitely prolonged agitation, he resolutely stepped into the political arena and in a succession of fiery sermons delivered in the cathedral declared in favor of the democratic principle as represented by the Grand Council. At once public opinion rallied behind him with such irresistible vigor that the necessary measures were passed with a minimum of delay and the new constitution completed before the end of the year. Its novel features, as already noted, were the Grand Council of approximately one thousand members and a small council or senate of eighty (the *Ottanta*); the features retained from the traditional system were the priors and gonfalonier of Justice with their two advisory colleges. By January, 1495, the new government was set agoing amidst extraordinary rejoicings. For the time being the *Popolari* or democratic party swept everything before it. That the Popolari were never called other than *Frateschi* (Friarists) or, more derisively still, *Piagnoni* (Weepers, Snivelers) by their opponents proves that they were confronted from the first with a very active ill-will. These opponents were well represented in the Grand Council and might, under favorable circumstances, achieve control of the commonwealth by being elected to the signory which, as in the past, was changed every two months. Luckily for the democrats their opponents were far from united. The most powerful group were the optimates, who because of their rabid antagonism to the ruling system were currently called *Arrabbiati*. Certain young men of the upper circles, not numerous but spectacularly active, were prepared at any moment to descend into the piazza and demonstrate against the puritanical friar; from their evil habits of life they were called *Compagnacci*. Although the Medici had suffered expulsion, they could still boast many followers, who, because they prudently avoided the light of day, were picturesquely called *Bigi* or Greys. Admitting that these enemies alone or in combination constituted a potential threat to the reconstituted republic, for the present at least they were harmless, owing to the general favor enjoyed by the new government. However, so great were the difficulties of that government that before long something was bound to go wrong and, as soon as that happened, the watchful opposition would be sure to leap into action.

The greatest peril to the government lay in the foreign field, for Florence lacked the power to play an independent role and was more or less at the mercy of all its neighbors. Ever since the invasion of Tuscany by the French it was very definitely at the mercy of Charles VIII, who to bind the Florentines to his side had planted garrisons in Pisa and in all the strongholds surrendered by Piero de' Medici. To make matters worse, Pisa had revolted, and other subject communities, such as Arezzo and Montepulciano, were preparing to follow suit. While the city owed these humiliations to the French sovereign and manifested great ill humor toward him, it was obliged to cling to the recently concluded alliance, if for no other reason than that it expected to be rewarded for its faithfulness with an early return of the occupied fortresses.

It must therefore be clear that the immediate destiny of Florence was indissolubly tied up with the destiny of the French expedition. We have followed Charles VIII to his occupation of Naples, up to which point he had been the very darling of Dame Fortune. But now the ever capricious lady suddenly deserted his banner. The first mishap was that, alarmed at the immense growth of French might, almost the whole European world combined together to deprive the king of the fruits of his victory. Spain and the emperor Maximilian of Germany were the heart of the movement, but three Italian states, Venice, the pope, and the shifty Lodovico of Milan gave an eager support to the cause. It was Lodovico on whom more than on any other Italian rested the responsibility for the French invasion. He had been, alas, only too successful in his purpose, and, filled with mounting fear of the ally who had waxed too great, he now completely reversed himself. The League, as the members of the anti-French combination called themselves for short, planned to raise an army in the rear of the French and thus shut off their retreat. One and all members of the League eagerly pleaded with the Florentines to join their ranks, for with Tuscany on their side they would have closed to Charles every avenue of escape. But the Arno folk could not be dissuaded from their view of the invincibility of the forces they had seen parade through their city a few months before. Consequently when Charles, obliged to beat a quick retreat from Naples in order to secure his communications with his homeland, passed again through Tuscany, he encountered a friendly reception from his faithful ally. Not till he attempted to cross the Apennines did the army of the League undertake to bar the way. On July 6, at Fornovo, the French king was obliged to attack a numerically superior foe who lay across his path. His desperate charges gave him the victory, and he continued his northward journey without further molestation until he reached home and safety. Almost as soon as he had left Naples behind, his Aragonese rival, young Ferrante II, reoccupied the kingdom and again set up his throne in its capital. A year after Charles VIII had entered Italy to turn the peninsula topsyturvy, he was back again on French soil, and Italy, relieved of his presence, to all superficial appearances resumed its former aspect.

So to its inner core, however, had Italy been shaken by the French incursion that it never again recovered from the shock. Let Florence, our immediate interest, illustrate the new risks that had been introduced into an already highly unstable situation. Before recrossing the Alps Charles VIII signed a new treaty with ambassadors of the republic, in which, in accordance with his earlier promise, he reassigned the Tuscan strongholds to the Red Lily. But whether the fault was the king's or that of his self-willed subordinates, the commandant of the Pisan fort surrendered it not to the Florentines but to the Pisans, while the commandants of Sarzana and Sarzanella surrendered to Genoa and the commandant of Pietrasanta to Lucca, in each case for the vulgar lucre of which no contemporary commandant could ever have enough. Of all its lost possessions Florence at this time reacquired only Livorno; and Livorno passed again into Florentine hands not owing to the loyal execution of their treaty by the French but in consequence of its resolute seizure by a Florentine captain.

No patriotic son of Arno doubted that trust and fidelity had been repaid by the French king with callous treachery. All this high-piled resentment, however, did not avail to bring about an abandonment of the French alliance. In Florentine eyes France led Europe in military might and would only have to reappear on the scene, as Charles VIII on leaving Italy had volubly promised to do the very next year, to scatter its enemies like chaff before the wind. Another reason for avoiding a rupture with the northern kingdom was of economic origin. France was still a leading market for Florentine goods and enterprise, which the government at Paris could destroy over night by directing the expulsion of the Florentine merchants from the kingdom. Finally, there was Savonarola. We have seen that he had from the time of his second sojourn at San Marco authenticated himself with the Florentines as a prophet sent by God by solemnly announcing the approaching punishment and reform of the church. When, following the death of Lorenzo de' Medici, the expedition of Charles VIII began dimly to take shape across the Alps, the friar became more definite in his language and proclaimed the French king as the tool by which God would effect the needed reformation. During the passage of the French through Tuscany, Savonarola repeatedly had speech with Charles and on these occasions never failed to utter the hortatory words his solemn faith imposed. "O most Christian king," he would say, "you are an instrument in the hand of the Lord who has sent you to cure the ills of Italy, as I have long since predicted. He sends you also to reform the church which lies prostrate on the ground. . . . Should you forget the work for which you are sent, the Lord will choose another to carry it out and will punish you with terrible scourgings. I say this to you in the name of the Lord." [4]

When we recall that these and similar words were addressed to a half-witted dwarf, whom an accident of birth had invested with the purple and who had come to Italy not to cure the country's ills but to take advantage of them for his selfish ends, we receive an impression of the immense gulf yawning between the substance of Savonarola's dreams and the realities of life from which there is no escape. Intent upon his inner voices, Savonarola completely overlooked the palpable insufficiency of the sovereign whom he summoned to great deeds. Had he employed his native shrewdness, which was excellent, he would quickly have reduced this imaginary Charlemagne to the simpleton he was. But native shrewdness enjoys no credit among prophets exalted by heavenly visions and commands. Being what he was, the friar went the narrow road traced by his convictions. It led unescapably to that martyrdom which he predicted for himself and which he craved. Every solemn commitment of his spirit, and not least among them his visionary misapprehension of the character of Charles VIII, contributed to the preordained catharsis. For even after steadily increasing numbers of Florentines had become disillusioned about Charles, Savonarola clung to him as the savior designate of both Florence and the corrupt church and used his immense

[4] Villari, Vol. I, Book II, chap. 2.

influence over the common people to maintain the French alliance. For his well-born enemies, the Arrabbiati, he had been ever since the revolution the man responsible for the new constitution and the democratic trend of the successive signories. As the years rolled by, with constantly increasing vehemence they charged him also with shaping the city's foreign policy. They raged at him as the secret ruler of the state, as that abhorrent thing, the hypocritical priest with an unslaked thirst for political power.

Although the charge of political ambition is still occasionally lodged against Savonarola in our day, it is undoubtedly based on a complete misconception. Fra Girolamo was a son of the Middle Ages, a logical product of the faith that the individual's leading concern on earth is the issue of life eternal, the issue of salvation. Not to leave bewildered man without guidance, God in his mercy has established the great institution of the church and committed to it the authority to save or to destroy. Never for a moment throughout his life did Savonarola doubt the divine power conferred upon the church. To his sorrow, however, and to the sorrow of all true believers, under a succession of worldly popes culminating in the abominable Borgia, Alexander VI, the church had grown so profoundly corrupt that it was threatened with estrangement from its mission. For a dedicated spirit like the friar, it was not difficult to become persuaded that the degenerate church must imperatively be renewed and that he was the man appointed by God to that end. To this central purpose, as wide as Christianity itself, was joined a purpose of more local import which grew out of his residence in Florence and his identification with the weal and woe of that particular community. On the immense following he had acquired on the Arno he made it his business to inculcate the need of daily living in the love and fear of God. This implied a reform of morals, which he regarded as the logical and unescapable concomitant to the reform of the church. It is possible that since the reform of morals could be inaugurated on the reformer's own initiative and without vexatious delays, it received at times greater attention in his sermons than the reform of the church. Essentially, however, Savonarola regarded the two reforms as inseparable and entertained no preference for one as against the other. Yet the fact stands out that, a minor and feeble member of the Catholic hierarchy, he made no headway with the reform of the vast institution of the church, while his attack on the evil customs of the Florentines brought him a notable success. Granted that it was ephemeral, as successes in this field have always been, still it constituted a seven-day wonder in his time and may not be passed over without notice.

A perusal of the friar's sermons will show that in attacking the evil daily practices of his Florentine fellow-citizens he unfolds the picture of a society essentially identical with that disclosed by puritanical preachers of every degree before and since his day. The Florentine men were reckless gamblers and blasphemers; their women decked themselves out in finery, painted their faces, and shamelessly displayed their physical charms. It would be absurd to maintain that these were novel transgressions or that it was a phenomenon of recent origin that the streets were infested with courtesans and that sodomy and other sexual perversities flourished. When and wherever men have built towns and developed an urban civilization, excrescences of the kind scourged in the friar's sermons have put in an appearance and have obstinately resisted eradication. Undiscouraged by past failures, Savonarola resolved to attack the reeking corruption of Florence with a view to creating a truly religious community fit to serve as a model for the rest of the evil world. Once upon a time, according to the official Christian doctrine, the Jews had been such a community ruled by the invisible Jehovah and led and admonished by his prophets. In Savonarola's ambitious design the Florentines were to be the chosen people of the modern world, acknowledging Christ as their king and the lowly prior of San Marco as Christ's prime minister.

Admitting again that never in history have the preachers of moral perfection made other than a temporary impression, we may fairly marvel at the measure of success achieved at Florence in his heyday by the Dominican friar. Courtesans and gamblers went into hiding; ribald street songs were replaced by pious hymns; men and women alike adopted a plain and modest dress and were untiring in their attendance at mass and sermon. Particularly remarked was the way the religious fervor took hold of the youths and children. Under the direction of the prior's most devoted follower, Fra Domenico da Pescia, they formed themselves into volunteer bands organized according to the parish in which they resided. They proclaimed themselves guardians of the town's morality and, roaming the streets of their quarter, induced gamblers to hand over the tools of their trade and women too fashionably attired to renounce their scandalous display. The plentiful, year-round merrymaking of the town had been wont to mount to a climax during carnival, which was characterized by a succession of disgraceful public orgies. Lorenzo de' Medici had fostered these practices, although to refer them to him as their author is a wildly partisan perversion of the truth. The cleansing of the city of its carnival excesses became a cardinal point in Savonarola's program of moral reform and in attempting to uproot them he wisely looked about for an equivalent. What were the usual sportive masquerades other than an indulgence of the flesh and a triumph of Satan? He, too, would have the people range the streets with songs upon their lips. But the songs would be religious lauds, and what had hitherto been a season of secular folly would be transformed into a joyous festival of the Lord. Then, on the last, the culminating day of the carnival he would send the whole population, men, women, and children, in religious procession through the streets to gather them at last in the duomo to receive the divine blessing delivered by the prophet's mouth.

In the year 1497 the friar added a feature to this carnival program, the rumor of which is loud in the world to this day. He ordered the children to make a house to house canvass to the end of persuading the occupants to surrender some small possession to which their heart was unduly attached. These "vanities" were piled together in a vast pyramid in the central piazza and the concluding act of the carnival, converted under the new dispensation into a season of penance, was the setting on fire of the inflammable heap, while trumpeters sounded a fanfare that made itself heard above the roar of the flames. This is the famous Burning of the Vanities, which was repeated the following year (1498), the last of Savonarola's life, when, in sign of the prophet's waning power, it was almost broken up by his enemies. There is little to recommend the ceremony to the sober judgment of mankind, and subsequent champions of moral reform have not seen fit to imitate it. But misrepresentations of the event fathered by the Dominican's enemies must be rejected. There is no proof whatever that valuable books and irreplacable works of art were sacrificed to the flames. The surrendered vanities were conceived as symbols of the worldly life, and there is good reason to believe that the bonfire, which, like all bonfires, delighted the hosts of children, consumed nothing more valuable than carnival masques, dice, obscene books, and lascivious pictures together with innumerable trivialities of dress and furniture.

To charge a man so exclusively set on creating an austere Christian society with political ambition is, let it be said again, flatly to misunderstand his type. Savonarola never sat in the Grand Council or the signory, he participated in no elections or party caucuses. Undeniably, however, these surface facts are not the whole story. For, though not a direct political agent, indirectly he figured in all the acts of government through his moral influence over the supporters of the democratic system, the Popolari. To this system he had committed himself at a critical moment with no idea of pleasing anyone other than the God in whom he put his faith. Fiercely hating tyranny because of its secret crimes and moral laxity, he wanted in the interest of the religious society which was his aim to close the gates forever on the Medici and justly concluded that the most effective way of achieving that result was a broadly based popular regime. In the same way his unwavering support of Charles VIII, in spite of its purely religious motivation, had unavoidable political implications. With every honorable intention to limit himself to the part of friar and prophet he was pushed into the arena of politics to sustain the cause for which he believed he was sent by God. As a result, although not intentionally a politician, he succeeded in offending powerful political forces, which by finally combining against him proved his undoing.

The undoing of Savonarola constitutes an intrigue so extraordinarily involved that full justice cannot be done it under many chapters. It will therefore have to suffice to assemble its leading elements and carry them forward to their tragic climax. The foremost as well as the most constant plotters against the friar were the great Florentine families, the optimates, loosely associated in the party of the Arrabbiati. They were well represented in the Grand Council and occasionally placed representatives in the signory, but for the first two years of the new government they were in such general disfavor that they were unable to injure Savonarola directly. Their impotence in their own community led them to resort to Rome, where, because of their wealth and social position, they had no difficulty in getting a hearing. Their plan was to work upon Pope Alexander VI and by filling him with alarm regarding the friar's program of ecclesiastical reform to persuade him, by virtue of the authority vested in him, to remove the offender from Florence or at the very least to condemn him to silence. In this early and still relatively harmless stage of the conflict there was as yet no desire to take Savonarola's life. Since, to their disgust, the plotters had but a doubtful success with Alexander, it will be necessary before going any farther to examine this celebrated personage somewhat more closely. Undeniably one of the most infamous pontiffs of history, he was not just that sum of all conceivable infamy as he has been often described and, taken as which, he becomes a devil incarnate and is no longer a man. Where there are so many proved iniquities we should not find it difficult to dispense with figments. Let it suffice that Alexander Borgia was addicted to all the lusts of the flesh; that he had many children into whose lap he did not scruple to pour the riches of the church; that he purchased his elevation to the papacy by open and scandalous bribery; and that, enthroned on St. Peter's chair, he sold, as it were under the hammer, all the dispensations, pardons, bishoprics, and cardinalates at his disposal. These abominations notwithstanding, he was a man of good intelligence and a capable administrator. It does not help our understanding of the papal policy toward Savonarola to conceive of its author as an ogre bent on indiscriminate mischief.

We bring Alexander into correct historical focus if we say of him that, like many other men of the culminating Renaissance, he had lost both his religion and his morals by his too exclusive pursuit of purely selfish advantage. With his grossly material outlook on the world he had no immediate interest in the friar who was making such a stir in nearby Florence by preaching the reform of morals and the church. Of course Alexander did not believe in either of these reforms; but what, versed in the cynic wisdom of the world, he did believe was that the Dominican's enthusiasm would soon evaporate and that, as in a score of similar cases of which he had had personal experience, in the end the forces of social inertia, than which there was nothing stronger in the world, would win the day. The feature of Savonarola's activity the pope liked least was the friar's assigning the role of reformer of the church to the powerful king of France. However, now that Charles had come and gone, even this dangerous vagary of the Ferrarese need not be taken too seriously.

Unable greatly to excite the Holy Father about the religious agitation of the Dominican, the Arrabbiati agents at Rome turned next to his political activity and at once met with a much livelier response. For politics, whether of the church or state, constituted Alexander's only genuine interest. In forcing his way during his recent campaign through the State of the Church the irresistible king of France had deeply humiliated the pope; and when the great league was formed to oblige the French to relinquish their Neapolitan prey, Alexander had not hesitated to join it. Since then his policy in regard to Charles VIII was clearly mapped out. He must hold with the anti-French combination in order by a solid front to dissuade the French sovereign from repeating his Italian adventure. And in regard to Florence, the one Italian state which by clinging obstinately to the French alliance extended a perpetual invitation to the northern invader to return to the assault, it was Alexander's opinion, which his neighbors of Venice, Naples, and Milan shared, that every available ounce of diplomatic pressure must be brought to bear on the Arno government to draw it into the anti-French league. We have already examined the situation and listed the reasons why Florence stubbornly refused to give up the French connection. While they may be said to have been inspired in the main by the public interest, indubitably one reason not of a public nature was Savonarola. In his capacity of missionary and prophet the friar inclined violently toward France and by his support made the French party in the government invincible.

As soon as Alexander was persuaded that Savonarola was a factor in the hateful foreign policy of Florence he was much more ready to consider taking measures against him. But as the information that reached him from his private agents in Florence revealed that even without the friar the government would persist in its pro-French attitude, he refused to commit himself to the Arrabbiati and handled the problem created by the inconvenient reformer after his own judgment. He tried repeatedly to draw Savonarola to Rome. However, when the Dominican, suspecting a trap, urgently but politely excused himself, the pope showed no particular resentment and let the matter drop. For almost two years the best efforts of the Arrabbiati to get Alexander to use his ecclesiastical power against Savonarola produced no appreciable result. Nonetheless, in these two years the friar was becoming increasingly outspoken in his denunciation of the church and its servants, priests and prelates alike; and although he carefully avoided mentioning names, he was sufficiently precise to leave no doubt in the mind of his hearers that he regarded the Holy Father as the greatest sinner of them all. Constantly annoyed by and frequently enraged against his merciless critic, the pope at last resolved on reprisals and on November 7, 1496, issued a brief by which he deprived the convent of San Marco of its independence and subordinated it to the provincial of the Tusco-Roman congregation. What lent the order a directly punitive character was that the independence of San Marco was a gift which Alexander himself had made to Savonarola only three years before. Had the new decree become effective, the friar could have been lifted out of San Marco and transferred from Florence to some small provincial town by the stroke of the pen of his new Dominican chief. This was of course the purpose of the order, which Fra Girolamo so clearly understood that he was resolved in his heart never to accept it. His dispatch of a remonstrance to Alexander was interpreted as open recalcitrancy and for the first time persuaded the pope that, unless he was prepared to surrender the leadership of the church to the friar, he must bring him to heel. But even though he was the omnipotent head of the Christian congregation, there were precautions to be observed in view of the attachment the Florentines manifested for their prophet and of the wisdom of not unnecessarily offending a civil government the pope and the other Italian powers were attempting to lure away from the French. Not till a change of popular sentiment had been effected and a gonfalonier of Justice headed the signory who was not of the Savonarolist persuasion would it be safe to proceed against the friar with the vigor to be expected from an authoritative pontiff.

To the pope's chagrin the signories of the winter of 1496–97 were as devoted to the prior as any that had gone before. During the January-February term of 1497 the tide seemed to run even more strongly in Savonarola's favor, inasmuch as Francesco Valori was elected to the post of gonfalonier of Justice. Valori was the most energetic statesman of the democratic party and so completely under the friar's spell that he held the prophet's divine inspiration to

be no less sure than the Day of Judgment. It was under his gonfalonierat that
the inverted carnival of 1497 culminated in the first Burning of the Vanities.
However, because of a natural reaction to these excesses, the next signory (of
the March-April term) was of Bigi or Medicean complexion; and the signory
after that was of even worse augury for the Piagnoni, for it was strongly
Arrabbiati. As in every republic, the mass of Florentine voters was subject to
these sudden fluctuations, which did not necessarily signify a change of fundamental opinion. Still the successive enemy signories were dangerous, since
Bigi and Arrabbiati, although hostile to each other, agreed in hating the democratic regime and its leading sponsor, the friar. By dispatching his November
brief against him Alexander had again drawn close to the Arrabbiati; and
when, early in the following May, certain extremists in the Arrabbiati ranks
started a riot in the crowded cathedral during one of Fra Girolamo's sermons,
the pope was delighted. The outburst was happily suppressed before it became
general, but with an Arrabbiati signory in the seat of power and a hostile
demonstration conducted under the very nose of the prophet, Alexander VI
persuaded himself that the time had come for a more energetic offensive. Consequently he now hurled his long-threatened decree of excommunication at the
friar, justifying his act on the ground of Savonarola's flagrant disregard of the
papal rescript of the previous November. On June 18, 1497, the document was
read with the usual impressive ceremonies in the leading churches of Florence.
Henceforth retreat on the part of the pope was not possible. It was war between the head of the church and his rebellious subject, a distressingly unequal
war, which the friar might sustain for a period but in which he would be
disastrously defeated the moment the Florentine people no longer lent him
their enthusiastic support.

While the events just recounted had occurred during an Arrabbiati signory,
that signory did not feel strong enough as yet to employ its ascendancy for a
final stroke against its enemy. In fact the aroused Piagnoni rallied their forces
so successfully in the Grand Council that the signories following that of the
May-June period were again favorable to the friar. Cheered by this renewed support, his indomitable spirit now resolved to scale the last height and to defy and
ultimately to depose his enemy, the pope, with the machinery supplied by
ecclesiastical tradition. On Christmas Day he administered communion to the
brothers of San Marco and, shortly after, he resumed his public preaching. A
more flagrant offense against age-old Catholic practice was not conceivable, for
by the renewed exercise of his ecclesiastical functions he boldly set the papal
excommunication at nought. At the same time he took a step even more offensive to the pope in that he opened negotiations with the princes of Christendom with a view to persuading them to call a General Council. The papal
sinner and criminal was to be brought to trial before the supreme bar of the
church. To be sure, this latter action of the friar's, which proceeded under cover
of the greatest secrecy, did not become generally known till long afterward; but
the flouting of the excommunication was a demonstration conducted in the public view and for this open defiance of the ancient ordinances of Christianity conservative Florentine opinion was not prepared. Again and again in the past the
city had on one ground or another resisted the Holy Father, but it had never

dreamt of challenging his ecclesiastical supremacy. With opinions clashing in the streets and squares more vehemently than ever, the timid and lukewarm among the citizenry began to leave the friar's camp; and when the elections for the March-April signory of 1498 took place the victory went in a decisive manner to Savonarola's enemies.

The pope could now play his last card. He declared that unless his disobedient subject be delivered into his hands for punishment, he would put the whole city under interdict. While in some ways the surrender of the friar's person might appeal to his local enemies as a convenient way of washing their hands of him, they had too keen an understanding of their countrymen to believe in its practicality. For, should they hand over the prophet to his Roman executioner, not only would his popularity flare up afresh but they would put such a stigma on their own name as would quickly bring their regime to an inglorious fall. They would have to take the matter of ridding the city of the fanatic into their own hands; and before taking his life they would have to bring him into discredit and, more particularly, they would have to deprive him of his halo as a prophet. While with vacillating thoughts they were pondering the thorny problem, an incident was created by the San Marco brotherhood itself, which with the sharp clairvoyance of hate they foresaw could, if skilfully manipulated, be made to bring about the desired result.

In speaking of the organized bands of children we had occasion to mention a disciple, Fra Domenico da Pescia, who stood next in authority at San Marco after Savonarola and who by his utter devotion to his chief had come to be regarded almost as his other self. To him the prophet character of Fra Girolamo was so incontrovertible that he was ready to prove it by going through fire. As the city was full of scoffers, Brother Domenico had been moved to repeat from time to time his offer of the fire test without any immediate effect until a friar of the rival Franciscan order took the matter up. It is highly probable that the Franciscan was persuaded to come to the front by a group of Savonarola's enemies, from whom he received a secret promise of protection from the consequences of his hardihood. The plan of the plotters was to have the current Arrabbiati signory take the affair in hand, go through with all the preparations for an old-fashioned ordeal by fire, work up the miracle-loving masses to the highest pitch of excitement, and then let them down abruptly by an adjournment which would be dishonestly laid to the door of Savonarola and his friars. In view of the blind and unsuspecting zeal of Fra Domenico, a zeal which he shared with the whole San Marco brotherhood, it was easy to get the intrigue under way. Not one of the two hundred and fifty brothers but envied Fra Domenico the honor of bearing witness before assembled Florence to the divine mission of their beloved master. For that the prior was the authentic messenger of God had by now become the basic article of their renewed Christian faith. Since he had prophesied again and again and the prophecy had always been fulfilled, it could not be other than that on this supreme occasion the Father Omnipotent would cool the ardor of the flames and permit the prophet's champion to walk through them unscathed. Although Savonarola had had nothing to do with the affair in its initial stages and apparently disapproved of it, he saw no way of breaking off negotiations after they had begun, as he could not possibly exhibit less faith in supernatural intervention in his behalf than did his followers. By the end of March there was talk in Florence of nothing else but the ordeal, until to appease the constantly waxing excitement the plotting signory, assuming the willing role of impresario, proclaimed that it should take place on Saturday, April 7.

On the afternoon of that day the great piazza before the palace of the priors presented an extraordinary sight. Opposite what is now called the Loggia dei Lanzi stretched a long rectangular heap of firewood with a passage in the middle through which, when the match had been applied, Fra Domenico da Pescia and his Franciscan challenger were supposed to walk to prove or disprove the prophetic claim of the prior of San Marco. The two champions, each surrounded by the chanting and praying members of his order, were gathered under the great stone vaults of the Loggia; the lordly signory, in its role of umpire, occupied the platform in front of the palace; and in the piazza pressed and from the windows and house roofs hung suspended a vast and wildly agitated mass of citizens. We call the period the Renaissance and glibly speak of it as pagan. Yet we should have to go back four hundred years in Florentine history, into the deep Middle Ages, to encounter a comparable spectacle. It was in the year 1068 that a Vallombrosan monk, celebrated after the event as Petrus Igneus, walked through the flames in nearby Settimo to attest the truthfulness of the charge of simony lodged against the bishop of Florence.[5] Gazing at the spectacle afforded on that April day of the closing quattrocento by the Florentine piazza a pessimistic philosopher might have been moved to affirm that life perpetually repeats itself and that there is nothing new under the sun. And yet, compared with the earlier ordeal, there was something new which, could our putative philosopher have known of it, might only have deepened his pessimism. This novelty was that the show that met his eye was a pure hoax arranged by a skeptical signory for selfish political purposes, and that this exalted body had no intention whatever of going through with the game. Accordingly, they welcomed one trivial objection after another presented by the Franciscans until the afternoon wore away with futile negotiations between the contesting parties. The packed and perspiring multitude was already showing signs of impatience when a heavy shower descended soaking everyone to the skin. More negotiations were followed by more delays until, as the day died, the signory announced that, owing to the lateness of the hour, the ordeal would have to be adjourned.

It did not require the whispers of the enemies of the friar to put the blame for the fiasco on his shoulders. Even his ardent followers were inclined to find fault with him, for they had worked themselves up to such a frenzy of faith that in their opinion Fra Domenico da Pescia should, if necessary, have been sent into the flames alone to provoke the confidently expected miracle. The first effect of the plotters had been achieved in the sudden decline of Fra Girolamo's favor following the disappointments of the day. To pursue their advantage they organized demonstrations around San Marco and by the evening of the next day (April 8), a Sunday, they had succeeded in assembling a mob which surged in frenzied excitement around the place, threatening to

[5] See chap. IV, p. 48.

set it on fire and level it with the ground. The first mood of the brothers, heartened by the crowding to their aid of numerous adherents from among the citizens, was to meet force with force. However, when commissioners from the signory appeared with a warrant for Savonarola's arrest, he promptly agreed to surrender in order to avoid bloodshed and civil war. Together with Brothers Domenico and Silvestro, his two closest associates, he was led through the seething, howling mob, which cuffed and spat upon him to vent its hideous spite, and thrown into prison.

Filled with rejoicing, the Arrabbiati pressed the signory to complete its triumph without delay. Composed as it was of the friar's enemies, that body needed no urging to pursue its advantage. It appointed a commission of the most ferocious opponents of Savonarola to subject him and his two fellow-prisoners to a criminal inquisition. The one certain statement this commission was determined from the start to get from its victim was the confession that he was an impostor. To this position the friar's enemies were forced by the fact that nothing less than the friar bearing witness against himself would serve to destroy the legend which had grown up around him. Accordingly, for several days in succession he was put to horrible, bone-racking torture after the monstrous criminal procedure of the day. Not till, unable any longer to support his sufferings, he left the path of truth and gave ambiguous answers to the questions put to him were his tormentors satisfied. On handing over the pathetic evidence they had thus secured to a notary for "editing," the unscrupulous scribe converted it into a clear confession of fraud and in this form published it to the world. The effect for the moment at least was overwhelming. Not only Christian Florence but Christian Italy as well, if it is permissible, at the turn of the century, to speak of such an entity, was stunned into silence and sorrow. The prophet was a confessed deceiver, the light that had risen over the land had gone out.

All that remained now was to put the friar out of the way before a reaction should set in in his favor. However, as he belonged to the clerical order, it was impossible to proceed with his execution without the consent of the pope. Alexander at first took the position that his honor required that the offender be delivered into his hands for trial at Rome; but when the signory made it clear that they would under no circumstances surrender their prey, he yielded and agreed to dispatch two commissioners to Florence to review the case in behalf of the church. When they arrived on May 20, the torture began all over again till a fresh body of incriminating admissions had been wrung from the three anguished victims. They were then declared guilty of heresy and handed over for punishment to the secular arm in accordance with the ancient, hypo-critical pretense that the church never spills blood. The verdict of heresy was precisely what the signory needed in connection with its campaign of destroying the reputation of its victim before crushing his life. No sooner had the church spoken than the government named the following day, which was May 23, as the day of execution. As the custom ran in such instances, the wretched men were to be first hanged and immediately afterward to be destroyed by fire.

Six weeks after the great spectacle which had proved such a sorry failure, the Florentines were offered another spectacle, which it was certain would not be a failure because the government that stage-managed both events was as firmly resolved to make a success of the one as it had been determined to ruin the other. Again the center of interest was a wooden pyre, from which, an unbroken mass of brush and logs, there reared itself with an ominous gesture a tall gallows with three arms, from each of which dangled a stout rope. The pyre in the center of the piazza was connected with the palace by an elevated wooden walk, over which the three victims were to proceed on their last journey. Against the gallows rested a ladder, on which stood the expectant executioner. At the appointed hour the three friars were conducted slowly from the palace across the platform to the foot of the ladder. They had recovered their courage and bore themselves with the dignified humility demanded by their faith. Fra Silvestro was the first to mount the ladder and have the noose adjusted to his throat. Fra Domenico came next; the last was Fra Girolamo. They could not yet have been dead as the hangman leaped to his torch and set his inflammable pile ablaze. When, some hours later, the fierce fire had spent itself, the charred scraps of what had once been men and pious Christians were gathered up by the city scavengers and tossed into the Arno to be carried away to oblivion and the sea.

Owing to two remarkable portraits by which the painter, Bartolommeo della Porta, has preserved the appearance of Fra Girolamo Savonarola, his features have been so often reproduced that they are perhaps better known than those of any man of his age. Carried away as a young man by the friar's call to repentance, Bartolommeo joined the Dominican order after the tragic end of his spiritual guide and ended his days in the hallowed precincts of San Marco. One of his pictures now hangs in the cell which Savonarola occupied as prior and which retains its simple, solemn character unchanged to this day. The painting, showing the friar in profile, displays a powerful hooked nose, a heavy, drooping lower lip, and a firm-set jaw. The deep hollow under the high cheek bone speaks of fasting and privations; the dark cowl drawn over the head almost to the eyes reveals a spirit withdrawn from the world, intent on the eternities. If Savonarola's sermons and writings had been swallowed up by Time and the most immediate remaining item of evidence regarding the man were this strangely haunting face, we should find it easy to convince ourselves that the charge launched against him by his enemies that he was an impostor is absurd. On this face are stamped austerity, truthfulness, and an uncompromising sincerity. It belongs to one who, having earnestly sought and found God, as earnestly preached him to his countrymen in the resolute hope of bringing them to the foot of the Cross. The owner of this face authenticates himself without effort as one of the long succession of the saints and martyrs constituting the church militant of Christianity.

On turning from the man to his mission an equally conclusive judgment is not possible. His two leading modern biographers, Villari and Schnitzer, while recognizing his radical antagonism to the main trends of his period, nonetheless concede him a considerable relevance in its general moral, religious, and political set-up. This view the present author is unable to share. Regardless of the depth, the sincerity, the rarely unified character of the friar, he sees him, in the language of modern biology, as a throw-back or, in terms more immediately relevant to history, as an anachronism. The plain and undeniable fact is that Savonarola lived his life among strictly medieval thoughts and feelings, and that with a vigor worthy of unstinted admiration he tried to revitalize them in an age, into the altered conditions of which they could no longer be fitted. To have had something more than the brief sensational success that attended his revivalist preaching it would have been necessary for Florence not merely to rid itself, as the reformer perpetually urged, of its gamblers and courtesans, of its wastrels and usurers, but also to close its banks and warehouses, to surrender its Tuscan conquests, to reduce itself once more to the dimensions of a country market, and, as a final measure, to wreck its Palazzo Pubblico and tear down its cathedral. Like the uncompromising heir of the Middle Ages he was, Savonarola preached that nothing mattered but the life beyond the grave and that the only proper concern of the sinful son of Adam during his mundane sojourn was salvation. In spite of the advance during recent generations of a civilization opposed to these ideals and energetically bent on taking possession of the earth and its fruits, there was still so large a residuum of medieval thought and feeling in the average Florentine that a large proportion of the citizens instinctively responded to Savonarola's impassioned call to repentance. No one, in view of the friar's failure and end, will doubt that he lit in their hearts a mere fire of straw. At the same time it is indisputable that his leading opponents, well-to-do merchants and religious skeptics, fell far below him in integrity of character and moral worth. If nonetheless they won the victory, it was because, accepting the new day which had arisen over Europe and which it was not in their power to turn back, they fought on the side of destiny for an expanding as against a stationary or a retreating civilization. In final historical analysis the issue between two contending individuals or groups does not and cannot reduce itself to the simple question of the moral worth of each, for in every such issue are involved also innumerable social and intellectual forces, whose strength and incidence are an inseparable part of the problem. It was the verdict of these latter forces that Savonarola was an impediment in their path. Therefore they swept him aside; but as he stood his ground unyieldingly, heroically, until the advancing hostile flood poured over him, he will always live in the memory of mankind as a soul that, refusing commerce with corruption, kept the faith.

XXVII. The Revived Republic: The Story of a Living Corpse (1498–1512)

S O COMPLETELY was Savonarola identified with Florence and so dominatingly did his figure for a period of almost four years rise above the turmoil of Italian politics that his individual eminence concealed from the general view the fact that the revived republic was woefully without power and authority. And yet such was the unchallengeable truth. Ever since that November day of the year 1494 when Charles VIII made a triumphant entry into the city, Florence had become a client of France and owed such security among its neighbors as it enjoyed to the distant French protector enforced by the nervous expectation of his early return to the scene of his meteoric glory. From a narrowly territorial angle the leading event of the passage of the French army through Tuscany had been the revolt of Pisa. Violently as Piagnoni, Arrabbiati, and Bigi might quarrel with each other as to the kind of government best suited to the city, in regard to the Pisan rebellion they were of a single mind and prepared unitedly to forswear liberty and life itself rather than to accept Pisan independence. But in the span of almost four years since Charles's expedition nothing of any consequence had been done to realize the purpose with which everybody declared he was animated. Calling loudly on Heaven to witness their violated integrity, when it came to action the Florentines had shown themselves feeble to the point of impotence. With all their spiteful neighbors lending open or secret support to Pisa, the rebel city had thus far mocked at the threats of the Red Lily to bring it again under its yoke.

As soon, however, as the distracting issues raised by Savonarola had been disposed of, at least temporarily, by his death, the government resolved to prosecute the Pisan matter with greater energy and intrusted a celebrated Italian condottiere, Pagolo Vitelli, with the commission to lay siege to Pisa till it was captured. Doubtless the death of Charles VIII, which by a curious coincidence took place on the very day of the famous ordeal by fire that did not come off, was a factor in the heartening spurt of governmental vigor. For Charles was morally pledged to turn Pisa over to Florence, and as long as he lived his Tuscan dependents were free to indulge themselves in the hope that he would some day become conscious of his responsibility and utter the Olympian word that would cow Pisa into surrender. With his death that dream was dispelled and, cheated of its French hopes, the government felt prompted for the first time to rely on itself alone. In choosing Vitelli as commander-in-chief of its forces it probably made as good a choice as the circumstances permitted.

In the approved manner of his hireling tribe Vitelli went about his task with such deliberation that months passed before Pisa was invested. Then, when after new delays, his cannon had made a breach in the walls and all Florence was joyously expecting from moment to moment to hear that the town had been taken by storm, the lame news reached the city that Vitelli had withdrawn to a safe distance in order to rest his exhausted troops. It was too much for the disappointed government and citizens. Commissioners were dispatched to the camp with orders to arrest Vitelli and bring him in chains to Florence. The condottiere, whose sole guilt probably was that he conducted war in strict accordance with the principles in which he had been reared, was tried on the charge of treason and executed (October, 1499).

At the very time the first assault on Pisa worthy of the name came to this lamentable end, the whole Italian situation was undergoing one of its frequent kaleidoscopic changes in the wake of a new French invasion. It was conducted by Louis XII (1498–1515), head of the Orléans branch of the royal line, who succeeded Charles VIII on the latter's demise without direct heirs. More a humdrum burgher than a victim, like his predecessor, of the glamorous romances of chivalry, Louis was nonetheless a king with a tradition to uphold; and no sooner had the crown been placed upon his head than he began preparations for a new invasion of Italy. In correction of his predecessor's mistaken strategy directed solely at the conquest of Naples, he resolved as a necessary preliminary measure on the seizure of Milan. This state lay just across the Alps from France and was the logical base for any military action conducted in the peninsula by an invader from the north. Should we assume that the geographical argument did not of itself suffice to direct the sovereign against Milan, there was the additional circumstance that, as duke of Orléans, Louis had been brought up in the tradition that the Lombard duchy belonged of right to him, since he was the heir of the Visconti predecessor of the upstart and usurping Sforza. Nor, in making his preliminary survey of the situation, did the king overlook the advisability of operating in Italy with Italian allies. While Florence could no doubt be counted on morally, the amount of calculable physical aid the badly shaken republic might give was highly problematical. It therefore greatly cheered Louis to receive an offer of help from another and far more important quarter.

Immediately on mounting the throne Louis XII had approached Pope Alexander VI in a strictly private issue, in which he required papal support. He wished to divorce his wife and marry Anne, the widow of his predecessor, in order to make sure that the province of Brittany, of which she was duchess, would remain merged with the royal domain. Save by special dispensation from the pope the desired divorce was impossible. Accordingly, Louis presented himself as a petitioner at Rome and found Alexander unexpectedly well disposed because that sharp bargainer, who never in his life gave anything for nothing, desired a return favor. He had a young son, Caesar, to whom, as to all his children, he was passionately devoted, and whom he wished to establish in the world as an independent prince. In theory this was not difficult, since he would be doing no more than following the example set by his immediate predecessors if he made over to Caesar one or another

of the many territories belonging to the State of the Church. A practical obstacle to this procedure, however, lay in the circumstance that the papal lands
were already held by rulers, euphemistically called vicars but really independent sovereigns, whose formal acknowledgment of the papal suzerainty did not
hinder them from doing very much as they pleased. If the pope wished to set
up his son as a ruler in Umbria or the Romagna, he could only do so by dis-
placing an existent tyrant; and in order to effect such a displacement he could
not dispense with military power. As soon as Louis XII approached the pope
with the request to grant him the dispensation, which would cut the bonds
tieing him to his queen, Alexander declared himself ready to strike a bargain.
Completely reversing himself in regard to the French, whom to keep out of
Italy he had thus far been unintermittently busy, he affirmed his willingness
not only to promote the divorce, but also to support the king's projected campaign against Milan if, in exchange, Louis would marry Caesar to a lady related, no matter how remotely, to the royal house and if, further, he would
lend young Borgia the French troops necessary to effect a lodgment by force
of arms in the State of the Church.

The bargain, advantageous to both sides, was struck with the result that
when in the late summer of the year 1499 the French again crossed the Alps,
the young and darkly handsome Caesar Borgia, recently married to a royal
relative and created, as an added favor, duke of Valentinois, rode proudly in
the train of the French monarch. So weak was the Milanese state that it required no more than the presence of the French army to produce its collapse.
Lodovico the Moor escaped capture by hurriedly crossing the Alps into Germany, and King Louis, after entering the capital as conqueror and planting a
garrison in its citadel, ended a pleasant, sight-seeing tour of northern Italy by
going home to receive the congratulations of his court. Taking advantage of
the opportunity afforded by the king's withdrawal, in February, 1500, the ever-
adventurous Lodovico staged a sudden return from Germany and for a few
days flattered himself that he had recaptured his duchy. It was a gross mis-
calculation, for, as soon as the surprised French had assembled their scattered
forces, the Moor's unpaid Swiss mercenaries deserted him and, unable this
time to escape the net flung about him, he was captured and transported for
safekeeping to France. There, some ten years later, he ended his life in a dun-
geon. No contemporary Italian with as much as a touch of patriotism can
have viewed the catastrophe of the Moor with any other feeling than that a
traitor had received his reward.

No sooner had the French effected the conquest of Milan than Caesar Borgia, in command of a body of royal troops, proceeded southward into the
Romagna in adventurous quest of a kingdom. He began with the towns of
Imola and Forlì, which did not yield to him without offering rather more resistance than Caesar had expected. Having organized their government, he
carefully scanned the scene with a view to deciding where and whom to strike
next. Already his first swift action had drawn the eyes of the peninsula on
himself. Instinctively the country sensed a political portent, and as the months
and years passed by, disclosing fresh and ever bolder aggressions committed
by the young condottiere, who had behind him both the pope and the king of

France, his figure gained in stature till it dwarfed all the other actors on the Italian stage. It does not fall within the scope of this book to trace the steps, by which young Borgia, usually called Valentino by his countrymen from his French ducal title, consolidated his successive brutal seizures and bloody conquests. Let it suffice to mention that in the course of little more than three years he succeeded in uprooting a score of petty tyrants planted in papal territory and in assembling his whirlwind gains into a single political unit. Technically, even after his conquests had been consolidated, they constituted not his personal realm but the State of the Church and owned the pope as their ruler. No one doubted, however, that Caesar was firmly resolved to keep as his property what he had seized, as it was also universally assumed that the pope, his father, was so completely under the son's domination that he was fully prepared to commit the monstrous felony of alienating the patrimony of St. Peter in order to supply his bastard with the territorial basis required for a self-perpetuating dynasty.

While all Italy followed these astonishing developments with a mind fluctuating between terror and fascination, even more than with Caesar Borgia's actions the country was intrigued by the personality of this latest military adventurer sprung from its fertile loins. For here surely was the summit, the super-condottiere, to whom his numerous lawless predecessors beginning with Ezzelino da Romagna were but stepping-stones. This suddenly risen Valentino was tall, handsome of feature, powerfully built. Although he had not been brought up to arms, he showed himself to have been born to them from the first moment that he assumed command. He had also the rare executive gift enabling him to penetrate at a glance to the core of a problem. Finally, hard as flint and pitiless as a beast of the jungle, he subordinated every human consideration to his dream of grandeur and was prepared to go through fire and wade through blood to reach his goal. Since there seemed to be no limit to Valentino's ambition, he spread an alarm through the small states of the peninsula which in the case of his most immediate neighbors, the Florentines, rose intermittently to panic. When we recall that the sons of the Red Lily had recently established a republic of a democratic pattern and that in their public conduct since that event they had exhibited a painful lack of self-assurance, we should not be surprised to learn that Duke Valentino's activities along the unprotected line of their eastern border gave them the gravest concern.

In the spring of the year 1501 the Borgian activities precipitated the first active crisis. Caesar suddenly crossed into Florentine territory with the ostensible purpose of passing through it in order to reach Piombino on the western coast. As eventually he actually arrived at that seaport, his avowal was not contradicted by the facts; nonetheless it is plain that in entering Tuscany on a seemingly harmless errand, his real plan was to test the military resistance of the Florentine state. He moved his forces down the Arno Valley with deplorable deliberation, permitted them to plunder at will the villages through which they passed, and closed his eyes to the monstrous acts of cruelty with which they punished the occasional reprisals of the tormented peasantry. To the indignant protests of the Florentine signory he responded with the cool offer to serve as their general for a modest annual return; and it was not till he had extorted a portion of his proposed salary from his anguished hosts that he finally took his departure. He might not have left at all if the Florentines had not, like himself, been allies of the king of France, and if they had not directed a clamorous appeal to that sovereign for protection.

No comment of Caesar's on his Tuscan transit of 1501 has come down to us, but that thenceforth he held the republic in contempt is proved by what happened a year later. In June, 1502, Arezzo followed the example of Pisa and revolted against Florentine supremacy. Montepulciano to the south had already done the same, and Pistoia, torn by bloody factions, was trembling in the balance. Only a strong Florence could succeed in holding its conquests together; the revived and hopelessly feeble republic was visibly dissolving into its constituent elements. No sooner had Arezzo proclaimed its independence than a number of Duke Valentino's subcommanders appeared upon the scene and fanned the flames of revolt till the whole upper Arno Valley seemed lost to the republic. Valentino himself lurked watchfully in the background awaiting developments. It was an immensely critical moment with nothing less than the very existence of the state hanging in the balance. And again, having no stomach for action, the only coin of courage, the pusillanimous government offered the sorry spectacle of going on its knees to the French monarch to save it from destruction. Thereupon Louis XII, happy to play the part of Italian Jove, gave orders to his Borgian ally to cease molesting his other ally, the equally beloved Florentines. To make it quite plain to Valentino that, while ready to support his original adventure in state-building, the king drew a line beyond which he did not intend to let his protégé go, he dispatched French troops into the upper Arno Valley, under whose authoritative direction the whole territory was restored to his faithful Florentine servants.

While this last-minute rescue released great demonstrations of joy at Florence, many thoughtful citizens, filled with apprehension by every phase of the outrageous Arezzo incident, were stirred to demand a change of system. The French king might not always be prepared to launch his august veto against a trespasser on Tuscan soil and, besides, it was a disgraceful derogation from the dignity of a free state to live by a monarch's favor, and he a foreigner. The trouble lay with the new constitution, perhaps with its main democratic feature, the Grand Council, perhaps with its swiftly changing executive and the consequent lack of continuity and firmness. That the butchers, bakers, and candlestickmakers constituting the majority of the Grand Council would ever be moved to decree its abolition or that they would agree to even the slightest curtailment of its authority was out of the question. However, the continued misfortunes of the state had gradually brought them around to the view that a new signory every two months, totaling six distinct governments for each calendar year, undermined the sense of responsibility and was the sufficient reason for the paralysis that overtook the rulers every time there was need of vigor. In the face of recent events and of the all but certain prospect of an early resumption by Caesar Borgia of his wanton aggressions, a majority came around to the view that a more steady executive was indispensable. Prolonged constitutional debates, which, as in 1494, were greatly influenced by the example of Venice, resulted in at least one capital change. In imitation of the Venetian doge, the gonfalonier of Justice was given an appointment for life. The new life appointee was to exercise substantially the same functions as the old gonfalonier, while to meet the undiminished Florentine thirst for office eight priors serving for two months, exactly as in the past, were to be associated with him in the signory.

When the election for the new head of the state took place in the Grand Council, the victory went to Piero Soderini, who entered on his duties on November 1, 1502. Soderini belonged to an old family of optimates and doubtless owed some of the votes that fell to his lot to the prestige of his name. But as the optimates, as a rule, were greatly feared and hated by the democratic majority, in the main his success was probably owing to his consistent defense of democratic principles. Not only had he never missed an occasion to show his respect for the Grand Council, but throughout his prolonged participation in public life he had always proved himself a stickler for strict constitutional forms. The sum, besides, in his private life of all the conventional virtues, he was just the man a body of small tradesmen and property-owners never fails to look up to as its ideal and to pick as its spokesman. That an executive of Soderini's type can render an important service to the commonwealth in ordinary, quiet times is certain. Unfortunately the times were neither quiet nor ordinary with the result that Piero Soderini's burgher virtues became a contributory factor in the ruin of the state.[1]

It is undeniable that the Florentine government gained in stability at home and in authority abroad with the assumption by Soderini of the gonfalonierat for life. For one thing, one man now held all the threads of policy continuously in his hands. A second advantage was that since Soderini was a capable administrator and hated slovenly finances, he succeeded in a surprisingly short time in putting the Florentine house in better order. It may even be said that the city entered on a period of improved security, although this blessing cannot by any stretch of the imagination be attributed to the new head in person, since it flowed from events with which he had nothing to do. The first of these events occurred some nine months after the gonfalonier's advent to power. On August 18, 1503, Pope Alexander VI died of the malarial fever which was endemic in Rome and annually levied an enormous toll on the population.[2] The doting father departed this life before the son had been solidly established in his conquered dominion. Even more destructive of Caesar's plans was the circumstance that, stricken by the racking fever at the same time as the pope, he lay for many critical weeks at the point of death. When he finally recovered, a man who was his match in energy, if not in his defiance of the moral

---

[1] Among the many diarists of the period Luca Landini perhaps offers most of that precious quality called local color. See his *Diario Fiorentino* published by I. del Badia (Florence, 1883). Luca was an apothecary and a Piagnone with a typical small shopkeeper outlook. When Piero Soderini was elected gonfalonier for life Luca was of course delighted and piously commented: "Veramente fu da Dio tale opera!"

Invaluable for this period is F. Guicciardini's youthful work, the *Storia Fiorentina,* published as Vol. III of the *Opere Inedite* (Florence, 1859).

[2] The piquant tale of the banquet at which the pope accidentally drank the poisoned wine intended for his guests has absolutely no basis in fact. That small defect will not keep it from being handed down from author to author to all eternity.

law, sat upon St. Peter's chair. This was Giuliano della Rovere, raised to the
cardinalate over a generation ago by that other Rovere, his uncle, the fourth
Sixtus. Having at last reached the goal of his ambition, the new pope, Julius II,
was not minded to let the State of the Church slip out of his hands into those
of a hated predecessor's despised bastard. He dispossessed Caesar of his conquests, and although after some hesitation he released Caesar's person, the
condottiere's fickle goddess, Fortune, had turned her back on him and, slowly
pushed into oblivion, he died a few years later (1507) in an obscure skirmish
in the Pyrenees.

A relative calm succeeded in the ever-troubled State of the Church as Julius
II directed his powerful energy to the task of appropriating Caesar's conquests
for himself and the papacy. At the same time the political storm which had
been raging ever since Louis XII had occupied Lombardy was temporarily
calmed by developments in the south of Italy. When Louis seized Milan in
1499, he looked upon his action as no more than the initial step toward the
total subjugation of the peninsula. The next step was to be the conquest of
Naples, to which his immediate predecessor had pointed the way. When
Charles VIII had been obliged to withdraw from that kingdom, the displaced
Aragonese dynasty had effected a quick return with the aid of its Spanish
relatives. On pondering the Neapolitan problem after his Milanese success
Louis came to the conclusion that he was not strong enough permanently to
hold the southern territory against the will of the king of Aragon and entered
into negotiations with him with a view to a peaceful settlement of their opposed claims. The king of Aragon was Ferdinand, husband of Isabella, queen
of Castile, and one of the most cunning and grasping sovereigns of his century. Ever ready to extend his sway, Ferdinand received his French rival's
overtures with the greatest alacrity. The result was a treaty signed at Granada
in November, 1500, by the terms of which Louis, in return for the northern
half of the kingdom of Naples, conceded the southern half to his rival. The
rights of the actual ruler received the consideration the strong are in the habit
of giving the weak, and he was coolly dropped on the ash heap of history by
being declared deposed.

There followed the occupation of the kingdom of Naples by French and
Spanish armies, with everything passing according to plan until the agents of
the two powers intrusted with the partition disagreed regarding the boundary
between their respective shares. From harsh words they passed to blows with
such precipitation that already by 1503 the two jealous partners were openly at
war. In the very months when Rome was disturbed by the death of Pope
Alexander and the election of his successor, the armies of France and Spain
were engaged in bringing their Neapolitan differences to a decision in the
field. It came with extraordinary swiftness, owing to the amazing military
talents of the Spanish commander, the famous Gonsalvo of Cordova. In the
month of December, on the banks of the Garigliano River, Gonsalvo all but
destroyed the French army and followed up his victory by taking possession of
the whole of the Neapolitan kingdom in behalf of his sovereign. As Louis
XII, involved in manifold difficulties with such neighbors close at hand as
Maximilian I of Germany and Henry VII of England, was unable to continue

the war in southern Italy, he came to terms with Ferdinand of Aragon, by which he surrendered his claim to Naples to his triumphant rival. Accordingly, the reduction of Italy by foreign powers begun in 1494 came to a temporary halt. France at Milan dominated the north; Spain at Naples ruled the south. Held as in a vise between them were the as yet unconquered states of Venice, Florence, and the papacy, together with such minor historical accidents as Siena, Lucca, Mantua, and Ferrara. The situation remained dangerously unstable; however, as long as France and Spain, exhausted by their recent efforts, kept the peace, the doomed peninsula might hope to enjoy a welcome temporary lull.

The general situation needed to be put before the reader in order to explain the improved position of the Florentine republic in the years immediately following Piero Soderini's assumption of power. In view of the narrated facts no further proof is required that the improvement did not follow from any contribution immediately ascribable to the gonfalonier. We put his case in a nutshell, when we say that he enjoyed beginner's luck; and he enjoyed the same luck also in another matter. In the precipitate retreat of the French following Don Gonsalvo's victory, Piero de' Medici, who was serving in the French ranks, met his death in the waters of the swift Garigliano. The worthless Piero had never ceased to harass the republic either by joining with its enemies or by plots of his own devising. Now that he was gone the Medici interests came into the safekeeping of Piero's two younger brothers, Giovanni, the cardinal, and Giuliano. Both of them were men of kindly disposition and superior intelligence, who saw the futility of trying to win their way back to the city they had lost by antagonizing its inhabitants. Not only did they cease from plotting against the government but more especially the cardinal, who was a great personage at Rome, went out of his way to extend a gracious hospitality to every Florentine who for one reason or another paid a visit to the papal capital. With the outlawed Medici giving no immediate anxiety, with Duke Valentino no longer rampant along the eastern border, with France and Spain at least temporarily quiescent, the problem which since its renewal the republic had never ceased to regard as its leading concern again came automatically to the front. This was the problem of rebellious Pisa. Soderini was aware that what the Florentines to a man expected of their new executive was the reduction of that port; and, eager to please them, he went about the business in the familiar way by hiring mercenary troops. Although he got the usual unsatisfactory returns, since there was nothing else to do he persisted in his efforts until one day a slight, studious-looking, ingratiating official in his employ let fall the arresting remark that he knew of a far more effective way of levying war.

The man whom our story now brings to the front is one of the most strikingly individual figures in the long panorama of Florentine political agents from Farinata degli Uberti and Giano della Bella to Rinaldo degli Albizzi and Lorenzo the Magnificent. He is Niccolò Machiavelli, descendant of an old but impoverished family, who in the year 1498, one month after the tragic end of the prophet Savonarola, received the appointment as head of the second chancellery and secretary of the war committee called the Ten. He was an alert and clever young man, twenty-nine years old, whose leading intellectual attribute was an inexhaustible interest in all the concerns of the state. Since in his double capacity of chancellor and secretary of the Ten all papers relating to both domestic and foreign affairs henceforth passed through his hands, he was free to indulge his peculiar taste to the limit. Before many months had elapsed he had gained an unrivaled insight into all the problems vexing the city. Even before Florence provided itself with a gonfalonier for life the secretary's special talents had won recognition and he had been enabled to enlarge his political experience by being sent on important missions to neighboring states. When Piero Soderini took over the executive, he was so greatly drawn to the official who was always primed with the decisive information on every subject that arose that he made use of him more than ever. In the autumn of 1502 Machiavelli was sent to spy out the plans of Duke Valentino, just then at the height of his career; and after the death of Pope Alexander in the following August the shrewd secretary was dispatched to Rome to study and report on the now fast sinking fortunes of the great adventurer. So satisfactorily did he perform these services that, on Soderini's express orders, he was sent repeatedly to Louis XII and Emperor Maximilian, and at least once to every Italian ruler, great or small, who in any way affected the Florentine destiny. Naturally Soderini consulted him also in the matter of the interminable Pisan war. Having pondered the problem closely for years, the secretary had come to the opinion that a radical change in Florentine military methods was unavoidable. His deliberate view was that it was pure folly to continue to trust the welfare of the state to mercenary troops. While freely consuming the substance of the citizens, not only did the hired condottieri fail to give wholehearted service, but on sufficient inducement they were always ready to betray their employers.

The condottiere system had long been a stench in the nostrils of every Florentine, but until Machiavelli came forward no one had ever proposed a remedy. When he first divulged his plan confidentially to his subordinates and cronies of the chancellery, they burst into amused laughter. When the gonfalonier heard of it, he, too, was convinced that it was utterly impracticable for the unanswerable reason that the Florentines of the beginning cinquecento no longer bore any resemblance to their medieval forebears. This was indeed the core of the issue; for what Machiavelli proposed was to return to the military system of the early republic, which was, as everyone was aware, that the citizens themselves, including the residents of the contado, supplied the army required for the protection of the state. It was almost two hundred years ago that the national army had expired to be replaced by the mercenary system which, whatever its early effectiveness may have been, had latterly become an intolerable burden. Only reluctantly and because of the desperateness of the situation was the gonfalonier persuaded to give the secretary's proposal a trial; and conscious of the certain opposition to the measure of the substantial burgher element, he turned by way of experiment to the more tractable countryside. First in one village and then in another the peasants were called together to undergo a brief period of military training. So promising were these beginnings that they did not fail to make an impression in the city and, spurred by the tireless secretary, Soderini at last ventured to bring the issue before the councils.

It was accounted a notable victory for the gonfalonier and his ingenious subordinate when, on December 6, 1506, a bill authorizing the establishment of a national militia was formally enacted. Owing as much to the fear of putting weapons in the hands of citizens, who might use them to levy civil war, as to the settled burgher dislike for military service, the bill limited the obligation to serve, at least for the time being, to the country residents. This was a serious flaw. Not only did it cut down the new militia to approximately ten thousand men, but it excused from a primary obligation of patriotism the very people who were the masters of the state and its leading beneficiaries. Machiavelli was aware of these and other drawbacks imposed by the existing frame of mind, but he persuaded himself that they did not count as against the capital advantage of providing the government with a reliable force capable of being brought into action with a minimum of expense and delay. Of course there remained such weighty questions as whether the necessary discipline and courage could be instilled into bands of unwilling peasant lads, and how the indispensable corps of devoted native officers was to be obtained. On the answer hung the success or failure of the new institution. As always in novel experiments, much would have to be left to time; and till time had spoken there was nothing an energetic statesman like Machiavelli could do but to labor incessantly in behalf of his plan. It was a great help that the organization of the new force fell into his hands. By the terms of the law of 1506 the national militia was put in charge of a commission of Nine; but as the Nine made Machiavelli their secretary, he became to all intents the civil head of the native forces, from which he expected the salvation of the republic.[3]

When elements of the new national militia were first employed in connection with the siege of Pisa, it was found that they were serviceable at less exposed points but that they could by no means be rated as the fighting equivalent of professional troops. The state had therefore to continue to employ mercenaries, although it was considered a cause for congratulation that from year to year their numbers could be reduced and the national units increased proportionately without imperiling the enterprise. We thus come to the spring of the year 1509 when, in connection with the latest developments in the general Italian situation, it became apparent that Pisa was about to fall. The general situation had by that year taken a new and, as usual, an unexpected turn. In view of the Franco-Spanish settlement of 1504 a reasonable forecast would have run to the effect that the peace of Italy would not be again disturbed until France and Spain should resume their struggle for peninsular control. For reasons having to do with events engrossing each of them at home, they adjourned the inevitable breach, each power contenting itself with the Italian territory in its possession. As a result, for the four years during which the

---

[3] The fundamental biography of Machiavelli is still that of P. Villari, *Niccolò Machiavelli e i Suoi Tempi*. 3 vols. Florence, 1877-82. The English translation is by Linda Villari, *The Life and Times of Niccolò Machiavelli*. 2 vols. London, 1898. The leading source for Machiavelli are his collected works (*Opere*) of which there are many editions. It would require a footnote of essay proportions to discuss even the recent literature on Machiavelli. An unusually illuminating character sketch will be found in R. Roeder, *The Man of the Renaissance*. New York, 1933.

truce between France and Spain continued, the leading disturber of Italy's always precarious peace was a native ruler, the new pope.

In Pope Julius II (1503–13) we encounter one of the most masterful of the great Renaissance personalities. On mounting the throne of St. Peter he at once identified himself with the purely secular policy which had distinguished his immediate predecessors, but he put behind it an impersonal majesty, of which they with their petty aims of family aggrandizement had not shown so much as a trace. As soon as he was able to rid himself of the incubus of Caesar Borgia, his single purpose came to be to bring the territories the duke had conquered under the control of the church, to which they rightfully belonged. The task was rendered difficult by the chaos precipitated in Umbria and the Romagna following the collapse of Caesar's power. Some of the dispossessed tyrants took advantage of the confusion to return to the towns from which they had been driven, while the republic of Venice, always recklessly eager to make up for its loss of sea power since the coming to the near east of the Turks by its expansion on *terra firma,* seized a considerable section of the adjoining Romagna. Julius II was not the man meekly to bear this succession of effronts. By breaking Caesar's power he had broken the immediately available sword of the church and he would have to put off action until he had succeeded in forging a new weapon. It was characteristic of his essentially military temper that he never thought of letting anyone but himself exercise the supreme command; and when at length he was ready to resume the interrupted task of consolidating the papal state, he took the field in person, armed beneath his flowing pontifical vestments from head to foot in flashing steel.

Although the warrior-pope enjoyed considerable success against the petty usurpers of his dominion, when it came to rich and arrogant Venice he was helpless. His frustration caused the mighty man to erupt like a volcano. He was a son of the Ligurian littoral, and just as characteristic of him as his sailor-like bluffness and honesty, was an impulsiveness that often hurled him forward on a path which he had no desire to travel. Blocked in the Romagna by the republic of St. Mark, he readily joined in a plot for the partition of the Venetian possessions on the mainland hatched out by the three towering sovereigns of France, Spain, and Germany. Grasping Venice, although certainly no more grasping than the rulers who combined against her, had made the mistake of giving offense to all three of them at the same time. The result was the league of Cambray of December, 1508, by which they revenged themselves on Venice by agreeing to blot the ancient republic from the map. It was this callous arrangement, to which the hate-blinded Julius II gave his consent on being promised the alienated Romagna lands as his share of the spoils. Hardly, however, had the campaign of the Cambray allies been inaugurated in the spring of 1509, when the pope was visited by compunctions. The overwhelming might of the league had in a first concerted rush all but suffocated the Venetians, thus enabling Julius to repossess himself of the lands he considered his own. Then, as his passions cooled and his judgment reasserted its empire, he was reduced to the role of spectator while three great foreign powers proceeded to divide among them the strongest of the few remaining independent states of the peninsula. His patriotic gorge rose at the sight until he could hardly wait to undo the mischief he had himself helped to wreak. He made a separate peace with the republic, of course prudently retaining what he had already seized. Immediately after, he went boldly over to the side of his threatened fellow-countrymen. It is certain that his action was a large factor in the recovery that the Venetians presently effected and by which they extricated themselves from the deadly net of Cambray. Not content with this contribution, with characteristic initiative the pope next attempted to give the war an entirely new turn by transforming it into a national struggle for the liberation of Italy from its foreign oppressors.

Before we follow the fortunes of the new struggle we shall have to return to the Florentine siege of Pisa. That the impoverished, desperate, and starving seaport had been able to resist its more powerful neighbor for so many years was nothing short of a miracle, partially explained by the disguised or open assistance afforded it by the many enemies of Florence. When the spring of 1509 arrived, Niccolò Machiavelli, who, although only a lesser official, was substantially in charge of the siege, recognized that the preoccupation of Italy with the attack on Venice by four great sovereigns furnished Florence an unequaled opportunity to push the siege without the probability of serious interference from any quarter. Accordingly, he drew his lines closer and closer around the miserable town, making more and more use of his national militia, until on June 8 the Pisans gave up their stubborn struggle of fifteen years' duration by opening their gates to the enemy. It was the greatest moment in the life of the revived republic. Its divided citizens forgot their hatreds as they gave themselves up to unrestrained manifestations of joy. Incoherent with rapture, one of his chancellery assistants dashed off a congratulatory note to his "honored Niccolò" at Pisa: "Everyone without exception has gone mad with exultation. There are bonfires all through the city, although it is still afternoon. Think what it will be like at night! . . . If I were not afraid of making you overproud, I would say that with your battalions you have conducted the work so well that it was none other than you who have re-established the Florentine state." [4] If on that June day of the year 1509, when Pisa surrendered, the struggling Florentine republic touched its apogee, the statement applies with equal force to the public career of Niccolò Machiavelli.

From these heights the descent was tragically precipitate for both. In the course of the following year (1510) the pope, as we have already noted, succeeded in converting the war of the league of Cambray into a struggle for the liberation of Italy. He naturally appealed to Florence to join the national movement. As the ever-fluctuating Emperor Maximilian before long declared his willingness to come to terms with Venice, and as Spain, although associated diplomatically with the league of Cambray, had not sent a single soldier into Lombardy from its south Italian listening-post, the liberation of Italy, as viewed by Julius II, might be effected by a union of Italian states against the original invader, France. However, to join in a struggle against France ran violently counter to Florentine tradition as well as against the settled predilections of the Gonfalonier Soderini. In regard to the problem presented by the pope's invitation the gonfalonier and his favorite man of affairs were perhaps for the

---

[4] Machiavelli, *Opere* (Passerini-Milanesi), Vol. V, p. 431, note.

first time since their association in the government of different minds. Machiavelli argued in favor of an opportunist policy, such as since his day has with a wholly unjustified implication of malignancy been called Machiavellian. The position of the secretary was that since Florence was a feeble republic confronted by more powerful states, it must not once and for all commit itself to any one of them but must be prepared to act according to circumstances. This view was not shared by Soderini, who was inflexibly resolved to keep Florence under the protecting wing of France. He argued that Florence had always been associated with France, that in the past France had regularly come out on top in the long run, and that to turn against France now in the interest of an Italian independence, for which nobody really cared, would be both folly and perfidy.

When the impulsive Julius first inaugurated his liberation campaign to the ringing nationalist cry *Fuori i Barbari!* (Put the barbarians out!) the refusal of Soderini and his democratic supporters in Florence to join hands with the pope brought no immediate injury to the city. The pope's original plan was to expel the French by means of a union of peninsular governments, that is, by an action limited to the nationally aroused Italians. It need hardly to be pointed out that the flaw in this plan was that it was based on something that did not exist, on an Italian national sentiment. Therefore the war that resulted in 1510 and continued through 1511 simmered down to a struggle of Venice and the State of the Church against Louis XII; and in such a struggle Florence could without running any grave risks decline the invitation to join the Italian cause. In fact, on narrow considerations of immediate safety it may even be said to have made the correct decision, for the best efforts of which the liberators were capable failed to shake the grip of the French on the fertile plains of Lombardy. Pope Julius filled his contemporaries with amazement as at the head of an army he swept across the area of conflict like a pagan Mars or heathen Thor. But the French had the heavier artillery and the more mobile troops, and sadly Julius had to admit to himself that with his countrymen refusing to participate in his great national undertaking his program for putting the barbarians out would have to be revised.

With his habitual lack of reflection the pope now invited Spain to come to his aid and concluded with it and Venice what he was pleased to call the Holy League (1511). It might much more appropriately have been called the Unholy League, since its purpose was to drive out the devil with Beelzebub. The allies renewed the invitation to the other Italian states to share in the great work; and now that the two great powers of France and Spain faced each other to determine, regardless of the pope's private expectations, which one of them was to be supreme in Italy, the choice Florence might make between them became a matter of the gravest import. However, the issue was not even debated on the Arno, for, hypnotized by its French tradition, the republic decided for Louis XII. A single campaign decided the new conflict. In April, 1512, there occurred a desperately fought battle between the French and the Spanish armies at Ravenna, and although it was finally won by the French, it brought them no advantage. Owing to pressure from many sides, the French troops were obliged to retreat from the Adriatic coast toward their base at

Milan, which, when their quarreling generals could agree on no plan, they were unable to hold. Withdrawing more and more precipitately, they ended by giving up Italy altogether.

When summer came the Holy League was in complete control of the peninsula. Thereupon the delegates of the victor states held a congress at Mantua, at which, after the son of the Moor, Maximilian Sforza, had been restored to the recovered duchy of Milan, the fate of Florence was made the order of the day. The unanimous verdict was to the effect that the republic, identified with the defeated French cause, should be abolished and the Medici brought back to the city. The leading member of the banished family was Cardinal Giovanni. He had vigorously co-operated with the pope in the affairs of the Holy League and might not improperly look upon the restoration voted by the congress as his personal reward. To carry out the judgment against Florence the victorious Spanish army under the viceroy of Naples, Raymond of Cardona, was ordered to cross the Apennines into Tuscany.

It would be an exaggeration, and therefore fallacious, to declare categorically that the republic might have been saved if it had possessed the foresight to have switched in good time from France to Spain. While it is true that in that case its existence might have been prolonged, it should by now be plain beyond dispute that in the altered circumstances of Italy an independent Florentine state, regardless of the constitution under which it might be operating, was no longer possible. Florence had become the helpless shuttlecock of France and Spain. Should by some chance the republic have escaped the doom pronounced at Mantua in 1512, it would irretrievably have met its end under different auspices a little later. Agreeing therefore that its demise was fated, we may nonetheless regret the manner of its passing, since it took place amidst manifestations of pusillanimity, cowardice, and base betrayal calculated to wreck the faith in human nature of the stoutest optimist. When the approach of the Spanish army was reported on the Arno, the councils on being summoned by the gonfalonier pledged themselves spiritedly and to a man to defend the popular government. Hardly had this courageous stand been taken, when the Spaniards were reported at Prato some ten miles away; and shortly after, on August 29, came the message that they had taken the little town by storm and were putting it to a murderous sack. The defense of Prato had been intrusted to the new militia re-enforced by a small band of mercenaries. Confronted by the Spanish veterans, the militia made a miserable showing by scattering in headlong flight as soon as the enemy, who possessed only two small, almost useless cannons, had made an inconsiderable breach in the walls. Poor Machiavelli! A single touch of war as conducted by foreign soldiers revealed the flimsiness of the national instrument he had forged with such high hopes for his country. The sharp disappointment caused by the militia added to the terror struck to the hearts of all by the merciless plunder of Prato produced a precipitate change of sentiment. A commission was hurriedly dispatched to Raymond of Cardona with instructions at all costs to come to terms with the general. It was a panic such as every people is liable to in similar circumstances and which only a resolute leader can stem. In Piero Soderini Florence had given itself an official head but that he was not even remotely a leader was now revealed to every jabbering shopkeeper. It sufficed for five impertinent young men to appear (August 31) in the gonfalonier's suite of rooms in the palace with the demand that he resign to overcome his resistance. Not only did he obediently evacuate the palace, but he fled from Florence with such haste that he did not again draw a quiet breath till he had set foot in the town of Ragusa on the farther shore of the Adriatic Sea. When he died some ten years later, still an exile whom papal charity permitted to reside at Rome, his one-time henchman and collaborator, Machiavelli, composed an epitaph for him which breathes such withering contempt that it must have scorched the dead man in his grave:

> La notte che morì Pier Soderini,
> L'alma n'andò dell' Inferno alla bocca;
> E Pluto le gridò: anima sciocca,
> Che Inferno! va' nel Limbo dei bambini.[5]

It did not require long negotiations on the part of the commissioners sent to the Spanish camp at Prato to come to a settlement with their unbidden guests. On the payment to them of 140,000 ducats and the readmission of the Medici to Florence as private citizens the guests agreed to take their departure. Since it was now the end of August and the signory was on the point of expiring, the Grand Council elected a new signory and appointed a new gonfalonier in place of the fugitive Soderini. Evidently the official view was that, save for the reintegration of the Medici, the government would go on much as before. With these matters settled, the Medici brothers, first Giuliano, and, some days later, Cardinal Giovanni, entered the city, the latter with appropriate pomp under escort of four hundred lances. According to the treaty the Medici were to have the position and rights of simple citizens. Undeniably, however, they had been brought back by Spanish bayonets and were protected in the city against violence by mercenaries smuggled into the palace and piazza. Under these circumstances could it be pretended with any show of reason that they were citizens on the same basis as the rest of the Florentines?

[5] On the night when Piero Soderini died, his soul descended to the mouth of hell; at which Pluto snorted: Silly soul, hell is no place for you; your place is in the limbo of babies.

XXVIII. Florence an Annex of the Papacy (1512–27)

THE status of the repatriated Medici was not long left undecided. It has already been pointed out that the two younger brothers of Piero had broken with his policy of violence not only because they recognized the folly of systematically antagonizing the Florentines, but also because, as men of peace, they were reluctant to resort to force and bloodshed. This was particularly true of the younger of the two brothers, Giuliano. Indeed Giuliano was unfitted by temperament to play a political role in a country so chaotic as Italy; and except for the fact that he was a gracious aristocrat with many friends in the literary and artistic circles of his country, he cannot be said to have been much of an asset to his family. The responsibility for the Medici fortunes therefore devolved exclusively on Cardinal Giovanni; and while he, too, was averse to unnecessary violence, he possessed a sufficiently robust nature to take action whenever a crisis arose and especially when the interests of his house were at stake. For Giovanni never forgot that he owed his cardinalate to his father, who had secured the son's appointment to the single end that the young prince of the church might use his ecclesiastical dignity to advance the family fortunes.

Cardinal Giovanni made a ceremonial entrance into Florence on September 14, 1512. Although, for safety's sake, he was attended by troops, he tried to give his homecoming an ecclesiastical rather than a political character. However, there was no escaping politics, for hardly had he taken his residence in the great palace of his family, which had stood empty and bare since the sack of 1494, when he was importuned by his friends to change the government. These partisans insisted that neither they nor the family to which they were pledged had any security under the existing regime. It required no long urging on their part to win over the cardinal. Two days later, on September 16, a parliament was called, and with Medicean mercenaries holding all the entrances to the piazza and letting only Medicean adherents pass, the proposal of the intimidated signory to the assembled people to appoint a balìa to "reform" the state was accepted by acclamation. It was the familiar device long practiced by the oligarchic cliques of the past and so thoroughly detested by the advocates of a free regime that the parliament had been solemnly outlawed in the days of Savonarola. The resort to the banished institution was made possible only by the threat to use force, and the same threat constituted the sanction behind the balìa. This all-powerful committee consisted of forty-five members (later increased to sixty-

five), all trusty Mediceans hand-picked by the cardinal. It went about its business of destroying the republic with the greatest good will. Not only did it
expressly abolish the numerous characteristic features of the constitution, more
particularly the democratic Grand Council, but yielding to the spirit of blind
partisanship, it even canceled the outstanding institutional creation of the
period just closed, Machiavelli's militia. The offense of the militia was not that
it had proved a poor prop of the state, but that it represented a concession to
popular principles.

This wreckage effected, the balìa at a somewhat more leisurely pace re-
established the Medicean system as it had operated in the days of Lorenzo the
Magnificent. Florence again acquired a senate of the Seventy, a council of the
Hundred, a signory of eight priors and a gonfalonier of Justice, in short, an
elaborate visible apparatus serving no other purpose than to mask a hidden
control. Actual authority lay with the Medicean balìa, which was made a permanent institution. It named the signory for each two months' period and
determined the foreign and domestic policy of the state. However, as the balìa
took its orders from the cardinal, Florence in effect again had a single ruler and
with some show of reason Lorenzo's son might persuade himself that his father's
age had returned.

Although the Medici on again entering Florence had no more than a feeble
following, it grew steadily under the cardinal's skilful nursing until his elevation to the papacy released such popular enthusiasm that opposition, or at least
all visible opposition, completely disappeared. Once more we must return to
Rome to take note of the position of Pope Julius II after the sweeping triumph
of the Holy League. The terrible old man, as his harassed and overworked
dependents called him, had actually achieved his purpose, for in fulfillment
of his slogan, *Fuori i Barbari,* he had driven the barbarian French out of Italy.
In so doing, however, he had greatly strengthened the hold on Italy of those
other barbarians, the Spaniards. Profoundly dissatisfied with this result, he let it
be growlingly known to whoever succeeded in catching him off his guard that
his next move would be to throw out the Spaniards after the French; but before
he got under way with this new and far more difficult undertaking, he was cut
short by death (February 13, 1513). Immediately on receiving the news Cardinal
Giovanni left Florence to join the conclave, from which he himself, in spite
of his youthful age of thirty-seven, on March 11 issued as pope. He took the
title Leo X.

Rarely has the election of a pope been attended by such high expectations.
Leo's fellow-townsmen on the Arno gave themselves up to wild demonstrations of joy, partly on personal, partly on patriotic, grounds, for the young
Medici was the first Florentine ever to achieve the papal honors. The last
endearing memories of the republic were forgotten, as all eyes turned toward
Rome, from which the common people confidently expected valuable favors
for their city and innumerable ambitious and selfish members of the ruling
class liberal benefits for themselves. Hardly less keen were the hopes aroused
by the new pope in the general body of the Italian literati. They saw in him
the embodiment of the culture of the age, a friend of the humanists, a patron
of the artists, and that rarity among recent occupants of St. Peter's chair, a

high churchman who was not soiled with the common vices of his age and who had never failed to show a scrupulous respect for ecclesiastical decorum. Leo promptly met these expectations of the publicists by casting himself for the role of Maecenas. Innumerable scholars, musicians, architects, and painters found employment at his hands. Although they constituted in the main a vulgar horde of sycophants and mediocrities, it will always be remembered in his favor that, included in his patronage, were also Raphael and Michelangelo. The fact is Leo X was a soft, genial personality, who loved movement and gayety and who, even when he glimpsed a high goal, lacked the moral fiber to pursue it for long. An examination of the striking portrait done of him by Raphael reveals the man more unerringly than the most searching words. The Leo of the famous canvas is a large, flabby man, whose native intelligence and cultivated taste have been all but destroyed by habitual self-indulgence.

It is impossible to take leave of the republic without paying our respects to the man who, although he never rose above a dependent political office, in the eyes of posterity looms as the most important figure in its employ between the death of Savonarola and the flight of Piero Soderini. Niccolò Machiavelli had worked hand-in-glove with the gonfalonier, and although he lamented his chief's pitiable collapse in the crisis of 1512, he never denied the obligations resulting from their long and close association. To their credit the Medici on their return did not practice a mean revenge, and, in the main, were inclined to let by-gones be by-gones. That they did not feel safe, however, with the sworn supporters of the past regime was natural, and accordingly they gradually pushed most of them out of office. Among the dismissed servants of the republic was the chancellor and secretary, Machiavelli, who two months after the Medicean triumph was deprived of all his functions. It was a terrible blow, for, as already noted, not in all probability since the world began has there been a man more interested in the state *per se* and more bent on finding out the procedures and measures that promote or hamper its welfare. Life to Niccolò was politics and outside of politics there was no life. To his mind, therefore, it was neither inconsistent nor unfaithful to tender his services to the Medici. They now represented the state, his ever-worshipful master, and he was as ready and anxious to serve that master under the new lords as he had been to serve him under Piero Soderini. Not impossibly Machiavelli might have succeeded in making himself acceptable to the restored rulers, had he not, while waiting for their suspicions to lose their first sharp edge, become the victim of a blind mischance. A young Florentine who, seduced by the revived pagan doctrine of tyrannicide, was engaged in evolving a plot for the murder of Giuliano and the cardinal, had written the names of possible supporters on a slip of paper and had afterward accidentally dropped it from his pocket. When the paper was picked up, the conspirator and his one accomplice were promptly arrested and executed. Unfortunately the name of Machiavelli figured in the list of sympathizers. He was taken into custody and, after the practice of the day, cruelly tortured in order to bring him to confession. As there was nothing to confess, nothing was elicited with the result that it was conceded by all, except the most rabid Mediceans, that he was not guilty.

The planned assassination was discovered in February, 1513, just as Cardinal Giovanni was preparing to hurry to Rome to the conclave. On his elevation to the papacy, he was inspired to publish an amnesty, by which Machiavelli and all the other suspects were set free. Thus was the ex-secretary officially cleared of specific charges but his person remained under a cloud. Influential friends did their best to plead his cause and to make his great talents once again available for the state; but his enemies were stronger than his friends and always succeeded in hindering his re-employment. Only very reluctantly did he persuade himself that his days of office-holding were over. Well, then, if fate blocked the path of active public service he would devote himself to a theoretic study of the state. He became a writer, one of the most distinguished in his chosen field in the long succession of the ages. Although his second life, as one may call it, was a second choice, it is in reality far more important than his first life, but it no longer belongs to Florentine political history. To this new Machiavelli, to Machiavelli the writer, we shall return when we take up the literary developments of the age.

When Leo X, the acknowledged and hardly any longer veiled ruler of Florence, became pope, he made the Arno city an annex of the papacy. Henceforth whatever foreign policy he would find it desirable to adopt as pope, he would impose on Florence as its own policy. No longer able, however, to exercise direct rule on the Arno, he was obliged to choose a Medici to serve as the visible head of the city. He may possibly at first have thought of Giuliano in this capacity. If so, he very soon changed his mind, for he permitted Giuliano to follow him to Rome and, apart from occasionally evolving an ambitious plan for his brother, he permitted Giuliano to live the obscure existence he preferred. The nearest Leo ever came to pushing his brother to the front was to have the French king give him a French princess to wife together with the title of duke of Nemours. Always in delicate health, the duke of Nemours died in 1516, and by this closing act leaped into an immortality for which no achievement of his active period offered the slightest warrant. The immortality was conferred by Michelangelo. On being commanded by Leo X to carve Giuliano's idealized figure for his tomb, Michelangelo wrought the seated warrior, who with lifted head eternally searches the horizon in the New Sacristy of San Lorenzo.

It is probable that Pope Leo never seriously considered any other Medici for the Florentine post than his nephew Lorenzo, only son of his brother Piero. Young Lorenzo was twenty years old on the repatriation of his family, a handsome, alert young man who, quite apart from any preference Leo may have had for him, was designated as the head of the state by the unwritten law of succession. So it was Lorenzo who was put in charge, although Leo, reluctant to trust the state to his nephew's inexperience, kept in the closest possible touch with Florentine affairs by an almost daily exchange of news and instructions through the mediation of Lorenzo's secretary. At the same time he never ceased plying the young man himself with counsel. "You must," he says in his earliest letter of advice, "introduce your own men as far as possible into all the principal magistracies. Seek to keep well informed as to what goes on among the members of the signory, making use to this end of Niccolò

LEONARDO DA VINCI AND VERROCCHIO. ANNUNCIATION. UFFIZI GALLERY (ALINARI).

LEONARDO DA VINCI. THE LAST SUPPER. FRESCO AT MILAN IN THE CONVENT OF SANTA MARIA DELLE GRAZIE (ALINARI).

left: LEONARDO DA VINCI. ADORATION OF THE KINGS. UFFIZI GALLERY (ALINARI).
right: LEONARDO DA VINCI. MONA LISA OR LA GIOCONDA. LOUVRE GALLERY. PARIS
(ALINARI).

left: MICHELANGELO. PIETÀ. MARBLE. ST. PETER'S. ROME (ALINARI). *right:* MICHEL-
ANGELO. DAVID. MARBLE. GALLERY OF THE ACADEMY OF FINE ARTS. FLORENCE (ALI-
NARI).

Michelozzi" (Machiavelli's successor, by the way, whom we thus see cast for the role of spy). "Above all, you must be sure of the Otto di Pratica and the balìa." [1] The Otto di Pratica were in control of foreign affairs and the balìa in control of everything. There is more to the same tenor, all of it interesting as an exposition of the Medicean system by a Medici, but not requiring reproduction in detail since we have long since become familiar with all the secrets the document lays bare.

Since, beginning with the year 1494, the history of Florence became inextricably tied up with the attempted conquest of Italy, we are obliged to take note of every capital move among the European powers affecting this issue. On Louis XII's being ejected from the peninsula in 1512 by the Holy League of Pope Julius II, he refused to abide by the consequences, and in the very next year renewed the attempt to gain a foothold in the plains of the Po. Although again defeated, he would again have returned to the attack, had he not died on January 1, 1515. His successor was Francis I (1515–47), a young man twenty-one years old, handsome, intelligent, and deeply persuaded that war was the only true business of a king. Without hesitation he made ready for still another invasion of Italy which, owing more to his undaunted spirit than to any other single factor, led to a dramatic overturn. By winning the battle of Marignano (September 13, 1515), Francis was able to oust young Duke Maximilian Sforza from Milan and repossess himself of the Milanese state. As Pope Leo X had maintained the political system inherited from his predecessor, he suddenly found himself at a disadvantage. He promptly sought an accommodation with the victor. The papacy, strengthened though it was at this time by the addition of Florence, was a feeble power compared with France or Spain and was obliged to steer its course carefully between them if it wished to avoid destruction. The frequent change of sides of Leo X (and of his predecessors and successors as well) was not so much due to the shiftiness of character charged against him by moralistic historians as to the need of every weaker organism to be watchfully alert in order not to be crushed by its stronger neighbors. Confronted with French predominance in northern Italy, Leo X quickly adjusted himself to the new situation and for the moment at least succeeded in doing so without giving offense to Spain. Spain was as determined as France to dominate Italy, but was less headlong than France, and frequently for several years in succession desisted from the pursuit of its Italian aims. Following the victory of Francis of 1515, the two countries actually signed a peace by which each acknowledged the other's position in the peninsula. This made it relatively easy for Pope Leo to maintain good relations with both powers; and, free under the circumstances to attend to matters close at hand, he took up plans to advance the fortunes of both the states intrusted to his care, the State of the Church and Florence.

A study of Leo's actions throughout his reign makes it perfectly clear that, as pope, he desired to continue his predecessor's policy of unifying the papal rule and that, as head of his house, he hoped to enlarge the Medicean state. The two aims were not necessarily incompatible, but they proved incompatible in Leo's case. For, precisely as with most of his recent predecessors, his family

[1] Villari, *Niccolò Machiavelli,* Vol. II, p. 204.

meant more to him than the crown of St. Peter. In spite of the stout besom wielded by Caesar Borgia and Julius II, there were still some petty tyrants left in Umbria and the Romagna. Some of these Leo dutifully got rid of, not hesitating to employ violence when milder measures failed. It is therefore possible to say of him that he contributed his bit to the consolidation of the State of the Church. In the crucial matter of the duchy of Urbino, however, he egregiously violated his papal obligations. This little mountain dominion was ruled by Francesco Maria della Rovere, a nephew of Pope Julius II. Sincere and honorable as Julius had proved himself on the whole to be, he was sufficiently touched with the nepotism he despised to find it impossible to brush Francesco Maria aside and bring Urbino directly under his rule. The problem evaded by Julius devolved on Leo, and Leo to his shame undertook to solve it in the interest of his house. In the year 1516 he declared Francesco Maria deposed in favor of his nephew Lorenzo, who, thus far no more than a citizen of Florence, now entered the high-titled world as duke of Urbino. The dethroned duke possessed enough of the energy of his stock to offer vigorous resistance to the papal army sent by Leo to establish his nephew in the disputed dominion, but in the end he had to yield possession to Lorenzo.

Embarked on the policy of raising his nephew to a higher eminence, Leo X next procured a French princess for him. Already Leo's brother Giuliano, who had died just before the launching of the Urbino venture, had been married to a woman related to the French ruling house. There had been a time when the Medici were considered audacious to look for spouses as high as the Roman house of Orsini. Under the guidance of Leo they became affiliated with the oldest royalty of Europe, the royalty of France. Young Lorenzo received a magnificent welcome on entering Florence with his foreign princess; and the rejoicings were repeated the following year (1519) when the princess gave birth to a daughter. This daughter was destined to reach the highest rung in the ladder of earthly honors, for she is the famous Catherine de' Medici, afterward queen of France and mother of three kings. To her parents, however, she was far from a bringer of good fortune. Her French mother died in childbed and her father on May 4, less than a month after her birth. His enemies affirmed young Lorenzo perished prematurely, the victim of his numerous vices, while his friends maintained just as positively that he was a man of promise, and that his death resulted from the ill health which was the aftermath of the strenuous Urbino campaign.

Whatever be the truth regarding Lorenzo's character and death, he was gone and with him went the fine plans spun by his papal uncle for his aggrandizement. Leo was not only saddened but deeply perplexed, for there was no legitimate male of his family left on whom to confer the rule of his native city. To win time for the consideration of the problem he dispatched his cousin, Cardinal Giulio de' Medici, to Florence to take over the government. This Giulio was the illegitimate son of the Giuliano, who had died in 1478 from nineteen dagger thrusts administered by the Pazzi conspirators. Born after his father's death, Giulio had been received into the Medici family by Lorenzo the Magnificent. He was destined for the church and, owing to his pleasant manners and lively intelligence almost as much as to the potent

Medici influence, he rose rapidly in his profession. His cousin Leo, who never let an opportunity pass to advance his family, made him a cardinal and found him so useful a personal agent that he intrusted the most important business of the papacy to his hands. No wonder that when the question of the Florentine succession arose, Leo should have sent Cardinal Giulio to the Arno as a sort of interim ruler. Giulio made a great success of this critical mission. He avoided the lordly airs with which young Lorenzo had latterly given offense, he lived in simple burgher style in the family palace, he conferred with the leading citizens on the conduct of affairs, and by taking pains not to overburden the budget of the city he won a very general approval.

At the very moment at which Leo was confronted with this latest phase of the Florentine problem, the Franco-Spanish relations entered a fresh period of disturbance. The first jolt to the recent truce was administered by the death in January, 1519, of Emperor Maximilian. When the seven German electors were called together to choose, according to custom, Maximilian's successor, they conferred the honor on the king of Spain. This was Charles, a youth of nineteen, who had entered on the rule of Spain three years before (1516) on the demise of his maternal grandfather Ferdinand. Charles, to be sure, did not owe his promotion to the empire to his being the king of Spain. He owed it to the fact that his father Philip, who died young, was the son of Emperor Maximilian, head of the house of Hapsburg and archduke of Austria. In other words, through the marriage of Joan, who, as the daughter of Ferdinand and Isabella, was the heiress of Spain, to Philip, who was the heir of Maximilian, their oldest son, Charles, brought the enormous possessions of both houses into his single hand. While at the time of Maximilian's death young Charles was already king of Spain, king of Naples, and lord of the Netherlands, what weighed with the German electors and German people was his being also a German prince, and he won the imperial election owing solely to this circumstance. In 1520 the new sovereign came from Spain to Germany to receive the crown and incidentally to look into the revolt against the rule of the Catholic church which had recently taken place, championed by an Augustinian friar by the name of Martin Luther. While the Lutheran movement is no affair of ours, we must not fail to bring it into our reckoning henceforth whenever we treat of international affairs. Inevitably it caused grave concern to Emperor Charles V, the new civil head of Germany; and while it occasionally troubled Leo X, the head of the church, owing to his care-free, secular nature he refused to let it distract him from the pursuit of the personal ends on which his attention was concentrated. Young Charles was a self-contained, taciturn youth of remarkable talents, as yet undisclosed either to himself or to others. Even before coming to Germany, he had resolved to reopen the Italian question. That signified war with France; and in preparation for that event he wished to secure for himself the help of the pope. Leo for his part was willing to accommodate Charles, in case the emperor would yield to him a share of the prospective Italian conquests. After the usual haggling, in May, 1521, an alliance was signed on this basis. While the pope was to receive a small territorial increase, the Milanese state, the hotly disputed apple of discord between France and Spain, was to revert to the emperor.

The new war between France and Spain began at once and led to still another of the dramatic reversals which had characterized the struggle of the two powers over Italy from the beginning. Merely by clever maneuvering and without the necessity of fighting a single battle, the Imperialists, as the many kinds of troops in the employ of Emperor Charles V were henceforth called, forced the French to abandon Milan and retreat in complete disarray toward the passes of the Alps. When the news of the triumph was brought to Pope Leo, he ordered a joyful celebration at which, extended far into a November night, he was seized with chills and fever. As he had never possessed great physical stamina, the attack made such rapid headway that in three days he was dead (December 1, 1521).

To the surprise of the whole world, the conclave elected a foreigner, a Fleming, as Leo's successor. The new pope owed his election to the influence among the cardinals of Emperor Charles, whose tutor he had been and with whom he was still closely associated. He took the name of Hadrian VI. He was an honest, austere, and learned cleric steeped in medieval conceptions so out of harmony with the semi-pagan ideas prevailing at Rome that he quickly became an object of general contempt and ridicule. It was his dream to reform the church; but before he had even begun to break down the resistance of his hostile environment, he was carried away by the fatal Roman fever, not much more than a year after mounting the papal throne.

The new conclave gave its vote to Giulio de' Medici, who adopted the title of Clement VII (1523–34). His recent successful conduct of the Florentine government had won him golden opinions, and because of his earlier service under Leo X at Rome no one was better acquainted with the diverse business of the papacy. In spite of personal and administrative merits considerably above those of his average predecessor, he was destined to be overwhelmed with such a succession of calamities as to make his reign one of the most disastrous in the long history of his office. Without any doubt these calamities were in large part the mere mounting to a peak of difficulties, which had been gathering momentum for generations past and for which his predecessors rather than himself were responsible; unquestionably, however, they fell upon him more crushingly than would have been the case had he not suffered from a fatal flaw of indecision. He had the habit, in the case of every issue that arose, of listening to many opinions; whereupon, after cautiously moving forward, he would hurriedly retrace his steps with the net result that he was back at his point of departure. We are aware that in his day the papacy was perilously suspended between the two aggressive powers of France and Spain. Clearly the interest of Clement VII was to maintain such a balance between them that, courted by both, he would not be obliged to become the dependent of either. He understood this perfectly, but his method of reaching his goal was to threaten to act without ever acting. While action, in the case of such a feeble power as the pope, will always involve risks, constitutional inaction and perpetual subterfuge lead to catastrophe with mathematical certainty. It is a curious circumstance that at the climax of his misfortunes Clement had among his advisers the two wisest political heads of Italy, his two Florentine fellow-countrymen, Francesco Guicciardini and Niccolò Machiavelli. After the Medici had permitted Machiavelli's talents to rust for ten years, this particular Medici, while still a cardinal, had added to his other merits the recognition that it was desirable by gradual stages to draw the former secretary back into the public service. But no good came to him from his two exceptional counselors. They urged with passionate and finally with frenzied insistence that a definite, virile stand be taken. They could not overcome the mental seesaw, for which the pope had a fatal preference and which ended by casting him for that least attractive of human roles, the deceived deceiver, the universal scapegoat.

Before following Clement to his downfall, we shall have to look into his handling of the Florentine problem. He was thoroughly familiar with the situation on the Arno, since from the death of the second Lorenzo to his own elevation to the papacy, that is, for a period of four years, he had exercised the rule in the city to the apparent satisfaction of most of the inhabitants. On withdrawing from Florence to take up his residence at Rome, he was obliged either to name another Medici in his place or to give the city back to the citizens by inviting them to re-establish the republic. He played with the latter solution, possibly to convey to the Florentines an impression of his great liberality. Considering that he was both a product of the individualistic Italian cinquecento and a typical Medici, it is much more likely that he never seriously entertained any other thought than to preserve the Florentine dominion for his family. The household situation that confronted him, however, was almost desperate. While there were some Medici females still alive, among them the little Catherine born in 1519, females had never counted in the Medici succession. With Leo X had expired the last legitimate male, and Clement VII, admittedly illegitimate, was generally regarded as the very last masculine shoot of the stock. There was indeed a younger branch of the family descended from old Cosimo's brother Lorenzo, but the two lines had quarreled and, like Leo before him, Clement VII did not view the younger branch other than as a house of strangers.

Faced with this situation, the pope disclosed the existence of two young Medici bastards, of whom till this moment the Florentines had had only the vaguest knowledge. One was Ippolito, supposed to be the son of Giuliano, duke of Nemours, by a woman of Pesaro, the other, Alessandro, putative son of Lorenzo, duke of Urbino, by a mulatto slave. Ippolito, about fourteen years old, was an exceedingly handsome and promising youth, but Alessandro, who was a year older than Ippolito and who had inherited the dusky skin, thick lips, and crisp hair of his mother, was regarded as almost a monster. After much dubitation, probably feigned, Clement VII sent these two youths to Florence to represent the house. While they were growing to manhood, Cardinal Passerini was set over them with authority to conduct the government in their name. The cardinal was as unhappy a choice as the two young men with the blot on their scutcheon. It irked the Florentines greatly to have a pair of dubious Medici suddenly dropped on them out of nowhere, while the boorishness, avarice, and small intelligence of Cardinal Passerini aroused an opposition which steadily gained in volume. Had it not been, however, for the catastrophe that overtook Pope Clement, it is not likely that the Florentines would have been encouraged once more to remedy the situation by rising in revolt.

Clement's catastrophe, as already said, was precipitated by the Franco-Spanish struggle over Italy, which had in 1521 entered a new phase when Emperor Charles V resolved to challenge the French occupation of Milan effected by King Francis I six years before. We have learned that Leo X had allied himself with Charles and had died in consequence of his exposing himself to the night air during the celebration of the first Spanish victories in Lombardy. With them the war was by no means over, for Francis I returned to the attack, without, however, scoring any notable success. In the autumn of 1524 he made a supreme effort and conducted a large and magnificently equipped army across the Alps into the Lombard plain. The Imperialists, outnumbered, gave way before him except for a small force of four thousand men who continued to hold Pavia. To this city King Francis laid siege, but it resisted him so stubbornly that the Imperialists were enabled to gather a relief army of Spanish and German troops. As it was contrary to King Francis' chivalrous code of conduct to retreat on vulgar considerations of safety, his forces were, on February 24, 1525, caught between the new Imperialist army and the garrison of Pavia and virtually annihilated. Francis himself was captured and carried a prisoner to Spain. The war came to an abrupt end with the Imperialists in unchallenged control throughout the peninsula.

The blow of Pavia fell almost as heavily on the pope as on France and its sovereign. During the preceding years Clement had been almost bled white by the continual and unrelenting demands of the Imperialists for subsidies. Sorely put out with them, he submitted to their exactions in the secret hope that the French would presently re-establish a balance of power, enabling him to reassert his independence. That hope was so completely blasted by Pavia that in his disillusioned eyes he was now himself no better than a Spanish prisoner. He made up his mind that his only possible escape was a national league of all the remaining Italian states backed by the power of France. That a nation so proud as the French would not accept the verdict of Pavia as final was accepted by Clement as certain. To be sure, little or nothing was to be expected from France while the king languished in captivity. Therefore it was welcome news to the pope when, a year after his capture, Francis came to terms with his jailer. By the treaty of Madrid (March 18, 1526) he gained his freedom in return for the surrender to Charles of all his Italian claims together with the duchy of Burgundy, a province of eastern France. Charles V was still young and inexperienced or he would not have believed for a moment that his rival would abide by terms of such crushing severity. It was no more than what the rest of the world expected when Francis, hardly back on French soil, entered into relations with the pope and the other Italian states with a view to renewing the war with Spain at the earliest possible moment.

Pope Clement met the urgent overtures of the French monarch with the greatest eagerness, although in the manner of the weak and timid he did his best to conceal from the emperor that he was about to desert him. As Clement controlled both the papacy and Florence, his act tied both states to the French

cause. Venice, too, was won over to the new league, and with this important addition the list of Italian allies was closed. It was still remembered
in the peninsula that the mighty Julius II had attempted to organize a national
movement for the expulsion of the invaders; but it was also remembered that
he had failed because, apart from an occasional enlightened individual, there
was no national sentiment to be found among the Italians. In plain truth the
anti-Imperialist league of 1526 was never anything more than a frail, hurriedly
patched-up improvisation. The French had gone ahead diplomatically before
they were militarily ready, and as a result, in spite of the lavish promises of
Paris, no French army appeared on Italian soil. The pope and Venice, aided
by the money of Florence, duly collected soldiers up to their limited capacity;
but owing to the inveterate suspicions dividing them, they could not be
brought to act on a common plan. Luckily the Imperialists were during the
year 1526 in almost equally evil case. It was characteristic of them throughout
this period that they lacked adequate funds, and that consequently, as soon
as a campaign was over, they would be obliged, in order to lighten their financial burden, to disband their troops. Charles could not therefore act promptly
in the face of the new danger. An advantage, however, that was bound to
tell in the long run was that he had a better political head than his rival,
Francis, and was served in the field by better commanders. During the winter
of 1526–27 he succeeded in again assembling German and Spanish troops in
northern Italy. In his opinion he would have only to possses himself of the
person of the pope for the whole conspiracy against his domination of Italy
to be completely disrupted.

It will not be possible to do more than indicate the strange vicissitudes of
the campaign of 1527. All the action that took place was supplied by a body of
German Landsknechts under their leader, Frundsberg, and an army of Spaniards under the duke of Bourbon, a French nobleman who had deserted his
king to join the enemy. Both armies were in a rebellious frame of mind owing
to arrears of pay and an incurable lack of provisions. To have stopped them
as they moved southward, plundering as they went, would not have been
difficult if the armies of the anti-Spanish league had been able to come to an
agreement. Instead of action, there was on the part of both generals and
governments nothing but bickering, bad faith, ineptitude, and cowardice. It
was the confession to the world of the complete political and military bankruptcy of Italy. Without being obliged to strike a single blow the Spaniards
and Germans, having united their forces, on May 4 reached the meadows outside the Vatican quarter. Two days later they had breached the wall and,
streaming over the bridges of the Tiber, held Rome at their mercy. The pope
and the cardinals were just able to save their lives by taking refuge in the
Castle of Sant' Angelo. Around them raged unchecked such a sack as the
Eternal City had not experienced even in the far days of the migrations.
Many of the German Landsknechts, as followers of Martin Luther, delighted
in venting their spite on the rich furnishings of the altars and on the persons
of great prelates, whom they held to extravagant ransom, while the Spaniards
in their house-to-house visits seized the gold, silver, jewels, and portable wealth
of every kind which the past generations had accumulated in the capital of

Christianity. The wild orgy ceased only when the pope accepted the terms dictated by the victors and in pledge of their fulfilment agreed to remain a prisoner in the Castle of Sant' Angelo at the discretion of the emperor.

The news of the capture of Rome reached Florence on May 11 and immediately produced a popular commotion. Ever since 1512 the city had made the best of the turn of chance that had converted it, through its renewed subjection to the Medici, into an annex of the papacy. Under Leo X the connection, distasteful though it was to the strong republican sentiment, had carried with it numerous compensatory advantages. These had continued for a time under Clement VII. They entirely disappeared, however, when the new pope's vacillating policy drew the plundering Imperialist hordes into central Italy and precipitated the awful Roman catastrophe. Immediately the old republican memories slumbering just below the surface of consciousness asserted themselves with elemental vehemence. There was nothing more to be expected from these latter-day Medici; besides, the only member of the family the citizens had reason to fear cowered, a broken man, behind the stout walls of his Roman prison. Cardinal Passerini, the unpopular personal representative of Clement in the city, was soon convinced that his position was hopeless. There was no violence to speak of, just a rising tide of irresistible opinion. Prudently yielding to its pressure, the cardinal on May 17 left the city accompanied by his two young Medicean charges.

Songs of thanksgiving sounded through the streets, as once again the yoke of tyranny was broken and the city enthusiastically assumed its republican vestments. Besmirched though they had been by the confirmed dishonest practices of knavish politicians, against every probability in this, the last phase of the free state, they took on once more the luster of their prime.

XXIX. Heroic End of the Republic (1527–30)

WITH a swiftness and spontaneity that testify to the abiding affection of the Florentines for the republican regime, the political arrangements imposed during the recent Medicean ascendancy were swept aside and replaced by the constitution elaborated after the expulsion in 1494 of young Piero de' Medici and sanctified for a large section of the population by the memory of Brother Girolamo Savonarola. The outstanding feature of this constitution was the Grand Council, to which over three thousand citizens were eligible and which was charged with the duty of electing the magistrates and validating the laws proposed by the signory. There were also set up again the smaller council of eighty members, the *Ottanta,* the *Dieci* or Ten charged with the conduct of war, and the signory of eight priors presided over by a gonfalonier of Justice. Instead, however, of conceding the gonfalonier a life-appointment, it was agreed that he should serve for one year only, but that at the expiration of his term he might be eligible for re-election.

When, on the last day of May, 1527, the Grand Council proceeded to vote on the new head of the state, its choice fell on Niccolò Capponi. Niccolò was the son of that Piero Capponi who, on the occasion of Charles VIII's occupation of the city, had spoken a word which had taken the hearts of the Florentines by storm. On the royal puppet's threatening to sound the trumpets summoning his soldiers to assault the town, Piero had cowed him with the bold reply: "And we shall ring our bells!" Other forebears of Niccolò had in their day played an equally important part in Florentine affairs so that the Capponi took rank among the greatest families of the city. Until recently Niccolò had figured as a partisan of the Medici; and although he had broken with them and been a prime mover in their most recent expulsion, he was so far from being their irreconcilable enemy that he openly favored sparing their partisans within the city the usual reprisals and planned, besides, to do his utmost to reach an accommodation with Pope Clement himself. In short, the gonfalonier was a moderate; and that a moderate was elected to the highest office of the state is conclusive proof that, at least in the first stage of the revolution, a considerable majority of the citizens were animated by peaceful sentiments and wished to come to terms with their former ruler, who, though momentarily a prisoner and not to be feared, nevertheless still was the pope and capable in the long run of rallying enormous resources to himself.

Undeniably, however, Florentine opinion, like opinion everywhere and always, was in a state of flux and might under changed conditions exhibit an entirely different complexion. Again let us note, there were in the town no political parties in our sense with an organization, officials, and a platform. There were merely voluntary groupings in the councils and magistracies determined in part by political principles, in larger part still by nothing more calculable than momentary emotional discharges. With this in mind we may speak of Capponi enjoying in the first place the support of the *Frateschi* or *Piagnoni,* composed in the main of the small shopkeepers who had constituted the solid kernel of Savonarola's following. That the gonfalonier was a man of sincere, if somewhat ostentatious, virtue grappled these people to him with bonds of steel. The Mediceans or *Palleschi,* still numerous in the city though now singing small, also gave their suffrages to a gonfalonier, whose main conviction was that the city must at all costs be pacified. A numerically feeble body of Optimates (*Ottimati*) were sworn enemies of the re-established democratic regime. While, owing to their insignificant representation in the Grand Council, they did not count for much, still they, too, were quick to sense that they were better off with Niccolò Capponi, socially if not politically of their own persuasion, than with any other available chief executive and lent him their somewhat equivocal support. Active, systematic opposition to the gonfalonier was reserved to the extreme democrats, whose animating principle was uncompromising hostility to the Medici. They went so far in their fear and hatred of the former ruling house that they received the name of mad men or *Arrabbiati.* Although the Arrabbiati, not to be confused with the Arrabbiati of the Savonarola period, commanded no great following, they embraced the most daring and vigorous youths of the city and furnish a good illustration of the disproportionate influence a coherent and spirited minority may attain in a society, the majority of whose members are as unwilling as they are unfit to accept responsibility. The capable head of this group was Baldasarre Carducci. Although himself an old man of grave bearing, he was as violent in his denunciations of the Medici as the young Hotspurs who frequented the piazza and the palace and was vociferously acclaimed by them as their leader.

While in view of the desperate Italian situation we may argue with a fair degree of assurance that the renewed republic was doomed, the fact remains and is forever memorable that, although it did perish after only three years, on the occasion of the second demise it went down gallantly with flying banners. Undeniably, too, the heroic exit of the later and, as the result proved, the last republic resulted as certainly from the fiery quality of its democratic temper, as this temper in its flaccid aspect had been the cause of the earlier disgraceful collapse. The strength of a democracy is an aroused popular emotion directed by competent leadership toward an inalterable goal. This strength the Florentine democracy of 1527 exhibited, bringing a glory to its last stand which nothing can ever dim. However, when, instead of acting bravely on impulse, the democracy was obliged to make important practical decisions in the business routine of each day, it developed violently opposed opinions and, after irritating debate, usually adopted the wrong course. Here lies, in part at least, the explanation of its failure; and a fateful decision taken in June, 1527, in the second month of its existence, will serve strikingly to illustrate how the lack of reflective discipline operated to nullify the emotional resolution of the embattled citizens.

For the new Florentine government looking out over the Italian world, the salient fact was that it would have to reckon with an attack by Pope Clement VII, even though that attack was not imminent since Clement was living in the Castle of Sant' Angelo as a Spanish prisoner. Filled to overflowing with passionate resentment against the emperor, Clement would hesitate to come to terms with that ruler, even though the orthodox Charles, in sympathetic response to his profoundly orthodox subjects, might be disposed to smooth the path for a reconciliation by offering notable concessions. However, concessions no matter how liberal would not be able to conceal the pope's virtual subjection to the emperor; and before Clement would submit to this humiliation, he would have to be assured that there was no longer the slightest prospect of his rescue from Spanish clutches by the intervention of France. For France was his sole hope; only France, as matters stood, possessed even the potential power to challenge the emperor's ascendancy in Italy, spectacularly declared to the world by the recent terrible sack of Rome. While it was therefore inevitable that the pope should look to France, the fact stood out that he had thus far been ill served by that power. For, having been persuaded by King Francis I to join the league of Cognac of 1526, Clement had been left without support when the army of the duke of Bourbon singled him out for attack. Hardly less angry with the king, because of his broken promises, than with the emperor, Clement still clung to Paris in the hope of escaping the dictation of Charles. Following the monstrous insult offered the head of Christendom by his brutal imprisonment, a wave of indignation had swept through the whole Catholic world. Himself carried along by it, King Francis hastened to express his devotion to the papacy, coupling it with the assurance that an army about to be dispatched across the Alps was evidence that he was at last done with delay. In sum, dissuading the pope from coming to terms with the emperor, Francis offered the alternative of a vigorous renewal of the war to the end of bursting open the papal prison by force. Thus hotly importuned by representatives of both France and Spain, Clement acted as he had always done. His many calamities had not changed his character by an iota. He refused to commit himself to either side, and with the indecision and ambiguity that had become his second nature awaited developments.

As soon as a new campaign loomed between France and Spain the Florentine signory, exactly like the pope, was exposed to the solicitations of both combatants. The struggle between the two powers over the control of Italy had now been going on for over thirty years and there was no telling how much longer it would last. What was already plainly apparent, however, was that Italy had lost its independence and was being slowly ground to pieces between an upper and a nether millstone. Its best hope under the circumstances was the early cessation of the terrible grinding process by the decisive victory of one power or the other. It did not much matter which, since in either case the peninsula would fall under foreign direction. As no Italian state, and certainly not Florence, possessed enough strength to count in the result, from a strictly peninsular point of view it was immaterial with which power Florence would elect to stand. From the point of view of the preservation of the republican form of government, on the other hand, the choice was of capital importance. For, if Florence should have the good fortune to align itself with the victor, it might with some measure of assurance count on its government being left undisturbed, whereas, in case it fought on the losing side, it would unescapably have to submit to such constitutional changes as the victor might see fit to impose.

Examined in this light, the foreign issue before Florence in the late spring of 1527 hinged on the question of which side would win, France or Spain. Conceding that it was impossible to forecast the outcome with certainty, we may nevertheless aver that ever since the campaign of Don Gonsalvo of Cordova there had been a firmness in Spanish policy and a vigor in Spanish arms which indicated that the ultimate victory would go to Spain. The Gonfalonier Capponi himself inclined to this view and a number of hard-headed friends lent him their support. They therefore advocated the alliance with Spain, especially as in their opinion, if Clement ever submitted to the emperor, he would stipulate as his very first condition that Florence should again be subjected to the Medici. According to the gonfalonier the best measure with which to parry that prospective blow would be for Florence to anticipate the pope by concluding an alliance with the emperor without delay. This cool calculation roused the Francophiles to fury. They pointed to the long tradition of friendship between the kings of the line of Capet and the Arno commonwealth, receiving their strongest support in the altered circumstances of the town no longer from the great merchants, as had once been the case, but from the honorable trade folk who, in spite of the thirty years that had passed since Savonarola had been reduced to ashes by a tragic miscarriage of justice, still tenderly cherished his memory and his words. A central point of the dead prophet's preachment, it will be recalled, had been that the reforms he advocated would be effected under the French aegis. By continuing to ascribe this protective role to France the large Savonarolist element of the population permitted itself to be swayed by a misguided and unreasoning sentiment. Unfortunately it was strong enough to turn the scales. The Spanish party, headed by the gonfalonier himself, was overwhelmed by the French party dominated by Frateschi sentiments, and on June 22, 1527, Florence recommitted itself to the French league of Cognac by agreeing to contribute an army of four thousand foot and four hundred horse to the common cause.

The decision was not immediately disastrous. Stung by the papal reproaches, King Francis in the late summer of 1527 sent a large army into Italy under the command of the very competent Lautrec. In the course of a few months this enterprising general succeeded in gaining a dominant position throughout northern Italy. As had frequently happened before, the Imperialists, whose chronically depleted funds regularly compelled them to dismiss most of their troops as soon as a campaign was over and to leave the remainder unpaid, were not prepared for the French thrust and gave way at every point. Pushing his advantage, Lautrec in the spring of 1528 drove southward into the kingdom of Naples and was, to all appearances, on the verge of capturing this chief Spanish stronghold when an incalculable event occurred. The contemporary historians, who have recounted the tenacious duel between France and

Spain over the possession of Italy, convey a puzzled impression that fate or the gods, indistinguishable from fate, fought all along on the side of Spain. In view of what happened in 1528 to Lautrec with victory almost in his grasp the modern historian is tempted to agree. While the French were laying siege to the city of Naples, a pestilence visited their camp which swung its scythe among them till the stricken handful of soldiers that was left beat a panicky retreat. Surrounded by the enemy among the mountains, this remnant was obliged to lay down its arms (August) and the campaign was over.

Although King Francis had tried to revive the faith of his Italian adherents by means of Lautrec's expedition and although the Florentines had yielded to his persuasions, the pope had obstinately remained deaf to the French pleas. We left Clement a prisoner in the Castle of Sant' Angelo at the mercy of the emperor. So great throughout the Catholic world was the scandal of this confinement that, after some six months, Charles agreed (December, 1527) to release the Holy Father on the strength of a few shadowy, unfulfillable promises. Thereupon Clement had made his escape to Orvieto, where he was comparatively free from imperial supervision. By this time the new French action in his behalf was well under way and, although Clement accompanied it with his secret prayers, he had too recently been personally terrorized by the Spaniards to risk any other official stand save that of neutrality. For once luck was with him, for, when in the summer of 1528 the French invasion of Naples ended, as we have seen, with the total destruction of the French army, Clement did not again, as in 1527, draw down on his head the imperial avalanche. Sadly no doubt but wisely he concluded that no further help was to be expected from France and that the time was at hand to make the best bargain in his power with the triumphant emperor. Charles was far away in Spain and the negotiations were greatly hampered by this circumstance; also the imperial and papal positions were at first separated by a wide gap, which it required much patient correspondence to close. Nonetheless already by the autumn of 1528 it was clear to every intelligent observer that pope and emperor had taken the preliminary steps toward a settlement, the aim and substance of which, so far as the Emperor Charles was concerned, would be the pacification of Italy under his hegemony.

With the give-and-take inevitable when two parties draw up a contract, it was patent that the pope would insist on being paid for his acceptance of Spanish preponderance in Italy with important benefits. In the forefront of these, according to everyone who had any knowledge of Clement's character, would be the restoration of the Medici to their native city. So thoroughly was this understood on the Arno that, no sooner had the rumor of negotiations between Rome and Madrid gone abroad, than the Florentines became convinced that the crisis hitherto latent between Clement and themselves was about to burst into the open. The period of domestic quiet was therefore over. Of course it had never been more than a relative quiet and, such as it was, may be ascribed to Gonfalonier Capponi's resolve to hold to a middle course. Never from the first day of the restored republic had the clash of opinion among the citizens ceased. Many acts of violence, which Capponi was helpless to repress, had occurred in consequence of the periodic overflowing of the animosity of the anti-Medicean Arrabbiati. A much more effective curb of their insolence, at least for the time being, than the soft-treading gonfalonier was the pestilence which had swept Florence and Italy in the years 1527 and 1528. We have already noted how in the summer of the latter year it wiped out the French army which had invaded Naples. It visited Florence in both years, although it was more virulent in 1527 than on its return. The number of deaths in the city and suburbs from both visitations is given, let us hope with the usual exaggeration in these matters, at 30,000, approximately one-third of the population! The famous Black Death which had raged at Florence almost two hundred years before had not been much more destructive. It comes to us with something of a shock to learn that at the height of the Renaissance, when the Italians had been engaged for some generations in revising their medieval outlook, they had done nothing whatever to improve the monstrous hygienic conditions of their towns. We are obliged to conclude that abstract intellectual activity is one thing and social reform directed by scientific inquiry quite another thing. In any case the recovery of classical antiquity, the main aim of Renaissance humanism, does not seem either to have stimulated medical knowledge or to have promoted the cause of public health.

An incident which occurred during the harrowing Florentine pestilence is commemorated by an intriguing inscription still to be read over the entrance to the Palazzo Pubblico. This inscription solemnly declares that the Florentine people recognize no other king than Jesus Christ. Already in Savonarola's time this curious sentiment had received official sanction and its revival during Capponi's gonfalonierat proves how living the memory of the great Dominican still was. The pious Capponi himself was so strongly under its ban that on February 9, 1528, apparently on the spur of the moment he made a speech to the Grand Council on the need of the citizens in their present affliction to put their trust in God. He imitated the hortatory manner of Savonarola even to repeating the prophet's actual words, and at the climax of his appeal threw himself on his knees calling on Heaven to have mercy. Immediately the whole assembly did the same, and before the rapture subsided the motion to make Christ perpetual king had been offered and carried.[1]

The upshot of the republic's first year was so favorable to the moderate policy of the gonfalonier that on the expiration of his term he was re-elected to office (July 1, 1528). Immediately after this event the pestilence destroyed the French army under Lautrec, the pope and the emperor began the maneuvering which foreshadowed their reconciliation, and a justified alarm stole its way into the hearts of the Florentines. From the moment of their return to the republic they had recognized the necessity of providing for their defense by re-establishing the militia, which, Machiavelli's proudest achievement, had been

[1] A recent thoroughgoing study of the years treated in this chapter is by C. Roth, *The Last Florentine Republic*. London, 1925. The bibliography on pp. xi-xii lists the leading printed and documentary authorities. The contemporary historians, Guicciardini, Segni, Nardi, Nerli, and Pitti, by treating this period each from his particular angle, build up an effective composite picture. The crown in this group, however, undoubtedly goes to Varchi, whose presentation is at the same time comprehensive and penetrating. Among the printed sources the most important are the reports of the Venetian ambassador, Carlo Capello. They have been published by E. Albèri, *L'Italia nel Secolo Decimosesto*. Florence, 1858.

abolished on the restoration of the Medici. It would have been a deserved recognition of merit to have again put Machiavelli in charge as secretary of the governing committee, but he had forfeited that honor by his recent acceptance of service under Pope Clement. As suspect to the republicans of 1527 as he had been to the Medici in 1512, he once again experienced the bitterness of finding himself tossed aside as a useless tool. He did not have to grieve long at this new misfortune, for, after a brief illness, on June 22, 1527, he came to the end of his many tribulations. With his successors lacking his tireless initiative the reorganization of the militia proceeded at such a leisurely pace that very little had yet been done when the crisis of 1528 descended upon the town. For reasons already explained the original militia law applied only to the country residents, the peasantry. Excited by the threat of war, the young enthusiasts of liberty within the walls clamored to be armed in their turn; and under pressure from them in November, 1528, the momentous forward step was taken of putting arms once more into the hands of the citizens. Ranged in the traditional sixteen companies (*gonfaloni*), they reached a total of four thousand men, who took upon themselves the unfamiliar obligation to march and drill with a zeal which put heart in all that beheld them. As the peasants, already enrolled, could be brought at need to about ten thousand foot, the two militias together constituted a far from negligible force, always provided they could be filled with the stubborn spirit of combat. Nobody doubted, however, that for a successful defense hired professional troops could not be dispensed with, and hesitatingly, for action under Gonfalonier Capponi proceeded with the greatest deliberation, the hiring of mercenaries and the providing of funds for their pay were taken under consideration.

Among the numerous measures made necessary by the coming struggle the most pressing of all was the strengthening of the city walls and the addition of such improvements as were imposed by recent changes in the art of war and the more general use of artillery. Pope Clement himself, before his overthrow, had set up a commission to consider the problem presented by the walls in the light of these innovations. The most conspicuous member of the commission was none other than our old friend Machiavelli. On being thus again absorbed into the service of the state, the former chancellor had elaborated a plan for a thorough overhauling of the Florentine fortifications. To be sure, not very much had been done by the time the revolution of 1527 terminated Clement's rule and Machiavelli's commission. Nor did the situation experience any immediate improvement under the republic. It required the slowly developing crisis of 1528 to make the fortifications the order of the day, while tangible results did not put in an appearance till the election in January, 1529, to the board of works, called the Nine, of Michelangelo Buonarotti. Like many other artists of the age, Michelangelo was also an engineer and was appointed to the Nine not to honor a famous fellow-citizen but for strictly professional reasons. A few months later, in April, he was given sweeping authority as governor of the fortifications and as such, elaborated a scheme of defense, the main feature of which has survived to our day. He took the position that the most vulnerable section of the vast urban girdle of brick and stone lay on the left bank of the river and that indispensable to a successful resistance was the inclusion of the hill of San Miniato within the system of defense. Accordingly, the work of fortifying San Miniato was begun and had well advanced when the general of fortifications suddenly ran away. In this strange evasion we are confronted with an episode in the personal history of the great artist which, in spite of the ready apologies of his biographers, will always be a blot upon his record. Apparently the constitutionally timorous Michelangelo was swept off his feet and stampeded into flight by rumors of treason among his associates. After an absence of some weeks he happily recovered his mental balance and was permitted to return under a pardon from the government. His removal from his post did not cause any alteration in the program he had worked out. In point of fact work on the fortifications was greatly accelerated following the artist's flight and was conducted with such thoroughness and industry that, when in due time the siege befell, Florence proved impregnable to direct assault.

While much of the hesitation and delay connected with the measures of military preparation may be ascribed to the paralyzing cross-currents of opinion inevitable in a democratic society, the most important individual cause of the unsteady course pursued was the head of the state, the Gonfalonier Capponi. It was explicable and pardonable that he should wish to spare Florence the harrowing experience of a siege, and it was at least intelligible that as a middle-of-the-road politician he should attempt to come to a peaceful understanding with Pope Clement. Unquestionably it would have to be a very secret understanding, for the violent anti-Mediceans of the Grand Council, to whom he was under constant suspicion on account of his moderation, had passed a motion expressly forbidding him to conduct negotiations on his own account with Rome. When he did so just the same, and when in April, 1529, an accident disclosed his disobedience, a tremendous storm was precipitated which swept him out of office. His followers were just strong enough to cause his life to be spared. A successor was at once elected and inevitably, under the circumstances, it was the leader of the Arrabbiati opposition, Francesco Carducci. Francesco was the younger brother of Baldassare Carducci, the original Arrabbiati head; and when late in 1528 Baldassare was sent as the republic's ambassador to France, Francesco had inherited his brother's position. The new gonfalonier must have proved a disappointment to his more extreme adherents, for, while conducting his office with an admirable firmness, he was so far from submitting to the violent spirit of party that he proved an excellent head of the state.

Not till June 29, 1529, were the long-drawn-out negotiations between the pope and the emperor brought to a conclusion by a peace and alliance signed at Barcelona. It bristled with concessions to Clement having as their object the return to his control of the State of the Church and the republic of Florence. A notable article revealed Clement's determination to establish the bastard Alessandro in the city as the representative of his house; and Charles's support of the plan was guaranteed by his promise to give to Alessandro his illegitimate daughter, Margherita, to wife. A month later (August 5) the emperor crowned his program of Italian and European pacification with the peace of Cambray. This is the famous Ladies' peace, so called from the circumstance that it was negotiated by the mother of Francis I and the aunt of Charles V acting for their respective relatives. The only feature of the Cambray document that immediately concerns us is that Francis gave up his Italian claims, thereby accepting the Spanish control of the peninsula. He made his surrender, unquestionably with the usual mental reservations, because his repeated defeats in the field had stripped him of his power of resistance. Granting that at the moment no other course was open to him, we have nonetheless no difficulty in understanding the indignation of the Florentines, whom he duped with promises of help to the very day the negotiations were completed and whom, even after the peace was signed, he privately encouraged to resist the Spanish hegemony with promises of help. With this monstrous deception of the trusting republic by Francis I the age-old intimacy of the two states so long united by a common interest and a common emblem came to a disastrous conclusion.

The treaties negotiated by the emperor with King Francis and Pope Clement respectively having cleared the way for the pacification of Italy under his control, in the late summer of 1529 Charles came by sea to Genoa attended by a formidable army and acclaimed by an expectant population. From Genoa he proceeded by slow stages to Bologna, where he set up his court for many months, during which he patiently negotiated a settlement of the many issues still awaiting adjustment between himself and the various Italian governments and among the contentious governments themselves. As a large part in the settlement had been assigned to the pope, Clement, too, came to Bologna, where he abode in close and friendly communication with his late enemy. To mark the triumphant conclusion of Charles's intervention, he was, by the terms of his recent treaty with the pope, to receive the imperial crown at the hands of Clement. This culminating event took place on February 24, 1530, amidst scenes of unrivaled magnificence. Thus during the winter of 1529-30 pope and emperor were the cynosure of all eyes and Bologna to all intents the capital of Europe. We must keep constantly before our eyes the congress of potentates and princes conducted just across the Apennines from Florence, if we would appreciate the isolation and also the heroism of the republic stubbornly bent on independence. For, with Pope Clement and King Francis reconciled with Charles, the many small states of the peninsula had no choice but to make the best terms possible with the emperor and accept him as the arbiter of the Italian destinies. The last state to come to heel was Venice. The republic of St. Mark was the final hope of the republic of the Baptist for support in its dire necessity. Turning a deaf ear to the frantic appeals of its Italian sister, in December, 1529, Venice reached a satisfactory, if selfish, settlement with Charles. The abandonment of Florence was complete.

To avoid a war, regarding the outcome of which there could be no reasonable doubt, the republic sent not one but several embassies to Charles to plead for an amicable settlement. Faithful to the obligations of his treaty with the pope, the emperor consistently referred the negotiators to Clement, and with the utmost reluctance they consented at last to treat directly with their adversary. It was a concession as futile as it was humiliating. The pope insisted on the restoration of his house to its traditional position, and as the Florentine government and people stood unbendingly by the restored republic the exchanges came to nothing. Reluctantly but unescapably the issue was referred to a decision in the field, for which pope and emperor had been prepared from the beginning. In the view of the two allies the war was the pope's war to be conducted at the pope's expense with forces put at his disposal by the emperor.

Owing to these hesitations and delays the papal war against Florence was slow in getting under way, and when it started in the autumn of 1529 reduced itself, in the main, to a single action, the siege of the city. A memorable feature of the siege, essentially the only feature worth remembering, are the resolution and valor displayed by the beleaguered citizens. While intrusting their defense, according to custom, to hired troops under the Perugian condottiere, Malatesta Baglioni, they supported the action of the professional soldiers by devoted service in the newly established militia. The commander of the besieging Imperialist host was the Prince of Orange. After a few preliminary maneuvers he paid tribute to the stalwart character of the defense which he encountered by recognizing his inability to take the city by storm. Thereupon he settled down to reduce it to surrender by starvation. As the emperor's captain-general had at his disposal a mobile field force two or three times as large as that of the republic, he had met with no resistance on his pouring into Tuscany by the upper Arno Valley and had been able to lead his army right up to the city walls. The strategy adopted by the Florentines was to let the enemy exhaust his strength in attacking the fortifications. A necessary corollary of this strategy, however, was that the defenders would have to bend every effort to retain command of the lower Arno Valley as far as Pisa to serve as a source of bread, meat, and the other necessities of life.

Under these circumstances it became clear to the Prince of Orange that he could not hope to force the city to its knees until he had cut it off from its markets. Relatively large as his army was, he did not have enough troops completely to encircle so considerable a town. He had therefore been obliged to content himself with investing that part of Florence which lay on the left bank of the Arno and to utilize such forces as he could spare to patrol the highways of the right bank in order to intercept the food caravans directed to the city. At the same time no opportunity was to be permitted to escape for seizing the fortresses in the lower Arno basin which served the Florentines as points of concentration and support. In this manner it came about that while the campaign, as already said, reduced itself to a siege, the successful resistance of the beleagured citizens depended on their keeping command of the fertile country extending westward to the sea. All the really crucial actions of the winter of 1529-30 turned about the effort of the Florentines to keep their grip on this area. While in the face of the large Imperialist re-enforcements continually pouring into Tuscany from the north the defenders slowly but steadily lost ground, they offered a stout resistance, all the high moments of which were due to a Florentine citizen, who in the daily skirmishes for control of the highways rose to amazing heights of gallantry. This surprising and unheralded hero was Francesco Ferrucci. If the republic went down in a blaze of glory, more than to the actual siege it owed this distinction to the struggle for the possession of the open country carried on by this resourceful, vigorous partisan.[2]

It is a curious circumstance that Florence, from whose fertile womb there had, in the course of the ages, issued so many sons of the rarest worth in every conceivable field of human striving, had never given birth to a soldier, who by his deeds in her behalf had shed a special luster on her long and troubled military annals. In her very last phase she made amends for this lapse with Francesco Ferrucci. Son of an impoverished father of good family, Francesco was, like the average middle-class lad of the city, apprenticed at an early age to a commercial firm but developed such aversion for the work in office and warehouse that he broke away from it in uncontrollable revolt. His mind was set on adventure, and after many hazards he was, although not till after the death of Giovanni de' Medici, absorbed into the latter's famous *Bande Nere*. Giovanni, a captain of great renown in his day, was, as his name suffices to declare, of Florentine birth; but never in his condottiere career, cut short by an early death, did he have the good fortune to fight under the lily banner. Such soldier glory as was his is therefore of a strictly personal nature. At best only in a roundabout way may he be considered to figure in Florentine military history through the circumstance that from his Black Bands a fellow countryman, Francesco Ferrucci, learned the art of war, which with a devotion beyond praise he put at the service of his city.

When the investment of Florence began, the war committee of the Dieci resolved to make use of Francesco's talents by employing him in the open country and gave him the command of Empoli. This small fortified town on the Arno midway between Florence and Pisa and commanding the entrance to the Elsa Valley was absolutely pivotal in the system of defensive warfare devised by the Ten. Not only did Ferrucci hold Empoli against attack but he tirelessly scoured the countryside for enemy raiders and kept an uninterrupted stream of supplies flowing to the beleaguered city. As the winter wore on his task became more and more difficult. The ever-increasing forces of the Prince of Orange took town after town in the disputed western area till the noose around the Florentine throat became steadily more galling. When still another body of Imperialists began to move in from the south, from the direction of Siena, with the plan of occupying the Elsa Valley, Ferrucci resolved to show them his teeth. The most audacious single action of his whole career was his recapture in April, 1530, of the hill town of Volterra. Although he fought like a lion to hold Volterra against repeated assaults, his long-drawn-out operations at a peripheral point of the scene of action proved a misfortune, for, taking advantage of his absence, an Imperialist troop surrounded and stormed the centrally located Empoli. The event occurred in June and was nothing short of decisive. The supplies which had been gradually failing during the preceding months now ceased entirely, and Florence was faced with that cruelest of alternatives, surrender or starvation. Not yet ready for surrender, the Dieci elaborated a last desperate plan of rescue, in which the liberator role was as-

[2] On the occasion of an anniversary celebration for Francesco Ferrucci a valuable collection of sources dealing with his career was published under the title: *Francesco Ferruccio e la Guerra di Firenze del 1529-30*. Florence, 1889.

signed to the native son whose brilliant defense of the open country had aroused an unbounded enthusiasm in every Florentine bosom.

The plan of the Ten was for Ferrucci to attempt with the forces at his command to come to the relief of Florence, which, now completely surrounded, was drawing a more anguished breath with every revolving hour. Although to his fine military intelligence the proposal must have appeared wildly utopian, he accepted it with the born soldier's invariable preference for action in every paralyzing crisis. Moving first from Volterra to Pisa, he swung thence northeastward in a wide circle along the foothills of the Apennines toward Pistoia in the hope of sifting unobserved through the enemy lines and reaching the city. Informed of the enterprise by intercepted letters, the Prince of Orange made all the arrangements necessary to smother his adversary before he should arrive at his goal. Accordingly, when, on August 3, Ferrucci with three thousand foot and three hundred horse tried to pass through the village of Gavinana in the mountains above Pistoia, he was met by several converging columns of Imperialists. One of the first victims of the ensuing ferocious struggle was the Prince of Orange himself. Several times was Gavinana taken and lost by the Florentines, but in the end the immense numerical superiority of the Imperialists decided the issue and the few surviving members of Ferrucci's expeditionary force were surrounded and captured. Among them was the wounded and exhausted leader of the troop. On being brought before a Neapolitan captain in the imperial employ he was set upon and murdered by this tiger in human form, in whom war had destroyed every sentiment of kindliness and mercy.

When the news of Gavinana reached Florence, the whole citizen body with the exception of a small band of frenzied young republicans knew that there was now no escape from surrender. The Florentine captain-general, Malatesta Baglioni, had been coming to this same opinion for some time past. He was a professional soldier as well as a foreigner and had never viewed the situation with the unbalanced enthusiasm of a hot, patriotic partisan. On first taking it on himself during the mounting difficulties of the spring of 1530 cautiously to advise the government to open negotiations with the Prince of Orange he had found some support among the leaders. It was hurriedly withdrawn as soon as the fiery young Jacobins of the piazza learned what was in the wind and staged a demonstration against the traitor element in the signory. The result was that Malatesta took the bit between his teeth and some time in either June or July entered into relations with the Prince of Orange on his own account. In any case he was in secret touch with his opponent before Francesco Ferrucci's great stroke was carried out; and it is not unlikely, although unproved, that the general of the Florentines contributed to the extinction of the Red Lily's last hope of rescue by stipulating not to attack the Imperialist camp while Orange was engaged in the man-hunt that ended with his own death at Gavinana, but also with that of his heroic opponent. By his independent negotiations the Perugian condottiere became a traitor, and no argument can free him from that blot, not even the argument that in his soldier's judgment Florence had arrived at the end of its tether and that, taken, as the next step, by the enemy at the point of the sword, it would be subjected to the nameless horrors of a sack. Following the blow of Gavinana, Malatesta pressed his negotiations with the successor of Orange more urgently than ever and gradually forced the distraught Florentine government to submit to his authority. The leading official of the city was no longer the radical Francesco Carducci. On January 1, 1530, he had been succeeded as gonfalonier of Justice by Raffaelo Girolami, who owed his election to the strong moderate opinion reasserting itself in the Grand Council. The gonfalonier as well as the other leading officials, such as the priors and the Ten, continued to make a public display of reluctance, but in their hearts they were far more willing to negotiate than they were prepared to admit in the face of the loudly declared determination of a handful of overwrought youths rather than surrender to let Florence be destroyed and its people be buried under the ruins. However, with negotiations once under way the sentiment in favor of peace quickly swelled to such irresistible proportions that the opposition was silenced and a treaty signed which brought the siege to a close.

The peace, signed on August 12, was not an abject surrender. It carried a number of palliative, face-saving articles, as, for instance, that the city submitted not to the pope but to the emperor, who within a stipulated number of months, on the understanding that its liberty should be preserved, was to determine the future form of its government. The truly determinative articles, however, declared that the imprisoned Medicean partisans should be set free and that the numerous exiled followers of the former ruling family should be permitted to return. If any Florentine was so blind to the realities of politics as not to know what these concessions signified he was destined to be promptly disillusioned. Only a week after the fateful peace the citizens, still dazed by the recent disaster, were summoned to a parlamentum—the old, old trick!— and under the usual duress granted supreme power (balìa) to twelve fellow-townsmen, all of them proved and tested Mediceans. Thereafter no Florentine with even the rudiments of an intelligence could doubt that on August 12 the republic had perished to be succeeded by the re-established regime of the Medici.

When in the years following the return of the Medici the disappointed and embittered citizens, who, whether strict republicans or not, stood together as enemies of tyranny, reviewed the tremendous crisis of the siege, they inclined with steadily increasing assurance to ascribe the disastrous conclusion to the treason of Malatesta Baglioni. With the patriotic bias unescapable in times of war they finally went so far as to persuade themselves they would have triumphed save for their false leader, and with mounting animosity they charged him with having diabolically plotted against the city he was supposed to serve from the very day he accepted his command. With all but complete unanimity the native-born historians of Florence of all periods have incorporated this viewpoint in their books. But it will not stand up under investigation. The judicial present-day writer will not even be prepared to concede that the late, eleventh-hour treason of Malastesta, which he accepts as proved, did more than slightly to accelerate the surrender which had become a military necessity. Florence fell not on account of Malatesta's betrayal, or Ferrucci's death, or of any other single incident of the siege, but because the completely isolated republic could not sustain itself in the long run against the overwhelming strength of the two allied world-powers, the pope and the emperor.

While this is the cold verdict of historical logic, we cannot thus impersonally conclude our story of the agony of Florence. With our generation still as with our earliest ancestors the heart is enthroned above the calculating intelligence; and if we still peruse with eagerness the records of the past, it is, in spite of the sage counsel of the philosophers, not so much to discover the safest course to be followed among the mazes of life as to lift up our spirit with examples of devotion to a great cause and with instances of a courage that does not flinch before sacrifice and death. Florence defended its independence against overwhelming odds because it believed that independence was a jewel beyond price. It is a relatively unimportant matter that for independence there were substituted in the minds of many the more elastic and ambiguous concepts of liberty and democracy. Undoubtedly these, too, elicited a genuine enthusiasm; but what leaped as a spark from heart to heart until a whole people was kindled to a self-forgetful blaze was independence. It was to retain the dignity of free political agents that the Florentines fought their hazardous fight; and while such a fight has always been accounted good in itself, what matters much more than its universally conceded goodness is how those who undertake it meet the challenge they invite. We have learned in these pages that the Florentines stood their ground undauntedly on the walls and in the field; that they cheerfully yielded up their money and possessions; that they uncomplainingly supported intolerable privations of body and of soul. In the light of such heroism their defeat loses its temporal sting, and we, its awed spectators, experience that elevation of spirit which permits us to see the siege of 1530 as the fitting end of a community, which had always lived adventurously and which owed its amazing achievements to its resolute pursuit during five centuries of an obstinate dream of self-realization.

XXX. The Cinquecento: Climax and Disintegration of Florentine Culture

B
Y THE beginning of the sixteenth century the cultural autonomy of Florence was drawing to a close. Not even in the fourteenth and fifteenth centuries, when its heart-beat was most vigorous, had Florentine culture been other than an offshoot of the ruling culture of the occident, within which it was embraced and with which it was in substantial accord. Like the culture of Venice, Padua, Siena, Ferrara, and like the similar cultures of the towns of the other European countries, it owed its existence to the social order of the Middle Ages with its innumerable independent political units. When these tiny polities began to be assembled into the large national wholes characteristic of the new, the modern social order, an inevitable consequence was that broad national cultures superseded the many provincial varieties that had germinated within the range of the European occident. To be sure, the political unification of Italy lagged considerably and, as we have seen, with tragic consequences behind that of France and Spain; but Italian cultural unification was another matter and by the sixteenth century had acquired a measure of coherence approximately equal to that of its politically more fortunate rivals. With the unconsciousness as well as with the irresistibleness of movements in the mental realm the separate cultures of the Italian towns were in the course of the cinquecento molded into a general Italian form. The cinquecento is therefore the last phase of a specifically Florentine culture. And like every final transformation it is both a culmination and a decline, that is to say, while marking the coming to a peak of forces which had been locally operative for many generations past, it also signifies their enfeeblement and disappearance. This double character of the cinquecento culture of our city is so important that it is indispensable to call attention to it at the outset. And since by about the year 1530, when the republic expired, the process by which the municipal culture was absorbed into the national culture was approaching completion, a second preliminary consideration may not be overlooked. It is that, culturally considered, the Florentine cinquecento embraces not the full century but only the first three decades, and that even its extreme manifestations hardly extend beyond the mid-century.

Vigorously as Florentine cultural expression had set in from about the middle of the dugento, it showed steady and cumulative development only in the Fine Arts, whereas in literature and thought the record was broken and uneven. Although we have already considered this phenomenon, it is proper that in this concluding review we should bring it once more into focus. Sprung from an indefinable inner urge, architecture, sculpture, and painting were subjected to extraneous influences in the course of their development which they managed to assimilate without impairment of the creative energy of their practitioners, while literature and thought, on the contrary, were overwhelmed from without until they were repeatedly threatened with extinction. Let us begin with literature and again take note that its first great figure was Dante. With its very first manifestation therefore literature reached its apex and from Dante's time may be considered to have been in uninterrupted decline. True, the decline was gradual since Dante was followed by Petrarch and Boccaccio and these two poets and writers boasted an original talent enabling them to strike out on important literary paths of their own. With Boccaccio's death at the end of the third quarter of the trecento Florentine literary creativeness came to a temporary close. Of course writing as such did not cease, especially of *novelle* or short stories, but with the single exception of Sachetti, a story-teller of an admirable raciness of speech and matter, the literature of the imagination remained negligible for a hundred years. Then in the age of the magnificent Lorenzo there was a revival championed by Lorenzo himself; but it would be a manifest exaggeration to attribute either to Lorenzo's work or to that of Poliziano much more than the fluency and elegance of a high cultivation. To bring the work of the latter group into comparison with that of the three giants of the trecento is to see it at once as the artificial production which, in the main, it was.

After Lorenzo, in the cinquecento, to which this chapter is devoted, there was only very sporadic achievement. Fortunately, imaginative literature attained a fresh and memorable utterance in other Italian centers, such as Ferrara and Naples, and therefore went marching on as a manifestation of national life, but the specifically Florentine contribution of this period may be set down as unimportant. The appearance of a few comedies by Machiavelli, among them the pungent *Mandragola,* does not alter this judgment. Refusing to adorn the *Mandragola* with the stolen finery of Plautus and Terence, Machiavelli developed his theme from its own inner necessities and sustained it with a dialogue which is the very echo of life. No less true is the statement that the play, an appalling parade of obscenities, reveals local manners so corrupt that we experience a sudden rush of sympathy with Savonarola's reforming zeal. Its considerable merits notwithstanding, the *Mandragola* proved an erratic flare, a mere will-o'-the-wisp, and founded a theater neither in Florence nor in Italy.[1]

An explanation of this aridity has already been attempted by referring it

---

[1] It seems impossible to pass over without mention a work which, although written in the third quarter of the sixteenth century, by virtue of its content and its spirit is inseparable from the age treated in this chapter. I am referring to the *Autobiography* of the artist, Benvenuto Cellini (1500-1571). It unfolds a picture of the writer's period which for directness of speech, spiciness of detail, and general animation is without example. Although in the universalized quality of his art as well as in the innumerable dislocations of his life Cellini definitely marks the replacement of a specifically Florentine by a general Italian culture, he is in his writing a Florentine of Florentines, who, owing to his having been born a man of the people, had the good fortune to escape the cramping effects of a humanistic education. The *Autobiography* is one of the most fascinating works of its kind within the whole range of European literature.

to the revival of classical antiquity with its imposed imitation of famous models and its exaltation of a dead over the living language of the people. That may not, however, be the whole story. If we cast a glance at other culture groups of the European occident, we encounter instances in which the creative impulse spent itself in a single meteoric flash, and other and even more numerous instances in which it exhibited a specializing tendency in favor of a particular form of expression. We are herewith broaching the mystery presented by the diversity and sporadic nature of regional and national traits. In spite of the impressive display made by Dante, Petrarch, and Boccaccio, it may well be that the Florentines were chiefly gifted in the direction of the Fine Arts; and it may also be that, originally gifted in literature, they quickly exhausted this strain. With the mere mention of this puzzling matter we are content to let it fall. It brings us to a *terra incognita,* for the critical penetration of which neither biology nor psychology have as yet succeeded in providing us with a reliable road map.

Since, regardless of the emotional origin of great literature, it cannot live without thought, we have already in earlier chapters gone into the intellectual history of Florence. With Petrarch there came the great change which we have called humanism and which unfortunately was narrowed by its literary champions to the single purpose of reviving classical antiquity. Its most valuable outcome was scholarship, which, aiming at improved texts and accurate knowledge, developed norms of criticism basic to the whole subsequent structure of human knowledge. Engaged in uncovering buried antiquity, the humanists came also upon the treasure of classical philosophy. From this discovery sprang the Platonic academy, which, although native to Florence, developed sufficient force to spread its influence throughout the dominion of Italian speech. However, the academy died with its promoters of the Laurentian age, and the brief reign of philosophy on the Arno came to an end. Philosophy itself, it need hardly be said, did not die; but it was left to other centers than Florence to free it from both its medieval and its classical leading-strings and by a fresh examination of the facts of experience to establish it on definitely modern ground.

There remains a field of literary expression embraced within the dominion of *belles lettres,* in which the Florentine cinquecento attained a high originality and distinction. It is the field of history, of which something has already been said in the Introduction. Its leading figures are Machiavelli and Guicciardini, but around these central luminaries there circles a stately body of satellites, each of which boasts an individual energy imposing consideration and respect. These lesser but still important historians are Nerli, Vettori, Segni, Nardi, Giannotti, and Varchi. The fragmentary history of the last phase of the Florentine democracy left by Jacopo Pitti is hardly of sufficient merit to win him a place among this group, although, as the warm champion of a lost cause, he will always command a partisan following. Regard for the proportions of this book makes it impossible to consider these minor authors individually. We must content ourselves with the sweeping statement that, while each in writing the history of his native city maintained a point of view imposed by his personal circumstances and experience, they one and all lifted themselves to the level of critical historians by subjecting their material to an independent examination. Considered as a group, together of course with Machiavelli and Guicciardini, they signify the arrival of a new, a modern variety of historiography.[2]

Bracketed as Niccolò Machiavelli (1469–1527) and Francesco Guicciardini (1482–1540) usually are, they represent such diametrically opposed approaches to history that an examination of their method tempts us almost to lose sight of their resemblances. Resemblances, however, there are, of which the most important derive from the circumstance that, Florentine contemporaries and functionaries, they went through an identical political experience. Their striking differences spring from the possession by each of an independent personality which moved him to react to his experience in a very particular way. Wounded and heart-sore over the sorrows of Italy, Machiavelli diligently searched the pages of the past for a remedy of her ills. The record was far from clear, but pondering it through long years, he finally concluded that if he should succeed in reducing the confusing multiplicity of events to compact generalizations, he might arrive at a cure and prove the physician and savior of his country. This search for general rules or principles makes the Florentine secretary not so much a historian as a political scientist. While at the command of the Cardinal de' Medici (the later Pope Clement VII) he wrote a history, the *Istorie Fiorentine,* if the truth be told it is, in spite of a certain spice of comment inseparable from a mind so vigorous as Machiavelli's, a rather stiff and lifeless affair. For convincing evidence of Machiavelli's genius we must go not to his narrative but to his reflective works, *The Discourses (Discorsi sopra la Prima Deca di Tito Livio), The Art of War,* and *The Prince.* They constitute in their sum the first fruits of a political science of a distinctly modern inspiration. Guicciardini, on the other hand, distrusted generalizations and frankly expressed his skepticism in regard to those set forth by his friend Niccolò. What chiefly struck Guicciardini about life and history was a variety and mutability so overwhelming that it was a hopeless undertaking to reduce the chaos to an ordered system. Frankly rejecting therefore Machiavelli's procedure of assembling the mass of instances into classes, he was content, like his classical predecessors whom he admired but did not copy, to be a narrative historian, albeit one equipped with sharp critical powers developed by wide reading and, immeasurably more valuable, by a practical, first-hand knowledge of the motivating forces of states and politicians.

We learned in an earlier chapter that it was only on being excluded from the public service that Machiavelli took up as a solace and a pastime the speculative considerations of government on which his fame mainly rests. However, at bottom much more of a practical than of a speculative turn of mind, he was less interested in government in general than in finding an answer to the specific question imposed on him by his own troubled experi-

---

[2] For an estimate of the significance of these men within the whole movement of European historiography see E. Fueter, *Geschichte der neueren Historiographie.* Munich, 1911. A French translation of Fueter appeared in 1914. See also J. A. Symonds, *Renaissance in Italy* ("Age of the Despots," chaps. V and VI; "Italian Literature," Vol. II, chap. XVI); M. Lupo Gentile, *Studi sulla Storiografia Fiorentina alla Corte di Cosimo I de' Medici.* Pisa, 1905.

ence: what kind of a government will end the ills of Florence and of Italy? This should always be kept in mind, as it constitutes his defense against the accusing voices which have never ceased to be raised against him. Without any doubt whatever the indignation which he has aroused is to a large measure due to a misunderstanding. Aligning Machiavelli with such earlier speculative thinkers on the state as Aristotle and St. Thomas Aquinas, his critics have represented the Florentine as engaged in formulating general rules applicable to human societies throughout the ages, whereas his sole concern was Florence and Italy at the particular moment of time when he, Machiavelli, was alive. While he desired to impress his readers with his wide knowledge and sound scholarship, he never for a moment disguised the fact that he was following an intensely practical quest. On this account he did not feel any obligation to preface his reflections with an exposition of the theories of his predecessors in the governmental field. Indeed he did not so much as mention either Aristotle or Aquinas, possibly for the reason that he had not read them, more probably because in his view they had no relevance for his investigation. This was particularly true of St. Thomas. Machiavelli belonged to the group of humanistic pagans who had made a clean escape from the world of Christian ideology. The Thomist view that state and church were divinely authorized institutions collaborating in the great task of helping the individual to attain salvation was to his mind too contemptible even to debate. The only guidance he accepted for his problem, save his own experience, was the practice of that great state of antiquity, Rome, for which, as he rejoicingly took note, religion was nothing more than an instrument of popular control, and which completely subordinated the whole citizen body to the solely conceivable purpose of a state, which is authority and power.

In *The Discourses* Machiavelli's plan reduces itself to an analysis of Roman policy to the end of determining the laws of the republic's successful rise to world-mastery; and in *The Art of War,* wherein he compares ancient Roman with recent Italian practice, he arrives at the conclusion that states cannot be maintained in power and honor except by the citizens themselves transformed into soldiers, that is, by what we would now call universal military service. With these two works *The Prince* forms a single unit of speculative thought, springing from the same preconceptions and unfolding according to the same method. However, while *The Discourses* and *The Art of War* have been accepted as excellent examples of a novel manner of interrogating history and have given no offense, *The Prince,* as already said, created a moral scandal which is as lively in the world today as it was when the work first appeared.

For the Italy of Machiavelli's time there was no escape from enslavement to foreign conquerors except through national unity, and there was no way of attaining national unity except through a prince or tyrant. This is the central doctrine underlying *The Prince,* and it is so unanswerable that it has not been and cannot be successfully disputed. Consequently this has not been the feature on which the critics have sharpened their indignation. They sharpened it in his time and have continued to sharpen it to our own day on Machiavelli's further position that the hoped-for super-tyrant, who will crush the many

small existing tyrants in order to fuse their states into a united Italy, is justified to resort to force, violence, and fraud to attain his end. In the writer's
eyes the nation-state was the political form to which western Europe was at
that precise moment manifestly tending. This being true, it was imperative
for Italy to follow the path which France, Spain, and England had already
taken; and in the winning for Italy of its sovereignty, than which there was
nothing greater in heaven above or on the earth below, the desiderated tyrant
was invited to balk at no measure calculated to help him reach his goal.

Since this is obviously not the place to discuss the truth and falseness, the
strength and weakness of Machiavelli's powerfully argued political tenets,
we shall content ourselves with making three statements which may serve
to explain why *The Prince* has remained a living document down to the
present generation. In the first place the treatise is the boldest and rudest
challenge of the specific ideology of Christianity which has ever been issued.
Seeing that Machiavelli did not even honor this ideology with a rebuttal, he
may have thought in his pagan self-assurance that it was dead. Should we
concede that he may have had some ground for this assumption so far as
Renaissance Italy was concerned, we should still have to insist that he was
most egregiously in error in regard to the rest of Europe. To prove the point
it will suffice to recall that at the very time that Machiavelli propounded his
doctrine of the state as power, Erasmus set forth a diametrically opposed and
strictly pacifist view in his *Plea of Peace* and his *Education of a Christian Prince*
and Sir Thomas More projected in his *Utopia* an ideal society patterned on
apostolic Christianity. Far more alive in his own time than our pagan Florentine was ready to admit, Christian ideology has maintained a vigorous existence through the centuries and has carried on a relentless war against him.
The second statement deals with the demonstrable realities underlying the
sovereign state, which was emerging in Machiavelli's day and which has held
the European stage ever since. This sovereign state is and has been a law to
itself: it dwells in a moral void. Its aim is power and it acts, on the whole,
exactly as Machiavelli affirms, with sole regard to its own welfare. Every
scientifically inspired study of the behavior pattern of the great powers during the four centuries that have passed since Machiavelli wrote must agree
that his description is astonishingly close to the facts. The third and last statement has to do not with Machiavelli's thought but with his person. While
maintaining outwardly the cold manner of a chemist engaged in laboratory
operations, he is sustained throughout his studies by a suppressed patriotic
emotion. At the close of *The Prince* it exceptionally bursts forth with the
vehemence of a volcano. Even today, four centuries after it was written, no
one can read this flaming peroration without a quickened pulse beat. To
modern Italians, therefore, not only is the Florentine secretary the man who
nursed the sacred concept *patria* at the moment when the very word became
taboo and the *patria* itself was locked in a Spanish prison, but he is also the
prophet of a national delivery, which after three hundred years of waiting
leveled the prison walls with the ground and enabled Italy once more to take
her place among the nations.

Guicciardini's reputation, which for many generations burned as brightly as that of his friend and fellow-citizen, has since the beginning of the nine-teenth century suffered a considerable eclipse, owing chiefly to the improved technique and enlarged scope of history in our day. As his youthful *Storia Fiorentina,* a lively presentation of penetrating judgment, was not published till 1859, Guicciardini owed his fame to a single work, the *Storia d'Italia,* which was the ripe product of his experience and which, following its first appearance shortly after his death, went through many editions. In this his-tory he treats of Italy between 1492 and 1534, which is to say, during the period of enslavement prepared for it by France and Spain. With the same unwavering hand as Machiavelli's he brushed aside the hollow public pre-tensions of statesmen to disclose the hidden kernel of their thought. Stripped finally of every illusion and no longer believing in the reality of anything but self-interest, he was left without so much as a trace of what even to the critics of Machiavelli constitutes the latter's saving grace: his patriotic ardor and romantic hope. Not only is the *Storia d'Italia* the first thoroughly realistic history of modern times, but it has the further merit of being the first clear exposition of the European political system as it emerged in Guicciardini's time and has continued without a break to the present day.

At the exact middle of the sixteenth century there appeared a history which testifies to that ever-widening genetic curiosity destined to become the per-haps leading trait of the modern mind. I am referring to the *Vite (Lives) de' piu eccellenti Pittori, Scultori, ed Architetti* by Giorgio Vasari (1511–71). It may be taken as a sign that the creative urge had passed its peak that Vasari, a fine critical historian but a less than mediocre painter, felt moved to assemble the record of a magnificent burst of expression while the evidence was still relatively fresh and crowded on his attention wherever he went in Italy. Although the minute criticism of the last one hundred years has corrected in-numerable small errors of fact of which the author was guilty, it has not suc-ceeded in pushing him from his pedestal. Vasari is still the one indispensable guide to the unfolding of the Fine Arts in Italy between Cimabue and Michel-angelo. His *Lives* are a classic in the same sense in which Machiavelli's *Prince* and Cellini's *Autobiography* are classics and very few other literary works, which are not poetry. If the *Lives* have achieved this permanence, they owe it to their author's zealous scholarship, sympathetic understanding, and literary artistry, a rarely occurring combination of gifts but regularly present when a work qualifying as the history of any human movement or interest achieves a measure of immortality.

In turning to the Fine Arts we shall not follow, as we have done for the earlier periods, the separate development of architecture, sculpture, and paint-ing. For a general sketch like this the procedure becomes unprofitable in view of the fact that the energy giving all three of these arts their cinquecento character issued in so overwhelming a measure from two men that an ex-amination of their contribution is the best conceivable introduction to the new phase of expression. The two men, who carried Florentine art to its apogee, and just as certainly initiated its decline, were Leonardo da Vinci (1452–1519) and Michelangelo Buonarroti (1475–1564). Of course they did not appear in the stark isolation that this setting forth of their names would suggest. The practitioners of the arts were probably numerically as strong in the cinquecento as in any earlier period, but, overborne by the two geniuses in their midst, they were drawn from their individual orbits into the dependence of declared satellites. Not improbably a decline, if not in the number, at least in the quality·of the individuals electing to follow the arts, had already set in by the turn of the century. How else account for the fact that, except in that most Florentine of arts, in painting, there was a decided dearth of men for whom we may claim a genuinely original gift? Where are the architects of the period? Where is the sculptor whom it is not absurd as much as to mention in the same breath with Michelangelo? In painting, on the other hand, we undeniably meet with a number of artists, who, regardless of the influence over them of the two titans, managed to maintain a fairly independent status. Outstanding among such would be Fra Bartolommeo (1475–1517), Andrea del Sarto (1486–1531), Pontormo (1494–1556), and Bronzino (1502–72). Let us salute them respectfully as we pass them by, intent upon our plan of making acquaintance with the age through the work of its two key-men.

While Leonardo interested himself in all the arts, including music, his influence on his contemporaries made itself felt chiefly in the realm of painting. The reason is simple: he *was* a painter. True as this statement is in the realm of objective fact, it tells us nothing of the spiritual significance of Leonardo, the real clue to his wide sway. His puzzling personality must already have begun to disclose itself when, at the age of thirteen, he entered on his apprenticeship in the *bottega* of Verrocchio. Under this excellent master he absorbed the aims and traditions of the Florentine school of painting and prepared himself to make that magnificent contribution to the art which we shall presently examine. However, presented as a free gift from the gods with a restless, inquiring spirit, he found it impossible to restrict himself to the role of an obedient apprentice. Not only was he compelled to subject the teaching of Verrocchio to a critical examination but he found himself driven by an instinctive and irresistible force to go behind every finished work of his master to the infinite forms of life from which Verrocchio and all his contemporaries as well, according to their own statement, derived their inspiration.

Whether Leonardo experimented with painting, or, as was traditional with every ambitious Florentine craftsman, with one or all of the other arts, he regularly found himself in the end brought face to face with nature. He was still a young man when the infinite variety of natural phenomena took possession of his mind. As through the advancing years he saturated himself with this bewildering multiplicity, he became convinced that it represented nothing more than the surface play of hidden principles, by the discovery of which the whole apparently chaotic universe would fall into an ordered system. Starting his observations with the art with which he had embarked on life and gradually extending them to all the cognate arts, he found himself in the end drawn into the realm of science and broadened his studies till they embraced anatomy, physiology, mathematics, astronomy, physics, botany, zoölogy, and mechanical invention. To keep this crowding wealth of material from getting out of hand he adopted the practice of recording it in the form of notes in private diaries, which, scattered at his death but partially recovered in our day, furnish us with the indispensable means of becoming acquainted with the incomparable energy of his inquiring spirit. It goes to show that, after all, it was painting that served as the point of departure for his studies, that only in this field did he sufficiently systematize his observations to enable a later editor to produce a continuous document, the admirable *Treatise on Painting*. In this work Leonardo frequently packs the central purpose animating him into pithy aphorisms. Such are: "Practice must always be founded on sound theory"; and again, "My works are the issue of pure and simple experience, which is the only true mistress." [3]

These statements, which are borne to us down the ages with the very quality of the master's voice, deserve the most careful consideration. While formulated in regard to painting, they affirm guiding principles laid down by Leonardo for his procedure in all his studies. And they tell us in no uncertain manner that, after having begun life as an artist rejoicing in his senses and trusting to a blind inner urge, he passed into the world of experimentation and reflection and became engrossed with the task of reducing experience, his only mistress, to the laws by which it might be comprehended and controlled. Before he had reached middle age his interest in the arts had dwindled till they had become no more than a function of his all-embracing thought. He became in essence a scientist, one of the greatest the world has ever seen, although less by reason of his measurable achievements than by his formulation of an effective scientific method and by his prophetic hints of discoveries, such as the geologic ages of the earth, and of mechanical inventions, such as the submarine and the airplane. In the eyes of the living generation, the mind of which has received its special imprint from the vast scientific development since the cinquecento, Leonardo looms as a pathfinder and forerunner. While no one will begrudge him his belated fame, the historian of the arts may be permitted to point out that he did not achieve his scientific eminence without a severe loss. Concerned more and more with theory and abstractions, he inevitably gave himself less and less to practice. The time came when he dawdled painfully over the few paintings that he was still willing to undertake and which in the end he usually abandoned in a half-finished state. In the last ten years of his life he did nothing at all but think and dream. The paralysis of the will, as most of his biographers have called this curious lethargy, has been treated by them as the "problem" of the master's later years, but it is hardly so inexplicable as they would have us believe. Leonardo's glory as an artist lies without any question in the adjustment which he effected of an amazing natural endowment, essentially irrational, to the demands of a supreme intelligence. He marks a sum-

[3] Quoted from pages 15 and 18 of the *Literary Works of Leonardo da Vinci Compiled and Edited from Original Documents* by J. P. Richter. 2 vols. London, 1883. These writings, together of course with Leonardo's paintings examined directly or in reproduction, constitute the best approach to the master. Among the innumerable literary guides the reader is referred to Vasari and to the moderns already mentioned, such as Berenson and Mather. No one can afford to miss the appreciation of the master by Walter Pater in his volume *The Renaissance*. Leonardo's drawings have received an incomparable analysis and are in part magnificently reproduced by Berenson in his *Drawings of the Florentine Painters*. 2 folio vols. London, 1903.

mit in the arts because he achieved a balance such as has been only rarely brought about between the rational and irrational elements present in all great and sustained expression. Then slowly, as his reason mastered his instincts, the balance was disturbed and the fire at the core of his being was banked and subdued. There is no evidence that he ever analyzed his case or regretted the multiplying inhibitions that palsied his hand. He went, like all of us, his fated way, in the course of which the scientist in him, become too strong, devoured the artist.

Having dealt with the total man, we now turn to his particular achievement in the art of painting. Its indubitable magnitude is enhanced by the relatively small number of his extant works. Many a respectable modern painter, Renoir for instance, probably turned out more pictures in an average year than stand to Leonardo's total credit. The earliest evidence of his hand is the angel at the left of Verrocchio's picture of the Baptism of Christ in the Uffizi gallery. In the same gallery is an Annunciation, in which, designed in the main by Verrocchio, he had a much larger share than in the earlier work by supplying the gracious Gabriel and the characteristic Tuscan landscape. Finally, the Uffizi has also the large unfinished Adoration of the Magi, by which Leonardo disclosed (1481) for the first time his new principles of composition. His other leading works are the Last Supper at Milan; the Virgin of the Rocks, the Virgin with St. Anne and the Infant Jesus, the Mona Lisa—these three at Paris.

Beginning with the very first work of the young apprentice, the angel of Verrocchio's Baptism, we catch the challenge of his genius. It flashes more effectively still from the Annunciation and, excitedly increasing in the Adoration of the Magi, reaches its peak in the works at Milan and at Paris. Let us consider what these creations in their totality bring us that is new, and let our attention turn first to the matter of technique. Leonardo has caught and improved on Masaccio's chiaroscuro, the infinitely subtle transitions from light to dark. A logical consequence of this addiction to tonal finesse was that he sacrificed the frank color planes of the Florentine tradition and threw his influence on the side of the new oil technique recently imported from northern Europe, since only oil was able to render the *sfumature,* the imperceptible gradations of light and shade at which he aimed. His second novelty is that he turned away from the simple-hearted realism of the quattrocento which had made the pictures of the period an enchanting mirror of the throbbing life of town and country. The reflective bent of Leonardo, which prompted him to look for uniformity behind the endless individualizations of nature, sent him on the quest for the ideal man and woman never actually to be met with but definitely implied in all existing human forms. The search for the type, a passionate and characteristic pursuit of classical art, has always involved the attempt to create as a counterpart to our fleeting mundane existence a super-realm of permanence, serenity, and beauty. While Leonardo never wholly abandoned the traditional native realism, of which there is still abundant evidence in the rich characterization of the apostles in so relatively late a work as the Last Supper, we already get a glimpse of the artist's sublimated vision in that very first angel of his in Verrocchio's Baptism. That delicate celestial

MICHELANGELO. CREATION OF ADAM. FRESCO IN THE SISTINE CHAPEL. ROME (ALINARI).

left: MICHELANGELO. JEREMIAH. SISTINE CHAPEL. ROME (ALINARI). *right:* MICHELANGELO. DELPHIC SIBYL. SISTINE CHAPEL. ROME (ALINARI).

MICHELANGELO. THE MEDICI CHAPEL OR NEW SACRISTY, SHOWING THE MONUMENT
TO LORENZO DE' MEDICI (ALINARI).

MICHELANGELO. MONUMENT TO GIULIANO DE' MEDICI.
MEDICI CHAPEL (ALINARI).

visitor, completely out of tune with the harsh literalness of the rest of the composition, carries the unmistakable Leonardesque note. Struck in every subsequent creation with increasing clearness, it achieved its perfection in the unmatched loveliness of the women and children of the Paris altar pieces.

The third important contribution of the master is a new style of composition. In his view the quattrocentists, his immediate predecessors, had been guilty of cluttering their pictures with too much distracting detail. However, the greater compactness at which he aimed was not to be won by a simple process of elimination. Master of mathematics that he had become, he recognized that every good picture that has ever been painted possessed a geometrical substructure, whether consciously or unconsciously introduced by the artist. As a reflective, highly analytical painter Leonardo isolated this tectonic core as part of that theory which, according to his already quoted dictum, was a prerequisite of effective practice. The result was the triangle which, subtly broken and varied with straight and curved lines, constitutes his fundamental pictorial pattern. If his contemporaries detected a monumentality in Leonardo's works which even Masaccio had not attained and which swept them off their feet, it derived from the firm tectonic configuration of his designs.

Simple courtesy demands that we do not pass the Mona Lisa by without paying brief homage to her impassioned reticence. She is Leonardo's one indubitable work of portraiture. In view of the fact that the task which in this case he assigned himself was the likeness of a particular woman, he was obliged somewhat to disguise his preference for the type. The lady was the wife of a Florentine citizen, Francesco del Giocondo, who would not have been the successful business man he was if he had been satisfied with a feminine abstraction. Nevertheless Leonardo's philosophic passion for the universal over the particular showed itself clearly in his representing his sitter withdrawn into the world of dreams, where she is no longer reached by the earth and its affairs. Her fleeting, inscrutable smile reveals a soul which, having done with doubt and fear, is rapturously at peace with God. Only mystics will respond pleasurably to this pictured transfiguration; but all lovers alike of good painting will linger over and be thrilled by the artist's consummate chiaroscuro, which in this instance at least, far from being just another technical conquest, serves as the vehicle of a wholly novel kind of psychological portraiture.

As fascinating and unfathomable in his character of genius as Leonardo, Michelangelo Buonarroti does not present the same personal problem by reason of an attempted conquest of experience by an advance along too many and often contradictory lines. At no time of his long life did he desire to be anything other than an artist; and if, in addition to sculpture, which he preferred, he also practiced painting and architecture, he did no more in this than follow an honored Florentine tradition and, what is still more important, regardless of his medium of expression, he unfailingly brought to bear upon it the same compact and unified personality. Articled as a lad to the painter, Domenico Ghirlandaio, he broke away from his master after a few years to take up the study of sculpture among the collection of ancient and modern masterpieces assembled by Lorenzo the Magnificent in his garden hard by the monastery of San Marco. Lorenzo himself encouraged the lad to follow his natural bent by providing him with bed and board in the Medici palace. Under no other guidance than his own unerring instinct he absorbed the Florentine tradition as manifested in its most rugged representatives, Giotto, Masaccio, Donatello, Pollaiuolo, and Signorelli. Their continuous problem had been the mastery of the human form at rest or in the endlessly varied movements of which it is capable. Beginning with Masaccio, they had come to closer grips with the body by stripping it of its vestments and studying it in the state of nature. Michelangelo, the latecomer, enjoyed the advantage of starting where his predecessors had left off. With a masterful will that leveled every barrier he concentrated on the naked human form till by tireless drawing from models and with the aid of anatomical studies conducted with the eagerness of a surgical apprentice, he acquired a mastery of this instrument such as we can unhesitatingly pronounce unique in the history of the arts. The nude and nothing but the nude became for Michelangelo the medium of artistic expression.[4]

His draughtmanship and plastic modeling directed exclusively at the human body constitute the technical basis of Michelangelo's art. The art itself sprang from the mighty spirit which surged within his small, ill-favored body and clamored for expression. Conceding that this spirit was his very own marked with the uniqueness of every great soul from the dawn of history, still we cannot but be struck with the character stamped upon it by his age, by the Renaissance. This period which in his youth was approaching its meridian had steeped a succession of Italian generations in thoughts and plans of subjugation of the earth. It had stimulated the human will to a veritable riot of competition in all the fields of action, and it had glorified the essentially antiChristian emotions, without the support of which the fierce mundane struggle could not have been sustained. Chanting the praises of *virtù,* the quality of undaunted manliness, the leading spokesmen of the age had summed up the medieval ideal of conduct as *bontà* (goodness) and had dismissed it contemptuously from consideration. It was the thoughts and ideas of his age which constituted the inner life of Michelangelo and which to have brought to their fullest and most concentrated expression is the explanation of his fame. In his view the human body, that most flexible of instruments, was the supreme medium for manifesting power in its material and, above all, in its innumerable and far more important spiritual aspects. It is an arresting circumstance that Buonarroti was personally a rather timorous man, whose consistent prescription for meeting a physical hazard was to run away from it. It is also true that he never even in play assumed the pagan religious attitude of so many of his cultivated contemporaries but remained throughout his life a true Christian believer and an earnest communicant of the Catholic church. There is a contradiction here between the man and the artist, which is not unex-

---

[4] In addition to such guides as Vasari, Berenson, Mather, the reader will find it advantageous to consult on Michelangelo one or another of the many biographies. Such are J. A. Symonds, *Michelangelo Buonarroti.* 2 vols. New York, 1893; C. Holroyd, *Michelangelo Buonarroti.* London, 1903. The Holroyd volume contains in translation the valuable contemporary life by Condivi, for which Michelangelo himself provided the material.

ampled and which it is not our business to resolve. It suffices for us, concerned exclusively with the Florentine's significance as an artist, that he used his marvelous technical mastery over the human body to render and exalt the resolution, the courage, the dignity, and the majesty of man under the ruling secular dispensation of the Renaissance.

Although his earliest works already have the touch of genius, we would not expect and do not get his full message at the start. He is engaged in finding himself in a group of works which we may assemble under the rubric of the Young Michelangelo. Among these are the Drunken Bacchus in the Museo Nazionale of Florence, the Bruges Madonna, and the Pietà at Rome. While exhibiting an excellent command of form, they indicate a lingering enslavement to the past and to the model. Already, however, it is apparent that the young sculptor desired to break away from the naturalist Florentine tradition and arrive at a more generalized version of the human body which would eliminate the distractions produced by a parade of individual idiosyncrasies. Since in the David (1504) he made in this respect a great forward stride, we may accept it as marking the transition from his first to his second phase. The David is a colossal figure representing the young shepherd at the moment of suspense preceding the discharge of the stone with which he will slay Goliath. He fixes his opponent with a level gaze; his whole body is taut with a stored power at the point of explosive release. While the David is a finely modeled body dramatically aglow with the idea that dominates it, it does not yet give us the entirely liberated Michelangelo. The head, hands, and feet are too large for the trunk and proclaim a carefully particularized and almost repulsively gawky adolescent, probably imposed on the sculptor by the actual youth who served him as a model.

It was not till the year 1508, when the artist undertook the frescos of the ceiling of the Sistine chapel at Rome that he achieved his rounded and matured style. Overruling Michelangelo's plea that painting was not his trade, Julius II, as lordly and, in his way, as typical a Renaissance figure as the artist, commanded that he slough his sculptor's skin to serve the pleasure of a pope. Amazing as is the fact that Buonarroti could thus transform himself, we accept his versatility without astonishment before the breath-taking miracle of this work. Besides, as, searching the slightly arched chapel vault, we become more familiar with the plan and its details, we have no difficulty in persuading ourselves that, although here is fresco painting even on the technical side of rarest excellence, it is the handiwork of one who has taught himself to think exclusively in plastic terms and who rigorously eschews pictorial effect. Not by a hair's breadth did Michelangelo in accepting an uncongenial medium depart from the sculptural quality imposed upon him by his genius. So complicated and elaborate is the design of this ceiling that it defies compact description. We shall have to content ourselves with few and distressingly futile words. The main, the central section consists of a series of nine scenes picturing the successive acts of Creation, the Fall of Adam, and the Flood. Around them runs a frame of twelve Prophets and Sibyls, who in the leaden days after the Fall nursed the faith of a Messiah destined to redeem mankind. The majesty of the Creator in his successive evocations of the world and its inhabitants, the relaxed supple vigor of Adam extending his hand to receive the divine spark, the massive dignity of the twelve heralds of redemption overcame and bewildered the spectators when the ceiling was uncovered. A new word, *terribilità,* was coined to express the awe which invaded the beholder before this unrivaled grandeur. Nor did the scenes from Genesis in their figured frame complete the undertaking. Beyond the inner there was a sweeping outer frame of lesser prophets and human ancestors of Christ reaching down to the arched window heads. Each single form of the vast composition was individually conceived and masterfully interwoven with the central panels into a varied and harmonious pattern. A census has revealed the presence in this vast picture book of three hundred and forty-three figures in every conceivable posture, each figure animated with that magic vigor by which art affirms itself to be not the imitator but the lord and the enhancer of life.

The only other work of Michelangelo's comparable to this masterpiece is the New Sacristy of San Lorenzo at Florence with the Medici monuments. This work, too, was evoked at the behest of a pope, the unhappy Clement VII, to whose honor it should always be remembered that, a man of unfixed and wavering purpose, he never wavered in his attachment to his great countryman's genius. Michelangelo's assignment was to construct the New Sacristy as a mausoleum or chapel to be filled with sculptured memorials of the more recent Medici dead. The building had been completed and the sculptural monuments were under way when the expulsion of the Medici in 1527 put an end to a labor, which was afterward never more than half-heartedly resumed. While what we now have is only a part of the original project, still it is for the lovers of Michelangelo the greatest shrine of art within the compass of his native city.

The chapel itself is a structure which shows that Buonarroti, working as an architect, reduced the classical principles revived by Brunelleschi to a greater precision and applied them with a greater freedom. By these innovations, according to Vasari, he prepared the way for the last or High Renaissance phase of this art, of which the cupola of St. Peter's at Rome, the work of Michelangelo's old age, is the finest single example. The New Sacristy is a medium-sized, rectangular structure crowned by a dome. Its inner walls constitute a handsome Renaissance decoration indented with numerous niches of a classical design. Had all these niches been filled with statues, as was originally planned, a most painful overcrowding would have been the result. It was probably not unfortunate that Michelangelo did not carry the work beyond the figures which commemorate the two princes, the duke of Nemours (Giuliano de' Medici) and the duke of Urbino (Lorenzo de' Medici). The two statues occupy opposite, elevated niches behind their respective sarcophagi, which rest upon the floor. On each sarcophagus repose two allegorical figures, one male the other female. They are known traditionally as Dawn and Twilight and Day and Night, and the most suggestive hint as to their significance was dropped by Michelangelo himself. Considered together, he is reported to have said, they represent "Time who consumes all things." Each prince with the tomb and its recumbent figures at his feet constitutes a composition employing the plastic idiom so magnificently realized for the first time in the Sistine chapel. Unalterably sure now of his purpose, the artist flatly refused to undertake portrait statues of the two dukes. With very little truth to fact he represented these rather insignificant Medici as warriors, and then, elaborating this concept, differentiated them respectively as the active and the thinking type of soldier. It is Giuliano who is the man of action, for his left leg, drawn back, shows that he is on the point of rising to issue a command, while Lorenzo, his chin dropped into his left hand and his face shadowed by his helmet, is brooding over problems which, vaster than war, plumb the depths of life itself. Every even fleeting consideration reveals the two princes as allegories, exactly like the male and female figures reclining on the tombs. So potent is this generalizing art and so unfathomable, let us add, is its secret that the two monumental compositions completely blot out for the beholder this multifold and confusing world to transport him on the wings of the imagination to a realm of beauty and permanence, which for Michelangelo, as for all thinkers of his mystic temper, is both the cradle and the goal of man.

It remains to justify an earlier remark to the effect that if Florentine art came to its efflorescence in Leonardo and Michelangelo, they too prepared the way for its decline. In this connection what we must never lose from mind is the subjugation these two titans effected of the contemporary practitioners of the arts. So complete a conquest as they made imposes the thought that the artistic vitality of the population was no longer what it had been. The followers of all the arts alike fell under the spell of the two magicians and, gathering around their works, searched them for the secret of the power with which they seemed to strike dumb whoever beheld them. To such an investigation by overawed admirers certain elements of a purely technical nature would not be slow to disclose themselves. It would, for example, be clear that Leonardo's chiaroscuro made for an intriguing mystery, and that his compositions owed their compactness to their tectonic, their triangular pattern. In the case of Michelangelo the *terribilità,* which prostrated the overwhelmed spectator, plainly emanated from his nudes monumentally conceived and violently agitated.[5]

The enumerated features lent themselves, one and all, to imitation. Industriously applied by sculptors and painters, they would give birth to a period of expression completely dominated by the recognizable outward characteristics of the two masters. It need hardly be expressly said, however, that a work composed on this copy-book recipe is bound to lack the vital spark. We recognize it at once as a piece of pretentious exhibitionism and turn away from it in disgust. Michelangelo in particular proved direct poison for the succeeding generation, which aped his lofty style and transformed it into a vulgar mannerism. The nudes of his followers tended to become bigger and bigger, their muscles more bulging, their movement more vehement till what emerged on canvas or in marble was a travesty utterly bare of meaning. Vasari, the excellent historian but execrable artist, is a fair illustration of the general degradation. He was the favorite painter of the new Medici lord of Florence, the grand duke Cosimo I, and not content to cover the walls of the great council chamber

---

[5] For an excellent analysis of the formal elements in the art of the two masters, so skimpily treated in this summary, see H. Woelfflin, *The Art of the Italian Renaissance.* New York, 1903.

of the Palazzo Pubblico with a series of hollow rhetorical compositions, he spilled a second series in even madder welter over the inner surface of Brunelleschi's cupola. In Vasari's own eyes he was with these empty declamations obediently following in the footsteps of Michelangelo, whom he idolized. Flying the flag of either Michelangelo or Leonardo or of both, the Florentine artists of the second half of the cinquecento plunged violently to destruction; but only by a prejudiced and too narrowly technical attack of the problem will the two leaders be made responsible for the disaster. Certainly the historically informed critic is bound to take another and a larger view. For him the problem of art is part of the general problem of the rise and fall of peoples, and in attempting to understand this tidal or, perhaps more truly, cyclic movement, he refuses to study it in isolation from the social, economic, and political situation. He must therefore insist on taking account of the sum of the influences operating in the Florentine area, and in order fully to understand Florence he must not fail to embrace all Italy in his consideration. Now the decline so manifest throughout Italy in the Fine Arts in the second half of the sixteenth century was at that same time overtaking every department of human activity. An ever-thickening fog was descending on the Italian cultural scene and blotting it from view; but as this disaster is a general and, in the main, a political event, which considerably transcends the history of Florentine art, we shall reserve consideration of it to our concluding pages.

Epilogue: The Great Lethargy

WHEN after the ever-memorable affirmation of their will to remain the masters of their destiny, the resolution of the Florentines was broken by the irresistible might of the two greatest lords of Europe, the pope and the emperor, it was clear that the city would become the prize of Clement VII in accordance with the terms of his alliance with his great secular rival. By making formal submission on August 12, 1530, to the emperor the city hoped to escape the noose that had been prepared for it, but the hope was one of those vain illusions to which the defeated have ever been prone to cling. A few days after the capitulation, on August 20, a parliament, held under the eyes of the victorious troops, conceded extraordinary power to a committee of Medicean partisans to reform the state. On that day and by that act was inaugurated the absentee rule of Clement VII; and its first measure was the extortion from his local enemies of the money promised by the treaty to the victorious troops and necessary to bring about their departure from the territory their savage forays had reduced to the extreme of misery. Fast on this measure there followed a long succession of similarly vengeful acts. In consequence the safeguards accorded in the treaty were canceled, the leading figures in the late uprising punished by exile, imprisonment, or death, and the terrorized citizens reduced to the abject docility which would enable the pope to lay such a yoke upon them as they should never again be strong enough to shake off.

After the unprecedented humiliations to which, since his mounting the chair of St. Peter, Clement had been subjected both at Rome and at Florence, he was prepared to proceed with a certain caution and to take one step at a time in order not unduly to imperil his renewed possession of his native town. Above all, for the present at least he was resolved to do nothing calculated to disturb his harmonious relations with Charles V, without whose co-operation he would not again have laid his hands upon Florence. As his representative on the Arno and as future lord of the Florentine dominion, he had fixed upon the youthful Alessandro; and on his first plotting with Charles in the treaty of Barcelona (1529) to reduce Florence to submission, he had already revealed his intention by having the emperor formally pledge to Alessandro as his bride Charles's illegitimate daughter, Margaret, although she was not yet of marriageable age. It will not be necessary to indicate all the steps by which the

513

way was smoothed for Alessandro's assumption of power. Not till the summer of 1531, on July 5 to be precise, did the young man enter the city, dispatched thither with the blessings of his prospective father-in-law and fortified by the charter, whereby the imperial overlord, in accordance with the power granted him by the articles of capitulation, regulated the government of Florence. The document declared Alessandro and his heirs after him to be the lawful heads of the state; however, by permitting the traditional constitution to remain in operation it conspicuously failed to provide against a repetition of the two previous risings against Medicean rule. In the eyes of Clement this was an intolerable concession to his opponents. He was in poor health and, in expectation of his early death, focused with fanatical intensity on achieving through the exercise of the vast power of the papacy, if nothing else within the wide range of his mental vision, at least the establishment in perpetuity of his family in Florence. Accordingly he resolved to sweep the old constitution, which after the frequent tinkering it had experienced was, if the truth be told, a rubbishy assortment of ruins, onto the ash-heap and to make an entirely new start. In conformity with orders sent by him from Rome, on April 27, 1532, the old constitution with its familiar and cherished executive of priors and gonfalonier was declared abolished and the state entrusted to Alessandro as hereditary duke exercising his power in connection with three bodies, to wit, a council of Two Hundred, a senate of Forty-eight, and an inner administrative committee of Four. In strict fact these bodies were, one and all, no more than window-dressing intended to conceal from a people still clinging to its dream of freedom that they had at last succumbed to that long threatening specter, *il governo d'un solo*. The republic had been definitely and, as it turned out, finally superseded by a monarchy, and young Alessandro was master and duke of Florence.

In spite of his illegitimate birth and his repulsive negroid appearance, the young duke at first won a certain amount of favor by seriously devoting himself to his duties. So rapidly did he consolidate his position that even the death in 1534 of his exalted sponsor, Clement VII, did not impair his hold on the state. Before long, however, his head was turned by his new eminence and he became the object of a very general aversion by engaging in indecent orgies and indulging an unbridled lust. Consequently, when on the night of January 5, 1537, he was murdered in his bed by his relative, Lorenzino de' Medici, not a single Florentine experienced even a passing regret. As he was the last male member of the older Medicean line, the succession to the duchy now passed automatically to the younger line, which descended from Lorenzo, the younger son of old Giovanni di Bicci.[1] In point of fact the murderer of Alessandro, young Lorenzino, was Alessandro's next of kin; but as he had made himself impossible by his deed and, furthermore, had sought safety in precipitate flight, the succession was claimed by Cosimo, the most immediately available male of the younger line. Cosimo was the son of the famous soldier, Giovanni delle Bande Nere, whose career had been cut short by death in battle at the early age of twenty-eight. Had there been an effective republican sentiment still to be found in Florence, the occasion of Alessandro's sudden removal

---

[1] See genealogical tree at end of this chapter.

might have been utilized to put an end to the young and as yet precarious regime of tyranny. As not so much as a single voice made itself heard in protest against Cosimo's assumption of power, the son of the condottiere encountered no difficulty in mounting the throne that had been vacated by Alessandro's murder.

The new duke was not yet eighteen years of age. He was a tall, vigorous youth, expert in every form of athletic exercise, handsome to look upon, of a penetrating intelligence, and prepared to give his energies ungrudgingly to the obligations of his office. In short, he was the kind of man whom Florence, become a tyranny, required if the tyranny was to be transformed into an established monarchical form of government. Cosimo reigned from 1537 to 1574 and in that period so thoroughly reorganized the state that at his death it presented itself to view in the character which it substantially retained for two centuries, retained in fact till the great changes precipitated throughout Europe by the French Revolution. He, the second duke, and not Alessandro, the first duke, is the true founder of the dynasty. If we agree, as agree we must, that the atmosphere in which republics thrive was no longer to be encountered in the cinquecento, and that not only in Italy but everywhere in Europe the stage was set for the advent of the absolute monarchy, we cannot deny that Cosimo is a notable political figure. The numerous Florentine exiles, victims of the catastrophe of 1530 and therefore champions of the republican idea, regarded him with an understandable detestation. They assiduously spread slanderous stories about him by which they so successfully blackened his character in the court of public opinion that he is still very generally held to have been one of the most sinister figures of his age. Let it be conceded at once that, engaged during a long reign in establishing his rule upon unshakable foundations, he committed many a hideous excess against his enemies. Similar excesses can be brought home to every sovereign of the period intent on the same kind of work, the statement being as true of the kings of such great states as Spain, France, and England as it is true of the smaller lords of the Lilliputian subdivisions of Germany and Italy. Within narrow Tuscan limits Cosimo is the "Prince," whom Machiavelli in his day attempted to wrest by prayer from the reluctant gods. If Cosimo was not able to operate on a national scale, as Machiavelli would have had his "Prince" do, that was not Cosimo's fault but the result of peninsular conditions reaching far back into the past. It is not likely that a student of the Renaissance acquainted with the forces operating in the field of political history will fail to accept him as an effective example of the tyrant type current in his age. To a striking degree, moreover, he exhibited the most characteristic traits of the outstanding rulers of his day. He relied chiefly on himself for counsel, was taciturn and sphinx-like; and while reasonably accessible to his subjects, especially of the lower orders, he practiced a cold aristocratic aloofness and made no effort to found his rule on a specious popularity. Conceding that Cosimo neither in his individual capacity nor as the representative of a new type of absolute sovereign is capable of eliciting a warm enthusiasm, we may yet attribute to him such a combination of qualities of will and mind that we cannot withhold from him a measure of sincere, if cold, respect.[2]

To put Duke Cosimo's achievement in a nut-shell he consolidated his state to a notable degree both within and without. The republic of Florence had never been anything other than a victorious town, powerful by reason of its population, wealth, and unrivaled energy, lording it over lesser towns, castles, and villages which by gradual stages had been reduced to obedience. By Cosimo's legislation Florentine citizenship was extended to the whole state; the ancient distinction between major and minor gilds was suppressed, as was indeed the far more fundamental distinction between gildsmen who enjoyed political rights and non-gildsmen who did not enjoy them; in short, the whole population was systematically reduced to an indistinguishable mass of subjects under a single master. This summary statement should serve to make clear that Cosimo envisaged not Florence but Tuscany as his inheritance. This same Tuscan outlook is also the key to his foreign policy. So long as the republic of Siena maintained a separate existence in southern Tuscany, his own state was, in Cosimo's eyes, no better than a torso. Firmly resolved to round off his dominion by the acquisition of Siena he adopted the only policy calculated to bring him success. This was to attach himself closely and unswervingly to that power, Spain, whose Italian hegemony had become the determining factor in the general peninsular situation. With the patience of a hunter stalking a deer, he bided his time, and on the occasion of a new war, in which France once again challenged the Spanish ascendancy and in which Siena, ever given to ill-considered, headstrong action, sided with France, the duke's help was welcomed by Emperor Charles V with open arms. As a result, when in the year 1555 Siena was captured after a ferocious and memorable siege, Cosimo could put forth an excellent claim to it as his share of the common spoils. On his taking over the Sienese state the duke, whose reputation as a competent autocrat had steadily mounted ever since his accession, was widely looked upon as the leading prince of Italy. He was therefore not succumbing to an inordinate ambition when he determined to mark his increased dignity and power by adopting a new title. In the year 1569 he proclaimed himself grand duke of Tuscany. By that act he swept from the public stage the last few properties recalling the old Florentine republic, which, having long lost the power to rouse men to action, now definitely took its place in the mausoleum dedicated to the memories of the past.

In earlier times than ours, when life moved at a more deliberate pace and boasted a greater dignity, it was customary for historians to mark the passing of the state which has engaged their attention with a solemn funeral oration, wherein they attempted to gather into a final estimate the manifold achievements of the polity which they had followed through its appointed cycle. Quite apart from the changed manners of our day which would make such a performance ludicrous, a review of the achievements of Florence coupled with an effort to define its place in the movements of European thought and life would

---

[2] The many contemporary historians, Varchi, Segni, Nardi, and Nerli deserve to be heard on the subject of Cosimo. The best modern presentation of Cosimo and the state he founded is by A. Reumont, *Geschichte Toscanas.* 2 vols. Gotha, 1876-77. A recent biography is by C. Booth, *Cosimo I Duke of Florence.* Cambridge, 1921.

be to squeeze into a dry summary the animated story, to which the many hundred pages of this book have not sufficed to do justice. We shall content ourselves therefore with a few words concerned with the significance for Tuscan
and Italian history in general of the disappearance of the Florentine republic.
The writer has not concealed his recognition of the considerable accomplish-
ment of Duke Cosimo in reshaping the broken administrative mechanism that
had come into his hands into a monarchical unit which succeeded in fitting
itself into the ruling European system of his day. But he is sharply indisposed
to leave his readers with the impression that he regards the grand duchy of Tuscany as marking in any other than a purely formal sense a continuation of the
republic to which it succeeded. In his view the republic expired with the heroic
spasm culminating in the siege of 1530; and if it did not again revive, that was
because the exceptional energies that had sustained the citizens for a span of
four amazing centuries had during recent generations gradually diminished
until with the famous siege they were finally and tragically dispersed. The
magnificent Florentine will-to-power, around which the history of the Red
Lily revolves as around its axis, can with arguments of an undeniable plausibility be ascribed to the pressure of external conditions calculable as "forces,"
such as the geographical situation of the town in respect of the communal revolution and the consequent economic stimulations which pricked the citizens to
an unwonted daring. But that would very decisively not be the whole story.
In the record of the Florentines there clearly is something akin to what,
vaguely enough, we call genius when manifested by an individual. Genius
falls where it chooses to fall; it is given and taken away. Nobody earnestly
contemplating the demise of the republic can come to any other conclusion
than that its peculiar genius or, if a less symbolical term is preferred, the historical energies of the citizens were by that catastrophe extinguished. Of course
the extinction did not occur with anything like the dramatic suddenness suggested by our statement. It was a gradual process which had unquestionably
set in some generations before 1530 and which even with the establishment of
the duchy was not complete, as the single name of Galileo, mathematician,
physicist, and astronomer, will suffice to prove. Substantially, however, the statement is true that in the year 1530 the spirit or genius or soul of Florence—
call it what you will—took its departure. The unfathomed event is reflected in
the uncertain terms employed to describe it. Physically the town survived, has
indeed survived to this day, but as a cultural manifestation it had reached the
end of the trail.

And yet, after admitting the presence of an incalculable factor in the fall of
this state, its historian, prompted to defend the rational and systematic character of his studies, cannot but insist on submitting the issue to an analysis.
The insistence becomes unescapable in the present instance, since the growth
and expansion of Florence has through many chapters and with abundant
detail been referred to a complex of forces, political, economic, social, religious,
and intellectual, which have been carefully identified and which never for a
moment ceased to operate. The judgment may be ventured that the incidence
of these various forces was most favorable to Florence in the fourteenth and
early fifteenth centuries, and that consequently this period marks the culmina-

tion, the indisputable heyday of the Arno community. A scrutiny of these same determinative agencies will disclose, beginning approximately with the rise of the Medici, a gradual shift in their volume and direction, with the result that Florence was progressively deprived of the advantages hitherto enjoyed and subjected to disadvantages of a cumulative vigor. Although scattered reference has already been had to these increasing handicaps, it is proper that the many circumstances revealing how Florence, originally so greatly favored and exalted by fortune, sank to the level of fortune's step-child, should be assembled into a co-ordinated picture.

The material prosperity of Florence, which rested mainly on the two pillars of its banking facilities and the trade in woolen cloth financed by its bankers, probably reached its highest level in the first half of the fourteenth century. The ability of the Florentines to sell their cloth profitably in all the markets of the world and particularly in France, Flanders, and England resulted from the cheapening of costs through the adoption of a capitalistic form of production and from an improved product due to the special skills developed by the local artisans. Inevitably these advantages disappeared in measure as competitors imitated the industrial organization of the Arno merchants and copied and in some cases even improved on the original Florentine techniques. By the fifteenth century the home production of the northern countries had already taken such a development that, had not the sons of the Baptist made a quick adjustment to the altered situation, they would with very little delay have seen the end of their material power. Still splendidly elastic at that time, they found a substitute for the vanishing woolen markets of the north by gaining admission for their goods to the markets of the Levant, while at the same time they tapped a fresh source of prosperity by calling into life a new industry, the manufacture of silk. However, in the course of the sixteenth century they were once again checkmated. On the one hand, France, from of old a leading economic dependency of the Arno city, developed an infant silk industry of its own; on the other hand, the woolen industries of Flanders, France, and England, already long escaped from their swaddling clothes, pushed their emancipation from Florentine production still further by the adoption of a high tariff policy. Unscalable tariff walls completed the rout which the successful imitation of Florentine business methods had begun.

If we now add to these blows the economic revolution precipitated by the Portuguese discovery of a sea-route to Asia and by the Spanish discovery of the western hemisphere, the main factors in the economic decline of Florence are before us. The situation is so entirely familiar to everyone that it would be tiresome to rehearse it in detail. With Asia and the Americas opened to exploitation western civilization was launched on a new era of an all but unbounded horizon. It followed that Europe, which for many centuries had contentedly spent its energies upon the Mediterranean, swung about, and turning its back on this ancient sea, faced toward the Atlantic. At the same time, as chance would have it, the Atlantic powers, Spain, France, and England, succeeded in reorganizing themselves into compact monarchies and, thus fortified, they prepared to appropriate the trade and all the many other advantages which the voyages of discovery had made accessible. The conversion of the republic of Florence into a grand duchy of Tuscany may not improperly be interpreted as an attempt to keep abreast of the contemporary and compelling movement of political consolidation. But that so feeble a state as the grand duchy could operate with effectiveness on the enlarged stage of the world and enter into rivalry with the Atlantic powers for the great Atlantic prizes was not to be thought of.

Since men do not live by bread alone there are other than geographico-economic reasons for the cinquecento Florentine and, let us add, the concomitant Italian decline. Humanism, still so extravagantly celebrated in many quarters in our day, had proved to be a very doubtful benefit to the self-styled heirs of Rome ever since Petrarch and his collaborators had given the movement the narrowly circumscribed character of a revival of antiquity. In its final sixteenth-century metamorphosis this Petrarchan humanism took the form of a command to its followers to imitate as slavishly as possible the letters and arts of the ancients. What this signified in the way of systematically cultivating a sterility which a laughably pretentious façade served to disclose rather than to conceal has been briefly expounded in the preceding chapter. We are asserting what cannot be successfully challenged when we declare that it was the arid imitative classicism of the cinquecento which first laid a disturbing palsy on the Italian spirit. But that the classical inhibition became an enduring paralysis followed from the impact of a movement of an entirely different nature. I am referring to the Counter Reformation. It is well known that the Counter Reformation first gathered strength in Spain and that its gradual subjugation of Italy was a consequence of the Spanish political hegemony, with the main stages of which we have become familiar. Developing into a movement fiercely repressive of the free exercise of the human mind, the Counter Reformation fashioned to its use in such institutions as the Inquisition and the Order of the Jesuits a set of instruments with which it was able, first, to check and, finally, to stifle the fiery initiative of the Italian spirit. With the second half of the sixteenth century the breath of that spirit became steadily more feeble until the whole nation quietly subsided into a kind of winter sleep. While there continued to take place here and there splendid individual manifestations of that creativeness with which this so highly endowed people had projected itself into the story of western civilization, taken as a whole the nation exhibited multiplying symptoms of a steadily advancing mortal lethargy. We may sum up the arresting event in the words with which the Italians themselves have long since formulated their national tragedy: Italy entered the prison of Spain and the Counter Reformation and had the key turned on its spirit for over two hundred years.

A history of Florence cannot fittingly close on a note of lethargy and death. To be sure, the republic, the concern of this book, died, as we have seen, and has had its end duly recorded. But from the physical corruption of the Florentine state the great achievements of that state, products of the not equally corruptible mind, have been largely immune. These mental achievements belong to every field of human endeavor, to government, justice, trade, industry, finance and, notably, far more notably, to those highest ranges of the spirit where literature and art bring forth their golden fruit. In the great works of the imagination handed down to us from the past of the human race we of to-day still recognize, as have all the generations who have gone before, spiritual manifestations which serve as a fountain of youth for our perpetual renewal. Surely the best of what the Florentine artists, writers, and thinkers have left behind is such a refreshing fount. Partaking of its vitalizing waters, we slough off the fetters of the flesh and rise to a realm of serenity and understanding than which our mortal state holds no higher reward.

THE HOUSE OF MEDICI

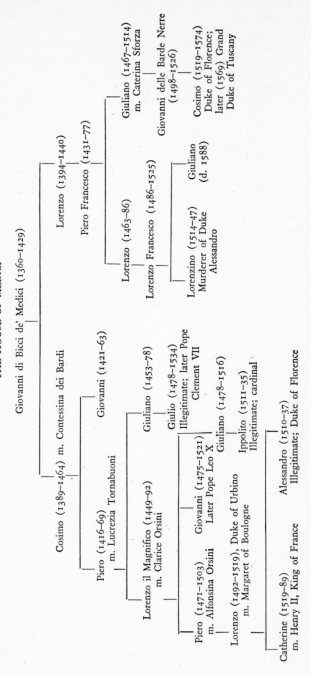

Giovanni di Bicci de' Medici (1360–1429)

Cosimo (1389–1464) m. Contessina dei Bardi

Lorenzo (1394–1440)

Piero Francesco (1431–77)

Lorenzo (1463–86)

Giuliano (1467–1514)
m. Caterina Sforza

Giovanni delle Barde Nerre
(1498–1526)

Cosimo (1519–1574)
Duke of Florence;
later (1569) Grand
Duke of Tuscany

Lorenzo Francesco (1486–1525)

Giuliano
(d. 1588)

Lorenzino (1514–47)
Murderer of Duke
Alessandro

Piero (1416–69)
m. Lucrezia Tornabuoni

Giovanni (1421–63)

Lorenzo il Magnifico (1449–92)
m. Clarice Orsini

Giuliano (1453–78)

Giulio (1478–1534)
Illegitimate; later Pope
Clement VII

Giovanni (1475–1521)
Later Pope Leo X

Giuliano (1478–1516)

Ippolito (1511–35)
Illegitimate; cardinal

Piero (1471–1503)
m. Alfonsina Orsini

Lorenzo (1492–1519), Duke of Urbino
m. Margaret of Boulogne

Alessandro (1510–37)
Illegitimate; Duke of Florence

Catherine (1519–89)
m. Henry II, King of France

INDEX

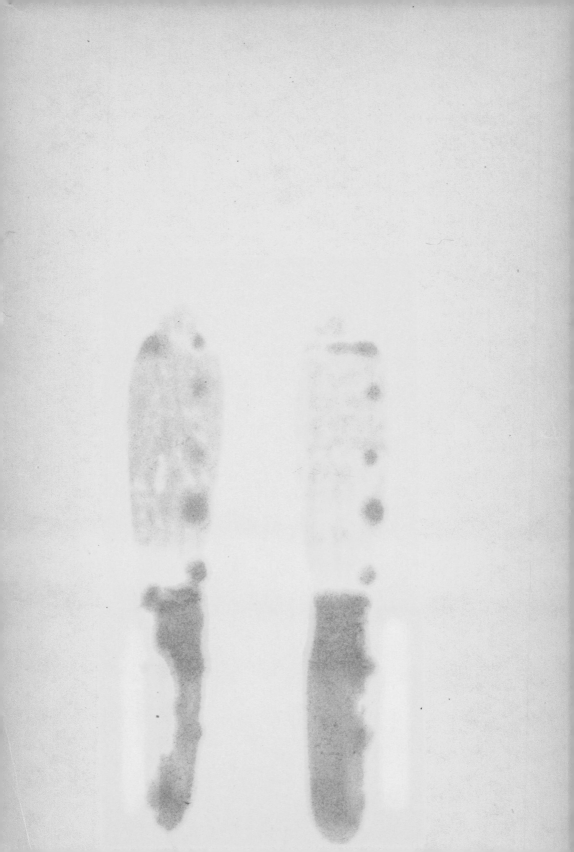

DATE DUE

GAYLORD   PRINTED IN U.S.A.